London in the Later Middle Ages

London in the Later Middle Ages

Government and People 1200–1500

CAROLINE M. BARRON

OXFORD
UNIVERSITY PRESS

Great Clarendon Street, Oxford OX2 6DP

Oxford University Press is a department of the University of Oxford.
It furthers the University's objective of excellence in research, scholarship,
and education by publishing worldwide in

Oxford New York

Auckland Cape Town Dar es Salaam Hong Kong Karachi
Kuala Lumpur Madrid Melbourne Mexico City Nairobi
New Delhi Shanghai Taipei Toronto

With offices in
Argentina Austria Brazil Chile Czech Republic France Greece
Guatemala Hungary Italy Japan South Korea Poland Portugal
Singapore Switzerland Thailand Turkey Ukraine Vietnam

Published in the United States
by Oxford University Press Inc., New York

First published 2004
First published in paperback 2005

British Library Cataloguing in Publication Data
Data available

Library of Congress Cataloging in Publication Data
Data available

Typeset by Hope Services (Abingdon) Ltd.
Printed in Great Britain
on acid-free paper by
Biddles Ltd,
King's Lynn, Norfolk

ISBN 0–19–925777–9 978–0–19–925777–5
ISBN 0–19–928441–5 (Pbk.) 978–0–19–928441–2 (Pbk.)

1 3 5 7 9 10 8 6 4 2

Preface

IF THIS BOOK has any heroes, they are those clerks who compiled the Journals recording the business conducted by the London aldermen and common councilmen, and so bequeathed to us the written record, by turns illuminating and enraging, that makes it possible to write anything at all about the medieval city of London. When I left university I thought I was interested in high politics, and began my long pilgrimage through the city's archives in the hope of throwing light on the activities of kings; the harvest was richer in cabbages. Here I deal with some of the themes I had already addressed in my doctoral dissertation—London's government and its relations with the Lancastrian kings—and, although my interests have come to range more widely over a larger field, I should at the outset acknowledge the book's origins, and recall how much I owe to May McKisack and Tom Reddaway.

This book has taken so long to write that it limps finally into harbour heavily in debt. It would be impossible to list all those who have helped me but many of them are to be found in the footnotes and the bibliography. I am deeply conscious of my dependence upon others who have laboured, and are labouring, in the London vineyard. Some friends were kind enough to take the trouble to read particular chapters and save me from tediousness or inaccuracy: for such acts of scholarly friendship I am grateful to Jim Bolton, Martha Carlin, David Carpenter, Penelope Corfield, Matthew Davies, Peregrine Horden, John Schofield, and Penelope Tucker. I am also grateful to the two anonymous readers to whom the Oxford University Press sent my original typescript: their reports were invaluable, albeit bracing. Stephanie Hovland skilfully designed and computerized the tables: Jessica Freeman compiled the bibliography and the map gazetteer: Betty Masters allowed me to print her unpublished material on civic officers (to which Jessica Freeman and Hannes Kleineke also contributed), and Anne Lancashire has supplied the scholarly and definitive list of the mayors and sheriffs. The Historic Towns Atlas Trust has kindly allowed me to use the London map of 1540, and to redesign it in a new format.

It has been my good fortune to supervise the doctoral theses of a number of scholars many of whom (as my daughter rather tartly pointed out some years ago) have written more books than I have. Whether their names appear in the bibliography or not, they have all contributed their scholarship, industry, and enthusiasm to this enterprise: Roger Axworthy, Virginia Bainbridge, Helen Bradley, Meriel Connor, Matthew Davies, Mark Forrest, Jessica Freeman, Matthew Groom, Julia Merritt, Elizabeth New, Stephen O'Connor, John Oldland, Andrew Prescott, Eleanor Quinton, Steve Rigby, Gervase Rosser, Marie-Hélène Rousseau, John Schofield, Jenny Stratford, Anne Sutton, Penny Tucker. All those named here have at different times contributed to the seminar on Medieval and Tudor History that Vanessa Harding and I have been running at the Institute of Historical Research since 1975. This book is, in a host of ways, indebted to all those who have attended that seminar over the years and generously shared their discoveries and ideas.

At times, when the end seemed out of sight, I have been particularly grateful for the persistence, friendship, and scholarly encouragement of Clive Burgess, Barrie Dobson, Vanessa Harding, Barbara Harvey, Peregrine Horden, and Joel Rosenthal. If I were, like Richard Whittington, to be in a position to found an almshouse, I would ask the inmates to pray for them all as my 'speciall lordes and promoters'.

No one will be happier to see this book finally between boards than my family. They did not write it, and at times they may even have delayed its completion, but without them it would not have been worth writing at all.

C. M. B.

Friday before the Feast of St Augustine of Canterbury, 2003

Contents

List of Figures

Figures 5.1–5.6
Compiled by Stephanie Hovland using information, slightly adjusted, from E. Carus-Wilson and O. Coleman, *England's Export Trade 1275–1547* (Oxford, 1963)

Figures 5.7–5.8
Compiled by Stephanie Hovland using: 1400–1500, information from M. K. James, *Studies in the Medieval Wine Trade* (Oxford, 1971), 108–116; 1500–1509, unpublished material kindly supplied by Professor Peter Ramsey; 1509–48, information from Georg Schanz, *Englische Handelspolitik gegen Ende des Mittelalters . . . Heinrich VII und Heinrich VIII* (Leipzig, 1881), 128–45

Figures 5.9–5.12
Compiled by Stephanie Hovland using: 1399–1482, information from H. L. Gray, 'Tables of Enrolled Customs and Subsidy Accounts 1399–1482', in E. Power and M. M. Postan, (eds.),

List of Tables

Abbreviations

(For full details of these manuscripts and published works, see the Bibliography.)

A Chronicle	*A Chronicle of London*, ed. H. N. Nicolas
Annales Londonienses	*Annales Londonienses* in *Chronicles of the Reigns of Edward I and II*
Annales Paulini	*Annales Paulini* in *Chronicles of the Reigns of Edward I and II*
Beaven	Beaven, *Aldermen of the City of London*
BIHR	*Bulletin of the Institute of Historical Research*
BL	British Library
Brooke with Keir	Brooke with Keir, *London 800-1216*
CLRO	Corporation of London Records Office
CChR	*Calendar of Charter Rolls*
CCorR	*Calendar of Coroners' Rolls*
CCR	*Calendar of Close Rolls*
CEMCR	*Calendar of Early Mayor's Court Rolls*
CFR	*Calendar of Fine Rolls*
CLibR	*Calendar of Liberate Rolls*
CP	HR, Common Pleas
CPMR	*Calendar of Plea and Memoranda Rolls of the City of London*
CPR	*Calendar of Patent Rolls*
Davies	*Merchant Taylors' Company*, ed. M. P. Davies
EconHR	*Economic History Review*
EETS	Early English Text Society
EHR	*English Historical Review*
Ekwall	*Two Early London Subsidy Rolls*, ed. E. Ekwall
Fabyan	Fabyan, Robert, *The New Chronicles*
French Chronicle	*French Chronicle of London*, ed. H. T. Riley (1863)
GL	Guildhall Library
Hughes	Hughes, A., *List of Sheriffs for England and Wales*
HR	Husting Rolls
HW	*Calendar of Wills...Enrolled in the Court of Husting*
Jor.	Journal. Manuscript series in CLRO
LB [A-R]	Letter Book. Manuscript series in CLRO
LB[A-L]	*Calendar of Letter Books of the City of London*
Liber Albus	*Liber Albus*, ed. and trans. H. T. Riley (1861)
Liber Albus (Rolls Series)	in *Munimenta Gildhallae*, ed. H. T. Riley (1859-62)

Liber Custumarum	in *Munimenta Gildhallae*, ed. H. T. Riley (1859-62)
London Assize of Nuisance	*London Assize of Nuisance 1301-1431*
LMAS	London and Middlesex Archaeological Society
LTR	*London Topographical Record*
Mayors and Sheriffs	*Chronicles of the Mayors and Sheriffs*, ed. H. T. Riley (1863)
Memorials	*Memorials of London*
MGL	*Munimenta Gildhallae Londoniensis*, ed. H. T. Riley (1859–62)
Nightingale	Nightingale, P., *Medieval Mercantile Community*
OED	*Oxford English Dictionary*, 2 vols. (Oxford, 1971)
Poss.Ass.	*London Possessory Assizes*
PRO	Public Record Office
PPC	*Proceedings . . . of the Privy Council*
Rep.	Repertory. Manuscript series in CLRO
Reynolds	Reynolds, S., 'Rulers of London'
Rot. Normann.	*Rotuli Normanniae*
RP	*Rotuli Parliamentorum*
Stow, *Survey*	John Stow, *A Survey of London*
Strype, *Survey*	John Strype, *Survey of the Cities of London and Westminster*
TLMAS	*Transactions of the London and Middlesex Archaeological Society*
TRHS	*Transactions of the Royal Historical Society*
VCH, London	Page, W., (ed.), *Victoria History . . . London*
WAM	Westminster Abbey Muniments
Williams	Williams, G. A., *Commune to Capital*

Introduction

THIS BOOK AIMS to provide an account of what might be termed 'public' London, that is, those areas which were of concern either to the king, or to the citizens communally, or, very often, to both. It attempts to examine the many ways in which those who lived in London learned how to construct and manage 'self-government at the king's command'; how they negotiated with demanding and very diverse kings and evolved ways of raising money, distributing burdens, accommodating different economic interests, controlling the use of communal space and resources, and protecting—and to some extent even enhancing—the health and welfare of all the city's inhabitants.

It is not the aim of this book, except incidentally, to analyse the private life of Londoners, which was done so brilliantly by Sylvia Thrupp over fifty years ago,[1] or to consider the role played by religion in animating a parish structure and providing, through Christian teaching on good works and the efficacy of *post-mortem* prayer, a notable series of charitable acts and attitudes of wide civic significance.[2] The study of the church in London, which played such a significant part in Professor Christopher Brooke's history of London in the period before 1200, has been, until recently, comparatively neglected for the later medieval period.[3] The only general survey is that by the various authors who wrote the very useful account to be found in the 1909 volume of the Victoria County History.[4] Since then a good deal of work has been done on particular religious institutions.[5] There is, moreover, much more work in progress: major studies of St Paul's cathedral, of the friars in London, and of the church in London in the early fourteenth century

[1] S. Thrupp, *The Merchant Class of Medieval London* (Michigan, 1948).

[2] See e.g. J. A. F. Thomson, 'Wealth, Poverty and Mercantile Ethics in Late Medieval London', in N. Bulst and J.-Ph. Genet (eds.), *La Ville, La Bourgeoisie et La Genèse de L'État Moderne (XII–XVIII siècles)* (Paris, 1988), 265–78.

[3] C. N. L. Brooke with G. Keir, *London 800–1216: The Shaping of a City* (London, 1975).

[4] Joyce Jeffries Davis wrote the account covering the years to 1348, and she, together with Eliza Jeffries Davis and Margaret Cornford wrote the account for 1348 to 1521, see W. Page (ed.), *The Victoria History of London*, i (London, 1909; rpt. 1974). See also C. Pendrill, *Old Parish Life in London* (Oxford, 1937): an excellent volume but vitiated by a lack of notes indicating his sources.

[5] On particular religious houses, see e.g. C. L. Kingsford, *The Grey Friars of London* (Aberdeen, 1915); B. F. Harvey, *Living and Dying in England 1100–1540: The Monastic Experience* (Oxford, 1993); D. Knowles and W. F. Grimes, *The London Charterhouse* (London, 1954); C. Paxton, 'The Nunneries of London and its Environs in the Later Middle Ages' (University of Oxford D.Phil. thesis, 1992); M. Rosenfield, 'Holy Trinity Aldgate on the Eve of the Dissolution', *Guildhall Miscellany*, 3 (1970), 159–73; C. Thomas, B. Sloane, and C. Phillpotts, *Excavations at the Priory and Hospital of St Mary Spittal, London* (London, 1997); J. Rohrkasten, 'The Origin and Early Development of London Mendicant Houses', in T. R. Slater and G. Rosser (eds.), *The Church in the Medieval Town* (Aldershot, 1998), 76–99; id., 'Londoners and London Mendicants in the Late Middle Ages', *Journal of Ecclesiastical History*, 47 (1996), 446–77.

are all in progress.[6] Popular religion and the important role played by the numerous London parish churches (of which some forty of the 107 parishes have surviving pre-Reformation records) is now receiving serious, rather than simply antiquarian, attention.[7] A synthesis of this work will demand, and should receive, a book of its own. Of course, churchmen and ecclesiastical institutions are frequently to be found in the pages of this book, and to separate church and state would be to misunderstand the interdependent structures within medieval society.

The mayor and aldermen of London were not a Gild Merchant, nor did they form a religious fraternity: they did not conduct their business within a religious framework, nor did they, in their official capacities, take part in a city-wide Corpus Christi procession as was common in other towns.[8] The annual mayor's riding to Westminster when the new mayor took his oath before the barons of the king's exchequer was an almost entirely secular occasion. It is true, however, that after the riding to Westminster and the formal procession and dinner, the mayor and aldermen customarily went to St Paul's where, in the middle of the nave, they prayed for the soul of Bishop William 'who, by his entreaties, it is said, obtained from his lordship William the Conqueror, great liberties for the city of London'.[9] The mayor and aldermen did not, on this occasion, go to the cathedral to pray, or to make offerings, at the shrine of St Erkenwald, the great saint of London but, rather, to give thanks for the relatively unsaintly bishop who had obtained an important charter of privileges for the citizens. The medieval mayors and aldermen of London give every indication of being, individually, pious men, but in their corporate activities their outlook appears to have been secular, and this book reflects that position.

It has become easier for historians to write about medieval London because in the last thirty years or so a great deal of new work has been accomplished and made available. In the years since the Second World War archaeologists have been able

[6] The History of St Paul's Cathedral is to be produced by a group of scholars working under the editorship of Professor Derek Keene; Dr Jens Rohrkasten is writing the history of the friars in London; David Rollenhagen of Cornell University is writing his doctoral dissertation on the 'Church in London *c.*1250–*c.*1350'.

[7] See e.g. C. Barron and J. Roscoe, 'The Medieval Parish Church of St Andrew Holborn', *London Topographical Record*, 24 (1980), 31–60; *Parish Fraternity Register: The Fraternity of the Holy Trinity and SS Fabian and Sebastian in the Parish Church of St Botolph without Aldersgate*, ed. P. Basing (London Record Society, 1982); C. Barron, 'The Parish Fraternities of Medieval London', in C. Barron and C. Harper-Bill (eds.), *The Church in Pre-Reformation Society* (Woodbridge, 1985), 13–47; C. Burgess, 'Shaping the Parish: St Mary at Hill, London in the Fifteenth Century', in J. Blair and B. Golding (eds.), *The Cloister and the World: Essays in Medieval History in Honour of Barbara Harvey* (Oxford, 1996), 246–86; *The Church Records of St Andrew Hubbard Eastcheap, c.1450–c.1570*, ed. C. Burgess (London Record Society, 1999); H. Combes, 'Piety and Belief in Fifteenth-Century London: An Analysis of the Fifteenth-Century Churchwardens' Inventory of St Nicholas Shambles', *TLMAS* 48 (1997), 137–52.

[8] M. James, 'Ritual, Drama and Social Body in the Late Medieval Town', *Past and Present*, 98 (1983), 3–29; M. Rubin, *Corpus Christi: The Eucharist in Late Medieval Culture* (Cambridge, 1991), esp. 243–71.

[9] *Liber Albus*, 23–4. This refers to William the Norman, bishop of London 1051–75, who appears to have been instrumental in securing William I's charter of privileges for London soon after William's coronation, see Brooke with Keir, *London 800–1216*, 28–9; *Regesta Regum Anglo-Normannorum: The Acta of William I (1066–1087)* ed. D. Bates (Oxford, 1998), 593, no. 180.

to uncover, particularly along the Thames waterfront, the cellars and structures of medieval houses and, in some cases, the foundations and walls of religious buildings, as well as the city wall and the layout of several medieval streets.[10] The work of Professor Derek Keene and his colleagues at the Centre for Metropolitan History has not only led us to consider London in a broader context but has also helped historians to look at the medieval city in new ways.[11] Many more of the rich sources for medieval London have been made available largely, but not exclusively, through the publications of the London Record Society which was founded in 1965: about half of the thirty-six volumes already published cover the pre-Reformation period. Much of this new material, both archival and archaeological, was brought together in the *British Atlas of Historic Towns* volume on the *City of London from Prehistoric Times to c.1520*, published in 1989.[12] The footnotes and bibliography of this book demonstrate the extent to which it is dependent upon the research done by other scholars who have worked, and are still working, on the history of London.

The records of the city of London are remarkably rich, well kept, and well published. William I's charter of *c.*1067 is still carefully preserved in the archives at the Corporation of London Records Office in Guildhall, together with much other remarkable material.[13] Fortunately for the historian much of this material has been carefully published, in particular the city's medieval letter books covering the years 1272 to 1498, the records of the mayor's court from 1298 to 1482, and the medieval wills (but not the deeds or legal cases) enrolled in the Husting Court.[14] Much of this book is based upon this material and also upon the evidence to be found in the unpublished volumes of the so-called 'Journals of the Common Council' which survive from 1416.[15] In fact these largely record meetings of the court of aldermen until 1495 when a new series, the 'Repertories', begins for the court of aldermen while the Journals continue to record only the meetings of the common council itself. In spite of the loss of almost all the chamberlains' records for the medieval period (and these included all the city's records of apprenticeships and entries to the freedom) it has been possible to build up a picture of the steps by which the citizens of London gradually worked out ways of organizing representative government and of recruiting and paying a civic

[10] For a bibliography of this archaeological work, see Keene's and Barron's bibliographies in P. Garside, *Capital Histories: A Bibliographical Study of London* (Aldershot, 1998), 23–6, 38–40.

[11] See the works of D. Keene, B. Campbell, J. Galloway, and M. Murphy, in Garside, *Capital Histories.*

[12] M. D. Lobel (ed.), *The City of London from Prehistoric Times to c.1520, The British Atlas of Historic Towns*, 3 (Oxford, 1989).

[13] See H. Deadman and E. Scudder, *An Introductory Guide to the Corporation of London Records Office* (London, 1994).

[14] *Calendar of the Letter Books of the City of London A–L*, ed. R. R. Sharpe, 11 vols. (London, 1899–1912); *Calendar of Plea and Memoranda Rolls 1324–1482*, ed. A. H. Thomas and P. E. Jones, 6 vols. (Cambridge, 1924–61); *Calendar of Wills Proved and Enrolled in the Court of Husting, London 1258–1688*, ed. R. R. Sharpe, 2 vols., (London, 1889–90).

[15] See C. Barron, 'The Government of London and its Relations with the Crown 1400–1450' (University of London, Ph.D. thesis, 1970); P. Tucker, ' Government and Politics, London 1461–1483' (University of London, Ph.D. thesis, 1995).

bureaucracy. The development of governmental institutions does not always make exciting reading, but the way in which they worked (or failed to work) was important to the inhabitants of London, who numbered perhaps 80,000 in 1300, 40,000 in 1400, 50,000 in 1500, and 200,000 in 1600.[16]

The city of London did not, however, speak with a single voice, even though the voice of the ruling elite, the aldermen, may have spoken most loudly. In fact there was a plurality of voices: the aldermen who were, certainly by the later part of the period, drawn from the merchants engaged in wholesale trade whether at home or abroad, the citizen artisans, and the householders who may not always have been citizens but who had a voice at the wardmote meetings; and then there were also the unenfranchised, the women, aliens, clerics (of whom there would have been thousands rather than hundreds in London),[17] members of the numerous aristocratic households in the city and, of course, boys and girls who often formed an important part of the workforce, but had no say in how their craft or trade or household was run, let alone in the government of the city.

The development of the city of London was moulded by a number of pressures. Of these the most obvious, and probably the most important, was the Crown. The grudging steps by which the Angevin and Plantagenet kings allowed the citizens of London a measure of control over their own affairs can be traced in the surviving royal charters. But these tell only part of the story of the complex daily negotiations that made up the pattern of Crown/city relations in these centuries. It has been attempted in Part 1 to consider these relations not only at the times of crisis for the monarchy, for example in 1259, 1327, 1399, or 1460, but also during the more ordinary years that lay between the crisis peaks.

Prosperity also moulded the forms of government in the city. The often-crucial role played by Londoners in national events, and their comparative autonomy within the body politic, derived from the city's ability to attract immigrants both from other parts of England and from overseas. They came to London because it was here that great fortunes could be made. The ways in which these fortunes were created, and the role played by the city corporately in fostering economic opportunities are examined in Part 2.

As the city grew in the years following the Norman Conquest of England, so it became increasingly necessary for the people crowded into the area bounded by the old Roman walls to work out systems of self-government, to regulate neighbourly behaviour in crowded conditions, to resolve competing claims upon common resources, and to provide some communal services to improve the quality of urban living. At the beginning of the thirteenth century, when the mayoralty was just ten years old, there are almost no surviving records to enable us to understand how Londoners governed themselves. A hundred years later, by 1300, there is a

[16] See Ch. 10.

[17] There were about 300 clerics attached to St Paul's Cathedral; see also *The Church in London 1375–1392*, ed. A. K. McHardy (London Record Society, 1977), from which it is clear that each of the 107 parish churches in London was served by a number varying from three to twenty clerics, and of this total, nearly 500 were chaplains of one sort or another: see esp. p. xiv.

wealth of written documentation, which becomes ever thicker as the centuries roll on. It was, however, in the thirteenth century that the city of London moved from government by memory to government by written record. The growth and transformation of London government is the subject of Part 3. But alongside this growth in the central governing structures in London, there was also developing, from the early fourteenth century, a parallel governing structure provided by the craft and trading organizations, known at first as guilds and later evolving into chartered companies. In addition there were also the hundred or so parishes, each with its own churchwardens, whose responsibilities extended beyond the care of the fabric and furnishings of the church to the lives and behaviour of the parishioners.[18] There were, therefore, in London a plurality of governing structures with complementary and competing areas of jurisdiction.

It was this plurality that determined the character of the response to the social problems created by urban life. In Part 4 two areas, nowadays considered to be the responsibility of government (whether local or national), are looked at in more detail: the regulation of the physical environment and the provision of welfare services. Here royal pressure, civic initiatives, craft concerns, religious preoccupations, and private charity can all be seen to play a part in providing the necessities of urban life. The government of London was not solely the responsibility of the mayor, aldermen, and civic bureaucracy: it depended also in a variety of ways upon the Crown, the church, and private individuals to make it work. And it did not always work well. This is not the story of relentless progress from the darkness of the twelfth century to the bright uplands of Tudor England. It is, rather, an account of competition, struggle, failure and success; an account of how successive Londoners in a particular 300-year period, through individual enterprise, debate, innovation, experiment, and set-backs, evolved ways of organizing and regulating competing aims and needs. Londoners are still struggling with these tasks.

[18] See C. Burgess, 'London Parishioners in Times of Change: St Andrew Hubbard, Eastcheap, c.1450–1570', *Journal of Ecclesiastical History*, 53 (2002), 38–63.

PART 1

City and Crown
The Reality of Royal Power

CHAPTER ONE

The Demands of the Crown

At the death of John in 1216 the Londoners were actively supporting Prince Louis of France against the late king's 12-year old son: to win over the Londoners was one of the many tasks facing William the Marshal, who had been appointed by the Council to act as the guardian of the king and the kingdom. Without the support of the city of London the kingdom would be lost to John's son. By contrast nearly three hundred years later, in 1485, the Londoners tamely acquiesced in the accession of Henry VII. By the end of the fifteenth century the city was better governed and more orderly than it had been in 1216 but, in the affairs of the kingdom at large, it carried less weight.

Throughout the period the Londoners (using the different voices of the mayor, the aldermen, or the commoners) maintained a continuous dialogue with the Crown. Over the years the matters for debate and negotiation changed: some issues were resolved and others came into prominence: some periods were comparatively harmonious and at other times the dialogue degenerated into a shouting match. Some periods are much better documented than others and this may give the impression of greater dialogue when it is simply that the sources are richer. Before 1272 there are almost no records surviving from the administration of the city and yet, in compensation, we have an extremely detailed 'insider' chronicle written by Arnald fitz-Thedmar who was an alderman of the city from *c.*1255 until his death in *c.*1272. This provides an insight into aldermanic faction which is available for no other period.[1] The sources are again very rich for the reign of Richard II when the faction fighting in London reached its zenith.[2] Do the controversies provoke more detailed records or do we perceive greater controversy because the records are richer? The relentless march of the annual chronicle can obscure not only the importance of general and continuing points of conflict between the Londoners and the Crown but also the significant changes as contentious issues of one generation give way to new disputes and concerns.

At the simplest level the king needed money and the Londoners wanted self-government which largely (albeit not completely) contributed to their ability to

[1] The Latin text of this MS (which is now in the Corporation of London Records Office) was edited, not very accurately as *Liber de Antiquis Legibus seu Chronica Maiorum et Vicecomitum Londoniarum*, ed. T. Stapleton (Camden Society, London, 1846) and later a more accurate translation was produced as *Chronicles of the Mayors and Sheriffs of London*, ed. and trans. H. T. Riley (London, 1863), 1–178. All references to fitz–Thedmar's chronicle will be taken from Riley's translation.

[2] See R. Bird, *The Turbulent London of Richard II* (London, 1949), xi–xv.

make money. These were not the only matters of debate and contention but they underlay many of the overt struggles and complex negotiations. It is worth remembering that what the Crown wrung from the city tended to be permanent, what the city won from the Crown was constantly subject to review and renegotiation. Even when the Crown appeared at its weakest as in 1263, 1311, 1388, or 1460, yet it always retained the power (*de iure* if not *de facto*) to take back all that had been conceded to the city and to govern it directly through appointed royal wardens who could collect and manage all the city's revenue. London was not a semi-autonomous city like Ghent, Augsburg, or Venice, and it was clear to all who was, ultimately, the cat and who the mouse.

The city of London was disadvantaged in its dealings with the Crown in that it did not speak with a single voice. It is true that during minorities the will of the Crown might be fragmented (as in 1216–27, 1377–86, 1423–44, 1483) and even when the king was of full age the magnates who opposed his policies might claim to speak for, or in defence of, the Crown. But for the city the problem was a chronic one for it was not a single person but a commune composed of many people who were expected to speak with one voice in pursuit of a common goal. In practice such harmony was rarely achieved and at periods the faction fighting among the aldermen reached fever pitch as in the 1380s. Moreover at times there were deep rifts between the governing aldermen and the common people of the city. When it suited him, a king might appeal over the heads of the aldermen (who comprised the official voice of the city) to the citizens at large (as did Henry III in 1257 and the Yorkist lords in 1459). But if the Crown could, on occasion, pick and choose to whom it spoke in the city, so the Londoners might support particular magnates or claimants to the throne in the risky hope of securing more advantages or privileges for the citizens, or for a particular group among them. But, on the whole, the Crown spoke with fewer voices than did the rulers of London: the king and his council were a smaller and more homogeneous group than the mayor, twenty-four aldermen and 40,000–80,000 inhabitants of the city. So the king had a distinct advantage in formulating and carrying out policy but, if push came to shove, the Londoners could muster a sizeable military force.

FINANCE

Most obviously the Crown needed money but the nature and extent of that need changed over the years. In the thirteenth century the Crown was struggling to find sources of revenue to augment the dwindling income from the diminished Crown estates and the unwieldy and contentious feudal revenues. John's efficient attempts to increase royal revenue during a period of inflation led to the drawing-up of Magna Carta in which the concerns of the Londoners, as well as those of the baronage, were carefully addressed. Clause 12 of the Charter laid down that financial aids were to be paid to the king only after they were agreed by the common counsel of the realm and to this clause was added, doubtless at the insistence of the

Londoners, that 'Aids from the City of London are to be treated likewise'.[3] This implied that the city of London was not required to pay the arbitrary royal taxation, known as tallage as other royal boroughs were bound to do, but would be expected only to offer the voluntary aid such as was asked of the king's tenants-in-chief. Not surprisingly this clause was omitted from the later reissues of the Great Charter yet the Londoners fought on, and persistently attempted to resist Henry III's demands for tallage. Without doubt this was the single most significant issue at stake between the Londoners and Henry III: between 1217 and 1268 tallage was levied from the Londoners fourteen times.[4]

The king, however, devised other ways, over and above tallage, of extracting money from the Londoners: 1,000 marks in 1253 for jostling the king's household servants;[5] 400 marks in 1256 in lieu of paying Queen's Gold,[6] and, of course, a swingeing fine of 20,000 marks in 1265 for having supported Simon de Montfort, followed by a further fine of 1,000 marks paid to the king's brother Richard of Almaine for damage done to his manors at Isleworth;[7] in 1269 the Londoners were obliged to contribute 100 marks for the new abbey at Westminster and 500 marks for the forthcoming crusade of Prince Edward.[8] When in 1257 it appeared that the aldermen might not agree to pay the sum demanded , the king appealed over their heads to the commonalty at large and ordered an investigation into those who had avoided contributing their due share to recent tallages.[9]

Although the king was, by and large, successful at extracting tallage from the Londoners it was clear that some new system of raising royal revenue needed to be developed. In the first place the Crown began systematically to levy a charge on goods passing in and out of English ports. The tax on the export of wool was at first levied intermittently,[10] but became a regular imposition from the 1270s and more general customs dues payable on imported wine (tunnage) and other imports and exports (poundage and petty custom) were gradually introduced and accepted. The export of cloth was not taxed until the 1340s. By the second half of the fourteenth century the export and import trade of England was, subject to the consent of Parliament, regularly taxed to provide income (some £30,000 p.a.) for the Crown. This taxation was not the subject of direct negotiation between the Londoners and the Crown but was mediated first through separate assemblies of merchants (1320s–1360s) and then through the Commons in Parliament.[11]

[3] J. C. Holt, *Magna Carta* (Cambridge, 1965), 321.

[4] G. A. Williams, *Medieval London from Commune to Capital* (London, 1963), 88–9; see S. K. Mitchell, *Taxation in Medieval England* (New Haven, Conn., 1951), esp. ch. 7.

[5] *Chronica Johannis de Oxenedes* ed. H. Ellis (Rolls Series, 1889), 195–6.

[6] *Chronicles of the Mayors and Sheriffs*, 25. For Queen's Gold, see M. Howell, 'The Resources of Eleanor of Provence as Queen Consort', *EHR* 102 (1987), 372–93, esp. 378; *CPMR 1323–64*, 156 n. 1.

[7] *Chronicles of the Mayors and Sheriffs*, 85, 98, 112.

[8] Ibid. 130.

[9] Fitz-Thedmar's enraged account of the way in which the king, through the agency of John Maunsel, turned the Londoners against their aldermen provides an excellent insight into royal tactics: ibid, 33–40.

[10] In 1268 the Londoners paid 200 marks to be free of the 'new custom': ibid, 114–15.

[11] Roger Axworthy, 'The Financial Relationship of the London Merchant Community with Edward III, 1327–1377' (University of London. Ph.D. thesis, 2000).

In parallel with the development of the royal taxation of overseas trade came the emergence of Parliament where the representatives of the shires and the boroughs met together with the lords and with the king himself to debate and discuss the business of the realm. Edward I used this body to provide the consent to direct taxation which could then be levied more widely, and more equitably, than the contentious feudal tallage. In the Parliament of 1275 the knights and burgesses agreed to a tax assessed at the rate of one-fifteenth of the value of moveable goods.[12] Such taxation was at first intermittent, and the king continued to collect tallage when he could, which led the Londoners to secure, in their charter of 1327, a confirmation of their right to pay taxes as other commons of the realm and to be free of all liability to tallage.[13] The assessments for the taxes on moveables were extremely laborious and this made them difficult to collect, so in 1334 it was agreed that the sum raised by the grant of one-tenth and one-fifteenth to the Crown should be standardized and raised by quotas to produce *c.*£34,000.[14] Although all boroughs were assessed at the rate of one-tenth, London, on the grounds that it had not been liable to tallage as other towns were, asserted its right to pay at the lower rate of one-fifteenth. As a result London contributed only £733 to the national total throughout the period. In relation to its wealth London was seriously undertaxed.

These developments in national taxation in the years 1272 to 1334, by eliminating the insistent royal demands for tallage from London, removed the most serious source of discord between the city and the Crown. Debates about financial support for the Crown were now transferred to Parliament: London paid what the Commons agreed and the king no longer demanded arbitrary tallage. But the king's financial thirst was not slaked. The Crown still expected gifts from the city and privileges, in the form of new and renewed charters, continued to be sold to the Londoners. Moreover, increasingly, the Crown needed loans of ready cash in anticipation of the Parliamentary taxes, which always took time to collect.

The Londoners were expected to provide gifts at royal marriages and coronations and on other special occasions. In 1305–6 the Londoners paid £2,000 when Prince Edward (the future Edward II) was knighted (a relic of the old feudal aid).[15] Henry IV was given 1,000 marks as a coronation gift and the French princess Katherine also received 1,000 marks and two silver-gilt basins when she came to England in 1421 for her marriage to Henry V and for her coronation.[16] Henry VI had £1,000 on his return to England after his coronation at Paris and he received a further £1,000 on his marriage to Margaret of Anjou in 1444.[17]

[12] See M. Jurkowski, C. L. Smith and D. Crook, *Lay Taxes in England and Wales 1188–1688* (London, 1998), esp. p. xxvi.

[13] *Historical Charters and Constitutional Documents of the City of London*, ed. W. de Gray Birch (rev. edn. London,1887), 57.

[14] Jurkowski et al., *Lay Taxes*, 38.

[15] *Annales Londonienses* in *Chronicles of the Reigns of Edward I and II*, ed. W. Stubbs, 2 vols. (Rolls Series, 1882–3), i. 146; *Croniques de London depuis L'An 44 Hen. III jusqu'à l'an 17 Edw. III*, ed., G. J. Aungier (Camden Society, London, 1844), 31 and n.

[16] 6 July 1400, PRO E401/619; 7 February 1421, CLRO Journal 1 fo. 88.

[17] 21 January 1432, *LBK*, 129–30; 26 August 1444, CLRO Journal 4 fo. 39^{v}, 40, 49^{v}.

On other occasions the London citizens had to buy their charters, which might be straightforward confirmations or might incorporate substantial new privileges. The important charter of 1319 cost the citizens £1,000.[18] Richard II charged the Londoners £10,000 for the restoration of their charter in the years 1392–7 (since the rulers of London were deemed to have committed an offence in failing to keep peace in the city this was a fine as well as a sale) and the contentious new charter of 1444 cost £1,000.[19] In fact the gift offered to a new king at his coronation was simply the price to be paid for the confirmation of earlier charters.

From the 1330s onwards the negotiations between the king and the citizens of London came to be dominated by negotiations about loans. In the thirteenth century the Londoners were tallaged and, on occasion, they provided gifts but it was the Jewish community and, later, the Italian companies who provided the ready cash to finance the day-to-day costs of the household and the king's relentless military expeditions. In the early years of Edward III it was still the Italians, in particular the Bardi and the Perruzzi, who financed the king but after their bankruptcies in the 1340s the city of London began to play an increasingly large part in financing royal government.[20] Some loans were provided by the city corporately, but many more were provided by individual Londoners such as Sir John de Pulteney or the mercer Adam Fraunceys. Often groups of London merchants were associated together in providing a joint stock loan for the king. But whereas interest was payable (as it had been to the Jews and to the Italians) on these 'private' loans, those provided by the city in its corporate capacity were interest-free. These loans were provided for the king because of his 'necessity'.[21] By Richard II's reign such corporate loans had become a regular feature of royal finance. Between October 1377 and March 1388 the Londoners corporately made seven loans to the king ranging in amount from £2,000 to £5,000. The failure of the city to lend any sum to the king in the next four years may well have contributed to Richard's displeasure and seizure of the city's liberties in 1392. The Lancastrian kings borrowed steadily and desperately from the city: there were corporate loans provided by London in thirty-eight out of the sixty years of Lancastrian rule.[22] From 1429 to 1450 these loans were authorized by Parliament in anticipation of the money to be collected from Parliamentary taxation. In this way the city of London had developed into a quasi-Bank of England. The timing, and the amount, of such loans could still be matters of dispute but the Londoners were able, if they had a

[18] *Croniques*, 40; *Annales Paulini* in *Chronicles of the Reigns of Edward I and II*, ed. W. Stubbs, 2 vols. (Rolls Series, 1882–3), i. 287.

[19] C. Barron, 'The Quarrel of Richard II with London 1392–7', in F. R. H. DuBoulay and C. Barron (eds.), *The Reign of Richard II: Essays in Honour of May McKisack* (London, 1971), 173–201; 7 June 1443, PRO E401/781.

[20] The city of London made five corporate loans on three occasions to the Crown between March 1340 and June 1346, see Axworthy, 'London Merchant Community', app. A.

[21] See G. L. Harriss, 'Aids, Loans and Benevolences', *Historical Journal*, 4 (1963), 1–19.

[22] C. Barron, 'London and the Crown 1451–61' in J. R. L. Highfield and R. Jeffs (eds.), *The Crown and the Local Communities in England and France in the Fifteenth Century* (Gloucester, 1981), 88–109, esp. 102.

reasonable excuse, to refuse to lend. Between 1448 and 1460 the city refused to lend to the Crown on seven occasions although they did provide loans fourteen times in those same years. The desperate situation in France led the Crown to make unprecedented demands.

By the fifteenth century a rich London merchant might be contributing to royal finances in several different ways: he paid customs dues on the goods that he imported and exported; he contributed to Parliamentary taxation assessed on the value of his moveable goods, and he might lend money to the Crown in three ways: as an individual creditor (e.g. Richard Whittington or John Heende), as a merchant of the Calais Staple whose members also provided corporate loans, or as a citizen of London contributing to the city's corporate loans.[23] Although areas of conflict and dispute remained there is none of the bitterness that characterizes the financial relations between London and the Crown in the thirteenth century. The replacement of arbitrary royal tallage by Parliamentary taxation was the single most important factor in securing better relations between London and the Crown in the later medieval period.

But the Crown was never anxious to be dependent upon London alone for finance and this need for plurality led the Crown to encourage and protect groups of alien merchants who wished to trade and, sometimes, to live in London and in other parts of England. The Londoners resented the presence of these privileged and distinctive outsiders and, on occasion, vented their fury and prejudice upon them. In the thirteenth century the Jews were not only important royal creditors but they also paid large sums of money to be allowed to remain and to do business in English towns. The Londoners used and abused them and, as the royal dependence upon the Jews decreased, so the protection of the Crown became less effective. In the lawlessness of the mid-thirteenth century the London Jewry was frequently attacked, for example in 1262 and again two years later when the Italians and the Cahorsins were also victims.[24] On these occasions the mayor and aldermen did their best to protect the Jews from the enraged mobs, for the city's rulers were bound to the king to protect merchant strangers in their midst. In 1287 the Crown itself imposed an impossibly heavy fine on the Jews and then, in 1290, came the final expulsion.[25] The Londoners would have liked the Crown to expel all aliens but it was unlikely to do this while the aliens were willing to pay for the privilege of being allowed to stay and to trade. Moreover alien merchants paid additional customs on the goods that they imported and exported (see figures in Ch. 5) and so were particularly valuable from the point of view of the Crown. Groups of alien merchants were expected also to provide loans at short notice and

[23] For London merchants lending to the Crown as members of the Calais Staple, see D. Grummit, 'The Financial Administration of Calais during the Reign of Henry IV, 1399–1413', *EHR* 113 (1998), 277–99.

[24] *Chronicles of the Mayors and Sheriffs*, 66. 'Chronicle of Thomas Wykes', printed with the Chronicles of Oseney Abbey in *Annales Monastici*, ed. H. R. Luard (Rolls Series, 1869), iv. 141; J. Hillaby, 'London: The Thirteenth-Century Jewry Revisited', *Jewish Historical Studies: Transactions of the Jewish Historical Society of England*, 32 (1990–2), 89–158.

[25] *Chronicles of the Mayors and Sheriffs*, 96; 'Chronicle of Thomas Wykes', 308, 311.

in this way they afforded an important source of financial support and prevented the Crown from becoming exclusively dependent upon the Londoners. The sophisticated business skills both of the Jews and of the Italians, and their aloofness, caused jealousy and resentment but the king consistently turned a deaf ear to London protests. Although the role of the Italians in royal finance diminished after the bankruptcies of the 1340s it never disappeared altogether: they lent substantial sums to Richard II in the 1390s[26] and the Caniziani, as agents of the Medici, played an important part in financing royal government in the reign of Edward IV.[27] Moreover the alien share of London's overseas trade (see Ch. 5) remained very considerable even at the end of the period. In the face of royal protection the Londoners could make no headway in eroding the privileges that alien merchants enjoyed in England. For example in 1402 Henry IV agreed that Genoese merchants would not be liable to pay the local tax, known as scavage, on the goods they brought from Southampton to London for sale. The Londoners challenged and fought this decision but had, in the end, to accept a compromise drawn up in 1455 whereby the Genoese paid an annual compounded sum of £28.[28] As Lancastrian finances worsened in the 1450s the Crown began to sell licences to Italian merchants which allowed them to export wool without passing through the Staple at Calais, and this provoked violence against the Italians living in London in 1456 and 1457. The ringleaders in these orchestrated attacks seem to have been mercers and, in particular, William Cantelowe who was imprisoned by the Lancastrians but was quickly knighted by Edward IV, which suggests that there may have been a dynastic as well as an economic motive behind the violence.[29]

The merchants from the northern European countries (collectively known as the Hanse merchants) who came originally from Cologne, but by the thirteenth century included men from Hamburg and Lübeck, occupied their own fortress/ghetto in the Steelyard on the Thames. They imported fish, timber, furs, wax, wood, and, on occasion, grain, and they largely exported cloth. These merchants were crucial to the economy of London but this did not make them loved. Some of the hostility that, according to his own chronicle, Arnald fitz-Thedmar encountered in his adopted city, may well have been due to his Cologne origins.[30] The numbers of Hanse merchants living in the Steelyard at any one time were small, perhaps twenty or thirty, but they enjoyed distinctive privileges: they were allowed to have a London alderman to act on their behalf and they were free from paying local tolls on goods brought to London for sale.[31] The Londoners were

[26] Helen Bradley, 'The Italian Community in London' (University of London, Ph.D. thesis, 1992), 214–15, 456–57.

[27] George Holmes, 'Lorenzo de'Medici's London Branch', in R. Britnell and J. Hatcher (eds.), *Progress and Problems in Medieval England: Essays in Honour of Edward Miller* (Cambridge, 1996), 273–85.

[28] C. Barron, 'The Government of London and Its Relations with the Crown 1400–1450' (University of London Ph.D. thesis, 1970), 372–8.

[29] J. L. Bolton, 'The City and the Crown , 1456–61', *The London Journal*, 12 (1986), 11–24.

[30] See J. P. Huffman, *Family, Commerce and Religion in London and Cologne: Anglo-German Emigrants c.1000–c.1300* (Cambridge, 1998), 189–95.

[31] Barron, 'Government of London', 368.

quite unable to secure reciprocal privileges in Hanse towns and the English kings made little serious attempt either to help the Londoners or to diminish Hanseatic privileges in England. Henry IV confirmed their charter and Edward IV issued them with royal protections in 1461 and again in 1463.[32] In 1462 when he confirmed the city's privileges, the king specifically preserved earlier royal grants 'to merchants of Almaine'.[33] It was, in fact, in Hanseatic ships that Edward and his supporters returned to England in 1471 after his brief exile, and so it is clear that the royal policy of dividing royal favour between native and alien merchants had been a wise one. It was in the interests of the Crown to preserve alien communities as alternative sources of revenue and other support and the Londoners were impotent to prevent this counter-challenge to their economic monopoly. It was only when the English merchants began in the 1530s to take over their own export trade using their own ships that the Italian and Hanse merchants were squeezed out, not by any decline in royal favour but by shifts in the patterns of trade. Only in the sixteenth century did the privileges enjoyed by alien merchants cease to be an issue between the city and the Crown.

MILITARY AID

Money was not, however, all that the king required from London. Attention has recently been drawn to the importance of towns in providing soldiers both for the late Anglo-Saxon kings and for their Norman successors. It may be somewhat anachronistic to think of medieval towns as non-military islands in the midst of warring feudal armies. These towns, even in the comparative security of well-governed medieval England had, on occasion, to defend themselves. The military character of London in the twelfth century was probably formed by the great magnates of the realm who lived for periods of time in the city. Robert fitz-Walter, one of the leaders of the opposition to John in 1215, was the lord of Baynard's Castle which, together with Montfichet's castle, controlled access to the city from the west.[34] To what extent the Londoners expected, in the thirteenth century, to array themselves in arms to fight, other than in the defence of the city, is hard to say. In 1232 fitz-Thedmar recorded that in August the citizens of London 'mustered in arms at Mile End, and (marched) well arrayed in the London Chepe' and this may be the origin of the later Midsummer Watch.[35] It was the events of 1263 and, in particular, Louis IX's arbitration at Amiens in favour of Henry III, that brought the Londoners into the field. Thomas Puleston was chosen as constable of the city's host and Stephen Bukerel its marshal. The army sallied forth in May 1264 and met the royal troops at Lewes where the London militia broke when charged by the

[32] *CPR 1399–1401*, 57, 140; *CPR 1461–67*, 261; *LBL* 18.

[33] Birch, *Charters*, 79.

[34] Williams, *Medieval London*, 6.

[35] *Chronicles of the Mayors and Sheriffs* 7; S. Lindenbaum, 'Ceremony and Oligarchy: The London Midsummer Watch', in B. A. Hanawalt and K. L. Reyerson (eds.), *City and Spectacle in Medieval Europe* (Minneapolis, 1994), 171–88.

well-trained cavalry of Lord Edward. The Londoners fled home but their ally and leader, Simon de Montfort, remained to claim the field for the baronial opposition. His victory, it has been claimed, was bought 'with the Londoners' blood'.[36] It is possible that at Lewes Edward realized the military potential of the Londoners: certainly in his reign the city began to equip men for the king's wars rather than simply to supply money. In 1276–7 the city provided a hundred arblasters for the wars in Wales,[37] but it seems to have been Edward II who particularly exploited this form of royal pressure: in 1317 the Londoners sent two hundred men-at-arms for the Scottish campaign and a further hundred men four years later.[38] In the autumn of 1321 Edward attempted to formalize the military obligations of the Londoners and the mayor, Hamo de Chigwell, was obliged to offer five hundred men to join the army sent to crush the rebellious Bartholomew Badlesmere at Ledes castle in Kent.[39] These military demands were deeply resented by the Londoners and Edward, in an unusually placatory gesture, wrote to the citizens in December 1321 to thank them and to assure them that the provision of armed footmen, 'so thankfully done, shall not be prejudicial to the said mayor and good men, their heirs and successors'.[40] But it is clear that Edward's demand for military help in 1321 (perhaps especially resented because the troops were not to be used against an external threat but, in effect, for faction fighting) certainly contributed to the Londoners' support for Isabella and Mortimer in 1326. In the new charter which the Londoners received in March 1327 it was conceded by the new king that the citizens should 'not be compelled to go or send to war out of the city'.[41] In the future kings might ask for military support but the Londoners were not obliged to provide it. The city certainly raised contingents to fight with Edward III's contract armies in France, but the increased professionalism of these armies may have discouraged the enthusiastic part-time London soldier. It is possible that the city was also developing its own non-militaristic ethos. Few London aldermen in the fourteenth century sought (or were offered) knighthoods while they were aldermen. In June 1381 the mayor and aldermen made an unimpressive military showing and when, in November 1387, Richard II asked the mayor of London what military help the city could supply in Richard's forthcoming struggle with the Appellant lords, the mayor Nicholas Exton and his fellow aldermen replied 'that the inhabitants of the city were in the main craftsmen and merchants, with no great military

[36] Williams, *Medieval London*, 225; *Chronicles of the Mayors and Sheriffs*, 66.

[37] *Croniques de London*, 14.

[38] *The Great Chronicle of London*, ed. A. H. Thomas and I. D. Thornley (London, 1938), 28; *Croniques de London*, 45.

[39] *Annales Paulini*, 298–300, where the rates of pay offered to the soldiers are recorded: 8*d*. for a 'balistarius', 6*d*. for an archer, 24*d*. for a knight, and 12*d*. for an esquire; Williams, *Medieval London*, 298–9; the French chronicle also describes these events and records that the Londoners had earlier in the year sent 380 men to the king at Worcester: *Croniques de London*, 42–5.

[40] Birch, *Charters*, 51; but it should be noted that in 1324–5 the Londoners sent 140 'hommes armez' to fight in Gascony: *Croniques de London*, 48.

[41] Birch, *Charters*, 55. Almost immediately after the granting of this charter, the city sent 100 well-armed men to fight against the Scots, 'but for shame, they did no good there and returned without honour': *Annales Paulini*, 333.

experience, and it was not permissible for them to devote themselves to warfare save for the defence of the city alone'.[42] On the whole the citizens confined their support for military ventures to the financial sphere but on occasion they did raise troops themselves. In 1436 when Calais was threatened by the duke of Burgundy the Londoners raised a hasty army and in 1449 they again provided 319 archers and 43 lancers to protect the town from the rapidly advancing French armies. Two years later a London contingent of some two hundred men was sent to Calais under the command of Sir Thomas Fyndern.[43] After the drift into civil war in the middle of the fifteenth century the Londoners tried hard to remain neutral and to avoid sending armed citizens to fight on either side. When in July 1460 the mayor and aldermen committed the city to the Yorkist cause by admitting their leaders into the city, they had a vested interest in a Yorkist victory. A contingent of Londoners, led by the mercer John Harowe, marched north to be defeated with York at Wakefield in December 1460: their second away defeat in two hundred years.[44] In 1471, however, the citizens effectively held the city for Edward IV against the challenge of the Lancastrian supporter Fauconberg and some real military skill was required to defend the city from his attack.[45] By the end of this period it is clear that the Londoners were not anxious to pay for the king's wars but they were even less eager to fight in them. For the aristocracy and the knightly classes fighting was a way of life, perhaps their *only* way of life, but the Londoners knew of other, and easier, ways of making a living and they tacitly accepted the need to pay someone else to do the fighting.

CIVIC PAGEANTRY FOR ROYAL OCCASIONS

The Crown had another use for the wealth and craftsmanship of the Londoners: it needed the city to provide impressive receptions for foreign visitors which would enhance the king's prestige and, at the same time, remind the Londoners of the authority and grandeur of their monarch. These welcome pageants might also be enjoyable, both for the participants and for the crowds lining the streets who might take time off work to admire the magnificence of others, and to scoop up some of the free wine. The first recorded royal reception in London appears to be the welcome provided for Eleanor of Provence in 1236 when she came to England for her coronation. The historian John Stow, writing at the end of the sixteenth century, provides a description of the festivities (although his source is unknown):

> the citie was adorned with silkes, and in the night with many pageants, and straunge devices there presented, the citizens also rode to meet the King and Queene, clothed in long gar-

[42] *The Westminster Chronicle 1381–1394*, ed. L. C. Hector and B. F. Harvey (Oxford, 1982), 217.

[43] C. Barron, 'Chivalry, Pageantry and Merchant Culture in Medieval London', in P. Coss and M. Keen (eds.), *Heraldry, Pageantry and Social Display in Medieval England* (Woodbridge, 2002), 219–41, esp. 227.

[44] Barron, 'London and the Crown', 98.

[45] C. F. Richmond, 'Fauconberg's Kentish Rising of May 1471', *EHR* 85 (1970), 673–92.

ments embrodered about with gold, and silks of diverse colours, their horses gallantly trapped to the number of 360, every man bearing a cup of gold or silver in his hand, and the kings trumpetters sounding before them: these citizens did minister wine, as Bottelers, which is their service at the coronation.[46]

When Eleanor of Castille came to England as the new bride of Prince Edward in June 1255 the citizens joined the king in going out of the city to meet her and 'the city of London was most nobly tapestried and arrayed'.[47] The hanging-out of tapestries seems to have become a characteristic feature of these thirteenth-century celebrations.[48] The preparations for the coronation of Edward I in 1274 appear to have been particularly elaborate: for the first time it was recorded that the conduit in Chepe flowed with red and white wine for all to drink.[49] When Queen Margaret came from France for her coronation in 1299 the mayor and aldermen rode out to meet her dressed in a common livery and 300 citizens also wore matching outfits. There were two wooden towers set up in Cheapside, each with eight spouts for the free flowing of wine, and the street was covered with cloths of gold.[50]

As time went on the receptions became more ambitious and elaborate and pageants were added to the festivities. When the city celebrated Edward I's victory over the Scots in 1298 there were several pageants including a remarkable one provided by the fishmongers: four silver-gilt sturgeons were borne aloft on four horses and they were followed by four silver salmons also carried on horses followed by forty-six knights riding on luces (sea-pikes), followed by St Magnus.[51] Andrew Horn, the city chamberlain, in writing about the reception for Edward II and his new bride Isabella of France, described the city as the 'new Jerusalem' and noted that the mayor, aldermen, and citizens displayed the arms of England and France on their liveries.[52] When the Londoners learned of the birth of the future Edward III on 13 November 1312 they took to the streets singing and the fishmongers again prepared a magnificent pageant in which a ship in full sail, bearing the arms of England and France, was carried through the streets of the city in front of the royal couple who were then accompanied back to Eltham with more singing and dancing.[53] Thus by the early fourteenth century all the customary elements in a royal 'entry' were already present: the mayor, aldermen, and citizens in special clothing;

[46] John Stow, *A Survey of London*, ed. C. L. Kingsford, 2 vols. (Oxford, 1908), i. 95.

[47] *Chronicles of the Mayors and Sheriffs*, 24.

[48] November 1255, Lord Edward welcomed to London; August 1256, king and queen of Scotland welcomed at London; February 1258, the king of Almaine to London: ibid. 25, 43–4.

[49] A detailed description of the preparations for the coronation at Westminster palace forms the last entry in fitz-Thedmar's chronicle: he died the next year: *ibid.* 178; 'Chronicle of Thomas Wykes', 259; *Croniques de London*, 13; see also D. Keene, 'London from the Post-Roman Period to 1300', in D. Palliser (ed.), *Cambridge Urban History of Britain* (Cambridge, 2000), 187–216, esp. 213–14.

[50] *Chronicles of the Mayors and Sheriffs*, 220.

[51] Stow, *Survey*, i, 95–6; the presence of St Magnus is explained by the fact that the celebrations took place on his feast day, 19 August. The church of St Magnus at the north end of London bridge was in the centre of the fishmongers' area. It is also possible that St Magnus's Scottish associations made him a particularly suitable saint to preside over festivities to celebrate a victory over the Scots.

[52] *Annales Londonienses*, 152.

[53] Ibid. 221; Riley, *Memorials*, 105–7.

a procession that included singing; the houses in the city hung with tapestries; the conduits flowing with wine and elaborate pageants appropriate to the particular person or occasion to be celebrated.

It is possible that there were written contemporary accounts of these celebrations that were circulated as early as the thirteenth century, and it may be something of this kind that Stow used for his account of the reception of Eleanor in 1236. It is clear that Thomas Walsingham had a written account of the coronation celebrations for Richard II in 1377 in which the conduit in Cheapside was transformed into the Heavenly City peopled by virgins and angels who scattered gold leaves and coins (presumably in limited quantities) and offered the king a golden crown and a cup of wine from the conduit.[54] This is also the first time that actors are recorded as taking part in these pageants, but it is not clear whether the king, or indeed the virgins, spoke. But in the elaborate reconciliation celebrations that marked the end of Richard II's quarrel with the city of London, the king and the queen certainly spoke and it seems clear that there was a newsletter account of the festivities as well as an elaborate Latin poem written by Richard of Maidstone describing all the four pageants and the royal response to them. This may have been commissioned by the king, but it is more likely that the Londoners paid for the verse account.[55]

In the fifteenth century civic receptions for the monarch at coronations and marriages or following victories abroad became quite commonplace and, to some extent, standardized. Elaborate accounts of the pageants and their meanings were circulated after the events and then found their way into contemporary chronicles. Moreover, the information from the chroniclers can now be augmented by traces of discussion and expenditure recorded in the city's own records. The magnificent reception offered to Henry V on his return from Agincourt is described in detail in the *Gesta Henrici Quinti* and noted in the accounts of the Bridgewardens who paid nearly £20 to decorate the Bridge with an antelope, a lion, St George, singing angels, and the figure of a giant 'to teach Frenchmen curtesy'.[56] The accounts of the Grocers' Company record payments of nearly £3 towards the costs of the minstrels who met the king 'at his coming out of France'.[57]

Perhaps the most detailed accounts have survived for the 'joyous entry' devised to welcome Henry VI in 1432 on his return from his coronation in Paris, where the apathy had been deafening. To ensure that the London reception was suitably

[54] [Thomas Walsingham], *Chronicon Anglie 1328–1388*, ed. E. M. Thompson (Rolls Series, 1874), 153–6.

[55] Richard of Maidstone's poem is printed in *Political Poems and Songs*, ed. T. Wright, 2 vols. (Rolls Series, 1859–61), i. 282–300; it is partially translated in E. Rickert, *Chaucer's World* (Oxford, 1948), 35–9; see also C. Barron, 'Richard II and London', in A. Goodman and J. Gillespie (eds.), *Richard II: The Art of Kingship* (Oxford, 1999), 129–54, esp. 152–3.

[56] *Gesta Henrici Quinti*, ed. F. Taylor and J. S. Roskell (Oxford, 1975), pp. xxxvii, 101–13. Lydgate's poetic account of the same event is printed ibid., 191–2; CLRO, Bridge House Accounts, ii. fo. 171; see Vanessa Harding, 'Pageantry on London Bridge', in B. Watson, T. Brigham and A. Dyson, *London Bridge: 2000 Years of a River Crossing* (London, 2001), 114–15.

[57] *Facsimile Account of the First Volume of the Ms Archives of the Worshipful Company of Grocers of the City of London 1345–1463*, ed. J. A. Kingdon, 2 vols. (London, 1886), i. fo. 115.

triumphant, the poet laureate, John Lydgate, was employed to write a long verse account of the 'Triumphal Entry' which, it has been justly said, provides a sharp test for 'the flexibility of our concept of poetry'.[58] It is likely that Lydgate was employed by the city to memorialize this elaborate series of seven pageants and so his poem is, in effect, a 'souvenir programme'.[59] But, the deviser of the series of pageants was, probably, the city's common clerk, John Carpenter, a learned man with an extensive library. Carpenter wrote his own, less lengthy, account of the pageants and procession, which he entered in the city's letter book.[60] Whereas the reception for Henry V in 1415 was religious in tone and liturgical in form, that for his son adopted a more didactic style, offering the young king instructions on the duties and attributes of the good ruler. The change of tone may be a response to the youth of the king, but it may also owe something to Carpenter, the learned and serious-minded common clerk. What is striking, however, is that on neither occasion is there any reference to chivalric heroes, or to figures from the popular tales of romance. The first London welcome to incorporate heroes from chivalric literature was that offered to Katherine of Aragon in 1501 when, in allusion to her intended husand, King Arthur featured prominently.[61]

What is also striking about the London shows is the extent to which they were literate: the pageants were provided with explanatory texts, which the king and bystanders were expected to be able to read 'withoute a spectacle'.[62] In addition to these visible explanatory captions, speech was used extensively from at least 1445 when Margaret of Anjou was welcomed to London with a series of pageants at each of which she was addressed in a manner both ingratiating and bossy. Whether she replied is not recorded.[63] What is also clear is that by the fifteenth century these elaborate pageants were neither spontaneous offerings to the Crown, nor were they voluntary. The citizens might attempt to haggle over the size of the gift offered during the welcome, or they might try to limit the number of pageants, but they were unable to avoid providing such festivities. Whereas in the fourteenth century London had provided such celebrations roughly every seven years, by the fifteenth century the demands came more frequently, about every five years. Although such welcomes were expensive (the pageants for Margaret of Anjou cost 500 marks and the citizens also had to offer her a gift of £1,000)[64] yet the building of the pageants, supplying the costumes and the liveries, the food and drink, the provision of tapestries and other hanging cloths, the fashioning of the gold and silver-gilt presents

[58] D. Pearsall, *John Lydgate* (Charlottesville, Va., 1970), 171. The poem is printed in *Great Chronicle*, 156–70. Lydgate based his poem on a Latin prose account written by John Carpenter, see Henry N. MacCracken, 'King Henry's Triumphal Entry into London: Lydgate's Poem and Carpenter's Letter', *Archiv für das Studium der neuren Sprachen und Literaturen*, 126 (1911), 75–102.

[59] Pearsall, *Lydgate*, 171.

[60] *LBK*, 138.

[61] S. Anglo, 'The London Pageants for the Reception of Katherine of Aragon in 1501', *Journal of the Warburg and Courtauld Institutes*, 26 (1963), 53–89.

[62] *Great Chronicle*, 163.

[63] G. Kipling, 'The London Pageants for Margaret of Anjou: A Medieval Script Restored', *Medieval English Theatre* (1982), 5–27.

[64] CLRO, Journal 4 fos. 44, 49^{v}.

for the honorands and the business generated for inns, taverns, and cookshops (not forgetting the scriveners, albeit not the spectacle-makers) must have gone some way towards compensating the citizens for the taxation involved. Indeed it could be argued that the frequent royal demands for pageants and processions eliminated the need in London for the kind of play festivals devised at York or Coventry or Chester to attract visitors and customers. In London the king called the tune, the city paid, and the crowds came.

Royal entries, victory processions, and marriages were occasions when the London craftsmen could display their wares to the king, the court, the aristocracy, country gentry, and foreign visitors. Much of the money raised by taxation in London found its way back into the pockets of London merchant suppliers and craftsmen. Many of the mayors of the thirteenth century who led the city in opposition to the payment of tallage were those who sold goods on a large scale to the royal household. Adam de Basing (mayor 1251–2) was 'an outstanding supplier of costly fabrics and luxury goods' to the royal household; John Gisors (mayor 1246, 1258–9) was a vintner whose wine 'flowed into the royal cellars', and the immigrant Henry le Waleys from Gascony (mayor 1273–4, 1281–4, 1298–9) sold wine to the average value of £300 a year to the royal household.[65] Richard II, who extracted some £30,000 from the Londoners in 1392, spent £13,000 on purchases for the Great Wardrobe in 1392–4, and almost all the goods were supplied by London merchants and craftsmen.[66] Kings and royal courtiers travelled abroad and developed sophisticated tastes for foreign luxuries and skills. If the king could not find among the Londoners the skilled craftsmen he needed, then he would encourage alien craftsmen to come to London and set up workshops in the city. Henry III brought craftsmen from the Cosmati workshop in Rome to work on the floor of Westminster Abbey, on the shrine of Edward the Confessor, and on his own tomb there.[67] Richard II encouraged Baldwin of Lucca to come to England to weave gold cloths[68] and Andronicus and Alexius Effomatus from Constantinople were allowed by Henry VI to remain in England in 1445 in order to practise their craft of making 'damask gold' or gold wire for embroidery.[69] The Crown needed the city of London to provide the skilled craftsmen and merchants who could create a magnificent and impressive royal court. In this area at least the needs of the Crown met an eager response from the Londoners, although it must be remembered that whereas all citizens contributed to royal taxation, not all benefited from royal patronage.

[65] Williams, *Medieval London*, 69, 72–3, 323–5, 333.

[66] PRO E101/402/13.

[67] P. Binski, *Westminster Abbey and the Plantagenets: Kingship and the Representation of Power 1200–1400* (New Haven, Conn., 1995), 93–104.

[68] L. Monnas, 'Fit for a King: Figured Silks shown in the Wilton Diptych', in D. Gordon, L. Monnas, and C. Elam (eds.), *The Regal Image of Richard II and the Wilton Diptych* (London, 1997), 165–77 esp. 171–2.

[69] J. Harris, 'Two Byzantine Craftsmen in Fifteenth-Century London', *Journal of Medieval History*, 21 (1995), 387–403.

A HEALTHY AND PEACEFUL CITY

If the king was to process through the city and to show it off to foreign visitors such as the Byzantine Emperor Manuel who came in 1402 or the Emperor Sigismund who visited Henry V in 1416, then it was important that London should look impressive and, in particular, that it should be clean.[70] In 1274 the mayor, Henry le Waleys, swept the butchers' and fishmongers' stalls out of Cheapside 'in order that that no refuse might be found remaining in Chepe on the arrival of his lordship the King'.[71] The rights of the ousted victuallers were voiced by Walter Hervi but, after 'wordy strife', le Waleys finally disposed of the popular champion.[72] Le Waleys was right: kings disliked dirty and smelly cities and Cheapside was the city's main processional way. The Black Death of 1348–9 heightened the awareness of the link between dirt and disease and the city appears to have taken serious steps to improve civic hygiene.[73] But by the later fourteenth century, as the standard of living rose and more fresh meat was consumed, so the health hazards posed by urban butchering became more acute. In 1369 Edward III sent a fierce writ to the Londoners complaining about the 'grievous corruption and filth' which arose in the city streets from discarded butcher's waste. The king demanded that beasts should be slaughtered outside the city at Knightsbridge or Stratford. Since this would have been difficult to implement and would certainly have led to a rise in prices, the mayor and aldermen prevaricated and their sloth in this matter may have been one of the many 'defaults' that led Richard II to seize the liberties of the city in 1392.[74] The city may well have taken this royal reprimand to heart because there seem to have been no royal complaints about dirt in London in the fifteenth century and there is considerable evidence of communal concern about street cleaning and public health.

Dirt may have been a hazard, but lawlessness was an even greater one. By his oath the mayor undertook to hold the city peaceably for the king and the taking of the city into the king's hand both in 1285 and again in 1392 was provoked by the unchecked lawlessness and violence on the streets of London. In the thirteenth century the assembling of the folkmoot in St Paul's churchyard was often the start of civic riot and disorder. In June 1285 the king ordered the dean and canons to enclose the area around the cathedral and incorporate it into the churchyard. This marked the beginning of the end of the folkmoot.[75] A certain amount of violence was acceptable but the mayor had to be able to establish his control and when he failed to do this the king would intervene. In 1267 a dispute between the goldsmiths and the tailors escalated into three nights of street fighting. The sheriffs imprisoned

[70] For a more detailed discussion of this, see Ch. 10.

[71] *Chronicles of the Mayors and Sheriffs*, 73.

[72] Le Waleys later created the Stocks market in 1283 at the east end of Cheapside as a place where butchers and fishmongers could sell their wares: Williams, *Medieval London*, 86–7; see Ch. 3.

[73] See Ch. 10.

[74] Riley, *Memorials*, 339, 356–8; Barron, 'Richard II and London', 143–4.

[75] *Liber Custumarum*, 338–46; Williams, *Medieval London*, 254.

thirty of the rioters and then brought them before the royal justiciar. Local juries declared that a number of the men had taken part in the riots and they were 'immediately hanged'. Fitz-Thedmar who described these events was shocked by the rioting but he was also taken aback at the severity of the punishment, for none of the men had actually been convicted of homicide, mayhem, or robbery and one of them had done no more than allow his house to be used by some of the rioters. But fitz-Thedmar acknowledged that this was done 'so that others, put in awe thereby, might take warning, so that the peace of his lordship the king by all within the city might be the more rigidly maintained'.[76]

A hundred years later, when craft rivalries reached fever pitch at the mayoral election in 1383, the supporters of the defeated candidate John de Northampton took to the streets. John Constantine, a cordwainer, urged the citizens to close their shops and rise in support of Northampton. He was brought to a summary trial and executed, and his head was displayed on Newgate. The author of the *Westminster Chronicle*, like fitz-Thedmar before him, was shocked at the severity of the punishment and noted that Constantine had been a man of godly life.[77] Richard supported the mayor in the measures which he took to keep the peace and prevent riots. It was in the interests of the Crown that the mayor and sheriffs should keep London under control: when the mayor, Simon de Swanlond, and the twenty-four aldermen were summoned to Woodstock in 1330 it was because the king wished to speak 'super pacem civitatis' and the Londoners assured the king that they would safeguard and hold the city for him.[78] Although Richard II took the city into his own hands for some months in 1392, on the whole the mayor and aldermen were able to keep the city peaceably for the king. There were no more great inquiries into the government and administration of justice in the city as had been held in 1321 and, after the 1380s, craft rivalries were contained and controlled. The artisan protesters of the 1430s and 1440s never posed a threat to mayoral control comparable to that of the 1380s (in part because, in the 1440s, the aldermen were not divided).[79] But the mayor and sheriffs had to be constantly vigilant to curb rioting before it got out of hand. The aristocratic rivalries of the 1450s certainly made their task more difficult, but they succeeded in avoiding the seizure of the city's liberties.[80] The evolution of responsible craft and trading companies with their own structures of authority may have helped in the maintenance of civic order.[81] In this matter the demands of the king were persistent and inescapable and so the maintenance of peace in London became crucial to the self-government of the city.

[76] *Chronicles of the Mayors and Sheriffs*, 105.

[77] *Westminster Chronicle*, 65; *LBH*, 231; *Memorials*, 482–3; *CPMR 1381–1412*, 50–1; *CPR 1381–85*, 391; Barron, 'Richard II and London', 146–7.

[78] *Annales Londonienses*, 251.

[79] C. Barron, 'Ralph Holland and the London Radicals, 1438–1444' in R. Holt and G. Rosser (eds.), *The English Medieval Town: A Reader in English Urban History 1200–1540* (London, 1990), 160–83.

[80] Barron, 'London and the Crown', esp. 94–5.

[81] See Ch. 9.

PATRONAGE

In the later medieval period the Crown made new demands upon the city: patronage and legitimation. The Crown sought patronage, in the form of appointments to civic offices, as an extra source of income. In the fourteenth century the king had occasionally sought to secure offices in London for members of his household but from the 1430s the pressure on the city mounted. In the first place the king sought the freedom of the city for servants in his household so that they might be able to buy goods easily and cheaply in the city. Since 1319 the control of entry to the freedom had lain with the city crafts but in the fifteenth century the king presented his servants to Common Council so that they might persuade a suitable company to sponsor them.[82] In 1437 Thomas Brown of the royal larder was admitted to the freedom as a chandler and John Elyngham, a royal valet, as a pinner.[83] Further requests for enfranchisement followed and were usually agreed.[84] Henry VI and his queen also wrote to the city to seek civic offices, usually comparatively minor ones, for their nominees. Robert Watson in 1440 was given the office of rent-collector of London Bridge at the king's request but the city was able to refuse the queen's demand in 1450 that Alexander Manning should be reinstated as warden of Newgate prison.[85] The mayor and aldermen were also able to reject the queen's nominee for the office of common serjeant and chose Thomas Urswyk instead.[86] Again in August 1461 the city was able to reject Edward IV's candidate for the office of common clerk and selected instead the able and industrious William Dunthorne.[87] Royal demands of this kind were growing in number and although the city was largely able to maintain its independence of action, the pressure was to mount under the Tudors.

But there was a further twist to royal inventiveness: again it was in the 1430s that the minority government of Henry VI developed the idea of creating and selling monopolistic offices in the city. The offices of gauger of wines, garbeller of spices, packer of cloths, and drawers of wine were created and sold to royal servants, creditors and job-seekers. Such officers were empowered to charge what they liked for carrying out inescapable services for merchants. In the fourteenth century the charge for gauging a tun of wine had been a penny; now, following the sale of the office of gauger to Thomas Multon in 1432, it had risen to fourpence. The governors of the city struggled ineffectively to regain control of these offices. Edward IV at first offered the citizens simply the disposal of the offices for the next six years, then during royal pleasure, and, finally, in 1478 when he was deeply in debt to the Londoners, he sold the disposal of these four disputed offices to the city in

[82] See Ch. 6.

[83] CLRO, Journal 3 fo.188.

[84] Barron, 'The Government of London', 464–5.

[85] *LBK*, 238; CLRO, Journal 4 fo.172; Journal 5, f. 16, 48, 51; *Letters of Queen Margaret of Anjou, Bishop Beckington and others*, ed. C. Munro (Camden Series, 86, 1863), 161–2.

[86] CLRO, Journal 5 fos. 112^{v}–113^{v}.

[87] Ibid. 6 fos. 46, 22^{v}, 7^{v}.

perpetuity.[88] But as one monopoly was recaptured, another was devised and the Lancastrian experiments were to bear fruit later, for the royal appetite for patronage was to prove voracious and the city, with its great wealth and ever-growing bureaucracy, proved to be a source of easy pickings. On the other hand the Londoners, who had fought since the twelfth century for self-government, were unwilling to see even the least of the city offices slip out of civic control.

LEGITIMATION

Several medieval English kings needed the help of the Londoners in order to make their rule legitimate and acceptable. In the mid-twelfth century the Londoners claimed that they had the right to elect the monarch and in 1135 they chose Stephen as king.[89] The proximity of Westminster, the usual place of coronation for English kings, tended to reinforce this claim. But the development of primogeniture diminished the role played by election: the Londoners might recognize and accept a new king but they did not choose him. By the fourteenth century sons succeeded fathers as kings of England and the Londoners were largely onlookers. In 1326, however, Isabella and Mortimer realized that if they were to be able to depose Edward II in favour of his son they would need the moral, as well as the physical, support of the Londoners. Isabella sent letters to the commons of London asking them to assist in the destruction of the king's enemies (i.e. the Despensers) and these letters were posted on the Cross in Cheapside and elsewhere in the city.[90] After a mob of Londoners had murdered Bishop Stapledon of Exeter on 15 October 1326 the city was fully committed to the deposition of the king. The Londoners, led by Richard de Betoyne (Bethune) who was elected mayor in November in place of the 'royalist' Hamo de Chigwell, together with John de Gisors, an alderman of twenty years' standing and an ex-mayor, played a leading role in the Parliament that met at Westminster on 7 January 1327.[91] When those summoned to Parliament seemed uncertain what course to take, Betoyne sent them an ultimatum: were they willing to join the city in the deposition of the king? On the morning of 13 January the lords rode to Guildhall and were there sworn by the mayor and the chamberlain of the city Andrew Horn, to stand by Isabella, queen of England and her son Edward, heir apparent, against the Despensers and Robert Baldock, to aid them with good counsel and to protect the liberties of

[88] Barron, 'London and the Crown', 99.

[89] C. N. L. Brooke with G. Keir, *London 800–1216: The Shaping of a City* (London, 1975), 84–5; M. McKisack, 'London and the Succession to the Crown during the Middle Ages', in R. W. Hunt, W. A. Pantin, and R. W. Southern (eds.), *Studies in Medieval History Presented to F. M. Powicke* (Oxford, 1948), 76–89.

[90] *Croniques de London*, 51–2; *Annales Paulini*, 315; *The Anonimalle Chronicle 1307–1334*, eds., W. R. Childs and J. Taylor (Yorkshire Archaeological Society, 1991), 122–35; for Isabella's letters, see *CPMR 1323–64*, 41–2; for a helpful discussion of the events of 1326–7, see Claire Valente, 'The Deposition and Abdication of Edward II', *EHR* 113 (1998), 852–81, esp. 853–62.

[91] Williams, *Medieval London*, 297–9.

London.[92] In the afternoon in Parliament those assembled agreed to replace Edward with his son and to send a deputation to the king of Kenilworth in which John de Gisors was a prominent member. Edward was persuaded to abdicate in favour of his son 'by the clamour of the whole people' but, as has been pointed out, 'that clamour had a distinct London accent'.[93] Without the support of the Londoners it would have been much more difficult for Edward III to be made king. Not only did the Londoners organize the physical attacks on the Despensers and their supporters, but they also played a role in devising the means to depose the king and to justify the election of his son. It was their actions that made the partisan victory of Isabella and Mortimer appear as an expression of the common will.[94]

The role played by the Londoners in 1399 was no less crucial, but they were not the instigators of Richard's deposition; only after Henry Bolingbroke had been in England for six weeks did the Londoners send a deputation to Chester to renounce their allegiance to Richard and confirm their acceptance of Henry as king.[95] There is no account of the events in London in the autumn of 1399 comparable to that in the *Annales Paulini* describing what happened in 1326. It is clear, however, that once the citizens had decided to support Henry Bolingbroke they did so wholeheartedly and gave him counsel, service in his first Parliament, and cheering crowds for his importunate coronation. The prior of St Botolph's, Colchester, sourly remarked that Henry was only made king by the rabble of London.[96]

But the Londoners were losing their taste for kingmaking. In the 1450s the citizens were reluctant to play a partisan role and their cautious neutrality is in marked contrast to their proactive role in 1326. But just as the murder of Stapledon was decisive in committing the city to the cause of Isabella, so the entry of the Yorkist lords into London on 1 July 1460 converted the city's ineffective neutrality into partisan support. The Londoners in the next nine months supplied loans totalling an unprecedented £11,000, they sent troops to fight with the duke of York at Wakefield in December 1460, and in March 1461 they joined with the retinues of the earls of March and Warwick to proclaim Edward of York king at Clerkenwell fields. Three days later they played their accustomed roles at the coronation of the new king.[97] In so far as they had the power to do so, the Londoners helped Edward to be a *de iure* as well as a *de facto* king.

92 *Annales Paulini*, 323; *CPMR 1328–1364*, 11–12. It is possible that Thomas, Lord Wake and John Stratford, bishop of Winchester, both supporters of Isabella, for political reasons contributed generously at Christmas 1326 to the repair of Guildhall chapel, see Riley, *Memorials*, 152.

93 Williams, *Medieval London*, 298. The Londoners have been characterized as 'junior partners' in these events, which may be true, but their corporate threat of street violence must have been significant, and they certainly secured some important privileges in their new charter in 1327: P. Nightingale, *A Medieval Mercantile Community: The Grocers' Company and the Politics and Trade of London 1000–1485* (New Haven, Conn., 1995), 157.

94 I am grateful to Anthony Moore for letting me read his unpublished Cambridge M.Phil. essay on 'London and the Crown in the Reign of Edward II, with Special Reference to the Period 1319–27'.

95 C. Barron, 'The Deposition of Richard II', in J. Taylor and W. Childs (eds.), *Politics and Crisis in Fourteenth-Century England* (Gloucester, 1990), 132–49, esp. 139–42.

96 J. H. Wylie, *Henry IV* (London, 1884), i. 420.

97 Barron, 'London and the Crown', 98–9.

In 1483 the Londoners appear to have acquiesced in Richard's usurpation: following the death of Edward IV on 9 April the mayor Edmund Shaa and the aldermen made the customary preparations for the coronation of his son Edward V but seem to have made no protest when Gloucester ambushed the young king and postponed the coronation.[98] Gloucester had no particular following in the city and he took steps to strengthen his case. Mayor Shaa provided his brother Dr Ralph Shaa, who conveniently preached at Paul's Cross on 22 June propounding the view not only that Edward IV's children were illegitimate because of the king's prior contract of marriage, but also that Edward himself was illegitimate. Two days later the duke of Buckingham appears to have been sent to Guildhall to point out the same disqualifying circumstances and to urge the undoubted virtues of the duke of Gloucester: a scene made famous by Shakespeare and in which the role of the mayor of London is far from heroic. On 26 June in response to a petition from the lords and commons, Richard accepted the crown and two days later the common council of London agreed to give the new king and his queen Anne a coronation gift of £1,000. The events of the summer of 1483 reveal that Richard was anxious to win the support of the citizens and took trouble to manipulate public opinion. The mayor and aldermen went along with Richard's usurpation but the London citizens refrained from spontaneous enthusiasm for Buckingham's speech on 24 June.[99] It seems unlikely that many Londoners believed in the legitimacy of Richard's takeover but they were prepared to acquiesce since they could see that there were advantages in having a strong ruler rather than a young boy. Edmund Shaa seems to have led the Londoners in a passive, if inglorious, role in the making of Richard III. The new king remained anxious about his reputation in the city and when, after the death of his wife Anne, it was bruited about in the city that he had murdered her in order to marry his niece Elizabeth (daughter of Edward IV and future wife of Henry VII), Richard took the unprecedented step of summoning the mayor and aldermen to meet him in the Priory of St John at Clerkenwell on 30 March 1485. He then asserted that

> It never came in his thought or mynde to marry in suche maner wise nor willyng or glad of the dethe of his quene but as sorye & in hert as hevye as man myght be, with muche more in the premyses spoken, for the whiche he then monysshed & charged every parson to ceas of suche untrue talkyng on parell of his indignacion.[100]

That Richard should have demeaned himself to make such a public protestation is suggestive of the perceived importance of a good political reputation in the city of London. Although Henry VII was also a usurper, he had the advantage of having only a dead, and not a living, predecessor. Following Henry's victory at Bosworth

[98] The best account of the events of 9 April to 13 July 1383, which includes the London material, is to be found in A. Sutton and P. Hammond (eds.) *The Coronation of Richard III* (Gloucester, 1983), 13–29.

[99] One author commented that a small number cried 'ye ye', more out of fear than love, *Great Chronicle*, 232.

[100] *Acts of Court of the Mercers' Company 1453–1527*, ed. L. Lyell and F. D. Watney (Cambridge, 1936), 173–4.

on 22 August, the mayor and aldermen had little difficulty in deciding to send a deputation northwards to greet king Henry and he was welcomed into the city in triumph early in September.[101] The first Tudor king owed little of his success to the support of London: the great age of the city as kingmaker was past.

[101] CLRO, Journal 9 fos. 85^{v}–87; D. J. Guth, 'Richard III, Henry VII and the City: London Politics and the "Dun Cow"', in R. A. Griffiths and J. Sherborne (eds.), *Kings and Nobles in the Later Middle Ages: A Tribute to Charles Ross* (Gloucester, 1986), 185–99.

CHAPTER TWO

The Needs of the City

It is not difficult to assess what the citizens required from the Crown because their desiderata were regularly catalogued in the series of charters that they were able to extract from kings throughout the period. It seems reasonable to assume that the primary concern of the Londoners was well expressed in the charter (or more properly, the writ) that they won from William the Conqueror early in his reign. By this grant the 'burgesses within London' were assured that 'every child shall be his father's heir, after his father's days'.[1] This meant that the succession to land and tenements in the city would not be subject to arbitrary royal intervention. In the medieval period the freedom of London citizens to bequeath their London property as they wished was never seriously challenged by the Crown, although in the thirteenth century there were test cases in which the nature and extent of the city's jurisdiction over wills were contested and refined.[2]

SELF-GOVERNMENT AND FREE ELECTION OF CITY OFFICERS

The city's main concern in the thirteenth century, and that which was most contested, was to maintain the right secured by charter from Henry I to elect its own sheriffs for London and Middlesex who were answerable directly to the Exchequer for the city's annual farm (or tax) of £300; and also the more recent grant made to the Londoners by John, probably under duress in May 1215, of the right to elect the city's mayor.[3] In 1227 Henry III confirmed both these rights for the Londoners: the mayor might remain in office at the end of a year or he could be re-elected for a further term at the will of the citizens. The king stipulated that the new, or re-elected, mayor was to be presented to him each year on his taking up office and, in the absence of the king, to his justices and he was to swear 'to be faithful to us'.[4] In 1253 the king agreed that the mayor might be presented to the barons of the

[1] W. de Gray Birch (ed.), *The Historical Charters and Constitutional Documents of the City of London* (rev. edn., London, 1887), 1; *Regesta Regum Anglo-Normannorum: The Acta of William I (1066–1087)*, ed. D. Bates (Oxford, 1998), 593, n. 180.

[2] See the case of Margery Viel in 1247, the right of the city to probate wills in 1258, the city's jurisdiction *vis à vis* that of the bishop of London in 1267: *Chronicles of the Mayors and Sheriffs of London, A.D. 1189 to A.D. 1274*, ed. and trans. H. T. Riley (London, 1863), 14, 44, 111; problems relating to intestacy in 1309–10, *Croniques de London depuis L'An 44 Hen.III jusqu'à l'an 17 Edw.III*, ed. G. Aungier (Camden Society, 1844), 35.

[3] Birch, *Charters*, 15, 19, 21.

[4] Ibid. 24.

Exchequer provided that when the king, or his son Lord Edward, was next at Westminster the mayor would then be presented to him personally. In the following autumn the mayor Nicholas Bat was presented at the Exchequer 'in the manner granted by the king'.[5] Henry III, however, frequently intervened in the citizens' choice either of the sheriffs or the mayors. In 1239 the Londoners elected Ralph Eswy and Reginald de Bungheye as sheriffs but the king appointed Simon fitz-Mary and when the citizens refused to accept him (he had served as sheriff in 1232-3), the king in turn refused to accept the elected mayor.[6] The barons of the Exchequer in 1321 made difficulties since one of the elected sheriffs was out of town and they refused to admit the other to office because the city charters specified that both sheriffs should be present.[7] Frequently Henry III rejected the Londoners' choice of mayor, as in 1240, 1245 and 1254. In 1323 Edward II ousted Hamo de Chigwell from the mayoralty and replaced him with the goldsmith Nicholas de Farndone.[8] Richard II, in the 1380s, let it be known who he wished to see elected as mayor (John de Northampton in 1381 and 1382, Nicholas Brembre in 1383–5, and Nicholas Exton in 1386) and when Adam Bamme died in office in 1397 Richard chose Richard Whittington as his successor without allowing the citizens to hold an election.[9] But intervention of this kind was becoming unusual and in the fifteenth century kings appear not to have intervened in mayoral elections.

The activities of the sheriffs and the mayors while in office were subject to frequent royal investigation and review. In his 'populist' charter of 1319 Edward II responded to some complaints about the current practices of the sheriffs. In future they were to take responsibility for their servants who were to be limited in number to two clerks and two sergeants; if deputies were appointed they were to be of sufficient standing not to need to abuse their office. Edward III's charter eight years later was friendlier to the sheriffs and allowed that they should not be unreasonably fined if prisoners escaped from their custody, and they were allowed to keep forfeited victuals and merchandise.[10] In fact the sheriff's office was gradually diminishing in importance as that of the mayor developed: whereas in the thirteenth century Arnald fitz-Thedmar in his chronicle headed each year with the names of sheriffs, by the mid-fourteenth century, when the *French Chronicle of London* was written, the name of the mayor preceded the names of the sheriffs. The fifteenth-century compilers of the London chronicles always began their annual entries with the name of the mayor followed by the names of the sheriffs.

The mayor's office was a hundred years younger than that of the sheriffs, and was in the thirteenth century much more frequently suspended by the king who might, as Edward I did in 1285, take the city's liberties into his own hands,

[5] Ibid. 34; *Chronicles of the Mayors and Sheriffs*, 21.

[6] Ibid. 8.

[7] *Annales Londonienses*, in *Chronicles of the Reigns of Edward I and II*, ed. W. Stubbs, 2 vols. (Rolls Series, 1882–3), 218–19.

[8] *Chronicles of the Mayors and Sheriffs*, 210.

[9] C. Barron, 'Richard II and London', in A. Goodman and J. Gillespie (eds.), *Richard II: The Art of Kingship* (Oxford, 1999), 147–8; ead., 'Richard Whittington: The Man Behind the Myth', in W. Kellaway and A. Hollaender (eds.), *Studies in London History presented to P. E. Jones* (London, 1969), 205.

[10] Birch, *Charters*, 46, 48, 54, 56-7.

allowing the citizens still to choose their sheriffs but denying them a freely elected mayor. Henry III frequently suspended the city's liberties, sometimes for quite short periods. For example in 1243 he kept the liberties in his hands for four months until the citizens had paid a fine of £1,000 for having harboured Walter Bukerel without licence.[11] In 1247 he also withdrew the liberties for another month because he was displeased at the city's handling of the case of Margery Viel. And in 1249 the king again seized the liberties because the citizens had resisted the claims of the abbot of Westminster to exercise jurisdiction in Middlesex.[12] In 1254 the city was punished with a fine of 600 marks and the removal of its liberties for a month for failing to keep the assizes of bread and ale, and in the following year the liberties were again forfeited for a month while the king pressed the city for payment of the Queen's Gold.[13] Further seizures followed in February 1257 because of irregularities in the collection of tallage in the city and for three years in 1266–9 following the civil war.[14] In 1271 the citizens were unable to agree on a mayor (most of the aldermen wanted Philip le Taillour but the common people, in fitz-Thedmar's terminology, shouted for Walter Hervi) and so the king chose Henry Frowike to act as warden while the factions fought it out.[15]

Edward I decided to be tough with the city: in June 1285 following a scandal in which Lawrence Duket had been murdered in St Mary le Bow church, the king took the city into his own hands and appointed Sir Ralph de Sandwich to act as warden. For thirteen years the city was governed by royal wardens and the Londoners recovered their liberties only on payment of a fine of 2,000 marks in April 1298.[16] From reading fitz-Thedmar's account of events in London in the thirteenth century it seems clear that the rulers of London (and fitz–Thedmar was one of them) were probably self-interested and violent men and the king had good reason to intervene in city government. The king was probably motivated as much by financial need as by concern for the well-being of the city. The Londoners were having to learn slowly and painfully how to develop a system of self-government and to devise local constituencies where public opinion might be effectively expressed. The thirteen years of rule by a royal warden 'broke the political monopoly of the dynasties' and 'changed the climate of the commons'.[17] But self-government was still not safe from royal displeasure and interference.

The Crown had another way of interfering in the self-government of London: it could send a group of royal justices 'in Eyre' to visit the city and investigate the way in which the city's rulers had governed it and administered justice on the king's behalf. Here again the royal motive may, in part, have been financial since fines could be exacted for any breach of charter or custom. The earliest recorded visit of

[11] *Chronicles of the Mayors and Sheriffs*, 10-11.

[12] Ibid. 14, 18.

[13] Ibid. 22–3, 24–5; for Queen's Gold, see Ch. 1 n. 6.

[14] Ibid. 34–40, 90–129, 192.

[15] Ibid. 153–60. Hervi finally won.

[16] *Annales Londonienses*, 93–4, 95–7; G. A. Williams, *Medieval London from Commune to Capital* (London, 1963), 254–5, 261; *Chronicles of London*, 39. The chronicler notes that the fine was so heavy that servants, as well as masters, were forced to contribute.

[17] Williams, *Medieval London*, 262–3.

such royal justices in Eyre (known as an 'Iter') to London took place in 1220–1, and was followed by another in 1226.[18] The records of the findings of the justices in 1244 and 1276 have survived, and they testify to the enthusiasm with which the royal justices set about their task, and to the range of fines that they exacted.[19] In 1285 the findings of the visiting justices led to the king suspending the government of the city and placing it, for thirteen years, under the direct rule of a royal warden (a procedure known as 'taking the city into the king's hand').

When the Londoners were allowed once more to govern themselves in 1298 they may have been particularly circumspect: there appear to have been no further visits from royal justices until 1321 when Edward II sent the royal justice Hervey de Stanton and his colleagues to look into every aspect of civic government. The justices continued their relentless investigations for six months 'bent on prising every privilege and penny out of the city'.[20] The mayor was deposed and a warden appointed and from then until the end of the reign, Edward continued to choose either wardens or mayors to govern the city so that 'the Londoners lived under an emergency regime of dubious legality'.[21] Queen Isabella on her return to England in November 1326 restored to the Londoners their freedom to choose their own mayor 'since before that time they had only had mayors by the king's grace, because the mayoralty had been lost at the Iter of the justiciars'.[22] The Londoners chose Richard de Betoyne and, after the crises of his father's reign, Edward III decided to work through the London mayors rather than against them.

In the charter granted to the city in March 1327 the powers of the mayor were strengthened for, in future, he was to act as one of the royal justices assigned to hear and deliver prisoners held in Newgate and he was also to serve as the royal escheator in the city.[23] In this new charter it was also granted by the Crown that the city's liberties would not be forfeited by a personal trespass or wrong judgement given by a city officer (as had been the case following the Iter of 1321): the officer was to be punished and not the city as a whole.[24] Later in his reign, in a Parliamentary statute, Edward defined those causes and conditions that might provoke the seizure of the city's liberties and when Richard II briefly took the city into his own hand in the summer of 1392 he was careful to observe the letter, if not the spirit, of the 1354 statute.[25] Apart from the few months in 1392, after the

[18] See R. R. Sharpe, 'Pleas of the Crown in the City of London', *Journal of the British Archaeological Association*, NS 3 (1897), 103–12; *Liber Albus*, i. 62–82.

[19] Year 1244, CLRO Misc. Roll AA, see *The London Eyre of 1244*, ed. H. M. Chew and M. Weinbaum (London Record Society, 1970); 1276, B L Add. Charter 5153 and CLRO. Misc. Roll BB, see *The London Eyre of 1276*, ed. M. Weinbaum (London Record Society, 1976).

[20] Williams, *Medieval London*, 287; *The Eyre of London 14 Edward II A.D. 1321*, ed. H. Cam, 2 vols. (Seldon Society, 1968).

[21] Williams, *Medieval London*, 287.

[22] *Croniques de London*, 55.

[23] Birch, *Charters*, 53, 55; H. M. Chew, 'The Office of Escheator in the City of London during the Middle Ages', *EHR* 58 (1943), 319–30. It might be argued that this strengthening of the powers of the mayor ran counter to the more 'populist' charter of 1319 in which the king had granted that the mayor should hold no other office 'belonging to the city' nor hear any pleas other than those of the mayor, Birch, *Charters*, 46.

[24] Ibid. 57.

accession of Edward III, Londoners were governed by mayors and sheriffs of their own choosing.

The London aldermen needed royal support: they did not always get it. Henry III and, to some extent, Edward II, had tried to gain control over the city by seeking the support of the 'common people' to counterbalance the influence of the wealthy merchants who dominated city government, but the later Plantagenets followed a policy of strengthening the power of the city's rulers rather than undermining them. Whereas the charter of 1319 had required aldermen to be elected every year without the option of re-election, in fact the aldermen of the city in the reign of Edward III served for life and the attempt to enforce the annual elections of aldermen in 1376–84 was brought to an end with royal support. During the artisan protests of 1438–44, the king supported the mayor and aldermen in their desire to become, not simply Guardians of the Peace but Justices, with power to hear and determine cases,[26] and the charter of 1444 which granted this was confirmed by Edward IV in 1462.[27]

The city wanted, indeed needed, the right of self-government but it had to learn by a long and hard process how to govern itself. In 1319 the citizens took their reforming needs to the Crown and Edward II agreed by his charter to a number of detailed regulations about the way in which the city was to be governed: the means of entry to the freedom, the custody of the common seal, the administration of London Bridge, the selection of some of the city's chief officers (chamberlain, common clerk, and common sergeant) and the fees to be paid to city officials. This was a city that demanded self-government and yet turned to the Crown to authorize the means of achieving this. The Crown in the first charter of Richard II's reign acknowledged that the citizens had come of age and could be left to govern themselves: 'If any customs in the said city hitherto held and used shall be in any part difficult or defective . . . the mayor and aldermen . . . with the assent of the commonalty of the same city, may appoint and ordain . . . a suitable remedy . . . provided, however, that such ordinance shall be profitable to us and our people and consonant with good faith and reason.'[28] In effect the Crown was now willing to allow to the city a measure of delegated authority to reform and streamline its own government: the government of the city had, as it were, come of age.

[25] *RP* ii. 258–9; *The Statutes of the Realm*, 10 vols. (London, 1810-28), i. 346-7; C. Barron, 'The Quarrel of Richard II with London 1392–7', in F. R. H. Du Boulay and C. Barron (eds.), *The Reign of Richard II: Essays in Honour of May McKisack (London, 1971)*, 185-6, 196, 201.

[26] C. Barron, 'Ralph Holland and the London Radicals, 1438–1444', in R. Holt and G. Rosser (eds.), *The Medieval Town: A Reader in English Urban History 1200–1540* (London, 1990), 173–6. In fact such commissions of the peace to urban governors had become increasingly common since the fourteenth century and it was anomalous that London's rulers were not so empowered, see E. Kimball, 'Commissions of the Peace for Urban Jurisdictions 1327-1488', *American Philosophical Society*, 121 (1977), 448–74. For a similar struggle in the city of York, see S. Rees Jones, 'York's Civic Administration 1354–1464', in S. Rees Jones (ed.), *The Government of Medieval York: Essays in Commemoration of the 1396 Royal Charter*, Borthwick Studies in History, 3 (York, 1997), 108–40 esp. 115–19.

[27] Birch, *Charters*, 75.

[28] Ibid. 70.

ROYAL SUPPORT FOR LAW AND ORDER: THE PROBLEM OF SANCTUARIES

The most serious threat to the city's right to govern its own affairs through officers chosen by the citizens, was posed by the problems of lawlessness and disorder. Neither the king nor the city's rulers wished to see the government of the city degenerate into anarchy, so in this respect their interests coincided. In the view of the citizens there were ways in which the king could help them to maintain good order in the city. Sanctuaries, or privileged places denied to civic officers, posed a serious challenge to law-keeping and there were numerous such havens within the city: not only the hundred or so parish churches but also an area known as Blancheappleton in the ward of Aldgate and, most significantly, the church and precinct of St Martin le Grand lying just north of St Paul's.[29] There were other sanctuary areas lying outside, but near, the city: Westminster Abbey, the Church and Priory of St Bartholomew, and, to the east of the city, the hospital of St Katherine. The existence of sanctuary was a problem for the Crown as well as for the city. One of the thieves who robbed the royal treasury at Westminster in 1303 fled to sanctuary in the church of St Michael Candlewick Street. Those who seized him from the church were made to do public penance in the city.[30] A Lombard who had fled to All Saints Gracechurch after a brawl had to be restored there after he had been dragged out and placed in Newgate on the mayor's instructions.[31] Both the king and the rulers of London, however grudgingly, acknowledged that the right of sanctuary extended to ordinary criminals, but by the fifteenth century there was considerable debate as to whether sanctuary might be claimed also by those accused of treason. In December 1451 the duke of York's chamberlain, Sir William Oldhall, was accused of treason and fled to sanctuary in St Martin's. Although he was dragged out by royal officers they were forced to restore Oldhall after the dean of St Martin's had protested vehemently at this breach of his rights.[32]

In the fifteenth century the problem seems to have become particularly acute. Several sanctuaries, especially those at Westminster, St Martin's, and Blancheappleton, developed as havens where debtors, aliens, and foreigners, shoddy workers, and those who had fallen foul of their craft organizations could set up shop and practise their trades immune from craft supervision and civic taxation, as well as from their creditors. The shops and houses from which these illicit businesses operated paid useful rents to the abbot of Westminster or the dean of

[29] See I. D. Thornley, 'Sanctuary in Medieval London', *Journal of the British Archaeological Association*, 2nd ser. 38 (1933), 293–315; G. Rosser, 'Sanctuary and Social Negotiation in Medieval England', in J. Blair and B. Golding (eds.), *The Cloister and the World: Essays in Medieval History in Honour of Barbara Harvey* (Oxford, 1996), 57–79.

[30] *Annales Londonienses*, 130–1.

[31] *Annales Paulini*, in *Chronicles of the Reigns of Edward I and II*, ed. W. Stubbs, 2 vols. (Rolls Series, 1882–3), 363.

[32] CLRO, Liber Fleetwood, fos. 179v–181v; J. S. Roskell, *The Commons and their Speakers in English Parliaments 1376-1523* (Manchester, 1965), 247, 360.

St Martin's.[33] In fact the church, the Crown, and the city all found the existence of sanctuary useful, but all wanted it controlled in their own interests. The city would have liked the king to have joined them in a more rigorous attempt to limit and contain the rights of sanctuaries. Thomas More vividly described the abuses of the sanctuaries at Westminster and St Martin's where unthrifty men ran into debt, women absconded with their husbands' plate, and thieves disposed of stolen goods.[34] In 1566 sanctuary was finally abolished when the desires of the Crown and the city combined to overwhelm the protests of the church.[35]

Southwark, at the south end of London Bridge, posed a problem for the rulers of London similar to that caused by the places of sanctuary. Here, in the five manors that comprised the borough of Southwark, criminals, shoddy workmen, aliens, and tax-shy craftsmen could live safely outside the jurisdiction of the city. The bailiffs of the manors held private courts leet that remained immune to outside, and especially to civic, authority.[36] The mayor and aldermen looked to the Crown to grant them jurisdictional powers in Southwark to deal with this problem but they were largely unsuccessful. In 1327 Edward III allowed the Londoners to choose their own bailiff to collect tolls and other revenues in the small manor at the Bridge head which belonged to the Crown (known as the Guildable manor) but there was no grant of jurisdiction.[37] Henry IV made good this deficiency in his charter of 1406, and the bailiff was empowered to bring criminals from Southwark before the civic aithorities, but the inhabitants of the Guildable manor continued to challenge the city's rights and these had to be exemplified in a new charter in 1444. But the support of the Crown, ever conscious of the rights of the lords of the other Southwark manors, was not consistently offered to the Londoners and the inhabitants south of the river were able, throughout the fifteenth century, to maintain an effective rearguard action against the city's claims. In the sixteenth century, however, Henry VIII bought extensive lands in Southwark and his son sold most of this property, including two further manors, to the city for just under £1,000 in 1550. The city amalgamated these holdings into the ward known as Bridge Without and this removed some, but not all, the anomalies of the administration of Southwark. But in this case it is clear that the city needed the support of the Crown in order to exercise jurisdiction in Southwark and the Crown granted only piecemeal and limited jurisdiction in ambiguous terms and, indeed, was willing to retract, or reinterpret, grants already made.

[33] G. Rosser, *Medieval Westminster* (Oxford, 1989), 155–8, 218–19; C. Barron, 'The Government of London and its Relations with the Crown 1400–1450' (University of London, Ph.D. thesis, 1970), 402–8; in 1457 the city rulers and the dean of St Martin's, with the active co-operation of the king, managed to draw up a set of regulations to govern the behaviour of those living in the St Martin's sanctuary: ibid. 407.

[34] Cited in Rosser, *Medieval Westminster*, 218–19.

[35] I. D. Thornley, 'The Destruction of Sanctuary' in R. W. Seton-Watson (ed.), *Tudor Studies Presented to A. F. Pollard* (London, 1924), 182–207.

[36] D. Johnson, *Southwark and the City* (London, 1969), 25.

[37] Birch, *Charters*, 59–60, 80–4; M. Carlin, *Medieval Southwark* (London, 1996), 118–27; Johnson, *Southwark and the City*, 49–50.

THE MAINTENANCE OF THE CITY'S PRIVILEGES: LEGAL AND ECONOMIC

Within the city itself, however, the Crown had, by a series of charters, granted quite considerable judicial privileges to the citizens: no citizen was required to plead outside the city, nor to submit to trial by battle. In 1227 the king confirmed the city's right to hold the court of Husting once a week where pleas relating to lands and tenements in the city and common pleas (all other pleas) might be heard, and wills probated.[38] As the business of the court developed, so the king allowed the citizens to hold the court on a second day in the week.[39] On occasion, the mayor and aldermen successfully argued that they could not be summoned outside the city to answer a royal writ: for example in 1273 when they were summoned to the Exchequer to explain why the sheriff had been deprived of his office (for taking bribes from bakers). In response to the protests of the Londoners the justices came instead into the city and sat to hear the case in the sanctuary of St Martin's le Grand.[40] The city was extremely sensitive on the issue of where royal justices might sit when they came on commission to London. When the royal justices of Trailbaston held sessions in the city between June 1305 and April 1307 they sat at the Guildhall but the judges who conducted the great Iter of 1321 sat in the Tower which must have aggravated the sense of menace in the city.[41] By the charter of 1327 the Crown granted that in future all inquisitions taken by royal justices 'shall be taken in St Martin's le Grand' i.e. the royal justices would sit in neutral territory.[42]

The king did not challenge the right of the mayor and aldermen to settle disputes about urban property, goods and chattels, and wills and debts in city courts, but he retained the right to send writs to enquire into miscarriages of justice or to query the procedures that had been followed. The city maintained that it might respond to such writs verbally by the mouth of the recorder and was not obliged to respond in writing. The administration of justice in the city was not, however, independent of royal justice but subject to it: if there was no cause for complaint then the Crown did not interfere. The citizens knew that if they wished to preserve their independent judicial activities then they had to maintain the effectiveness and impartiality of the city courts.

On occasion they needed more extensive powers to deal with threats of riot or lawlessness. When the cordwainer John Constantine appeared in February 1384 to be about to provoke a riot, he was precipitately seized, tried, and summarily executed. The mayor and aldermen secured retrospective royal authority for this act, which exceeded their judicial powers which did not, at this time, extend to the trial

[38] Birch, *Charters*, 29. [39] Ibid, 40. [40] *Chronicles of the Mayors and Sheriffs*, 18, 167–8.

[41] *Calendar of London Trailbaston Trials under Commission of 1305 and 1306*, ed. R. B. Pugh (London, 1975), 10; Cam, *The Eyre of London*, pp. xxii–xxv.

[42] Birch, *Charters*, 58. The Crown retained the right to hold inquisitions in the Tower. In future the justices of gaol delivery for Newgate prison almost always sat in St Martin's.

and execution of criminals.[43] It was the need to be able to take rapid action to deal with incipient lawlessness that, doubtless, led the mayor and aldermen to seek a new charter in 1444 which would empower them to act not simply as guardians but also as justices of the peace within the city.[44] The powers that the mayor and aldermen received under this new charter were similar to those already secured by numerous other governing bodies in other towns in England. It is clear that in the administration of justice the Londoners needed the help of the Crown both to protect the autonomy and independence of the city courts and also to support the wider judicial powers exercised by the mayor and aldermen.

The Londoners also sought the help of the Crown in maintaining their distinctive trading privileges. The most important privilege was secured by Henry I's grant that 'all the men of London shall be quit and free, and of all their goods, throughout England, and the ports of the sea, of and from all toll and passage and lastage and all other customs'.[45] In the early twelfth century such tolls were not substantial. However, the freedoms granted to the Londoners in this charter were to become more significant as the Crown developed its own taxation of the overseas trade of England. In 1269 the Londoners had to pay Lord Edward 200 marks to be free of paying customs taxes that had been granted to the Italians.[46] But clearly the Londoners could not shelter behind their charter and avoid paying the customs dues granted in Parliament from the 1270s onwards. They did, however, continue to claim the right to sell their goods freely throughout the towns and fairs of England without being liable to pay local dues and taxes. Many of the letters written under the mayor's seal in the period 1350-70 were sent in defence of the goods of London citizens that had been wrongfully seized by local officers for the non-payment of local taxes.[47]

Londoners needed the support of the king not only to protect their freedom to trade on favourable terms in other English towns but also to control the markets within London to ensure that they were run by Londoners for Londoners. This meant the exclusion of foreigners and aliens from trading within the city except with London citizens, that is, they were not to use the facilities of London to trade among themselves. It was, as we have already seen, the policy of the Crown to encourage the alien merchants within the realm.[48] In the view of the Londoners, if alien merchants were to have access to the London markets then they must pay for that privilege. The charter of 1319 confirmed that merchants who were not citizens of London could not sell their wares retail within the city or suburbs, i.e. they could trade only as wholesalers and the profitable retail market was to be the

[43] *Memorials*, 482–3; *The Westminster Chronicle 1381–1394*, ed. L. C. Hector and B. F. Harvey (Oxford, 1982), 65; *CPR 1381–5*, 391.

[44] Barron, 'Ralph Holland', 173–82.

[45] Birch, *Charters*, 3.

[46] *Chronicles of the Mayors and Sheriffs*, 114–15.

[47] *Calendar of Letters from the Mayor and Corporation of the City of London c.1350–1370*, ed. R. R. Sharpe (London, 1885). These are the only letters under the mayor's seal to have survived from the medieval period.

[48] See Ch. 1.

monopoly of the London citizens.[49] The first charter of Edward III in 1327 restricted the activities of the merchant strangers yet further: they were compelled to sell their goods within forty days and, while they remained in the city they were required to board with a citizen and not to keep their own 'households or societies'.[50] In this way it was hoped that alien merchants could be kept under surveillance and prevented from selling their goods to anyone but a London citizen, and this practice whereby London citizens hosted Italian merchants certainly continued into the fifteenth century.[51]

But it was in the interests of the Crown to open up the opportunities for alien merchants to trade freely in England. The Statute of York of 1335 abolished all the restrictions that had been placed on aliens trading in England but, two years later, Edward III confirmed the ancient privileges of the Londoners 'the foresaid statute for the said merchants made to the hurt of the liberties and customs of the city notwithstanding'.[52] But in 1351 the provisions of the Statute of York were reimposed upon London and from this date until the end of the century the issue of whether aliens (and Englishmen who were not London citizens) could trade freely within the city was a matter of serious dispute between the Londoners and the Crown and, indeed, between different groups of Londoners. But for long periods (1351–76, 1378–82, 1388–99) the Crown withdrew the privileges of London and allowed outsiders to trade freely in the city.[53] The extent of the Londoners' concern over this royal interference in their accustomed privilege is a good indication of the extent to which the citizens needed the Crown and the damage that the king could inflict when he chose to exercise his prerogative.

Although Magna Carta had established that the standard weights and measures of the realm were to be those of London, the issue of the use of authorized weights and balances was of concern to the citizens in the thirteenth century.[54] Henry III confirmed that goods brought to the London market by alien merchants were to be weighed at the king's beam which was controlled by a London citizen (usually a grocer) and those who failed to do this were to be fined.[55] In 1319 the control of weights and scales was granted to the city by royal charter and from this time onwards the officers who administered the great beam (for heavy goods) and the small beam (for silk and lighter goods) were chosen by the mayor and aldermen or, from the mid-fourteenth century onwards, by the members of the most appropriate city company.

There were numerous privileges that the king could grant or withold that affected the economic well-being of the city. For example the king claimed the right, in London as elsewhere, to seize goods needed for the royal household and

49 Birch, *Charters*, 48; see Ch. 4.

50 Ibid. 54–5.

51 H. Bradley, 'The Italian Community in London *c.*1350–*c.*1450' (University of London, Ph.D. thesis, 1992), 132–7, 262–4.

52 Birch, *Charters*, 62.

53 The best account of this long and complicated story is to be found in P. Nightingale, 'Capitalists, Crafts and Constitutional Change in Late Fourteenth-Century London', *Past and Present*, 124 (1989), 3–35, esp. 9–16; see also Barron, 'Richard II and London', 140–2.

54 *Chronicles of the Mayors and Sheriffs*, 27, 37, 75.

55 Ibid. 123–4; Birch, *Charters*, 41.

to pay for them later at below market value or, on occasion, not at all. In 1262 the constable of the Tower seized 100 quarters of wheat from a vessel belonging to Thomas de Basinge before it reached the wharf and paid 2*d.* a quarter less for it 'than it would have sold for when brought ashore'. The city contested this action on two grounds: that the whole water of the Thames came under the jurisdiction of the city and also that the king had no right to prisage of corn before the vessel reached the wharf.[56] By the reign of Edward III this was a less contentious issue as the king raised money by Parliamentary taxation to pay for the supplies needed for war, but the charter of 1327 granted that the constable of the Tower would no longer take prises of vessels coming to the city and the king's purveyor would not seize goods without making 'due payment' and only with the 'good will of the seller'.[57]

Henry III also (and probably deliberately) damaged the economic prosperity of the Londoners by granting to his favoured abbey of Westminster the right to hold a fair around the feast of the Translation of St Edward (13 October) during which time not only was the business of all other fairs in England suspended but the shops of London were to be closed for the fortnight of the fair.[58] In spite of the Londoners' attempts to bribe the king into relaxing the privileges that he had granted to the abbey he refused to do so and the annual fair was a source of considerable profit to the monastery in the later thirteenth century. The Londoners' response to this challenge was to take over the fair and by the end of the century almost all the shops and stalls in the fair were leased to Londoners. But fairs were gradually going out of fashion as the more permanent shops and warehouses took their place.[59] In fact the wealth of the Londoners enabled them to dominate the local fairs and markets and so Edward III's concession in his charter of 1327 that neither he nor his heirs would, in future, grant any market rights 'within seven miles in circuit of the city' was probably not of great significance by that date.[60] The issue had, in fact, been resolved in practice years before.[61]

In their dispute with Henry III over the prise of vessels in 1262 the city claimed wide jurisdictional powers in the Thames. In their attempts to keep the waterway free for the passage of boats, and to regulate fishing, the Londoners needed the support of the Crown. As early as 1197 Richard I had granted that all fish weirs (which projected into the water and impeded the passage of boats) were to be removed from the Thames, and this was confirmed in Magna Carta.[62] In 1237 the Crown formally granted the city the jurisdiction over the waters of the Thames from Staines downstream as far as the Medway and this was not seriously challenged during the later medieval period.[63] But it was not easy for the mayor and

[56] *Chronicles of the Mayors and Sheriffs*, 55–6.
[57] Birch, *Charters*, 55, 57.
[58] Rosser, *Medieval Westminster*, 97.
[59] See Ch. 4.
[60] Birch, *Charters*, 58.
[61] Rosser, *Medieval Westminster*, 97–115.
[62] Birch, *Charters*, 9; this clause was confirmed by John in his charter for the city in 1199 with the addition of the Medway to the Thames, and it was this enlarged provision that was incorporated into Magna Carta: ibid. 13; J. C. Holt, *Magna Carta* (Cambridge, 1965), 325–6, clause 33.
[63] See *CPMR 1381–1412*, 71 n. 2; D. Keene, 'Issues of Water in Medieval London', *Urban History*, 28 (2001), 161–79, esp. 167–8.

aldermen to carry out this jurisdiction effectively. In 1327 they were empowered by the king to take away all weirs in the Thames and the Medway and 'to have the punishments thereof to us belonging'.[64] The concern about weirs was provoked not only by problems of navigation: there was also anxiety that the nets being used were of such a small gauge that fish were caught before they had grown sufficiently and, in this way, stocks were being depleted. On occasion weirs were destroyed and illegal nets were brought into Cheapside and publicly burnt.[65] But even with royal support the mayor and sheriffs did not have the resources effectively to police the Thames all the way from Staines to the Medway, and all that could be done was to make periodic raids, burn nets, and punish offenders and then let them go again. By the fifteenth century the city employed a waterbailiff to supervise the river and, on occasion, they mounted armed excursions to seize illegal nets and destroy weirs, usually comandeering young men of the city companies to sally forth in an armed flotilla.[66] Sometimes they encountered armed resistance: at Northfleet in Kent the weir was defended by archers and armed men who shouted 'Hence traitors of London', frightening away the citizen militia.[67] In order to carry out a form of Thames conservancy the city needed not only the support of the Crown, which it largely had, but also greater resources than it could consistently muster for this work of policing. The problems the citizens encountered in trying to exercise their jurisdiction over the Thames waters provide a good example of the ways in which the lawful needs of the Londoners might come into conflict with equally lawful rights elsewhere.

It was crucial to have the support of the king but the city operated within a complex network of royal grants, to the citizens themselves and to others, and also those rights reserved to—and exploited by—the Crown. London was populous and wealthy but it was constantly thrown onto the defensive by a Crown served by eagle-eyed lawyers anxious to protect and enhance the rights of their royal master. In a series of charters from the twelfth century the Londoners had gained some important rights of self-government, judicial immunities, and economic advantages over other towns, but all these could be challenged, redefined, or simply withdrawn. New privileges and new exemplifications of old ones were constantly needed to deal with changing circumstances, the rise of overseas trade, the pervasive role of the Italians and other alien merchants, and the growing needs of the Crown to finance expeditionary forces abroad. The city frequently had to defend its rights while the Crown was able to withdraw privileges or redefine them. New charters cost money. The citizens haggled and bargained and employed clever lawyers to pit their wits against the royal justices. Much of the evidence and the negotiations depended not upon written evidence (although that became increasingly important) but upon the spoken word. But while the rulers of London struggled to hold their own against the frequent royal challenges, the ordinary business

[64] Birch, *Charters*, 54.

[65] *Chronicles of the Mayors and Sheriffs*, 7–8, 22.

[66] For the waterbailiff, see Ch. 8.

[67] 4 and 5 October 1454, CLRO, Journal 5 fos. 196^{v}., 197; see generally, Barron, 'Government of London', 357–65.

of the city had to go on, the Londoners had to be fed, the markets opened, goods made and sold, bodies buried and ships harboured and loaded. On reading the action-packed chronicles written by fitz-Thedmar, or Andrew Horn, or the monk of Westminster, one is bound to wonder how the ordinary business of the city was conducted amidst such constant and distracting struggles with the Crown. In part this was made possible by the growth of a civil service in London which could continue to conduct business even when the conflict between the Crown and the city was most fierce.[68] But in those struggles the two sides were not evenly matched. The opportunities which the Londoners enjoyed to make money and to govern their own affairs ultimately depended upon the good will of the Crown.

68 See Ch. 8.

PART 2

City and Prosperity
The Creation of Wealth

CHAPTER THREE

The Economic Infrastructure

London was important to the Crown because of its wealth: this is why the relations with the city of London took up a considerable amount of the time both of English kings and of their counsellors. It was not simply convenient for the king to get on with the city of London: it was crucial. The population of the city of London may have been as high as 80,000 in 1300 which was probably four times greater than its nearest competitor, Norwich.[1] Perhaps 1.5 per cent of the population of England lived in London in 1300, and this may have risen to 2 per cent by 1500 as the city increased its share of a declining national population. London was not immune to the demographic decline that affected England from the early fourteenth century and accelerated rapidly after the Black Death of 1348–9, but it was not so badly affected as other parts of the country and continued to attract immigrants, thus aggravating the problems of other English towns that lost their inhabitants to the brighter attractions of the capital city. The population of London in 1400, at 40,000, may have been half that of a century earlier, but the wealth of the city had not suffered a comparable decline. In 1334 the taxable wealth of London was reckoned, at £11,000 (2% of the total national assessed wealth), to be five times greater than that of its nearest competitor Bristol.[2] By the 1520s, when there was a new assessment of the country's taxable wealth, London was found to be eleven times wealthier than Norwich and seventeen times wealthier than Bristol.[3] Certainly the prosperity of London did not develop at an even pace throughout the medieval period: but what is striking is that in spite of the demographic setbacks, a marked recession, and bullion famine of the middle years of the fifteenth century, the city continued to prosper. How did this come about? To what extent was London blessed by good fortune and to what extent was this comparative prosperity the result of the good management of the city's natural advantages?

The wealth and importance of London were sustained amidst the ebb and flow of political events and natural disasters by its situation on a major river, navigable

[1] D. Keene, 'A New Study of London before the Great Fire', *Urban History Yearbook* (1984), 11–21; id., 'London from the Post-Roman Period to 1300', in D.Palliser (ed.), *The Cambridge Urban History of Britain,* 3 vols. (Cambridge, 2000), i. 187–216, esp. 195. For a more conservative estimate, see P. Nightingale. 'The Growth of London in the Medieval Economy', in R. H. Britnell and J. Hatcher (eds.), *Progress and Problems in Medieval England* (Cambridge, 1996), 89–106 esp. 97–8.

[2] See A. Dyer, 'Ranking Lists of English Medieval Towns', in Palliser, *Cambridge Urban History,* 747–70, esp. 755–7.

[3] J. Sheail, *The Regional Distribution of Wealth in England as Indicated by the 1524/5 Lay Subsidy Returns*, ed. R. W. Hoyle, 2 vols. (List and Index Society, 1998), i. 52.

well into the heartlands of England, at the lowest bridging point of that river and, in consequence, at the nerve-centre of the English road system. It was a seaport and also a river port serving a rich hinterland.

In spite of its inland situation, London was an overseas port and much of her wealth depended upon the export and import of goods from many parts of Europe and, indeed, further afield. Many of her most prosperous merchants were engaged in overseas trade, and the wealth and the wool of England attracted merchants from foreign countries: Italians, Hanse merchants from around the Baltic, Flemings, men of Holland, the French, especially the Gascons, Spaniards, and Portuguese. The survival of royal customs accounts from the late thirteenth century when exported wool was systematically subjected to custom charges, makes it possible to chart, however imperfectly, some of the patterns and trends in the overseas trade of London (and, of course, of other ports also), the ships in which the cargoes were transported, and the names of the merchants who paid the custom due. The richness of this material may, however, have led to an exaggerated emphasis on overseas trade at the expense of the other, but less well-documented, sinews of economic activity in London.

By 1200 London was well established at the centre of a national distributive network: the river Thames provided a national artery along which goods travelled westwards to Reading, Henley, and, perhaps less regularly, to Oxford.[4] In 1476 Goddard Oxbryge, the Stonor family's agent in London, had loaded a barge travelling to Henley with raisins, saltfish, spices, two brass pots, a pair of pavenys (perhaps peacocks?), and a mustard quern and a gown for Lady Stonor. The barge was leaving London on the Thursday (May 9) and was expected in Henley on the following Monday or Tuesday 'at the fardyst'.[5] Downstream goods could be taken to the ports along the Essex estuary, or to the north Kentish towns such as Rochester, or they could travel further by sea to Ipswich, Lynn, Boston, Hull, or Newcastle.[6] Some shipping hugged the Kentish coast and transported goods to Sandwich or even, if the goods were heavy, further west to Portsmouth, Exeter, and Plymouth.[7] But the road system was also well developed and goods that needed to travel between Southampton and London did so by road and not by water.[8] The

[4] See R. B. Peberdy, 'Navigation of the River Thames between London and Oxford in the Late Middle Ages: A Reconsideration', *Oxoniensia*, 16 (1996), 311–40.

[5] C. Carpenter (ed.), *Kingsford's Stonor Letters and Papers 1290–1483* (Cambridge, 1996), no. 164; in May 1478, William Somer, the bargeman at Queenhithe, took wine, salt, stockfish, herrings, a basket of glass and two wicker baskets with bowls, on board to be delivered at Henley: ibid., no. 209.

[6] In 1448–9 Sir John Fastolf had fish, malt, oats, and grain brought to London by sea from Yarmouth: Magdalen College Archives, Fastolf Estate paper 171/13. For the coal trade with Newcastle, see B. Dietz, 'The North East Coal Trade 1550–1750: Measures, Markets and Metropolis', *Northern History*, 22 (1986), 280–92.

[7] Bells made in London foundries were distributed widely in England: Johanna Hill supplied bells for the church at Manaton in Devon, see C. Barron, 'Johanna Hill (d.1441) and Johanna Sturdy (d.*c.*1460), Bell-Founders' in C. M. Barron and A. Sutton (eds.), *Medieval London Widows 1300–1500* (London, 1994), 99–111, esp. 105.

[8] H. S. Cobb, 'Cloth Exports from London and Southampton in the Later Fifteenth and Early Sixteenth Centuries: A Revision', *EconHR* 31 (1978), 601–9, esp. 602.

Romans had established Londinium as the centre of a radiating road system and that system was largely still in place in the medieval period.[9] The Gough map of *c.*1363, drawn up in the west of England, demonstrates clearly the central, indeed dominating, importance of London in the national river and road networks.[10] It has been suggested that the road system of medieval England 'brought every part of the country within a fortnight's ride of London'.[11]

It is clear therefore that the natural advantages of the situation of London as both an inland and an overseas port, first recognized by the Romans, had ensured the city a measure of political importance. Since the seventh century London had been the seat of a bishop and since the reign of Edward the Confessor (if not earlier) it was adjacent to one of the richest monastic houses, lavishly patronized by the English kings. The Normans had recognized and promoted the pre-eminence of London by building the Tower to dominate the city, and Westminster Hall as the centre of their peripatetic government. In the course of the twelfth century Westminster (but, in effect, London) took over from Winchester as the administrative centre of England.[12] Bishops and abbots were beginning to establish town houses in London or nearby in Southwark or Westminster, in order to be on hand to advise the king and to secure his patronage, but also to be able to use their houses as bases for the sale of surplus produce from their estates and for the purchase and storage of goods to supply the needs of their rural communities.[13] But just as Winchester, in the course of the twelfth century, lost out to London, so London might well have lost out to another English city in the course of the later medieval period. That it did not may be attributed in part to its natural advantages, to a measure of support from the Crown but, above all perhaps, to the efforts of the Londoners themselves, who took care, albeit fitfully and inconsistently, to maintain and to develop the 'economic infrastructure' of the city, that is, the facilities that promoted the easy exchange of goods and attracted buyers and sellers to London.

All medieval merchants and craftsmen, whether outsiders or the Londoners themselves, who used the London market for the sale of goods, did so at a cost. These 'transaction costs' included the hidden expenses of searching for customers and travelling over a long distance, the overt tolls charged to enter the city, and the charges for setting up stalls or using the markets.[14] London, like other towns, established the prices that could be charged for certain products (particularly

[9] M. D. Lobel (ed.), *Historic Towns Atlas: The City of London from Prehistoric Times to c.1520* (Oxford, 1989), 1–5 and map 'Situation of London'.

[10] E. J. S. Parsons, *The Map of Great Britain circa AD 1360 known as the Gough Map* (1958, rpt. Oxford, 1996).

[11] F. M. Stenton, 'The Road System of Medieval England', *EconHR* 7 (1936–7), 1–21, esp. 21.

[12] G. Rosser, *Medieval Westminster 1200–1540* (Oxford, 1989), 16–32.

[13] C. Barron, 'Centres of Conspicuous Consumption: The Aristocratic Town House in London 1200–1500', *London Journal*, 20 (1995), 1–16.

[14] D. C. North provides the theoretical framework in 'Transaction Costs in History', *Journal of European Economic History*, 14 (1985), 557–76. North's argument is developed, and effectively applied to medieval markets and towns, by M. Kowaleski, *Local Markets and Regional Trade in Medieval Exeter* (Cambridge, 1995), 179–221.

foodstuffs) and regulated the times when goods might be sold and the required quality of the product. On the other hand the size of the London market considerably reduced the expense of searching for customers, and the city also provided comparatively easy access to credit. In London, too, there were courts for resolving commercial disputes, registering debts, and pursuing debtors. In this way the London market might be attractive, even to those traders who had to travel quite long distances. But the rulers of London had a difficult balancing act: they had to address the concerns of all the city's inhabitants to ensure an adequate supply of reasonably priced goods (especially food); they had to provide some privileged access to the city's markets for the citizens who paid civic taxes; and they had to secure for outsiders, whether from other parts of England or overseas, a safe and profitable environment in which to make sound commercial transactions. These different objectives were not easily compatible but in this period the city's rulers, on occasion prodded into action by the king, taxed, regulated, inspected, and admonished the thousands of men and women who bought and sold within the mayor's jurisdiction. The successful commercial environment of medieval London was not the result of chance: it was created, sustained, and enhanced by the co-operative efforts of the Crown, civic regulation, and private charity.

We have already seen how the city attempted to maintain the Thames waterway free for navigation within the area of the city's jurisdiction, that is from Staines in the west to the Medway in the east.[15] On the whole the river appears to have been successfully maintained for river traffic and overseas shipping. The Fleet river was certainly navigable as far as Holborn Bridge, if not further. When a jury enquired into the tributary of the Fleet which surrounded the prison in 1355 they declared that the ditch there should be ten feet wide and have sufficient water in it to float a vessel freighted with a tun of wine.[16] The river Lea was also navigable deep into Hertfordshire.

But it was not sufficient for the city simply to keep the waters of the Thames flowing smoothly: it was also necessary to provide public harbourage for the ships bringing goods to unload for sale. By the thirteenth century much of the northern shore of the Thames was tightly developed from the Fleet estuary in the west to the Bridge in the east. The development of the riverside area between the Bridge and the Tower took place rather later. Much of the waterfront was occupied by small private wharves built first of wood, but then increasingly rebuilt in stone: some had jetties built out over the water. Here small craft could tie up and unload their cargoes. Many ships anchored in midstream and discharged their cargoes into lighters or small craft. The only public quays, or wharfs, were at Queenhithe above the Bridge and at Billingsgate below. At these two 'harbours' the water was sufficiently deep for quite large ships to tie up, and as the reclamation on adjacent properties extended into the river on either side of them they became increasingly like inlets, or docks. Before the stone bridge was built, Queenhithe was the most important of the city's two public quays. The 'hythe' originally belonged to the

[15] See Ch. 2. [16] *LBG*, 49.

king although it appears to have been customary for the revenues derived from it to be assigned to the queen, hence its name. In 1246, Richard earl of Cornwall, Henry III's brother, leased Queenhithe to the mayor and citizens of London for an annual payment of £50.[17] From this date onwards it became the responsibility of the citizens to maintain the harbour and also to administer the market that developed there for the sale of corn, fish, and salt. The citizens were, of course, entitled to collect the various dues that were paid by ships using the hythe, and to charge a tax on goods brought there for sale.[18] The bailiffs appointed by the city to administer the hythe and collect the tolls were frequently accused of extortion,[19] but in spite of their activities goods continued to be unloaded at Queenhithe. In 1357, however, the city had to impose a special levy on all merchants in order to rebuild the hythe and cleanse the entrance to the haven.[20] Ten years later a further surcharge was imposed in order to clean and repair the 'roumland' there, that is the open space at the dock where ships unloaded their cargoes.[21] In 1471, however, it was the Fishmongers' company that 'of theire propre costes' agreed to enlarge Queenhithe,[22] and in the following century the grocer Sir John Lyon (d. 1564) left £100 towards the cost of building a market house at the wharf so that goods (in particular grain) might be stored there between unloading and sale.[23] Here we see clearly an instance of the many public/private partnerships that maintained and improved the city's economic facilities.

Billingsgate, the civic wharf that lay below the Bridge, was less ancient than Queenhithe and less important until the development of large ships made it difficult for overseas shipping to pass through London Bridge. It was not until 1400 that the city secured at Billingsgate the same rights to charge tolls that it had enjoyed by royal licence since the mid-thirteenth century at Queenhithe.[24] But as the demand to unload goods at Billingsgate developed, so it became necessary for the city, in the middle of the fifteenth century, to spend the very large sum of £1,000 in purchasing land from the estate of Sir Thomas Haseley to extend the Billingsgate wharf.[25] The improvements must have been successful, for two years later the city found it necessary to try to ensure that an equal number of boats unloaded their goods at the two wharfs.[26] The appearance of Billingsgate is well known from the famous miniature (dated *c.*1500) that prefaces the poems of Charles duke of Orleans in the BL Royal manuscript. This depicts an open arcaded

[17] 12 October 1246, *LBC*, 15 and n. 2.

[18] For a list of the various and immensely complex charges, see *The London Eyre of 1244*, ed. H. M. Chew and M. Weinbaum (London Record Society, 1970), 108–12; *Liber Albus*, 209–14.

[19] See e.g. 1303, *CEMCR 1298–1307*, 150–1; 1365, *CPMR 1364–81*, 29.

[20] 6 December 1357, *LBG*, 97.

[21] Ibid. 221.

[22] *CPMR 1458–82*, 70–1 and *LBL*, 137.

[23] *Hugh Alley's Caveat: The Markets of London in 1598*, ed. I. Archer, C. Barron, and V. Harding (London Topographical Society, 1988), 9, 75, 95–6.

[24] 25 May 1400, *Cal. Charter Rolls 1341–1417*, 403.

[25] Barron, 'Government of London', 226; Haseley, who died in 1449, may have given the city the first option to buy this land from his executors, see J. S. Roskell, L. Clark, and C. Rawcliffe, *The House of Commons 1386–1421*, 4 vols. (Stroud, 1992), iii. 307–10.

[26] *LBL*, 45–8.

building which was probably built for storing goods once they had been unloaded.[27] Billingsgate, like Queenhithe, was also a market, as well as a wharf, and the city appointed not only bailiffs for both markets but also men to measure coal, salt, grain, and oysters.[28] So, by the end of this period, the city was providing two deep wharfs, with unloading and storage facilities, and adjacent markets to facilitate river- and seaborne trade. The city thus attempted to ensure that access to London by water, whether from within England or overseas, was comparatively easy and that when the ships reached London there would be wharves available where merchants could unload, store, and sell their produce.

In some ways it was harder for the Londoners to ensure that there was easy access to the city by road since no part of the national road network lay under their direct control. But in building a stone bridge to span the Thames in place of the earlier wooden one, the citizens of London in the late twelfth century were making a considerable investment in their economic future. Peter of Colechurch appears to have begun work on the new stone bridge in about 1176 and the work was completed by 1209, probably earlier.[29] We know little of how the work was funded or organized since no civic records survive from that date.[30] But the work was pious in purpose and Peter of Colechurch may not have been insensible to the economic advantages of dedicating the chapel at the centre of the bridge to London's home-grown saint, Thomas Becket, martyred in 1170. Indeed it may have been Becket's martyrdom that presented the economic opportunity for such an expensive enterprise. By 1189–90 there were at least five separate Bridge guilds run by London aldermen whose purpose, one may surmise, was to raise money for the building programme.[31] Once it was built the Bridge was maintained, rather like a monastic house, by the income from a landed estate given, over the years, by many different Londoners, but most of it acquired by the middle of the fourteenth century.[32] This income was supplemented by the tolls charged to traffic crossing the Bridge, and to ships that required the drawbridge to be raised.[33] In addition the enterprising mayor, Henry le Waleys, had built a covered market for the sale of meat and fish in 1283 and the income from leasing the stalls was paid to the Bridge.[34] So this asset, of immense economic importance to the city, was funded and maintained by pious endowment and corporate civic enterprise. The Bridge, which seems to have antedated the formation of a permanent civic bureaucracy,

[27] *Hugh Alley's Caveat*, 53, 84.

[28] Barron, 'Government of London', 582–6.

[29] C. N. L. Brooke with G. Keir, *London 800–1216: The Shaping of a City* (London, 1975), 110.

[30] See B. Watson, 'The Construction of the Colechurch Bridge', in B. Watson, T. Brigham, and A. Dyson, *London Bridge: 2000 Years of a River Crossing* (London, 2001), 83–92.

[31] G. Unwin, *The Guilds and Companies of London* (London, 1908), 48.

[32] *London Bridge: Selected Accounts and Rentals 1381–1538*, ed. V. Harding and L. Wright (London Record Society, 1995), pp. ix, xvii; P. E. Jones, 'Some Bridge House Properties', *Journal of the British Archaeological Association*, 3rd series 15 (1953), 59–73; When Rochester Bridge collapsed in 1381 a new bridge had to be funded and built: this was done by means of private charity and the creation of a landed estate, see R. Britnell, 'Rochester Bridge 1381–1530' in N. Yates and J. M. Gibson (eds.), *Traffic and Politics: The Construction and Management of Rochester Bridge AD 43–1993* (Woodbridge, 1994), 43–106.

[33] *Liber Albus*, 205–7; *London Bridge*, pp. xx–xxi.

[34] Ibid. xx.

was run separately from the government of the city. Two Bridgemasters (or Bridgewardens) were elected each year (although they could be re-elected and serve for several years in succession) by the citizens, to maintain the Bridge and administer the estates that had been given to it. In accordance with the charter of Edward II the Bridgewardens were not to be aldermen, and they were to be chosen 'at the will of the commonalty'.[35] The records of the Bridge House Estate are extant from the mid-fourteenth century (unlike the city's other financial records they were not burnt in later fires) and provide a detailed picture of the income and expenditure of the Bridgewardens.[36] It would seem that, by and large, the income from various sources was adequate to provide for the continual maintenance that Peter of Colechurch's bridge needed to face the double assaults of heavy carts above and rushing tidal waters beneath. But, in the fifteenth century, age took its toll: in 1435 the Bridge was declared to be 'in a ruinous condition' and in January 1437 the tower at the Southwark end of the Bridge collapsed, destroying two of the nineteen arches as it did so.[37] The normal income was insufficient to meet the large repair bill and so the city agreed to raise a civic tax of 500 marks for the work.[38] It is clear that the fabric of the Bridge continued to cause concern and matters were not helped by the attack during the revolt in 1450 when Cade's supporters cut the ropes that kept the drawbridge raised so that they might enter the city. By 1476 it had become impossible to raise the drawbridge without further essential repairs to the stonework and it would seem that, after this date, the drawbridge was not raised again.[39] This meant that larger boats could no longer pass upstream to Queenhithe (which became the haven for inland Thames traffic), thus accelerating the development of the harbours downstream for the use of overseas shipping. But whatever the difficulties, the elected Bridgewardens, assisted when necessary by the city's rulers, managed to maintain London Bridge as the crucial artery linking London to southern England. There was no other Bridge across the Thames until much further upstream at Kingston.

It was not, however, sufficient for the city to provide access by water and by road; important as that was, there had also to be convenient and appropriate places provided for the sale of both imported and London-made goods. Most exchanges of goods took place in the open, and by the thirteenth century it is likely that certain places were already designated in the city for the sale of meat, fish, grain, and other foodstuffs. Many of these open-air markets continued throughout the medieval period.[40] There were detailed regulations about where goods might be sold, when the markets could be open, who could buy when, and the prices at which goods (especially foodstuffs) could be sold. There were severe punishments (usually the pillory) for those who sold unwholesome or putrid food, or short-changed the customer. It was crucial to the city that food supplies should be brought into London for sale in order to feed the population, which had little

[35] Birch, *Charters*, 49.
[36] *London Bridge*, pp. xxiv–xxvii.
[37] 27 July 1435, *LBK*, 191; *London Bridge, 2000 Years*, 129–30.
[38] Ibid. 131–2; Barron, 'Government of London', 190.
[39] *London Bridge*, pp. xxi–xxii.
[40] *Hugh Alley's Caveat*, 3–4.

means of feeding itself, so the venues had to be made attractive to the sellers.[41] In all the city maintained eight markets, four on either side of the Walbrook, where meat, fish, grain, and general goods might be sold. In addition, at Smithfield lying outside the city to the north, the city had maintained a market for livestock since the twelfth century.[42] But these comparatively primitive facilities were supplemented from the thirteenth century onwards by a series of covered markets.

The first of these owed its existence to the energetic mayor, Henry le Waleys, who in 1283 secured a site adjoining St Mary Woolchurch on which to construct a market building known as 'le Stokkes' where meat and fish could be sold and the income from rents used to maintain London Bridge.[43] This seems to have been a successful venture and in 1381–2 the stalls leased there to fishmongers and butchers brought in an annual revenue of just over £100 to help to maintain the Bridge. Above the market stalls were small chambers which were let to drapers selling cloth and, in 1404, to a schoolmaster.[44] But the building, after a hundred years of use, had to be reconstructed: the author of the *Great Chronicle* records under the year 1409: 'Also this same yere the Stokkes was newe bygonne to make And in the next yere folowyng complete and full ended and made'.[45] It is possible to gain some idea of the appearance of this rebuilt Stocks market from the drawing made by Hugh Alley, *c.*1598: here it can be seen that the butchers displayed their wares on rails beneath an overhanging pentice whereas the fishmongers used trestle tables or 'boordes'. Above the stalls were two floors of chambers which were let out to chaplains and assorted tradesmen.[46] But in spite of the rebuilding, the income that the Bridge derived from the Stocks declined: this may have been the result of the development of other markets, or of retail shops, within the city, but the Stocks market building remained in use up to the time of the Great Fire when it was rebuilt as a vegetable market.[47] The market owed its existence to the enterprise of one Londoner who devised a way of facilitating the sale of meat and fish while, at the same time, creating revenue to maintain London Bridge. The market was never the direct responsibility of the mayor and aldermen but, when necessary, they would take action to protect the interests of the market, in particular against the encroachments of the adjacent church of St Mary Woolchurch.[48]

It was a hundred years before the city acquired another market house. Again the benefactor was an individual London citizen who worked, in conjunction with the Crown, to provide a building where wool could be weighed and stored, and the wool custom paid, prior to its export abroad. John Chircheman, a Norfolk man who was making a small fortune in London, in 1376 bought the quay called the

[41] *Hugh Alley's Caveat*, 5–7.

[42] Ibid., 93–4.

[43] *Liber Custumarum*, i. 274–8; *CPR 1321–1324*, 425–6; H. A. Harben, *A Dictionary of London* (London, 1918), 554.

[44] *London Bridge*, pp. xx, 37.

[45] *The Great Chronicle of London*, ed. A. H. Thomas and I. D. Thornley (London, 1938), 88: see account by D. Keene, 'The Walbrook Study: A Summary Report' (unpublished manuscript, 1987), Appendix 118/17.

[46] *Hugh Alley's Caveat*, 33, 63, 89.

[47] Ibid., 89; *London Bridge*, p. xx; Barron, 'Government of London', 229.

[48] Ibid., 229–30.

Woolwharf which lay just west of the Tower. On this site, in the course of the next five years, he constructed a new Custom House 'for the quiet of merchants . . . to serve for the tronage (weighing) of wools in the port of London'.[49] In the following year Chircheman added some rooms over the 'counting house' together with a latrine. Archaeologists have found the walls of the hall (or counting house) where the tron, or scales for weighing the wool were kept, which measured 24 × 10 metres, and also the remains of a timber drain which could plausibly have formed part of Chircheman's latrine.[50] To recover some of his outlay, in 1382 Chircheman was able to purchase the office of tronager of wool in London from which he drew the profits until his death.[51] The building of the new custom house was not a civic enterprise but rather a joint venture undertaken by a London grocer in partnership with the Crown. It was convenient for merchants to be able to bring their wool to one fixed place to have it weighed and customed ready for export, but it was also in the interest of the Crown to be able to collect the London wool subsidy in one place. Indirectly the city benefited because if the facilities for weighing and storing the wool were good in London, then merchants would bring their wool to the city, rather than to other ports, for export.

Perhaps encouraged by Chircheman's enterprise, the city decided, in the 1390s, to create a covered market for the sale of woollen cloth. In 1396 the mayor and aldermen purchased the Blackwell Hall property which lay to the south-east of the Guildhall 'ad opus communitatis civitatis' and there, during the first mayoralty of Richard Whittington (1397–8) was established a market house where all 'foreign' (i.e. non-citizen) merchants were required to bring their cloths for sale.[52] The market was to be open every week, from midday Thursday until midday on Saturday and it was here that all sales and purchases of cloth involving those who were not freemen of London were to take place. There is very little evidence to tell us how the market was run, or what it looked like, but it is clear that merchants could rent chambers there, or cupboards, or simply chests (hucches) by the year or by the month or even for a day. The rents from these lettings were collected by the keeper of Blackwell Hall who paid over the money to the city chamberlain.[53] John Stow wrote that the building was aligned north-south 'in forme of a noble mans house' and constructed over vaults of Caen stone. By 1587 the market hall had become so 'ruinous and in daunger of falling' that it was pulled down and a new hall built on the same site.[54] The enterprising Londoners of the late fourteenth century had perceived the need for London merchants to gain control over the burgeoning sales of woollen cloth, not only in the city itself but

[49] *CPR 1381–1385*, 149.

[50] T. Tatton Brown, 'Excavations at the Custom House Site, City of London, 1973', *TLMAS* 25 (1974), 117–219, esp. 138–41, 145; ibid. 26 (1975), 103–70, esp. 109–10, 113–15.

[51] *CPR 1381–1385*, 149, 154, 299.

[52] CLRO, Husting Deeds 125 (61), (65); 124 (57); *CPR 1396–99*, 13; *Memorials*, 550–2; *LBH*, 449–50.

[53] See the fifteenth-century oath of the keeper of Blackwell Hall, *LBD* 200; for the names of some fifteenth-century keepers of Blackwell Hall, see Barron, 'Government of London', 588.

[54] Stow, *Survey*, ii. 286–9; recent archaeological work in the area has largely confirmed Stow's description, see N. Bateman, *Gladiators at the Guildhall* (London, 2000), 75–9.

nationally. By providing a central and convenient market where cloth could be stored safely, and sold when convenient, the Londoners ensured that the city became the national market for the sale of cloth: here Venetians, Florentines, and Hanse merchants could purchase more than enough cloth to fill the holds on their return journeys, and likewise country producers could be sure of finding a market for their cloths.[55] Such easy access to an assured market must have easily outweighed the charges to be paid to the keeper of the Hall. This office soon fell under the control of the Drapers' company which was allowed to choose the keeper although his 'admission, confirmation and removal' remained in the power of the mayor and aldermen.[56] It is clear that this supervision was not simply nominal: a foreign draper and a London fishmonger, who in 1451 transacted a deal in the fishmonger's house instead of openly at Blackwell Hall, were brought before the mayor and aldermen.[57] It seems likely that it was only by providing a convenient market in Blackwell Hall that the Londoners were able not only to attract cloth sales to London but also to maintain their asserted right to participate in all the commercial transactions that took place in the city.

The convenience of covered and localized places in which goods might be inspected before being offered for sale doubtless became more apparent in the course of the fifteenth century: if the drapers found it convenient to keep an eye on cloth sales, then it is not surprising that other groups of craftsmen saw advantages in similar arrangements. In 1435 the wardens of the turners pointed out to the mayor and aldermen that foreign turners were making bushel and other measures out of green wood which then shrank, thus reducing the size of the measure. It was agreed that the foreign turners should be required to sell their wares in the housing under the newly built mayor's court on the north side of the Guildhall where their goods might be inspected by the wardens of the London turners.[58] Two years later they were joined by the foreign tanners who brought tanned hides into London to sell: their goods were to be stored in the market house under the mayor's court so that they could be inspected and taxed before sale. It may have been that the smell was unpleasant because five years later the mayor and aldermen decided that the sale of tanned goods should be moved elsewhere in the city although, perhaps because there was no suitable venue, the market for hides was still being held at Guildhall in 1453.[59]

The years 1390 to 1420 were marked by a series of major, and costly, civic ventures: the acquisition and development of Blackwell Hall as a market for cloth in the 1390s, the rebuilding of the Guildhall begun in 1411, and also, in 1409–11, the city acquired the great hall of the Neville family, the Leadenhall in Cornhill.[60] All these

[55] The city had to defend its right to insist that all retail commercial exchanges in London must involve a London citizen, *LBI*, 54 n.1.

[56] 1405, *LBI*, 41; for the Drapers' ordinances, see A. H. Johnson, *The History of the Worshipful Company of the Drapers of London*, 4 vols. (London, 1914–22), i. 258–62.

[57] 6 April 1451, the fishmonger was Richard Phippes: CLRO, Journal 5 fo. 56.

[58] *LBK*, 193–4.

[59] *LBK*, 227, 285–6.

[60] Alice Neville died in 1394 and, presumably, the city then began negotiations to acquire Leadenhall which involved the purchase not only of the building and site, but also of a royal licence to alienate the

ventures were associated to some degree with Richard Whittington, although the development of the Leadenhall building as a 'civic complex' did not take place until long after his death. Although Leadenhall belonged to the Neville family until it was finally acquired by the city in 1411 it had been leased by them to the city and had been in use as a market earlier. It was here that poulterers and cheesemongers were expected to sell their wares, although it is not clear whether this was a street market or whether the vendors sold their wares inside the old Leadenhall building.[61] But in 1439, perhaps as work on the Guildhall complex was drawing to a close, the city decided to develop the Leadenhall site, ostensibly as a granary but also, as the building plans got under way, as a market, chapel, and school as well. The moving spirit behind this remarkable new building was the draper Simon Eyre, elected as mayor in 1445, who saw to the rapid completion of the great quadrangle by 1453. It seems clear from Eyre's will, drawn up in 1457, that his main concern by that date was for the chapel and the three schools—of song, grammar, and writing—that he had established there. The schools did not flourish, but the great quadrangle continued to be a building of importance to the city. In 1455 common council ordered that the market for poultry, victuals, grain, eggs, butter, and cheese which used to be held at (*apud*) Leadenhall should now be held within (*infra*) the new granary constructed there by Simon Eyre.[62] In 1463 it was decided that lead nails and 'worsted cloth' were to be stored and sold there and, before the end of the century wool and tanned leather were added to the list of goods.[63] Recent work by archaeologists has revealed just how magnificent Simon Eyre's building was: parts of the site have been excavated, and the discovery of moulded stones surviving in the infill of the houses built on the site in the 1790s when the old Leadenhall building was demolished, has made it possible to reconstruct Eyre's 'great work' there.

> It was one of the most important civic buildings in the late medieval City. Its role was to provide free-standing for non-citizen food vendors at ground level, while the upper floors acted as storehouses for grain. The former market courtyard was greatly enlarged by the provision of a covered arcade (seld) to keep the market people and their wares dry. By enlarging the market and supplying it with free shelter, a well and a chapel, the supply of food from the country for the city would have been increased and prices lowered.[64]

The size and the quality of the building indicates the vision of Simon Eyre, of the master mason John Croxton, and of the city's rulers. It is difficult now to be sure whether the main purpose of the building was to serve as a granary, a market hall, or a chapel and school, or all three. When the commons of the city petitioned

land in mortmain, see M. Samuel and G. Milne, 'The "Ledene Hall" and Medieval Market' in G. Milne (ed.), *From Roman Basilica to Medieval Market* (London, 1992), 39–50, p. 41; *LBI*, 92–3.

[61] *Hugh Alley's Caveat*, 9–10; *Memorials*, 405–7; see A. H. Thomas, 'Notes on the History of the Leadenhall, 1195–1488', *London Topographical Record*, 13 (1923), 1–22.

[62] CLRO, Journal 5 fo. 235.

[63] Samuel and Milne, 'The "Ledene Hall" and Medieval Market', 45; *LBL*, 251; Stow, *Survey*, i. 155–6.

[64] M. Samuel. 'Reconstructing the Medieval Market at Leadenhall', in Milne, *Roman Basilica to Medieval Market*, 114–25, esp. 123.

common council in 1519 against the leasing out of Leadenhall, they listed several of the purposes that it then served: as a place of assembly for the citizens, as a storehouse for city armoury and stores of timber for repairing civic buildings, for assembling civic pageants, for handing out alms to the poor, and as a marketplace for the men and women who came to the city to sell victuals so that they might keep themselves and their wares dry and 'to encourage them, and all other to have the better will and desire the more plenteously to resort to the said Citie to victual the same'.[65] The Leadenhall was not leased, but fifteen years later there was another plan, this time to use the building as a Bourse for the assembly of merchants. At just this period the first custom-built exchange was constructed in northern Europe in Antwerp to a design that closely resembled the London Leadenhall.[66] By providing dry, secure places where sellers could store and sell their goods and purchasers could see and compare what was offered, the city was creating the infrastructure that encouraged those with goods to offer to bring them to London, assured of a place to sell and customers to buy.

The markets thus created were not entirely free: rents were, of course, paid to lease the stalls and the city stringently controlled the measures, the quality of the goods offered, and, in the case of food, the prices that might be charged. At the bottom end of the market both dry and liquid measures used for selling goods within each ward were the responsibility of the ward alderman who was to inspect and seal all such measures four times a year.[67] Although such injunctions were aimed at protecting the customer they also protected the reputation of the honest vendor. At the markets at Queenhithe and Billingsgate, the city appointed, in addition to the warden of the market, men who were to be the official measurers of coal, grain, oysters, and salt, and these men charged for their services.[68] Although this charge increased the transaction costs for the vendor, the assurance of an acknowledged weight or quantity must have attracted buyers.[69] Magna Carta had established that the weights and measures used in the city of London were to be those used throughout the kingdom and the Londoners took pains to ensure that their primacy in establishing national standards was observed.[70] In the fifteenth century the statutes of 1429 and 1438 enacted, among other matters, that every town was to have its own common balance with sealed weights and measures to comply with those kept in the king's Exchequer.[71] When required to do so, Robert Otele, who was elected mayor in 1434, refused to take an oath to maintain the new statute on the grounds that the standard weights and measures of London took precedence over those in the Exchequer.[72] He successfully maintained that the

[65] Stow, *Survey*, i. 158–9.

[66] Samuel, 'Reconstructing the Medieval Market', 125.

[67] *Liber Albus*, 290.

[68] Barron, 'Government of London', 583–7.

[69] See Kowaleski, *Local Markets and Regional Trade*, 189.

[70] Magna Carta, Clause 35, 'Let there be one measure of wine throughout our kingdom and one measure of ale and one measure of corn, namely the London quarter, and one width of cloth whether dyed, russet or halberjet, namely two ells within the selvedges. Let it be the same with weights as with measures': J. C. Holt, *Magna Carta* (Cambridge, 2nd edn. 1991), 461.

[71] *The Statutes of the Realm*, 10 vols. (London, 1810–28), ii. 174, 241–2, 282–4.

[72] Barron, 'Government of London', 233.

king's weights and measures (and hence the national standards) were the weights and measures of London, displayed in the Guildhall. In his charter of 1268 Henry III had allowed that 'no merchant stranger or other, may buy or sell any wares, which ought to be weighed or troned, unless by our beams or trone, upon forfeiture of the said wares'.[73] So the city's great balance, or trone, was known as 'the King's trone' or the 'King's Common Beam'.[74] The choice of the office of keeper of the Great or Common Beam belonged to the city but by the middle of the fourteenth century the choice, in practice, fell to the newly formed company of grocers and pepperers.[75] From 1417 the Great Beam was kept in a special 'weigh house': first at the 'Barge' in Bucklersbury and then at a house on the north side of Cornhill given to the Grocers' company for this purpose by Sir Thomas Lovell (d. 1528).[76] Whereas heavy goods (which included spices) were weighed at the Great Beam, lightweight goods (less than 25lb), particularly silk of all kinds, was weighed at the Small Beam. This fell completely under the control of the Mercers' company and, unlike the Great Beam, there are very few references to the Small Beam among the civic records in the fifteenth century. But although the mercers chose the weigher of silk (as he had come to be called) and gave preference in appointment to a 'decayed' member of the livery, their choice was then presented to the city's chamberlain for approval. After this the balance-beam and the weights that belonged to the 'fellowship of the Mercery' were delivered into his charge.[77] Here can be seen clearly the evolution of a process to be discerned in several aspects of civic regulation, where the city fought the king to be allowed to regulate the economic life of the city and then, having secured such control by royal charter, devolved the responsibility to the most appropriate city company. The company had then to ensure that they weighed fairly and charged moderately so that merchants and tradesmen had no cause to complain to the mayor about their activities. But a respected and reliable system of weighing and measuring facilitated the exchange of goods and minimized the likelihood of disputes and legal cases.

The city of London was not able to feed itself: it relied on its ability to suck food supplies into the city from the surrounding region and, in some cases, from further away still.[78] Non-citizen food suppliers were not allowed to operate in a free and competitive market: the places where they could sell their produce and the

[73] Birch, *Charters*, 41. [74] Barron, 'Government of London', 232. [75] Ibid., 235–8, 581.

[76] *HW* ii. 635–6; Stow, *Survey*, i. 192; P. Nightingale, *A Medieval Mercantile Community: The Grocers' Company and the Politics and Trade of London 1000–1485* (New Haven, Conn., 1995), 386, 522.

[77] A. Sutton, 'The Mercery Trade and the Mercers' Company of London, from the 1130s to 1348' (University of London Ph.D. thesis, 1995), 362–5; Barron, 'Government of London', 233–4.

[78] The extent to which the need to feed London warped the agrarian economies of counties at a considerable distance from London has recently been analysed by the innovative work of the 'Feeding the City' project, see D. Keene, 'Medieval London and Its Region', *London Journal*, 14 (1989), 99–111; B. Campbell, J. Galloway, D. Keene, and M. Murphy, *A Medieval Capital and its Grain Supply: Agrarian Production and Distribution in the London Region c.1300*, Historical Geography Research Series, (London, 1993); J. Galloway, 'One Market or Many? London and the Grain Trade of England' in id. (ed.), *Trade, Urban Hinterlands and Market Integration c.1300–1600* (Institute of Historical Research, London, 2000), 23–42.

times when it could be displayed for sale were carefully controlled, as was the price. Every year from the time of Edward I the mayor and aldermen had been accustomed to decide the prices of grain, bread, salt, fish, and wine brought for sale in the city or marketed by the citizens themselves. In the course of the fourteenth and fifteenth centuries they extended their price regulation to include beer, meat, and poultry.[79] It was a fiercely controlled economy and yet the existence of price controls does not appear to have discouraged merchants, wholesalers, and food producers from bringing their goods to feed London. The demand must have been sufficiently assured to make the journey worthwhile and the returns measurable and comparatively secure. Much of civic regulation was aimed at excluding the middleman and bringing the producer into direct contact with the consumer. In the medieval period, when London was comparatively small, this was a realizable goal, but as the city quadrupled in size in the sixteenth century the role of the middleman developed to meet the logistical problems of getting the supplies into the city, and this, inevitably, contributed to the rise in prices caused also by a number of other factors. As the crafts developed their corporate organizations in the course of the fourteenth century, so the mayor and aldermen delegated to the sworn masters and wardens the responsibility for policing the wares offered for sale by their members. But the city's rulers retained, and on occasion exercised, their residual responsibility: for example William Page, a poulter, who had sold geese and piglets on a Sunday in 1444, and at unreasonable prices, was fined 6*s.* 8*d.* by the court of aldermen.[80] By the middle of the fifteenth century the wardens of the bakers (somewhat reluctantly), the brewers, salters, fishmongers, butchers, poulters, and vintners were all consulting the mayor and aldermen about shortages and problems in supplying goods, and about transgressors of all kinds. Even the fishmongers had had to accept the abolition, in 1400, of their monopoly of the retail sale of fish in the city in the interests of ensuring a better and cheaper supply of this essential commodity.[81]

It is interesting to note that from the second half of the fourteenth century, when living standards in London are generally agreed to have been rising, the mayor and aldermen began to regulate the prices at which ready-cooked food might be sold: in 1378 the prices for roasted fowl of all kinds were established and two years later the mayor and aldermen turned their attention to the less than savoury bits and pieces of rabbits and geese that were cooked into pies by the

[79] See Kowaleski, *Local Markets and Regional Trade*, 187–9.

[80] 30 May 1444, ordinance against Sunday trading, *LBK*, 293; 2 October 1444, Page in court, CLRO Journal 4 fo.43.

[81] For the civic control of food prices in London, see Barron, 'Government of London', 239–57, 570–8; Campbell, Galloway, Keene, and Murphy, *A Medieval Capital and its Grain Supply*, 104–7; S. Thrupp, *A Short History of the Worshipful Company of Bakers* (London, 1933), Ch. 2; P. E. Jones, *The Worshipful Company of Poulters of the City of London* (2nd edn., London 1965), chapters 5–7; J. Steven Watson, *A History of the Salters' Company* (London, 1965), 19; A. Crawford, *A History of the Vintners' Company* (London, 1977), 26–27; P. E. Jones, *The Butchers of London* (London, 1976), 106–7; M. Ball, *The Worshipful Company of Brewers* (London, 1977), 14–15, 23, 34–5, 40–4.

pastillers or pie-bakers.[82] They were concerned not only about prices but also to ensure a wholesome product. It may have been a desire to regulate the sale of cooked food in the city more effectively that led the mayor and aldermen, from the 1440s, to choose two aldermen each year to oversee the activities of hostellers, brewers, cooks, pie-bakers, and hucksters to ensure that they sold their goods at the agreed prices and that they did not keep their establishments open longer than the permitted hours.[83] But on special occasions, such as the festivities at midsummer, cookshops might stay open longer: in 1410 the king's sons, Thomas and John, were eating supper in a cookshop in Eastcheap after midnight on midsummer eve and were drawn into a brawl, which led to the imposition of a 9 p.m. curfew on the city.[84]

If the city was to attract traders and wealthy customers into London to do business then they must be provided not only with hot meals but a place to sleep at night. From the late thirteenth century there are references to hostellers in London and their activities began to be regulated by the mayor and aldermen.[85] By the mid-fourteenth century named commercial inns appear, such as The George in Lombard Street and The Bell in Holborn.[86] In Southwark and Westminster by 1400 inns were ubiquitous: twenty-two innkeepers were listed in the Southwark poll tax of 1381.[87] In London many country gentlemen and knights who, like the Stonors, had acquired a London inn, now leased it out and stayed at public inns—The Woolsack or The Sword in Fleet Street—when they had business to transact in London. The Pastons never bought a London inn but stayed at The George at Paul's Wharf where Thomas Green the landlord and his wife received and forwarded messages and collected parcels.[88] The growing importance of this crucial service industry was recognized, perhaps, in 1473 when the wardens of the 'mistery of hostelers' asked the permission of the mayor and aldermen to be known in future as 'the craft and mistery of Innholders'.[89] Although providing bed and breakfast for travelling salesmen was an important part of the innholder's job, the stabling and feeding of horses were probably even more important. The new ordinances that the innholders presented to the mayor and aldermen for approval in 1483 were concerned, not with the comfort of their human customers, but with the price and quality of hay and horsebread.[90] However, to provide stabling for horses was as important to the commercial well-being of the medieval city as the provision of car parks is now for modern towns. If the visitor with business to

[82] *Memorials*, 426, 438; see M. Carlin, 'Fast Food and Urban Living Standards in Medieval England', in M. Carlin and J. Rosenthal (eds.), *Food and Eating in Medieval Europe* (London, 1998), 27–51, esp. 38–40, 49.

[83] Barron, 'Government of London', 256–7.

[84] Cited by Carlin, 'Fast Food', 51 n. 112.

[85] *LBC*, 84.

[86] Lobel, *Historic Towns Atlas*, 66, 75.

[87] M. Carlin, *Medieval Southwark* (London, 1996), 192–200, esp. 193; G. Rosser, *Medieval Westminster* (Oxford, 1989), 122–33.

[88] See Barron, 'Conspicuous Consumption', 12.

[89] *LBL*, 112; in an earlier petition presented to the mayor and aldermen in 1446 the craft was known as that of the 'Hostillers', *LBK*, 316–18.

[90] *LBL*, 209; see Carlin, *Medieval Southwark*, 200.

transact could stay at a known address where his customers or business associates would know where to locate him, then his business could be transacted more quickly and efficiently.

Many of the transactions conducted in these inns and hostelries would not have been cash sales but rather transactions involving credit or deferred payment: it was important to the vendor to be able to offer credit and to have a reasonably secure method of recording and recovering debts. The city had to be able to facilitate transactions in these ways, as much for the small tradesman as for the large-scale overseas merchant. As early as 1221 the citizens had assured the royal justices that they would in future provide 'piepowder' courts to hear 'the plaints of persons passing through the city who cannot make any stay there' in relation to debt or injury: this court would comprise the mayor and sheriffs assisted by two or three aldermen and they would sit daily if necessary.[91] It would seem that, at first, the courts held by the sheriffs were the most favoured by foreigners for commercial pleas to such an extent that in 1230 the citizens complained that their own pleas were being delayed.[92] But by the later fourteenth century the mayor's court began to remove cases concerning the law merchant from the sheriffs courts because such actions 'according to the custom of the city ought to be finished and terminated in the Chamber before the mayor and aldermen having knowledge of the law merchant'.[93] Few records remain to indicate how the city, in the thirteenth century, held its piepowder courts, and there are not many records for the later period either.[94] But it is clear that the city of London had a procedure for dealing with these cases and this may well have influenced those who drafted the statutes at the end of the thirteenth century.

The Statute of Acton Burnell (1283), which was subsequently strengthened by the Statute *de Mercatoribus* (1285), provided a procedure whereby debts could be registered as bonds before the mayors of London, York, and Bristol and at other 'good towns' and at fair courts. These courts kept rolls of debts (recognizances) and gave the creditor a copy. If the debtor defaulted, the mayor or sheriffs could imprison the debtor and seize his lands and chattels to the amount of the debt.[95] The whole procedure was swift and, in most cases, effective.[96] In the *Carta Mercatoria* of 1303 the king reiterated the principle of speedy justice for all merchants in accordance with the Law Merchant, and in all commercial disputes between domestic and alien merchants half the jury was to be composed of men of

[91] *Liber Albus*, 59. [92] *CPMR 1381–1412*, p. xii. [93] Ibid. xiv.

[94] For a discussion of the surviving material, see Elizabeth Bennett, 'Debt and Credit in the Urban Economy: London, 1380–1460' (University of Yale, Ph.D. thesis, 1989), 98, 139, 144.

[95] See 1283 Statute Acton Burnell, *English Historical Documents 1189–1327*, ed. H. Rothwell (London, 1975), 420–2; J. Kermode, 'Money and Credit in the Fifteenth Century: Some Lessons from Yorkshire', *Business History Review*, 65 (1991), 475–501, esp. 484–94; J. H. Munro, 'The International Law Merchant and the Evolution of Negotiable Credit in Late Medieval England and the Low Countries', in *Banchi Pubblici, Banchi Privati e monti di pieta nell' Europa preindustriale* (Societa Ligure di Storia Patria) NS 31 (Genoa, 1991), 49–80.

[96] Year 1285, royal injunction to city to hold daily courts for 'foreins', *Liber Albus*, 257; for the dating of the different sections of the Liber Albus, see W. Kellaway, 'John Carpenter's Liber Albus', *Guildhall Studies in London History*, 3 (1978), 67–84.

the nationality of the alien. It was already London custom by the early fourteenth century that where alien merchants were involved, half the inquest should be 'de sa lange'.[97] This principle was reasserted in the Statute Staple of 1353, which also extended the registration of debts to any town where a mayor of the staple had been appointed. The juries in these courts were to consist of the mayor, two constables (or sheriffs), and a jury of domestic and alien merchants.[98] The 1353 statute established fifteen staple towns and, in the case of London, transferred the staple from London to Westminster, in what may have been an intentional policy of cutting the city down to size. But, in practice, since the mayoralty of the Westminster Staple was usually held by a London citizen (in the case of William Walworth in 1380, by the London mayor himself) the shift of location had little effect in practice.[99] Cases arising out of debt transactions recorded at the Westminster Staple court may well have been heard in the mayor's court of London which was careful to try cases, where appropriate, in accordance with the Law Merchant.

It seems likely that the London courts, well before the various Edwardian statutes, were providing for the speedy resolution of commercial disputes and a satisfactory means for recording debts and, when necessary, for calling the debtor effectively to account. The two London courts which, by the fourteenth century, were recording debts and dealing with the pursuit of debtors were the sheriffs' and the mayor's court. More material has survived from the mayor's court, but some analysis of the use made by litigants of the two courts is possible. On the whole the debts pursued in the sheriffs' court involved larger sums of money: nearly 50 per cent of the debts recorded between 1391 and 1393 involved amounts of more than £50. By contrast, half the suits for debt in the mayor's court between 1388 and 1456 involved sums of less than £4.[100] As might be expected a high percentage of the creditors in both courts were Londoners, but it is clear that the sheriffs' court was used for registering the debts owed to Londoners by men from other parts of England, whereas 90 per cent the debtors recorded in the mayor's court were Londoners (many of them were artisans and labourers).[101] Clearly by the later fourteenth century it was predominantly Londoners who used the city courts to record debts and pursue debtors, yet a substantial number of those who came from outside London to do business in the city with Londoners chose to use the sheriffs' court and 16 per cent of the creditors using the mayor's court were aliens (particularly the Hanse merchants). So it is clear that by the later fourteenth century the city was providing a useful 'debt collection service' to supplement that provided in the Staple courts and, in addition, complicated commercial disputes could be heard quickly and expertly in the mayor's court.

It was also important for the Londoners to develop negotiable credit instruments, whereby debts might be assigned to others and bills of exchange sold on, or

[97] *Liber Albus*, 191, for date see Kellaway, 'Liber Albus', 77.

[98] Munro, 'The International Law Merchant', 53–4; *CPMR 1323–64*, 259 n. 3; Bennett, 'Debt and Credit in the Urban Economy', 117–22.

[99] *CPMR 1364–1381*, 277; *CPMR 1381–1412*, pp. xvi–xvii.

[100] See Bennett, 'Debt and Credit in the Urban Economy', 139–40, 144–5.

[101] Ibid. 142, 147.

used to settle debts, so that in a period when banking facilities were minimal and bullion in short supply, goods could continue to be traded in the absence of cash payments.[102] Written obligations appear to have been bought up and assigned to third parties in London as early as 1307 and in a case in 1436 it was recognized that the bearer of a commercial bill, provided that he had been assigned the rights in the bill, might be acknowledged as having the same rights in law as the original principal: i.e. the courts (in this case the mayor's court) accepted the existence of a legally transferable credit instrument and the bearer might sue as if he were the principal.[103] If such negotiable instruments were developed and used in the London mayor's court as early as the fourteenth century, then the city was offering to merchants, whether Londoners or aliens, a means of facilitating trade in difficult times.[104] And there is no doubt that there were some hard times. In the middle years of the fifteenth century there was a severe depression in European trade caused, in part, by a shortage of bullion.[105] This shortage led to a contraction in credit as governments took protectionist measures. The Lancastrian government first, in the Bullion Ordinance of 1429, demanded payment for all exported wool in bullion, and restricted the amount of credit that merchants could offer to their overseas buyers. These measures simply aggravated the problem and the recession began to lift only as bullion, mined in southern Germany, began to seep into the European economy. From about 1450 we can observe a rise in the output of coin from the London mint, and this in turn improved commercial optimism and credit. It was not until about 1470 that the exports of English cloth began to rise from the plateau they had occupied since 1420, and it is only in the 1480s that the imports of wine, and the income from Poundage and Petty Customs regained the levels of the first decades of the century.[106] It has been argued that this prolonged recession 'made it difficult for merchants at the periphery to compete with London'.[107] Although the Londoners had attempted to devise ways in which they could make credit available not only to overseas merchants but also to provincial traders, in the end, the greater resources of capital in London 'as well as its

[102] See *CPMR 1381–1412*, pp. xxxvi–xl.

[103] Munro, 'The International Law Merchant', 71–5; see *Select Cases Concerning the Law Merchant 1251–1775*, ed. H. Hall, 3 vols. (Selden Society, 1932), iii. 117–19.

[104] Munro suggests that London practice in these matters may have influenced the developments in Bruges and Antwerp in the early sixteenth century, 'The International Law Merchant', 75.

[105] P. Nightingale, 'England and the European Depression of the Mid-Fifteenth Century', *Journal of European Economic History*, 26 (1997), 631–56; Nightingale sees the problems developing from the late fourteenth century, see her 'Monetary Contraction and Mercantile Credit in Later Medieval England', *EconHR* 43 (1990), 560–75; John Hatcher, while acknowledging the role played by the bullion shortage, sees the mid-century depression as deeper, and lasting longer, than other historians: 'The Great Slump of the Mid-Fifteenth Century', in R. Britnell and J. Hatcher (eds.), *Progress and Problems in Medieval England: Essays in Honour of Edward Miller* (Cambridge, 1996), 237–72.

[106] See figs. 5.4, 5.7, 5.9, and 5.11.

[107] Kermode, 'Money and Credit in the Fifteenth Century' 476. Wendy Childs has demonstrated that, in spite of the statutory restrictions, credit continued to be used to facilitate home and overseas trade throughout the middle years of the century, '"To oure losse and hindrance": English Credit to Alien Merchants in the Mid-Fifteenth Century', in J. Kermode (ed.), *Enterprise and Individuals in Fifteenth-Century England* (Stroud, 1991), 68–98.

geographical advantages, ensured that it survived the recession better than its rival ports' and went on to widen the gap between the city and the other towns in England in terms of both population and wealth.[108]

In all these ways the Londoners, acting together or as individuals, accepted a measure of responsibility for creating an attractive commercial environment: they ensured access to the city by water and road, they provided public quays where goods could be unloaded, warehouses for storage, and market places, both open and covered, where goods could be sold. There were civic officials who weighed and measured goods, oversaw sales and, in many cases, established the prices at which goods (especially foodstuffs) might be sold. There were, moreover, local courts (in addition to the Staple courts) where debts might be recorded and pursued, and in the mayor's court expert judges were on hand to hear and determine cases speedily in accordance with the Law Merchant. In these ways the Londoners attempted to attract tradesmen and merchants from other parts of England, and from abroad, to come to London to buy and sell. What goods they had to sell and what role the Londoners themselves played in their manufacture and distribution within England and abroad—in short, the ways in which the Londoners created the wealth that maintained the commercial facilities and kept the city far ahead of all other towns in England—will be explored in the next chapter.

[108] Nightingale, 'England and the European Depression', 647.

CHAPTER FOUR

The Manufacture and Distribution of Goods

MANUFACTURING INDUSTRIES

IN SIXTEENTH- AND seventeenth-century London 'nearly three-fifths of the occupations of Londoners involved some form of production of goods'.[1] This included 'transforming raw materials into meat, bread and light' which 'were mainstream economic activities'.[2] Much of this production of goods was carried out by men (and women and children) who were not members of the organized and recognized craft or trade associations, namely the city companies. The situation was the same in earlier centuries: many workmen lived in the suburbs and so avoided company control, or they practised such specialized crafts (e.g. the leather bottlemakers) that company control was unnecessary and irrelevant. The study of the city companies can reveal something of the organization and success of the larger groupings of craftsmen, but such a study can tell only part of the story.[3]

The records used in the study of manufacturing in sixteenth-century London utilized the occupational descriptions to be found in the burial registers of fifteen London parishes covering the years 1540 to 1600 (a total of some 2,388 persons).[4] A comparable study has been attempted using the wills enrolled in the Commissary Court of London between 1374 and 1486 (a total of 4,516 persons, excluding clergy (768) and those, such as knights, gentlemen, and widows (1,363) who were described by rank rather than occupation).[5] As far as possible the broad classifications established in the sixteenth-century study have been followed in the analysis of the fifteenth-century wills. These classifications have been largely followed in comparable studies of the occupations of other English towns (York, Worcester, Coventry, and Southwark) and all the percentages have been included in Table 4.1. That London was an industrial city is evident from the complaints voiced in civic ordinances and by neighbours when they gathered together at the ward meetings. Industrial activity in the medieval period was small-scale and

[1] A. L. Beier, 'Engine of Manufacture: The Trades of London', in A. L. Beier and R. Finlay (eds.), *London 1500–1700: The Making of the Metropolis* (London, 1986), 141–67, esp. 150.

[2] Ibid. 146; D. Keene, 'London from the Post-Roman Period to 1300', in D. Palliser (ed.), *Cambridge Urban History of Britain* (Cambridge, 2000), 187–216, esp. 200.

[3] See Ch. 9.

[4] Beier, 'Engine of Manufacture'.

[5] See Table 4.1 for an explanation of the use made of this source and its limitations.

domestic: it took place in the home, the yard, or the street outside the shop and it was, inevitably, a frequent source of grievance to neighbours.[6] The repeated civic regulations and the complaints of indignant neighbours bear witness to the volume and diversity of industrial activity in medieval London.

Clothworking was from the thirteenth century, and most probably earlier, England's prime industrial activity. In the twelfth century London was an important centre of clothworking and the weavers were among the earliest craft groups in the city to secure a royal charter and, by implication, a measure of co-operative action.[7] But the weavers seem not to have been popular and they were unable to prevent their craft from falling into the hands of the entrepreneurial group of middlemen known as burrellers, who appear to have owned the wool, which they then put out to weavers, fullers, and dyers.[8] In spite of protectionist civic legislation, cloth appears to have been sent out of the city to Stratford and elsewhere to be fulled.[9] By 1321 it was asserted that the restrictive practices of the weavers had led to a decline in the number of working looms in the city and in 1335 their monopoly was ended. Any freeman was now to be allowed to set up a loom in his house.[10] But comparatively few appear to have done so. The fact is that the making of cloth was moving out of towns and into the countryside. But clothmaking was not entirely banished from London. Dyers, fullers, shearmen, tapissers,[11] and weavers all elected men for the common council in the 1370s and all, except the tapissers, had company halls by the early sixteenth century, although the shearmen and the fullers found it necessary to join forces in 1528 in order to secure a position among the 'Great Twelve' as the clothworkers.[12] It seems likely that what may have been an important industrial activity in London in the twelfth and thirteenth centuries developed into an entrepreneurial trade in which Londoners bought up unfinished cloth in the countryside and brought it to London to be finished and sold. The wealth of the London dyers in the fifteenth century attests to the importance of this aspect of the finishing trade in the city.[13] Such cloth as was actually made in London was probably of mediocre quality and largely for local consumption. It is clear that York, Oxford, Worcester, and Coventry all had a higher percentage than London

[6] See Ch. 10. [7] See Ch. 9.

[8] See E. Miller and J. Hatcher (eds.), *Medieval England: Towns, Commerce and Crafts 1086–1348* (London, 1995), 112–3.

[9] Years 1297–8, *LBC*, 51–2; 1310, *LBD*, 239–40; 1379, *LBH*, 37.

[10] *Liber Custumarum*, 416–24; also F. Consitt, *The London Weavers' Company* (Oxford, 1933), 26–8.

[11] Tapissers were specialized weavers who largely made figured cloth, see E. Crowfoot, F. Pritchard, and K. Staniland, *Textiles and Clothing 1150–1450* (2nd edn., Woodbridge, 2001), 70–1; they appear as a separate company at intervals between 1376 and 1485 but probably joined forces with the weavers by the end of the century, see Table 9.1.

[12] See Ch. 9 and Table 9.1. It may be indicative of the decline of the clothmaking industry in London that whereas in the 1370s the cardmakers (who made the wooden boards with nails attached to them that were used for carding wool) were sufficiently prosperous to elect representatives to the common council, yet they disappeared entirely in the fifteenth century.

[13] A large thirteenth-century dyeworks has been excavated at Swan Lane, see J. Schofield, *Medieval London Houses* (London, 1994), 218; Crowfoot, Pritchard, and Staniland, *Textiles and Clothing*, 19–20; see also J. R. Oldland, 'London Cloth-Making, *c.*1270–*c.*1550' (University of London, Ph.D. thesis, 2003).

TABLE 4.1. DISTRIBUTION OF CRAFTS AND TRADES IN LONDON COMPARED WITH OTHER TOWNS (%)

	York 1381 Poll Tax[1]	Oxford 1381 Poll Tax[2]	Worcester, 1377 & 1381 Poll Taxes[3]	Southwark 1381 Poll Tax[4]	London wills 1374–1486[5]	Coventry 1522–24 Subsidy[6]	London 1540–1600 Burials[7]
Victuals	15.8	27.2	22	23	22.5[8]	15	8.9
Leather	15.0	14.7	17	13[9]	11[8]	10.6	9.1
Textiles	11.6	13.5	15	11	5	17.1	22.4 (Textiles and Clothing together)
Clothing	8.4	11.9	10	12[9]	11.5[8]	15.3	
Mercantile	15.5	4.7	6.8	—	13.5[8]	10.6	12.8
Metal	12.8	6.2	7.3	3	13.4[8]	9.7	9.1
Building	3.6	7.0	7.6	6[10]	5.5	6.7	8.4[11]
Wood	5.7	3.2	2.3	0.7	2.7	4.0	—
Transport	2.6	2.7	0.7	6	2.3	—	6.4
Armaments	2.1	1.6	2.0	0.5	1	—	18 (Armaments, Chandlers and Others together)
Chandlers	0.4	2.0	2.0	0.5	2.3	—	
Others	6.4	5.3	7.3	25[12]	9.2	11.1	
Total (100%)	2,193	1,535	410	534	4516[13]	568	2388

[1] Poll Tax, see J. P. Goldberg, *Women, Work and the Life Cycle in a Medieval Economy: Women in York and Yorkshire 1300–1520* (Oxford, 1992), 45–6.

[2] Ibid.

[3] C. Barron, 'The Fourteenth-Century Poll Tax Returns for Worcester', *Midland History*, 14 (1989), 1–29 esp. 11.

[4] Calculated from M.Carlin, *Medieval Southwark* (London, 1996), App. 1, Poll Tax Return 1381, 259–69.

[5] Calculated from *Index to Testamentary Records in the Commissary Court of London, 1374–1488*, ed. M. Fitch (London, 1969). These wills represent half of those enrolled in the church courts in London in these years: the wills enrolled in the Archdeaconry Court are lost from 1416 until the sixteenth century. I am very grateful to Dr Jane Martindale for invaluable help in compiling this table.

[6] C. Phythian-Adams, *Desolation of a City: Coventry and the Urban Crisis of the Late Middle Ages* (Cambridge, 1979), apps. 3c and 3d.

[7] A. L. Beier, 'Engine of Manufacture: The Trades of London', in A. L. Beier and R. Finlay (eds.), *The Making of the Metropolis: London 1500–1700* (London, 1986), 141–67, esp. 148, 164.

[8] Grocers (151) have been included with 'Mercantile' rather than with 'Victuals'. Vintners (90) have been included with 'Victuals', Leathersellers (32) and Skinners (172) with 'Leather', and Goldsmiths (148) with 'Metal', although all four crafts contained a significant 'Mercantile' element, as did the Tailors (369) who have been placed with 'Clothing'. The Haberdashers (66) have been classed as 'Mercantile'.

[9] Carlin, *Medieval Southwark*, includes shoemakers, cobblers, and glovers under 'clothing' not, as in other calculations, under 'leather'.

[10] If Labourers are added from 'Others' the number rises to 13.5.

[11] If Labourers are included (currently in 'Others') the figure rises to 13.3.

[12] If Labourers are subtracted the number falls to 17.

[13] From this total of London wills have been excluded those of Servants (28), Dames (7), Armigers/Esquires (69), Freewomen (2), Gentlewomen (70), Husbandmen (50), Knights (40), Spinsters/maidens (11), Widows (1052), Yeomen (44), Clergy of all kinds (768).

of workers employed in the textile industry. In Worcester and Coventry the percentage was three times greater than that of London, which reflects, also, their less diversified economies. It may be that much of the clothmaking in London took place in Southwark where 11 per cent of the workers in 1381 were involved in the textile trade as shepsters (female shearmen) and, above all, as spinsters.[14]

As in all medieval English towns, the working of leather (the ubiquitous plastic of medieval society) was widely practised in London. The tanning of cattle hides and the tawing of other skins were carried on all over the city often to the annoyance of neighbours.[15] The craft of skinners comprised both the merchants who imported the furs and put them out to tawyers, and also the craftsmen who stitched together the newly tawed furs. Adam Wenlock, a London tawyer, employed nine men and joined the Corpus Christi fraternity of the merchant skinners.[16] But relations were not always so harmonious between the retailing skinners and the dependent craft of tawyers. Tanners and tawyers (sometimes known as whitetawyers) both sent representatives to the common council in the 1370s but their importance appears to have declined in the fifteenth century and, in particular, the tanners virtually disappeared.[17] It may be that the tanners were driven out of the city by the hostility to their trade and it is possible that they followed the butchers' slaughterhouses into the city suburbs. There is evidence that Londoners sent large numbers of hides by boat to be tanned in Maidstone in Kent and Barking in Essex, and then the tanned hides would be reurned to the city to be made up into leather goods.[18] Tawing, however, continued and there is evidence of more specialized leatherworking such as could only flourish where there was a large consumer market. This large London market explains the demand for bottlemakers, cofferers, pouchmakers, sheathers, leathercutters, and leatherdyers. As in all towns cordwainers (or shoemakers) were ubiquitous and swallowed up the lesser craft of cobblers. The surviving shoe fragments found in archaeological excavations in London testify to the skills of these craftsmen who produced sophisticated shoes with elaborate points and fine tooling and fretwork in the leather. At the other end of the market they produced complicated pattens, shoes with wooden soles and

[14] See Table 4.1; figures derived from an analysis of the Southwark poll tax, M. Carlin, *Medieval Southwark* (London, 1996), 259–69.

[15] See M. Kowaleski, 'Town and Country in Late Medieval England: The Hide and Leather Trade' in P. J. Corfield and D. Keene (eds.), *Work in Towns 850–1850* (Leicester, 1990), 57–73 ; D. Keene, 'Tanners' Widows, 1300–1350' in C. Barron and A. Sutton (eds.), *Medieval London Widows 1300–1500* (London, 1994), 1–27.

[16] E. Veale, *The English Fur Trade in the Later Middle Ages* (Oxford, 1966), 88.

[17] See Table 9.1: the tanners do not appear as an organized group in the city after 1381; only seventeen tanners enrolled wills in the Commissary Court between 1374 and 1488, whereas there were fifty-three tawyers in the same period, see *Index to Testamentary Records in the Commissary Court of London 1374–1488*, ed. M. Fitch (London, 1969), 211, 213–14. A number of alien (German) tawyers and their servants were assessed for the subsidy in 1483, see J. L. Bolton, *The Alien Communities of London in the Fifteenth Century* (Stamford, 1998), 136.

[18] See J. Galloway, 'Town and Country in England, 1300–1570', in S. R. Epstein (ed.), *Town and Country in Europe 1300–1800* (Cambridge, 2001), 106–31, esp. 126.

leather straps, and, for a time in the fifteenth century, the pattenmakers were able to operate as an independent craft.[19]

A very large number of craftsmen in London worked in making and decorating clothes. The most common craft designation among the London testators in the years 1374 to 1488 was that of tailor.[20] These men ranged in their activities from the merchant tailors who took part in overseas trade, such as Sir John Percyvale who became mayor of London in 1498[21] to men who were paid by the day to work in the shops, and wardrobes, of other men.[22] The work of the ubiquitous tailors was supplemented by a host of specialist craftspeople such as embroiderers, silk-women,[23] girdlers, cappers or 'hurers', and glovers. The fragments of their work that have been found in excavations bear witness to their remarkable skills—and eyesight.[24] The London tailors lived all over the city but there was a particular clustering of them along Fleet Street in the parish of St Dunstan in the West where they were close to their gentlemen lawyer and civil-servant customers.[25] But, important as the clothing was in the economy of medieval London, it is clear that it became even more notable in the sixteenth century: whereas 11 per cent of London craftsmen in the fifteenth century were working in the clothing trades, by the second half of the next century the percentage had doubled to 22 per cent.[26] These figures demonstrate the remarkable development of London as a centre of 'conspicuous consumption' and as the fashionable capital of England in the Tudor period.[27] The clothing trade now included such specialized workmen as bodice-makers, buttonmakers, and hatband-makers but, not surprisingly, vestment-makers are no longer to be found amongst the London craftsmen.[28] Even if London became more conspicuously a centre of conspicuous consumption in the sixteenth century, yet even in the medieval period it was to the city that the aristocracy and knightly families would come to buy their clothes. In 1382 on one of his annual visits to London Sir John Dinham from Devon bought red and green cloth which he had made up by the tailor John Bourwill into gowns for himself and his wife and also his squire at a total cost (cloth and making-up) of £14 14*s.* 4*d.*[29] It is interesting that Dinham remained loyal to Bourwill and always used him to

[19] F. Grew and M. de Neergaard, *Shoes and Pattens* (London, HMSO, 1988), 35, 82–8, 91–101.

[20] There were 369 tailors, calculated from Fitch, *Commissary Wills*; the next most common craft was that of brewers, with 317 testators.

[21] M. P. Davies, 'Dame Thomasine Percyvale, the "Maid of Week" (d.1512)', in Barron and Sutton, *Medieval London Widows*, 185–207, esp. 193–6.

[22] See M. P. Davies, 'The Tailors of London and their Guild *c.*1300–1500' (University of Oxford, D.Phil. thesis, 1994), esp. ch. 6.

[23] See Crowfoot, Pritchard, and Staniland, *Textiles and Clothing*, 130–45.

[24] Ibid. 150–98.

[25] Davies, 'The Tailors of London', 224–6 and map p. 46.

[26] See Table 4.1.

[27] F. J. Fisher, 'The Development of London as a Centre of Conspicuous Consumption in the Sixteenth and Seventeeth Centuries', *TRHS* 30 (1948), 37–50, rpt. in F. J. Fisher, *London and the English Economy, 1500–1700*, ed. P. J. Corfield and N. B. Harte (London, 1990), 105–18.

[28] Beier, 'Trades of London', 164.

[29] Cornwall Record Office, AR 37/41/1: I am grateful to Dr Hannes Kleineke for a transcript of this document. Between 1379 and 1394 the Dinhams paid Bourwill a minimum of £19 for tailoring work, but the accounts are by no means complete, see H. Kleineke, 'The Dinham Family in the Later Middle Ages' (University of London Ph.D. thesis, 1998), 127–9.

make up his clothes in London: a custom of loyalty that is to be found also among other royal and aristocratic patrons.

It is hardly surprising that woodworking crafts, such as joiners, turners, and coopers, were comparatively little in evidence in London since there was no local supply of wood, although the specialized 'armaments industry' of fletchers and bowyers continued to be important well into the middle of the sixteenth century. Although it is likely that there was a concentration of skilled building craftsmen such as carpenters and masons in and around London, they may simply have maintained a base, or storehouse, in the city and otherwise moved around the country wherever the work was to be found. The famous architects/masons, William Ramsey (d.1349) and Henry Yevele (d.1400) were important in the city, but they were certainly not continuously present.[30] Only masons and painters sent men to the common council in the late fourteenth century, yet by the early sixteenth century the carpenters, glaziers, and tilers were also prominent crafts with their own halls (see Table 9.1). This development may reflect the rise in population which created, by the mid-sixteenth century, an unprecedented demand for housing in London. Moreover the Court and the aristocracy, influenced by Continental tastes and practices, were making more specialized demands for their houses and palaces near London.

The most distinctive industry in medieval London was that of metalworking, both by virtue of the numbers of men engaged in the metal crafts and for the number of organized groupings of specialist workers.[31] In the late fourteenth century the armourers, brasiers, cardmakers (wooden bats with metal spikes for carding wool), cutlers, founders, goldsmiths, ironmongers, lorimers (makers of the metal parts of horse harness), pewterers, pinners, plumbers, smiths, and spurriers all sent representatives to the common council, and in the fifteenth century yet more specialized groups sometimes appeared, such as the bladesmiths, coppersmiths, latteners, and wiresellers (see Table 9.1). For the most highly specialized work it was necessary to use London craftsmen: Richard II in 1394 employed the coppersmiths, Nicholas Broke and Godfey Prest to make the two gilt latten effigies for the tomb in which he was to be buried in Westminster Abbey with his queen, Anne of Bohemia.[32] The finest incised memorial brasses were made in London workshops from where they were transported all over England.[33] The craftsmen who worked the brasses, which appear from the 1270s onwards and became immensely pop-

[30] J. Harvey, *English Medieval Architects: A Biographical Dictionary to 1550* (2nd edn., Gloucester, 1984), 242–5, 358–66.

[31] On metalworking in London, see D. Keene, 'Metalworking in Medieval London: An Historical Survey', *The Journal of the Historical Metallurgy Society*, 30 (1996), 95–102.

[32] See P. Lindley, 'Absolutism and Regal Image in Ricardian Sculpture', in D. Gordan, L. Monnas, and C. Elam (eds.), *The Regal Image of Richard II and the Wilton Diptych* (London, 1997), 61–83, esp. 62–9. When Broke died in 1425 he bequeathed 300 barrels of 'auricalco' (copper brass), see C. Blair, 'Copper Alloys' in J. Blair and N. Ramsay (eds.), *English Medieval Industries* (London, 1991), 81–106, esp. 81–3.

[33] P. Binski, 'Monumental Brasses', in J. Alexander and P. Binski (eds.), *Age of Chivalry: Art in Plantagenet England 1200–1400* (London, 1987), 171–3; J. Blair, 'Purbeck Marble', in Blair and Ramsay (eds.), *English Medieval Industries*, 41–56.

ular in the fourteenth century, seem to have formed a specialized, but subordinate, craft to that of the marblers, the men who made the marble slabs or tomb chests on which the brass was placed. When the marblers presented ordinances to the mayor and aldermen for approval in 1486 they claimed to speak for everyone who 'maketh any stone-werk of marbyll, laton werke or coper werk' in the city.[34] Monumental brasses were also made outside London but their quality did not touch that of the London craftsmen. In the same way, although bells were made elsewhere in England, most of the bells hung in the church towers of later medieval England were made in London by men who were originally known as potters but, by the later fourteenth century, as founders. Although the founders were numerous (thirty-eight testators in the fifteenth century) and well established, yet not all of them had the considerable resources needed to cast bells: such men would cast a range of brass and latten goods such as candlesticks, pots, bowls, and kitchen utensils. Only a few founders had premises that were sufficiently large and secure to make bells and these bell workshops were, clearly, large-scale enterprises by medieval standards.[35] The bell foundry outside Aldgate whose business history can be traced for over a hundred years was run, in the early part of the fifteenth century, by Richard Hill and then, for a short period, by his widow Johanna. In their workshop they employed four apprentices, six servants, one 'bell maker', a clerk, four other men, and two female servants. This was a substantial workforce and the survival of twenty-three of Richard's bells (from a twenty-five-year working life) and of seven of Johanna's bells from a period of less than a year when she ran the foundry, testifies to their considerable industrial output and to the range of their market. Their bells are found in East Anglia and the south-east, but also as far west as Gloucestershire and Devon.[36] The fact that London bells travelled considerable distances suggests that the London industry was of national, and not just local, importance.

Johanna Hill may have cast a bell for the village church of Manaton in Devon in return for a supply of tin. By the 1420s half of all the tin mined in Devon and Cornwall was being transported to London, much of it to be made into a range of pewter goods.[37] The pewter made in London was reckoned to be the finest in Europe; an Italian visitor in 1497 commented that English pewterers 'make vessels as brilliant as if they were of fine silver, and these are held in great estimation'.[38] The first reference to a pewterer in London occurs in 1305 and the craft developed rapidly. Ordinances were drawn up in 1348 and it has been estimated that, in the early fifteenth century, London pewterers were working some 60 tonnes of ware a year which means that some 200,000 individual items of domestic pewter were

[34] *LBL*, 233–4.

[35] Blair, 'Copper Alloys', 89–93; for a discussion of the excavation of a foundry workshop in the intramural parish of St Mary Axe, see E. Howe, *Roman Defences and Medieval Industry* (London, 2002), 48–60, 64.

[36] C. Barron, 'Johanna Hill (d.1441) and Johanna Sturdy (d.*c*.1460), Bellfounders', in Barron and Sutton, *Medieval London Widows*, 99–111.

[37] J. Hatcher, *English Tin Production and Trade before 1550* (Oxford, 1973), 137.

[38] *A Relation . . . of the Island of England . . . c.1500*, ed. C. A. Sneyd (Camden Society, 1847), 11.

being produced annually in London workshops.[39] Exports of English pewter rose dramatically in the course of the fifteenth century (15–20 tonnes p.a. by 1400; 45–50 tonnes by the 1430s; 90 tonnes in 1466-7) and it ranked second in total value after cloth among English manufactured exports.[40] The craft was numerous: in 1456 there were forty-one liverymen, fifteen freemen, thirty-five journeymen, and ninety-seven apprentices: a total of nearly 200 craftsmen, not including the women who doubtless also worked in the trade. In the following year there were fifty-six workshops in London and twelve of these contained a master and three other workmen. The largest, that of Thomas Dounton, comprised eleven apprentices and seven journeymen, apart from Dounton himself. This is the largest craft workshop yet discovered in medieval London.[41]

The other metal-working industry in which London craftsmen enjoyed not only a national, but also a European, reputation was that of goldwork. From the reign of Edward the Confessor the skilled engravers of coin dies had been concentrated in London, and the link between London goldsmiths and the minting of royal coins in the Tower of London ensured the national significance of the London craftsmen.[42] Their highly skilled work was known and admired by visitors from the twelfth century to the sixteenth when Italian visitors marvelled at the fifty-two goldsmiths' shops in Cheapside filled with silver vessels of all kinds so that 'in all the shops in Milan, Rome, Venice and Florence put together, I do not think there would be found so many of the magnificence that are to be seen in London'.[43] Of course, many of the men calling themselves goldsmiths (148 testators between 1374 and 1488) were probably not craftsmen themselves but rather shopkeepers, or employers of craftsmen. Many of these craftsmen who worked in London were, in fact, aliens: in particular, Germans.[44] There were twenty-seven alien goldsmiths assessed for the subsidy in 1483. But there were, of course, also English craftsmen: John Orewell (who was the king's engraver) made a silver-gilt crozier for the abbot of Bury St Edmunds in 1430, and a silver font for Canterbury Cathedral Priory seventeen years later.[45] When Thomas Bourgchier was elected bishop of Worcester in 1435 he ordered a large amount of new plate for the episcopal table, including

[39] R. F. Homer, 'Tin, Lead and Pewter', in Blair and Ramsay, *English Medieval Industries*, 57–80, esp. 70.

[40] Ibid. 73; *The Overseas Trade of London: Exchequer Customs Accounts 1480–81*, ed. H. S. Cobb (London Record Society, 1990), p. xxv, and see index s.v. 'pewter'.

[41] Homer, 'Tin, Lead and Pewter', 71.

[42] M. Campbell, 'Gold, Silver and Precious Stones', in Blair and Ramsay, *English Medieval Industries*, 106–66, esp. 146; the small group of specialized craftsmen who actually struck the coins were known by the mid-fifteenth century as 'coiners', had their own guild run by a 'provost', and largely lived in Shoreditch and Islington, see J. Freeman, 'The Mistery of Coiners and the King's Moneyers of the Tower of London, *c.*1340–*c.*1530', *The British Numismatic Journal*, 70 (2001), 67–82.

[43] *A Relation . . . of the Island of England*, 42–3.

[44] Bolton, *Alien Communities*, 137.

[45] M. Campbell, 'English Goldsmiths in the Fifteenth Century', in D. Williams (ed.), *England in the Fifteenth Century* (Woodbridge, 1987), 43–52, esp. 51–2; see also T. F. Reddaway and L. Walker, *The Early History of the Goldsmiths' Company, 1327–1509* (London, 1975), 300.

twelve silver dishes, twelve salvers, and two chargers from William White, a London goldsmith.[46] Very little of this fine work survives although the reliquary given by Johanna, the second wife of Henry IV to her son Jean, duke of Brittany in 1412, now in the Louvre, was probably made in London as was the magnificent crown that travelled to Bavaria in the trousseau of Blanche, daughter of Henry IV, and is now in Munich.[47] Within the goldsmiths' craft in London were found a range of specialists: jewellers, coiners, finers, and gold-wire drawers who made the wire used for ornamentation on jewellery and vessels and also stitched onto vestments, altar cloths, and rich clothing. The skill of wire-drawing may have been stimulated by immigrants from Constantinople who brought their specialist knowledge to the cities of western Europe after the fall of the Byzantine Empire to the Turks.[48] Nor were these crafts exclusively male. Anne, the wife of John Framlingham, appears to have practised the 'craft of werkyng of wyre called Goldwyre drawyng' in London in the 1470s for which she had the use of a surprising variety of specialized tools.[49]

Goods of all kinds were manufactured in medieval London by a remarkably wide range of craftsmen and women. Clearly there were more specialist craftsmen in London than in any other English town. Among the 'other' crafts in Table 4.1 which accounted for 9 per cent of the manufacturing workforce were those associated with writing (bookbinders, limners, and parchmentmakers), with music (harpmaker, lutemaker, and organmaker) and the important craft of transforming animal horns into transparent sheets for lanterns and windows.[50] Taken altogether the manufacturing industries in London in the fifteenth century accounted for some 50 per cent of the workforce. If, however, we include those who transformed raw materials into meat, bread, and drink among the manufacturing, or producing, crafts then the figure rises to 75 per cent which is comparable to that for London in the later sixteenth century.[51]

The absence, or comparative insignificance, of certain industries in London should be noted. The textile industry is comparatively unimportant within the manufacturing sector of the London economy, although more cloth may have been made in London than in any other town in England. It is clear that a certain amount of clothworking, particularly dyeing and shearing, took place in London or nearby. Certainly there were a notable number of spinners and shearmen in

[46] Worcester Record Office, 009:1 Box 175, Doc. 92475; William White was not a particularly notable goldsmith: he became warden in 1457 and died in 1461.

[47] Campbell, 'Gold, Silver and Precious Stones', 130, 137, 154 and n.; Alexander and Binski, *Age of Chivalry*, no. 13.

[48] J. Harris, 'Two Byzantine Craftsmen in Fifteenth-Century London', *Journal of Medieval History*, 21 (1995), 387–403.

[49] *CPMR 1458–82*, 112–13; cf. the tools that Johanna Reynold, a widow and a foundress, left to her apprentice in 1482, GL Commissary will register 9171/6 fo. 350.

[50] A. Macgregor, 'Antler, Bone and Horn', in Blair and Ramsay, *English Medieval Industries*, 355–78; there were sixteen horners and one lanternmaker among the fifteenth-century testators

[51] Beier, 'Trades of London', 150.

Southwark. Again there was comparatively little shipbuilding in medieval London, although there was a guild of shipwrights from the late fourteenth century.[52] They appear to have been a very small mistery, living in the area known as Pettywales, lying between the Custom House and the Tower of London in the parish of All Hallows, Barking. Although in 1294–5 the London shipwrights were able to gather fifty men to build an oared galley at the command of the king, their normal work seems to have been building the river–going craft known as 'shouts', the safe and steady boat-of-all-work on the Thames.[53] The comparative novelty of the craft may be suggested by the entry in the Bridgewardens' accounts in 1381 when wages of 8*d.* a day were paid to '2 carpenters called *shipwrights*' but by 1460, led by Alan Fenne, a group of shipwrights was employed to mend the boats used by the Bridgewardens and also to build a boat called a 'cokke'. Fenne was paid 8*d.* a day, but the others received less. By 1537 the daily pay for the leading shipwright, Hugh Yonge, had risen to 11*d.*[54] It is possible that this industry was located downstream from the city, perhaps near the hospital of St Katherine: certainly by the sixteenth century the craft had moved eastwards to Shadwell and Wapping where there was the space needed to construct the ever-larger ships of the Tudor mercantile marine. But in the medieval period much of the shipping that came into the port of London was built in Holland or Flanders.[55] The rest was probably built in other English ports where timber was more accessible. The remarkable development of the ship-building industry in London was to come at the end of the sixteenth century.[56]

Another craft that seems to have been absent from London was the making of domestic pottery tableware (plates, bowls, and jugs); it has been estimated that two-thirds of the pottery used in London in the late-medieval period was made in Surrey, much of it at Cheam and Kingston.[57] Archaeologists have excavated as many as sixteen kilns at Kingston where the characteristic 'Surrey White Ware' was produced in quantity for the London market from the middle of the thirteenth century, replacing the pottery that had formerly been made in London. The development of this specialized local industry supplying, and dependent upon, the

[52] 13 February 1388, the men of the craft are found acting together in the transfer of an apprentice, see flyleaf of GL MS 4600. The guild elected masters between 1428 and 1433, *LBK*, 78, 143, 149, and there are a few shipwrights' wills.

[53] I. Friel, *The Good Ship: Ships, Shipbuilding and Technology in England 1200–1520* (London, 1995), 39–41.

[54] *London Bridge: Selected Accounts and Rentals, 1381–1538*, ed. V. Harding and L. Wright (London Record Society, 1995), 17, 143–4, 192–3.

[55] V. Harding, 'Cross-Channel Trade and Cultural Contacts: London and the Low Countries in the Late Fourteenth Century', in C. Barron and N. Saul (eds.), *England and the Low Countries in the Late Middle Ages* (Stroud, 1998), 153–68, esp. 162–3.

[56] B. Dietz, 'Overseas Trade and Metropolitan Growth', in Beier and Finlay, *London 1500–1700*, 115–40, esp. 127–8.

[57] J. Pearce and A. Vince, *A Dated Type-Series of London Medieval Pottery:* p. 4, *Surrey Whitewares* (LAMAS, 1988); P. Miller and R. Stephenson, *A Fourteenth-Century Pottery Site in Kingston upon Thames, Surrey* (London, 1999), 5–12, 40–1.

London market provides a graphic illustration of the ways in which the metropolis influenced the economies of small towns within its region.[58]

Likewise roof and floor tiles do not appear to have been made in the city. Tiles were made in elaborate and dangerous kilns in the countryside such as those at Cheam in Surrey, or Penn in Buckinghamshire.[59] Archaeologists have excavated a roof-tile kiln at Keston in north-west Kent and another at Woolwich.[60] Although there may have been some tilemaking in the Smithfield and Moorfields areas to the north of the city, the London tilers were probably suppliers and fixers of tiles, rather than the makers.[61] Although they do not appear in the city's records acting together as an organized craft until the second half of the fifteenth century, yet they seem to have become quickly established and had their own hall near Bishopsgate by 1475.[62] As tile came increasingly to replace thatch as the preferred form of roofing for London houses, and as the number of houses grew dramatically in the sixteenth century, so the tilers became an important city craft. Bricks were certainly not made within the walls of London but, like tiles, they came to be made in the environs of the city as the demand for them grew in the sixteenth century.[63] The only two medieval London brickmakers whose wills have survived both lived in the parish of St Mary Matfelon lying outside the city to the north-east.[64]

It is clear that London was a great industrial centre where goods of all kinds were fashioned from metals, leather, wood, wool, linen, bone, horn, and other animal by-products into an extraordinarily wide range of consumer goods, for London was also a massive consumer society. A quarter of the fifteenth-century testators analysed in Table 4.1 were not producers of goods, but rather consumers: these included the merchants (13.5%), those involved in transport (2.3%), and, in the category of 'other', there were fifty-six officials (or civil servants) of various kinds and 115 'professionals', such as scriveners, surgeons, schoolmasters, and attorneys. There were also a number of men who pursued a variety of trades which were certainly not manufacturing: men such as barbers, horse-dealers, haymongers, grooms, and drovers. In addition to the 25 per cent of the four and a half thousand testators classified as consumers, there were a large number of testators who do

[58] For a more general discussion of this point, see D. Keene, 'Small Towns and the Metropolis: The Experience of Medieval England', in J. M. Duvosquel and E. Thoen (eds.), *Peasants and Townsmen in Medieval Europe: Studia in Honorem Adriaan Verhulst* (Ghent, 1995), 223–38.

[59] J. Cherry, 'Pottery and Tile', in Blair and Ramsay, *English Medieval Industries*, 189–209, esp. 193–4; E. Eames, *Medieval Tilers* (London, 1992). For the fourteenth-century Penn tiles found in excavations in London, see Howe, *Roman Defences and Medieval Industry*, 78; B. Barker and C. Thomas, *The London Charterhouse* (London, 2002), 97.

[60] Howe, *Roman Defences and Medieval Industry*, 78.

[61] L. F. Salzman, *Building in England Down to 1540: A Documentary History* (Oxford, 1952), 229–30; E. Levy, 'Moorfields, Finsbury and the City of London in the Sixteenth Century', *London Topographical Record*, 26 (1990), 78–96, esp. 83, 93; D. Moss, 'The Economic Development of a Middlesex Village', *Agricultural History Review*, 38 (1980), 104–14.

[62] M. D. Lobel, (ed.), *Historic Towns Atlas: The City of London from Prehistoric Times to c.1500* (Oxford, 1989), 96.

[63] Howe, *Roman Defences and Medieval Industry*, 80.

[64] John Caunton (d. 1479) and Christopher Hall (d. 1536), both brickmakers, see Fitch, *Commissary Wills*, i. 40 and ii. 120.

not appear at all in that analysis of the commissary wills. The consumer market in London was swollen by the presence of large numbers of clergy (768) and those people who were described by their rank rather than their craft, such as esquires (69), gentlewomen (70), knights (40), and yeomen (44). In addition there were over a thousand testators who were described simply as widows. We cannot assume that these women were not, in fact, producers and it is likely that a number of them (perhaps as many as half) should be rightly categorized as craftswomen. If half of these widows are transferred to the manufacturing Londoners we arrive at a rough calculation that of some 6,500 testators dying in London in the period 1374–1488, 60 per cent were engaged in some form of industrial activity and 40 per cent were professionals, officials, clergy, or those with livelihoods from estates outside London. It was, to a very considerable extent, this large, and largely wealthy, consumer market that was the engine which drove the industrial activity of medieval London.

THE DISTRIBUTIVE TRADES

The inland trade of London was as important to its economy as the much better-documented overseas trade, and yet it tends to be neglected. There was no centralized taxation of sales, and so there are very few records. Yet the inland trade was crucial in bringing goods to London for export and in distributing imported wares, or goods manufactured in London.

Londoners could not be certain that all their customers would come to the city to buy the goods that were made and sold there or the alien goods that were brought into their warehouses by overseas trade. It was crucial that the citizens should develop, control, and exploit distributive or inland networks and, indeed, many made their fortunes in this way. It has been asserted that: 'Even overseas trade depended upon a network of transactions within the country and exotic goods from distant lands needed a pre-existing distributive apparatus in order to find their way to English customers; and goods destined for export, especially those that were small men's produce, had to be collected and bulked before they were put to sea.'[65]

In the thirteenth century London merchants played a leading role in the inland trade of England, but not a dominant one. Since large quantities of imported goods flooded into London, largely brought in ships from the Low Countries (e.g. wine, fruit, manufactured goods, spices, and Flemish cloth) it is not surprising that London merchants, if not themselves the importers, stored and resold the goods. In this early period much of the distribution of these imported goods was done by the London merchants who took the goods to provincial towns or, more usually, to the great regional fairs held at St Ives, Lynn, Boston, or Stourbridge (near

[65] E. Miller and J. Hatcher, *Medieval England: Towns, Commerce and Crafts 1086–1348* (London, 1995), 143.

Cambridge), Bury St Edmunds, or St Giles's fair at Winchester.[66] In the late twelfth and thirteenth centuries the London citizens appointed wardens to act for them in cases arising during the fairs at Winchester and Boston and probably also at other regional fairs, and so important were these two fairs that the London Husting court was closed for their duration.[67]

Henry I's charter granted that:

All the men of London shall be quit and free and all their goods, throughout England and the ports of the sea, of and from all toll and passage and lestage [port duty] and all other customs . . . And if any shall take toll or custom of any citizen of London, the citizens of London in the city shall take of the borough or town, where toll or custom was so taken, so much as the man of London gave for toll and as he received damage thereby.[68]

In this way the citizens of London were freed from paying local tolls throughout England. If London citizens were forced to pay such tolls, or if their goods were forfeited for their failure to do so, then the mayor and aldermen would intervene to uphold the rights of the London citizens. In the late twelfth century the London merchants boycotted the market at Bury St Edmunds for two years in support of their claims to toll exemption but, in the end, they had to come to a compromise with the redoubtable abbot Samson.[69] In 1301 ten casks of wine belonging to Adam de Scaylesworth, a Northampton merchant, were seized in London in retaliation for the seizure of goods belonging to Richard Poterel, a London citizen, which, it was claimed, had been bought in the Northampton market without paying toll.[70] Clearly there were problems of proof and it became customary for London citizens to travel with letters or certificates testifying to their status as freemen of London.[71] For the middle years of the fourteenth century there survives a roll of the letters that were sent out under the seal of the mayor of London and addressed to mayors and bailiffs of towns in England and abroad, to defend the persons and the goods of London citizens. The letters reveal the extended tentacles of London's distributive trade: vintners were taking wine to Colchester, Bristol, Cambridge, Winchelsea, Rye, and Northampton; woolmongers were operating in Gloucester, Bristol, Reading, Sleaford, Oxford, and Edington in Wiltshire. As might be expected, much of the trade of London merchants was in the Home Counties and in the towns and markets of the Midlands, but it extended also to the north and

[66] Ibid. 171–2; E. W. Moore, *The Fairs of Medieval England* (Toronto, 1985), 12–22.

[67] G. A. Williams, *Medieval London from Commune to Capital* (London, 1963), 82, 138, 144; Veale, *The English Fur Trade*, 119–20 and n. 1; *Liber de Antiquis Legibus seu Chronica Maiorum et Vicecomitum Londoniarum*, ed. T. Stapledon (Camden Society, 1846), 207.

[68] *Historical Charters and Constitutional Documents of the City of London*, ed. W. de Gray Birch (rev. edn. London, 1887), 3–4; the charter also laid down that all debts owed to Londoners were to be paid in London, and the goods of those owing them money might be distrained either in London or elsewhere. On the authenticity of this charter, see C. N. L. Brooke, G. Keir, and S. Reynolds, 'Henry I's Charter for the City of London', *Journal of the Society of Archivists*, 4 (1973), 558–78.

[69] R. Gottfried, *Bury St Edmunds and the Urban Crisis: 1290–1539* (Princeton, NJ, 1982), 85.

[70] 6 July 1301, *CEMCR 1298–1307*, 115.

[71] 23 June 1327, certificate for Poncheus Portinari of Florence, freeman of London, who, as such, ought to pass free of toll in England, *CPMR 1323–64*, 27.

west.[72] William Servat, a wealthy Cahorsin merchant who had become a citizen and settled in London, sold his wine to Durham priory in the early fourteenth century and in 1475 William Vernon, another London vintner, sold his wine in a string of towns in eastern England and his business extended as far north as Newcastle.[73] London merchants were transacting business in Yorkshire and buying property there from the middle years of the fourteenth century and, by the last quarter of the fifteenth century, they had managed to squeeze the Yorkshire merchants out of the lucrative export trade in cloth. As has been aptly observed, 'London's commercial tentacles were lengthening'.[74]

But whereas in the twelfth and early thirteenth century London citizens had taken their goods to fairs, whether to sell to the very rich such as the king and members of the aristocracy, or to middlemen who would service the local markets, this pattern changes in the fourteenth century. By 1300 the fairs were in decline and instead of the goods being taken to the customer, the customer was coming to the towns, and particularly to London to seek the goods he (or she) needed. There were several factors that contributed to the decline of the great fairs. In part their importance had depended upon the presence of alien merchants who brought foreign cloth and wine for sale there. Gradually English cloth seriously dented the market for imported cloth and so alien merchants no longer found easy markets at the English fairs. Commerce was, therefore, diverted 'from periodic fairs to towns in which trading was a continuous activity'.[75] The great days of the great fairs had owed much to the dominant role played by these alien merchants in many branches of English commerce. A telling instance of the shift away from the great fairs may be seen in the case of the woad merchants from Amiens, Corbie, and Nesle who, in 1237, had agreed to pay £50 a year to the city of London in return for trading privileges. This sum was to be handed over in three instalments at the times of the fairs at St Ives, Boston, and Winchester. When the agreement was revised in 1334 the amount was reduced to 50 marks payable in two instalments (2 February and 8 September) but there was now no mention of the fairs. Presumably the money was now to be paid at London.[76]

From the early twelfth century abbots and bishops had begun to acquire town houses in London and their example was followed by the lay aristocracy. By 1300 there were at least forty-four aristocratic town houses in London, and by 1540 there

[72] J. Masschaele, *Peasants, Merchants and Markets: Inland Trade in Medieval England 1150–1350* (London, 1997), 119–20.

[73] *Account Rolls of the Abbey of Durham*, ed. J. T. Fowler, 3 vols. (Surtees Society, 1898–1901), ii. 494; M. K. James, *Studies in the Medieval Wine Trade*, ed. E. Veale (Oxford, 1971), 189–90.

[74] J. Kermode, 'Money and Credit in the Fifteenth Century: Some Lessons from Yorkshire', *Business History Review*, 65 (1991), 475–501, esp. 496–7; see also ead., *Medieval Merchants: York, Beverley and Hull in the Later Middle Ages* (Cambridge, 1998), 252–3.

[75] Miller and Hatcher, *Towns, Commerce and Crafts*, 175; see also G. Rosser, *Medieval Westminster 1200–1540* (Oxford, 1989), 109–15; R. Britnell, *The Commercialisation of English Society 1000–1500* (2nd edn., Manchester, 1996), 90; Moore, *Fairs of Medieval England*, 204–22 .

[76] *Liber Albus*, 361, 364.

were about seventy-five.[77] The great men of the realm (who were also the richest men) found it useful to have a permanent base in London to serve as a hostel when summoned to advise the king, or his council or, increasingly, at meetings of Parliament held at Westminster; as a storehouse for produce from their country estates, or for goods bought in London, and for servants (and their horses) on business in London.[78] The great lords would send heavy duty 'chariots' to London loaded with produce to be sold, and ready to return with goods bought in the city for their country castles and manors.[79] So the carts were no longer sent to the great fairs, but to London. Moreover the richest lords, from the early fourteenth century, began to buy separate houses in London to serve as storehouses, known as wardrobes. Henry de Lacy, earl of Lincoln, in 1302–4 bought a house near Cheapside that had belonged to the Jewish family of Master Moses and his son Hagin to use as his wardrobe, and the king had a wardrobe in London from 1311. But later in the century, he bought the great house that had belonged to Sir John Beauchamp in the London parish of St Andrew, near the Thames, and this became the home of the Great Wardrobe.[80] The development of royal and aristocratic wardrobes in London is symptomatic of the shift from fairs to shops. In London the servants of kings and nobles could purchase wine, silk, spices, weapons, saddlery, jewellery, and cloth, and then store them. Here in London also could be hired men to work in the wardrobes (e.g. tailors) for short periods of time to respond to a particular need. In consequence the London merchant no longer needed to take his goods out of the city to sell them: instead the buyers came to his shop and warehouse. Moreover in London only citizens could buy and sell goods retail. Alien importers who had not purchased the freedom of the city were debarred from selling directly to the customer. They could sell only to London citizens. It is easy to understand, therefore, why the London merchants who were involved in overseas trade and had imported goods to sell (e.g. the drapers, grocers, and mercers) were so concerned in the 1370s and 1380s to maintain the city's chartered privileges, popularly known as the franchise.[81]

The geographical range of the business of London merchants can be seen in the distribution of their debtors. London skinners did business with men as far north as York and as far west as Exeter. Moreover, two Exeter skinners thought it

[77] C. Barron, 'Centres of Conspicuous Consumption: The Aristocratic Town House in London 1200–1500', *London Journal*, 20 (1995), 1–16; Schofield, *Medieval London Houses*, 34–8.

[78] The importance of these London hostels, and the London market, is suggested by the carrying services demanded of villeins by their lords for bringing goods from manors to London; see the southern manors of the bishops of Ely, or the tenants of Holy Trinity Caen at Felstead, Miller and Hatcher, *Towns, Commerce and Crafts*, 150.

[79] C. Dyer, 'The Consumer and the Market in the Later Middle Ages', in id. *Everyday Life in Medieval England* (London, 1994), 257–81, esp. 262–3; Barron, 'Centres of Conspicuous Consumption', 5–6.

[80] D. Keene, 'Wardrobes in the City: Houses of Consumption, Finance and Power', in M. Prestwich, R. Britnell, and R. Frame (eds.), *Thirteenth Century England*, 7 (Woodbridge, 1999), 61–79.

[81] See P. Nightingale, 'Capitalists, Crafts and Constitutional Change in Late Fourteenth-Century London', *Past and Present*, 124 (1989), 3–35, esp. 9–16; see Ch. 2.

worthwhile to join the yeoman fraternity of the London skinners.[82] A London mercer in the 1470s was owed money by men in Salisbury, Glastonbury, Coventry and Manchester.[83] It is clear that tailors also were doing business throughout the length and breadth of England: in the fifteenth century 26 per cent of tailors' debtors came from the West Country, 15 per cent from the eastern counties, and 14 per cent from the northern counties. London, the Home, southern and midland counties accounted for the remaining 45 per cent.[84] It is clear that not all this business was transacted in London. Indeed, the story of the tailor Henry Galle who, when travelling in Cornwall on business, saw and fell in love with a young Cornish girl from the village of Week St Mary and brought her back to London as his bride, suggests the itinerant nature of some London business.[85] But it seems likely that much of the business that led to debt litigation was transacted in London. A study of this litigation in the Court of Common Pleas around the year 1400 indicates the magnetism of the London market, and the extent of its influence, which was especially marked in the Home Counties and the Midlands.[86] Using the evidence of debts it can be suggested that London's 'distributive region' expanded between the early fifteenth century and the later sixteenth as the Londoners tightened their grip on the inland trade of England.[87] In 1393 the London grocers claimed that they sold pepper in London to lords and also to 'gentz paissantz',[88] and in 1406–7, 41 per cent of the total outlay of the bishop of Salisbury was spent on goods (fish, wine, jewellery, and spices) purchased in London and brought back to Salisbury in carts.[89] John Lord Dinham, or his son, or one of their servants, made a minimum of twenty-two trips to London between 1379 and 1394 to buy cloth, clothes, and armour. On what appears to have been a Christmas shopping expedition, their steward John de Baucombe brought back brasil dye, saffron, ginger, and scarlet cloth in December 1386.[90] The wealthier the household the more likely it would be that the steward, or the lord himself, would come to London to purchase goods. More modest, or more distant, households would make most of their purchases locally, but would send to London for particularly important goods. The Arundell family of Lanherne in Cornwall bought livery cloth in London in 1466–7, although

[82] Veale, *The English Fur Trade*, 71 and n. 3. For the fraternity, see Ch. 9.

[83] S. Thrupp, 'The Grocers of London: A Study of Distributive Trade', in E. Power and M. Postan, *Studies in English Trade in the Fifteenth Century* (London, 1933), 247–92, esp. 277.

[84] Davies, 'The Tailors of London', 256–7. The tailors may have been unusual in the range of their business. A survey of all debt certificates recorded under the statute staple between 1390 and 1459 suggested that as many as 66% of debts to Londoners were in fact owed by people who came from London and the Home Counties: see Elizabeth Bennett, 'Debt and Credit in the Urban Economy in London, 1380–1460' (University of Yale, Ph.D. thesis, 1989), Table 17, pp. 163–4.

[85] Davies, 'Thomasine Percyvale', 185–9.

[86] J. Galloway, 'Market Networks: London Hinterland Trade and the Economy of England', *Centre for Metropolitan History: Annual Report 1997–8* (Institute of Historical Research, London, 1998), 44–50. See also D. Keene, 'Changes in London's Economic Hinterland as Indicated by Debt Cases in the Court of Common Pleas', in J. Galloway (ed.), *Trade, Urban Hinterlands and Market Integration c.1300–1600* (London, 2000), 59–81.

[87] Ibid. 70–1.

[88] CLRO, LBH, fo. 284^{v} (not in *LBH*, 400–1), cited by Thrupp, 'Grocers', 273.

[89] Dyer, 'Consumer and the Market', 260.

[90] Cornwall Record Office, AR 37/48.

all their other needs were supplied locally.[91] By the end of the fourteenth century the 'high end' of the Exeter fur trade had settled in London and, moreover, expensive and elaborate saddles were no longer made locally, but purchased in London.[92] There were, of course, certain goods that could only be found in London, such as the fine set of silver tableware that Thomas Bourgchier, newly elected bishop of Worcester, bought from a London goldsmith in 1434.[93] From the beginning of the fourteenth century for about a hundred years, it is clear that London merchants, shopkeepers, and craftsmen could sit in their London shops and wait for the passing trade to stop at their doors. But in the fifteenth century the situation began to change.

The 'gentz paissantz' were not, however, exclusively great lords and wealthy customers: they were also modest middlemen who bought up goods in London to take back to provincial towns for resale, like the Winchester mercer who bought his stock of thread, belts, and points from the London mercer, John Baddeby.[94] Peddlars and chapmen filled their packs in London for their journeys across England. The largest group of men who owed money to the London mercers in *c*.1400 were chapmen who came to London 'to collect consignments of cloth and other goods from the mercers, which they retailed in their home town or region'.[95] Thomas Gryssop, a chapman from York, in 1446 had in his pack eleven London coffers, seven London glasses, two London purses, and a London girdle. He owed money to four Londoners including a capper and a spicer.[96] The London mercers, however, took a very haughty attitude to the peddling of goods around the country and in 1376 had forbidden members of the company to attend any fairs or markets outside the city.[97] The mercers were confident that the customers would come to them, and the grocers followed suit: in 1420, and again in 1455, they forbade their members to take goods out of London for sale in the countryside under threat of heavy fines, although for a time in the 1440s the company relaxed this policy of compelling the distributive trade to come to London and allowed grocers to take their goods to provincial markets and fairs.[98] But the expectation was that country merchants from the smaller towns of England, and the mobile chapmen, would come to London to purchase their stock-in-trade and, in this way, the transaction costs were borne by the provincial merchants and chapmen.[99] It was this confidence in the centralizing magnetism of London that led the mayor and

[91] H. L. Douch, 'Household Accounts at Lanherne', *Journal of the Royal Institution of Cornwall*, 2 (1953), 25–32, esp. 27.

[92] Kowaleski, *Local Markets and Regional Trade*, 158.

[93] Worcestershire Record Office, 009:1 Box 175, doc. No. 92475.

[94] I. Archer, *The History of the Haberdashers' Company* (Chichester, Sussex, 1991), 3.

[95] Galloway, 'Market Networks', 48; see also maps in Keene, 'Changes in London's Economic Hinterland', 75.

[96] H. Swanson, *Medieval Artisans: An Urban Class in Late Medieval England* (Oxford, 1989), 147.

[97] A. Sutton, 'The Shop-floor of the London Mercery Trade, c.1200–c.1500: The Marginalisation of the Artisan, the Itinerant Mercer and the Shopholder', *Nottingham Medieval Studies*, 45 (2001), 12–50, esp. 35.

[98] Thrupp, 'Grocers', 274; Nightingale, *Mercantile Community*, 448–9.

[99] R. Britnell, 'Urban Demand in the English Economy, 1300–1600', in J. Galloway (ed.), *Trade, Urban Hinterlands and Market Integration*, 1–21, esp. 14.

aldermen in 1396 to acquire Blackwell Hall, and to set it up as a national market for the sale of English cloth.[100] The Datini agents in London (1380–1410) travelled to the Cotswolds in search of the best wool to feed the Florentine cloth industry, but they were able to buy English cloth as and when they wanted it easily in the London market.[101] The pre-eminent position of London as a port for overseas trade and its focus as a centre of royal government made it possible for London merchants largely to dictate the terms on which they sold goods. There were, moreover, considerable fortunes to be made in the distributive trade: Simon Eyre, a London draper who came originally from Brandon in Suffolk, made a great deal of money. He never appears in the London customs accounts either as an exporter or importer. He bought goods from Italian importers, and he probably also purchased English cloth which he sold on to alien and other exporters. It is certain that he became extremely wealthy since he was able to contribute substantially to the building of the new Leadenhall market, granary, and school in the 1440s and he left a considerable fortune at his death in 1458.[102]

But the complacency of the stay-at-home London merchants was challenged by the rise of the haberdashers. Increased *per capita* wealth following the Black Death led to a rise in consumer demand, not just in London but throughout England, for goods such as purses, caps, buttons, combs, decorative bells, cosmetic implements, points for shoes, gloves, games, pens and paper.[103] These were the goods that, in the early fourteenth century, had been stocked by mercers but their company forbade them to take such goods into the countryside. The haberdashers saw the gap in the market and having no such rules, happily took similar wares around the markets and fairs of England. The mercers discovered that they were losing business to the enterprising haberdashers and in 1479 they revoked their ban on their members taking goods to country fairs since 'many parsones abydyng at hom [i.e. in London] be gretely hurte in lesyng of theire custumers, that used and cam unto this Citie and here bought theire ware, that nowe be served of the haberdisshers and other haunting suche fayres and markethes'.[104]

When the mayor of London considered the issue it was found that whereas seventeen crafts agreed with the mercers and wished to keep the focus of their trade in the city, eleven crafts definitely refused to stay away from fairs and markets.[105] In spite of the reservations of the mercers and the grocers, the free market economy finally triumphed and London merchants, led by the haberdashers, took the 'small goods' trade out into the highways and byways of England.[106] In fact, by the

[100] See Ch. 3.

[101] H. Bradley, 'The Datini Factors in London 1380–1410' in D.Clayton, R. Davies, and P. McNiven (eds.), *Trade, Devotion and Governance: Papers in Later Medieval History* (Stroud, 1994), 55–79, esp. 60.

[102] See Ch. 3.

[103] Archer, *Haberdashers*, 1–3.

[104] 21 July 1479, *Acts of Court of the Mercers' Company, 1453–1527*, ed. L. Lyell and F. Watney (Cambridge, 1936), 116.

[105] Ibid. 115; Sutton, 'Shop-Floor', 36.

[106] The mercers continued to agonise over the problem, and wanted to force all other companies to refrain from going to fairs, but they failed in this, Lyell and Watney, *Acts of Court*, 142, 157; the mayor and aldermen adopted the mercers' point of view and in 1487 forbade freemen to take goods to fairs, but this ordinance was very rapidly suspended since it was, presumably, found to be unenforceable, *LBL*,

second half of the fifteenth century, the mercers were more concerned with wholesale trade and with the export of English cloth and were probably not unduly troubled at losing the 'bottom end' of their trade to the dynamic haberdashers. On the other hand the haberdashers were not content simply to play the role of the 'pedlar's friend': they too wanted a share in the lucrative export of woollen cloth, and in their new charter of incorporation in 1502 they claimed the title 'merchant haberdashers'.[107] Although they were forced to drop the offending claim to 'merchant' status, yet the haberdashers secured eighth place in the hierarchy of the 'great twelve' city companies. This achievement in itself bears telling witness to the wealth and importance of the distributive trade within the London economy.

240–2 and n. 2; in 1487 Parliament annulled the restriction on selling goods in markets and fairs, *The Statutes of the Realm*, 10 vols. (London, 1810–28), ii. 518; Sutton, 'Shop-Floor', 37.

[107] Archer, *Haberdashers*, 17–18.

CHAPTER FIVE

Overseas Trade

THE THIRTEENTH CENTURY

BY 1200, AND indeed well before, London was an international port. As early as the eleventh century regulations had been drawn up in London to govern the trading practices of visiting German, Danish, and Norwegian merchants.[1] The regulations mention wine, cups of gold and silver, precious stones, luxury cloth, and linens from Constantinople and Regensburg, armour from Mainz, linen and fustian, wax, pepper, cumin, and grain.[2] Fitz-Stephen, writing of his native city in the 1170s, described the exotic goods that poured onto the London wharves in lyrical (and classical) terms: Arabian gold, spices and incense, weapons from Scythia on the Black Sea, palm oil from Babylon, gems from Egypt, silk from China, wines from France, and furs from Russia and Norway.[3] It is possible that Fitz-Stephen was here indulging in some literary licence, but there is no reason to doubt that alien merchants were bringing exotic goods into London and that their activities were regarded with a certain amount of suspicion and hostility by the native merchants who wanted themselves to control and exploit the overseas trade.

Wine was probably the major commodity imported into London in the thirteenth century and, after the loss of Normandy and Anjou, almost all of this wine would have come from Gascony. In England, unlike other parts of Europe, the Gascon wine merchant encountered little competition from dealers in Rhenish wine. 'When the Englishman of the thirteenth or fourteenth century referred to wine he had in mind only the wine of Gascony.'[4] Imported wine was subject not only to a royal tax of 2–4*s.* a tun, but also to the royal right of prise and purveyance. The wine had also to be gauged by the royal gauger who charged 1*d.* a tun for his services.[5] In the thirteenth

[1] M. Bateson, 'A London Municipal Collection of the Reign of John', *EHR* 17 (1902), 480–511, 707–30, esp. 495–502; the dating of these regulations is difficult, they may be eleventh century, or perhaps early twelfth, see C. N. L. Brooke with G. Keir, *London 800–1200: The Shaping of a City* (London, 1975), 267 n. 2.

[2] Ibid.; T. H. Lloyd, *Alien Merchants in England in the High Middle Ages* (Brighton, 1982), 9–10.

[3] Text of Fitz-Stephen printed in *Elenchus Fontium Historiae Urbanae*, ed. S. Reynolds, W. de Boer, G. MacNiocaill (Brill, 1988), 45–83, esp. 80. Although Fitz-Stephen may have been inspired (certainly in his use here of hexameter verse) by a passage in Virgil's *Georgics*, i. ll. 57 *et seq.*, yet he has clearly added appropriate information relevant to London. There is nothing in Virgil about wines from France, or furs from the northern countries; cf. D. Keene, 'London from the Post-Roman Period to 1300' in D. Palliser (ed.), *The Cambridge Urban History of Britain* (Cambridge, 2000), 187–216, esp. 197.

[4] M. K. James, *Studies in the Medieval Wine Trade*, ed. E. Veale (Oxford, 1971), 71.

[5] Lloyd, *Alien Merchants in England*, 56–87.

century most of the Gascon wine was imported by Gascon merchants who had to sell the wine wholesale to London distributors. An analysis of the recognizances for debt recorded in the city's Letter Book A between 1276 and 1284 shows that 48 per cent of all the debts involving aliens were with merchants from south-west France and reflects the dominant role played by the trade in imported wine in the economy of London.[6]

It was in the king's interest to help the Gascon merchants and, while he taxed their imports, he encouraged them to come to England. In 1280 Edward I extended the time that they could remain in England from forty days to three months and, when the Londoners complained, the king responded by allowing the Gascons to sell to anyone and not just to London citizens. When the privileges of London were suspended in 1285, the alien wine importers were given yet more privileges: they were allowed to live permanently in the city and to trade retail, in effect to enjoy all the privileges of the London citizens.[7] It was this marked royal support for the Gascons that led the London vintners into closer co-operation with each other and so to the formation of the vintners' fraternity.[8] This could not, however, prevent Edward I's grant of a charter to the Gascons in 1302 which, in return for a new custom of 2*s.* payable on every tun of imported wine, exempted the Gascons from all other exactions including the royal prise of wines. The charter also granted the Gascon merchants the right to live freely where they pleased in England without being required to lodge with English hosts; moreover, they could sell wine wholesale wherever and to whomsoever they liked throughout the kingdom and their contracts were protected by law with provision for speedy justice in case of need.[9] The king was at war with France and had need not only of Gascon wine, but also Gascon loyalty and he had little reason to protect the interests of the Londoners.

London was, and remained, the main English centre for the Gascon wine trade. In 1290–91 over 50 per cent of all the wine ships put into London: by 1350 63 per cent of the wine entering England came through London.[10] The Londoners resented the privileges the Gascons enjoyed and challenged and harassed them at every turn: in 1309 the king ordered the arrest of seventeen Londoners for persistent attacks upon the Gascon merchants. But although the king continued to support the Gascons the daily vexations made their life increasingly difficult and they began to divert their trade elsewhere to the markets of northern France and Flanders. Even before the outbreak of the war with France in 1337, the Gascons were already retreating from the English market and their place was being taken by London merchants.[11] At the beginning of the fourteenth century English merchants were handling no more than a quarter of the wine laded in Gascony for

[6] W. Childs, *Anglo-Castilian Trade in the Later Middle Ages* (Manchester, 1978), 16.

[7] Lloyd, *Alien Merchants*, 89.

[8] E. Veale, 'The "Great Twelve": Mistery and Fraternity in Thirteenth-Century London', *Historical Research*, 64 (1991), 237–63, esp. 252–3.

[9] James, *Wine Trade*, 71–2; see *The Red Book of the Exchequer*, ed. H. Hall, 3 vols. (Rolls Series, 1896), iii. 1060–4.

[10] Calculated from the tables in James, *Wine Trade*, 95, 98.

[11] Ibid. 74, 82–3.

England, yet by 1330 the London citizens alone were importing as much as all the Gascon merchants. In 1350–1, 62 per cent of the wine coming into London was imported by Londoners and only 38 per cent by the Gascons.[12] By dogged unpleasantness the Londoners had managed to capture the wine import trade from the Gascons, although the misfortunes of war made it a much less profitable trade than it had been in the glory days of the late thirteenth century when men like Henry le Waleys (d.1302) and William Servat from Cahors (d.*c.*1319) had made their fortunes by importing wine and selling it to the royal household.[13]

London's most significant trading partner, after Gascony, was Spain. Thirty-one per cent of the debt recognizances of 1276-84 involved merchants from Spain.[14] The main imports from the Iberian peninsula were skins, furs, and leather and in 1283 special brokers were appointed to deal with negotiations between Spanish merchants and the Londoners who purchased their wares.[15] In the early years of Edward I there was a group of about thirty Spanish merchants trading in London and, in spite of a breach between England and Castille in the 1290s, the trade seems to have been restored by the early fourteenth century.[16] There is evidence of a small Spanish colony in London in the 1320s[17] and the merchants of Spain were granted by the king exemption from paying murage, pavage, and pontage in London in 1331.[18] But the Spanish trade was shattered by the outbreak of war in 1337 when the French made an enduring alliance with Castille. The trade with Spain was, therefore, largely in abeyance until the later fifteenth century.

The earliest London trade with 'German' lands appears to have been with the Rhineland (Mainz and Cologne) and the Cologne merchants may have established their own Guildhall in Thames Street as early as 1155, although it now appears that they did not receive their trading privileges in London until 1175.[19] As the German people pushed eastwards they brought towns such as Lübeck, Danzig, and Riga into their trading alliance and these merchants were known as Esterlings. They received privileges from Henry III in 1237. After a series of disputes between the Cologne merchants and those from Hamburg and Lübeck, in 1281 they finally united as one Hanse of Almain based on their guildhall in Thames Street in the Vintry which, by 1382, was known as the Steelyard.[20] But whereas the German and

[12] Ibid. 81, and calculated from app. 13.

[13] G. A. Williams, *Medieval London* (London, 1963), 142–3, 333–5; A. Sutton, 'Merchants, Music and Social Harmony: The London Puy and its French and London Contexts *c.*1300', *London Journal*, 17 (1992), 1–17, esp. 9–11.

[14] See n. 6.

[15] *LBA*, 206–7; these brokerage regulations refer to imported leather, basan (lower quality leather made from sheepskin and sometimes dyed red), cabern (goatskins), baldred (cheaper white leather), and cumin (from Castile and Leon).

[16] Childs, *Anglo-Castilian Trade*, 15–18.

[17] *Two Early London Subsidy Rolls*, ed. E. Ekwall (Lund, 1951), 266.

[18] *LBE*, 269.

[19] M. D. Lobel (ed.), *Historic Towns Atlas: The City of London from Prehistoric Times to c.1520* (Oxford, 1989), 76; J. L. Bolton review of Natalie Fryde, *Ein mittelalterlicher deutscher Grossunternehmer, Terricus Teutonicus de Colonia in England, 1217–1247* (Stuttgart, 1997), in *German Historical Institute London: Bulletin*, 21 (1999), 30–4, esp. 32.

[20] Lobel, *Historic Town Atlas*, 94; for an account of the steps by which the Cologne merchants finally joined forces with the men of the Baltic towns, see Lloyd, *Alien Merchants*, 129–33; T. H. Lloyd, *England*

Baltic merchants may have resolved their internal disputes, the Hanse merchants were to be in a state of near-continuous conflict with the city of London over the obligations that the merchants were expected to shoulder in the city. In return for contributing to the costs of the upkeep of Bishopsgate and for maintaining the watch there, the Hanse merchants were excused from contributing to murage.[21] They also elected their own alderman who, after he had been presented to the mayor and accepted, was allowed to hold a court for the Hanse merchants and to act on their behalf.[22]

The merchants from the northern Baltic and, in particular, the Norwegians traded directly to the east coast ports of Hull, Boston, and Lynn, but the Hanseatics who came to London had usually come via the ports of the Low Countries and so included in their cargoes manufactured goods as well as the more usual raw materials from the Baltic lands. Their imports included stockfish, herring, masts and spars, timber for building, other wooden goods (e.g. bow staves, troughs, gates, and chairs), resins of trees (e.g. pitch, bitumen, and tar), ashes (made from hard woods for the textile industry), beeswax, grain (not only in years of dearth),[23] iron from Sweden, and zinc and copper from central Europe.[24] Skins of all kinds were imported by Hanse merchants in large quantities and especially into London. Many of the skins came from Russia and were exported via Novgorod; weasel and ermine skins came from Finland and Estonia; martens from Sweden, and squirrel skins from the central European forests of Lithuania, Poland, and Hungary, which travelled north to Danzig. The Hanse merchants would move all these skins westwards to Hamburg, and thence to Bruges and London.[25] On their return voyages they took corn, cloth, honey, and lead, but the balance of trade must have been in their favour. England needed the goods imported by the Hanse merchants more than the Hanse needed trade with England and this imbalance was to be the cause of the bad relations between the trading partners which were particularly serious in the fifteenth century.

The thirteenth century appears to have witnessed the rise and fall of the London-Picardy trade route. At the beginning of the century woad was produced in the area around Amiens and exported to London for use in the then-flourishing clothmaking industry. In 1237 the men of the woad-producing towns of Amiens, Corbie (*c.*12 km east of Amiens) and Nesle (45 km south-east) formed themselves into a guild or hanse. In return for the sizeable annual contribution of 50 marks to the city's farm, the merchants were allowed to store woad in the city for sale, to take it (and also garlic and onions, which they imported) elsewhere in England and to sell it to non-citizens. They were also exempted from murage, pontage, and

and the German Hanse (Cambridge, 1991), 16–21; Derek Keene, 'Du seuil de la Cité à la transformation d'une economie morale: L'Environment hanseatique à Londres entre XIIe et XVIIe siècle', in J. Bottin and D. Calabieds (eds.), *Les Étrangers dans la Ville* (Paris, 1999), 409–24, esp. 413–19.

[21] See Ch. 10.

[22] June, 1282, *Liber Albus*, 417–19.

[23] In accordance with the agreement of 1282, the Hanse merchants could sell their grain in their hostels and granaries within forty days, ibid. 418.

[24] Lloyd, *Alien Merchants*, 146–56.

[25] E. Veale, *The English Fur Trade in the Later Middle Ages* (Oxford, 1966), 74.

pavage and could choose the measurers of woad and the brokers who negotiated the deals.[26] But the seizure of the woad merchants' supplies in England in 1295, and the decline of the London clothmaking industry discouraged the Picardy merchants from bringing their wares to London.[27] By 1334 the merchants of Corbie and Nesle were refusing to contribute to the communal annual payment and the men of Amiens renegotiated the agreement on their own behalf with the Londoners.[28] Although the Anglo-Picardy trade certainly declined as another casualty of the war with France, yet in the fifteenth century the merchants of Amiens still found it worth their while to pay for the right to trade freely in London.[29]

The Italians began to arrive in substantial numbers in England in the 1220s: the first merchants came from Florence, Lucca, Siena, Piacenza, Pistoia, and Genoa. By the early fourteenth century there were also merchants from Milan, Padua, Pisa, Asti, and—by 1319—Venice.[30] Stangely enough, in the light of later conflicts, it is interesting to note that in this early period their presence seems to have caused very little trouble: there are few records of the hostilities and conflicts that marred the relations between the Londoners and the Hanse and the Gascons in the second half of the thirteenth century.[31] It may be significant that there are very few Italian debts recorded on the Recognizance rolls between 1276 and 1284.[32] This suggests that there may have been little trading between the Londoners and the Italians, the bulk of whose business may have been with the royal household. The Italians used their own capital (only occasionally augmented by the revenues from papal taxation) to purchase wool direct from the producers (especially the Cistercian houses) and also to lend to the king.[33] The Riccardi, the Frescobaldi, Antonio Pessagno, and the Bardi all rose and fell as royal bankers and creditors between the 1290s and the 1320s.[34] The difficulties and dangers of royal banking seem not to have deterred the Italians, in part because they were desperate for English wool.

26 *Liber Albus*, 201, 360–2; see E. Carus-Wilson, 'La Guède française en Angleterre: un grand commerce du Moyen Âge', *Revue du Nord*, 35 (1953), 89–105.

27 Ibid. 96–101; Woad continued to be imported via other English ports, Hull for Yorkshire, and Lynn for Lincoln, Banbury, and Norfolk: Lloyd, *Alien Merchants*, 75.

28 *Liber Albus*, 362–8.

29 Payments from Amiens are recorded intermittently between 1409 and 1431 and again in 1445, so it is clear that the trade was not entirely moribund, see C. Barron, 'The Government of London and its Relations with the Crown' (University of London Ph.D. thesis, 1970), 147 and n. 2; Carus-Wilson notes that woad was now imported also from the Low Countries, Germany, Lombardy, and Languedoc, 'La Guède française', 101–4.

30 Lloyd, *Alien Merchants*, 169.

31 Lloyd detected a rise in hostility to the Italians in London during the reign of Edward II, ibid. 30; this has been challenged by S. Dempsey, 'The Italian Community in London During the Reign of Edward II', *London Journal*, 18 (1993), 14–22.

32 See n. 6.

33 Lloyd, *Alien Merchants*, 169–70.

34 Ibid. 166–203; M. Prestwich, 'Italian Merchants in Late Thirteenth and Early Fourteenth Century England', in [Centre for Medieval and Renaissance Studies, University of California, Los Angeles], *The Dawn of Modern Banking* (New Haven, Conn., 1979), 77–104; W. E. Rhodes, 'The Italian Bankers and their Loans to Edward I and Edward II', in T. F. Tout and J. Tait (eds.), *Historical Essays by Members of the Owen's College* (Manchester, 1907), 137–67; N. Fryde, 'Antonio Pessagno of Genoa, King's Merchant of Edward II of England', in *Studi in memoria di Federigo Melis*, 4 vols. (Naples, 1978), ii. 159–78.

Earlier in the thirteenth century the trade in the export of English wool had been dominated by Flemish merchants, but by the 1270s they had lost out to the Italians. At first the Italians took the wool and, using English or northern European shipping, had exported it to the Low Countries and thence to the Flemish looms or, by the overland route, to Italy.[35] By the 1320s, however, the Italians were using the sea route: in 1307 a group of Milanese merchants sent wool in carts from London to Southampton to be taken from there by ship direct to Italy.[36]

The Italians imported into England 'mercery' (i.e. silk, cloth of gold, gold wire, cut velvet and other luxury fabrics) and spices from the Mediterranean basin, also sugar, fruits both fresh and dried, and alum that was crucial in the process for dyeing cloth. From the sophisticated industrial centres of northern Italy they brought glass, paper, and fustian. The numbers of Italian merchants in London were never large and, in this early period, their trading and banking concerns were complementary to those of the Londoners. Later, as the London merchants became more sophisticated and adventurous, they would come to resent and challenge the dominant role that the Italian merchants occupied in royal finance, and as importers and suppliers of luxury goods.

There is no doubt that England's most important trading partners were the Low Countries, especially the county of Flanders and the duchy of Brabant. The Flemish cloth industry depended crucially upon the import of English wool, to the extent that England, in the course of the thirteenth century, was converted from exporting finished cloth to exporting wool. The English cloth industry did not disappear, but it produced goods for the lower end of the market and for home consumption. By the first two decades of the thirteenth century Englands' average annual export was between 25,000 and 30,000 sacks of wool (see fig 5.1). In return large quantities of Flemish cloth were imported into England: in the early fourteenth century alien merchants alone brought in 12,000 cloths each year.[37] The competition of Flemish cloth drove the English clothworkers out of the towns and into the cheaper countryside. Although the picture was to change in the later medieval period, in the century following the imposition of a regular tax on wool exports (i.e. from 1280) less than half the English wool export passed through the port of London (see fig 5.2).

The export trade in English wool and the import trade in Flemish cloth was of great importance to England and to Flanders and was also the cause of much conflict. This was the result less of economic than of the political rivalries of the kings of England and France in which the counts of Flanders found themselves caught between these two warring nation states. In the thirteenth century (as later) the trade between England and the Low Countries was characterized by embargoes, acts of piracy, and short-term agreements.[38] Italian merchants played an important role in the export of English wool, but London merchants were not entirely absent

[35] Lloyd, *Alien Merchants*, 200.

[36] PRO E122/68/23–4.

[37] J. L. Bolton, *The Medieval English Economy 1150–1500* (London, 1980), 159.

[38] Lloyd, *Alien Merchants*, ch. 5; C. Barron and N. Saul (eds.), *England and the Low Countries in the Late Middle Ages* (Stroud, 1995), Introduction, 1–4.

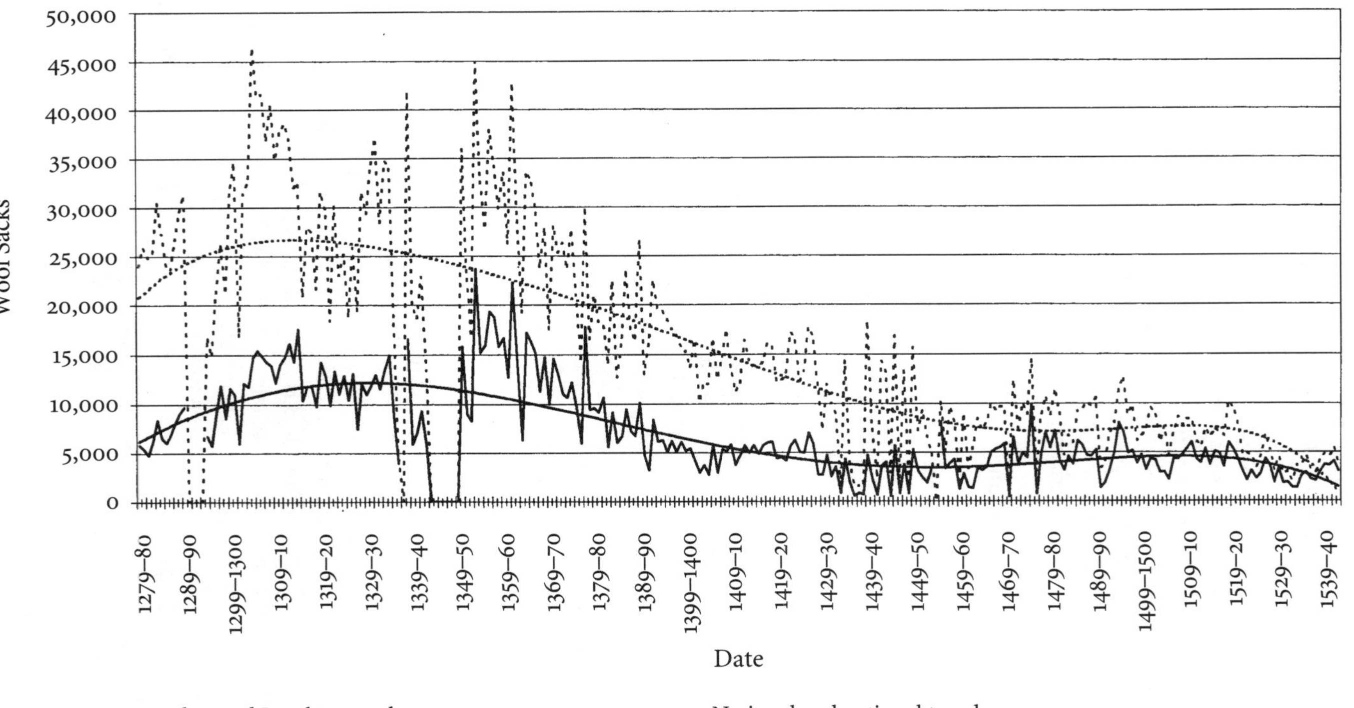

FIG. 5.1. England's raw wool exports: total amounts of the raw wool export trade, 1279–1543.

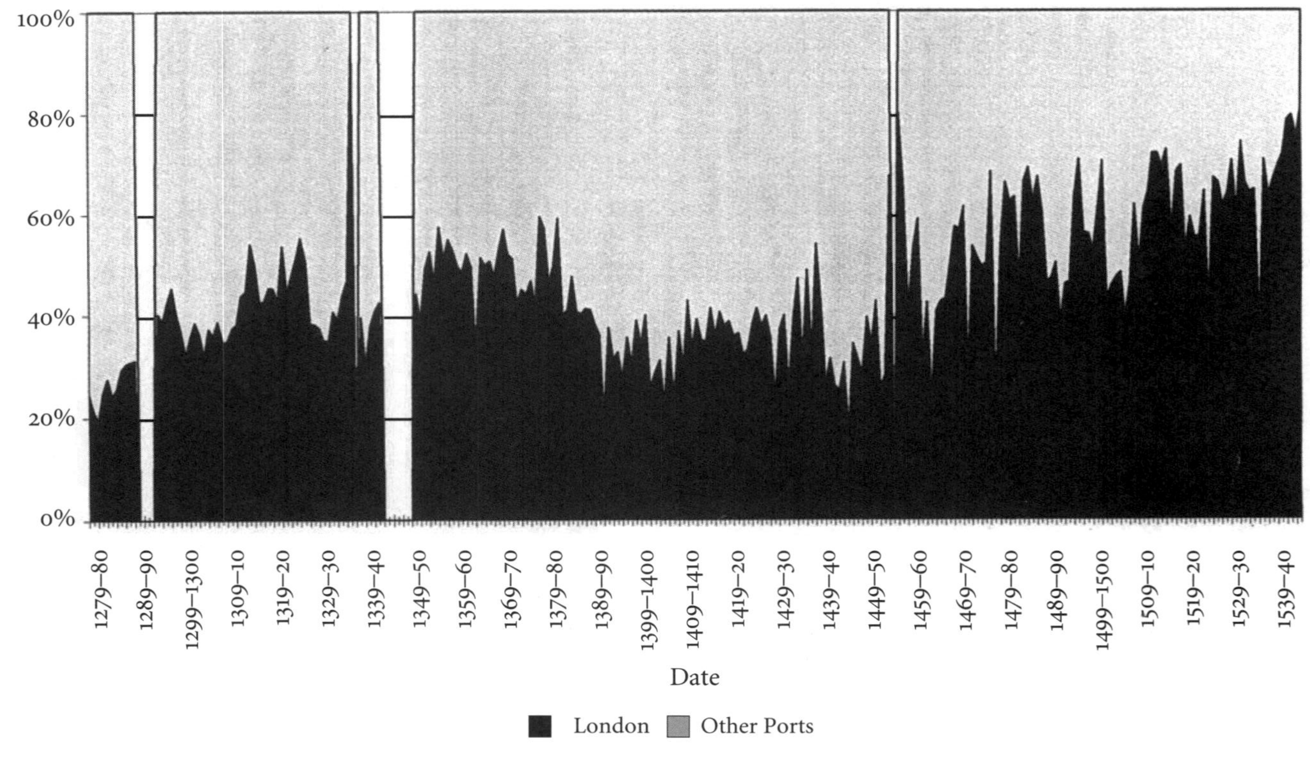

FIG. 5.2. England's raw wool exports: London's share of total exports, 1279–1543

from the export of their country's major product.[39] At the beginning of the fourteenth century English wool belonging to a group of London exporters was seized in Ghent as part of a series of economic reprisals.[40] But the alien domination of the wool export trade was to be short-lived. Between 1300 and 1337 a group of English merchants, many of whom were Londoners, adopted a more or less corporate organization to export wool, and to do this using a Staple abroad that at first moved around but, from 1313, was fixed at Saint-Omer in Picardy.[41]

There may, at one time, have been a Flemish *Hanse* in London,[42] and in the 1240s there was a *Hanse* at Saint-Omer to which towns in the locality belonged specifically to trade with England,[43] yet it seems that comparatively few Flemings or Brabanters came to London as merchants to buy wool, or to sell cloth. They were industrialists and were content to stay at home and leave the transport of their raw materials, and the sale of their products, to others. The Flemings who came to England came as craftsmen: they did not form a mercantile community in London as the Italians and men of the *Hanse* towns did. The Flemings and Dutch however, were, also present as shipmasters, and although the men who owned the cargoes were Italians or Germans, yet the goods crossed the English channel in Flemish or Dutch bottoms. In 1275 the sheriffs of London were able to seize twenty-eight ships from Holland and Zeeland in the Thames in retaliation for English goods seized abroad.[44] The shipmasters filled their holds for the outward voyage not only with cloth but also with miscellaneous goods such as timber, latten table ware, tiles, woad, and onions. On the return journey there was room for little apart from the bulky sacks of wool. But, as in the other areas of English trade, native merchants began to take a much more active part in the wool and cloth trade with Flanders in the early fourteenth century.[45]

There is no doubt that by 1300, and probably by 1200, London was an important European port: merchants from Picardy, the Hanse towns, Spain, and Italy found it worth their while to spend periods of time in London. Flemish, Hanse, Brabanter, and Dutch ships filled the reaches of the Thames both above and below the bridge. What is surprising is the comparatively low profile of London merchants themselves. Much of England's wool crop was exported from England by alien merchants in alien ships. Enterprising merchants from Italy, Spain, and around the Baltic brought their goods to London and, en route, collected manufactured goods from Flanders to swell their cargoes. England appears to have been the passive goose laying golden eggs for the benefit of others. In the thirteenth century the economy of England was in a 'colonial' phase: the raw materials of wool and grain were exported in return for the import of not only luxury items but also

[39] A. Sutton, 'The Merchant Adventurers of England: Their Origins and the Mercers' Company of London', *Historical Research*, 75 (2002), 25–46, esp. 32.

[40] T. H. Lloyd, *The English Wool Trade in the Middle Ages* (Cambridge, 1977), 101–2.

[41] Bolton, *Medieval English Economy*, 193–4; Sutton, 'Merchant Adventurers', 29–33.

[42] For a discussion of the various theories about this, see Lloyd, *Alien Merchants*, 105–6.

[43] E. Perroy, 'Le Commerce anglo-flamand au XIIIe siècle: Le Hanse flamande de Londres', *Revue Historique*, 252 (1974), 3–18.

[44] *CPR 1272–81*, 25, 89; *CCR 1272–9*, 246; PRO E159/50 m. 2^{v}.

[45] Lloyd, *Wool Trade*, 112.

Gascon wine, and cloth and metal goods manufactured in Flanders. Alien merchants played a remarkably prominent role in English overseas trade.

The reasons for the prominence of the aliens may, in part, be political, and the role of the Londoners may be of significance here. The Angevin kings had been deeply suspicious of the commune of London, and the Londoners returned the suspicion by siding with the barons against John in 1215 and against Henry III in the civil wars of 1258–65. The hostility of the London merchants may, therefore, have encouraged the English kings to look favourably upon alien merchants who were malleable, taxable, and expendable. Groups of alien merchants could be used by the Crown as counterweights to the power and pretensions of the Londoners.[46]

It seems to have been the policy of Edward I, in particular, to encourage alien merchants and to challenge the privileges of the Londoners, as has already been noted in the cases of the Gascon and the Hanse merchants. The issues at stake seem to have been the local taxes (e.g. pontage, murage, pavage, and scavage) to be paid by alien merchants, whether they should be allowed to sell retail as well as wholesale, and the length of time that they might be allowed to remain in England to sell their goods.[47] When Edward I took the city into his own hand and removed the citizens' right of self-government, he issued ordinances that made notable concessions to alien merchants who were wanting to sell their goods in London. In particular he ordained that alien merchants who were of good standing in their own countries and who wished to live in London, were to be admitted to the freedom. In this way aliens would be able to live in the city and to do business as citizens.[48] Not only did Edward wish to support the aliens as an antidote to the pretensions of the Londoners, but he knew also that they were a source of revenue. In 1275 the 'Ancient Custom' had been imposed on all wool, woolfells, and hides whether exported by denizen or alien merchants. Then, in 1303, Edward issued the *Carta Mercatoria*, which enlarged and defined the privileges of alien merchants: they were to be allowed to keep their own hostels and live where they wished; they were to be free to trade wholesale and all alien goods were to be free of the local taxes of murage, pontage, and pavage (note that the aliens were not exempted from the payment of scavage)[49] throughout the king's dominions; royal weights and measures were to be used in all towns and fairs; speedy justice was to be made available for the settling of disputes in accordance with the law merchant and, in London, if the Mayor and sheriffs failed to provide such speedy justice, then the king would appoint a special royal justice to hear the case.[50] In return for these extensive privileges the aliens agreed to pay a differential rate of custom on their wool, woolfell and hide exports, i.e. to pay at a higher rate than denizens. In addition the alien merchants agreed to pay a 'new' or 'petty' custom on other goods that they imported or exported: there were to be specific duties paid on cloth, wine, and wax and an *ad valorem* duty of 3*d.* in the pound on all other wares.

[46] See Ch. 2.

[47] Lloyd, *Alien Merchants*, 22.

[48] *Liber Custumarum*, ii. 104–6; Williams, *Medieval London*, 191.

[49] See Ch. 9.

[50] For the text of the *Carta Mercatoria*, see N. B. Gras, *The Early English Customs System* (Cambridge, Mass., 1918), 259–64 .

The results of the *Carta Mercatoria* were manifold and not all of them anticipated. Alien merchants, now discriminated against, albeit privileged, began to seek denizen status in order to avoid paying the higher rate of customs dues, which may explain the growing concern among mercantile groups in London, especially the mercers, about the need to control entry to the city's freedom.[51] What Edward had done, in return for income which benefited the Crown, was to dispense with the local taxes that had been extracted from aliens for local use, and to allow aliens to trade much more freely in areas that had customarily been closed to them. In effect he had overridden many of the chartered privileges granted by his forebears in order to generate revenue by encouraging aliens to trade in England. The Londoners, however, refused to accept that the *Carta Mercatoria* overrode their own privileges: in particular they insisted that aliens should not be free to sell to non-citizens, nor to sell retail and that they should follow London weighing practices.[52] It appears that some kind of compromise was reached in 1309 whereby the alien merchants and the Londoners came to an arrangement about the way in which goods should be sold by weight in the city.[53]

The differential rates in the wool custom, and the new customs on other goods, did discourage some alien merchants and there is a noticeable decline in alien imports in the second decade of the fourteenth century.[54] But the pro-alien policies of Edward I also had the effect of galvanizing the fractious and fragmented London merchant community into greater co-operative action in the face of this new threat to their livelihoods. They began to work together to protect their distributive trade and to gain a greater share of the overseas trade passing in and out of London. Political events were moving in their direction as the English kings, particularly Edward I and Edward III, began to pursue increasingly nationalistic policies and so could rely less on alien merchants and needed to promote native merchants whose interests more easily coincided with national ambition. The Hanse merchants and the Italians continued to be important in the commercial life of London, and although their share of the export trade in wool and cloth gradually declined (see figs. 5.3 and 5.6), they were not to be completely eliminated from the overseas trade of London until the sixteenth century.

The free market economy that had, largely, characterized the overseas trade of London in the thirteenth century was slowly changing into a protectionist one. Alien merchants now had to pay a higher rate of custom on the wool they exported and they alone had to pay customs on the other goods (including cloth, wine, and wax) that they imported or exported. The native merchants now had an advantage over their alien rivals in the conduct of overseas trade but the *Carta Mercatoria* had given aliens a chance to penetrate the distributive trade within England by allowing them to do business almost as freely as native merchants in English towns and fairs.

[51] See Ch. 3, and *LBD*, 280–1, 283.

[52] See their protest in 1305, *LBC*, 127–9.

[53] *LBD*, 209–10.

[54] Lloyd, *Alien Merchants*, 31.

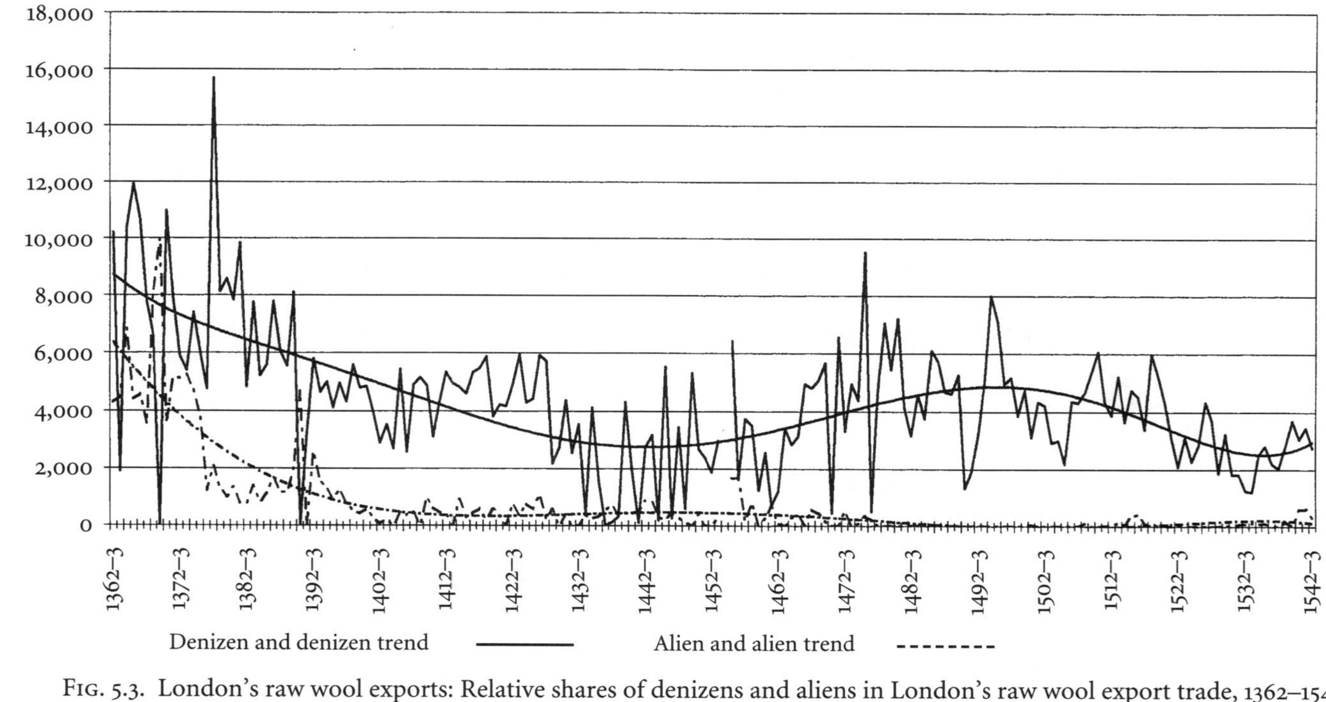

FIG. 5.3. London's raw wool exports: Relative shares of denizens and aliens in London's raw wool export trade, 1362–1543

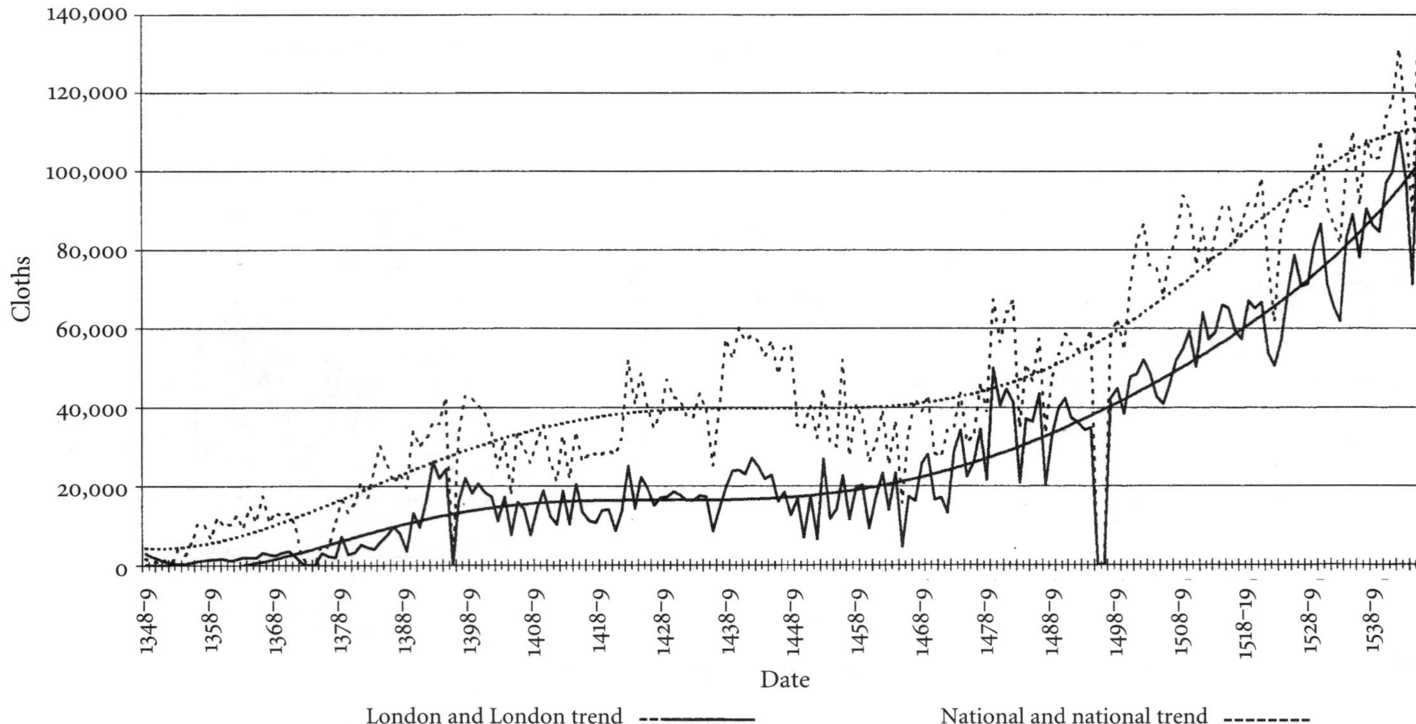

FIG. 5.4. England's cloth exports: London's share of the cloth export trade, 1348–1543

Not surprisingly, the Londoners argued that if aliens were to be allowed to trade in England as if they were native merchants, then they should contribute to civic taxation as other London citizens. The *Carta* had released aliens from certain specific local taxes, but it was vague about many other forms of taxation. The alien merchants in London claimed that they were immune from *all* forms of taxation. When the king in 1304 demanded a tallage from London and all other places within the royal demesne, the London assessors tallaged the aliens along with the citizens. The names of the aliens who protested are recorded in the enrolled Exchequer account.[55] This is unlikely to be a complete list of all the aliens living at that time in London but it does reveal something of the topographical distribution of the different alien communities. There were thirty-five aliens living in Vintry ward, most of them from Gascony and largely operating as individuals. In the adjoining Dowgate ward there were thirty German merchants (presumably living in the Steelyard) together with some men from the Low Countries, such as Terry le Villein from Ypres who was very highly assessed. There were fewer foreign merchants living in the central wards, but they were noticeably wealthier. In Cordwainer ward there were a dozen or so merchants from Spain, Italy, and Provence, and the very wealthy Italian companies were to be found in the wards of Cheap and Langbourne. There were a few aliens in the wards of Candlewick Street and Walbrook, so it would seem that foreign merchants were living in only eight of the city's twenty-four wards.[56] This clustering of Italians in the central wards of the city and of Hanse merchants along the Thames was to persist throughout the medieval period.[57]

THE FOURTEENTH CENTURY

The more co-operative attitude of the London merchants, together with the warlike policies of the English kings, combined to change the pattern of English overseas trade in the first half of the fourteenth century. Although the Italians and the Hanse merchants remained prominent players, the Gascons,[58] Spaniards, and woad merchants from Picardy had largely disappeared from the English commercial stage by 1350. The growing importance of the native English merchants was recognized by the Crown by making their imports and exports also liable to the payment of custom. In 1333 a new subsidy was raised on exported wool, in

[55] Lloyd, *Alien Merchants*, pp. 2, 227–23; M. Jurkowski, C. L. Smith, and D. Crook, *Lay Taxes in England and Wales 1188–1688* (London, 1998), 26–7.

[56] Lloyd, *Alien Merchants*, pp. 2, 227–31.

[57] H. L. Bradley, 'The Italian Community in London *c.*1350–*c.*1450' (University of London, Ph.D. thesis, 1992), ch. 1; S. Jenks, 'Hansische Vermächtnisse in London ca.1363–1483', *Hansische Geschichtsblätter*, 104 (1986), 35–111.

[58] Alien imports of wine to England dropped from over 8,500 tuns in 1322–3 to just over 2,000 in 1350–1, see James, *Wine Trade*, 34; by 1400 alien and denizen imports together reached about 10,000 tuns a year, see fig. 5.7; this was half the amount that had been imported into England a hundred years before: Bolton, *Medieval English Economy*, 290.

addition to the existing 'Ancient Custom' with the result that native merchants paid only 13*s.* 4*d.* for each sack exported when alien merchants paid 23*s.* 4*d.*[59] Moreover all alien merchants since 1303 had had to pay a tax on each cloth exported while the denizen merchants had not been liable to this. From 1347, however, when the new cloth custom was imposed, denizens were no longer exempt.[60] In addition from the 1340s denizen merchants became liable to pay tunnage (a charge on imported wine) although this was not regularly charged until the early fifteenth century, and also poundage, an *ad valorem* duty on imported and exported goods payable by all merchants, whether alien or denizen, at the rate of 12*d.* in the pound. The systematic inclusion of native merchants among those liable to pay these new and adapted customs duties is suggestive of the growing importance of native merchants in the overseas trade of England. Since these charges were to be paid by Englishmen as well as aliens (who, it might have been argued, were paying in return for royal protection), it became increasingly important that these grants of indirect taxation should be brought under Parliamentary control and should not be imposed at the whim of the king. Edward III tried hard to prevent this erosion of royal financial autonomy. At first he attempted to come to financial arrangements with the merchants by summoning them to meet separately from the other estates in Parliament, but this was successfully resisted by the shire knights and, in 1360, Edward was forced to agree that, in future, the indirect taxation of overseas trade should, like direct taxation, be subject to the approval of the Commons and Lords assembled in Parliament.[61] As English merchants pushed up their share in the export trade in wool (by 1362 about 45 per cent of all English wool was exported through the port of London and 70 per cent of this wool belonged to denizen merchants, see figs. 5.2 and 5.3) so they were able to buy a voice in Parliament and to play a national political role.

The success of the English merchants in recapturing a large share of their own wool export was due, in part, to their corporate organization and to the creation of a Staple town through which all wool for export was required to pass. In 1303 the Staple town had been fixed at Saint-Omer, but in the course of the fourteenth century the Staple moved to other European towns and, for periods of time, it was also based in one or more English towns. From 1389, however, it was fixed permanently at Calais.[62] The Company of the Staple, a broadly based group of about two hundred merchants who were mainly Londoners and were led by their own

59 *Medieval English Economy*, 194.

60 In fact the Hanse merchants successfully claimed that they were liable to pay only the old custom that had been agreed in the *Carta Mercatoria*, so they ended up paying at a rate lower than that now charged to native merchants. Italians, who paid the old custom of 1303 and the new custom of 1347, bore the heaviest charges. Because of these three different rates, it is possible, in the case of cloth exports, to see how much is being exported by Hanse merchants, denizens, and other (largely Italian) aliens, see fig. 5.6.

61 G. Unwin, 'The Estate of Merchants 1336–65', in id. (ed.), *Finance and Trade under Edward III* (Manchester, 1918), 179–255; see A. R. Myers, *English Historical Documents 1327–1485* (London, 1969), 444; R. L. Axworthy, 'The Financial Relationship of the London Merchant Community with Edward III 1327–77', (University of London, Ph.D. thesis, 2001), 235–45, 251–6.

62 Lloyd, *Wool Trade*, 231.

mayor, organized the wool trade to their own advantage; and they lent money to the Crown as advances on the wool custom they would be expected to pay on their exports.[63] From the 1370s the Crown began to make money by selling, usually to Italian merchants, licences to avoid the Calais Staple and this, not surprisingly, became a source of friction between the Crown and the Staple merchants.

But in the middle decades of the fourteenth century, before the Staple was finally fixed at Calais, the English wool trade went through several convulsions as Edward III attempted to manipulate it to raise ever more money for his armies and his allies in the Low Countries. By the early 1340s Edward III had bankrupted his Italian financiers and turned instead to his native English merchants. In the 'affair of the Dordrecht bonds' in 1337 the king 'seized' 10,000 sacks of English wool at Dordrecht, paying for it with bonds that promised the English merchant owners exemption from customs on future wool exports.[64] Needless to say this was an extremely unpopular move, and the king's second experiment was scarcely more popular. In 1343 the English customs were farmed (we should now say 'privatized') to a syndicate of English merchants who paid the king a handsome sum in advance but then found themselves unable to recover their initial outlay.[65] It was in the aftermath of these disastrous experiments that Edward came to realize that if he was to be able to gain access to the new wealth of these native English financiers, he would have to do so through Parliament. In this way royal finance became less arbitrary, but more secure. The middle years of the fourteenth century were, however, exciting times for enterprising and adventurous Englishmen who began to experience the pains and pleasures of high finance.

The war was a forcing ground for capitalists, and in the hothouse conditions of those two decades of speculation (1340–60) fortunes were rapidly amassed and as rapidly lost, and great men rose like meteors and, like meteors, disappeared into the night.[66]

Not all these early financiers were Londoners: William De La Pole was a merchant of Hull, and John de Wesenham and Thomas de Melchbourn came originally from Lynn, but Reginald de Conduit and Simon and Thomas de Swanlond were Londoners.[67] These men were all involved in the unhappy experiments of the 1330s and 1340s, but there were other important London merchants who avoided taking part in these ventures and were still able to make their fortunes: such men

[63] D. Greaves, 'Calais under Edward III', in Unwin, *Finance and Trade*, 313–50; S. O'Connor, 'Finance, Diplomacy and Politics: Royal Service by Two London Merchants in the Reign of Edward III', *Historical Research*, 67 (1994), 18–39, esp. 29–30; Bolton, *English Economy*, 294–9.

[64] E. B. Fryde, 'Edward III's Wool Monopoly of 1337: A Fourteenth-Century Royal Trading Venture', in id., *Studies in Medieval Trade and Finance*, 8 (London, 1983), 8–24; O'Connor, 'Finance, Diplomacy, Politics', 19.

[65] E. B. Fryde, 'The English Farmers of the Customs 1343–51', in *Studies in Medieval Trade*, 10 (1983), 1–17; O'Connor, 'Finance, Diplomacy and Politics', 20–1.

[66] E. Power, *The Wool Trade in English Medieval History* (Oxford, 1941), 114.

[67] For Wesenham, see *A Calendar of the Cartularies of John Pyel and Adam Fraunceys*, ed., S. O'Connor (Camden Society, 1993), 26 n. 127; for de Conduit and de Swanlond, see A. B. Beaven, *The Aldermen of the City of London*, 2 vols. (1908–13), i. 382, 384; S. Thrupp, *The Merchant Class of Medieval London* (Michigan, 1948), 333, 368; Axworthy, 'The London Merchant Community', 235–48 and App. E.

as the draper Sir John de Pulteney, the builder of Penshurst Castle in Kent, who died in 1349, and the vintner Henry Picard who, during his mayoralty in 1356–7, entertained four kings to dinner at his house in London.[68] The wool custom was a major source of royal revenue by the mid-fourteenth century and those who were drawn into royal finance were often repaid by tallies drawn on the wool custom revenue, and so these royal creditors, if they were not already wool exporters, were likely to become involved in that trade. Adam Fraunceys, a mercer and mayor of London in 1352–4, lent money to the Crown on thirty-four occasions between 1339 and 1371, sometimes on his own and sometimes in partnership with another mercer, John Pyel, or with other Londoners. He was deeply involved in the export of wool and in 1365–6, the only year for which a detailed account survives, he exported over 500 sacks.[69] Although it is possible to see, with hindsight, that the volume of wool exported declined steadily from the middle years of the fourteenth century, yet London's share of that declining export was higher (at 50%) in the period 1350–80, than it was to be again until the second half of the fifteenth century (see fig. 5.2). It was wool that was the foundation of most substantial London fortunes in the fourteenth century.

Important as was the export of wool, the development of the English cloth industry and its reorientation for export were the significant developments for the future. By the middle years of the fourteenth century the home cloth industry had recaptured the home market: Flemish cloth was no longer imported in large quantities.[70] In 1331 Edward III had encouraged Flemish weavers to settle in England to pursue their craft and, five years later, he prohibited the export of wool to Flanders in order to starve the Flemish looms and so drive the men of Ypres, Bruges, and Ghent into an alliance with England against France.[71] From the introduction of the export tax on cloth from 1347 it is possible to chart the steady rise of the cloth export from just under 5,000 cloths in 1347 to 40,000 by the end of the century (see fig. 5.4). London's share in this trade, which had originally been quite modest at about 10 per cent rose to nearer 40 per cent by 1400 (see fig. 5.5). English cloth was exported to Gascony, southern Germany (via Antwerp), the Mediterranean, and, particularly—largely by the hands of the Hanse merchants—to the countries around the Baltic. English cloth was of medium quality and was cheaper than Flemish cloth, so it catered for the mass market which developed rapidly in the years of prosperity for the wage-worker that followed the Black Death of 1348–9.

Although Englishmen were controlling a greater share of the wool and cloth exports, yet these goods were not being exported in English ships. There was certainly an English mercantile marine for Edward III was able to impress ships to

[68] Stow, *Survey*, i. 106; other important London exporters in the mid-fourteenth century were Henry Vanner, vintner, William Baret, grocer, and John Buris and William Welde, drapers, ex inf. Dr Eleanor Quinton.

[69] O'Connor, 'Finance, Diplomacy and Politics', 37–9; id., *Cartularies*, 7–8.

[70] Eleanor J. P. Quinton, 'The Drapers and the Drapery Trade of Late Medieval London, *c.*1300–*c.*1500' (University of London, Ph.D. thesis, 2001), 170–82, 196–9.

[71] Barron, 'Introduction', in Barron and Saul, *England and the Low Countries*, 3, 13.

transport his armies to France, but most of the London cross-channel trade was conducted in Dutch, or Flemish, vessels.[72] The port of London was certainly busy. It has been estimated that the total number of ships visiting London (both for overseas and coastal trade) may have been about 750 a year, that is fifteen ships a week, or two a day, in the 1390s.[73] There is evidence that some Londoners, most notably fishmongers, owned ships, or part-shares in them, but it seems clear that most Londoners were less likely to own ships than to buy space in ships belonging to others.[74]

By the end of the fourteenth century London had gained a significant role in the overseas trade of England: about 30 per cent of English wool and 50 per cent of English cloth was exported from London (see figs. 5.2 and 5.5); 40 per cent of imported wine was unloaded on the Thames wharves (see fig 5.8) and 50 per cent of the revenue from Petty Custom and Poundage payable on all other imported and exported goods was accounted for by the London collectors (see figs 5.10 and 5.12). It is clear that the port of London was already moving towards the commanding position, indeed perhaps stranglehold, that it was to achieve in the course of the next century.

THE FIFTEENTH CENTURY

The seemingly inexorable rise in the number of English cloths exported continued into the fifteenth century. In the mid-years of the fifteenth century about 50,000 cloths a year were exported from London (see fig. 5.4) and although there was a slight drop in the period 1450–80 (a knock-on effect of the trade recession and bullion shortages of the mid-century), after that the number of cloths exported rose steadily to 80,000 by 1500, and to 120,000 by 1540. London's share of this national export hovered around 45 per cent but after 1470 it rose to 60 per cent and by 1540 had reached a staggering 85 per cent (see fig 5.5).

The growth of the English cloth export trade was due to two interrelated developments: the rise to prominence of Antwerp as the nexus of European trade and the formation of the Company of English Merchant Adventurers to handle the export of English cloth. The dukes of Burgundy ruled a diverse 'empire' which included the county of Flanders with its weaving towns of Ghent and Ypres, and the duchy of Brabant with the great port of Antwerp at its heart. The Flemings wanted a ban on the import of English cloth in order to protect their own cloth-making industries, whereas the Brabanters were desperate to import English cloth in order to supply the southern German markets via Cologne, and the Hollanders and Zeelanders wanted English cloth to sell to north Germany and around the

[72] V. Harding, 'Cross-Channel Trade and Cultural Contacts: London and the Low Countries in the Later Fourteenth Century', ibid. 153–68, esp. 162.

[73] Ibid. 155.

[74] William de Bernes, a fishmonger, had a share of a *craer* called 'Andreu of London' in 1348–9, and John Longeneye, also a fishmonger, had a share of a *creyer* in 1383, *HW*, i. 611; ii, 233.

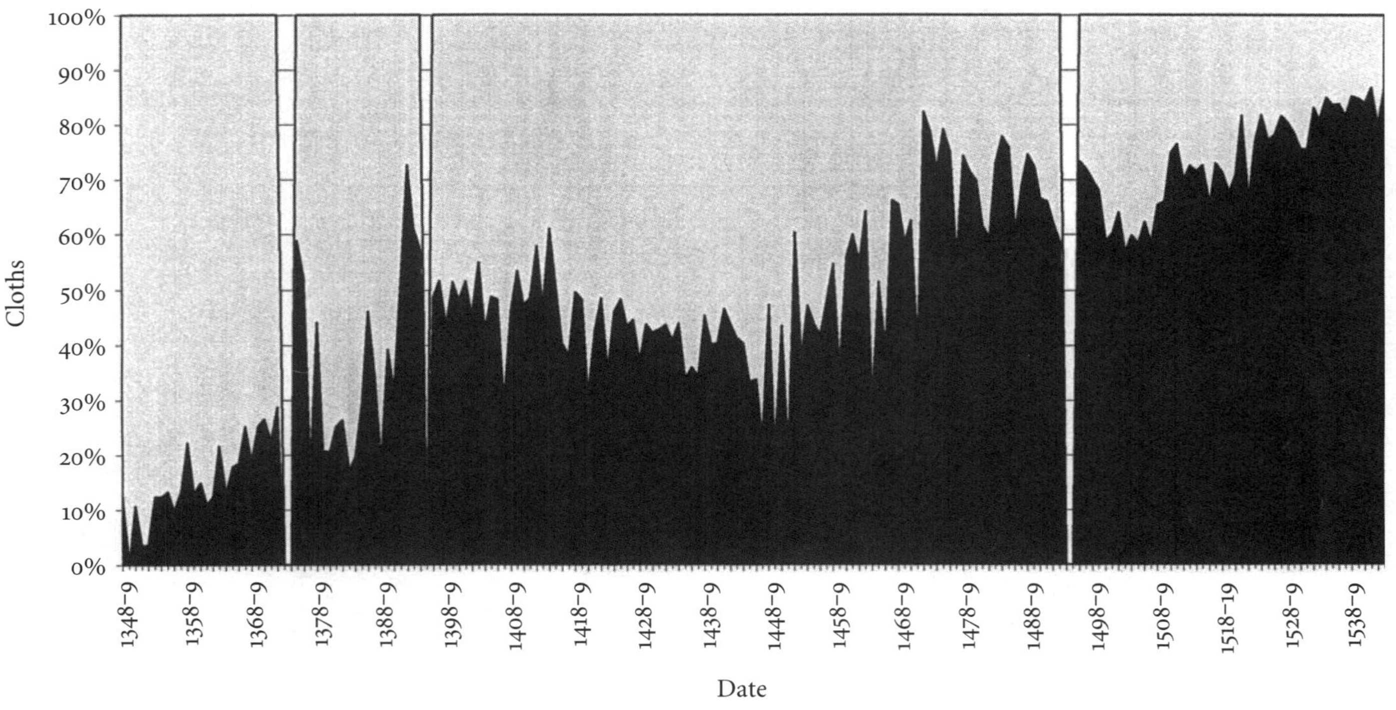

FIG. 5.5. England's cloth exports: London's share of total exports, 1348–1543

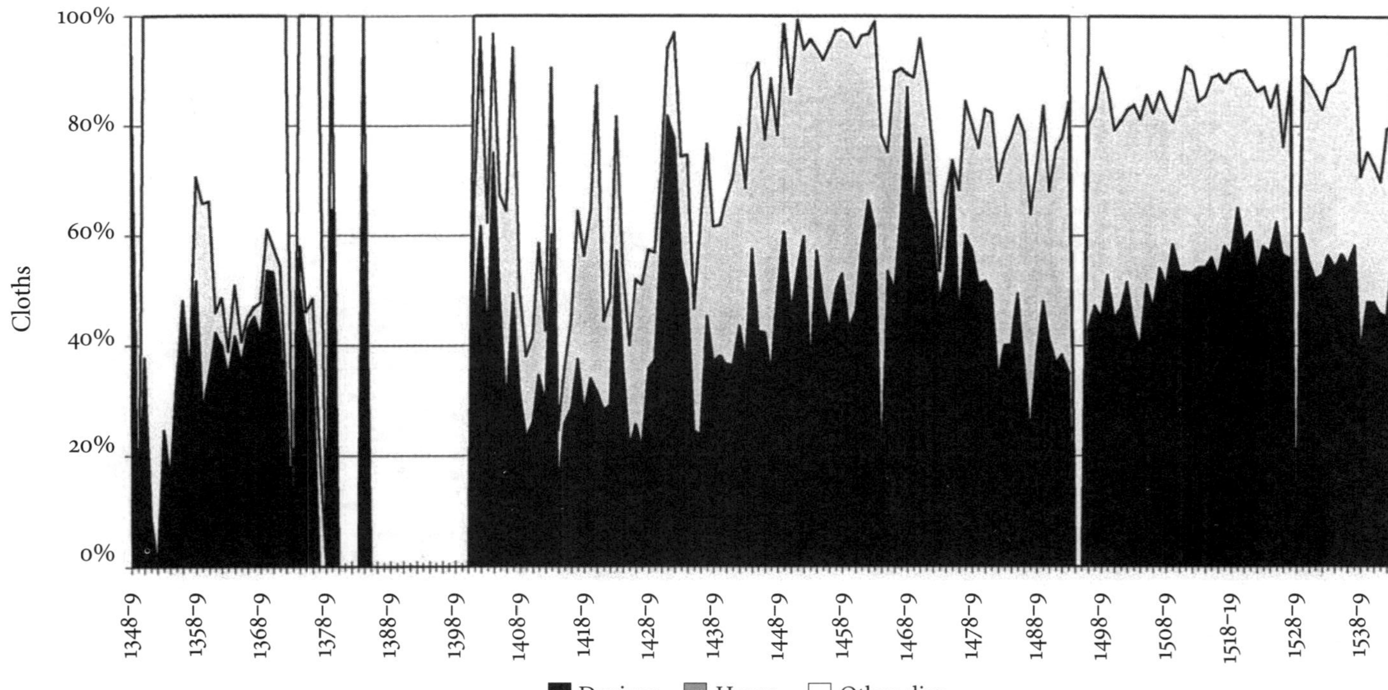

FIG. 5.6. London's cloth exports: relative shares taken by denizens, the Hanse, and other aliens, 1348–1543

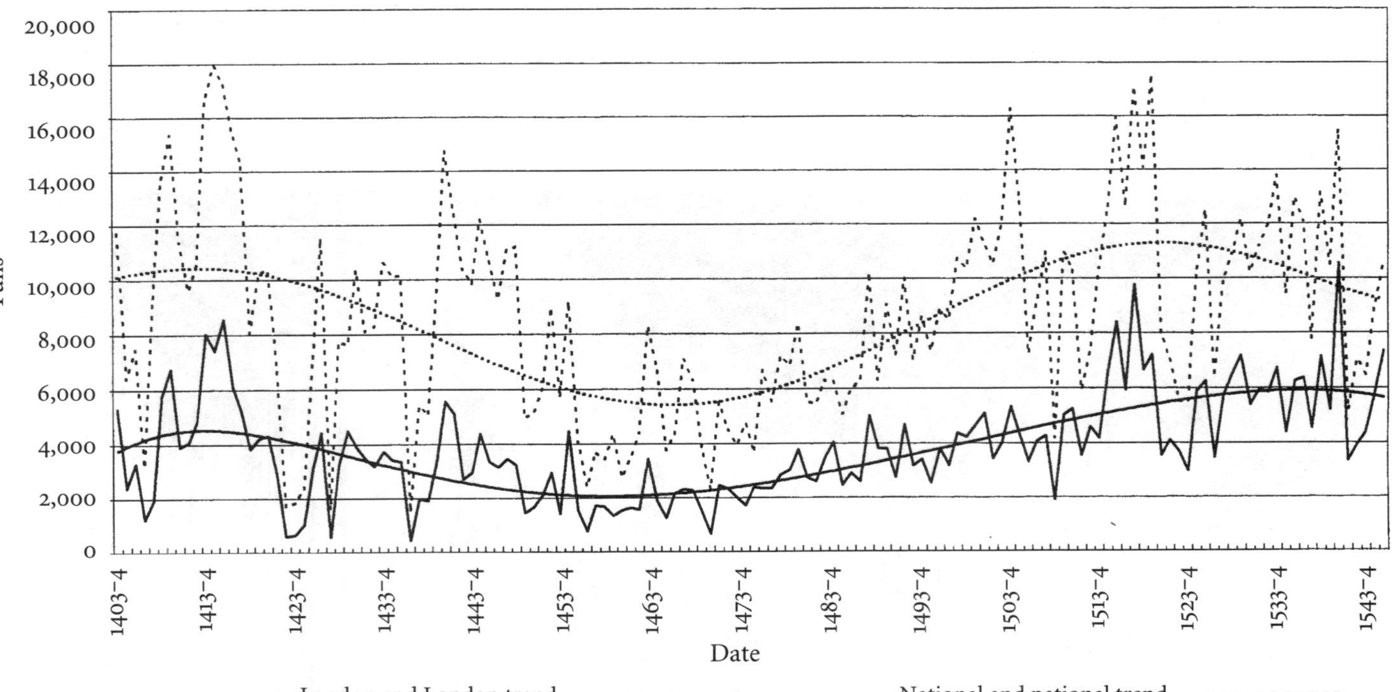

Fig. 5.7. England's wine imports: London's share of the wine import trade, 1403–1547

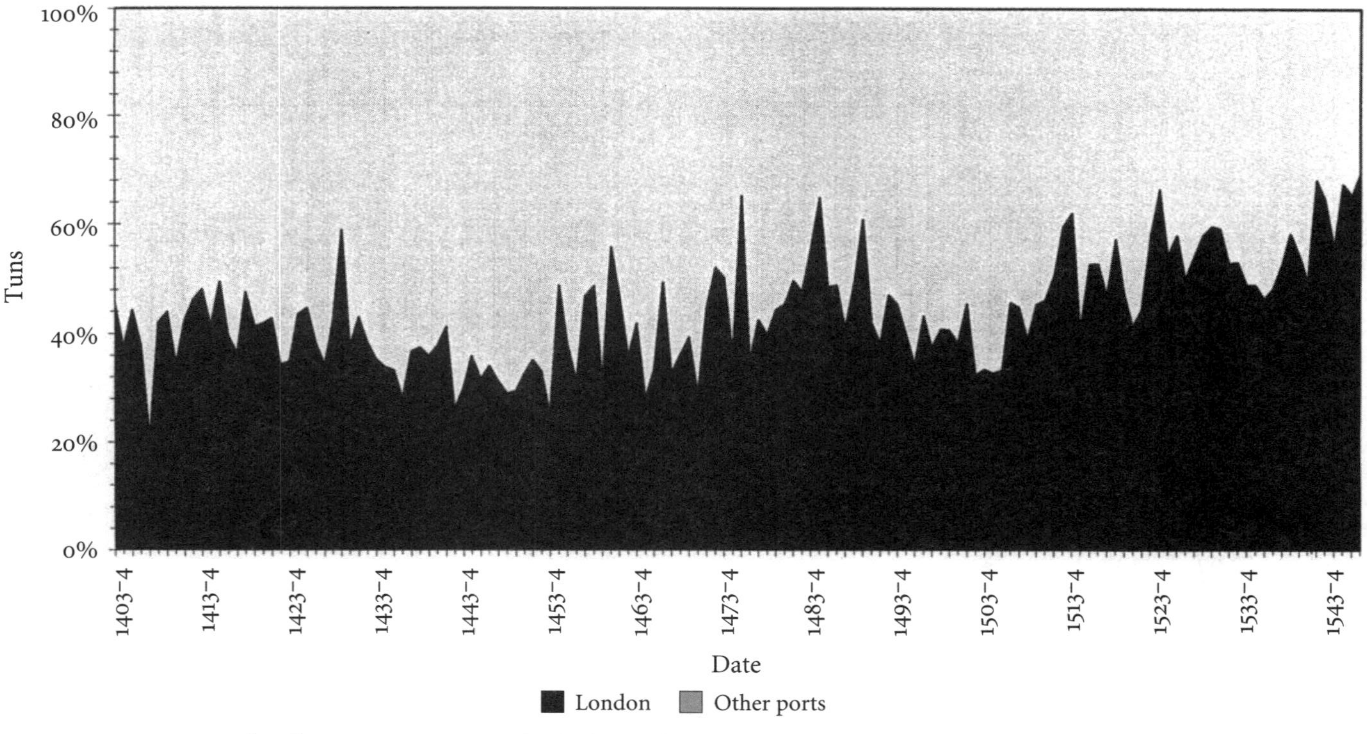

FIG. 5.8. England's wine imports: London's share of total imports, 1403–1547

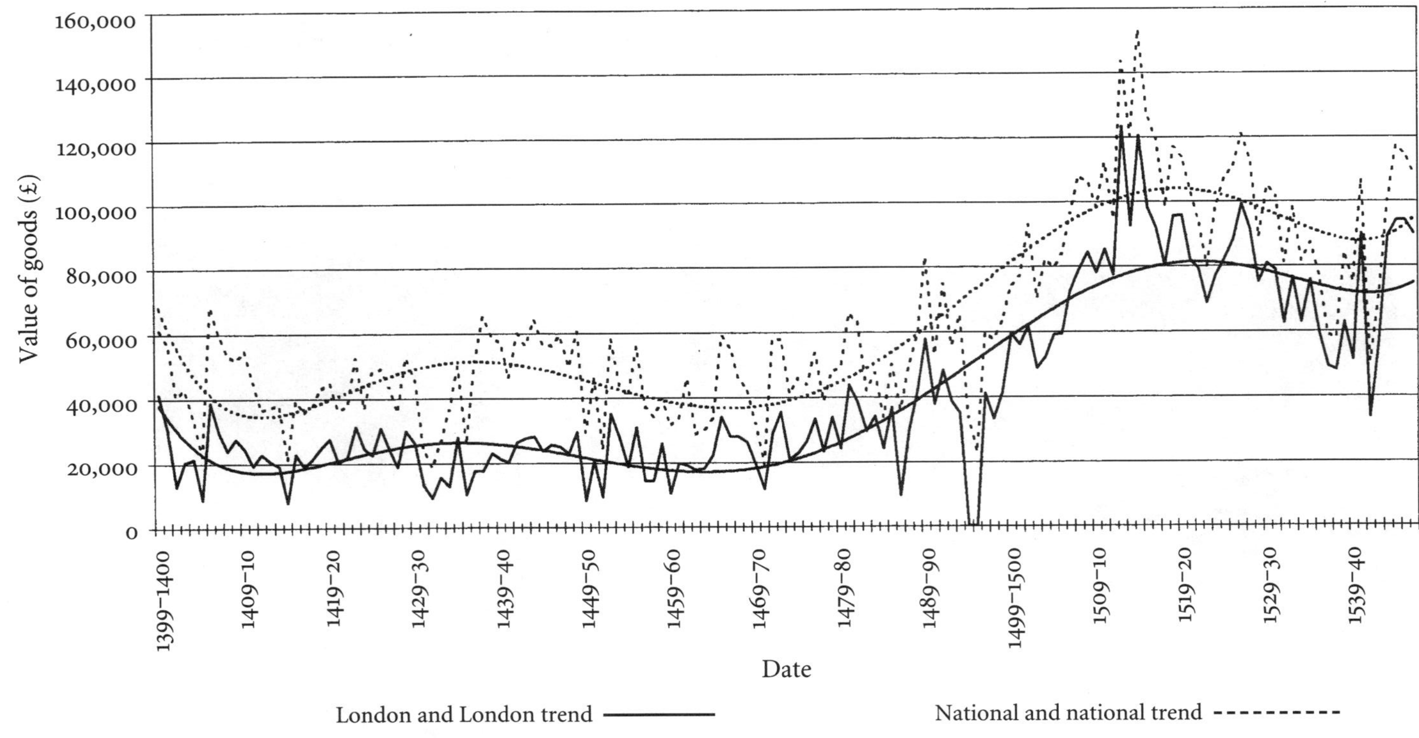

Fig. 5.9. England, total value of goods liable to petty custom: national trends, 1399–1547

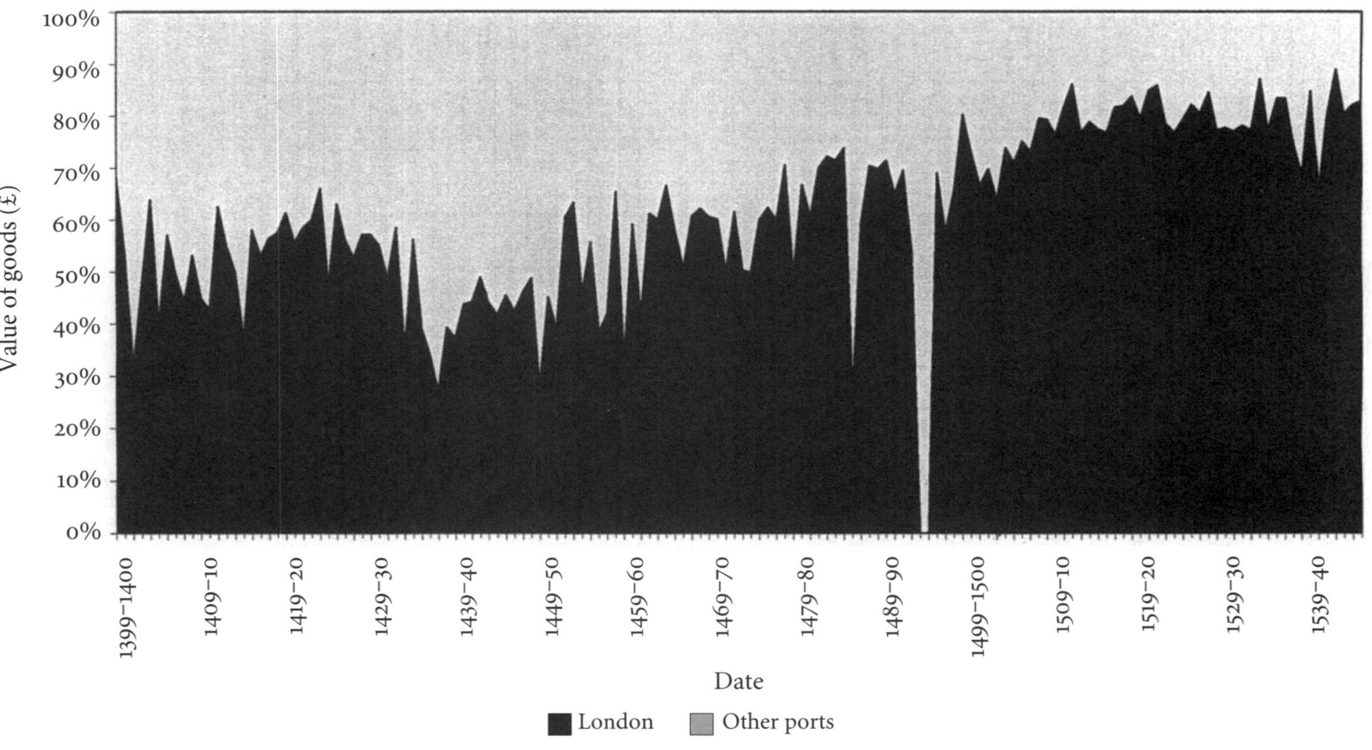

Fig. 5.10. England, total value of goods liable to petty custom: London's share, 1399–1547

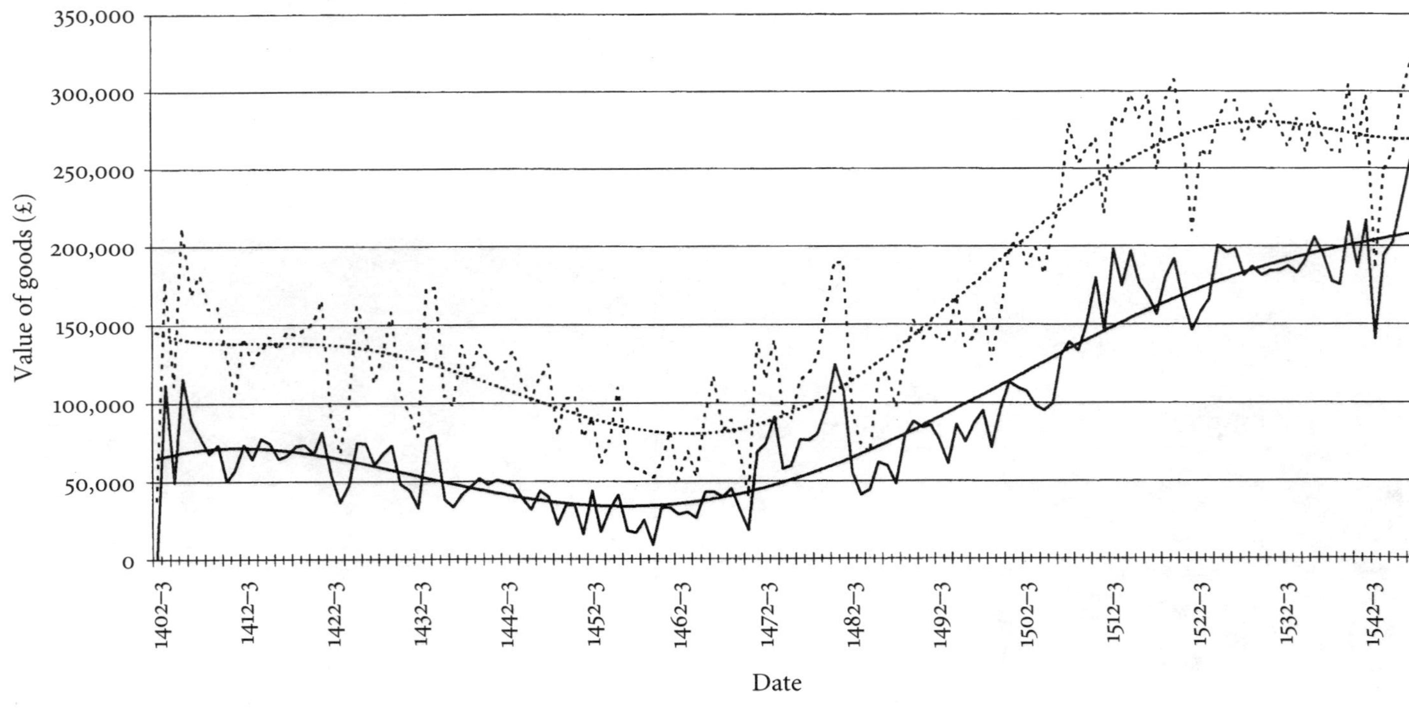

FIG. 5.11. England, total value of goods liable to poundage: National trends, 1402–1547

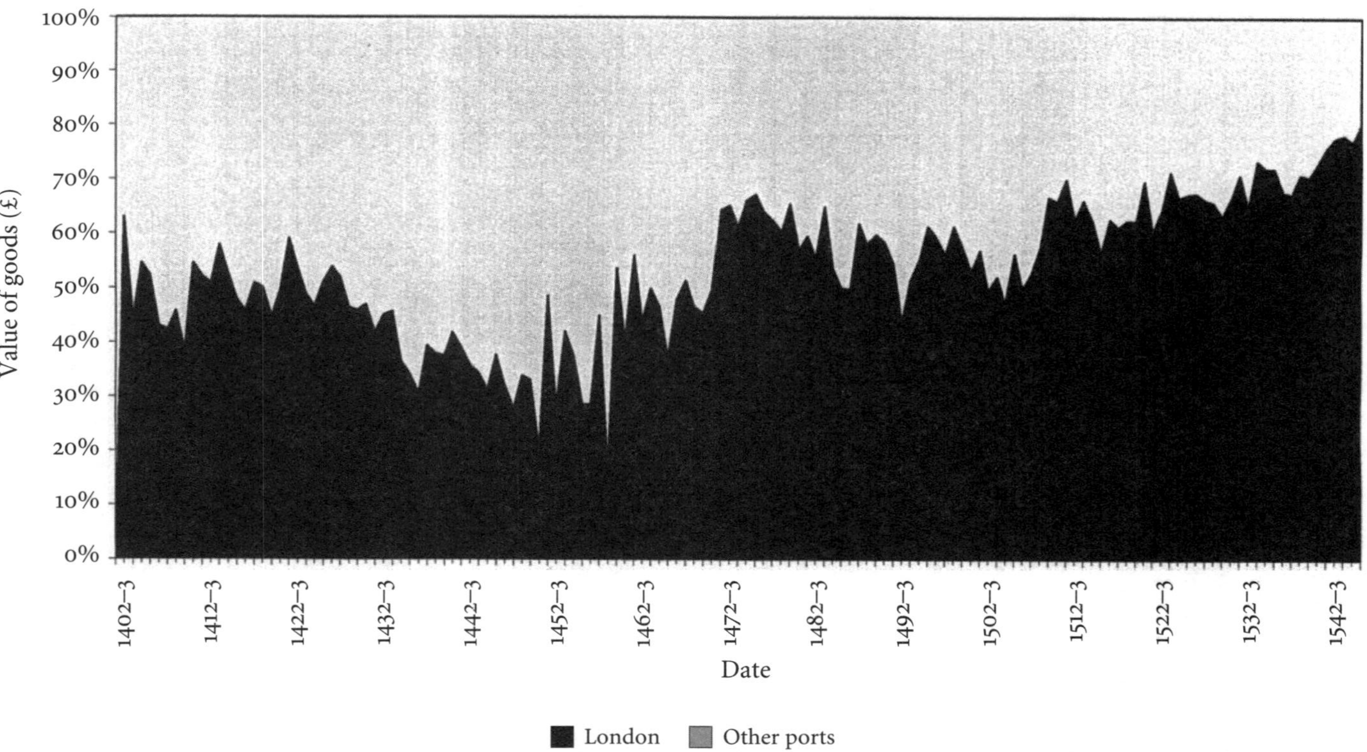

FIG. 5.12. England, total value of goods liable to poundage: London's share, 1402–1547

Baltic. Although there were periods when the duke banned the import of English cloth (1434–9; 1447–53; 1464–7) these bans seem not to have been effective and, in the end, the Burgundian dukes decided to let the Flemish weavers go to the wall.[75] The merchants of Antwerp were anxious to secure supplies of English cloth: large quantities of silver were being mined in Thuringia, Saxony, and Silesia, and as a result the merchants of Nuremberg and Augsburg had become extremely wealthy and eager to buy the comparatively heavyweight English cloth. Antwerp was, indeed, the nexus where German silver was exchanged for English cloth.[76] In the early fifteenth century much of the English cloth exported to Antwerp was finished and dyed there to the requirements of the German markets. This crucial development of the Cologne–Antwerp–London trade route was co-terminous with the growth of the organized company of the Merchant Adventurers.

Groups of merchant adventurers—merchants who traded abroad in goods other than wool—appear in England in the late thirteenth century but, from the middle of the fifteenth century, such groups in London had become closely associated with the Mercers' company and their main trading concern was the export of cloth.[77] Merchant adventurers might, however, belong to other companies such as the Grocers, Drapers, or Haberdashers, but their purpose was to charter vessels jointly to take cloth to the four great Antwerp markets and to fashion common resistance to royal subsidies. In spite of Edward IV's Letters Patent of 1462 which allowed the adventurers to meet together and to choose their own governors in Holland, Zeeland, Brabant, and Flanders to settle disputes and to make 'reasonable ordinances', yet the organization in London remained informal.[78] In 1486, however, the mayor and aldermen of London decided that they would choose each year two lieutenants, one from the Mercers and the other from one of the other crafts 'frequenting the parts of the duke of Burgundy', and these two men should organize fleets, arrange the contributions paid by participants, and select the place of assembly.[79]

There were, perhaps, eighty to one hundred and fifty London adventurers at any one time and they formed a regulated, rather than a joint stock, company; that is, they traded as individuals but the Fellowship charted the ships, fixed the rates charged for carriage, and determined when the fleet sailed. In spite of the attempts of other English towns, especially York, to maintain their own independent companies of Adventurers, the London group inexorably gained a dominant role which was recognised by Henry VII when, in 1495, he sent out John Pykering, a mercer and the governor of the London company, with royal authority over all the

[75] Ralph Davis, 'The Rise of Antwerp and its English Connection 1406–1500' in D. C. Coleman and A. H. John (eds.), *Trade, Government and Economy in Pre-Industrial England: Essays to F. J. Fisher* (London, 1976), 2–20, esp. 8; Barron, 'Introduction', Barron and Saul (eds.), *England and the Low Countries*, 9.

[76] Davis, 'The Rise of Antwerp', 8–12.

[77] Sutton, 'Merchant Adventurers', 28–9, 34–6.

[78] *CPR 1461–7*, 187.

[79] CLRO, Journal 9, folios 101, 103^{v}.–103; E. M. Carus-Wilson, 'The Origin and Early Development of the Merchant Adventurers Organization in London as Shown in Their Own Medieval Records', in ead., *Medieval Merchant Venturers* (London, 1954, 2nd edn. 1967), 143–82, esp. 158.

English adventurers in the lands of the duke of Burgundy.[80] By Letters Patent of 1505 all the English Adventurers were welded into a single company under one governor with twenty-four assistants, and although there were representatives from other towns among the assistants, the policy of the company was directed by the Londoners, a majority of whom were mercers.[81] The London base of the English Adventurers was Mercers' Hall: abroad the company had a less settled existence and did not fix upon a particular town, although much of their business was transacted with, and through, Antwerp.

While the London merchants were able largely to monopolize the export of English cloth and to drive out the merchants from other towns, they were less successful in expelling the alien merchants from their role as cloth exporters. Between 40 per cent and 50 per cent of all the cloths exported from London were owned by alien merchants among whom the Hanse merchants were particularly prominent and that substantial share had not notably diminished before 1540 (see fig. 5.6). A very significant number of English cloths not only left London as alien cargoes but also left in alien ships. In 1480–1 less than half the ships using the port of London were English. A substantial amount of the trade with the Low Countries was conducted in ships from Holland, Flanders, Zeeland, and Brabant. There were also quite a large number of Hanse ships from Hamburg and Danzig that brought in the usual Baltic imports of timber, ashes, tar, pitch, wax, furs, stockfish, and flax in return for cargoes of English cloth.[82]

The London Customs accounts for 1480–1 reveal the continuing presence and importance of the Italian trade into London. A Venetian galley brought in spices, soap, expensive cloths, carpets, silk, and glassware to a value of over £600 and carried away cloth, pewter, calfskins, 'cotton russet', and tin.[83] Genoese and Florentine merchants also brought in cargoes using Spanish and Portuguese ships. It is clear that in spite of the bankruptcies of the mid-fourteenth century the Italians had not left the English commercial scene. They had largely, but by no means completely, conceded their role in royal finance to native English financiers, but they (e.g. the Borromei) were still to be found in London providing financial services such as letters of exchange and funds for ransoms as well as engaging in overseas trade. They maintained their interest in English wool and now brought carracks or galleys by sea to English ports to collect the wool and, to

[80] Ibid. 173–4. In 1478 the merchants of York, Hull, Beverley, Scarborough, Whitby and 'others in the north' complained about John Pykering who had been appointed by the London company as governor in Brabant, Holland, Zeeland, and Flanders, *The York Mercers and Merchant Adventurers 1356–1917*, ed. M. Sellers (Surtees Society, 1918), 75–80.

[81] Carus-Wilson, 'Early Development of the Merchant Adventurers', 115; Sutton, 'Merchant Adventurers', 44–5.

[82] *The Overseas Trade of London: Exchequer Customs Accounts 1480–1*, ed. H. S. Cobb (London Record Society, 1990), p. xi; D. Burwash notes a rise in the volume of English shipping using the port of London from 31% in 1465–6 to 41% in 1519–20, *English Merchant Shipping 1461–1540* (Toronto, 1947), 148.

[83] *Overseas Trade of London*, ed. Cobb, p. xli.

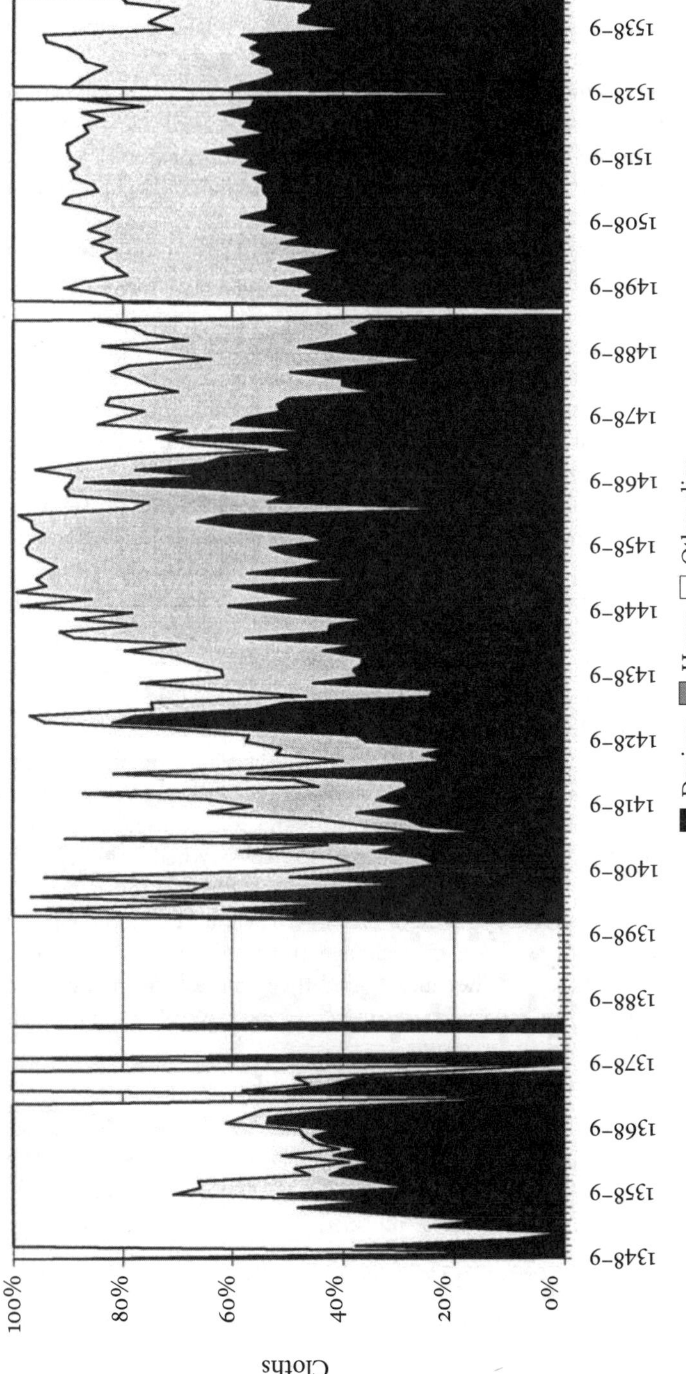

Fig. 5.6. London's cloth exports: relative shares taken by denizens, the Hanse, and other aliens, 1348–1543

a lesser extent, cloth. The Genoese galleys and Florentine carracks came to Southampton and Sandwich (effectively London's outports) and there collected Cotswold wool, whereas the Venetians had, from the 1390s, sent their galleys to London. Here they sold spices from the East, expensive cloths that they had imported from China or had manufactured in their own silk factories and took away wool and cloths that they had bought at the London cloth market at Blackwell Hall.[84] The hostility to the Italians that erupted on the streets of London in the 1450s may have had several causes. Some merchants found it easier than others to weather the trade slump and recession of the mid-century and to those who were struggling the Italians presented an obvious target for their discontent. Moreover, it has been pointed out that the Italians had been comparatively absent from the English scene since the later fourteenth century, with the result that their re-emergence provoked resentment.[85] In the 1450s, when English merchants were compelled to sell their wool through the Calais Staple, the Italians were able to purchase licences to bypass the Staple and to take their wool by sea to Italy.[86] The hostility to the Italians may also have been provoked by the popular, if misguided, belief that they brought into England expensive, unnecessary, and luxurious items. The author of the *Libelle of Englyshe Polycye* (1436) characterized Italian imports as:

> Apes and japes and marmusettes taylede
> Nifles, trifles, that litell have availed.[87]

It was believed, wrongly, that the Italians took away goods of less value than those they imported and, in this way, contributed to the bullion shortage in England. There is no doubt that there was such a shortage in England in the period 1430–50, but this famine was not unique to England, occurring throughout Europe. In any case, it has been shown that the Italian trade with England was well in balance: the total value of Italian exports in 1438–9 was more than double the value of their imports. The Venetians, who largely operated in London, seem to have spent more money than the other Italian merchants. Moreover, 33 per cent of Italian imports were of those raw materials that were crucial for the making of English cloth, such as alum and woad.[88] There is no doubt, however, that in London the Italians formed a small, elite, and prosperous group of about fifty to sixty men, almost all of whom lived in the two wards of Langbourn and Broad Street, worshipped together in the house of the Austin Friars, and stayed only for short periods. Their

[84] G. Holmes, 'Florentine Merchants in England', *Econ.HR* 13, (2nd series, 1960–1), 193–208, esp. 198; H. Bradley, 'The Datini Factors in London, 1380–1410', in D. Clayton, R. G. Davies, and P. McNiven (eds.), *Trade, Devotion and Governance: Papers in Later Medieval History* (Stroud, 1994), 55–79, esp. 59–61.

[85] Holmes, 'Florentine Merchants', 199.

[86] J. L. Bolton, 'The City and the Crown, 1451–61', *London Journal*, 12 (1986), 11–24, esp. 16.

[87] *The Libelle of Englyshe Polycye*, ed., G. Warner (Oxford, 1926), ll. 348–9.

[88] Bolton, *English Economy*, 313–14; and see E. Fryde, 'The English Cloth Industry and the Trade with the Mediterranean *c.*1370–*c.*1480', in M. Spallanzani (ed.), *Produzione Commercio e Consumo dei Panni di Lana*, 2 vols. (Florence, 1976), ii. 343–67.

time in London was seen as an 'exile' and was imposed on young men by the various firms to which they belonged.[89] But in spite of the popular resentment of their undoubted wealth and importance, in fact the Italian element of English trade was declining: between 1420 and 1460 their share of the import trade dropped from 29 per cent to 20 per cent, and of the export trade from 25 per cent to 21 per cent. The value of their imports dropped from £310,000 to £189,000, and of their exports from £415,000 to £217,000. The diminishing role played by the Italians may have been due less to English entrepreneurial skills than to the difficulties they were facing in the Mediterranean from the Turks (who had, for example, taken the principal alum works in Phocea in Asia Minor from the Genoese early in 1455) and from warfare among the different Italian states.[90]

The gap, if gap it was, left by the Italians in the English overseas trade was filled, in part, by the Spanish who in small numbers began to trade again with England even before the formal end of the Hundred Years War. The Spanish merchants were to be found lodging with Londoners (in particular the mercers Richard Rich and John Church) in the 1440s and there are other indications of modest, albeit 'firm and regular' trade between England and Spain in these years.[91] In 1466 Edward IV concluded a treaty of perpetual alliance with Henry IV of Castille which included important commercial clauses: merchants of the two countries were to be treated as denizens (and hence pay the lower rate of custom) and they could lease houses and negotiate their own sales.[92] This agreement came at a time when European trade was reviving after the recession of the mid-century: Spanish wine (to replace that from Gascony) was brought into London and cloth, especially ready-dyed cloth, was exported. The names of 260 Spaniards appear in the London customs accounts between 1460 and 1483, together with numerous Spanish ships, and it has been estimated that twenty to thirty Londoners were, in these years, involved in the Spanish trade.[93] In 1480–1 twenty-one Spanish ships left the port of London carrying over 300 cloths: in return they were importing iron, salt, sugar, wine, and fruits, both fresh and dried.[94] There is no doubt that cloth was, in fact, the major English export to Spain and that London played a predominant role in that trade.[95]

Those Londoners with interests in Spain extended them also to Portugal.[96] In 1480–1 Portuguese ships were to be found trading into the port of London. They brought in 300,000 oranges, sugar, and cork and exported the usual cloth, together with some pewter and calfskins.[97] One of those who exported cloth to Portugal

[89] H. Bradley, 'The Italian Community in London *c.*1350–*c.*1450' (University of London, Ph.D. thesis, 1992), esp. chs. 1 and 7, and map following p. 30; J. L. Bolton, *The Alien Communities of London in the Fifteenth Century* (Stamford, 1998), 6.

[90] Bolton, *English Economy*, 307, 314.

[91] W. Childs, *Anglo-Castilian Trade in the Later Middle Ages* (Manchester, 1978), 51.

[92] Ibid. 53.

[93] Ibid. 61; and see Quinton, 'Drapers and the Drapery Trade', 258–63, 274–6, 280.

[94] *Overseas Trade of London*, ed. Cobb, p. xli.

[95] Childs, *Anglo-Castilian Trade*, 90.

[96] See W. Childs, 'Anglo-Portuguese Trade in the Fifteenth Century', *TRHS* 2, 6th series, (1992), 195–219.

[97] *Overseas Trade of London*, ed. Cobb, p. xli.

that year was Sir Edward Brampton, the son of a Lisbon merchant, converted Jew and naturalized Englishman, who lived in Broad Street ward, together with three Portuguese servants.[98] The success of the London mercantile community had always been due in part to the alien merchants who lived and traded within the city, even if subject, on occasion, to jealousy and abuse. The years between the end of the Hundred Years War and the onset of the Reformation eighty years later may well have been a halcyon period for alien merchants who wished to live and trade peaceably in London. In a time of political neutrality and economic prosperity, London could flourish as a truly cosmopolitan city.

CONCLUSION

It is possible to discern some clear trends in the development of the overseas trade of London between 1200 and 1500. The Londoners themselves, provoked by alien intervention and royal manipulation, began, before the end of the thirteenth century, to organize themselves into 'interest groups' in order to resist both the aliens and the Crown. At first groups such as vintners or skinners formed their associations in order to control the sale of alien imports and to dominate the distributive trade within England. But they then moved on to form larger groupings to control the export trade: the Merchants of the Staple in the early fourteenth century to control the export of wool and, in the fifteenth century, the formal Company of Merchant Adventurers to organize and control the burgeoning export of English cloth. These two 'export' companies were successful largely because they were supported by the Crown.

In the thirteenth century the king had taxed overseas trade by ad hoc impositions such as the maltote on wool, and he had taxed alien merchants who, in effect, paid the Crown for the right to trade in England. The trading position of alien merchants was formalized in the *Carta Mercatoria* of 1303 which laid down both their privileges and their financial obligations. But although the king continued to favour and to protect alien merchants as a source of revenue, and as a useful antidote to the pretensions of English merchants, he also increasingly found it useful to negotiate with a single group (such as the staplers) and to allow them, in effect, to monopolize the export trade and to pay a higher rate of custom for the privilege, as well as providing loans in the form of advances on the customs revenue. Gradually the 'colonial' economy of thirteenth-century England, where the major exporters of English goods were alien merchants, and the major export was the raw material, wool, gradually shifted in favour of native merchants and manufactured cloth. The Hanse merchants, however, retained their privileges well into the sixteenth century. English kings, most notably Edward IV, found them to be useful allies and the preferential customs rates that they enjoyed attracted them to trade in England. English merchants were never able to penetrate the Baltic,

[98] Ibid. 94, 124, 158; Bolton, *Alien Communities*, 73 n. 117, 74.

nor to receive privileges in Hanse towns comparable to those that the Hanseatics enjoyed in London.[99] In the later fifteenth century the Hanse merchants were still exporting almost as much cloth from London as were the English merchants (see fig. 5.6).

So, by 1500, English merchants had gained control of a large, but not a complete, share of the English overseas trade. However, more and more of that trade was passing through London and, although Bristol, Southampton, and some of the other southern ports still enjoyed a decent overseas trade, the east coast ports had lost out almost completely to London.[100] The alien participation in English overseas trade had, by the late fifteenth century, largely returned to the pattern of the later thirteenth century: the French and Spaniards who had been absent during the Hundred Years War were once more bringing in cargoes and the role of the Italians was again reduced. Although there were signs of a growth in the English mercantile marine, yet in London in 1480 over 50 per cent of the ships entering the port were alien: another indication that England had not yet fully emerged from the chrysalis of a colonial economy.[101]

The most striking development in this period is, or course, the rise of the English cloth industry, which had flourished in the early thirteenth century but had been checked by the precocious development of the industry in the weaving towns of Flanders. It became easier to export the raw material and to import the finished product. But this situation began to change in the early fourteenth century, in part because of royal interference in the free export of wool, and the native cloth industry once encouraged began to develop rapidly in the comparatively peaceful environment of England, while the Flemish cloth towns suffered from internal strife and ducal interference. Only domestic-quality cloth appears to have been manufactured in London on a large scale, and yet by the late fourteenth century high-quality cloth made in other parts of England was being brought to the London market at Blackwell Hall for sale, and much of it was being sent abroad through the port of London. In return for this cloth, and also for wool, a variety of foreign goods from Italy, Flanders, and the Baltic countries poured onto the wharves and into the storehouses of London merchants.

Some of the imported goods were the raw materials needed in the manufacture of cloth: dyes such as woad, madder, brasil, vermilion, and grain; mordaunts such as potash and alum; fuller's earth and teasels for carding wool: other raw materials fed other industries: metals, timber, wax, and furs. Yet other imports were essential foodstuffs such as salt, spices and drugs, wine and fruit. But the imports to London reveal the extent to which the economy of England was undeveloped since, from the fourteenth century, goods manufactured in the Low Countries had been brought into London: Dutch beer, earthenware pots, brass cooking ware, linen kerchiefs and tablecloths, bricks, and wooden clogs. By the 1480s these

[99] Bolton, *English Economy*, 308.
[100] Lloyd, *England and the German Hanse*, 163–4, 228, 274.
[101] *Overseas Trade of London*, ed. Cobb, p. xxxviii.

manufactured goods were flooding into the city: altogether half a million yards of linen, together with tablecloths, napkins, and towels were brought in; also metal kitchenware of all kinds, armour, 900 books, 300 gross of spectacles, 28,600 girdles made of leather and silk and 46,000 knives.[102] Many of these goods were not of the quality of comparable goods made by English craftsmen upon whom high standards (and high prices) were enforced by guild regulations. But the imported goods were cheaper. In 1464 and again in 1484, statutes were passed that prohibited the import of a wide range of manufactured goods in order to protect the livelihoods of craftsmen and women in London and other English towns. Few prosecutions seem to have arisen from these acts, but that does not mean that these imported goods did not threaten the livelihoods of craftsmen who were, moreover, beginning to feel the effects of the slow rise in population which by the 1520s was to convert the prosperity of the fifteenth-century wage-earning craftsmen into mass underemployment.

The English economy was in many ways undeveloped: the Italians had far more sophisticated business practices and the craftsmen of the Low Countries produced goods in far greater quantities (and, sometimes, of far higher quality) than English craftsmen. The English mercantile marine was small and English merchants only rarely ventured abroad but chose to trade with those alien merchants who sailed to England and took the risks and the profits. But the situation was changing and the English merchants were cultivating those skills which would, in the next century, take them on trading ventures, in English ships, to all parts of the known world. London's share of English overseas trade had steadily increased in the fitful course of the fifteenth century: by 1500 60 per cent of English wool and 70 per cent of English cloth was exported from London and 65 per cent of the other goods (apart from wine) on which custom was paid passed through the port of London. The dramatic rise in English overseas trade was to come in the sixteenth century, and London's share of that trade also rose dramatically. By 1540 more than 80 per cent of all English customed goods, as well as wool and cloth, were being traded through London. (see figs. 5.2, 5.5, 5.10, and 5.12). The picture by this time was very different from that of 1300 when London merchants had shared the overseas trade of England with large numbers of alien merchants and with numerous other English ports.

[102] Ibid. pp. xxxv–xxxvii.

PART 3

The Government of London

CHAPTER SIX

The City Courts

AT THE BEGINNING of the period the structure of civic government appears tentative and confused: ad hoc arrangements mixing public and private authority, elected and hereditary officials, informal and formal offices. By the end of the period the records are more copious, the structure is clear, the duties and remuneration of office holders defined, and there is a dramatic proliferation of lesser officials and of committees, both the hallmarks of a successful and developing administrative bureaucracy. The city functioned through a mixture of honorary (and honoured) officers (mayor, sheriffs, and aldermen) and paid civil servants such as the recorder and common clerk. All these were served by households of clerks or serjeants. The distinction between the executive and judicial and legislative functions of government was not clearly defined: the men who made up the courts of aldermen and common council, for example, drew up civic legislation, administered it in their wards and judged and punished transgressors. Complaints against civic government, although quite numerous in the thirteenth and fourteenth centuries, seem to be remarkably infrequent in the fifteenth century in spite of a burgeoning volume of records.

THE ADMINISTRATION OF THE WARD

The basic unit of civic government was the ward: until 1394 there were twenty-four of these and in that year the large ward of Farringdon was divided into two, bringing the number of wards up to twenty-five.[1] The ward may well have been in existence as early as the eleventh century yet in the thirteenth century many wards still bore the names of their alderman rather than a topographical description.[2] Their origins in private judicial sokes were not yet overlaid by a superstructure of communal activity.[3] But there is no doubt that by the end of the thirteenth century the wardmote, that is the gathering together of all the men of the ward both householders and hired servants, had become an integral and essential element in city government.[4] By

[1] *LBH*, 407–8.

[2] C. N. L. Brooke with G. Keir, *London 800–1216: The Shaping of a City* (London, 1975), 162–70; G. A. Williams, *Medieval London from Commune to Capital* (London, 1963), 32–3; *CPMR 1413–37*, pp. xxx–xli.

[3] In 1275 there were eighteen sokes in one ward: Williams, *Medieval London*, 80–1.

[4] *Liber Albus*, 32–5.

the end of the fifteenth century the city companies began to be used by the city government for administrative purposes, and in the sixteenth century demographic pressure led to the fragmentation of the wards into precincts. The parish also developed as an administrative unit and it was the precinct and the parish that became the crucial sub-units of civic government. But in the medieval period it was the ward, its wardmote and alderman that provided the essential substructure of city government.

By 1246 the enquiries into purprestures (the illegal enroachments on, or enclosures of, land) were conducted on a ward-by-ward basis.[5] But by about 1290, or a little earlier, the wards had acquired the names by which they are still known and aldermen no longer gave their own names to their wards: in fact the wards had become institutionalized.[6] When the new royal taxation, assessed on chattels, was introduced in the 1290s the assessments were made in the wards.

An alderman may have summoned a wardmote only when it was necessary. It seems to have become customary for aldermen to hold at least one wardmote annually and to bring the indentures and inquest verdicts from the wardmote to the special court held by the mayor on Plough Monday (the Monday after Epiphany).[7] At the wardmote, those who attended would elect a jury, perhaps of twelve men, who in the thirteenth century may have acted as councillors or advisers to the alderman. Such men may have been considered as the *probi homines* or the good men of the ward. In the 1280s a list of the reputable men of each ward who had been sworn to consult with the aldermen was entered into the city's Letter Book.[8] In 1305 twelve good men of the ward of Chepe came to court to protest about the building activities of Master Stephen the surgeon in their ward. The sheriffs were ordered to produce Master Stephen at the next court.[9] As the common council developed in the course of the fourteenth century these local *probi homines* may have been transformed into the ward's common councilmen.[10] But there was still a need to elect also a number of jurymen to present offenders even if these were no longer the same men who acted as advisers to the aldermen. At the end of Henry VI's reign the ward of Aldersgate had twelve jurymen, although the number later in the sixteenth century varied from fourteen to sixteen.[11] It seems to have been customary for the jurymen to go with their alderman to the Plough

[5] *The London Eyre of 1244*, ed. H. M. Chew and M. Weinbaum (London Record Society, 1970), 136–52 (this volume contains records of the perambulations of the city in both 1244 and 1246).

[6] *LBA*, 209; A. B. Beaven, *The Alderman of the City of London*, 2 vols. (1908–13), i. 235–7.

[7] *c.*1385, precept to the aldermen to hold a wardmote before the feast of Epiphany and to bring the list of defects to the following Plough Monday court, *LBH*, 276; cf. 1390, 1391, ibid, 361, 368. Similar precepts are recorded almost annually from 1410 to 1437. In 1447 it was decided that by virtue of an annual precept from the mayor the alderman could hold as many wardmotes as seemed necessary during the year: CLRO, Journal 4 fo.180.

[8] *LBA*, 209–10; this list is not dated, but it follows a list of aldermen for the different wards that can be dated before 1287 when John of Northampton ceased to be the alderman for Aldgate ward.

[9] 11 September 1305, *CEMCR 1298–1307*, 225.

[10] See below n. 65.

[11] In 1584/5 the men of Aldersgate ward decided to examine the old records of their ward which were kept in a chest in Trinity Hall (the old guild hall of the fraternity dedicated to the Holy Trinity in St

Monday court, but in 1486 it was decided that the alderman alone should come bringing the indentures and verdict but leave the jurymen behind 'in order to avoid the dangers of the large numbers of people attending the hall'.[12]

It may be that the wardmote sometimes met in the house of the alderman; it would seem that the men of Aldersgate ward met in the hall belonging to the Trinity guild and the wardmote of Cripplegate in 1423 met in the hall of the brewers' craft.[13] The precepts to the aldermen defined the purpose of the wardmote: ward officers and common councilmen were to be elected, precautions taken against fire and rioting, and streets guarded, lighted, and cleaned. Recent civic legislation would be read out and, after the jurymen were elected, a series of articles were put to them and they were then required to list the transgressors within the ward: those who were immoral, or night walkers, or who kept houses of ill repute; those who threw dung or rubbish out into the street or blocked the public highways with extensions to their houses; those who ignored the price controls on bread or ale; all these were catalogued and their names and offences were written down. The written document took the form of an indenture; one half was kept in the ward and the other half was kept by the alderman until he presented it to the mayor at the Plough Monday court.[14]

Unfortunately very few of these indentures survive. Those that were presented to the Plough Monday courts in 1373, 1422, and 1423 were kept with the Mayor's records for these years, but the experiment—if so it was—was discontinued. The series of presentments, however fleeting, provide an interesting insight into bad neighbour relations in the London wards of the 1420s.[15] Fifteen of the indentures for Portsoken ward survive for the reign of Edward IV and by the reign of Elizabeth I the ward of Aldersgate had a virtually complete series of indentures from the last year of Henry VI's reign kept in a chest.[16] No other ward records survive before 1571 although a draft of the inquest for Broad Street ward in 1523 survives among the Letters and Papers of Henry VIII. Thomas Cromwell had a house in Throgmorton Street in that ward and the inquest return is heavily corrected in his hand: thus far had grassroots democracy fallen beneath the pen of a great lord.[17] Those who were

Botolph's church) and to note the indentures. At that date such indentures—or records of meetings of the wardmote—survived in an almost complete series from 1461, but the Elizabethan wardmen decided to preserve only the barest details, providing little more than the names of the aldermen and the jurymen, GL, MS 2050/1.

[12] *LBL*, 238. If a juryman died during his year of office, then the alderman was empowered to choose a man to fill the vacancy; he was not required to summon a meeting of the wardmote for this purpose, CLRO, Journal 4 fo. 180.

[13] *LBD*, 215–16; *Parish Fraternity Register: The Fraternity of the Holy Trinity and SS Fabian and Sebastian in the Parish Church of St Botolph without Aldersgate*, ed. P. Basing (London Record Society, 1982), pp. xxv–xxvi; *A Book of London English 1384–1425*, ed. R. W. Chambers and M. Daunt (Oxford, 1931), 148.

[14] *Liber Albus*, 37–8.

[15] *CPMR 1364–81*, 156–7; *CPMR 1413–37*, 115–41; 150–9.

[16] CLRO, Portsoken presentments, 1465–83; 1507–8; GL MS 2050/1, Aldersgate wardmote book.

[17] PRO, State Papers SP/1/29, printed in *Letters and Papers of Henry VIII*, iii. p. 2. no. 3657. The inquest was held before the alderman and the presentments were made by a panel of thirteen jurymen (including Thomas Cromwell) 'indifferently chosen' who presented their information according to

absent from the wardmote were fined fourpence, which was paid into the city chamber for general city purposes although sometimes the proceeds might be devoted to a particular project such as the building of Guildhall. Sometimes the wards were allowed to keep the money to buy firefighting equipment or to reward ward officers.[18] These ward officers were extremely important; they were chosen by the wardmote, but worked under the ward alderman and were sworn to their offices before the mayor and aldermen.

The most senior officer was the beadle.[19] In 1321 when the king held his great judicial enquiry in the city the ward beadles played an important role: their duties and dress were carefully laid down and they were enjoined to be 'smart, handsomely turned out, freshly shaven and shorn' in order, no doubt, to impress the royal judges and promote a favourable impression of the city.[20] According to his oath the beadle was expected to ensure that there was no immorality in the ward, no peace-breaking, and no selling of goods contrary to mayoral precepts.[21] But his duties did not stop there. On several occasions the beadles were instructed to assist other ward officials in keeping the streets clean, although this was not their usual duty.[22] Sometimes they acted as local policemen reporting illegal gatherings of suspect persons.[23] They seem to have been of some standing in city government and stood at the apex of the local government pyramid in the ward. It is rare to find a beadle under a cloud: only three seem to have got into trouble, one for insolence, one for disobedience and a third for attempting to run a protection racket. In this last case, William Mayle, who was the beadle of Billingsgate ward, on discovering a case of adultery, instead of bringing the offender to court, accepted a bribe of 16*s.* 8*d.* which he divided among his associates and then spent the remainder on food and drink.[24] On the whole, however, the beadles seem to have been men of some standing within their communities.

The constables were more numerous and probably less responsible than the beadles to whom they were subordinate. The constables appeared for the first time in 1365 and after that date occur frequently in the records as the maids of all work in the wards.[25] There were probably about 200 constables operating at any one time in the city: in 1422 the small ward of Bassishaw had two constables while the large extramural ward of Farringdon Without had twenty-one.[26]

parishes. Thomas Cromwell signed the presentment first followed by six other signatures; the other six did not sign, although three made marks.

18 *Liber Albus*, 32–5; 23 October 1434, *LBK*, 181–2; CLRO, Journal 3 fos.55^{v}, 56; 14 March 1413, fines for absence from the wardmote to be devoted to the rebuilding of Guildhall, *Memorials*, 591.

19 See *CPMR 1413–37*, p. xxiv.

20 *The Eyre of London, 14 Edward II AD 1321*, ed. H. M. Cam, 2 vols. (Selden Society, 1968–9), 8.

21 A fourteenth-century copy of the beadle's oath in French, *LBF*, 126; a fifteenth-century version in English was copied into *LBD*, 193–4; *Liber Albus*, 34, 272–3.

22 In 1332, the ward beadle in Cripplegate was instructed to keep the streets clean, *CPMR 1323–64*, 97; cf. similar instructions in 1345, 1366, 1417, *LBF*, 125; *LBG*, 208; CLRO, Journal 1 fo.39. In 1372 ward beadles, underbeadles, and constables were listed and their street-cleaning duties defined, *CPMR 1364–81*, 150.

23 Year 1418, CLRO, Journal 1 fo.38; 1431, *LBK*, 132.

24 24 August 1376, *CPMR 1364–81*, 222–3, 15 July 1439, CLRO, Journal 3 fo. 18; 6 May 1461, Journal 6 fo. 53^{v}.

25 Year 1365, *LBG*, 198; cf. 1366, 1372, 1390, *LBG*, 208; *LBH*, 361; *Memorials*, 522.

26 *CPMR 1413–37*, 116.

By the fifteenth century constables took an oath on taking up office and their tasks included the pursuit of offenders, raising the hue and cry, and arraying panels of juries.[27] On occasion they forcibly entered houses, although after 1440 they were to do this only in the presence of an alderman.[28] In 1465 William Willoughby, a constable of Bread Street ward had to pay twenty shillings to a man whose doors he had broken down and whom he had then 'unjustly imprisoned'.[29] Frequently they were expected to accompany the aldermen of the ward in carrying out vigils and because of the physical demands made on constables they had to be strong in wind and limb. Thomas Darlington was rejected as constable for Langbourn ward by the Plough Monday court in 1451 because he had a malformed hand.[30] The duties were often dangerous: constables could be wounded when they attempted to break up street fights, or assaulted when collecting taxes or entering hostelries to pursue offenders.[31] On occasion the behaviour of the constables was found to be negligent or provocative. John West, for example, the constable of Billingsgate in 1459 was sent to prison for causing a riot against the chamberlain.[32] But the role of the beadles and constables in pursuing fornicators and adulterers must have exposed them to a good deal of abuse and hostility; nearly a hundred arrests of such transgressors (many of whom were unbeneficed priests) are recorded in London between 1400 and 1460.[33] It is hard to assess the public attitude to these arrests—were the constables seen as heroes or spoilsports?

A ward officer known as the scavenger also appeared first in 1364; he was particularly responsible for the repair of pavements, fire precautions, and street cleaning.[34] In the 1290s the city had required wards to elect four men to look after the pavements and to ensure that they were free of dung and in the early years of the fourteenth century the oversight of the city's streets was delegated to six specially elected paviours.[35] But it may have been realized that the task was better dealt with at the local ward level and so in 1365 ward scavengers were specifically enjoined to survey pavements and ensure that they were clean and in good repair. By 1390 the precept to the alderman specifically mentioned his duty to see that scavengers were elected;[36] the number elected might vary from ward to ward: Bassishaw and Lime Street, for example in 1421 had only two scavengers each and Farringdon Within had thirteen.[37]

[27] *Liber Albus*, 271; *LBD*, 192–3.

[28] Year 1440, CLRO, Journal 3 fo. 41^{v}; 2 May 1442, the city guaranteed to pay constables for any expenses incurred in the execution of their office, CLRO, Journal 3 fo. 133^{v}; *LBK*, 269.

[29] CLRO, Journal 7 fo. 103.

[30] CLRO, Journal 5 fo. 52^{v}.

[31] Year 1390, *Memorials*, 522; 1444, CLRO, Journal 4 fo. 132^{v}; Journal 5 fo. 163.

[32] 16 February 1459, CLRO, Journal 6 fo. 149^{v}; cf. cases of constables being imprisoned, 1450, 1458, 1461, ibid. 3 fo.31; ibid. 6 fos. 222^{v}, 53^{v}.

[33] Seventy arrests are recorded between 1400 and 1439, *LBI*, 273–87; a further 28 prosecutions are recorded in the Journals between 1421 and 1460.

[34] Oath of scavengers, *Liber Albus*, 272; *LBD*, 10, 192. For the Londoners' increased concern about the cleanliness of the city, see Ch. 10.

[35] *LBA*, 183; 1302, 1311, 1316, *LBC*, 115; *LBD*, 312; *LBE*, 55.

[36] *LBH*, 361; further references to scavengers in 1366, 1372, *LBG*, 208, 300; 1373, *CPMR 1364–81*, 164.

[37] *CPMR 1413–37*, 116.

The last officer to join the ward hierarchy was the raker; his role was much more menial and his work was not considered to be sufficiently important to require him to be sworn, like the other ward officers, before the mayor and aldermen. There is no oath recorded for rakers and their names do not appear in the lists of ward officers in 1372 and 1422. When they first appear in 1357 it is clear that they were, simply, street-sweepers.[38] The first wardmote precept that enjoins the men of the ward to elect a raker comes in the year 1414, and they are again referred to in precepts of 1422 and 1437, but such officers are not listed in 1422 along with the other ward officers.[39] By the reign of Edward IV the Portsoken ward records list the name of the raker along with the other ward officers. His task was to clear away refuse and so ensure that water could flow down channels in the street. The city authorities tried to provide tips to which rakers could take the rubbish from the ward but they were often to be found simply dumping the refuse in the next ward or placing it strategically so that the force of water would carry it beyond the bounds of their responsibility.[40] As with the other ward officers, these men were paid out of sums levied in the ward, although the men of Coleman Street maintained that a raker should be paid 26*s.* 8*d.* annually by the city chamberlain since he was responsible for cleaning out the grates at London Wall and Lothebury where the Walbrook tributaries trickled south towards the Thames.[41] But rakers, like the other ward officers, were usually paid by levies within the wards and in some of the surviving churchwardens' accounts payments were recorded for contributions towards the salaries of these officers.[42]

There was another ward officer elected by the wardmote whose duties were of a rather different kind. Aleconners were supposed to be summoned whenever ale was brewed in the ward, to ensure that it was of the right quality, sold in the correct measures, and priced according to civic custom. Since ale was brewed frequently the task of the aleconners must have been quite laborious, if, perhaps, enjoyable; for their efforts they received half the forfeitures and fines for transgressing ordinances.[43] Aleconners may have been an innovation in 1377 when they seem to have been elected and sworn for the first time and the names of several ward aleconners are recorded.[44] The wardmote precept of 1390 instructed the men of the ward to elect aleconners but this injunction was not repeated again until 1417. Perhaps the practice was found to be unsatisfactory or unworkable; no aleconners were listed with ward officers in 1422, and in 1440 common council enjoined that aleconners should be elected 'as hitherto accustomed' which may suggest that the practice had lapsed.[45] But although the names of aleconners

38 *Memorials*, 299.

39 *LBI*, 131; *LBK*, 5–6, 215; *CPMR 1413–37*, 116.

40 Year 1378, *LBH*, 108; 1384, *CPMR 1381–1412*, 71.

41 *CPMR 1413–37*, 117; the ward of Coleman Street had a point since it was in the interests of the whole city that the Walbrook should flow cleanly through the centre of the city.

42 *Medieval Records of a London City Church (St Mary at Hill)*, ed. H. Littlehales (EETS, 1905), 67, 412; *The Church Records of St Andrew Hubbard, Eastcheap c.1450–c.1570*, ed. C. Burgess (London Record Society, 1999), 18–19.

43 *Liber Albus*, 34, 274; *LBH* 157.

44 *LBH*, 71; *CPMR 1364–81*, 256.

45 Year 1390, *LBH*, 361; *LBI*, 191; *LBK*, 243; and see CLRO, Journal 3 fo. 53^{v}.

appear only once in the Portsoken ward records of Edward IV's reign, by the sixteenth century it would seem that all wards were electing 'tipplers' (as they had come to be called) to guarantee the quality of ale brewed in the ward. In 1510 the ward of Aldersgate nominated as many as forty-six tipplers.[46]

It is difficult to tell from the limited evidence how long ward officers remained in office. It would seem that there was a considerable turnover among the more numerous constables and scavengers but that the beadle and raker each held office for a period of years. At least twelve of the beadles listed in 1422 were still in office in 1428 and William Seggesle was beadle of Lime Street for at least nine years, Henry Sewardby at Tower ward for ten years and Richard Chapman at Queenhithe for sixteen years. The Portsoken records of Edward IV's reign suggest that the beadles and rakers may have been appointments during good behaviour whereas constables and scavengers viewed their jobs as short-term employment and as tasks they might take on in the hope of moving on to better things. The evidence is not extensive but it does appear that, at least in the second half of this period, the ward constituted an effective unit of local government and provided a means whereby the (male) inhabitants were able to voice their grievances and articulate their anger at unsociable neighbours. Here also in the ward the alderman came into contact with the needs and concerns of those whom he both represented and governed.[47]

THE FOLKMOOT AND THE HUSTING COURT

By the fourteenth century it was doubtless in wardmotes that grassroots democracy operated in medieval London. But in the early days all the freemen of the city had been accustomed to gather at least three times a year in the folkmoot, summoned by the great bell of St Paul's to meet on open ground lying to the north-east of the cathedral. The growth in population in the thirteenth century rendered the folkmoot impracticable; there is evidence that the folkmoot was still summoned in the middle of the thirteenth century,[48] yet by 1321 the king's justices were told that the folkmoot was now closed.[49] In the later part of the thirteenth century the site of the ancient folkmoot seems to have been taken over by St Paul's Cathedral and enclosed as part of the precinct.[50]

[46] GL, MS 1499.

[47] For a more detailed discussion of the wards of medieval London, see C. Barron, 'Lay Solidarities: The Wards of Medieval London', in P. Stafford, J. L. Nelson, and J. Martindale (eds.), *Law, Laity and Solidarities: Essays in Honour of Susan Reynolds* (Manchester, 2001), 218–33.

[48] Folkmoots in 1227 and 1242, *The London Eyre of 1244*, ed. H. M. Chew and M. Weinbaum (London Record Society, 1970), 16, 63; Williams, *Medieval London*, 35–6; D. Keene, 'London from the Post-Roman Period to 1300' in D. Palliser (ed.), *The Cambridge Urban History of Britain* (Cambridge, 2000), i. 187–216, esp. 205.

[49] *Eyre 1321*, ed. Cam, pp. li, 32.

[50] R. Macleod, 'The Topography of St Paul's Precinct, 1200–1500', *London Topographical Record*, 26 (1990), 1–14, esp. 10–11.

In the place of the folkmoot there grew up a number of other courts, some judicial, some deliberative, and some a mixture of both. As the business of the city grew in complexity new courts rose and fell in response to different needs. The Husting court may well have been as old as the folkmoot: its purpose was, at least by the thirteenth century, more specifically judicial. All citizens had access to the Husting court and in the eyes of the Parliamentary legislators of the fifteenth century it was still viewed as the most open, most democratic, of the city's many courts.[51] Originally the court probably had both a 'governmental' and a judicial role but, as other courts developed, the Husting by 1300 came to be considered primarily as a judicial court and as a court of record. At the beginning of the thirteenth century the Husting court had theoretically met every Monday, and heard all pleas except those of the Crown (these were the more serious offences and crimes) but, with the multiplication of actions that could be initiated by writ and the increasing volume of business, it became necessary to divide the work of the Husting court. In 1244, it was decreed that pleas relating to land and all other pleas (i.e. common pleas) were to be heard on alternate weeks.[52] In 1260 it was decided that pleas relating to dower, and to customs and to services were to be heard with the common pleas.[53] Writs of novel disseisin were first read in the Husting court before an assize was held. The records of such assizes might be brought into the Husting court for permanent record or as a result of a writ of error.[54] As the business of the court grew so it sometimes became necessary to hold sessions on Tuesdays as well as Mondays. Six aldermen had to be present as well as the recorder who gave judgments by word of mouth.[55] A man who was summoned to the Husting five times and failed to appear could be declared an outlaw.[56] The importance of the Husting court as the premier judicial court and court of record in the city is evident in the seriousness with which its records were kept. The earliest London records are those rolls onto which deeds and wills were enrolled: these survive from 1252. Twenty years later, coincident with the accession of Edward I, the two series of rolls, those of pleas of land and of common pleas, begin. These rolls are the work of a body of competent scribes who wrote careful Latin in

[51] C. Barron, 'London and Parliament in the Lancastrian Period', *Parliamentary History*, 9 (1990), 343–67, esp. 344–5.

[52] *Eyre 1244*, 95–6; Williams, *Medieval London*, 82.

[53] *Chronicles of the Mayors and Sheriffs of London, A.D. 1188 to A.D. 1274*, ed. and trans. H. T. Riley (London, 1863), 48.

[54] *CPMR 1437–57*, 3 n.1; *London Possessory Assizes: A Calendar*, ed. H. M. Chew (London Record Society, 1965), pp. xiii n. 3, xvii–xviii; 56; Plaints of nuisance were also first brought to the Monday Husting court, *London Assize of Nuisance 1301–1431*, ed. H. M. Chew and W. Kellaway (London Record Society, 1973), p. xiii.

[55] For the history of the Husting court see *EMCR 1298–1307*, pp. xiii–xx; *CPMR 1323–64*, 210 n. 2; P. E. Jones, 'The Court of Hustings', *The Law Journal*, 93 (1943), 285–6; *Liber Albus*, 162–70; *Iter 1321*, pp. i, li–liii; P. Tucker, 'London's Courts of Law in the Fifteenth Century: The Litigants' Perspective', in C. W. Brooks and M. Lobban (eds.), *Communities and Courts in Britain 1150–1900* (London, 1997), 25–41.

[56] *CPMR 1413–37*, 51–2; in the fourteenth century outlawries declared in the Husting court were recorded in the rolls of the pleas of land or common pleas. In the fifteenth century special outlawry rolls were compiled of which that for 1415–17 has survived, CLRO, Misc. Roll KK.

a skilled hand. It has been suggested that the keeping of the records of the Husting court may go back to the 1230s and that the more systematic record-keeping from the 1250s may have come about because of pressure from the royal justices following the royal judicial enquiry of 1244.[57]

There is no doubt that the city collectively valued and continued to make use of the records of the Husting court over prolonged periods. In the fourteenth century various calendars and indexes to deeds and wills were made.[58] It is not clear how the Husting court was 'serviced' and whence came the body of skilled clerks who kept the records. In 1302 the sheriffs were expected to provide clerks to enrol the pleas in the Husting court and in 1380 Henry Perot, clerk, was responsible for filing documents among the Husting rolls.[59] But by the fifteenth century it looks as if the records of the Husting may have been kept by the same group of clerks who were responsible for keeping the records of the other city courts; that is, by this date there had emerged a city secretariat under the overall supervision of the common clerk.[60]

It would seem that at times it was customary to discontinue holding sessions of the Husting court in the summer. In 1321 the royal judges were critical of this practice but it appears to have persisted, for in 1416 it was decided that the Husting court should be held throughout the year and not close for the month of June when Londoners were thought to be absent from the city at St Botolph's fair at Boston.[61] There was some debate in the fifteenth century as to whether the Husting should meet out of law terms and the mayor and aldermen in 1446 were empowered to hold sessions during these times if it seemed advisable.[62] Perhaps the aldermen were anxious to be able to absent themselves from the city during the unhealthy summer months if they could and there may have been genuine concern about the inadvisability of holding sessions of the Husting court when the central courts and the Chancery were not operating. But the Husting court was far from being the only court that the aldermen might have been expected to attend during the summer months.

THE COURT OF COMMON COUNCIL

To take the place of the folkmoot and the Husting court as the 'communal organ' of civic government there began to emerge, slowly and awkwardly, the body that

[57] G. H. Martin, *The Husting Rolls of Deeds and Wills, 1252–1485* (Cambridge, 1990); *Calendar of Wills Proved and Enrolled in the Court of Husting, London 1258–1688*, ed. R. R. Sharpe, 2 vols. (London, 1889–90).

[58] e.g. CLRO, Misc. MM, Calendar of Husting Rolls of Common Pleas, 1327–1376; from 1448 onwards there is a series of Husting books which record brief notes of cases heard each week. Between 1438 and 1448 some notes relating to cases in the Husting court were entered in the city Journals but, when Journals were begun in 1448 it may then have been decided to begin a separate Husting book.

[59] *LBC*, 106; *London Possessory Assizes*, ed. Chew, 56.

[60] The second most commonly encountered hand in the Husting Book 1448–81 is one that is frequently encountered also in the Journals of the period. I owe this information to Dr Penny Tucker.

[61] *Eyre 1321*, ed. Cam, 35; *Memorials*, 637–8. The fair was, in any case, in decline by the fifteenth century.

[62] *LBI*, 64; CLRO, Journal 4, fos. 34v, 113, 150v.

by the later fourteenth century was to be known as the court of common council. The creation of the common council, as a representative body in the government of the city, is the achievement of the fourteenth century. From the late thirteenth-century *probi homines* were, on occasion, associated with the mayor and aldermen and the better, more learned, citizens were becoming an accepted elite among the thirteenth-century citizenry.[63] The wards seem at this early date to have formed the constituencies: in the earliest list of councilmen that has survived, from about 1285, each ward provided two men and this was again the pattern in 1322.[64] But in 1317 when 'good men' of the city came to confer with the aldermen the numbers from the wards ranged from five from Aldersgate to seventeen from Farringdon.[65] These early ward councilmen were bound by an oath and may have formed a kind of inner council or standing committee to take the place of a larger body of freemen from the wards. It may be for this reason that in 1322 their election was said to have had as its purpose 'saving the commonalty trouble'.[66] But it is clear that two was not always the number of ward representatives and, on occasion, the number could rise to twelve producing a body of nearly 300 men.[67] Nor was the ward uniformly considered to be the appropriate constituency: it was the consistent aim of the more 'radical' elements in civic politics in the fourteenth century to secure election by the misteries or craft guilds rather than by the wards. In October 1326, after the murder of Bishop Stapledon, a meeting of citizens was summoned whose members had been elected by the misteries.[68] Clearly this was a special meeting summoned by the mayor and aldermen who, in a time of crisis, felt the need for a wide base of support: the decisions of the meeting were to be shown to 'the Commonalty' (i.e. the whole body of the citizens) before being implemented. But it is clear that the experiment of 1326 did not at once become common practice. In 1346 and 1347 when meetings of common council were called the members were elected by the wards; in 1346 133 men were chosen who were fined for absence. Most of the wards elected six men, but six elected fewer and Lime Street chose only two men. The next year it was laid down that the wards were to elect twelve, eight, or six according to their size.[69]

The radical group, composed presumably of men of the lesser artisan crafts, disliked ward elections because the richer men of the ward, who were usually members of the greater overseas trading companies such as vintners, drapers, or grocers, tended always be elected and so produced a common council weighted in favour of the 'mercantile' interest. By contrast, election by craft ensured that even the most modest crafts had a say in the city's deliberations. In 1377, for example, the bakers, the cordwainers, the curriers, the pouchmakers, the tanners, the tawyers, the brasiers, the cardmakers, the pinners, the painters, the fusters, the

[63] Williams, *Medieval London*, 36–7; Keene, 'London from the Post-Roman Period', 205.

[64] *LBA*, 209–10; *LBE*, 174.

[65] *LBE*, 80–1; this is only a partial list of the wards, all of them to the west of Walbrook.

[66] 1 November 1322, *LBE*, 174. In 1321 a committee of twenty-four 'ex communi consilio' was appointed to help to frame the responses to be made to the royal justices, *Eyre 1321*, ed. Cam, 7.

[67] Williams, *Medieval London*, 37–43.

[68] *CPMR 1323–64*, 15; see Chapter 1.

[69] Year 1346, *LBF*, 162; *Memorials*, pp. liii–lv; 1347, *LBF*, 304.

joiners, the woodmongers, the horners, and the tallowchandlers among other modest crafts all sent representatives to the common council.[70] Indeed it was possible for the members of the lesser, or artisan, crafts to outnumber the men sent by the mercantile companies. The radical party had its way in 1351 and 1352, and again from 1376 to 1384.[71] Forty-nine companies took part in the elections of the early 1380s but there were problems: men who were not elected and summoned came to the meetings and it was necessary to ordain that those who misbehaved should not be re-elected.[72] The difficulties of the new method led to a hybrid system of election using both constituencies in 1379 and 1380 and then in 1380 the wards were asked to discuss what would be the best way of electing the common council.[73] Inevitably, perhaps, power flowed back to the wards and in February 1384 it was decided that the elections to the common council should take place in the wards since recently the decisions in common council had been carried, it was claimed, 'by clamour rather than by reason'. It was agreed, however, that there should be no more than eight men from any one craft. This restriction, a sop to the lesser crafts, must have been difficult to administer and it was abolished five years later.[74] The decisions of 1384 mark the coming of age of the common council of London. The wards were finally decided upon as the unit of election but they were to be represented in proportion to their size, so wards were to elect six, four, or two men within fifteen days after 12 March each year. Councilmen were to take an oath and to be fined forty pence for absence from meetings which were to be held at least once a quarter. On the other hand a common councilman was excused service on inquests, except in pleas of land where his presence was essential, and also from serving on city watches unless he chose to do so.[75] After the excitements of the 1380s there seem to have been few changes in the next century: the common council settled down into its secure and defined place in the government of the city and came, like the House of Commons at the national level, to play an essential role in the process of civic administration and decision-making.

Although common councilmen had to be elected every year there was no reason why a man should not be re-elected as long as he was willing to serve and the ward would have him. The four men who were serving as common councilmen for Portsoken ward in 1460 were still acting in 1466, and a third of the men serving

70 *CPMR 1364–81*, 243.

71 Year 1351, *LBF*, 237–9; 1352, *LBG*, pp. xxix, 3; 1376, *LBH*, pp. iii–viii, 35, 38–44; *CPMR 1364–81*, 256; 1377, *CPMR 1364–81*, 243, 256; 1382, *CPMR 1381–1412*, 29–31; on the wider significance of the constitutional changes in the City in 1376–7, see C.Barron, *Revolt in London: 11th to 15th June 1381* (London, 1981), 14–16.

72 March 1377, *LBH*, 59, 60.

73 Year 1379, *Memorials*, 435; 1380, *LBH*, 155, 156; in January 1383 those who were elected to common council were exonerated from serving on inquests, *LBH*, 209. The privileged status of common councilmen was reiterated in 1423, 1426, and 1440, CLRO, Journal 2 fos. 8ᵛ, 62; ibid. 3 fo. 69ᵛ.

74 Year 1384, *LBH*, 227–8; 1389, ibid., 347.

75 29 January 1384, *LBH*, 227, cf. ibid. 237–40, 277, 279–81, 347; *CPMR 1381–1412*, 91–2; precepts to the aldermen to cause common councilmen to be elected in wardmotes to be found in 1387, 1388, *LBH*, 300, 322; the question whether to fine common councilmen who were absent from meetings goes back to 1321 when it was decided that they should not be fined but all decisions taken in their absence were to be binding, *LBE*, 147; cf. 1346, *LBF*, 304; 1354, *LBG*, 23; *Memorials*, 274.

on the council in 1458/9 were still there in 1460/1.[76] When election by wards was reintroduced in February 1384 the number of common councilmen was fixed temporarily at four men per ward, or ninety-six in total,[77] although a complete attendance was rarely recorded and in June 1384 there were as few as sixty councilmen present.[78] It is likely that the size of the council was enlarged in the later 1380s, and by the time that John Carpenter was compiling the *Liber Albus* in 1419 the numbers to be elected were not six, four, and two as in 1384, but sixteen, twelve, eight, and four which would produce a larger body.[79] There are few records of attendance in the fifteenth century but in October 1441 the common council was summoned to deal with the contentious matter of the office of common weigher. Ninety-three men were present which suggests that the full complement was already enlarged.[80] By March 1454 an attendance list of common councilmen numbered 104, and by 1458/9 the official number appears to have risen to 188.[81] It would be interesting to know what lay behind the decision in effect to double the size of the council between 1422 and 1441 (or 1454). The decision demonstrates a move to broaden the basis of government, which stands in marked contrast to several other towns where the electorate and the councils were becoming narrower and more elitist.[82]

A common councilman was expected to be 'sufficient' but otherwise the wardmote was free in its choice, although the presumption was that a man should be a freeman. In 1427 however it was decided to restrict membership to men who had achieved the freedom of the city by birth, apprenticeship, or office, that is, no one who had purchased the freedom was to be eligible for the common council.[83] On being elected, a member of common council had to take an oath to be true to the king, to come when summoned (unless he had a reasonable excuse), to give good and true counsel, to maintain no man's cause contrary to the good of the city, to stay at the meeting until the mayor departed and to keep the council's secrets.[84]

[76] CLRO, Portsoken Ward Presentments; one of the Portsoken common councilmen, William Stalon, appears to have served, probably continuously, from 1460 until 1483. For the 1458/61 lists of the members of the common council, see CLRO, Letter Book D, fos. lxxv–lxxvi and discussion below.

[77] *LBH*, 227–8; it should be noted, however, that 'it was further suggested' that the number of common councilmen from each ward should be proportionate to their size, six, four, or two, calculated in such a way as to bring the total number of common councilmen up to ninety-six; *CPMR 1381–1412*, 122–4, 132–3; the common council elected by the misteries had been larger: in August 1376 there had been 153 men present, *LBH*, 41–4.

[78] *CPMR 1381–1412*, 53–4; compare this number, and the attendance list of seventy in March 1385, with the ninety-four councilmen on the summons list for October 1384, by which time the wards were electing between two and six common councilmen each, ibid. 54–5, 84.

[79] *Liber Albus*, 36.

[80] CLRO, Journal 5 fo. 99^{v}.

[81] 21 March 1454, CLRO, Journal 5 fo. 155; this list of wards with their allocated number of common councilmen has been copied into Letter Book D fo. 75; the lists of common councilmen tentatively dated to 1458–9 and 1460–1 are to be found in the same volume on fos. 70^{v}–74^{v}, 75–6^{v}.

[82] See S. Rigby, 'Urban "Oligarchy" in Late Medieval England', in John A. F. Thomson (ed.), *Towns and Townspeople in the Fifteenth Century* (Gloucester, 1988), 62–86; J. Kermode, 'Obvious Observations on the Formation of Oligarchies in Late Medieval English Towns', ibid. 87–106.

[83] Precept to elect 'sufficient men', e.g. 1410, *LBI*, 89–90; 1427, CLRO Journal 2 fo. 90; 1446, Journal 4 fo. 119^{v}.

[84] *LBD*, 192; *Liber Albus*, 36–7.

Absent members were noted by the clerk of the chamber and fined.[85] A serjeant of the chamber summoned members to meetings, giving them a day's notice. On special occasions the common council would wear a common livery: for the reception of Margaret of Anjou in 1445 they wore red and for the coronation of Edward IV they chose a light green to distinguish themselves from the men of Coventry who had also selected green.[86]

In the fourteenth century knowledge of meetings of common council can be gained only from the Letter Books or mayor's court rolls, hence it is only exceptional meetings that have left any record. From 1416, however, there survive the Journals that record the day-to-day proceedings of both the court of aldermen and the court of common council. The first meeting which is unambiguously described in the Journal as a meeting of the common council was recorded on 20 April 1417.[87] After this date references become more numerous although the business is rarely recorded in as much detail as that of the court of aldermen. It would appear that the council—following the 1384 ordinance—did meet about once a quarter, but from 1439 onwards the recorded number of meetings averages fourteen a year and from 1451 to 1462 the average jumps again to seventeen meetings a year. But the initiative lay still with the court of aldermen and it was that body which decided when it was necessary to summon a common council, and to seek thereby a broader basis of support.[88]

The Journals tell us little about how meetings were conducted. John Carpenter, however, in the *Liber Albus* describes how the serjeant of the chamber took the register and notes that business was not to be delayed for latecomers. When the sense of the meeting could not be obtained by consensus, each member was to be separately questioned on oath, which must have been an extremely time-consuming procedure.[89] When in October 1441, the common council met to discuss whether the office of the common weigher should be placed in commission or not, all ninety-three members present were listed and the letter 'p' for 'placet' or 'np' for 'non placet' was written against the name of each man to signify support or not for the proposal.[90] Members were expected not to discuss the business of the council outside meetings and when in 1427 it was found that a matter had been revealed to the duke of Gloucester which was contrary to the city's interests it was decided that anyone who acted in this way in future should be fined £20 and lose his freedom.[91]

The scope of common council business was very wide. By the fifteenth century no tax could be imposed on Londoners without the consent of common council

[85] *LBH*, 237–40; *Liber Albus*, 36; the 1384 fine of 40*d.* appears to have reduced to 24*d.* by 1419. 17 August 1453, the mayor, aldermen and common council decided that any common councilman who was absent from the next meeting of the council (summoned to deal with a royal request for money) should be fined the large sum of 6*s.* 8*d.*: CLRO, Journal 5 fo. 117ᵛ.

[86] Year 1444, CLRO, Journal 4 fo. 52; 1461, ibid. 6 fo. 54.

[87] Ibid. 1 fo. 18ᵛ.

[88] e.g. 24 September 1448, court of aldermen decided that the common council should meet on the following Friday, 27 September, CLRO, Journal 4 fo. 225ᵛ.

[89] *Liber Albus*, 36.

[90] CLRO, Journal 3. fos. 99ᵛ–100.

[91] 24 and 26 May 1427, ibid. 2 fo. 93; 21 May 1428, ibid. fo. 109ᵛ.

although the court of aldermen might first prepare the ground. Common council not only agreed to the tax, but members of the council would also be appointed to serve, jointly with aldermen, on the committee appointed to receive the money and, in the case of a royal loan, to examine the security offered by the Crown. Common councilmen often acted as the assessors for their wards. If the money raised was for a civic purpose, they would be appointed to audit the final account. The omnicompetence and omnipresence of members of the common council in all financial aspects of city government in the fifteenth century is unquestionable, particularly during the Lancastrian period. Difficult or tricky negotiations with the king or his council would be referred to common council; the election of the city's MPs in practice took place there (although the formal election was in the Husting court) and proposed city projects which would cost money would be discussed, such as the building of Guildhall, the purchase of land to enlarge Billingsgate quay, the repair of London Bridge and the prosecution of the city's dispute with the clergy over the payment of tithes. It was the forum where disputes between city crafts could be most easily settled and proclaimed: in 1445, it was the common council that decided that if the plumbers and latteners (makers of latten, a metal compound similar to brass) continued to refuse to finish off work begun by members of the other craft, then foreign plumbers and latteners who had to be brought in to do such work would be made free of the city.[92] In September 1378 it had been decided that strangers were not to be admitted to the freedom of the city without the consent of common council and although this ruling was not strictly adhered to, and men were admitted to the freedom by the court of aldermen, yet it was far more common for admissions to be made in meetings of common council. Moreover regulations about the freedom were almost always made in common council.[93]

Not surprisingly the citizens at large were concerned that land that belonged to the city should not be leased out nor the common seal of the city placed on documents that might have consequences for the commonalty, without general consent. These were contentious matters in the fourteenth century and in 1312 it was decided that the common seal was to be kept in a chest under six keys, three to be held by aldermen and three by nominees of the commonalty.[94] This number was reduced to four, two aldermen and two commoners, by the charter of 1319. The seal was to be available to rich and poor alike without any charge for its use.[95] Where the names of fourteenth-century keepers are recorded they usually consist of the mayor, and alderman, and two commoners.[96] In 1376 the 'radical' party altered the common seal by the addition of a star, perhaps to invalidate earlier and, in their view, illegal grants and, perhaps, to signify the arrival of a new order.[97] By

[92] 17 September 1445, ibid. 4 fo. 95; cf. the compromises made between the girdlers and the cordwainers over the assay of leather, July 1424, ibid. 2 fos. 13, 20^v; *LBK*, 114–15; dispute between the fusters and saddlers settled in common council in 1424–5, CLRO, Journal 2 fos. 27, 45, 45^v; *LBK*, 37.

[93] *LBH*, 109.

[94] *LBD*, 283; Williams, *Medieval London*, 272, and cf. 1321, *LBE*, 149; *Liber Albus*, 317.

[95] *Historical Charters and Constitutional Documents of the City of London*, ed. W. de Gray Birch (rev. edn. London, 1887), 48.

[96] Years 1363–4, 1364–5, 1365–6, *LBG*, 334; *LBH*, 36, 62, 219.

[97] *LBH*, 36–7; *Memorials*, 400.

1427 there seem to have been six keepers of the common seal, usually the mayor, two aldermen, and three commoners, and after 1452 the mayor, one alderman, and four commoners. The six men who held the keys, three to the inner chest and three to the outer chest, were known as keepers of the common seal or keepers of the common chest. It is likely that the keepers of the common seal were chosen at meetings of the common council but this is only definitely the case on three occasions.[98] In 1312 the citizens had asked that the common seal should not be used for purposes that burdened the commonalty without their consent. When the common seal was used on letters during the dispute with the city clergy over tithes this was done with the assent of the common council. In the same way a written obligation to repay alderman Simon Eyre the sum of £315 4*s.* 4*d.* in 1452 was sealed with the common seal in a meeting of the common council.[99]

It would be wrong, in the fifteenth century, to see the court of common council in conflict with the court of aldermen. Like the Commons and the Lords in Parliament, the interests of the two bodies were very similar and there were few issues that provoked a clash of wills. The choice of city officers might have proved contentious but seems not to have been. Perhaps the aldermen, mindful of the clashes and frictions of the later fourteenth century, trod warily and took careful notice of commoner feelings. The choice of the common serjeant-at-law lay with the common council which is not surprising since he was their spokesman (cf. the Speaker in the Commons), as did the choice of the common weigher.[100] The choice of the waterbailiff and the common huntsman also lay with the common council and when the court of aldermen in 1457 decided to offer the post to John Green they did so with the proviso 'as far as it was in their power' and three days later the common council ratified the appointment.[101] More important, perhaps, was the choice of the common clerk which also lay within the common council's sphere of influence. As this post grew in importance so the court of aldermen found it harder to stand aside from the election. In 1438 common council chose Richard Barnet as common clerk and the court of aldermen, unhappy with the choice, put him on probation for a year.[102] Barnet's successor, Roger Tonge (alias Spicer) was dismissed on 5 August 1461 for his many offences against Edward IV (that is, for his Lancastrian sympathies) in a meeting of common council and his successor was finally chosen at a common council meeting .[103]

The spirit of co-operation and compromise that pervades the relations between the court of common council and the court of aldermen in the fifteenth century found further expression in the growing number of joint committees. They begin in the 1430s with joint committees to investigate ways of raising money for the

[98] 6 May 1444, CLRO, Journal 4 fo. 24; 17 October 1452, CLRO, Journal 5 fo. 90ᵛ; 26 January 1461, CLRO, Journal 6 fo. 188ᵛ.

[99] 10 October 1452, CLRO, Journal 5 fo. 89ᵛ; see J. A. F. Thomson, 'Tythe Disputes in Later Medieval London', *EHR* 78 (1963), 1–17.

[100] B. Masters, 'The Common Serjeant', *Guildhall Miscellany*, 11 (1967), 379–89, and Ch. 8.

[101] CLRO, Journal 6, fos. 116ᵛ, 118, 118ᵛ; see Ch. 8.

[102] CLRO, Journal 3, fos. 164, 164ᵛ. In fact Barnet remained in office until 1446.

[103] 15 August, 25 September, October 1461, CLRO, Journal 6 fos. 46, 22ᵛ, 7ᵛ.

Leadenhall granary and to deal with renewing the city's piped supply of fresh water. These were followed by joint committees to deal with repairs to London Bridge, to improve the city's walls and ditches, and to examine encroachments on the common soil. Groups of aldermen and common councilmen acted as feoffees for some Bridge House lands or for the property bought from Sir Thomas Haseley's executors in order to enlarge Billingsgate quay. In fact from the 1440s onwards it is clear that any important city project, and especially those that involved the raising and spending of money, was likely to be organized by a joint committee of aldermen and common councilmen. Many councilmen would, of course, in their time become aldermen but there is evident here a spirit of shared concern and a tangible effort to spread responsibility beyond the small body of aldermen to a wide body of responsible *probi homines* anxious to play their role in city government. The enlargement of the common council, its more frequent meetings and the increasing use of joint committees are also to be dated to the 1430s and 1440s. The change seems to be more deeply rooted than one simply of record-keeping.

THE COURT OF ALDERMEN

However important were the wardmotes, or the Husting court and the court of common council, each expressing ideas of equality and participation by freemen in a self-governing process, yet it was without doubt the aldermen who really governed the city during these centuries. It is true that the hereditary or proprietary view of aldermanic office gave way—by the end of the thirteenth century—to a concept of elective office; moreover in the course of the fifteenth century the aldermen took the common councilmen increasingly into partnership in the development of a more sophisticated decision-making process; yet the aldermen governed the city because they spent most time on its affairs and the court of aldermen was, without doubt, the nerve centre of city government through these centuries.

The office of alderman can be traced back to the early eleventh century, and by the early thirteenth century the division of the city into twenty-four wards each headed by an alderman was already at least a century old.[104] The early aldermanries bore the character of sokes, areas of private jurisdiction, and like the sokes might be passed from father to son within a small group of ruling dynasties: for a time the hereditary clashed with the elective principle in determining succession to aldermanries. But by 1249 the electoral process was firmly established. The *probi homines* of the ward made their choice and presented him to the mayor and other aldermen: if he was acceptable to them he was then sworn and admitted.[105] The

[104] S. Reynolds, 'The Rulers of London in the Twelfth Century', *History*, 57 (1972), 337–57, esp. 339 and n.; Williams, *Medieval London*, 30.

[105] Ibid. 34; 1293, the aldermen were elected by the 'wealthier and wiser' men of the ward, *LBC*, 11. This procedure for electing an alderman can be seen in practice in the case of Bassishaw ward in

presumption was that the alderman so chosen would remain in office for life. But the mid-thirteenth century process of election of an alderman did not remain unchanged in the following centuries.

The charter of 1319 specified that aldermen should be elected annually and not re-elected, but this requirement seems to have been honoured only in the breach.[106] The idea, however, of aldermanic responsibility to the ward electorate remained in the consciousness of radical Londoners and when, in the aftermath of the Good Parliament of 1376, constitutional changes were the order of the day, the return to the annual election of aldermen was introduced. Moreover it was not the intention that an existing alderman should simply be re-elected, rather there was to be a complete turnover of aldermen every year, although a man could be brought back to the aldermanic bench after a year's absence. Clearly the new system was fraught with difficulties and introduced an unwelcome instability in city government. The 'conservatives' tried hard to move back towards the old system, first by referring the matter to Parliament, then in 1392 by securing that aldermen might be re-elected every year, and then, finally, a complete return to the *status quo ante* was achieved in 1394 when aldermen were, once again, elected for life.[107]

After the turbulent experiments of the 1370s and 1380s it was clearly thought to be advisable to lay down procedures for the election of aldermen in the wards and, in order to curb any attempt to force an unacceptable candidate upon the court of aldermen it was decided in 1397 that the men of the wards should select at least two candidates from whom the mayor and aldermen would choose one.[108] The number of candidates to be presented was raised to four in 1402.[109] Once the Journals begin in 1416 some light is thrown on the actual practice of aldermanic elections. In 1420 when John Botiler was chosen for Farringdon Within, three candidates were presented to the court but when Thomas Wandesford was elected for Vintry six years later there were only two candidates.[110] In 1429 Stephen Broun was selected for Aldgate from two candidates but in the same year the men of Castle Baynard presented four men and Thomas Walsingham was chosen.[111] When the Journals are again extant after a seven-year gap the presentation of four candidates seems to have become the norm. After 1436 whenever the Journals record the names of candidates, there are always four of them.[112] The court claimed and exercised the right to reject all the candidates presented. Sometimes the court

1310: *LBD*, 14. There are, however, some traces left of the old proprietary principle in the case of the ward of Farringdon, Williams, *Medieval London*, 32; *LBA*, 11 and n; the ward of Aldersgate was known, in 1277, as the ward of John de Blakethorn, ibid. 15–16.

[106] Birch, *Charters*, 46. [107] Beaven, *Aldermen*, i. 392–402. [108] *LBH*, 436; *Memorials*, 545.

[109] *LBI*, 18, reiterated in 1420, ibid. 241.

[110] Year 1420, CLRO, Journal 1, fo. 78^{v}; 1426, ibid. 2, fos. 67^{v}, 68; cf. the presentation of two candidates in the same year when Robert Otele was chosen, ibid. fo. 78.

[111] Ibid. 2 fos. 131^{v}, 133.

[112] In 1436 the men of Langbourn ward were told to present four suitable candidates, *sub pena*: ibid. 3 fo. 126. In 1480 it was laid down that the men of the ward were only allowed to present two existing aldermen among their four candidates: *LBL*, 175.

maintained that none of the candidates was 'sufficient',[113] and in 1448 the court rejected the four candidates presented by the men of Lime Street ward on the grounds that not all the candidates were of sufficient standing, with the result, probably intended, that the choice of the aldermen would thereby have been restricted.[114] Clearly the court, by its use of the veto, kept a firm control over its membership and resisted any attempt to force its hand.[115]

When candidates were presented to the court the choice of a new alderman was usually arrived at by common agreement and the Journal clerk records that the choice was made *nem. con.* But on eight occasions between 1436 and 1462 the court had to resort to voting. The voting cannot have been secret for the clerk has noted, above the name of each alderman present, the initial letter of the candidate for whom he voted.[116] On one occasion, in 1458, the votes were equally divided between Thomas Oulegrave and Richard Flemyng and the mayor gave his casting vote in favour of Oulegrave, which, in the light of Oulegrave's later behavior, may have been an error of judgement.[117]

The ordinance of 1397 had laid down that candidates for vacant aldermanries were to be reputable and discreet, and fit both in morals and in worldly goods to be judges and aldermen of the city.[118] In 1413 it was further decided that an alderman must have been born in England of an English father; and four years later he was also required to live in the city.[119] Although doubtless many men were anxious to become aldermen there were others who were equally anxious to avoid office. In 1415 the future mayor John Gedney tried to refuse office as an alderman and had to be coerced into acceptance by a spell in prison. The justification for this harsh approach was that if he avoided office, then others would try to follow his lead.[120] John Carpenter, writing a few years after the Gedney episode, envisaged that there might be those who would try to refuse office after being chosen and he suggested that they should be coerced by the threat of losing their freedom.[121] John Paddesle, who had been chosen as alderman for Farringdon Within in February 1428 had failed to come to take his oath a month later. The court decided that if he did not do so he would be imprisoned and his house sequestered. He was soon sworn.[122]

[113] 24 July 1444, *LBK*, 295–6; 29 November 1456, CLRO, Journal 6 fo. 87^{v}; 22 November 1457, ibid. 6 fo. 185^{v}; 12 February 1458, ibid. 192^{v}; 17, 26 November 1460, ibid. 268.

[114] 1 April 1448, ibid. 4 fo. 213^{v}.

[115] There is only one recorded case in the fifteenth century, that of Philip Malpas, where the king appears to have tried to intervene in the election of an alderman; for a discussion of the circumstances surrounding the election of Malpas as an alderman, see C. Barron, 'The Government of London and Its Relations with the Crown 1400–1450' (University of London, Ph.D. thesis, 1970), 494–9.

[116] CLRO, 29 August 1438, Journal 3 fo. 166; 26 April 1446, ibid. 4 fo. 125^{v}; 16 July 1451, ibid. 5 fo. 60; 19 July 1452, ibid. 78^{v}; 24 October 1454, ibid. 202; December 1457, ibid. 6 fos. 186–7; 9 March 1458, ibid. 194^{v}; 3 April 1458, ibid. 195.

[117] 3 April 1458, ibid. 6 fo. 195; see p. 147.

[118] 1 August 1397, *LBH*, 436.

[119] Year 1413 *LBI*, 117; *Memorials*, 654–5. The restriction to the sons of Englishmen may have been intended to prevent upstart immigrants such as Richard Lyons, impeached by the Good Parliament in 1376 and murdered in 1381, from reaching aldermanic office.

[120] *Memorials*, 601–3.

[121] *Liber Albus*, 35.

[122] CLRO, Journal 2 fos. 107^{v}, 109^{v}.

The demand that the prospective alderman should be sufficient was not a meaningless phrase. It cost money to be an alderman and this was explicitly recognized in 1469 when it was decided that unless a man had goods, chattels, and 'hopeful' (that is, recoverable) debts amounting to £1,000 he would not be able to serve as an alderman and could be discharged.[123] By his oath the alderman undertook not to sell food (bread, ale, wine, fish or flesh) by retail, either personally or through his apprentices or servants. Perhaps retail trade was thought to be a little beneath the dignity of an alderman, but it also took time and the alderman had to be about the city's business. In 1437, Thomas Bernewell, a fishmonger who had been chosen as alderman of Queenhithe ward four years earlier, petitioned to be discharged from office on the grounds that he could not make a living unless he was able to sell fish retail. His petition was granted.[124] This wealth requirement inevitably limited membership of the court of aldermen to members of the 'mercantile' companies and excluded artisans whose wealth was related less to capital and more to the skill of their own hands. Throughout these centuries the men who became aldermen came almost exclusively from the companies of grocers, mercers, fishmongers, drapers, goldsmiths, skinners, vintners, and ironmongers.[125] Even among these companies membership was not evenly distributed: in the fourteenth century the drapers, fishmongers, grocers, and mercers tended to dominate the court and the pattern continued into the next century although the fishmongers became less conspicuous and the mercers emerged as pre-eminent. In 1446 it was decided to limit the members from any one company to six unless there were no suitable candidates from another company.[126] This decision shows an awareness of the problems caused by a particular interest taking over the court.

There is no doubt however that the duties of aldermanic office were such that they would have taken up too much time for a man also to have been earning his living by daily toil.[127] The duties were by no means negligible: the alderman presided over the wardmote and acted as a judge, deciding whether, for example, in a case of affray the suit was a Crown plea or not.[128] He had considerable duties in relation to Crown pleas, and when the great royal judicial inquiry into the activities of civic officials took place in 1321, each alderman had to produce a roll listing all the pledges and attachments relating to pleas of the Crown in his ward and was responsible for summoning those listed to appear before the royal justices.[129] In

[123] *LBL*, 85; this ruling may have been provoked by the case of Stephen Fabyan who had twice resisted election on the grounds of insufficiency and had been imprisoned for his contempt, see ibid. 79.

[124] Year 1437, CLRO, Journal 3 fo. 190. Simon Seman, a vintner, who served as an alderman from 1422 to 1433, unsuccessfully petitioned to be allowed to sell goods retail, 28 September 1426, ibid. 2 fo. 84^{v}.

[125] Beaven, *Aldermen*, i. 329. Members of these companies were heavily involved in wholesale and overseas trade; the fishmongers tended to be ship-owners. All these companies had, of course, an artisan element.

[126] 31 May 1441, CLRO, Journal 3 fo. 86^{v}; 25 February 1446, ibid. 4 fo. 118.

[127] For an indication of the tasks an alderman might be expected to shoulder see his oath, *LBD*, 205, and the precepts to the aldermen in January 1378 and April/May 1379, *LBH*, 84–5, 128–9.

[128] Williams, *Medieval London*, 28.

[129] *London Eyre, 1244*, ed. Chew and Weinbaum, 102–3; *Eyre, 1321*, ed. Cam, 6.

the twelfth and thirteenth centuries the aldermen were doomsmen, or *judices*, men skilled in the law who gave judgments and rulings. Probably, as time passed and the law of England became more skilled and professionalized, this legal function became less marked, although aldermen together in their court did pronounce judgments and something of this concept of an alderman as a man skilled in the law is to be found in the considerable use made of aldermen as arbiters in the fifteenth century.[130] Moreover, in a general sense, the alderman was responsible for maintaining law and order in his ward although it was the beadles and constables who saw to the practicalities of this. But the alderman was not completely remote from the rougher side of peacekeeping. In 1440 the court decided that no constable was to make a forcible entry into a house for any cause, except in the presence of the ward alderman.[131]

In times of crisis the aldermanic office could assume a quasi-military character. In order to keep the peace within and/or defend the city from without, the court would decide on daily and nightly patrols and each alderman would be allocated a time for his patrol or a section of the city walls to defend.[132] For the first time, in 1377 (perhaps as a result of the 'democratization' of aldermanic elections) it was decided that each alderman should have a pennon 'bearing his arms in relief' specifically in order to enable him to lead 'his men whithersoever commanded for the defence of the city' and this injunction was repeated in 1386.[133] Dramatically the aldermen led the city troops in battle in 1450: in the famous 'battle of the bridge' between the Londoners and Cade's rebels, the London defenders were led by the alderman and sheriff William Hulyn. One London alderman, the goldsmith John Sutton actually lost his life in the battle when Cade and his supporters were driven out of the city.

Doubtless the duties of an alderman were not usually as dangerous as they were in the summer of 1450. But as the ward was an essential unit of civic government, so the ward alderman was the linchpin in effective government. All civic regulations were put into operation via the ward (as opposed to the companies, which, however, from the late fifteenth century onwards became increasingly important agents of civic control) so the alderman was the man of all work. He was responsible for collecting all taxes and levies in his ward and for keeping the relevant taxation lists; he presided at the wardmote; he was responsible for the strangers who were staying in his ward and he frequently acted as a witness and his seal was

130 In 1303 the aldermen gave judgment as to whether certain properties could lawfully be bequeathed by testament, and the dissenting opinion of one alderman was noted, *LBC*, 119; for aldermen acting as arbitrators, see *CPMR 1437–57*; 10, 17; *CPMR 1458–82*, 1, 43, 49, 63, 65; for arbitration in the fifteenth century, see C. Rawcliffe, '"That Kindliness Should be Cherished More, and Discord Driven Out": The Settlement of Commercial Disputes by Arbitration in Later Medieval England', in J. Kermode (ed.), *Enterprise and Individuals in Fifteenth-Century England* (Stroud, 1991), 99–117.

131 *CPMR 1413–37*, pp. xxviii–xxx; 28 April 1440, CLRO, Journal 3, fo. 41v.

132 18 July 1440, CLRO, ibid. fo. 47v; also the measures taken to deal with the rising of Jack Cade in 1450; Barron, 'Government of London', 485, 500–1; see also the measures taken by the city in 1460–61, C. Barron, 'London and the Crown 1451–61', in J. R. L. Highfield and R. Jeffs (eds.), *The Crown and the Local Communities in England and France in the Fifteenth Century* (Gloucester, 1981), 95–6.

133 *LBH*, 65, 286.

constantly used to authenticate deeds.[134] Moreover his tasks were not merely routine ones: in 1321 when the dreaded visit of the royal itinerant justices was impending, the aldermen of Langbourn and Tower wards were made responsible for erecting, at their own expense, the benches and seats in the Tower to be used for the judicial sessions.[135] These multifarious activities required multifarious records; lists of Crown pleas and of taxpayers, wardmote indentures, and lists of strangers and their hosts. These records were the personal property of the aldermen which may explain why so few of the individual ward records have survived: in 1304 an alderman complained that he had been robbed and the stolen goods consisted not only of personal valuables but also the chest containing the records of his ward, 'the charters, letters obligatory, tallies, rolls and memoranda', in effect, 'the documentary witnesses to an intense and ceaseless administrative life of his ward'.[136] It seems likely that the alderman would have had some clerk or personal secretary to help him with these duties. John Carpenter in the *Liber Albus* refers to the alderman's clerk who was expected, for example, to be present to help compile the list of presentments at the wardmote.[137]

By the fifteenth century it seems to have become customary for aldermen to choose deputies to act for them in their absence, or illness. In 1384 aldermen appointed deputies to act for them while they were absent at the royal court at Reading, and John Carpenter refers to the wardmote being held in the presence of the alderman 'or his deputy'.[138] In 1425 Robert Tatersale asked the court of aldermen if Thomas Ayer and then John Whatele might act as his deputy while he was away from London on business.[139] On occasion aldermen chose others—perhaps more sound in wind and limb—to carry out their peacekeeping vigils. By 1438 the deputy was sufficiently accepted on the administrative scene for a writ addressed to the alderman to enjoin him—or his deputy—to hold a wardmote to discuss finance.[140] It is impossible to know whether the men of the ward had any say in the choice of the alderman's deputy: what seems to be clear is that although the court of aldermen was usually consulted about the appointment of a deputy yet no deputy ever attended the court of aldermen: he acted as the alderman's deputy within the ward but he had no wider delegated authority. By the sixteenth century all aldermen seem automatically to have appointed deputies.[141]

Attendance at the meetings of the court of aldermen must in fact have absorbed a great deal of time. The Journals that survive from 1416 record meetings both of the court of aldermen (and mayor's court) and of the court of common council. It is likely that record-keeping in these early years was unsystematic. In Journals 1 and 2, which cover the years 1416 to 1429, the court of aldermen met on average

[134] As early as 1231, the alderman was made responsible for ensuring that all strangers who stayed more than three nights in the ward were incorporated into the frankpledge system, *London Eyre 1244*, ed. Chew and Weinbaum, 103; For the use of the seals of aldermen, see *CPMR 1437–57*, 159, 160, 165, 175, 184, 185; *CPMR 1458–82*, 159, 161, 163, 175.

[135] *Eyre 1321*, ed. Cam, 5.

[136] Williams, *Medieval London*, 31; *CEMCR 1298–1307*, 164.

[137] *Liber Albus*, 33.

[138] *LBH*, 246; *Liber Albus*, 32.

[139] 13 June, 28 July 1425, CLRO, Journal 2 fos. 44^{v}, 48^{v}.

[140] 19 January 1438, ibid. 3 fo. 183^{v}.

[141] I. Archer, *The Pursuit of Stability: Social Relations in Elizabethan London* (Cambridge, 1991), 67.

fifty-four times a year, or roughly once a week. When the Journals resume in 1436 the court appears to be meeting much more frequently: the average number of meetings in the period 1436–46 was ninety-three per year; in 1446–56, 102, and in 1456–62 (when Journal 6 ends) the average was 103; that is, by the third decade of the fifteenth century the court was meeting about twice a week.

Obviously the more troubled the political scene, the more meetings were held. In the years 1453 to 1455, the court averaged three meetings a week, and again in the years from 1459 to 1461. The mayor usually attended all the meetings of the court during his term of office—hence John Norman as mayor appears to have attended all the 165 meetings held in 1453–4 and William Hulyn was equally assiduous in attending all the 147 meetings in 1459-60.[142] The sheriffs also attended quite regularly but the court seems to have tolerated a good deal of absenteeism among the aldermen provided that they turned up for crucial or difficult meetings. At times aldermen were away on business or were ill: John Michell attended his last meeting of the court on 20 November 1437 and yet remained an alderman until his death in July 1444; Henry Frowyk was also absent in the last two years of his life (1456–8), as was John Hatherle (1459–61), and Nicholas Wyfold (1454–7). It is likely that they were unwell or, in some cases, they may have withdrawn from civic life to their country estates.[143] In the fourteenth century aldermen who stayed away from the elections of the sheriffs or the mayor (for fear of being elected to office) were heavily fined but such strictures seem not to have been necessary in the fifteenth century.[144]

Since the burdens were so onerous, it is not surprising that it was not easy either for a likely man to escape election or, once elected, to be able to resign from office. Obviously if a man was too poor to be able to continue to hold office he was discharged.[145] The usual grounds for being excused from service were old age or ill-health.[146] In 1418 Alan Everard was dismissed from his aldermanry because of his increasing deafness.[147] Two men in the fifteenth century were excused simply because they had served for a long time: Stephen Broun had served for thirty-one years and Nicholas Wotton for more than forty.[148] It may be that the developing custom of appointing deputies enabled men to continue to serve even when they were necessarily absent from the city on business. Hence whereas in the fourteenth century it had been possible to be excused because of pressure of business abroad, such excuses were no longer offered or accepted in the following century.[149] The

142 Barron, 'Government of London', app 1A.

143 Year 1417, aldermen enjoined to live in the city, *Memorials*, 654–5.

144 Year 1346, *LBF*, 304; 1354, *LBG*, 23.

145 Thomas Bernewell was discharged for poverty in 1437 and Stephen Forster in 1458, CLRO, Journal 3 fo. 190; ibid. 6 fo. 191; Stephen Fabyan was discharged for insufficiency in 1468, *LBL*, 79.

146 Year 1330, John Poyntel, alderman, allowed to retire because of his age: *LBE*, 243; Barron, 'Government of London', 73.

147 *Memorials*, 661.

148 February 1460, CLRO, Journal, 6 fo. 198; 1446, ibid. 4 fo. 123^{v}.

149 Year 1322, Henry Nasard quitted his office as an alderman because he was employed on the king's service, *LBD*, 316; cf. two similar cases in 1322, *LBE*, 172. In 1376 John Wroth gave up his aldermanry because of the pressure of business abroad, *LBH*, 48. On two occasions in the fifteenth century aldermen were discharged from office in order to pursue litigation in which they were involved, Barron, 'Government of London', 73 and n. 4.

answer to enforced absence was not dismissal but a deputy. But there were certainly occasions when aldermen were dismissed from office: the three aldermen—Adam de Bury, John Pecche, and Richard Lyons—who were impeached in the Good Parliament of 1376 were subsequently dismissed from office by the court of aldermen.[150] Ralph Holland, the radical alderman of the 1430s, was deprived of office by his fellow aldermen in 1443, and the political upheavals of the 1450s and 1460s probably account for the dismissal of Philip Malpas in 1450 and Thomas Canynges in 1461.[151] But as the fifteenth century progressed there are ominous signs of that flight from office-holding that was to become the curse of provincial towns in the early, and of London in the later, sixteenth century.

It cost money to escape from the obligations of aldermanic office but increasingly men were prepared to pay for their release and when the city was in need of funds such windfalls were hard to refuse. Thomas Walsingham, elected alderman of Castle Baynard ward in 1429, had to pay for the glazing of the great east window of the new Guildhall in order to secure his discharge;[152] John Derby who wanted to be discharged in 1454 because he was involved in complicated lawsuits had to pay the substantial fine of £50 but was allowed to continue to wear the aldermanic livery; Thomas Canynges who was dismissed 'for contumacy and disobedience' had to pay a £40 fine and there was no suggestion that he might continue to share the livery.[153] But the price for buying oneself out of office seems to have risen for John Fisher secured his discharge in 1483 only after contributing 400 marks to the various building projects then afoot in the city.[154] In 1524 Alderman George Monoux struck a somewhat strange bargain with his colleagues: in return for a tenement that he gave to the city, lying to the east of the Bridge House in Southwark, the court agreed that Monoux should be able to continue to serve as an alderman but not be liable to serve as mayor nor—and this is perhaps more surprising—be expected to attend the court of aldermen except for extremely urgent business. In short, if a man was able to offer the city something it really wanted, then he could more or less dictate his own terms and, in this case, have his cake and not have to eat it.[155]

It is not surprising, perhaps, that men were anxious to avoid office: the business and expenses were considerable and the perquisites were few. An alderman might enrol his own deeds, recognizances, and will in the Husting court free of charge and he was also allowed to enrol his apprentices without paying the customary fee to the chamberlain. Furthermore he received a share of the fine paid by the

150 *LBH*, 38; Barron, *Revolt in London*, 14.

151 C. Barron, 'Ralph Holland and the London Radicals, 1438–1444', in R. Holt and G. Rosser (eds.), *The Medieval Town: A Reader in English Urban History 1200–1540* (London, 1990), 180–1; Barron, 'Government of London', 494–9; Canynges fined £40 and dismissed from office, 5 December 1460, 13 January 1461, CLRO, Journal 6 fos. 279ᵛ, 286.

152 22 April 1429, CLRO, Journal 2 fo. 132ᵛ; *LBK*, 109.

153 19 October 1454, *LBK*, 312; Barron, 'Government of London', 73 n. 4; Canynges had been refused a discharge, 5 December 1460, CLRO, Journal 6 fo. 279ᵛ.

154 *LBL*, 208.

155 M. Carlin, 'The Urban Development of Southwark, *c*.1200–1550' (University of Toronto, Ph.D. thesis, 1983), 360–1.

wardmote defaulters and one or two other customary payments.[156] Once elected as an alderman for a particular ward, he seems to have been able to move to another ward which fell vacant without, on occasion, any reference to the men of the wards in question.[157] But there is no doubt that the main perquisite of aldermanic office was prestige, and the power that goes with such prestige. From the thirteenth century aldermen were known as *barones* and they accorded themselves the rank and dignity commensurate with that of peers of the realm, although when the House of Commons emerged in the later thirteenth century the alderman MPs for London sat as commoners not as peers. But it is clear that a knighthood—that important step towards gentility—was more likely to come the way of an alderman than an ordinary Londoner. Such knighthoods were quite rare in the fourteenth century and no London alderman, not even Richard Whittington, was knighted in the fifty-year period following the Peasants' Revolt in 1381. William Estfeld appears to have been knighted in the 1430s and he was followed, at some distance, by William Cantelowe at the Coronation of Edward IV.[158] From 1461 onwards a very high proportion of London aldermen were knighted—perhaps because Edward IV needed money; perhaps because there were changes in the common perception of a knight: no longer a fighting warrior but, rather, a man of a certain rank in society who had lands and estates sufficient to produce a reasonable gentry income.[159] There is no doubt that to be an alderman of London was, by the end of the fifteenth century, an acknowledged means of converting mercantile wealth into landed gentility.

Moreover the city itself—and of course the aldermen were frequently the voice of city opinion—took steps to protect the alderman in the exercise of his duties and to punish those who slandered him or demeaned the high office which he held. Perhaps it is odd that whereas the hereditary principle was, in the course of the twelfth century, established in England and both the Crown and the great tenancies-in-chief passed from one generation to another by hereditary right, the aldermanries of London moved in the opposite direction—from being hereditary they became elective. London ceased to be ruled by a group of hereditary families and was ruled instead by men elected by their fellow citizens as being worthy of respect and office. A man who physically attacked an alderman, or who insulted or slandered him, was tried not in the wardmote but in the mayor's court. The traditional punishment for striking an alderman was the loss of the offending hand, but this punishment, though threatened, seems not to have been carried out during this

[156] Williams, *Medieval London*, 31; for the free enrolment of apprentices, see cases in 1311, *LBD*, 132, 150; it may be doubted whether aldermen still received the wardmote fines in the fifteenth century.

[157] In 1320 there seems to have been a general post among aldermen, see *LBE*, 11; Barron, 'Government of London', 68–9.

[158] Beaven, *Aldermen of London*, i. 254–5; *LBK*, 231 n. 3; on the political significance of Cantelowe's knighthood, see J. L. Bolton, 'The City and the Crown, 1456–61', *London Journal*, 12 (1986), 11–24.

[159] See C. Barron, 'Chivalry, Pageantry and Merchant Culture in Medieval London', in P. Coss and M. Keen (eds.), *Heraldry, Patronage and Social Display in Medieval England* (Woodbridge, 2002), 219–41.

period.[160] But perhaps because of the threat of such a punishment most recorded attacks on aldermen were verbal rather than physical and these offences were sharply punished either with fines or imprisonment. A brewer's servant who insulted the alderman of his ward in 1375 was brought into court and committed to prison on the grounds that 'all citizens . . . are bound to honour, as far as possible, their superiors and the aldermen'. Four days later he was released at the request of the alderman whom he had slandered.[161] Geoffrey Lovey was imprisoned in Newgate in 1413 for cursing and slandering the alderman Thomas Fauconer not once, but twice, and Thomas Mayneld was also imprisoned there, two years later, for threatening William Sevenoke, the alderman of Tower Ward, with the fate of Nicholas Brembre.[162] Mayneld was later released at the request of Sevenoke and it is clear that the image of 'the merciful alderman' was also an important one. But Clement Bishop, who called Nicholas Jamys 'a false extortioner' in front of a great many people, was condemned to the pillory for this offence. In fact he was later pardoned the pillory but had to provide a £10 bond for his good behaviour. Fining and imprisonment were the more usual punishments for those who publicly insulted aldermen and so brought their office into disrespect.[163]

But the city was concerned also with the positive side of office; the alderman was to have an appropriate household (as a lord had his retinue) and in 1475 it was thought necessary to limit the size of the retinue that an alderman might bring to the mayoral election: he was to be allowed only one servant to carry his gown.[164] Above all, perhaps, it was the livery that marked an alderman out from his fellow men; it was the livery that provided the outward and visible sign of the special status of the wearer. The first reference to the livery occurs in 1307 when the aldermen were to be clothed in a common livery for the coronation of the young king Edward II.[165] By the middle of the century the aldermen had new liveries twice a year—at Whitsun and in October when the new mayor rode to Westminster to take his oath.[166] By 1441 it is clear that the aldermen also bought a new communal livery for Christmas so that there were three new liveries to be purchased each year.[167]

[160] *CEMCR 1298–1307*, 6; *CPMR 1413–37*, pp. xxviii–xxx; in 1387 the punishment would have been imposed but for the intercession of the alderman concerned: *Memorials*, 490–2; a man who attempted to kill an alderman in 1311 was pardoned, *LBD*, 260–1; cf. a case in 1388: *Memorials*, 506–7.

[161] *CPMR 1364–81*, 199; cf. 1343, *CPMR 1323–64*, 197, and 1388, *Memorials*, 506–7; *LBH*, 329–30.

[162] Years 1411 and 1413, *LBI*, 114; *Memorials*, 575–7, 592–3, 595–6; 1415, *LBI*, 132; *Memorials*, 605–6; for other cases when aldermen were insulted, see *LBH*, 259, 323; *Memorials*, 500–2.

[163] 18 September 1427, CLRO, Journal 2 fo. 100; 1461, Thomas Barley was sent to prison for speaking shameful words about John Yonge, the alderman of Farringdon Without, CLRO, Journal 6 fo. 25ᵛ; 1469, Peter Peckham was fined £20 for insulting the alderman of Tower Ward: *LBL*, 89; 1478, William Capel, a future aldermen, threatened the former mayor Robert Drope and claimed that if he was imprisoned he would break out with twenty other men. The mayor and aldermen imprisoned him in Newgate nonetheless, ibid. 161–2.

[164] 13 September 1475, *LBL*, 133.

[165] *LBD*, 247.

[166] In 1358 the aldermen were enjoined not to give away their twice-yearly liveries within a year of receiving them, *LBG*, pp. xxv–vi, 93; *Liber Albus*, 31.

[167] The aldermen took trouble to decide on the colour of the Christmas liveries: scarlet in 1441, blood red in 1444 and 1446, violet in 1452 and brown/blue in 1459: CLRO, Journal 3 fo. 98; ibid. 4 fo. 50ᵛ; ibid. 5 fo. 92ᵛ; ibid. 6 fo. 141. In 1468 the livery cloth was described simply as 'ray' and no colour is mentioned: *LBL*, 81.

Although the decision about colour and cloth was taken by the court, each alderman was responsible for purchasing his own gown. It may well be that the cloth was often bought in bulk to ensure uniformity of colour. In 1339 a small committee of four was appointed to buy the Whitsun livery cloth for the mayor, aldermen, and sheriffs and this was the procedure followed in the fifteenth century also.[168] In 1421 the liveries cost each alderman fifty shillings and if a man was required to buy three liveries a year that would cost him £7 10*s*. annually, which was a tidy sum. In 1382, during the period when aldermen were elected annually and so perhaps had less incentive to provide themselves with aldermanic livery, John Sely, the alderman of Walbrook, appeared in a cloak that lacked the requisite lining of green taffeta and as a punishment was condemned to entertain his fellow aldermen to dinner—which is likely to have cost him more than the price of a properly lined livery gown.[169] The liveries were not worn once only: it is not clear whether the aldermen usually walked around the city dressed in their communal livery, nor whether it was worn at the normal meetings of the court; but it was certainly worn whenever the aldermen gathered in any formal way. In 1440 the court decided that for the forthcoming election of the sheriffs on 29 September the aldermen should wear the last livery but one, that is the livery of the previous Christmas, and for the mayor's election on 13 October they should wear the last livery, that is the Whitsun one.[170] We have some idea of the appearance of the liveries: in 1382 the livery that alderman Sely had failed to buy consisted of a cloak with a silk lining. The mid-fifteenth century heraldic drawings of the London aldermen show them wearing pink cloaks lined with grey silk marked out in squares with brown lines.[171]

In meetings of the court of aldermen or common council matters at issue might be debated and discussed and, indeed, decisions taken. But in order to make these decisions effective the city relied upon a host of civic officers: these were, broadly speaking, of two kinds; on the one hand there were unpaid officers who were elected annually, such as the mayor and the two sheriffs, and, on the other hand, the permanent salaried officers such as the recorder, chamberlain, and town clerk together with a host of lesser officers who may conveniently be classified as the civic serjeantry (this term includes men who were yeomen or valets). It was these salaried men who comprised the 'civil service' of the medieval city.

168 *CPMR 1323–64*, 105; *LBL*, 81.

169 Year 1382, *LBH*, 188; *Memorials*, 466. On occasion the aldermen treated themselves to liveries at the city's expense. In May 1441 it was decided that the chamber should pay each alderman 100*s*. for his livery – presumably for Pentecost – out of the profits of brokerage, CLRO, Journal 3 fo. 85, 88^{v}.

170 20 September 1440, CLRO, Journal 3 fo. 59.

171 K. Scott, *Later Gothic Manuscripts 1390–1490*, 2 vols. (London, 1996), i. pl. 333; ii. 245–7.

CHAPTER SEVEN

The Annually Elected Officials: Mayor and Sheriffs

THE MAYOR, HIS COURT AND HOUSEHOLD

THE MAYOR STOOD, albeit only for a year, at the pinnacle of civic government: within his small domain of three square miles he was a king with many of the powers and some of the prestige of that office. Inevitably the monarch at Westminster viewed his wealthy rival with some suspicion. But just as the mayor exercised his rights and privileges by virtue of royal authority delegated to him, so the wardens and masters of civic companies also exercised their powers of search and correction by the authority of the mayor.[1] The duties and tasks that fell to the mayor were multifarious; therefore he had to be not only wealthy, but wise and impressive to impose order within the city and to carry weight with the great men of the realm outside it. Not all those elected to the office were capable of exercising it: Adam Stable was unable to keep order in the city and was peremptorily removed from office by Edward III in March 1377. And the unimpressive Thomas Oulegrave, 'a replete and lumpish man', fell asleep during the Guildhall trial of Sir Thomas Cook in 1468, causing the duke of Clarence who was sitting on his right to say 'Sirs spekyth sofftly ffor the mayer is on slepe.'[2] Such incidents can hardly have enhanced the reputation of the office but, luckily for the city, most of London's elected mayors were more attentive to their duties.

To be eligible for the mayoralty a man had not only to be an alderman but also to have served as sheriff so that he might already have tried out his 'governance and bountee' before he became mayor.[3] Not everyone wished to stand at the pinnacle of civic government and shoulder the costs and responsibilities. On occasion aldermen stayed away from the annual meeting of 13 October, when the mayor was chosen, in order to avoid being elected.[4] The burdens of office were considerable

[1] See Ch. 9.

[2] *LBH*, 60–1; *The Great Chronicle of London*, ed. A. H. Thomas and I. D. Thornley (London, 1938), 206.

[3] *Liber Albus*, 399, referring to ordinance of 1385; *LBH*, 277.

[4] *LBF*, 304–6; the city attempted to eliminate this absenteeism and imposed fines for absence. In 1416 the court of aldermen condemned the practice whereby aldermen who were likely candidates for the mayoralty but did not wish to be elected would organize citizens, together with their apprentices and

yet in the thirteenth century some men held office for several years at a time—but these were the years when office was still, in effect, the perquisite of a few families. Even in the fourteenth century, however, it was customary for men to hold the mayoral office for more than one year: the radical John of Northampton had been mayor for two years, 1381–3, when he was displaced by his rival Nicholas Brembre who held office during 1383–6. It may have been the wish to avoid the creation of new political 'parties' under particular individuals that led to the decision in 1389 to allow no one to serve as mayor for more than one year at a time, and no one to be re-elected to the office until five years had passed.[5] The emphasis here is on preventing men from holding office for too long, but by the time John Carpenter was writing in the early fifteenth century there was more concern about imposing undue burdens on a single man. No one was to be compelled, against his will, to serve for a second term as mayor, and in 1424 the court of aldermen extended the gap between terms to seven years and stipulated that no one who had served for two terms should serve again.[6] The decision may have been provoked by Richard Whittington's third term of office in 1419–20. It was certainly unusual, by this time, for a man to serve three times, hence the extraordinary message that Dick was supposed to have heard from the bells of London: 'Turn again, Whittington, thrice Lord Mayor of London.'

The method of electing the mayor was a matter of some contention in this period. When the mayoralty was first instituted by royal charter in 1215 the Londoners had asked for election by open folkmoot, but what King John in fact granted was election by the barons of London, however that term might be interpreted.[7] As the population of the city grew rapidly in the thirteenth century an open 'folkmoot' election was found to be impracticable and, perhaps, also undesirable. By the time that elections were recorded in 1293 'the whole commonalty of the city' assembled for the mayoral election, 'namely from each ward the wealthier and wiser men'.[8] It would appear that each ward was expected to produce twelve such men, who were regarded as the *probi homines* of the ward. Indeed if each alderman came accompanied by twelve *probi homines* there would have been nearly three hundred men present for the mayoral election. But it is clear that the more radical citizens resented this limitation of their power to choose their ruler

serving-men, to come to Guildhall on the day of the mayor's election and shout loudly for some other candidate, and in this way would avoid the office themselves: *Memorials*, 635–7. This ordinance shows how far the situation had changed from the vigorous competition for the mayoralty in the 1380s to be seen from the testimony of Thomas Usk.

[5] *LBH*, 347.

[6] *Liber Albus*, 20; 8, 13 October 1424, CLRO, Journal 2, fo. 23; *LBK*, 33–4. At first the common council did not accept that a man should not serve more that twice, but finally did so, 8 April 1435: ibid. 197. John Reynwell who served as mayor in 1426–7 was excused from serving a second term in 1444, and in 1445 was excused altogether from serving again, 9 October 1444, 17 September 1445, CLRO, Journal 4, fos. 43^{v}, 95.

[7] M. Bateson, 'A London Municipal Collection of the Reign of John', *EHR* 17 (1902), 480–511, 707–30, esp. 726; *Historical Charters and Constitutional Documents of the City of London*, ed. W. de Gray Birch (London, 1887), 19.

[8] *LBC*, 11.

and the demands for 'free elections' and a wide-ranging franchise reappeared at intervals throughout the fourteenth and fifteenth centuries.

The king was brought in on the side of authority and issued a writ in 1315 limiting the election of the mayor to those who were summoned to attend.[9] This, not surprisingly, produced the complaint to the royal justices in 1321 that all the civic elections, and especially that of the mayor, were rigged by a small group.[10] But the weight of royal and judicial authority was lent to those who wished to limit attendance at the mayor's election to those who were summoned: in 1346 six, eight, or twelve men were to accompany the alderman to the mayoral election, depending on the size of the ward, and then, four years later, it was decided that four men from each ward would be sufficient. By 1370 exact numbers were dropped but it was reiterated that only those who were summoned might come and they were to be of the better class of citizens, or 'sufficient'. In 1406 it was specifically stated that members of the common council were to attend.[11] Obviously these restrictions, however necessary in practice, were a matter of contention when there was dissatisfaction, for whatever reason, with city government. In 1383 it was claimed that Nicholas Brembre had packed the election with his supporters and had thereby ousted Northampton from the mayoralty. When Ralph Holland led the artisan protest movement in the 1430s and 1440s one of the main planks in his radical platform was a challenge to this restriction of the franchise in mayoral elections to those who were summoned. As early as 1426 Ralph Holland protested against the restrictive writs arguing—wrongly—that they were new and fabricated and not included in any of the city's ancient books. In fact such writs, as we have seen, can be traced back at least to 1315, but it may be that the custom of proclaiming such restrictions had lapsed for some years and so when the ancient ordinances were promulgated early in October 1426 they were seen as innovations. Holland was the rejected candidate as mayor in 1439, 1440, and 1441: not surprisingly the mayor and aldermen were concerned to ensure a docile electorate at the elections in 1442. Fearing trouble the mayor and aldermen obtained a new royal writ to control elections from the king and this was proclaimed together with the ancient writ of 1315 lest anyone should fear that the restrictions were novelties. Similar precautions were again taken in the following year, 1443, and William Cottisbrook, a grocer and one of the radicals, objected to the royal writ and argued that an elected mayor was not the mayor of those who had not elected him, hence those who had been excluded from the election were entitled to withdraw their obedience to the mayor.[12] There was a widespread belief among the artisan agitators that the royal writ was a fabrication. In fact the protest movement fizzled out in the autumn of 1443 but the aldermen took no chances and in the following year not only was the

[9] *LBD*, 24–6, cf. pp. xxi and 22–3.

[10] *The Eyre of London, 14 Edward II AD 1321*, ed. H. M. Cam, 2 vols. (Selden Society, 1968–9), i. 43; the group of four confederates who controlled mayoral elections (among other things) were named as William de Hackford, Walter de Gorst, Peter de Hatfield, and Roger de Depham.

[11] Year 1346, *LBF*, 304; 1350, ibid. 223; 1370, *LBG*, 265–6; 1406, *LBI*, 34.

[12] Cottisbroke was himself elected chamberlain by the commonalty in the same year, see Ch. 8.

mayor's election confined to those who were summoned but the door of the Guildhall was closed during the election.[13] After this tumultuous period when the mayoral election became the forum for radical discontent, the issue of the restricted electorate appears no longer to have been a burning one. In 1467 the role of the city companies in mayoral elections was recognized for the first time when it was decided that the elections of both the mayor and the sheriffs were to be by the members of the common council, the masters or wardens of the companies dressed in their liveries, and other good men (*probi homines*) especially summoned. Eight years later the good men especially summoned were dropped and the election was to be carried out by the 'good men of the common council' together with the masters and wardens and liverymen of the companies.[14] The evolution of the franchise for the election of the mayor from a broad spectrum of all freemen in the early thirteenth century to the respectable citizens represented by the members of the common council and the wardens and liverymen of the companies by the end of the fifteenth century, is an interesting indicator of the twin developments characteristic of civic government: on the one hand the body of aldermen became less oligarchic and more open to newcomers; on the other hand, the electorate became restricted to the better sort of citizens, the prosperous and respectable.

It would be interesting to know more about what actually happened once the *probi homines* were assembled in the Guildhall and the door was shut. In the thirteenth century it seems that the aldermen probably chose the mayor for the succeeding year and those who were summoned simply approved or ratified the choice—providing the popular acclaim which was as necessary for a mayor of London as for a king of England. In 1328 the record expressly makes the process clear: 'The mayor and aldermen retired to the chamber [that is, away from the main Guildhall] to make the election for themselves and the commonalty according to custom.' When the aldermen had made their choice the recorder returned to the hall and announced the result of the election. In fact not all the commoners present were willing to accept the aldermen's candidate, Hamo de Chigwell, a fishmonger who had already served three terms as mayor, and called instead for the pepperer, Benedict de Foulsham (Fulsham). A group of 'wiser citizens' persuaded both candidates to stand down and the pepperer, John de Grantham, was chosen instead.[15] But by the early fifteenth century the procedure had changed: John Carpenter in the *Liber Albus* described how the commoners who were present in the Guildhall chose two aldermen whom they presented to the court of aldermen for their choice as to which should be the next mayor.[16] The custom of selecting from two candidates presented by the commonalty must go back at least to 1406 when the Letter Book records that Drew Barentyn was the rejected candi-

[13] C. Barron, 'Ralph Holland and the London Radicals, 1438–1444', in R. Holt and G. Rosser (eds.), *The Medieval Town: A Reader in English Urban History 1200–1540* (London, 1990), 160–83, esp. 163–4, 176–8.

[14] *LBL*, 73, 132.

[15] *CPMR 1326–64*, 72–3.

[16] *Liber Albus*, 20.

date when Richard Whittington was chosen.[17] But, after this, until 1439 the Journals and the Letter Books record only the name of the successful candidate. In 1439, however, and in the two successive years, the name of the rejected candidate was recorded: on all three occasions it was the alderman Ralph Holland. It may be that it was Holland himself who demanded that his failure should be minuted. When Holland was rejected for the third time, the 'handycrafty' men who were in the body of the Guildhall protested loudly and shouted at Robert Clopton, the aldermen's choice, 'Nay, not that man, but Rawlyn Holland.' Their commotion could only be silenced when the ringleaders were rounded up and sent to prison. So unusual were these events that several of the London chronicles provide accounts of the riot, from which it is clear that it was customary for the retiring mayor—in this case, John Paddesle—to lead the successful candidate out to the assembly and to present him for their acclaim.[18] It was the city recorder who acted as returning officer and counted the votes cast by the aldermen for the two candidates; and it would seem that the ballot was secret but perhaps verbal rather than written.[19] The Journals do not, after 1441, again record the names of the rejected candidates until 1457 when they are recorded for the succeeding four years.[20] In order to prevent one company dominating civic government as the mercers looked likely to do it was decided in 1475 that the two men nominated for the office of mayor should not belong to the same company.[21] By the end of the fifteenth century the election of the mayor seems to have been much less contentious: perhaps because his power was waning; perhaps because the aldermen and *probi homines* had finally gained control of the procedure and could ensure that it ran smoothly.[22]

Once the mayor was elected he had fifteen days to wait before taking his oath at Guildhall on 28 October. The original oath was in French and it is likely that in the

[17] *Memorials*, 565.

[18] Barron, 'Ralph Holland', 167–70.

[19] *Liber Albus*, 19; 13 October 1426, the city was without a recorder, so it was decided that the prior of Holy Trinity, the *ex officio* alderman of Portsoken ward, should examine the votes cast and faithfully report who had secured the most, CLRO, Journal 2, fo. 85^{v}.

[20] CLRO, Journal 6, fos. 180^{v}, 234^{v}, 163, 271^{v}.

[21] *LBL*, 132.

[22] On occasion a mayor did not complete his term: in 1342 John de Oxenford died in office and a new mayor, Simon Fraunceys, was immediately elected: *LBF*, 74, 77; *Memorials*, 212–13; when Adam de Bury was removed from office by Edward III in January 1366, the aldermen quickly elected John Lovekyn to take his place: *LBG*, 205; March 1377, Adam Stable was removed from office at the instance of John of Gaunt and a new election was held: *LBH*, 61; in the 1380s Richard II seems to have let the Londoners know whom he favoured as the next mayor of London and first Northampton and then Brembre was elected 'rege favente': C. Barron, 'Richard II and London', in A. Goodman and J. Gillespie (eds.), *Richard II: The Art of Kingship* (Oxford, 1996), 129–54, esp. 146–8; when Adam Bamme died in office in 1397, Richard II simply appointed Richard Whittington as his successor without allowing the Londoners to have any choice in the matter: C. Barron, 'Richard Whittington: The Man Behind the Myth', in W. Kellaway and A. Hollaender (eds.), *Studies in London History* (London, 1969), 197–248, esp. 205; in the fifteenth century London mayors had the good sense to avoid dismissal during their term of office, although two died of the sweating sickness in 1485 and new elections took place within the week: *LBL*, 226–7.

thirteenth century the mayor was assumed to be able to understand and speak Anglo-Norman, but there are fifteenth-century copies in both French and English, which suggests that the general command of Anglo-Norman was waning in London.[23] On the following day the mayor rode to Westminster to be sworn before the king or the barons of the Exchequer.[24] The day of 29 October was probably the most important in the civic year when the whole city was *en fête*. The mayor would be joined on his journey by members of all the city companies dressed, certainly by the fifteenth century, in their liveries and accompanied by minstrels.[25]

The pageantry became more elaborate as time went on and in 1453 it was decided that the mayor should go to Westminster by barge rather than ride down the Strand. It is not clear what were the reasons for this change (although John Carpenter suggests that in the past mayors had either ridden or gone by water) but it seems to have been popular, for the commonalty asked six years later that the mayor should always in future go by barge to take his oath.[26] Although the Londoners obviously favoured this change it seems not to have been welcome at Westminster and the lord chancellor and the duke of Somerset sent a royal serjeant at arms to the mayor and aldermen to ask them to revert to the old custom of riding to Westminster.[27] But the city would not budge on this point and all medieval mayors after John Norman in 1453 went by barge to take the oath. Although the city had other rituals and processions—for example the midsummer watch and the Christmas festivities—yet the mayor's journey to Westminster was the most important event in the civic cycle. The mayor and aldermen were dressed in new liveries and when the business of the day was done, the mayor gave a banquet at his home, or at a company hall or, after the new kitchens were built in 1501–5, at Guildhall.[28] Then he visited St Paul's to pray at the tomb of Becket's parents and finally rode home along Cheapside in a torchlight procession. The carnival atmosphere of the 'mayor's riding' is suggested by the need in 1481 to prohibit any 'disguysyng or pageoun' on the route from the mayor's house to the Thames 'like as it hath been used nowe of late afore this tyme'.[29] This day of civic ceremony had always been important but as the Reformation stripped away the religious ceremonies from civic life, so those that were essentially secular like the 'mayor's riding' took on an enhanced significance.[30]

[23] French oath, *Liber Albus* (Rolls Series), 306; fifteenth–century copies of the oath in French and in English, *LBD*, 11 and n. 4, 34–5.

[24] The king was usually there in person to hear the oath but, in 1459, he was prevented by virtual civil war, *Liber Albus*, 22–4; *LBK*, 396.

[25] See e.g. the restriction in 1409 that limited the number of minstrels who might accompany the mayor to Westminster to three bands at the most: *LBI*, 78; In 1368 the mayor elect failed to turn up for the oath-taking and so another alderman was hastily chosen and was given 100 marks' reward for his public-spirited behaviour: *LBG*, 234, 240.

[26] *Great Chronicle*, 186; *Liber Albus*, 19.

[27] 8 and 18 October 1453, CLRO, Journal 5, fos. 124^{v}, 126; the chroniclers attribute this change to the personal whim of the mayor elect for 1453, John Norman, hence the song of the Thames watermen, 'Rowe thy boat Norman', *Great Chronicle*, 186–7.

[28] C. Barron, *The Medieval Guildhall of London*, (London, 1974), 32.

[29] *LBL*, 187.

[30] M. Berlin, 'Civic Ceremony in Early Modern London', *Urban History Yearbook*, (1986), 15–27.

The new mayor would have realized by the close of the first day, if he had not realized it already, that he was in for an expensive year. There was no salary attached to the office but there were a few perquisites and privileges. In 1358 he was allocated the profits of pesage—the charge made for weighing goods offered for sale in the city—and 1463 it was decided that the mayor should be entitled to half the profits of fines in the mayor's court.[31] In the fourteenth century the mayor had claimed as custom 50 marks from the merchants of the three north French towns of Amiens, Corbie, and Nesle who enjoyed certain special privileges in the city, but it is doubtful whether this was ever paid on a regular basis.[32] If the mayor's expenses were particularly heavy the commonalty might agree that he should be reimbursed from the revenues of the chamber as they did in 1350 when he was allocated the very substantial sum of £100. But the mayor enjoyed some non-financial perks; the butchers provided him each year with a boar's head, he received four casks of the best red wine of Gascony, and many of the city companies provided him with annual gifts to ensure his friendship.[33] If the mayor wished he could transfer automatically to any aldermanry that fell vacant during his term of office and at the end of his term he might request civic posts for those who had served him well. [34]

The rewards might seem meagre (although they amounted to a minimum of £50 by the later fifteenth century) when compared with the responsibilities. The mayor's overriding responsibility, both to the citizens and to the king, was to preserve peace in the city. Moreover he had a general oversight of all civic officials; he had to ensure that trade was carried out in accordance with civic ordinances, he had to act as arbitrator and judge and to play the leading role in civic and religious rituals.[35] His oath stressed his responsibilities to the monarch. One of these responsibilities was that of acting as the royal escheator in the city which involved gathering in, listing, and valuing the goods of convicted criminals.[36] By the end of the period the office was carried out by a deputy who did not change from year to

[31] Year 1358, *LBG*, 103–4; 1364, ibid. 167; 1463, *LBL*, 38; in 1515 the fines in the mayor's court amounted to £60 – and by this period they were declining—so the mayor would have received about £30 from this source, see CLRO, Book of Fines, fos. 1–7. I am grateful to Dr Penny Tucker for this information.

[32] *CPMR 1323–64*, 179; in 1369 the city confirmed that the mayor was entitled to £20 from this source: *LBG*, 245; and see Ch. 5. By the late fifteenth century the mayor also received an annual payment from the bakers of white bread, 7 September 1480, CLRO, Journal 8, fo. 232.

[33] The boar's head was given in return for land that the butchers rented from the city in St Nicholas Shambles, *LBF*, 84; originally the mayor had the right to make six men free of the city, but this provoked royal displeasure and so, in 1434, the privilege was transmuted into four casks of wine: *LBI*, 64, *LBK*, 34–5, 180; the brewers' clerk noted in his book that William Crowmere (mayor 1423–4) 'wolde nought receyve no gifftes ne rewardes of the same craffte yn all his tyme' but promised to be a good friend to the craft without gifts 'and so he was', *A Book of London English 1384–1425*, ed. R. W. Chambers and M. Daunt (Oxford, 1931), 182.

[34] C. Barron, 'The Government of London and Its Relations with the Crown 1400–1450' (University of London, Ph.D. thesis, 1970), 81–2.

[35] In 1375 the mayor, William Walworth, went about the city in person to check on the prices at which poultry was being sold, *CPMR 1364–81*, 205.

[36] In 1319 the city refused to allow the royal escheator to exercise his office in London: *LBE*, 88; the first charter of Edward III in 1327 made the mayor the royal escheator *ex officio*: Birch, *Charters*, 55; see H. M. Chew, 'The Office of Escheator in London in the Middle Ages', *EHR* 58 (1943), 319–30.

year, and so this particular burden fell on other shoulders.[37] The same charter of 1327 which appointed the mayor of London as royal escheator in the city also appointed him *ex officio* a justice of gaol delivery at Newgate.[38] He was, thus, by the end of the period, the king's chief agent in the city, supervisor and director of the sheriffs, escheator and a royal justice.

Since the tasks that fell to the mayor were so crucial to the city it was accepted that he might, if he were ill or absent, need to appoint a deputy or *locum tenens*. As early as 1298 the mayor Henry le Waleys appointed deputies while he was away in Scotland, and there are references to mayor's deputies in 1300 and again in 1311 and 1312 when the mayors were ill.[39] By the fifteenth century mayors seem not to have absented themselves on business (since they now served for only a year it was, perhaps, reasonable to expect them to remain in the city during their year of office) but both Robert Large (mayor 1439-40) and Thomas Chalton (mayor 1449-50) had to appoint deputies because they were too ill to carry out their duties themselves. They were, however, expected to meet the expenses incurred by their deputies acting on their behalf.[40]

The most important single duty that fell to the mayor was the task of presiding over the mayor's court. This court developed during the thirteenth century, and although it emerged later than either the husting or the sheriffs' courts, it rapidly became an important member of the triumvirate of city courts. The earliest surviving rolls of the court date from 1298 and it is clear that it developed in part to respond to the need for rapid and specialized justice appropriate to a commercial community.[41] The speed with which cases could be dealt with is well illustrated by a case in 1419 where an alien merchant was permitted to make a peremptory oath to the truth of the matter in dispute and the issue was settled the same day.[42] By the later fourteenth century the court was virtually omnicompetent (it could not, however, deal with cases involving the ownership of land) and many of the surviving cases relate to actions between citizens, often about debt or apprenticeship or broken contracts of various kinds.[43] All cases in the mayor's court were begun

[37] In 1456, John Byron was chosen to act as sub-escheator, CLRO, Journal 5, fo. 177; in 1468 it was decided to elect a sub-escheator every year whom the mayor could not remove; *LBL*, 81.

[38] G. A. Williams, *Medieval London from Commune to Capital* (London, 1963), 82; *Eyre 1321*, p. lvi.

[39] *LBB*, 76, 89, 213; *LBC*, 67; *LBD*, 77, 289; in 1327 the mayor again had a locumtenens, *London Assize of Nuisance 1301–1431*, ed. H. M. Chew and W. Kellaway (London Record Society, 1973), 65.

[40] Robert Large was described on 14 July 1440 as 'iam infirmus' and he chose William Estfeld to carry out his duties for him, CLRO Journal 3, fos. 46, 47v; Thomas Chalton, did not attend the court after 8 July 1450 and Thomas Catteworth acted as his deputy during the aftermath of Cade's revolt; 12 August 1450, a committee of eight aldermen was appointed to negotiate with Chalton about the costs incurred by his deputy: CLRO, Journal 5, fo. 43v.

[41] See Ch. 3.

[42] 3 July 1419, *CPMR 1413–37*, 68–9.

[43] There are rolls of the mayor's court surviving from 1298, but these are superseded in the mid-fourteenth century by rolls, known as the plea and memoranda rolls, which are a mixed bag of copies of writs, civic memoranda of various kinds and some, presumably selected, records of cases heard in the mayor's court; for the history of the mayor's court, see Williams, *Medieval London*, 83; *CEMCR 1298–1307*, pp. ix–xlv; *CPMR 1381–1412*, pp. vii–xli; P. E. Jones, Introduction, *CPMR 1437–57*, pp. vii–ix; id. 'The City Courts of Law, Mayor's Court and Sheriffs' Courts', *The Law Journal*, 93 (1943), 301–2; P. Tucker, 'The Early History of the Court of Chancery: A Comparative Study', *EHR* 115 (2000), 791–811, esp. 794–5.

either by an oral bill or by a written bill of complaint and a number of these written bills survive from the late fourteenth century. It is clear from these that the business of the court was far more extensive than the surviving records would suggest.[44] It was important that the jurisdiction of the court, particularly when dealing with cases of law merchant, should be both speedy and comparatively private. When the mayor and aldermen sat as the court of aldermen to deal with the administrative business of the city they used the inner chamber of the Guildhall, and here they dealt with cases according to the law merchant and, later, with equity cases.[45] The ordinary business of the mayor's court—that is, common law cases between citizens—usually took place in the outer chamber of the Guildhall. There may have been some suspicion about sessions of the mayor's court that took place in the inner chamber, for in 1409 there was an attempt to restrict such 'secret sessions'.[46]

The most interesting development of the mayor's court in the fifteenth century was its use as a court of equity.[47] This development runs parallel to the development of the equitable jurisdiction of the chancellor, which emerges at the end of the fourteenth century. In 1414 a judgment in the mayor's court found that a tenant owed his landlord a certain rent *de racionis equitate* and in the course of the fifteenth century the mayor's court is to be found settling, in detail, comparatively trivial matters and applying reason rather than the strictures of the law to the solution of problems. In this way the court was adapting to the needs of the community that it served.[48]

It is difficult to assess the quality of justice to be found in the mayor's court. Verdicts depended upon the reliability of juries and 'oathhelpers' or, in cases decided according to the law merchant or equity, upon the wisdom and fairness of the mayor and aldermen themselves.[49] Inevitably there were complaints about delays, but these seem to be less noticeable in the fifteenth century.[50] It may well be that delays in the administration of justice in London—as elsewhere – may have contributed to the discontent that provoked the rising of 1381. Some Londoners appear to have joined the rebels in desperation when their cases were hopelessly entangled in the city courts.[51] Certainly there were criticisms of judgments in city

[44] The surviving original bills of the mayor's court are to be found in CLRO, mayor's court files of original bills, MC1/1–3A, with dates ranging from the 1360s to the 1450s; the Journals from 1416 onwards also include notes of sittings of the mayor's court and there are many cases recorded that do not find their way onto the surviving rolls.

[45] See case in 1378, *CPMR 1364–81*, 248–9 and n.; ibid. 283 and n.

[46] *LBI*, 80 and n. 2.

[47] E.g. a case in 1428, *CPMR 1413–37*, 214–15.

[48] *CPMR 1413–37*, pp. viii–ix, 32; for an award concerning which of two households should pay for the cleansing of a shared privy, see *CPMR 1437–57*, 36–7.

[49] Juries on occasion, perhaps inevitably, might give false verdicts or could be suborned, e.g. 1298, *CEMCR 1298–1307*, 13; 1364, a case of jurors being threatened: *CPMR 1323–64*, 267; 1344, a case in which abuse of oathhelpers (i.e. character witnesses) led to a miscarriage of justice: ibid. 210.

[50] E.g. criticism that the business of the court had been dealt with more speedily in the days of the royal warden: *CEMCR 1298–1307*, 146; attempts to speed up the processes in 1365 and 1463: *LBG*, 198; *LBL*, 38–9.

[51] C. Barron, *Revolt in London 11th to 15th June 1381* (London, 1981), 5; ead., 'The Quarrel of Richard II with London 1392–97' in C. M. Barron and F. R. H. DuBoulay (eds.), *The Reign of Richard II: Essays in Honour of May McKisack* (London, 1971), 173–201, esp. 174–5; cf. *CPMR 1381–1412*, 228–30.

courts, and those who uttered such criticisms were usually sent to prison for their pains: William Lytherpol was committed to prison in 1365 after claiming that the mayor and aldermen would not listen to him or do him justice and in 1445 Robert Edolf was also imprisoned for saying that the mayor gave false judgments.[52] In 1387 William Hughlot was moved to declare that the court of the Guildhall was the worst in the kingdom and in 1459 William Hubbard 'scandalously' voiced the opinion that the mayor's court was not a court of record but a court of favour.[53] The court not surprisingly insisted on seemly behaviour and punished the use of bad language and lack of respect for the judges, such as Walpole's description of the mayor's sergeant as a 'false harlot' and of the mayor, John Hadle, as 'outwardly the finest talker but inwardly the falsest' of all the four previous mayors.[54] The office of mayor was always accorded great respect in the city for the mayor not only carried great responsibilities—at the Eyre of 1244 he was the city's spokesman and by his answers the commonalty would stand or fall—but he also personified the city's self-respect and self-importance.[55] Although his title of 'Lord Mayor' seems not to have come into official use until the early sixteenth century, the mayor was referred to as *dominus maior* as early as 1283 and his actions were said to have been carried out *per dominum*.[56] Such courtesy titles were accorded to men of status: ordained clergy were also known as *dominus*. But as English came increasingly to be the language of the civic courts so an English phrase evolved to describe the mayor of London. In 1414 a petition was addressed 'To oure Worshipfull Lord Mair of the Citee of london. Like un to youre soverain discrecioun . . .' and from this date onwards the phrase 'lord mayor' crops up at intervals in the city's records.[57] Sometimes the epithets are more homely but equally emphatic: 'oure honurable and worthi Mair' well expresses the citizens' attitude to their elected leader.[58]

It may well be that the mayor was not, in fact, held in greater reverence as time went on, but there is no doubt that the office came to be invested with greater ceremonial. This is well demonstrated by the emergence of the mayor's esquire (as any knight would have a squire to serve him) who was gradually transformed into the mayor's swordbearer. In the early fourteenth century the mayor had a household composed simply of serjeants,[59] but by 1381 the mayor's esquire has emerged

[52] *CPMR 1364–81*, 14; *CPMR 1437–57*, 82; similar accusations of partiality were made against the mayor in 1441, ibid. 46; in 1463, *LBL*, 22.

[53] Year 1387, *Memorials*, 490–4; *LBH*, 295; April 1459, CLRO, Journal 6, fos. 154^{v}, 155^{v}.

[54] Year 1395, *CPMR 1381–1412*, 228–30; 1311, *Memorials*, 81; 1365, *CPMR 1364–81*, 17.

[55] *The London Eyre of 1244*, ed. H. M. Chew and M. Weinbaum (London Record Society, 1970), 5.

[56] *LBA*, 64, 73; *Assize of Nuisance* 1.

[57] *CPMR 1413–37*, 17 and n. 1. There are also references to 'lord mayor' in 1429: ibid. 224; 1440, *LBK*, 246; 1457, 1461, 1462, *CPMR 1458–82*, 2, 17, 28. For a discussion of the title 'Lord Mayor' see *LBG*, xxiv and A. B. Beaven, *The Aldermen of the City of London*, 2 vols. (1908–13), ii. pp. xxviii–xxxi.

[58] Year 1431, *CPMR 1413–37*, 253.

[59] Year 1309, *LBD*, 13–14; in 1368 it was decided that the mayor's serjeants, and their servants, should be sworn to assist in maintaining the oath to the king and the city that the mayor took, *LBG*, 226; it is not clear which royal charter had granted to the city of London the right to have a sword borne before the mayor, but in 1387 the city of Coventry was granted this right *ad modum Londoniensium*: *Knighton's*

as distinct from the rest of the serjeants and in 1381, when the mayor William Walworth rode out with Richard II to meet Wat Tyler, John Blyton 'that bore the mayor's sword of London' accompanied him and confronted Wat Tyler in the famous scuffle that led to Tyler's death and Richard's heroic role.[60] Clearly Blyton was the mayor's swordbearer, but after he relinquished his office in 1394 he was described simply as 'late the mayor's esquire'.[61] John Credy and John Hastings who succeeded Blyton were also described as mayor's esquires, but in 1425 the duke of Gloucester and other lords visited the city and the clerk of the Journals records that on this occasion the mayor and his swordbearer took precedence over the duke and his swordbearer.[62] This event may have provoked the city into appointing John Pencriche the next year specifically as the 'mayor's swordbearer' and all his successors in office were so called.[63] The swordbearer's oath was also, probably, drawn up at this time.[64] The transformation from serjeant to swordbearer was marked by a rise in salary. John Carpenter noted that the mayor's esquire was entitled to 40*s.* from the chamber *et nient plus*, but Pencriche in 1426 was allocated 53*s.* 4*d.* p.a. and a further reward of 6 marks.[65] Twenty years later Power was allowed 'a suitable servant' at the expense of the chamber: thus did officialdom burgeon.[66] The role of the mayor's swordbearer was primarily ceremonial, in an increasingly ceremonious society: in 1441, for example, the mayor's swordbearer led the duke of Gloucester and other lords into Guildhall for a special judicial session, and in July 1445 the ambassadors from the French king were met at London Bridge by the mayor and *bourgois* and a gilt sword was carried before the mayor.[67] It may just be coincidence but in the same year—1381—in which we find the first unambiguous reference to the mayor's swordbearer the mayor also, apparently for the first time, acquired a seal designed especially for his use.[68] After he had taken his oath at Guildhall the new mayor was handed the seal of his office,

Chronicle 1337–1396, ed. G. Martin (Oxford, 1995), 392; on the mayor's household, see B. Masters, 'The Mayor's Household before 1600', in Hollaender and Kellaway, *Studies in London History*, 95–114.

[60] *Chronicle of London*, ed. H. N. Nicolas (London, 1827), 74.

[61] *LBH*, 433; Blyton seems to have been closely identified with John of Northampton and when the mayor was disgraced in 1384, Blyton was sent to Corfe Castle, ibid. 229, 232. But when he finally retired from office the city gave him a lodging over Aldersgate and a garden for life as well as a pension of 100*s.* p.a.: ibid. 433.

[62] 5 June 1425, CLRO, Journal 2, fo. 44; John Credy came from Devon and left a will written in English, see *The Fifty Earliest English Wills in the Court of Probate*, ed. F. J. Furnivall (EETS, 1882), 73–7; J. S. Roskell, L. Clark, and C. Rawcliffe, *The House of Commons 1386–1421*, 4 vols. (Stroud, 1992), ii. 689.

[63] 9 July 1426, CLRO Journal 2, fo. 78^{v}; for subsequent swordbearers, see App. 2 (vii).

[64] *LBD*, 197.

[65] *Liber Albus*, 44; 1426, CLRO, Journal 2, fo. 78^{v}; his successor in office, Richard Power, was appointed on the same terms: ibid. 3, fo. 136^{v}.

[66] *LBK*, 320.

[67] 4 March 1441, CLRO, Journal 3, fo. 78; see the account of the reception of the count of Vendôme in London, July 1445, in *Letters and Papers Illustrative of the Wars of the English in France during the Reign of Henry VI*, ed. J. Stevenson, 2 vols. (Rolls Series, 1861–4), i. 101–2, 156–7. Questions of precedence were taken very seriously, see e.g. the care with which the scribe of the Journals described the royal visits of 1425 and 1427: CLRO, Journal 2, fos. 44, 93.

[68] *Memorials*, 447–8; the seal matrix of 1381 remained in use until 1910 by which time it had become extremely worn.

which was kept in a purse placed in the charge of the swordbearer.[69] The seal was used on mayoral precepts (for example, those instructing aldermen to hold their wardmotes) and occasionally on important 'civic' letters, but its most frequent use seems to have been authenticating private documents 'for better evidence and security'.[70] Each time the seal was used the swordbearer was entitled to receive a fee.[71] In addition all the mayor's swordbearers were provided with houses: John Blyton was given a house over Aldersgate and John Credy was housed over Cripplegate, but the later swordbearers, John Pencriche, Richard Power, and John Morley were all housed over the gate at Guildhall and this became the usual home of the swordbearer.[72]

The swordbearer was the most important member of the mayor's household yet the references to his housing make it clear that he did not live with the mayor—the office had, as it were, moved out of the household. But the mayor also maintained, at his own expense, a corps of valets and serjeants.[73] Since the mayor chose and paid these men, they had no official role and the city was not responsible for them. Yet although their jobs were impermanent, several mayor's serjeants moved on to permanent posts as serjeants of the chamber, so that a period of serving the mayor might provide an *entrée* to a permanent job.[74] After 1436 it was decided that the mayor should have three permanent serjeants, known as serjeants-at-mace who should, as it were, provide a permanent civil service to serve each mayor in succession. Obviously the annual fluctuations of the mayor's household had not been found conducive to good and stable government.[75] These permanent serjeants-at-mace were paid 40*s*. a year, granted a livery, and provided with houses; like the sheriffs' serjeants they had to be sworn on assuming office.[76]

69 *Liber Albus*, 21.

70 Seal used to authenticate documents: *CPMR 1381–1412*, 235; *CPMR 1413–37*, 190, 258, 301; *CPMR 1437–57*, 1, 50; seal used for 'civic' purposes in writing to the archbishop and citizens of Cologne, 8 October 1453: CLRO, Journal 5, fo. 124^{v}.

71 On 27 and 28 October 1440, it was decided that letters written under the mayor's seal should be composed by the common clerk and enrolled, CLRO, Journal 3, fos. 64^{v}, 65. The swordbearer received 12*d*. each time the seal was used, although in 1456/7 the Mercers' company paid him twice that sum to attach the mayor's seal to a letter to the earl of Warwick: Mercers' Company Hall, wardens' accounts, fo. 191.

72 Barron, 'Government of London', 137 n.5; *LBL* 68.

73 John Carpenter noted that the mayor was to be served by three serjeants (including the esquire or swordbearer) whom he paid himself, although they were also entitled to 40*s*. p.a. from the chamber: *Liber Albus*, 44. In 1419 it was decided that the mayor should choose the four valets of his household who had been most diligent and they were to receive 2 marks each as a reward, CLRO, Journal 1, fo. 66^{v}.

74 Barron. 'Government of London', 141 and n. 3.

75 *LBK*, 203; Barron, 'Government of London', 82, 569.

76 *LBD*, 204–5; housing granted to mayor's sergeants-at-mace: 1305, *LBC*, 144; 1467, *LBL*, 70; *CPMR 1458–82*, 47; Barron, 'Government of London', 142 and n. 3; in 1482 it was decided that before becoming one of the mayor's three serjeants-at-mace a man must first have served as a sheriff's serjeant-at-mace: *LBL*, 191.

THE SHERIFFS, THEIR COURTS AND HOUSEHOLDS

The sheriffs' office was one of great antiquity; the citizens of London had been choosing their own sheriffs for nearly a hundred years before they finally secured the right to elect a mayor.[77] But the mayor excelled the sheriffs in importance and prestige, and by the end of the fourteenth century the shrievalty was considered to be a necessary testing ground before a man embarked on the mayoralty. In the words of John Carpenter, the sheriffs were to serve as the eyes of the mayor.[78]

But the sheriffs were important for, in many senses, they did the mayor's dirty work for him. The sheriffs were elected on 21 September. Just as the mayor came to be elected by a gathering, not of all citizens but of a selected group of *probi homines*, so too from at least 1301, and probably earlier, the electorate at the choice of sheriffs was also limited. But in the case of the sheriffs, unlike that of the mayor, there seems to have been no recorded protest. On this occasion, one sheriff was chosen by the commonalty and the other sheriff by the mayor.[79] There seems to have been the same reluctance—perhaps with better cause when the tasks that fell to the sheriff are considered—to be chosen for office, and it was necessary to threaten likely candidates who absented themselves from the election with heavy fines.[80] John de Caustone, who was elected sheriff in 1324, failed to turn up on 28 September to take his oath. He was promptly deprived of his freedom.[81] On the other hand, before the sheriffs were sworn, at least in the early fourteenth century, they were expected to provide pledges to guarantee their financial responsibility.[82]

On 28 September the new sheriffs came to the Guildhall to take their oath which was detailed and comprehensive: to guard the counties of London and Middlesex; to see to the keeping of the assizes of bread and ale; to execute royal writs only after showing them to the mayor and city counsel; to carry out the mayor's reasonable wishes, and—this seems like an afterthought—to undertake not to farm (that is, let) the county of Middlesex or the gaol of Newgate.[83] On the day following their swearing at Guildhall the sheriffs went to Westminster to be presented and sworn before the barons of the Exchequer. It was to them that, in the course of the year, they would be rendering account for the various financial obligations of the city to the king, most notably the annual farm of the city of £300: that is, the sheriffs paid a lump sum to the Crown rather than answering for all the different sums of

[77] C. N. L. Brooke with G. Keir, *London 800–1216: The Shaping of a City* (London, 1975), 207–13.

[78] Year 1385, *LBH*, 277; *Liber Albus*, 42; Williams, *Medieval London*, 28–9.

[79] Year 1328, one sheriff was chosen by the mayor and one by the commonalty: *CPMR 1323–1364*, 69; and see Beaven, *Aldermen*, ii. pp. xxxvii. Usually the mayor chose an alderman and the commonalty chose a commoner—often a man on the way to an aldermanry.

[80] Year 1350, *LBF*, 306. There is evidence that men were unwilling to serve earlier in the century, in 1303, 1305, and 1309: *LBC*, 174, 176, 180.

[81] *LBD*, 32–3: he was subsequently restored to the freedom.

[82] Lists of sheriffs and their pledges from 1278: *LBA*, 194; and see *LBC*, 175.

[83] *Liber Albus*, 306–7 (oath in French); another copy of the oath in English (fifteenth century) copied into *LBD*, 206–7.

money that they might collect on behalf of the Crown. In the early fourteenth century, however, the citizens claimed, for a time successfully, that their elected sheriffs should be admitted by the barons of the Exchequer, but that they were not obliged to be sworn before them.[84]

The sheriffs originally rode to Westminster wearing new liveries and accompanied by members of the various city companies and minstrels. But in 1389 it was decided, for reasons of economy, that the journey should be by water and that the sheriffs should wear their old liveries and not buy new ones.[85] Certainly the journey continued, even by water, to be one in which the city companies took part and payments for the expenses involved in the 'sheriffs' riding' appear in almost all the surviving fifteenth-century company accounts. It would seem that the cost of the barges was originally borne by the city, but in 1439 it was decided that the sheriffs should pay for their own barges.[86] The sheriffs' riding was obviously overshadowed, as was the office itself, by the more splendid and significant mayor's riding that took place a month later.

If a sheriff died during his year of office the king tried, on occasion, to appoint a successor, but the city fought to maintain its right to elect, even in these circumstances.[87] John Bryan the newly elected sheriff in 1418, died twelve days after being sworn: his death by drowning, in the Thames, was quite dramatic:

> hit fortuned so for hym that with Inne vij nyght after that he hadde I-rede and toke his othe at Westm. He felle in to tempse as he wold have esed hym self, as men seyth, be yonde be seint Katerynes, comyng fro the bentenent whech that tyme was atte Stratford, nat with stondyng that all his sergians were there with hym, the weche sergeantys with help of the millenere thast there was tokyn hym up with an hoke, but forsothe afterward hadde he neuer gode day but peyned and dyed with ynne the sevenyth.[88]

In 1467 Henry Bryce died in office and his successor, alderman John Stokton, paid £100 to ensure that he did not have to serve as sheriff a second time.[89]

On the day that the sheriff took his oath at Guildhall, the retiring sheriffs were supposed to bring all the records of their term of office into Guildhall.[90] But this seems rarely to have happened because the sheriff was personally responsible both for his financial and judicial acts during his shrievalty, and so he was inclined to hang on to the records and, if he delivered them up at all, it was usually after some

[84] *LBD*, pp. xiii–xv; in 1329 the king conceded that the sheriffs should not be compelled to make an oath at the Exchequer except when they came, at the end of their term of service, to render their accounts, *LBF*, 227.

[85] Year 1389, *LBH*, 347–8; *Memorials*, 515–16. The decision to transfer the mayor's journey from riding to going by barge did not come until nearly sixty years later—see above, n. 26.

[86] 15 October 1439, CLRO, Journal 3, fo. 25.

[87] Years 1311 and 1312, Peter de Blakeneye and Richard de Welleford died during their term, *LBD*, 17–18, 20–1; see Beaven, *Aldermen*, ii. pp. xxxix.

[88] Harley MS 3775, printed in C. L. Kingsford, *English Historical Literature in the Fifteenth Century* (rpt. New York, 1972), 295.

[89] *LBL*, 71; when William Wyking died in 1481, a new election was held the next day: ibid., 186.

[90] *Liber Albus*, 44–5.

considerable lapse of time.[91] The city's records are full of injunctions to sheriffs, apparently rarely successful, to bring their records into Guildhall.[92] The city does seem, however, to have been quite successful in retrieving from the sheriffs the records of the possessory assizes for which the sheriff was responsible but, apart from these, there now survive in Guildhall very few records relating to the sheriffs' office.[93] There are, for example, almost no surviving records of proceedings in the sheriffs' court, unlike the series of mayor's court rolls.[94] There are signs that cases heard before the sheriffs were sometimes, by the mid-fifteenth century, being entered on the rolls of the mayor's court.[95] To compensate for the lack of material relating to the activities of the sheriffs, there is, of course, a certain amount of material relating to the London sheriffs among the royal records, particularly those of the Exchequer.[96]

It was, in part, because he was both a royal agent and a civic official that the sheriff's duties were so wide-ranging. Moreover, his two masters were not always in harmony. As a royal agent each sheriff was responsible for answering at the Exchequer for half the city's farm (i.e. £150 each) and the chamberlain might help the sheriff by providing necessary records or documentation.[97] Sometimes the sheriffs—like sheriffs elsewhere—paid royal creditors direct from the revenue they had collected and brought the sealed receipts into the Exchequer in lieu of cash.[98] The king might demand that they should execute traitors, or heretics, or erect scaffolds for duels or simply declare royal proclamations at the appointed places in the city. The sheriffs were responsible for the execution of the heretics William Sawtre in 1401, Sir John Oldcastle in 1417, and the Lollard priest, Richard Wyche, in 1440. The sheriff was expected to arrest criminals in the city and to summon witnesses to appear when the criminals were tried.[99] When criminals failed to appear the sheriff had to distrain their goods; when they were convicted he had to execute

[91] The records of the shrievalty of Simon Wynchcombe (sheriff 1383–4) were not brought into court until 1428: *LBK*, 76.

[92] Year 1303, ordinance requiring the sheriffs to hand over their rolls of *novel disseisin* and *mort d'ancestor* on leaving office: *LBC*, 14; repeated 1304, ibid. 108; 1356 and 1365, *LBG*, 72, 199; 1375, *CPMR 1364–81*, 201 and n.; 1382, *LBH*, 175–6.

[93] For the surviving assize of nuisance records for the period 1340–1451, see *London Possessory Assizes: A Calendar*, ed. H. M. Chew (London Record Society, 1965).

[94] There survive in the Corporation of London Records Office two groups of records of the sheriffs' court, a roll of actions covering July to September 1320, together with the record of one case from 1318 (Misc. Roll CC) and a roll of cases transferred from the sheriffs' court to the mayor's court, known as *querelae levatae*, 1406–08. The latter are not in fact rolls but individual scraps of paper, covering 45 cases in all. One register of writs received by the sheriffs in 1458–9 survives in the CLRO.

[95] E.g. 1461, 1469, *CPMR 1458–82*, 23, 66.

[96] Barron, 'Government of London', 90.

[97] Year 1336, the chamberlain handed over documents for the sheriffs to render account at the Exchequer: *LBE*, 300. The settling of the sheriffs' account might take some years: William Marowe and William Cantelowe, sheriffs 1448–9, were still trying to settle their account with the Exchequer in 1451 because there were desperate debts totalling nearly £222; see PRO E199/27/28.

[98] Some of the receipts sealed by the individuals who were paid by the London sheriffs survive for the reign of Henry VI, PRO E101/573 parts 1 and 2. On occasion the London sheriffs paid the royal justices, see, for indentures covering the years 1430–48, PRO E101/571/41.

[99] *Eyre 1244*, 103.

them or extract a fine.[100] In addition, he had overall responsibility for the prisons and prisoners in the city.

Moreover, the sheriffs of London were sheriffs not only for the city, but also for Middlesex. By his oath the sheriff was not allowed to farm the county but clearly it would have been an impossible task to administer both the county and the city, and so from at least 1322 the sheriffs had been accustomed to appoint an undersheriff for Middlesex.[101] One of the most notorious undersheriffs of Middlesex during these years was the author Thomas Usk, a clever clerk who acted as John of Northampton's secretary and then gave evidence against him, wrote *The Testament of Love,* and was executed by the Merciless Parliament in 1388.[102] The job may not have been, at least by the later fifteenth century, a very prestigious one, since it was decided in 1482 that the undersheriff should live either in Middlesex or London and have property to the comparatively modest annual value of 10 marks.[103] It seems to have been held by young men at the beginning of their climb up the legal ladder. The dual role of the sheriffs, responsible both for London and for Middlesex was problematic, although the link between the city and the county that lay closest to it stretched back to the Anglo-Saxon period. It was difficult for the London sheriffs to exercise effective control over affairs in Middlesex. They left the arrest of men there to local constables and the profits of office (e.g. deodands) usually went to the local manorial officials rather than to the sheriffs. The situation was full of anomalies and in effect the London sheriffs controlled the shrievalty in so far as they collected the royal revenues. But they made little attempt to ensure law and order in the county: this was largely left to local agents. The abbot of Westminster, for example, was able to appoint his own coroner.[104]

The sheriffs received, by the fifteenth century, at least two hundred writs a year ordering them to arrest, distrain, or to take securities for the peace from individuals, together with orders to start the process of outlawry. In addition, there were a similar number of writs ordering them to return details of cases brought in the

[100] On occasion, of course, sheriffs abused their power: in 1299 sheriff Thomas Sely was successfully sued for falsely distraining the goods of a Coventry merchant, Adam de Shepeye: *CEMCR 1298–1307*, 41–2.

[101] Year 1322, William de Norwich was the deputy of the sheriffs in Middlesex: *LBE*, 167–8.

[102] Usk was appointed undersheriff of Middlesex in 1387 at the king's request, see *LBH*, 316–7; for Usk's career and his 'appeal', see P. Strohm, *Hochon's Arrow: The Social Imagination of Fourteenth-Century Texts* (Princeton, 1992), 145–60.

[103] *LBL*, 196. 25 October 1454 Robert Beaufitz sworn as undersheriff of Middlesex and Robert Broker as his bailiff: CLRO, Journal 5, fo. 202^{v}. In 1454 the king agreed that prisoners taken in Middlesex could appear at the Newgate sessions of gaol delivery rather than at separate Middlesex sessions, CLRO, Journal 5, fos. 196, 199. For most of the fifteenth century the office normally passed annually between the King's bench clerks, but from the early 1460s the city started to intervene in these appointments, several times appointing John Stokker, the common huntsman, see M. Blatcher, *The Court of King's Bench 1450–1550* (London, 1978), 42–3; CLRO, Journal 7, fo. 155^{v}.

[104] Some surviving rolls of the abbot of Westminster's coroner are listed in R. F. Hunnisett, 'The Medieval Coroners' Rolls', *The American Journal of Legal History*, 3 (1959), 352–4; ex inf. Professor Andrew Prescott. The King's Bench records suggest that the London sheriffs presided over their own sessions for Middlesex, if the headings to the Kings Bench indictments (PRO, KB9) can be considered reliable, ex inf. Dr Penny Tucker.

city courts, with or without the defendant's person, to one of the central courts, chiefly chancery.[105] The recording of these writs, not to mention acting upon them, was a heavy burden, and it is not surprising that there were considerable delays in executing the writs and that men did not welcome a year as sheriff of London.

One reason for the delay in executing royal writs was that quite often action by the sheriff might have led him to infringe the city's liberties. For this reason by his oath he was required not to make a return to any royal writ 'touching the estate and franchise of the city' without first showing it to the mayor and city counsel (probably the recorder) for their advice.[106] In the fifteenth century the city had a prolonged quarrel with the Crown over the privileged position of St Martins le Grand where fugitives from justice could take sanctuary and craftsmen could work free of civic regulation. As servants of the city the sheriffs removed escaped prisoners from the sanctuary of St Martins, and as servants of the king they were instructed to restore them. In such a case the sheriffs expected the common council to indemnify them if they upheld the city's case against the Crown. In November 1459 the sheriffs were unable to return a royal writ because it stated that St Martin's Lane lay within the liberty of the church whereas the city maintained that the lane was a common lane and not part of the liberty of St Martins.[107]

As far as the king was concerned the sheriffs had both financial and judicial responsibilities, but from the point of view of the city the sheriffs' duties were predominantly concerned with maintaining law and order. To carry out these tasks each had a large household and his own court. The sheriffs' court may have been the oldest, and was probably the busiest, judicial court in the city.[108] Appeals from the sheriffs' court continued to be heard in the Husting court but the practice seems to have stopped by, or in, 1321, probably after the Eyre. At least from the late fourteenth century on, litigants could choose to have their case transferred to the mayor's court, using the procedure known as *querela levata*.[109] The court was divided into two 'sides', one for each sheriff, and there were normally two sessions per week on each side of the court. One, the routine session, was held in the sheriffs' counter (the sheriffs' office and prison for those awaiting trial in their courts), the other, the full

[105] CLRO, Sheriff's Register, covering the year 1458–9, contains over 230 writs, excluding exigents, and the section containing chancery writs *corpus cum causa*, which is mentioned on fo. 37, is missing. On average at least 130 *corpus cum causa* writs issued out of chancery to the London sheriffs each year between 1460 and 1480. I am grateful to Dr Penny Tucker for this information.

[106] Year 1454, sheriffs' clerks instructed not to return any writ touching the state of the city, or for delivery from Newgate prison, or any writ whereby the city might be 'burdened': CLRO, Journal 5, fo. 194v.

[107] Year 1459, CLRO, Journal 6, fo. 169; cf. the care taken in 1457 about responding to a royal writ dealing with the royal demand for soldiers to be raised in the city: Journal 6, fos. 124, 181v, 182v.

[108] For the early history of the sheriffs' court see A. H. Thomas, *CEMCR 1298–1307*, pp. xiv–xv, *CPMR 1381–1412*, pp. xii–xiv; P. E. Jones, 'The City Courts of Law, Mayor's Court and Sheriffs' Courts', *Law Journal*, 93 (1943), 301–2; *Eyre 1321*, i. pp. liii–liv, lxxxi; *ibid.* ii. 252–7. In 1385, the practice with regard to holding the sheriffs' court was described, *CPMR 1381–1412*, 113–116, and see 1383, an order forbidding sheriffs to hold any court except assizes on Saturdays: *LBH*, 213.

[109] See *CPMR 1381–1412*, 265.

court, at Guildhall.[110] Sometimes the court in the counter was held before the sheriffs' deputies, the undersheriffs; a practice that seems to have become commonplace by the early sixteenth century.[111] The business of the sheriffs' court covered a wide range, both civil and minor criminal jurisdiction: debt cases, forgery, mercantile disputes, trespass, theft, and cases involving foreigners, that is, exactly the same range of cases as was covered by the mayor's court.[112] The sheriffs were also responsible for holding the royal assizes of *novel disseisin* and *mort d'ancestor*, cases in which a complainant would acquire a royal writ to instruct a sheriff to hold an inquiry into a dispute about possession: the plaintiff was alleged to have been dispossessed by an unlawful intruder and was seeking reinstatement. In practice the majority of plaintiffs adopted the city's own remedy, known as *freshforce*, which permitted them to initiate an inquiry by making an oral complaint in the form of *novel disseisin* or *mort d'ancestor* before the sheriffs or mayor and aldermen, providing that the alleged dispossession had occurred no more than forty weeks previously. The records of these 'possessory assizes' held before the sheriffs and coroner, in theory, were supposed to be brought into Guildhall and kept there.[113]

On the day that the sheriffs took their oath at Guildhall they received also their most onerous obligation, namely the custody of the prisoners in the city prisons. The retiring sheriff handed over the responsibility for the prisoners by indenture and he was, doubtless, pleased to be relieved of the charge.[114] At the same time the keepers of the city gaols came to Guildhall to swear fidelity to the new sheriffs.[115]

The oldest city prison was Newgate where all prisoners were held pending the sessions of gaol delivery carried out by the royal justices who, from 1327, included the mayor.[116] Clearly the conditions were far from attractive and a telling witness to the deadly environment is provided by the number of cases of deaths in Newgate brought before the coroners in the first half of the fourteenth century.[117] It is probable that the decision in 1356 not to allow the sheriff to farm the office of

[110] The counters were usually located near Cheapside but seem to have moved from house to house, depending upon the individual sheriff: see M. D. Lobel (ed.), *Historic Towns Atlas: The City of London from Prehistoric Times to c.1520* (Oxford, 1989), 70.

[111] e.g. 1291, *Memorials*, 27; in 1460 the court of aldermen instructed the undersheriffs, rather than the sheriffs, to ensure that attorneys who were not sworn did not appear in the sheriffs' court, CLRO, Journal 6, fo. 262^v.

[112] Types of cases are derived from the part-roll for 1320 (CLRO, Misc. Roll CC) and from the forty-five cases of which records survive in 1406–8 (CLRO, Sheriff's Court rolls). In the part-roll for 1320, debt cases (56%), trespass (25%), account (8%), covenant, detinue, 'threats', and a few others (e.g. *abdracionis* of a horse) make up the rest. I am grateful to Dr Penny Tucker for this information.

[113] *Possessory Assizes*, pp. xiv–xviii. See also *Eyre 1244*, 104; *Eyre 1321*, i. pp. lxx, xciv; *Calendar of Letters from the Mayor and Corporation of the City of London c. 1350–1370*, ed. R. R. Sharpe (London, 1885), 104.

[114] *Liber Albus*, 45. Here only the gaol of Newgate is mentioned, which suggests that the regulation antedates the establishment of Ludgate prison in 1378: *LBG*, 31 n. 2.

[115] *Chronicles of the Mayors and Sheriffs of London, A.D. 1188 to A.D. 1274*, ed. and trans. H. T. Riley (London, 1863), 26.

[116] *CPMR 1323–1364*, 48 n. 1.

[117] For the history of Newgate prison, see M. Basset, 'Newgate Prison in the Middle Ages', *Speculum*, 18 (1943), 233–46; R. B. Pugh, *Imprisonment in Medieval England* (Cambridge, 1968), 103–9; *Calendar of Coroners' Rolls of the City of London 1300–1378*, ed. R. R. Sharpe (London, 1913), xvii, 53, 136; London Coroner's Roll for 1316–1317, PRO, JUST2/94A.

keeper of Newgate was an attempt to improve conditions since a salaried officer had less temptation to behave extortionately than one who was free to make out of the prison what he could.[118] But the physical conditions of the prison were clearly of the harshest. A prisoner who was thrown into the 'deepest part' died of a broken neck; a woman was put into the 'lowest part' until she paid the extortionate keeper 48*s*.; and the references to parts of the prison known as *Bocardo* and *Juliansboure* where a man claimed to have been tortured, have a sinister ring.[119] The appalling conditions at Newgate prompted humanitarian Londoners to two courses of action: one was to rebuild and refurbish the prison itself and the other, in 1378, was to provide a separate prison for London citizens at Ludgate. Newgate of course had a dual function, as a prison and as a city gate. In 1406 Richard Whittington appears to have paid for a separate tower or chamber to be built at the prison to house women, and then between 1423 and 1431 the whole gate and gaol were pulled down and rebuilt.[120] But even when it was rebuilt the state of the prison was a source of continual anxiety to the aldermen and the gaol was further damaged during Cade's revolt in 1450. Pious Londoners left bequests to the inmates (as to all prisoners in city prisons) and in 1382 Hugh Tracy, a chaplain, bequeathed a breviary for the use of clerks and priests imprisoned in Newgate, although one might think that a square meal or some bedding would have been more welcome.[121] In 1462 contributions were solicited for the repair of the prison and this was to be the continuing pattern throughout the medieval period and beyond.[122]

It is difficult to judge whether the keepers of Newgate gaol were particularly unattractive men or whether the job was an impossible one to administer humanely. Keepers were dismissed for oppressions and extortions and the detailed ordinances passed by common council vividly suggest the abuses in which keepers indulged: the gaolers were not to take alms intended for prisoners, to monopolize the sale of food to inmates, to charge undue sums for the hire of beds, or demand extortionate fees when delivering prisoners.[123] These fifteenth-century ordinances demanded that gaolers should be elected and sworn annually but there is little evidence that that took place.[124] Unfortunately, the prisoners may have had to stay in the prison for quite a long time. It is not clear how often the justices came on commissions of gaol delivery, although they were supposed to come at least once a year.[125] To what

[118] Year 1356, *LBG*, 74.

[119] *Eyre 1244*, 72; *Eyre 1321*, ii, 108; 1382, *LBH*, 204; 1370, *CPMR 1364–1381*, 119.

[120] Year 1406, *LBI*, 49–50, *LBK*, 19, 39, 49, 119. While the prison was being rebuilt the prisoners were housed in the sheriffs' counters.

[121] *LBH*, 185; *Memorials*, 461–7.

[122] April 1462, CLRO, Journal 6, fo. 62ᵛ.

[123] Year 1341, the keeper was dismissed for oppressions: *CPMR 1323–1364*, 135, and see Barron, 'Government of London', 98–9. In 1378 all who had grievances against the officials of Newgate gaol were invited to bring them to the mayor and aldermen, *LBH*, 112; 1431, 1434, *LBK*, 124–7; 1463, *LBL*, 41–3; see *Letters of Queen Margaret of Anjou, Bishop Beckington and others*, ed. C. Munro (Camden Society, 1863), 161–3.

[124] Barron, 'Government of London', 99.

[125] In 1471 it was decided that the sheriffs should pay the costs of the annual commission of gaol delivery at Newgate: *LBL*, 101.

extent the sheriffs might have been able to curb the excesses of the gaolers and ameliorate the conditions of the prisoners is difficult to judge: the building and the system may have made disease, extortion, cruelty, and corruption inevitable.

The administration of Ludgate prison seems to have been rather better. It appears to have been established in 1378 to provide a prison for citizens of London who were convicted of crimes other than felony and maiming, but it was envisaged that the prison would be predominantly used for freeman debtors.[126] Although the sheriff was responsible for the prison, by 1414 common council appears to have been choosing the keeper. In 1440 it was formally decided that the sheriff should choose and pay the keeper of Ludgate gaol as he did Newgate.[127] But, even at Ludgate, within ten years of the foundation of the new prison there were complaints about the 'evil and extortionate' rule of the prison by the keeper, John Botlesham, who had diverted alms intended for the prisoners and then punished those who complained by putting them in irons.[128] It may have been as a result of Botlesham's activities that the city in 1393 issued regulations about the behaviour of gaolers at both Newgate and Ludgate: no one was to be required to pay for lamps or beds while in the gaol nor were they to pay more than 4*d.* to the goaler at their release, but the gaolers were entitled to take a reasonable sum as surety for removing the fetters of prisoners.[129] In the reign of Henry IV the prisoners petitioned the future Henry V to secure for them five years' freedom during which they could pay off their debts. A situation in which debtors were placed where they were unable to work to pay their creditors was clearly unsatisfactory, but the absurd solution of imprisonment for debt remained for a further five hundred years.[130] The situation in Ludgate prison must have improved after the 1380s since in 1419 it was decided to close the gaol because many people—some of them prostitutes—had taken to living there 'upon the ease and licence that there is therein'. The Ludgate prisoners were moved to Newgate, but there more than sixty of them died within fifteen days so it was hastily decided to reopen the prison 'seeing that every person is sovereignly bound to support, and to be tender of, the lives of men'.[131]

It was found necessary again to close the prison for a time in 1431 and when it was reopened new ordinances were promulgated to try to reform some of the abuses to which prisoners were subjected.[132] Of considerable importance to the health of the prisoners was the introduction of a new water supply brought directly to the prison through the efforts of Thomas Knolles and the new gaoler Henry

[126] *LBG*, 31 n. 2; *LBH*, 97, 208, 213.

[127] Year 1384, 1386, *LBH*, 253, 292; Barron, 'Government of London', 99–100 and n. 1.

[128] Year 1388, *CPMR 1381–1412*, 158–9. In 1409 the keeper, William Kingscote, refused to hand over Ludgate to the new sheriffs, so he was discharged, and then reinstated, *Memorials*, 574, 579.

[129] *LBH*, 402; *Liber Albus*, 524.

[130] *Anglo Norman Letters & Petitions*, ed. M. D. Legge (Oxford, 1941), 31–2.

[131] *LBI*, 215, 227; *Memorials*, 673–4, 677; CLRO, Journal 1, fos. 57^{v}, 65^{v}; Stow, *Survey*, i. 37; *The Brut, or the Chronicles of England*, ed. F. W. Brie (EETS, 1906), 444.

[132] *The Brut*, 456; *Great Chronicle of London*, 155; *LBK*, 124–7, 183.

Dene, who himself paid to improve the prison privy.[133] Early in 1454, however, there was a fire near Ludgate and this may have prompted the then mayor, Stephen Forster, to take an interest in rebuilding or enlarging the prison. Although Forster died in 1458 his widow Agnes took up this work of charity. It is not clear how long the work took but there was a further set of ordinances promulgated in 1463 at the instance of Dame Agnes Forster 'for the ease, comfort and relief of the poor prisoners'. Among other improvements the ordinances stipulated that each year a committee should be appointed composed of two clergymen and two commoners in order to hear complaints from prisoners.[134] The water supply was further improved when it was decided to pipe off some of the city's water supply at the Great Conduit and bring water first to Ludgate and thence to Newgate further north.[135] Finally in 1477 the chapel at Ludgate, which had been destroyed by the building work of Forster's executors, was to be rebuilt and a fraternity established there to pray for, and minister to, the inmates.[136]

The remaining prisons for which the sheriffs were responsible were the two counter prisons, one for each sheriff, normally located in or near the Poultry and Bread Street.[137] The counters were the sheriffs' offices where the routine administrative sessions of their courts were held, and also served as prisons run by porters who were sworn into office like other city officers. In 1393 it was decided that the sheriffs were not to farm the running of the counter prisons and the sheriffs themselves, rather than the prison porters, were to pay the running costs of the prison. Prisoners were to pay one penny for a bed but nothing for 'suetz' and they were to be allowed to choose to stay in the counter prison rather than go to Newgate or Ludgate, except in cases of felony and trespass. If they stayed in the counter they were to pay between 4*d.* and 12*d.* a week towards the upkeep of the prison.[138] This pleasant way with prisoners must have got out of hand for in 1419 it was decided that prisoners, once they had been tried and sentenced, could not remain in the counter prison even for a night.[139] In fact the administration of the counter prisons was the immediate responsibility of the sheriff and the more remote, but perennial, concern of the mayor and aldermen, who continued to issue reforming ordinances throughout the fifteenth century.[140] When Sir Robert Plumpton fell on hard times early in the reign of Henry VIII he was sent to the counter prison in Poultry, then in the

[133] Indentures dealing with the water supply, 1436, 1442, *LBL*, 4; 1441, *LBK*, 254–5 and CLRO, Journal 3, fo. 82^{v}.

[134] *Six Town Chronicles of England*, ed. R. Flenley (Oxford, 1911), 108; Stow, *Survey*, ii. 175, *LBL*, 40–3.

[135] Year 1475, *CPMR 1458–82*, 92–3.

[136] Year 1477, ibid. 114–16. It is not clear whether this work was ever carried out.

[137] For the origin of the counter prisons, see Pugh, *Imprisonment*, 109–11.

[138] *Liber Albus*, 522–3. One reason for the new regulations may have been the uncertainty over responsibility for escaped prisoners, if the counter was farmed: 1385, *CPMR 1381–1412*, 92–8.

[139] 18 December 1419, CLRO, Journal 1, fo. 66^{v}.

[140] The porters of the two counter prisons were indicted by the wardmotes: 1421, *CPMR 1413–37*, 137, 151; 1431, *LBK*, 124–7, 183. 14 December 1448, two aldermen appointed to investigate the state of the counters, Newgate and Ludgate: CLRO, Journal 5, fo. 3^{v}; curates and commoners appointed (2 each), 1463: *LBL*, 40–3 (articles of government in accordance with Agnes Foster's request); 1488 ordinance to regulate the four prisons, *LBL*, 250.

charge of Hugh Reading and his wife. Sir Robert was accompanied by a servant and the Readings charged 4*d.* for food for Sir Robert and 2*d.* for that of his servant; he seems to have had a chamber to himself and in August his wife came to stay with him. The total expenses from 24 April to 5 August 1510 amounted to £7 4*s.* 10*d.*[141] Obviously Sir Robert was a knight and not completely destitute, and he was not a criminal, but the picture revealed in his accounts is a far cry from the inhuman conditions disclosed by the various inquiries in the thirteenth century.[142] Perhaps the endless attempts by the city rulers to impose some checks upon the malpractices of the gaolers and porters had finally borne some fruit.

The counter was the centre of the administrative bureaucracy of the sheriff, at least from 1375 when its existence is first recorded. William Gedyngton, a skinner, who was 'so swelled up with pride' that he refused to go to speak with the sheriff 'at his Compter' was promptly imprisoned for forty days for his presumption.[143] From the thirteenth century the shrieval staff had always been large: apart from the gaolers of the prisons, the sheriffs required the services of their undersheriffs, and other clerical staff headed by the secondary, together with a host of sergeants and valets to do the strong arm work.[144] In 1311, somewhat surprisingly, the 'cook to the sheriffs of London' was admitted to the freedom of the city at the request of the sheriffs.[145] The size of the shrieval staff caused problems and the court of aldermen tried at intervals to impose a limit on the number of servants and their fees and to organize their duties.[146]

The clerical household was composed of clerks who registered writs received, kept the records of the sheriffs' court and of the possessory assizes, kept accounts for the sheriff to present at the Exchequer, and wrote the necessary returns to royal writs. The dependence of the sheriff—who might well be ignorant of Latin—upon the ability of the clerical staff is obvious—particularly at the beginning of the period. In 1300 Adam de Hallingberi, who had been sheriff in 1295-6, was sued for failing to execute a judgment. He pleaded that he was a layman, that is illiterate in Latin, and asked for the help of his clerks. The importance of the sheriffs' clerks is demonstrated by the fact that in the early fourteenth century their oath was recorded in the city's Letter Book.[147] In the course of the fifteenth century a hierarchy of clerks emerged: each sheriff had an undersheriff, a secondary, and a clerk of the papers, together with the lesser and untitled clerks.[148] As with so much civic government, it was the last quarter of the fourteenth century during which the shrieval clerical hierarchy emerged. At first the sheriff seems to have chosen the undersheriffs each year and some may have served successive sheriffs. They were,

141 *The Plumpton Correspondence*, ed. T. Stapleton (Camden Society, 1839), p. cxviii.

142 See *Eyre 1244*, 72, 99; *Eyre 1321*, ii. 108.

143 Year 1375, *CPMR 1364–81*, 211.

144 The role of the secondary as head of the sheriffs' clerical administration only emerged gradually in the course of the fifteenth century, see B. Masters, 'The Secondary', *Guildhall Miscellany*, 10 (1968), 425–33.

145 Year 1311, *LBD*, 76; Williams, *Medieval London*, 93.

146 Williams, *Medieval London*, 93; 1358, *LBG*, 72–4; 1375, 1393, *LBH*, 12, 402; 1486, *LBL*, 235–6.

147 *CEMCR 1298–1307*, 100; *LBF*, 125.

148 Year 1393, *Liber Albus*, 519; for a list of undersheriffs, see Appendix 2 (ii).

like the rest of the shrieval entourage, sworn to office.[149] But in 1441 it was decided that, since the office was of such importance, it would be better if the undersheriffs were chosen by the common council and served during good behaviour.[150]

The duties of the undersheriff were extensive: he was to the sheriff what the recorder was to the mayor, namely an experienced civil servant and, increasingly during the fifteenth century the legal adviser who provided the professional knowledge which the annual and amateur sheriff lacked. According to his oath the undersheriff was expected to administer the law impartially, to enrol pleas for reasonable payments, to give no judgment contrary to civic ordinance, to amerce fairly, to account to the chamberlain for the sums collected, and to return no royal writs without first consulting the mayor and counsel of the city.[151] Until about 1500 the undersheriff acted as courtholder to the sheriff, managing all sessions of the sheriffs' court and the possessory assizes, checking that bills were correctly written, that attorneys and other legal advisers were duly appointed and were permitted to appear before the court, and ensuring that pleas and judgments were correctly proclaimed and entered in the court records. Thereafter, these functions were taken over by a new officer, the prothonotary, and the undersheriff's main task was to preside over the sheriffs' court in the counter; in the longer term, undersheriffs were to take over entirely from the sheriffs as presidents of their courts.[152] Presumably the undersheriffs were paid by the sheriffs, since there is no city record of their salary, although once they were chosen by the common council one might expect them to have been paid by the chamber. Obviously the undersheriff was entitled to a share of the various fines and amercements, and also the fees for enrolments, that came his way in the sheriffs' court.

But the decision by the common council in 1441 that they should choose the undersheriffs reflected the fact that this officer was no longer exclusively the servant or underling of the sheriff. His tasks extended beyond the court that he served and beyond the terms of his oath. Thomas Burgoyne, who was an undersheriff from 1434 until 1470 served on a number of city committees, was sent on deputations to the king, and in 1445 was chosen as one of the city's MPs.[153] As the job became more important, so more able men were attracted to it: several moved on to serve the city as recorder and ultimately a number of undersheriffs—Burgoyne, John Fray, John Markham, and John Fortescue—rose to be royal justices.

While the most senior of the sheriffs' clerks 'took off' and became an important civic legal officer, the second clerk, or 'secondary', became effectively the head of the sheriffs' clerical household. The office is mentioned as early as 1356 when the

149 *LBL*, x; oath, *LBD*, 3, *Liber Albus*, 317–8.

150 Year 1441, CLRO, Journal 3, fos. 88^{v}, 89; *LBK*, 257. In 1450 it was decided that the undersheriffs should be elected annually but this, as in the case of the chamberlain, meant, in fact, an annual approval by the commonalty, 2 October 1450: CLRO, Journal 5, fo. 47^{v}, and see Barron, 'Government of London', 104; the election of undersheriffs is recorded in 1463 and 1485: *LBL*, 35–6, 227.

151 *LBD*, 3; *Liber Albus*, 274–5.

152 *London Possessory Assizes: A Calendar*, ed. H. M. Chew (London Record Society, 1965), p. xiii; the undersheriff had a clerk: ibid. and *LBK*, 345.

153 Barron, 'Government of London', 166–7.

secondaries were supposed to be elected annually but it seems that they in fact remained in office during good behaviour.[154] They were sworn to office and they were senior to the two clerks of the papers and to the numerous other clerks known sometimes as 'clerks of the counters' or sheriffs' clerks, whose numbers fluctuated. In the early fourteenth century the sheriffs had been allowed four clerks each but the numbers rose on occasion to six or nine.[155] In 1416-1 the two sheriffs had eleven clerks sworn and it is likely that the clerical staff expanded remorselessly as the 'written word' took over from 'memory' and as the population of the city began once more to grow.[156]

The counters were not simply full of clerks assiduously copying up records of cases and entering royal writs into registers. There were considerable numbers also of serjeants and valets or grooms. Each sheriff was supposed to have only four serjeants in the early fourteenth century but the number had grown to ten or eleven for each sheriff by the time they came to be sworn in 1416, and in 1452 the commonalty asked that the sheriffs should be limited to twelve serjeants each. There was concern that they should be men of substance since if there were a good many of them they could not get a living except by 'extortion and oppression of the common people'.[157] In spite of the limitation to twelve serjeants, the number seems frequently to have been exceeded and in 1460 the sheriffs were allowed to have as many sergeants as they wished provided that all those who were chosen for office were freemen of the city.[158] But four years later the restriction to twelve serjeants was reimposed.

The serjeants' tasks included summoning people to court, assembling them for inquests and general policing of the city streets on the sheriff's behalf.[159] Certain sums were allocated to them for particular tasks which they performed, but they did not receive a salary and were dependent upon rewards from the sheriffs themselves, and whatever they could make from the office.[160] Clearly the situation was not very satisfactory and was open to abuse. Doubtless it was because of the possibilities of abuse that in 1481 the sheriffs' sergeants and valets were forbidden to sell ale retail.[161] The attempts to regulate the size of the sheriffs' household reflect the anxiety felt about the activities of their servants. In the fourteenth century the recorded complaints relate mainly to brutal behaviour and unjust exactions from

[154] Year 1356, *LBG*, 7; for regulations governing numbers and conduct in office, see *Liber Albus* (Rolls Series), i. 519–25, promulgated in 1393/4, *LBH*, 402, and 1486, *LBL*, 235. In 1494 it was decided that secondaries were to remain in office during good behaviour, i.e. there was no need for ritual annual elections, *LBL*, 300–1.

[155] Williams, *Medieval London*, 93.

[156] Year 1452, commonalty wanted the sheriffs limited to four clerks each (the secondary, the clerk of the papers, and two others apart from the undersheriff and his staff, CLRO, Journal 5, fo.77.

[157] Williams, *Medieval London*, 93; 1404, sheriffs to have eight serjeants each: *LBI*, 32–3; 1416, 1417, 1424, CLRO, Journal 1, fos. 1^{v}, 39^{v}, ibid. 2, fo. 28^{v}; 1452, ibid. 5, fo. 77^{v}; *LBK*, 345–7.

[158] October 1453, each sheriff to have two serjeants and one clerk more than allowed by ordinance, CLRO, Journal 5, fos. 122^{v}, 130; decision to remove the limitation, 22 September 1460, Journal 6, fo. 267.

[159] e.g. 18 July 1440, CLRO, Journal 3, fo. 47^{v}.

[160] 14 April 1367, at an assize of *novel disseisin* the jury awarded 100*s*. to the plaintiff of which 20*s*. was to be given to the sheriffs' clerks, and 6*s*. 8*d*. to the serjeants, *Possessory Assizes*, 42.

[161] *LBL*, 182.

victuallers.[162] The job obviously could be dangerous: when Richard Parys, one of the sheriff's serjeants, came to collect a fine from Thomas Parker, he was told that if he entered the house, Parker would sheath his dagger in his bosom.[163] During the period 1416–63 seven of the sheriffs' servants were dismissed and eight were sent to prison. Their offences included arrest contrary to civic ordinances, assault, acting before being sworn to office, disparaging the recorder, ignoring a mayoral precept, attacking a prisoner, packing a jury, and releasing prisoners without authority.[164] But some were rewarded: Nicholas Ivory, a valet, was granted 13*s.* 4*d.* when he was mortally ill 'for his good services and many costs when in his office for the honour of the city'.[165] Several were promoted, however, to become, for example, esquires of the mayor, a royal serjeant-at-arms, waterbailiff, or bailiff of Middlesex.[166] In addition to the serjeants, the sheriff's household also included valets: their numbers are not specified and their particular task seems to have been to requisition horses and carts for civic purposes.[167] To be a member of a sheriff's entourage was probably not an attractive job: the work was dangerous and unpopular, combining the roles of law enforcement officer, rent collector and taxman, and the remuneration was uncertain and inadequate. But the sheriffs' servants also came into contact with men of influence and authority in the city and could hope to be promoted to offices of greater status and more legitimate reward.

CONCLUSION

The office of sheriff was much older than that of the mayor and, in the thirteenth century, the sheriffs were still men of considerable importance in London. This can be clearly seen from the way in which Arnald fitz-Thedmar starts each year in his chronicle with the names of the sheriffs rather than that of the mayor. The sheriffs had a financial responsibility to the Crown that the mayor never had. But, by degrees, the mayor's office grew in importance and it was the day of his, rather than the sheriffs', riding to Westminster to take his oath that became the premier event in the civic ritual year. Moreover, the mayor's court was more prestigious than those of the sheriffs: not because of the value, nor indeed the number, of cases tried in the mayor's court, but because of the role it played in the development of mercantile law and equitable jurisdiction in the city.

Thus, by the late fourteenth century, the mayor was likely to be an older man who had already served as sheriff and had been an alderman for some years.

[162] December 1312, *LBE*, 13; 1321, it was said that unlawful fines had been collected from the butchers at Eastcheap, *Eyre 1321*, ii. 265; in 1379 and 1382, invitations to complain against the sheriffs' staffs were publicly proclaimed: *LBH*, 133, 199; in 1391, a serjeant was dismissed for negligence in allowing a prisoner to escape: *CPMR 1381–1412*, 179.

[163] 28 July 1453, CLRO, Journal 5, fo. 116.

[164] See Barron, 'Government of London', 110–11.

[165] 5 May 1458, CLRO, Journal 6, fo. 242.

[166] Barron, 'Government of London', 111 and n.

[167] The valets were not to take the horses and carts of those bringing goods to London to sell, but only those horses and carts which were plying for hire: *Liber Albus*, 319; for their duties generally, see ibid. 47; *LBI*, 115 (where they are described simply as 'officers'). But they were sufficiently important to be sworn to office—to behave as loyal men: *Liber Albus*, 319.

Sheriffs, by contrast, were younger men at the start of their civic careers: some were not yet aldermen when they were elected to the shrievalty and a few never became aldermen. Their tasks were more physically demanding than those of the mayor and although John Carpenter described them as the 'eyes' of the mayor he might as well have said that they were his strong arms, for they were, in effect, senior city police officers for their year of office.

The mayor remained, at the end as at the beginning of the period, the most important person in the city. But he no longer served for years at a time as he had done in the thirteenth century: the honour, the labour, and the expense were now distributed more widely amongst the aldermanic class. Few men served more than once, and to be three times mayor of London was extremely rare by the fifteenth century. Perhaps because the officer changed every year the office itself took on a greater ritual significance. The mayor acquired an esquire to carry his sword and his seal and a permanent household of three serjeants paid at the city's expense. Edward IV recognized this elevated status by increasingly conferring knighthoods on London mayors. Yet the elaboration of the outward and visible trappings of the mayoralty concealed an inward waning of effective power and authority. The explosion of London's population in the sixteenth century was to render the powers vested in the mayor of London almost useless since he could not enforce order and discipline upon a population that spilled out beyond the limits of the city's judicial authority. So power—if not prestige—passed down to the aldermen and their deputies, to the masters and wardens of the city companies, and, ultimately, in the sixteenth century to vestries where men struggled to implement national legislation and civic ordinances in their own neighbourhoods and communities. The fifteenth century may well have marked the apogee of mayoral power, when the city was small enough for many to participate in government and for the governors, be they aldermen, or the mayor, or the civic bureaucracy, to know and be known.

Whereas most mayors had served as aldermen, sheriffs were comparatively inexperienced and, indeed, not all aldermen were well prepared for the tasks they had to undertake once they became mayor. In order to help these comparatively inexperienced and annually elected officers there grew up a sophisticated London civil service. The sheriffs had particular need of trained help because of the complex judicial and financial relationship between the city and the Crown, hence the development of the important office of undersheriff and the significant clerical support staff headed by the secondary. Those who served the mayor as members of his household also became more permanent and were seen to be civic officials rather than members of a mayor's personal retinue. In this way there grew up a trained city bureaucracy able to support and advise the inevitably amateur governors of London as they attempted to rule the city in an increasingly professional world. The mayors and sheriffs of London remained of great importance as expressions of civic pride, as exemplars, and as energizing agents, but their success depended upon the creation and maintenance of an effective and professional civic bureaucracy.

CHAPTER EIGHT

The Government of London: A Civic Bureaucracy

Apart from the three annually elected and essentially amateur offices of the mayor and sheriffs, the city was also served by a permanent civil service or town hall bureaucracy. In the thirteenth century there were two particularly prominent civic civil servants, the chamberlain and the common clerk.[1] The common serjeant, who was very important as the city's prosecutor and legal adviser, emerged early in the course of the fourteenth century but was never as important as the recorder. Indeed by the fifteenth century it was the recorder who was the highest paid and the most prestigious member of the civic hierarchy, and aspiring lawyers who held the office of common serjeant would hope to be promoted to that of recorder in due course.[2]

THE RECORDER

Not surprisingly the recorder's office emerges at the same time as the legal profession itself takes shape. The office (although not the title) seems to have appeared first in 1298, although the first recorder *eo nomine* was John de Wengrave who was appointed in 1304 at the substantial salary of £10 p.a. His duties were primarily concerned with running the Husting court and he was to receive 20*d.* for every deed or testament enrolled there.[3] Six years later it was decided that Wengrave should have an extra £5 p.a.[4]

From the 1320s it seems to have been customary for a man to be elected as recorder and admitted to an aldermanry almost simultaneously: William de Haldene was admitted to the freedom and sworn as alderman of Tower ward and as recorder of the city all on the same day, 29 June 1365.[5] But, with the development

[1] G. A. Williams, *Medieval London from Commune to Capital* (London, 1963), 93–6.

[2] E.g. Gregory de Norton, common serjeant 1319–27, recorder 1329–39; John Tremayne, common serjeant 1388–90, recorder 1390–2; Alexander Anne common serjeant 1423–36, recorder 1436–8; Robert Danvers common serjeant 1441–2, recorder 1442–50; Thomas Billing common serjeant 1443–9, recorder 1450–4; Thomas Ursewyk common serjeant 1453–4, recorder 1454–71.

[3] For a list of recorders, see App. 2 (i); *LBC*, 132–3; *The Eyre of London, 14 Edward II AD 1321*, ed. H. M. Cam, 2 vols. (Selden Society, 1968–9), i, pp. xxvii and n. 3, 15.

[4] *LBD*, 233; 1329, Gregory de Norton the recorder was also to receive an extra £5, together with the same livery as that worn by the aldermen: *LBE*, 242–3; *Memorials*, 177–8.

[5] *LBG*, 193.

of the legal profession, it became necessary, perhaps, to have an expert lawyer to act for the city. When William Cheyne was chosen as the city's recorder in 1377 he was not made an alderman and from this date recorders never served also as aldermen. The recorder was, however, seen as the servant and ally of the court of aldermen and shared their livery.

In the fifteenth century we know something of how the recorder was chosen. Usually the aldermen came to an unanimous decision: sometimes they voted. In 1426 John Symond received 13 votes while his rival scored only 3.[6] In 1450 Thomas Billing was elected at the meeting of the commonalty where the sheriffs were chosen, but the clerk of the Journals was careful to note that the recorder had been elected by the mayor and aldermen alone.[7] On one occasion in 1440 the king tried to intervene in the election of the recorder, but since the royal candidate was not named, it is not possible to know if the royal influence prevailed.[8] By the early fifteenth century the recorder was receiving a salary of £66 13*s.* 4*d.* p.a.—a considerable increase on the £10 of a hundred years before, and a vivid testimony to the growing prestige and worldly success of the legal profession.[9] Not only did the recorder wear the alderman's livery but he also had a clerk who was entitled to wear the same livery as the serjeants who served the chamberlain.[10] On occasion the recorder's salary was in arrears but, on the other hand, if he served the city well he might receive a pension.[11]

Although in the early fourteenth century the recorder's duties had been primarily located in the Husting court, by the following century his brief was much wider. According to the terms of his oath he was to be skilled in law and to sit with the mayor when he heard pleas and delivered judgments. If complaints about the justice in the city's courts were brought to the royal justices sitting at St Martin's, the recorder had to defend the city by making a verbal report on the process in question. He was required to see to the recording and enrolment of pleas in the Husting court, to administer the same law to rich and poor alike, to care for orphans and to keep the city's secrets.[12] It is possible to check the assiduousness with which the recorder attended meetings of the court of aldermen and mayor's court, for the names of those present were noted in the Journals from 1416. It is

[6] CLRO, Journal 2, fo. 86. When Thomas Cokayne was elected as recorder on 27 October 1438, 'p' for 'placet' was written over the name of every alderman present except one, CLRO, Journal 3, fo. 163v.

[7] CLRO, Journal 5, fo. 46v.

[8] 6 and 13 July 1440, John Bowys was sworn as recorder: CLRO, Journal 3, fos. 45v, 46.

[9] In 1378 the recorder had complained about the inadequacy of his salary and had pointed out that he derived very little income from the enrolment of deeds and wills in the Husting court, and nothing like the £120 from that source that he had been promised. He was, instead, granted 40 marks, i.e. £26 13*s.* 4*d.*, in addition to his yearly fee of £40, which brought his total salary to £66 13*s.* 4*d.*, *LBH*, 100.

[10] *Liber Albus*, 42–3.

[11] Robert Danvers, the recorder in 1442–50, was still owed 100 marks in March 1452, CLRO, Journal 5, fo. 72v.; John Barton in 1422 received a pension of £10 a quarter and John Bowys, when he was old and infirm in 1442 was allowed 20 marks a year, CLRO, Journal 2, fo. 1; ibid. 3, fo. 41.

[12] *Liber Albus*, 42–3, 308–9; oath, *LBD*, 33. In 1440 the recorder had to defend the city's right to respond verbally to the royal judges at St Martin le Grand: CLRO, Journal 3, fos. 34, 41v; *CPMR 1437–57*, 38.

extremely rare for the recorder to be absent from meetings of the court. His skilled legal knowledge, and the fact that he did not come and go every year as the mayor did, must have meant that the influence of the recorder on civic government could be very considerable. It was, perhaps, because of his impartiality and continuity in office that the recorder also acted as returning officer at the mayor's election. When, in October 1426, the city was without a recorder, the prior of Holy Trinity Aldgate (and *ipso facto* alderman of Portsoken ward) was chosen to examine the votes cast and report faithfully as to who had been chosen.[13] The recorder was also used on civic deputations: for example, Robert Danvers was sent in July 1444 with others to report to the lord chancellor at Chiswick about the response of the mayor and aldermen to the king's request for a loan.[14] The services of the recorder were also frequently required as an arbiter in disputes between citizens, or as a witness at the acknowledgement (or registration) of their deeds and wills.[15] Three of the fifteenth-century recorders also served the city as MPs.[16]

On occasion recorders were accused by aggrieved litigants of failing to be impartial. In 1417, John Barton, who was both the city's recorder and, at the time, the steward of St Albans abbey, which was then at loggerheads with the town of Barnet, was accused of treating William Redehead unjustly because he came from Barnet.[17] But such accusations appear infrequently. The main problem, from the point of view of the mayor and aldermen, was to secure the sole and undivided attention of the city's recorder. By 1378 it had been expressly laid down that the recorder was not to receive any fee or livery from another lord or client, that is, the city did not want its recorder to be retained by anyone else, although if John Barton was still the steward of St Albans abbey in 1417, two years after his election as the city's recorder, then this ordinance had not been completely effective.[18] But Alexander Anne who had been recorder for two years seems to have been criticized for not giving the city his undivided loyalty and his successor was appointed on the express condition that he accepted no fee except that of the city.[19] When Thomas Billing became a serjeant-at-law and found that he could be profitably employed at Westminster, and on assizes elsewhere, he resigned his office as recorder.[20] In fact Billing went on to become a justice of the King's Bench in 1464 and, ultimately, chief justice from 1469 to 1481. Billing was one of five fifteenth-century London recorders who moved on to royal judicial office and by this period it is clear that the recordership of London was becoming a recognized stage in the *cursus honorum* leading to the judicial bench.[21] The court of aldermen paid the recorder a high

[13] *Liber Albus*, 21; CLRO, Journal 2, fo. 85v.

[14] 17 July 1444, CLRO, Journal 4, fo. 34v.

[15] As arbiter, see *CPMR 1413–37*, 2, 39, 177; *CPMR 1437–57*, 48; as witness to acknowledgements, ibid. 118, 126, 137.

[16] John Bowys was MP in 1442; Thomas Billing in 1449; Thomas Urswyk in 1463, 1467 and 1470: A. B. Beaven, *The Aldermen of the City of London*, 2 vols. (London, 1908–13) , i. 272.

[17] CLRO, Journal 1, fo. 12v; in 1455, Thomas Shelley, a mercer, accused the recorder of being 'chief counsel' with Shelley's opponent, Simon Dawdeley: CLRO, Journal 5, fo. 254.

[18] *LBH*, 100.

[19] 15 and 21 October 1438, CLRO, Journal 3, fo. 163, 163v.

[20] 3 October 1454, CLRO, Journal 5, fo. 196.

[21] John Prestone, recorder 1406–15, justice of the common pleas 1415–28; John Fray, recorder 1420–6, baron of the Exchequer, 1425, chief baron, 1436–48; Robert Danvers, recorder 1442–50, justice of the

salary—the highest of any civic officer—and while they recognized that he would be likely to move on to royal service, during the time he was employed by the city the aldermen expected his undivided attention.

THE CHAMBERLAIN

The chamberlain's office was older than that of the recorder but never achieved the elevated status of the legal office.[22] In the earlier period the Crown had appointed chamberlains for London. The office appears first in 1237 and, more clearly, in the reign of Edward I when so much in city government was being crystallized or defined.[23] The households of great lords usually had two chamberlains—perhaps to act as a check on each other's activities—and so it was with the city of London until 1300 when it was decided to have only one chamberlain.[24] Throughout the period it would seem that the chamberlain received only £10 p.a. for his labour for the city, in marked contrast to the rich salary of the recorder which rose from £10 in the early fourteenth century to nearly £70 at the end of the fourteenth century.[25] In part this difference reflects the kind of fees that skilled lawyers could command elsewhere. But there was another difference: the lawyer was a professional who was expected to devote his whole time to the business of the city; the chamberlain, on the other hand, was an amateur in the sense that he continued to practise his craft or trade while acting as chamberlain. An analysis of the thirty or so men who are known to have acted as chamberlain from 1300 onwards reveals that, as one might expect, most of them were drawn from the mercantile companies: mercers (7), grocers (6), fishmongers (5), goldsmiths (3), apothecaries (2), drapers (2), and one each from the cornmongers, ironmongers, woolmongers, corders, skinners, and, in the fifteenth century, a tailor, Robert Colwyche, in 1463 and, perhaps more surprisingly, a painter, William Milbourne, in 1492. It may be because the chamberlain was an amateur—not quite as amateur as the mayor and sheriffs, but more so than the recorder and common clerk—that his household developed comparatively early, as we shall see. The chamberlain was not provided with a house (doubtless he already had one of his own), nor was he given a livery or any perquisites.[26] If he discharged his office faithfully he might be given a reward for good and diligent service. When John Sturgeon left the chamberlain's office in 1454

common pleas 1450–67; Thomas Urswyk, recorder 1454–71, chief baron of the Exchequer 1471–9; Humphrey Starky, recorder 1471–83, chief baron of the Exchequer, 1483–6.

22 For a study of the origins and responsibilities of the office, and for a list of the chamberlains, see B. Masters, *The Chamberlain of the City of London 1273–1987* (London, 1988); for a list of chamberlains, see App. 2 (iv).

23 Masters, *The Chamberlain*, ch. 2; Williams, *Medieval London*, 91, 94.

24 *LBA*, p. v; for examples of two named chamberlains serving together, see 1237, ibid. 15; 1298, *LBB*, 70, 78; 1300, *LBC*, 65; Masters, *The Chamberlain*, 4–5. It may have been exceptional to have two city chamberlains serving together, even before 1300.

25 Years 1311–12, he was to receive £10 p.a.: *LBD*, 313; the same in 1336: *LBE*, 291, and in the early fifteenth century: *Liber Albus*, 47–8.

26 Masters, *The Chamberlain*, 87.

after four years' service he was rewarded with an annual robe at Christmas and a 'golden handshake' of £22 16*s.* 8*d*, although £12 of this was, in fact, the reimbursement of money that he had himself spent on the city's affairs.[27]

In the thirteenth century the chamberlain appears to have been chosen by the mayor and aldermen, but from 1304 there was a more 'popular' element in his selection and in 1310 the chamberlain was elected by the mayor, aldermen, and commonalty.[28] Edward II's charter of 1319—the city's 'Great Charter'—confirmed that the chamberlain should be elected and removable at the will of the commonalty.[29] Since the duties of the chamberlain were predominantly financial this measure of democracy is understandable and runs parallel with the increasing participation of the commons in providing consent to royal taxation. The chamberlain was usually re-elected every year (although he might serve for several years consecutively), and after 1404 it was decided that the annual election should take place at the same meeting (of the mayor, aldermen and common council) held on 21 September, when the sheriffs, bridgewardens, and auditors were chosen. An initial experiment to prevent the re-election of a chamberlain who had served for two years was abandoned as impractical.[30] It is likely that the mayor and aldermen continued to influence the election of the chamberlain: John Bederenden, for example, was re-elected as chamberlain in 1423 on the advice of the mayor and aldermen.[31] Moreover, when the commonalty tried to elect William Cottisbrook as chamberlain during the artisan troubles of 1443, the aldermen reinstated John Chichele in office and in the following year re-elected him to office without consulting the commonalty.[32] Although John Middleton was officially elected chamberlain by an 'immense commonalty' in 1449, the Journal entry makes clear that it was the mayor and aldermen who *voted* for Middleton, who received 15 of the 18 votes cast.[33] Then in 1491 it was decided that the mayor and aldermen should nominate two men, from whom the commonalty were to choose one as chamberlain—that is, the reverse of the procedure whereby the commonalty nominated two aldermen from among whom the aldermen chose one as mayor.[34] So, although this officer had originally been chosen by the citizens at large, by the end of the period the aldermen had secured the right to select two candidates, one of whom the commonalty would select to serve as chamberlain for the next year.[35] The author of the *Great Chronicle* argued that the old system had produced chamberlains who were 'nedy men and unhable for the office' which had 'doon the Cyte

[27] 27–28 September 1454, CLRO, Journal 5, fo. 194, 194ᵛ.

[28] Year 1310, election of Luke de Haveryng, *LBD*, 237; cf. the election of John le Mazeliner by the commonalty in November 1311, ibid. 275; Masters, *The Chamberlain*, 15–16.

[29] *Historical Charters and Constitutional Documents of the City of London*, ed. W. de Gray Birch (rev. edn. London, 1887), 49.

[30] Year 1414, *LBI*, 33, 35; *Liber Albus*, 48; Masters, *The Chamberlain*, 17–18. The chamberlain's election at the September meeting is not recorded in the Letter Book during the period 1408–17: *LBI*, 68–9, 189.

[31] 13 September 1423, CLRO, Journal 2, fo. 8ᵛ.

[32] C. Barron, 'Ralph Holland and the London Radicals, 1438–1444', in R. Holt and G. Rosser (eds.), *The Medieval Town: A Reader in English Urban History 1200–1540* (London, 1991), 160–83, esp. 174–5.

[33] 21 September 1449, CLRO, Journal 5, fo. 15; *LBK*, 328–9.

[34] *LBL*, 279; Masters, *The Chamberlain*, 19, 20 n. 26.

[35] Year 1491, *LBL*, 279.

noo good nor worshypp'.[36] At the same time it was decided that the two bridgewardens, who had customarily been elected by the commonalty at the same time as the chamberlain, should now be chosen from a panel of four preselected by the aldermen.[37] In this way the aldermen gained a measure of control over the selection of those who had the oversight of the city's finances and corporate estates. It may have been the increasing complexity of city finance that led the aldermen to intervene in this way in the selection of the chamberlains and bridgewardens. Over the centuries many wealthy Londoners had bequeathed lands to the city and to the Bridge for charitable and pious purposes so that the city's property portfolio had grown considerably, and the role of the chamberlains and bridgewardens as estates bursars and rent collectors had developed apace. The size of the task now presented to the chamberlains—in spite of the development of the highly professional financial bureaucracy—was extremely demanding and complex, and required an expert rather than a gifted amateur.

The chamberlain, like all medieval finance officers, was held personally responsible for the city's money which passed, or should have passed, through his hands. This personal responsibility was made clear by the appearance before the mayor and aldermen of the executors of dead chamberlains, accounting for the revenues of the office and obtaining acquittances. Andrew Horn served as chamberlain from 1320 until his death in 1328 and in 1329 his executors produced their accounts and were acquitted.[38] In this early period the accounts were audited spasmodically and at irregular intervals. In 1373 a committee of two aldermen and two commoners was appointed to audit the chamberlain's account, and it seems to have been in the 1370s that it was decided that there should be annual audits and that a certain number of aldermen and commoners, usually but not invariably at this stage two aldermen and four commoners, should be elected each year to audit the accounts.[39] Perhaps the audit was not found to be a sufficient check upon the activities of the chamberlain for in 1448 for the first time the elected chamberlain, the mercer John Middleton, was required to find 'sufficient security' before taking up office.[40] In the following year he, together with five others, produced security to four aldermen, the recorder and the common serjeant-at-law.[41] Five years later

[36] *The Great Chronicle of London*, ed. A. H. Thomas and I. D. Thornley (London, 1938), 245.

[37] Masters, *The Chamberlain*, 18–19.

[38] Year 1329, *Memorials*, 176. Similarly the executors of Thomas de Maryns (chamberlain 1336–49) rendered account in 1349: *LBF*, 196. The executors of John de Cantebrigge (chamberlain *c.*1359–74) settled his account in 1374: *LBG*, 332, 333. John Dode (chamberlain 1313–18) was not acquitted on his account until 1322: *LBE*, 169–70. Some of the acquittances for their accounts for the early chamberlains were also recorded, e.g. Nicholas Pycot's executors were acquitted in October 1313: *LBE*, 12. Thomas Prentiz who was removed from office was acquitted on his account, but had to pay 100*s*.: *LBE*, 92.

[39] Year 1373, *LBG*, 316; 1378, *LBH*, 102; 1379, four aldermen and eight commoners elected: *LBH*, 136; 1380, ibid. 153; 1381, four aldermen and four commoners: ibid. 168; 1382, ibid. 198; 1383, two aldermen and two commoners, ibid. 219. John Carpenter records that the chamberlain was to account every year between the feasts of Michaelmas (September 29) and SS Simon and Jude (October 28) before two aldermen and four commoners: *Liber Albus*, 48. See Masters, *The Chamberlain*, 8, and also *Chamber Accounts of the Sixteenth Century*, ed. B. Masters (London Record Society,1984), pp. x–xi.

[40] 21 September 1448, CLRO, Journal 4, fo. 228.

[41] 23 September 1449, CLRO, Journal 5, fo. 15^{v}.

the new chamberlain, Thomas Thornton, a draper, had to provide sureties of £1,000 shared with four other drapers, which suggests that the city's revenue at this date must have been very considerable and that the opportunities for the temporary deployment of capital may also have proved very attractive.[42]

Almost all the chamberlains' accounts for the medieval period have been destroyed either in the great fire of 1666 or in a fire in the chamberlain's office in the late eighteenth century. A few of the accounts, summarized from the more detailed originals, were copied into the city's Letter Books between 1330 and 1346 and provide a partial, but nevertheless welcome, view of the activities of the chamberlain at that period.[43] The chamberlain's duties were listed in the *Liber Albus* and defined by his oath: they are further revealed in the fourteenth-century accounts and in the fifteenth-century Journals. According to his oath the chamberlain was required to protect the rights of orphans, to safeguard the city's records, to accept no-one into the freedom except in accordance with the city's ordinances, and to maintain, and as far as possible increase, the profits from the city's lands and rents.[44] The oath does not cover all the tasks that fell to the chamberlain but it includes some important aspects of his work.

Presumably the primary duty of the chamberlain, although it was not defined in his oath, was to collect the city's revenues and to spend them properly and in accordance with due instructions. There were many sources of revenue, for example fines from victuallers who transgressed the various assizes, but the city's steadiest sources of income were the fees paid by masters when they enrolled the indentures of their apprentices, and by the apprentices themselves when they had completed their term and wished to be entered as freemen of the city.[45] Judging by the numbers of apprentice and freedom entries in the years 1309–12 when the records were entered in the city's Letter Book D, the sums must have been quite considerable: they brought in about £80 a year at this period.[46] Since the freedom of London was a coveted status there must have been pressure on the chamberlain to enter men in the freedom rolls illegally, for a small consideration. Hence the clause in the oath. Since the chamberlain saw apprentices at the beginning of their term when their indentures were enrolled, it seems to have fallen to him to hold a court at which apprentices could complain about their masters.[47] Although apprentices continued to turn to the chamberlain for redress, it is clear that in

[42] 30 September 1454, ibid. 195; in 1474 William Philip, a goldsmith, also had to provide recognizances of £1,000 when he was elected chamberlain: *CPMR 1458–83*, 82.

[43] Year 1330 account, *LBE*, 247; 1331–2, ibid. 270–71; 1332–5, ibid. 292; *c.*1337, *Memorials*, 196–8; 1337–9, ibid. 206–7; 1339–40, *LBF*, 54–5; 1343, ibid. 89; 1343–6, ibid. 154; and see Masters, *Chamber Accounts*, pp. x–xi. There is also a list of rents due to the chamber dated before 1304, *LBC*, 237–9.

[44] *Liber Albus*, 309–10.

[45] The chamberlain could also charge for enrolling deeds and indentures in the city's Letter Books. This source of income produced 7*s.* 6*d.* in 1366–67, *LBG*, 212, 218; 25s in 1367–68, *ibid.*, 233; 17*s.* 6*d.* in 1368–69, *ibid.*, 251; 10*s.* in 1369–70, *ibid.*, 267.

[46] *LBD*, 35–96 (freemen), 96–179 (apprentice enrolments and the freedom entries of former apprentices); Masters, *The Chamberlain*, 8, 13.

[47] For evidence of this court at work, see meetings of 7 and 11 February 1299, among the records of the mayor's court: *EMCR 1298–1307*, 46–8; see also *CPMR 1323–64*, 123 and n.

particularly difficult cases the parties increasingly had recourse to the jurisdiction of the mayor.[48]

The responsibility of the chamberlain for the city's lands and tenements could be onerous. He was expected to collect the rents—a task he usually deputed to one of his serjeants[49]—and also to maintain the properties in question. It is, perhaps, because of the chamberlain's responsibility for repairs that he answers in his accounts for stores of wood and stone kept in and around Guildhall yard.[50] The city's lands could be leased under the seal of the chamber (first recorded in 1325) or, more usually in the later period, under the city's common seal.[51] It is unlikely that the chamberlain would lease city properties without consulting the mayor and aldermen.[52] The chamberlain's work as 'estates bursar' tended to increase as pious Londoners bequeathed estates to be administered by the city for pious purposes. The former mayor, John Philipot (d.*c.*1389), left to the city substantial properties in Cheapside, Lombard Street, Pudding Lane, around Lambeth Hill, and near Queenhithe.[53] Fifteenth-century bequests by another former mayor, John Reynwell (d.1445) and by the former common clerk, John Carpenter (d.1442) brought in additional properties. Some of this property was earmarked for specific purposes: John Carpenter's bequest was used to support the schooling of four Guildhall chapel choristers.[54] In 1356 Adam Fraunceys and others had endowed the Guildhall chapel and college with lands. These properties were to provide an income out of which the chamberlain was to pay the salaries of the chaplains.[55] Land around the city wall, which was traditionally common land (or common soil, as it was known), was enclosed as commercial gardens and leased. In 1425 Moorfields was divided up into allotments and leased 'for the better profit of the community'.[56] On occasion the chamberlain was required to defend the common land from encroachments, as in 1453 when the rector and parishioners of St Botolph's Billingsgate tried to extend the east end of their church onto the common soil.[57]

[48] See S. Hovland, 'Apprenticeship in Later Medieval London, *c.*1300–*c.*1530', (Univ. of London, Ph.D. thesis, forthcoming), chapter C. 2.

[49] In 1375, William Greyngham, who had been a serjeant of the chamber since 1345, was granted a pension of 40*s.* and was described as 'sometime collector of rents of the chamber': *LBF*, 124; *LBH*, 15. In In 1454, John Sturgeon (chamberlain 1450–4) had paid John Deye £2 13*s.* 4*d.* p.a. to collect the rents due to the city from the tenements bequeathed by Sir John Philipot, grocer (d.1384): CLRO, Journal 5, fo. 194, 194^{v}.

[50] *LBE*, 304; in 1358 it was agreed by the mayor that the chamberlain himself should repair the weigh-house at Aldgate and have in return the use of the solar above the house, *LBG*, 103–4.

[51] Masters, *Chamber Accounts*, p. xxxii, n. 80.

[52] In 1359, with the assent of the mayor and aldermen, the chamberlain leased a new garden in the parish of St Giles Cripplegate, which had been lately enclosed by the mayor, for 10s p.a.: *LBG*, 121.

[53] *HW*, ii. 275–7.

[54] Masters, *Chamber Accounts*, pp. xiii, xxv–xvii; Masters, *The Chamberlain*, 7, also *CPMR 1458–82*, pp. ix–xiv .

[55] 2 July 1417, CLRO, Journal 1, fo. 24; C. Barron, *The Medieval Guildhall of London* (London, 1974), 23.

[56] 29 September 1425, CLRO, Journal 2, fo. 53.

[57] 10 May 1455, CLRO, Journal 5, fo. 241^{v}; *CPMR 1437–57*, p. ix.

The chamberlain was not solely responsible for city orphans, that is the fatherless children of London freemen (indeed the common serjeant had a particular responsibility in these matters), but he often took charge of the goods bequeathed to the orphan while the child remained a minor. The executors would hand over to the chamberlain the goods bequeathed to the child; he might entrust these goods to the child's guardian, whose appointment had to be approved by the mayor and aldermen, and, on coming of age, the orphan would come to court to acknowledge receipt of the goods.[58] Since all orphans were allocated to a guardian, the chamberlain in the medieval period rarely had possession of the goods for long, although on occasion the chamberlain himself might act as guardian and so be responsible more directly for the stewardship of the goods.[59]

The chamberlain's responsibility for the city's records came in the course of this period to be shared with, and then largely transferred to, the common clerk. Since the chamberlain was largely responsible for the city's cash, it is hardly surprising that valuable documents were also entrusted to him: royal tallies, title deeds, bonds, and obligations. His general responsibility for the city's records is suggested by the fact that the written records of financial matters, for example recognizances of debt taken before the chamberlain in the years 1276–1312,[60] or the entries of apprentices and freemen in 1306–9, or the summarized city accounts in 1330–46, were all entered in the city's main memoranda books, the Letter Books. When Nicholas Pycot died (chamberlain 1300–4) his executors brought into court numerous important documents relating to the city's financial affairs.[61] Andrew Horn, who became chamberlain in 1320, was already familiar with the city's records and compiled his famous custumal *Liber Horn* in 1311 *before* he became chamberlain. His career suggests that a knowledge of city records, custom, history, and law was considered to be an important qualification for a chamberlain at that date.[62] But by the time John Carpenter (admittedly a common clerk himself) was compiling his *Liber Albus* in the early fifteenth century, the responsibility for the records was shared between the chamberlain and the common clerk. A man who wished to consult the records had to ask permission of either the chamberlain or the common clerk; if the request seemed reasonable then a chamber clerk would show him the records and provide a copy as required, for a fee. A clerk who allowed unauthorized persons to see the records was to be severely punished.[63]

[58] Such acknowledgements appear frequently in the city's Letter Books, see Masters, *The Chamberlain*, 10–11.

[59] E.g. Andrew Horn assumed the guardianship of William le Fullere in 1315: *LBE*, 52; *Memorials*, 117–18; Masters, *The Chamberlain*, 11; see Ch. 11.

[60] Recognizances of debt were sometimes taken before the chamberlain at his own home, rather than at Guildhall, and for this he received 2*d*. for each pound of debt acknowledged, e.g. *LBA*, 26–9, 79, 225.

[61] Year 1315, *LBE*, 48.

[62] Masters, *The Chamberlain*, 23–5; J. Catto, 'Andrew Horn: Law and History in Fourteenth-Century England', in R. H. C. Davis and J. M. Wallace-Hadrill (eds.), *The Writing of History in the Middle Ages: Essays Presented to R. W. Southern* (Oxford, 1981), 367–91.

[63] *Liber Albus*, 48. In 1453 it was decided that an enquirer might only have a copy of a record made if the chamberlain or common clerk agreed, CLRO, Journal 5, fo. 135.

Precious documents and objects continued to be entrusted to the chamberlain in spite of the encroachments of the common clerk—for example, the indenture between the mayor and the royal treasurer in 1417 about the Spanish sword that the king had given to the Londoners as security for a loan.[64] After John Chichele ceased to be chamberlain in 1449 he was instructed to hand over a chest that contained books, evidences, and tallies belonging to the city which he had accumulated during his fifteen years in office.[65] But since the chamberlain was responsible for all the city's moneys until his account was audited and he was acquitted, it is understandable that he might wish to hang on to some of the documentation.

But, as with all the city's officials, the tasks performed by the chamberlain were not confined to those specified in his oath. The fifteenth-century Journals reveal that the chamberlain might attend the court of aldermen (but only infrequently, unlike the recorder who attended regularly) and could be appointed to serve on committees—particularly those that dealt with the raising and spending of money on civic projects, such as the rebuilding of Newgate gaol and prison in the 1450s.[66] When John Hill was chamberlain he found that he was expected to collect rush-boats and use the contents to get the city's streets cleaned; John Bederenden in 1425 had to collect aulnage (tax on cloth), and John Sturgeon was expected to provide samples of cloth for the aldermen's liveries and then to see to the ordering and making of the gowns. On another occasion in 1455 the chamberlain was instructed to resolve the quarrel that had arisen between the cobblers and the cordwainers. In short he was expected to act as a general city public servant and carry out faithfully a range of tasks that might be allocated to him.[67]

Since the chamberlain was essentially an elected amateur, it was particularly important that his household was staffed with competent men. John Carpenter explains that the chamberlain was to be served by three serjeants, who were to be elected and removed by common council (that is, the chamberlain did not choose his own household). These serjeants were to receive a salary of 40*s.* p.a. each and were to have a share of the fees for enrolling entries to the freedom. They were entitled to two liveries a year, like the members of the mayor's household, at the cost of the chamberlain himself. If a serjeant were negligent he was to be fined 40d at the first offence, 6*s.* 8*d.* at the second, and 10*s.* at the third. But if his crimes were 'outrageous' then he was to be removed from office The role of the chamber serjeants as described by Carpenter seems to be corroborated by the fourteenth-century records: the first recorded chamber serjeant was sworn in 1303 and, where salaries are recorded, the amount provided was 40*s.* On occasion chamber serjeants were generously pensioned.[68] In the fourteenth century, some chamber serjeants were granted housing: in the early 1300s, chamber serjeants Joice

[64] 2 October 1417, CLRO, Journal 1, fo. 35.

[65] 8 October 1451, ibid. 5, fo. 63v.

[66] Barron, 'Government of London', 98.

[67] Ibid. 121–2.

[68] John Juvenal is recorded as a serjeant of the chamber in 1299, but he was sworn to the office in 1303: *EMCR 1298–1307*, 29, 35; *LBC*, 126; 1314, Robert de Mounceny admitted as sergeant of the chamber at a salary of 40s p.a., *LBD*, 315; 1322, Joice Botedieu, serjeant of the chamber, retired on a pension of 40*s.* p.a., *LBE*, 161; 1365, Richard de Merstone, likewise: *LBG*, 204; 1375, William de Greyngham, likewise: *LBH*, 15.

Botedieu and Philip de Merdele were granted the 'gates' of Bishopsgate and Ludgate; in 1375 John Cobbe was given the houses at the Tower postern with the custody of the gate there, and William Wircester and Philip Walworth were granted rooms over Ludgate in 1378.[69] The tasks of the serjeants are less easy to pin down but it is clear that they were employed in collecting rents from city property, and Philip Walworth was responsible for sealing cloth in the city.[70] It would appear that the chamber serjeants were the elite among the civic serjeanty, perhaps because they were elected by common council and not chosen by individual chamberlains; moreover they were paid out of the chamber and held their jobs for life provided they behaved with propriety. John Cobbe who had been a serjeant to the mayor in 1375 was admitted as a serjeant of the chamber, which suggests that the chamber office was considered to be superior, or more desirable.[71]

It is likely that the chamber serjeants had some clerical or financial skills. Thomas de St Alban who was a chamber serjeant in 1360 later became the deputy coroner and John Strecche who was a serjeant in about 1375 was elsewhere described as a scrivener.[72] John Carpenter noted that the roll-call at meetings of the common council was taken by a serjeant of the chamber, although those who were absent were to be noted by 'a clerk of the chamber in a roll which he holds in his hands'.[73] The office of clerk to the chamberlain gained a new significance when David de Cotesbroke was appointed as controller, and granted a salary of 100*s.* p.a.—more than twice the salary of the chamber serjeants.[74] John Carpenter does not mention a salary but notes that the chamber clerk was entitled to half the fee paid for the enrolment of entries to the freedom, and also to whatever sum for his work the auditors of the chamberlain's annual account considered appropriate.[75] These men must have been extremely experienced, and they held the job for life. When Richard Osbarn retired from office in 1437 after serving since the beginning of the century he was provided with a house, an annual robe and a pension of £6 13*s.* 4*d.*[76] The growing importance of the office was recognized in 1454 when Robert Langford who had been in the chamberlain's office since 1437 and had succeeded William Chedworth as chamber clerk in 1450 was, on 28 September 1454,

[69] *c.*1310, *LBC*, 183; *LBH*, 2, 97; John Bandy on retirement in 1477 received a yearly gown and was to be allowed to eat and drink daily in the mayor's household 'as a serjeant of the mayor' for his lifetime: *CPMR 1458–82*, 108.

[70] In 1375, William de Greyngham retired and was described as 'sometime collector of rents of the chamber': *LBH*, 15; 1380, Philip Walworth appointed to seal cloths, to receive 2*d.* for a whole cloth and 1*d.* for smaller ones, *LBH*, 146.

[71] Year 1375, *LBH*, 14.

[72] Year 1360, *LBG*, 113; *London Possessory Assizes: A Calendar*, ed. H. M. Chew (London Record Society, 1965), nos. 48–9; *LBH*, 6.

[73] *Liber Albus*, 36.

[74] Masters, *The Chamberlain*, 27; 1311–12, *LBD*, 275, 276, 313. In 1380 John Marchaunt who was clerk of the chamber, also received 100*s.*: *LBH*, 163. William Chedworth, who was appointed in 1437, also received 100*s*: CLRO, Journal 3, fo. 191; for a list of chamber clerks/controllers, see App. 2 (v).

[75] *Liber Albus*, 43.

[76] CLRO, Journal 3, fo. 188^{v}. Osbarn had been provided with a fifty-year lease on a city house, but he had contributed 20 marks towards the costs of building it and paid 40*s.* p.a. rent for it: *LBI*, 6–7, 10–11.

sworn as controller and clerk to the chamberlain.[77] When John Hert succeeded Langford in 1478 it was laid down that he alone was to make up the chamber accounts and no other chamber clerk was to do this work. So by the end of the fifteenth century it is evident that the primary task of the controller was the preparation of the city's annual accounts.[78] But the Journals make it clear that a variety of tasks might fall on the controller's shoulders, such as organizing street cleaning, levying and disbursing money, attending the court of aldermen, acting as clerk to city committees, joining deputations sent to the king, or acting as an arbiter or executor. The chamber clerk (or controller) had acquired important and useful skills and his services were, not surprisingly, frequently in demand.[79] There were clearly close links between the chamberlain's clerk and the common clerk. John Carpenter acted as feoffee for Richard Osbarn (chamber clerk 1400–37) and in his will requested prayers for William Chedworth (chamber clerk 1437–45). Robert Langford (chamber clerk 1450–78) also acted as one of Carpenter's executors.[80]

The responsibilities shouldered by the chamberlain must have been considerable and the rewards were comparatively meagre. What, one wonders, attracted men to the office? Several chamberlains moved on to become aldermen and many, especially in the fifteenth century, served the city as MPs.[81] There is some evidence that a man who became chamberlain had already shown some interest in city finance or record-keeping. Andrew Horn had written or compiled his various books and custumals before his election as chamberlain in 1320. By the fifteenth century some proven ability in civic government or finance seems to have been the norm. Several fifteenth-century chamberlains had served first as auditors of the annual accounts or as common councilmen and had been active on various committees.[82] It seems to be clear, however, that some men took on the job of chamberlain in the hope of thereby becoming an alderman. John Sturgeon, a mercer, was a common councilman by 1437, served on numerous committees, and in 1445 was one of the city's MPs. He became chamberlain in 1450, but perhaps he was too ambitious: in 1446 he was accused of having written on a wall three times 'John Sturgeon alderman', and this ambition he never realized.[83] Both John Chichele and Thomas Thornton, though selected by wardmotes as candidates for aldermanries, were never selected by the court of aldermen. Only three of the thirteen

[77] CLRO, Journal 5, fos. 47, 194v.

[78] The rewards allocated to John Hert, the clerk of the chamber in 1492, were carefully specified and must have amounted to a tidy annual income. He was also to have under him a clerk paid by the city: *LBL*, 287.

[79] Barron, 'Government of London', 123; Richard Osbarn, described as 'clericus camerarii civitatis London' was appointed as the supervisor of the will of the wealthy and pious widow, Dame Margery Nerford, in 1417, see *Wills, Leases and Memoranda in the Book of Records of the Parish of St Christopher le Stocks in the City of London*, ed. E. Freshfield (privately printed, London 1895), 9.

[80] *HW* ii. 484–5; *CPMR 1458–82*, pp. ix, 128 n. 1, 130.

[81] Masters, *The Chamberlain*, 105–9.

[82] Barron, 'Government of London', 124–5.

[83] 24 January 1446, his accusers asserted that he had done much harm to the city as an MP: CLRO, Journal 4, fo. 119v.

fifteenth-century chamberlains, in fact, became aldermen. John Middleton, a mercer, was chamberlain in 1449 and a year later became sheriff and so relinquished the chamberlainship. He was presented as an alderman on three occasions before being finally selected for Faringdon Without in March 1456.[84] Robert Colwyche, a tailor, was elected chamberlain in 1463 and eleven years later became alderman of Faringdon Without—the most difficult ward, and the least popular.[85] The fact, however, that chamberlains were presented by wards as possible aldermen, although then rejected by the aldermen, may suggest that these men were more popular with the citizens at large than they were with the aldermen themselves. The chamberlain was elected by the citizenry and may have been viewed as dangerously populist by the aldermen.

THE COMMON CLERK

The third in the triumvirate of city officers, after the recorder and chamberlain, was the common clerk. He was not an amateur like the chamberlain but a permanent and paid officer, and he appears to emerge from the mists in the thirteenth century. The first common clerk whose name we know is Ralph Crepyn who is referred to as 'principal clerk of the city' in 1274–5.[86] But when Hugh de Waltham was elected in 1311 he was described as 'clerk of the commonalty'. He received a salary of 100*s.* p.a., that is, he was placed on the same level as the chief clerk to the chamberlain (the later controller).[87] Waltham's successor, elected in 1335, was also paid 100*s.* but when John de Shirbourne was chosen in the same year his salary was doubled to £10. John Carpenter, who had been recently elected to the office of common clerk, when he compiled the *Liber Albus* in about 1419, was particularly careful to describe the rewards and duties of the office. Although the salary remained still at £10 p.a. Carpenter noted that the common clerk also received 10*d.* for every deed or will enrolled in the Husting, 2*s.* for every deed enrolled in the mayor's court rolls, and 6*d.* for every writ drawn up for assizes of nuisance and freshforce.[88] Early common clerks may have been poorly remunerated—Hugh de Waltham's salary was two years in arrears in 1329[89]—yet the fifteenth century

[84] CLRO, Journal 5, fo. 56^{v}, 61; Journal 6, fos. 33, 26.

[85] CLRO, Journal 7, fo. 39; 1474, Journal 8, fo. 74.

[86] B. Masters, 'The Town Clerk', *The Guildhall Miscellany*, 3 (1969), 55–74, esp. 55. Ralph Crepyn [alias de Alegate], 'clerk of the city'; [Record Commission], *Rotuli Hundredorum temp. Hen. III & Edw I.*, 2 vols. (London, 1812), i. 428; John de Bauquell/Batequell/Banquell/Bankwell, 'clerk of the city', 1284: *LBA*, 161; and 'clerk deputed to receive recognizances', 1298: *CEMCR 1298–1307*, 27; for a list of common clerks, see App. 2 (vi).

[87] Years 1311–12, *LBD*, 275.

[88] *Liber Albus*, 47–8. Carpenter noted that the aldermen enrolled their deeds without payment. For the role of the common clerk in the assizes, see *Possessory Assizes*, p. xvii; *London Assize of Nuisance 1301–1431*, ed. H. M. Chew and W. Kellaway (London Record Society, 1973), p. xlv. During the period when John Carpenter was common clerk, an average of seventy-two deeds and wills were enrolled yearly in the Husting, which would, therefore, have brought a further 60*s.* p.a. into the pocket of the common clerk.

[89] *LBE*, 236.

clerks seem to have been both well rewarded and well regarded. John Marchaunt (common clerk, *c.*1399–1417 and John Carpenter's predecessor) was granted a house over the middle gate of Guildhall, and Roger Spicer (common clerk 1446–61) received a special reward of nearly £30.[90] John Carpenter (common clerk 1417–38) was given a special reward of 10 marks which may have been for his work in compiling *Liber Albus*, or for his work as an MP.[91] On the other hand, surviving records of the various companies make it clear that the common clerk was well placed to make a little extra money on the side by helping companies to draw up petitions for presentation to the mayor, writing letters, or offering good advice and counsel. John Carpenter, for example, was paid 20*s.* by the brewers in 1420 for offering counsel, and for other services he had performed for them.[92]

Carpenter wrote that the common clerk, like the chamberlain and common serjeant-at-law, was elected by common council and removable at its pleasure.[93] When John de Shirbourne was elected common clerk in 1335 he was said to have been chosen by the mayor, aldermen, and commonalty, although it is likely that in the fifteenth century the more amorphous body of the commonalty, which contained all the freemen, was replaced by the more limited constituency of the common council.[94] Once elected, the common clerk swore to defend the city's rights and liberties, to enter all the pleas in the Husting court and in the various assizes, to keep the city's secrets, and to keep safely the city's possessions entrusted to him. No records were to be shown that might harm the city, nor were those that contained a person's rights to be concealed.[95] It is difficult to know how faithfully the common clerks carried out these tasks, but only one was dismissed, and that was Roger Spicer who lost office in August 1461 because of his Lancastrian sympathies, although until then he had worked hard on the city's business.[96]

The developing role of the common clerk in the creation and safekeeping of the city's records can be charted over the two centuries. The common clerk had from the first been involved in writing up the assizes and keeping the Husting rolls. During the royal judicial inquiry in 1321, he was instructed, together with the mayor's clerk and the sheriffs' clerks, to make notes on matters raised during the inquiry 'lest for lack of notes they should be forgotten'.[97] Moreover, as early as Hugh de Waltham's tenure of the office (1311–35) the common clerk was the custodian of some of the city's legal records—for example, the roll of the royal inquiry of 1244.[98] But the city custumals seem to have been in the custody of the

90 Barron, 'Government of London', 127 and n.; Masters, 'Town Clerk', 58–9.

91 10 June 1440, CLRO, Journal 3, fo. 44. Hugh de Waltham (common clerk 1311–35) in 1324 was awarded 60*s.* for his efforts in securing repayment of a loan to the king: *LBE* 196; William Dunthorne was paid over £100 for compiling 'Liber Dunthorne': Masters, 'Town Clerk', 59.

92 Guildhall Library MS 5440, Brewers' Account Book 1418–1440, fos. 25–26^{v}. See Barron, 'Government of London', 127–8 for other examples of company *douceurs* to common clerks.

93 *Liber Albus*, 47.

94 *LBD*, 275; *LBE*, 5, 290; *LBG*, 232; *LBH*, 8; *LBI*, 179–80; CLRO, Journal 3, fo. 164, ibid. 4, fo. 149; ibid. 6, fo. 7^{v}; see Ch. 6.

95 *Liber Albus*, 311–12.

96 5 August and 23 October 1461, CLRO, Journal 6, fos. 262, 82.

97 *Eyre 1321*, i. 7.

98 *Eyre 1244*, p. xiii.

chamberlain, and it was a future chamberlain, Andrew Horn, who saw to the compiling of a civic custumal, the *Liber Horn.* But by the early fifteenth century the custody of city records seems to be entrusted less often to the chamberlain and more often to the common clerk. John Carpenter was given the custody of financial obligations of various kinds and when the records of the shrievalty of Simon Wynchcombe (sheriff 1383–4) were finally brought into court in 1428, they were handed to Carpenter for safekeeping.[99] Moreover when John Middleton (chamberlain 1449–50) brought into court various documents relating to the Reynwell bequest of lands to the city, these were handed over, not to the chamberlain, but to the common clerk.[100] Similarly, when William Dunthorne was elected common clerk in 1461 it was decided that the chamberlain should hand various books and records over to him.[101] This transfer was made complete in the following year when the mayor and aldermen decided that all the records in the chamberlain's possession were to be handed over to the common clerk who was to have complete responsibility for them.[102] At the same time the common clerk seems to have been given more complete control over the business, the clerks, and the records of the mayor's court. He was to act as registrar of the court and keep a record of the various fines.[103]

It is also clear that it was becoming the duty of the common clerk not simply to keep the records safe, but also to compile them. John Carpenter assembled the *Liber Albus*, some of which he took from existing city custumals and other parts he himself wrote.[104] William Dunthorne in 1474 put together another custumal that carried his name, the 'Liber Dunthorne'.[105] It seems as if both Carpenter and Dunthorne composed these books of their own volition, perhaps out of rage at being unable to find their way around the city's numerous books and records. John Carpenter clearly had access to the city's Letter Books, for many of his precedents are derived from that source. Indeed, the common clerk appears also to have been responsible for compiling the Letter Books as well as the Journals. He may not have written the Journals himself, but they seem certainly to have been put together under his supervision. Since there is no noticeable change of hand in the period when Roger Spicer was in Rome, it would seem that the rough notes that comprise the Journal were the work of some of Spicer's clerks. On the other hand Journal 3, which covers the years 1436–42, shows several signs of having been in the custody of Richard Barnet who became common clerk in 1438. There are three entries in the volume that record not civic business but private transactions involving Barnet himself. Moreover, Journal 4, which covers the years 1442–47 and hence four years of Barnet's tenure of the office since he was replaced in 1446, also

[99] 11 August 1428, *LBK*, 76.

[100] August 1456, CLRO, Journal 6, fo. 104.

[101] October 1461, ibid. 7^{v}.

[102] *LBL*, 17.

[103] 1462, *LBL*, 15; 1463, *LBL*, 38. In May 1462, it was decided that a letter and acquittance arising out of a case in the mayor's court were to be kept by the common clerk, in the upper chamber where the records were kept in a certain chest: *CPMR 1458–82*, 27–8.

[104] See W. Kellaway, 'John Carpenter's Liber Albus', *Guildhall Studies in London History*, 3 (1978), 67–84.

[105] Masters, 'The Town Clerk', 59.

has a couple of private Barnet entries.[106] Clearly the Journals were compiled in the office of the common clerk although none of the other common clerks used the city's Journal book in quite this cavalier fashion. Interestingly Barnet in one of these private entries—an obligation to 'J.W. gentleman'—describes himself as 'secretary of the city' and this is indeed what the common clerk had become, the secretary, and the filing clerk.[107]

Like the other civic officials the duties of the common clerk were not confined to those listed in his oath. He is found attending meetings of the court of aldermen and serving on committees: he drafted letters and precepts sent out under the mayor's seal, and he was used as an envoy. Richard Barnet was sent on a deputation to the lord chancellor at Chiswick in July 1444 and Roger Spicer was sent to Windsor in 1448.[108] Four years later it was decided to send Spicer to Rome to prosecute the city's case against the claims of the London clergy who were demanding increased tithes. On his way to Rome Spicer was imprisoned by the archbishop of Cologne and he did not finally return to England until the autumn of 1454 after an absence of two years.[109]

The lives of most of the common clerks were, however, more humdrum. The office, unlike that of the recorder, seems to have been the pinnacle of ambition rather than a stepping-stone to greater things. The common clerks were not, however, amateurs like the chamberlains, but industrious professionals who had worked their way up the civic secretariat. Roger de Depham was one of the sheriffs' clerks before he was elected common clerk in 1335 and John Carpenter had worked for his predecessor John Marchaunt before himself becoming common clerk.[110] In the *Liber Albus* Carpenter is careful to specify that the common clerk was entitled to sustenance for his clerks from the chamber (although he does not specify how many clerks or how much sustenance) and by his oath the common clerk was responsible for the reliability of his clerks.[111] By the 1460s there were four clerks serving in the common clerk's office and by the early sixteenth century their duties were carefully laid down.[112]

[106] For details of these entries see Barron, 'Government of London', 131 and nn. 1, 2.

[107] CLRO, Journal 4, fo. 235^{v}.

[108] 17 July 1444, ibid. 34^{v}; 16 March 1448, ibid. 213.

[109] Barron, 'Government of London', 32; J. A. F. Thomson, 'Tithe Disputes in Later Medieval London', *EHR* 78 (1963), 1–17.

[110] 25 January 1335, *LBF*, 5. It should be noted, however, that Depham (d.1359) did move on to become recorder 1339–59: *LBF*, 30; *HW*, ii 7.

[111] *Liber Albus*, 48, 311–12.

[112] Year 1463, there were to be no more than three (clerk-)attorneys in the mayor's court and the common clerk was to ensure this; 1464, to be no more attorneys than the four clerks sitting in the mayor's court, as formerly accustomed, the common clerk to name the fourth if he wished: CLRO, Journal 7, fos. 19, 74v; *Calendar of Letters from the Mayor and Corporation of the City of London c.1350–1370*, ed. R. R. Sharpe (London, 1885), pp. xxv–xxvi; for a description of their duties, see 17 May 1537, CLRO, Repertories 9, fo. 251^{v}; and see Barron, 'Government of London', 127 n. 2 for names of some fifteenth-century clerks in the common clerk's office.

THE COMMON SERJEANT-AT-LAW

Whereas the recorder's office had grown in importance from the late thirteenth century onwards the office of common serjeant-at-law (or common pleader) appears by contrast to have declined in importance. From the start it seems to have been, very often, a stepping-stone to more prestigious legal office: of the thirty serjeants-at-law in this period, seven became recorders and nine became under-sheriffs.[113] Although the office later slipped down the civic hierarchy, when it first appeared in 1319 it had ranked among the top city posts. The common serjeant was the legal spokesman for the freemen of London and was originally elected by all the freemen but, like the common clerk, he had come to be chosen by the common council.[114] Moreover the aldermen did not always stand aloof from the election: on 11 November 1437 the court of aldermen chose John Wilton as common serjeant and four days later he was duly elected by common council.[115] His fee had originally been 100*s.* p.a. but by the early fifteenth century it had doubled to £10.[116] On occasion the common serjeant might be granted a city house. Ralph Strode, Chaucer's friend, was granted a mansion over Aldersgate while he was in office.[117] According to his oath the common serjeant was to be loyal and discreet as other officers and assiduous in the city's service, but, in particular, he was to 'pursue, save and maintain' the rights of the city;[118] in effect his task was to keep a check not only upon the activities of the executors and guardians of orphans, but also on the activities of the chamberlain, especially when he was acting as the guardian of the goods of orphans.[119] There is considerable evidence that he acted and prosecuted on behalf of city orphans, especially in the fourteenth century.[120] By his oath the common serjeant was also expected to attend the mayor, aldermen, and commons for city causes and business whenever he was required.

Like the other city officers the common serjeant attended occasional meetings of the court of aldermen and served on committees: he might act as an arbiter or

[113] B. Masters, 'The Common Serjeant', *Guildhall Miscellany*, 2 (1967), 379–89; for a list of common serjeants-at-law, see App. 2 (iii).

[114] *Liber Albus*, 47; William de Iford was granted the freedom and elected common serjeant in 1330 in Husting, which may support the notion that all freemen were involved in the election: CLRO Husting Roll, CP54, m. 6^{v}. I owe this reference to the kindness of Dr Penny Tucker.

[115] CLRO, Journal 3, fo. 188, 188^{v}. 13 September 1443, the court of aldermen decided that the common council should meet the following Thursday, September 19, specifically to elect a common serjeant, CLRO, Journal 4, fo. 4.

[116] Year 1319, Gregory de Norton to be paid 100*s.*: *LBE* 20; John Carpenter states that the common serjeant was paid £10: *Liber Albus*, 47.

[117] *LBH*, 15. Two years later he was granted the house for life: *ibid.* 83. In the political turmoil of this period he was deprived of the house in 1382/3, then in 1384 compensated for the loss of the house (worth 4 marks p.a.): ibid. 208, 245. Alexander Anne (common serjeant 1423–36) was granted a house over Aldgate: CLRO, Journal 2, fo. 132.

[118] *Liber Albus*, 310.

[119] Masters, 'Common Serjeant', 380.

[120] e.g. Iford in 1343: *CPMR 1323–64*; 162–3, Briclesworth in 1363 (marrying orphan without licence): *LBG*, 163, Wentbrigge in 1368: *LBG*, 230; and Morice was described in 1356 as 'The common pleader who prosecutes for orphans': *LBG*, 79.

draft indictments.[121] But his main task was to act as the city's 'Director of Public Prosecutions' as he did in 1421 when the city prosecuted a number of men who were accused of usury.[122] Sometimes the common serjeants were sent on errands for the city—Thomas Billing, for example, was sent to Calais with £1,000 in 1438.[123] But for most of the men who held the office of common serjeant in the period 1300–1500 it was merely a stepping-stone on the way to more lucrative legal office either in the service of the city or the Crown. To be a spokesman for the city's orphans was, doubtless, to be like a barrister nowadays who works on legal aid—it provided good experience and modest pay for those who hoped ultimately to move higher up the legal ladder.

THE COMMON SERJEANT-AT-ARMS (COMMON CRIER)

The common serjeant-at-arms, or common crier, was an altogether much more humble office than any so far discussed. It required no particular skill, but, as it would seem, simply a loud voice. John Carpenter described his duties and remuneration: he was to be in constant attendance upon the mayor and was to receive a salary of 60*s.* p.a., or more, if the auditors of the city's accounts thought he deserved it. He was entitled to the robe or cloak that a new alderman was wearing on the day he was sworn to office or the sum of 6*s.* 8*d.* A cry throughout the city carried out for the sheriffs was to cost 12*d.* and the sheriffs were expected to provide the common crier with a suitable horse 'for the honour of the city'. Moreover, for each will proclaimed at the Husting and each plea terminated there he could demand 4*d.* or a fee. He was elected by the common council and removable at their pleasure.[124] John Carpenter tells us more about the activities of the common crier than it is possible to derive from other sources. The office seems to have emerged towards the end of the thirteenth century when the election of Thomas Juvenal was recorded in 1291.[125] Juvenal was given the house over Aldersgate, although towards the end of the fourteenth century the lodging over Cripplegate may have become the recognized 'tied cottage' of the common crier: at least three later common serjeants occupied those lodgings.[126] Although the duties as described by John Carpenter sound sufficiently time-consuming, yet John Combe (common crier 1417–60) was able to act both as bailiff of Southwark, and as deputy coroner, while carrying out his tasks as common crier.[127] But the common serjeant was also

[121] Barron, Government of London', 134 n. 1.

[122] *CPMR 1413–37*, 134 and n. 1; Gwen Seabourne, 'Controlling Commercial Morality in Late Medieval London: The Usury Trials of 1421', *Journal of Legal History*, 19 (1998), 116–42.

[123] 28 March 1438, CLRO, Journal 3, fo. 176^{v}.

[124] *Liber Albus*, 49; for a list of common serjeants-at-arms, see App. 2 (viii).

[125] *LBA*, 123.

[126] No date but probably 1310–11, Juvenal was granted the Aldersgate house: *LBC* 183; 1375, 1385, John Watlyngton to have the mansion at Cripplegate: *LBH*, 2, 252; John Combe (1417–60) and John Asshe (1460–85) also had the Cripplegate house, CLRO, Journal 2, fos. 107, 132, ibid. 4, fo. 97, ibid. 6, fo. 219^{v}.

[127] John Combe was bailiff of Southwark (1421–60) and deputy coroner (1421–5), see M. Carlin, *Medieval Southwark* (London, 1996), 291.

employed on comparatively menial tasks such as retrieving escaped prisoners, summoning people to attend court, and carrying civic messages.[128] He also acted as the city's mace-bearer. The first mention of the city's mace appears to be in 1338, when the king requested the city to allow the common serjeant/crier, Robert Flambard, to appoint a deputy to discharge 'loffice de porter la mace' as Flambard was otherwise occupied as the king's serjeant-at-arms.[129]

THE WATERBAILIFF

The office of waterbailiff emerged in the late fourteenth century. John Salesbury, one of the city's serjeants, was appointed in common council in 1385 to survey nets used in the Thames and to ensure that they were of the correct mesh, that is, that the holes were large enough to allow young fish to swim through.[130] His successor in 1387 was appointed to the office of 'keeper of the water of the Thames and surveyor of nets'.[131] The office was sufficiently established by the early fifteenth century for the king to intervene to appoint a man as waterbailiff, although the duties and oath were not recorded in Carpenter's *Liber Albus*, written *c.*1419.[132] A copy of the oath was, however, copied into the Journals in 1447 and specified that the waterbailiff was to search the waters of the Thames and Medway that fell within the city's jurisdiction, to remove illegal weirs and nets and to bring offenders into court.[133] In fact the city was quite active, albeit sporadically, in trying to remove fish weirs and confiscate illegal nets and, since the city's conservancy extended as far west as Staines and as far east as the Medway, the waterbailiff had a wide area to patrol.[134] To help him he had a valet who was paid 4 marks p.a., the same amount as the mayor's valets, and the waterbailiff himself received £5.[135] There were, of course, perquisites: John Houghton (waterbailiff 1431–45) was given a house over Aldgate and his successor William Veyse was made free of the city in 1446.[136] Common council elected the waterbailiffs but it seems to have been an

[128] Barron, 'Government of London', 135 and n. 3.

[129] *LBG*, pp. xxiii–xxiv; 2 November 1338, *CPMR 1323–64*, 178; in 1354 the city received a royal charter granting it the right to bear maces in the city and outside on certain conditions: Birch, *Charters*, 63–4; L. Jewitt and W. S. Hope, *The Corporation Plate and Insignia of Office*, 2 vols. (London, 1895), ii. 90–6.

[130] B. Masters, 'The Mayor's Household before 1600', in W. Kellaway and A. Hollaender (eds.), *Studies in London History*, 95–114, esp. 102; for a list of waterbailiffs, see App. 2 (ix).

[131] *LBH*, 253, 314.

[132] Year 1413, *LBI*, 120–1; although the city objected to the appointment of William Talworth by the king, he was still in office ten years later: CLRO, Journal 2, fos. 21^{v}.25^{v}; Barron, 'Government of London', 136, 565.

[133] February 1447, CLRO, Journal 4, fo. 166^{v}. The oath is not recorded in *LBD* where a large number of the civic oaths were copied in the fifteenth century. For the extent of the city's jurisdiction over the Thames waters, see Barron, 'Government of London', 357–65; Masters, 'Mayor's Household', 101–2; V. Harding, 'The Port of London in the Fourteenth Century: Its Topography, Administration and Trade' (University of St Andrews Ph.D. thesis, 1983), 3–10.

[134] See Ch. 2; Barron, 'Government of London', 103.

[135] Years 1431, 1434 *LBK*, 133, 182.

[136] House over Aldgate, 17 February, 2 June 1457, CLRO, Journal 6, fos. 92v, 124; William Veyse free of the city, 21 August 1446: ibid. fo. 144.

office in which the Crown or members of the aristocracy were interested, perhaps because the activities of the waterbailiff extended outside the limits of the city's jurisdiction and so collided with the interests of the landowners along the Thames banks. Three of the four fifteenth-century waterbailiffs held office at the instance either of the king or of Humphrey, duke of Gloucester.[137] William Veyse who had been appointed at the instance of Henry VI in 1445 was dismissed twelve years later for neglecting his duties.[138] The waterbailiff's work was doubtless rather unpleasant, certainly it was dangerous, for indignant weir owners might tackle the waterbailiff rather than see their weir dismantled, and fishermen were not inclined to hand over their nets without a protest.[139]

THE COMMON HUNT

The office of the common hunt has certain characteristics in common with the waterbailiff: it first appears in the last quarter of the fourteenth century and it was usually held by outsiders. The tasks also took the occupant beyond the bounds of the city's jurisdiction since the city claimed hunting rights throughout Middlesex, hence the officer came into contact with local gentry and landowners. Not surprisingly the common hunt was in 1384 one of a group of four sent to carry out a search of the Thames. But the men who held the office of common hunt seem to have come from more gentlemanly backgrounds than the waterbailiffs, and they were remunerated more generously. John Charneye, the first common hunt, in 1379 was paid a salary of £10 p.a. and was allocated the same livery as the chamber serjeants who were the elite of the civic serjeantry. He had been deputy-marshal of the bishop of London's household, which may be significant since it was on the bishop of London's lands at Stepney that the Londoners claimed their principal hunting rights.[140] Thus to make the bishop's marshal the city's common hunt may have been an astute move.[141] Charneye, when he held the office, was entitled to have the profits from the leasing of 'stations' to market people around the Cross in Cheapside. When in 1382 this income was found to be inadequate, the common hunt was granted an additional £5.[142] The common hunts were chosen by the common council or the freemen at large (for example, John Tyler was elected by

[137] Barron, Government of London', 136 and n. 2.

[138] 7 October and December 1457, CLRO, Journal 6, fos. 180, 186.

[139] See Ch. 2.

[140] In the late thirteenth century the Londoners had been in conflict with Richard de Gravesend (bishop of London 1280–1303) over their claims to hunting rights in Stepney: *LBC*, 5; *Memorials*, 28; see P. Taylor, 'The Estates of the Bishops of London from the Seventh Century to the Early Sixteenth Century' (University of London, Ph.D. thesis, 1976), 181; for a list of the common hunts, see App. 2 (x).

[141] Charneye was deputy coroner of London 1380–8 and in 1383 became coroner of Middlesex. In the 1390s he succeeded Thomas Usk (d.1388) as undersheriff of Middlesex and was to be found also in the retinue of Baldwin de Radyngton, one of Richard II's household knights: *CPR 1388–92*, 125; *1391–6*, 453: ex inf. Professor Andrew Prescott.

[142] Years 1379, 1382, *LBH*, 131–2, 138. Likewise John Stokker (common hunt 1463–1500) was granted an additional 5 marks p.a. The grant to Stokker was not, however, to be taken as a precedent, 1465: *LBL*, 59.

an 'immense commonalty' on 5 April 1448), but the court of aldermen, as usual, seems to have arranged matters in advance. When the court chose John Green in 1457 they took trouble to ensure that their choice should remain secret until the common council had agreed.[143] It is easier to know who the common hunts were and what their remuneration was than to know how they earned their money. Although John Green (common hunt 1457–9) was allowed to have a deputy, his successor William Sudbury was instructed to exercise the office himself. Their chief task was to exercise the city's dogs and horses and maintain the kennels and stables.[144] The kennels in the late fifteenth century were near Moorgate where the disgusting smells of the dog food offended the neighbours and passers-by.[145] The common hunts often seem to have been gentlemen from the 'Home Counties'. John Courteney (common hunt 1417–23) came from Aynesford, Kent and John Green (1457–9) came from Essex, although William Sudbury (1459–63) was the son of a London grocer.[146] It is equally uncertain where the city hunted: traditionally the citizens had hunting rights throughout the county of Middlesex which included Stepney. Moreover the common hunt, backed by the mayor and some of the more stalwart aldermen, rode off in 1460 to assert the Londoners' rights to hunt over the lands of the Cistercian Abbey of Stratford Langthorne in Essex.[147] The development of the office of common hunt in the late medieval period is suggestive of that gentrification of the mercantile community that was taking place in the Lancastrian period. The line between a merchant and a gentleman was becoming blurred as gentlemen like the Stonors stooped to trade in wool and apprenticed their sons to mercers; and successful merchants aimed to eat and hunt like gentlemen and buy country estates to back their claims to knighthood.[148]

THE SERJEANT OF THE CHANNEL

The last, and probably the most humble, of the city's serjeants was the serjeant of the channel. Again the office emerges in the last quarter of the fourteenth century: in 1385 a serjeant was appointed for the first time to survey the streets and lanes of the city and keep them free of rubbish.[149] The office was obviously novel because John Carpenter has nothing to say about it. But there is a fifteenth-century copy of the serjeant's oath that enlarges his fourteenth-century brief to include waterways

[143] *LBK*, 231; 24 March, April, 4 April 1457, CLRO, Journal 6, fos. 116^{v}, 118, 118^{v}.

[144] John Tyler was granted 10 marks towards the cost of repairs to various buildings carried out while he was common hunt (1448–57): 28 October 1457, CLRO, Journal 6, fo. 182.

[145] Masters, 'Mayor's Household', 101.

[146] He was the son of John Sudbury, and was a serjeant-at-mace in 1467–8: *CPMR 1437–57*, 11; PRO, C244/104, m. 155.

[147] 21 April 1458, CLRO, Journal 6, fos. 210, 214, 215. Taylor, 'The Estates of the Bishop of London', 175–91.

[148] See C. Barron, 'Chivalry, Pageantry and Merchant Culture in Medieval London', in P. Coss and M. Keen (eds.), *Heraldry, Pageantry and Social Display in Medieval England* (Woodbridge, 2002), 219–41.

[149] October 1385, *LBH*, 275; see Ch. 10; for a list of serjeants of the channel, see Appendix 2 (xi).

as well as streets and requires the serjeant to fine offenders and to account to the chamber for the sums so collected.[150] When William Horn was admitted to the office in 1422 he was specifically instructed to clean the banks of the Thames as well as the markets at Leadenhall and St Nicholas Shambles.[151] It is not clear what salary the serjeant of the channel received but he must have been paid something.[152] He was allowed to have a valet who was paid £1 in 1461 so the serjeant's salary can hardly have been less than £4.[153] The choice of serjeant of the channel seems to have lain with the court of aldermen and there are signs that, in spite of the unattractive nature of the work, the office was in demand.[154] The office of serjeant of the channel was often held in conjunction with another office: Henry Snowe (serjeant of the channel *c.*1468–1472) and John Hall (serjeant of the channel 1472–7) were both chamber serjeants.[155] The development of this office indicates the concern in London about the cleanliness of the city—in the aftermath of the plagues of the fourteenth century—and the developing awareness that the problem had to be tackled on a city-wide scale and could not be left simply to the enterprise of individual wards.[156]

THE CORONER

The final addition to the city's complement of officers was the coroner. In 1478 the city finally acquired the right from the Crown to choose its own coroner.[157] The first city-appointed coroner, on the death in 1483 of the last coroner who had been granted the office by the king, was Robert Cartleage, a mayor's court clerk.[158] Before the city acquired control of the office, it had been combined with that of king's chamberlain, later king's butler, and, since the king chose the butler, he had, *ipso facto,* also chosen the coroner of London.[159] From 1279 the butler was allowed

[150] Nicholas (*recte*, Richard) Foche was sworn in 1390: *LBH*, 355; oath of serjeant of the channel: *LBD*, 201; see Masters, 'Mayor's Household', 163 and n. 6.

[151] *LBK*, 5. John Horncastle in 1457 was similarly instructed: CLRO, Journal 6, fo. 188; *LBL* 11.

[152] When John Hall was admitted in place of Henry Snowe as serjeant of the channel in 1472, he was granted 'the accustomed fee': CLRO, Journal 8, fo. 32^{v}.

[153] In 1457 the valet was paid 6*s.* 8*d.*, in 1460, 13*s.* 4*d.*, and in 1461, £1: CLRO, Journal 6, fos. 123v, 215v, 82.

[154] 27 October 1461, court of aldermen decided that Richard Green should have the office after John Horncastle (appointed December 1457): ibid. 81.

[155] Snowe, chamber serjeant 1472: ibid. 8, fo. 32^{v}; mayor's serjeant 1479: *CPMR 1458–82*, 125; Hall, mayor's serjeant, fl. 1473–80: ibid. 80, 81, 87, 95, 127,141; chamber serjeant 1477: CLRO, Journal 8, fo. 161^{v}.

[156] See Ch. 10.

[157] Birch, *Charters*, 90–3; C. Barron, 'London and the Crown 1451–61', in J. R. L. Highfield and R. Jeffs (eds.), *The Crown and Local Communities: England and France in the Fifteenth Century* (Gloucester, 1981), 88–109, esp. 99–100; for lists of coroners and deputy coroners, see App. 2 (xii) and (xiii).

[158] He probably died in 1485, being succeeded in October of that year by another mayor's court clerk, John Green, who was himself dead by December. Thomas Butside, who succeeded Green, had been a sheriffs' clerk, and he was chosen by the common council: CLRO, Journal 9, fos. 88^{v}; *LBL*, 229 and n.; in 1490 Butside was admitted to the Scriveners' Company: F. W. Steer (ed.), *Scriveners' Company Common Paper 1357–1628* (London Record Society, 1968), 23–4.

[159] See W. Kellaway, 'The Coroner in Medieval London', in Kellaway and Hollaender, *Studies in London History*, 75–91, esp. 77.

to appoint a deputy to exercise the office.[160] Since no coroner's (or deputy-coroner's) rolls survive for the period after 1378 it is difficult to know how busy the deputy coroner was, but in the earlier period there was an average of about forty deaths a year in London that required coroner's inquests, although in particular years the totals could be much higher. In 1315–16, the year of the great famine, eighty-five deaths were investigated.[161] The office was not a sinecure. Even though the king's chamberlain and butler was allowed to appoint a deputy coroner, and rarely held inquests himself, this did not always get round the problem that hearings of the possessory assizes, at which the coroner, or his deputy, presided together with the sheriffs, were held up waiting for the deputy coroner to arrive. In 1399 the city was empowered to proceed with hearings in these assizes even in the absence of the coroner or the deputy coroner.[162] By his oath the coroner was sworn to serve the king and city; to be impartial and incorruptible; to keep a true record of the cases he had dealt with and to deliver a copy of this record annually to the common clerk; to hold no inquest without the sheriffs or their deputies; to be ready to assist the mayor; to ensure that no suspect persons were placed on inquests; and to preserve the king's right and the city's liberties.[163]

CONCLUSION

As might be expected the way in which London was governed developed remarkably in the years between 1200 and 1500. Areas of concern changed: some offices declined in importance as others come into prominence. In part the changes that can be observed may simply reflect the volume of material available. At the beginning of the thirteenth century there are no records surviving of the administrative or legal business of the city yet by the end of the period there are the legal records of the court of Husting, individual documents and extracts from the records of the mayor's court, the city's Letter Books (which in the early volumes contain much material relating to the chamberlain), and, perhaps most useful of all, the city Journals and the Repertories, the minutes of the meetings of the court of aldermen and the court of common council. Inevitably therefore it is easier to understand the machinery of London government in the fifteenth century than in the fourteenth and thirteenth centuries when it is often quite hard to comprehend exactly what is happening. Some records were considered, like those of the sheriffs, to be private and so few of them ever found their way into Guildhall. Some have been lost, although surprisingly few as the result of sheer neglect or lack of interest. The chamberlains' annual accounts, together with all the apprentice

[160] 26 November 1279, *LBB*, 280.

[161] Calculated from *Calendar of Coroners' Rolls of the City of London 1300–1378* ed. R. R. Sharpe (London, 1913), covering the years 1300–1, 1321–6, 1336–9; Kellaway, 'Coroner', 81.

[162] *LBB*, pp. v–vii, *Coroners' Rolls*, ed. Sharpe, pp. vii–xv; Kellaway, 'Coroner', 83–4. Many of the men who were appointed to act as deputy-coroners were clerks or attorneys in the city courts.

[163] Fifteenth-century copy of the oath in French: *LBD*, 1; another version is recorded in *LBK*, 28.

and freedom registers, were burnt, but in general the city has always been careful to preserve its records. In the course of this period the responsibility for maintaining and preserving the city's records shifted from the chamberlain to the common (or town) clerk of London, who is still officially the keeper of the records: the city's archivist today is the deputy to the town clerk.

At the beginning of the fourteenth century the city of London appears to have employed a civil service of about eight people who were paid a total of £41 p.a. (this figure does not include the various serjeants and valets in the households of the mayor and sheriffs who were paid by the officials themselves); by 1485 the city was employing at least twenty-four civil servants and the known salary bill (the salaries of seven of the civil servants are not known) was £140, perhaps £200 altogether.[164] This swelling of the payroll reflects the more organized and interventionist civic government that had emerged by the end of the fifteenth century: concern for street cleaning had led to the creation of the serjeant of the channel and concern for the conservancy of the Thames had led to the creation of the city's waterbailiff. Moreover, concern for the condition of the city's defences led to the creation of another civic officer: in 1478 Edward Stone was appointed as the master of the works of the city.[165] He was provided with two clerks to help him, and while they received 6*d.* for every day spent on the city's business, Stone received 12*d.* His successor in office, John Coke, received 40*s.* a year, but the office, which seems to have begun as an emergency measure in 1478 arising from the concern over the dilapidated state of the city walls, was not established permanently until the mid-sixteenth century.

Moreover the greater professionalism of city government, developing within the context of greater legal skill and expertise, required that the city employ the best lawyer it could afford as its recorder. Hence the recorder's salary was almost a third of the city's total salary bill. He had overtaken the common serjeant-at-law as the city's senior legal officer. The common serjeant, together with the chamberlain and the common clerk, was paid at the comparatively modest rate of £10, but the recorder was in a class of his own: the city needed him to defend its interests against the wiles of the king's justices and the common lawyers.

At the beginning of the period the most important judicial court had been the city's court of Husting and the courts of the sheriffs were also important. In the course of the fourteenth century the mayor's court with its flexible and rapid juris-

[164] Masters, *The Chamberlain*, 8, where the salary bill in the early fourteenth century is estimated at about £50 p.a.

[165] B. Masters, 'The City Surveyor, the City Engineer and the City Architect and Planning Officer', *Guildhall Miscellany*, 4 (1973), 237–55, esp. 238. Before this the city had employed master masons who seem to have worked almost exclusively on city business: John Croxton (d. 1447) supervised the work on the new Guildhall and the repairs to the Cross in Cheapside, overhauled the city's piped water supply and played a part in the rebuilding of Leadenhall, see J. Harvey, *English Medieval Architects* (Gloucester, 1984), 76; Barron, *Medieval Guildhall*, 25–31, Mark Samuel, 'Reconstructing the Medieval Market at Leadenhall', in G. Milne (ed.), *From Roman Basilica to Medieval Market* (London, HMSO, 1992), 114–25, esp. 123–5. Croxton appears to have been succeeded in this role by Master William Cliff who was employed by the city on the water supply and on works at the Guildhall chapel and at Leadenhall: CLRO, Journal 3, fo.11; ibid. 4, fo. 14^{v}.; ibid. 5, fo. 236^{v}.

diction, capable of dealing with mercantile law and giving decisions in equity on its informal side, developed as an important civic court, but even in the fifteenth century the sheriffs' court was probably entertaining ten times as many civil actions as the mayor's court, and it handled almost all the law-and-order type of offences.[166]

On the one hand the folkmoot, the open-air gathering of all citizens, disappeared and even its amorphous successor the commonalty was found to be impracticable and so was superseded by a more select body of citizens. In its place, hammered out on the anvil of bitter civil conflict in the fourteenth century, there was fashioned the common council, whose members were elected by the wards and whose role in the decision-making process was, by the fifteenth century if not earlier, assured. All taxation had to be agreed by the common council and many civic offices, such as those of the common clerk, the common serjeant-at-law, the common hunt, the undersheriffs, and the waterbailiff, came to be chosen by that body. But there was another body whose composition must have corresponded closely to that of common council but was not the same. That was the gathering that met twice a year, once to elect the sheriffs, the chamberlain, the bridgewardens, and the auditors, and once to elect the mayor. These meetings originally, in the thirteenth century, were expected to include all the citizens. Not surprisingly such meetings could be rowdy and unsatisfactory and so by degrees, helped by the Crown, the mayor and aldermen secured a limitation of those who might attend: only those who were summoned might come. Finally, in 1467, only the masters and good men of the city companies were to attend, together with members of the common council. This spread the electorate among the companies—both mercantile and artisan—but ensured that only their most substantial and reputable members could come to Guildhall for the elections.[167]

So the creation of the more democratic common council (*c.*180 men in the mid-fifteenth century) as an essential element in civic government was countered by a contraction in the ability of the lesser citizens (i.e. those who were not liverymen of their companies) to participate in civic elections. But such a man could still take part in the deliberations of his wardmote and help there to elect the common councilmen and select the ward candidates for the office of alderman when it fell vacant. Although the court of aldermen retained a right of veto, yet the system of hereditary aldermanries of the thirteenth century had gone for good: no longer was it possible to bequeath the office of alderman in a will as Nicholas de Farndone had done in 1334 when he left 'le Aldermanrie' of Farringdon Within and Without

[166] Chancery was certainly receiving ten times as many petitions relating to sheriffs' court cases as mayor's court cases in the period 1461–83; as far as mayor's court civil cases are concerned, numeration on the surviving bills indicates that it was entertaining 200 plus cases a year by the early 1440s, approaching 300 by the late 1440s, and nearly 400 by the mid-1450s. The value of contested assets in the sheriffs' court was similar to that of those contested in the mayor's court, although it *may* be true that more important people used the mayor's court from preference, see P. Tucker, 'Relationships between London's Courts and the Westminster Courts in the Reign of Edward IV', in D. E. S. Dunn (ed.), *Courts, Counties and the Capital in the later Middle Ages* (Stroud, 1996), 117–38.

[167] *LBL*, 132.

to John de Pulteney.[168] The aldermen were still the most important men in the city government but their ranks were open to all comers, although artisans were less likely to be able to afford the office than wholesale merchants. The work of the aldermen became increasingly demanding; meetings were more frequent, committees (often joint with common councilmen) were more numerous, and deputy aldermen began to make an appearance at the end of the period. So also did knighthoods, which had been rare until the mid-fifteenth century and then became the frequent reward of those who had passed the mayoral chair and lived to enjoy their dotage.

But the exclusion of some citizens from the elections of the mayor and sheriffs and other civic officers, and their replacement by councils composed of *probi homines* could certainly be seen as oligarchic. This trend, however, needs to be set against the growth of other governing institutions within the city: the parishes and the craft guilds.[169] It is clear that in London, as elsewhere, parishioners were taking responsibility, as churchwardens, or as the masters of religious fraternities or 'lights', for the running of many aspects of parish life. There were a hundred or so parishes in London, so at any one time in the fifteenth century at least 1,000 men would have been involved in some way in collecting money, overseeing building works, administering charity, and organizing religious services. The considerable administrative tasks that were placed on parochial officers in the sixteenth century made use of a system of local self-regulation that had been in place much earlier.[170] But in London, as in other large towns in England, there was a further governing structure, that of the craft guilds. By the end of the fifteenth century there were probably fifty guilds, or companies, in London which had serious governing structures, as opposed to evanescent and unreliable ones.[171] All Londoners were parishioners (although only adult males appear to have held parochial office); all London householders attended the meetings of the wardmotes; all citizens belonged to a craft association of some kind. By the end of the fifteenth century the craft associations had developed into important institutions, often incorporated, usually endowed with lands, and their members were willing and able to assist the mayor and aldermen in the business of governing the city.

[168] *HW* i, 388–99; in fact Richard le Lacer, and not Pulteney, succeeeded Nicholas as alderman.

[169] See C. Barron, 'London 1300–1540', in D. Palliser (ed.), *Cambridge Urban History of Britain*, 3 vols. (Cambridge 2000), i. 395–440, esp. 400–5.

[170] See C. Burgess, 'Shaping the Parish: St Mary at Hill, London in the Fifteenth Century', in J. Blair and B. Golding (eds.), *The Cloister and the World: Essays in Medieval History in Honour of Barbara Harvey* (Oxford, 1996), 246–86; *The Church Records of St Andrew Hubbard Eastcheap c.1450–c.1570*, ed. C. Burgess (London Record Society, 1999), pp. xxvii–xxx.

[171] The small group of London shipwrights (probably only twenty at any one time) tried several times to organize a craft fraternity but, clearly, failed; see R. Wright, 'The Shipwrights of Medieval London, 1250–1500' (Royal Holloway, University of London, MA thesis, 2001), esp. 30.

CHAPTER NINE

From Guilds to Companies

GUILDS, LIKE COMMITTEES, have a long and varied history. There were guilds in London in Saxon times but, as the population of London grew, so did the numbers of guilds and other forms of association. Men and women associated together in groups for a variety of purposes and with varying degrees of formality: only in rare instances have these early associations left behind any record of their existence. Of those groupings that later developed into the city's livery companies, only three, the mercers, the grocers, and the merchant tailors, have any administrative records before 1400. Several companies have earlier deeds, often acquired much later when the company bought, or was bequeathed, an urban property. But the absence of records may be revealing and may suggest that the history of the organized craft and trade guilds cannot in most cases be taken back much beyond their surviving records. Certainly there were craft associations earlier but they seem to have been, for the most part, largely informal, and their continuous history only really begins towards the end of the thirteenth century.

THE CRAFTS BEFORE 1200

By the beginning of the thirteenth century it is clear that men (and women) who practised the same craft, or traded in similar goods, tended to live near each other. The tanners lived near the upper Walbrook stream within the walls and had a guildhall in Broad Street;[1] the vintners lived together near the Thames in the Vintry; the goldsmiths' 'aurifabria' was at the corner of Cheapside and Friday Street; the cordwainers gathered together at the 'corveiseria' which had its focus in the later Cordwainer Street south of Cheapside; the mercery lay along the south side of Cheapside and the drapers gathered rather further to the west.[2] By 1246 the butchers were to be found where their markets were later, along the street inside

[1] *The Cartulary of Launceston Priory*, ed. P. Hull (Devon and Cornwall Record Society, 1987), 93–4; D. Keene, 'Tanners' Widows, 1300–1350' in C. Barron and A. Sutton (eds.), *Medieval London Widows* (London 1994), 1–27 esp. 9.

[2] C. N. L. Brooke with G. Keir, *London 800–1216: The Shaping of a City* (London, 1975), 277, 278, and n. 1; D. Keene, 'Introduction', in J. Imray, *The Mercers' Hall* (London, 1991), 8; the Spicery in West Cheap is mentioned in 1278–9, H. A. Harben, *A Dictionary of London* (London, 1918), 541; the Saddlery near St Vedast church by 1280, ibid. 515; the Cutlery by 1311–2, ibid. 193.

Newgate and at Eastcheap.[3] Not all these groupings of traders and craftsmen gave their names permanently to London streets, but the widespread use of such names in thirteenth-century London (and doubtless earlier also) is a good indication of the way in which people of the same occupation lived in close proximity to each other and so were likely to have combined intense rivalry with the formation of common policy on matters of common concern.

It is not necessary, however, to depend solely upon street names to indicate the existence of groupings of people of the same, or related, trades. A particular threat to the livelihood of the group, or some perceived advantage in association, or a brush with royal tax collectors or judges, might propel members of the group into formalizing their association by use of the written document. In the 1150s Henry II confirmed a charter which his grandfather had granted to the weavers (*telarii*) of London: only those who belonged 'in eorum gilda' were to be allowed to practise the craft and this monopoly extended to Southwark and other places near London. The gildsmen agreed to pay the king 2 marks (£1 6*s.* 8*d.*) each year.[4] It seems likely that the London weavers were attempting, by this manœuvre, to fend off the challenge posed by entrepreneurial weavers who were anxious to exploit the growing demand for English cloth. In 1202 King John, who was by this date receiving 18 marks annually from the weavers, agreed to revoke the weavers' charter in return for an annual payment of 20 marks from the Londoners.[5] At about the same time (1155) the London bakers (*bolengarii*) paid a mark into the Exchequer 'for their gild' and they continued to pay this regularly at least until 1178. It is likely that they, like the weavers, had secured a right of monopoly by royal charter in return for which they made this annual payment.[6]

As the population of London rose in the twelfth century, so there was a glut of labour and a scarcity of work. This may, in part, explain why such craftsmen as the weavers and bakers joined together to preserve their livelihood by the use of exclusion tactics, and they found in the Angevin kings rulers who were only too anxious to profit from their economic discomfort. In 1180 nineteen 'adulterine' or unchartered guilds were fined at the Exchequer because they had failed to pay the king for the right to associate.[7] Four of these guilds were, clearly, craft associations: the goldsmiths, the pepperers, the butchers, and the *pararii* (cloth workers). The rela-

[3] *The London Eyre of 1244*, ed. H. M. Chew and M. Weinbaum (London Record Society, 1970), 139, 148; for the location of the various metal-working crafts, see D. Keene, 'Metalworking in Medieval London: An Introductory Survey', *Journal of the Historical Metallurgy Society*, 30 (1996), 95–102 esp. 96–7.

[4] *Elenchus Fontium Historiae Urbanae*, ed. S. Reynolds, W. de Boer, and G. Mac Niocaill (Leiden, 1988), 74–5; see also F. Consitt, *The London Weavers' Company* (Oxford, 1933), 180–1.

[5] *LBC*, 55; Henry III appears to have granted a new charter to the weavers in 1243: *Liber Custumarum*, i. 48; E. Carus-Wilson, 'The English Cloth Industry in the Late Twelfth and Early Thirteenth Centuries', in ead., *Medieval Merchant Venturers* (London, 1954), 211–38. esp. 225; Consitt, *Weavers*, 4–5.

[6] S. Thrupp, *A Short History of the Worshipful Company of Bakers* (London, 1933), 2.

[7] *Elenchus*, 84; G. Unwin, *The Gilds and Companies of London* (London 1908), ch. 4. Unwin's book was reprinted in 1963, with an introduction by William F. Kahl (pp. xix – xlvi) that attempts to place Unwin's work in the context of nineteenth-century writing on guilds, and to assess his influence on later studies of the guilds and government of London.

tive wealth of these associations is reflected in the size of their fines: 24 marks, 16 marks, and 1 mark each paid by the butchers and the *pararii*.[8] But men did not associate together simply for economic objectives, and these groups of craftsmen may have had other ends in view. Early in Henry II's reign the canons of St Martin le Grand confirmed a charter for the *gilde sellariorum* (guild of saddlers) which established the saddlers as *confratres* of the canons, and admitted them to all the spiritual benefits of the house.[9] In return for the right to be buried, with due ceremony, in the house, to receive prayers while alive and after death, and to be able to call on 'aid and counsel', the saddlers agreed to attend masses, especially on the feast day of St Martin, and to remember the canons in their wills. In this way the saddlers, who lived nearby, were able to act together to secure spiritual benefits for themselves and their heirs. The economic motivation of the weavers and the spiritual concerns of the saddlers were both characteristic aspects of associations of craftsmen in London throughout the medieval period.

Before 1200, therefore, there is firm evidence for the corporate activity of weavers, saddlers, bakers, goldsmiths, butchers, pepperers, and *pararii* in London. It has been customary to view these early associations with a sceptical eye and to point out their evanescent character. Certainly it is hard to prove that—for example—the guild of saddlers which associated itself with the canons of St Martin le Grand in the reign of Henry II was the direct ancestor of the group of saddlers who in 1308 acted together to protest about the poor workmanship of the fusters who made wooden saddle trees.[10] But the evidence for corporate or conjoint activity in the twelfth century should not be underestimated: corporate fines have to be collected from the group members; officers have to be appointed to police a monopoly; the saddlers had four wardens (called *echevins*) and the agreement with the canons of St Martin le Grand was drawn up with them and all the elders (*seniores*) of the guild, which presumes that there was some kind of organizing hierarchy. Some crafts, like the tanners, already at this early date had guildhalls of their own, and the saddlers must have had some common space in which to keep their communal documents. The few fragments of information that have survived about the London guilds in the twelfth century suggest that there were more of them, and that they may have been more sophisticated, than is now easily discernible.

The absence of a guild merchant in London is notable. Such merchant associations existed in many English towns in this period (e.g. Oxford, Lincoln, Winchester, Leicester, Ipswich) yet the great merchants of London seem not to have felt the need to form such an association.[11] These merchants were general

[8] Some of the other fifteen gilds may well have been craft associations, but they are defined as being 'of the Bridge', or in relation to a particular alderman.

[9] Westminster Abbey Muniments, 13184; G. Martin, 'The Early History of the London Saddlers' Guild', *Bulletin of the John Rylands University Library of Manchester*, 72 (1990), 145–54; K. M. Oliver, *Hold Fast, Sit Sure: The History of the Worshipful Company of Saddlers of the City of London 1160–1960* (Chichester, 1995), 2–6.

[10] Ibid. 18, 31.

[11] See *Elenchus*, 66, 73, 96, 98, 101.

traders, and so may have been less inclined to confine themselves, by association, with a single community and their economic strength may have made the need for allies less acute.[12]

THE THIRTEENTH CENTURY

As the records become richer in the thirteenth century, so there is more evidence of corporate activity on the part of the London craftsmen, victuallers, and merchants. But the signs of this activity may not be simply a trick of the records. The informal associations of craftsmen and merchants were subject to 'a variety of forces, some working on them from within, others of royal or municipal origin' and it was these 'which gave them shape'.[13]

In some cases it was royal pressure that forced, or encouraged, men of the same trade to co-operate. The goldsmiths were made responsible for ensuring that gold and silver coinage was of the right standard: in 1238 six goldsmiths were selected by the mayor to ensure that royal decrees were observed.[14] From the late twelfth century the fishmongers and vintners were subject to price and quality control administered by the mayor and aldermen on the king's behalf.[15] In some cases the pressure seems to have come from the mayor and aldermen on their own initiative; from the 1240s the butchers were organized into selling their wares only in the two authorized markets of Newgate and Eastcheap and they were subject to civic regulation.[16] The activities of the bakers were regulated from at least 1276, and it may well have been the city's interference in the wage rates of carpenters that provoked them into forming their own 'parliament' in 1298.[17] Some groups of craftsmen banded together because they had come into conflict with other craftsmen: in 1300 the *burellers* (cloth merchants) got together to complain to the mayor and aldermen about the high prices being charged by the weavers, and the tailors were bound together in common opposition to the activities of the tawyers.[18] In 1298 representatives of the crafts of weavers, tailors, *burellers*, dyers, and fullers

[12] E. Veale, 'The "Great Twelve": Mistery and Fraternity in Thirteenth-Century London', *Historical Research*, 64 (1991), 237–63, esp. 239.

[13] Ibid. 262.

[14] Ibid. 243–5; and refs. there cited; see also a case in 1279 when a group of goldsmiths complain to the mayor about the illicit practices of another goldsmith, *The London Eyre of 1276*, ed. M. Weinbaum (London Record Society, 1976), 105; A. Sutton, 'The Silent Years of London Guild History before 1300: The Case of the Mercers', *Historical Research*, 71 (1998), 121–41, esp. 131.

[15] Veale, 'The "Great Twelve"', 249, 240; Sutton, 'Silent Years', 131.

[16] *Eyre 1244*, 139, 148, 153; *LBA*, 217; see Ch. 10.

[17] *LBA*, 215–16; ibid. 184; *Liber Custumarum*, i. 99; *CEMCR 1298–1307*, 25. At about the same time, 1298–9, the blacksmiths may have combined together to raise their wages and/or prices, although they claimed to have more innocent motives: ibid. 33–4. In 1299–1300, the spurriers formed a confederacy to regulate apprenticeship and the sale of goods, and to establish a monopoly: ibid. 52.

[18] For the weavers/burellers, see *EMCR 1298–1307*, 53–5; *LBC*, 60; *Liber Custumarum*, i. 121–6; *LBA*, 218–19; for the tailors/tawyers, see R. B. Pugh (ed.), *Calendar of London Trailbaston Trials under Commissions of 1305 and 1306* (London, 1975), 95–6, 103, 105; *The Eyre of London, 14 Edward II AD 1321*, ed. H. M. Cam, 2 vols. (Selden Society, 1968–9), i. 77.

were summoned before the mayor and aldermen to reach an agreement about the regulations for fulling cloth in the city (in effect, that it was not to be sent away to be fulled at the mills at Stratford).[19] As early as 1268 there is evidence that the cappers had formed an association to maintain the standard of cap production and to protect their market from the incursion of cheaper caps made of wool and 'flock'.[20] Sometimes associations were formed because of pressures from within the craft itself. In the late thirteenth century the skinners drew up regulations to define good workmanship in their craft and to control the 'lesser' craftsmen and journeymen who worked for the 'greater' skinners on a piecework basis.[21] There was trouble also between the master cordwainers and the journeymen (serving workers, *servientes operarii*) of the craft who brought a plea of trespass against the masters whom they accused of having bound themselves together by oath to lower the wages of the journeymen cordwainers. The masters pleaded that they had been forced to reduce the wages because of the influx of debased French currency and the shortage of food, but they claimed that they had not taken a common oath. A jury found for the masters and the journeymen were enjoined 'to work well and faithfully, and to serve their masters and the people', and not to demand more than the customary charges.[22] It seems likely that it was some similar discord within the craft (and desire for greater profits) that led the fruiterers in 1304 to take an oath not to buy any fruit from London gardens until after June 24 when there would be a glut which would bring down the wholesale price.[23]

In the case of the greater mercantile trades, for example the pepperers (later the grocers), the mercers, and the drapers, the impetus that drove them towards common action and association seems to have come from outside. The pepperers who lived in the area of Soper Lane banded together to attempt to gain control of the Great Beam (used to weigh spices) and to resist the claims of alien merchants.[24] The drapers, who exported wool and imported cloth, had little formal association although they could promote a common cause against the clothworkers whose goods they sold.[25] The drapers' main concern, however, was to exclude aliens and foreigners from the retail sale of cloth in the city, and there are other signs of their more formal association in London in the early years of the fourteenth century.[26] The mercers, many of whom were men of great wealth, and importance seem not to have acted together as a group before 1304. They may have been anxious to control the Small Beam (used for weighing silk) and so were unhappy at the

[19] *LBC*, 51–3.

[20] *LBD*, 271–3; *Eyre 1321*, ii. 166–9.

[21] Veale, 'The "Great Twelve"', 245–6. Doubtless in response to this control from above, the journeymen (*famuli*) of the skinners in 1303–4 formed a *confederacionem*, with their own 'common box' or fighting fund, *CEMCR 1298–1307*, 153–4.

[22] Year 1303, ibid. 148–9.

[23] Ibid. 157–8.

[24] Veale, 'The "Great Twelve"', 253–4; P. Nightingale, *A Medieval Mercantile Community: The Grocers' Company and the Politics and Trade of London 1000–1485* (New Haven, Conn., 1995), esp. ch. 6; see Ch. 3.

[25] Years 1226, 1244, *Eyre 1244*, 225, 323.

[26] Veale, 'The "Great Twelve"', 245; E. Quinton, 'The Drapers and the Drapery Trade of Late Medieval London *c*.1300–*c*.1500' (University of London, Ph.D. thesis, 2001), 18–36.

prospect of a royal—and perhaps ignorant—appointment. It has been suggested that what brought them together was a common concern about the control of apprenticeship and, thereby, the route to the freedom of the city.[27]

In the course of the thirteenth century, therefore, many more groups of craftsmen and merchants came to act together, sometimes informally through neighbourly proximity and sometimes more formally through the responsibility for organizing the craft, or supervising price controls or workmanship, a responsibility that might be delegated by the mayor and aldermen or by the Crown. There was no single path towards formal organization that was followed by all groups, nor was there a single economic imperative. As has already been argued 'different groups set up and used different forms for different reasons at different times'.[28]

THE STRUGGLE TO CONTROL THE FREEDOM

The intense competition and craft rivalry, the hostility to foreigners and aliens, the attempts at protectionism and monopolies, all bear witness to the pressures on the economy of London at this period. In about 1300 the population of London reached a peak of *c.*80,000–100,000 (a figure not to be touched again until the third quarter of the sixteenth century): there is evidence of overcrowding, shortage of work, and poverty.[29] In a situation where there was not enough work to go round, the issue of access to the freedom became of crucial importance, for only those who were freemen were allowed to sell their goods retail in the city or, apparently, to practise their craft there. William de la Foreste, a smith, was sued on a writ of trespass in 1298 because he had traded in the city with foreigners for ten years 'like a freeman' to the damage of the reputable men of his trade. William admitted that he was not a freeman but claimed that he dealt only with freemen and that he was a 'handicraftsman and not a merchant' which would imply that he believed that foreign artisans were not bound by the same rules about dealing with other foreigners as were foreign merchants.[30] What seems clear is that those who had, by whatever means, gained access to the privileges of citizenship did not wish to share those privileges with others who were not freemen (and who did not share in the communal costs, such as contributing to royal tallages).

[27] Year 1304, settlement of differences between Roger de Paris and the Commonalty of the Mercery of London, and John le Mirourer: *LBC*, 138–9; Veale, 'The "Great Twelve"', 260; Sutton, 'The Silent Years', 121–41.

[28] Veale, 'The "Great Twelve"', 237; cf. D. Keene, 'Guilds in English Towns, AD 1000–1500', in B. Ranson (ed.), *Power, Resistance and Authorities: Aspects of Guild Organisation in England* (Department of Sociology, Hong Kong Baptist University, 1997), 28–43, esp. 35–6.

[29] See Ch. 11.

[30] *CEMCR 1298–1307*, 49. William de la Foreste was again in trouble in 1305 when he struck the beadle of Cornhill ward. His anvil and bellows were later seized to compensate the beadle, but it seems likely that craft jealousy may have lain at the root of the charges against William: ibid. 174.

In the city's Letter Book D there are listed the names of all those who gained the freedom of the city in the years 1309–12: 907 men and two women.[31] Of these 657 (72%) had bought their freedom at sums ranging from five shillings ('because he was poor') to two pounds. The remaining 252 (28%) had reached the freedom via apprenticeship and were presented by a master, or his widow, or by a group of men who were prepared to certify that one had served his apprenticeship and had properly learnt his craft. The record of those who had purchased the freedom was kept in each ward and controlled, therefore, by the alderman. It would seem that, at intervals (as in 1312) the city chamberlain required the aldermen to bring their ward lists of freemen (together with the fees that had been collected) to Guildhall so that the names could be entered in a central register. Under this system the freedom of the city could have been purchased with comparative ease, and citizen traders and craftsmen would have been able to exercise very little control over the admission to the freedom of those who would go on to practise their craft in the city, unless they entered by apprenticeship. The power to sell the freedom appears to have lain with the aldermen in the wards and these men were, almost exclusively, rich wholesale merchants and victuallers.

Clearly this situation was unsatisfactory for the craftsmen and, at a meeting summoned by the mayor in December 1312, the aldermen and 'good men from every mistery' agreed that in future strangers who wished to become free of the city would have to be certified by merchants or craftsmen of the business which they wished to pursue.[32] This brought to an end the free-for-all-who-would-pay entry policy to the city freedom: now only those who were sponsored by citizen merchants or craftsmen would be allowed to purchase the freedom. It seems clear that such a change was the result of group activity on the part of different crafts and, in its turn, the new regulation encouraged people of the same craft or trade to associate together in sponsoring (or not) a prospective citizen.[33] In June 1319 Edward II granted to the city an important charter which came later to be known as the 'Great Charter'. Among other clauses it was laid down that foreigners and aliens were to be admitted to the freedom only on the surety of six men of the mistery or trade which they wished to practise, thus giving the stamp of royal authority to the decision of seven years earlier.[34] One consequence of this greater 'craft' control over entries to the freedom by redemption (or purchase) was that apprenticeship became the much more usual route to the freedom.[35] The craftsmen and traders

[31] This paragraph is derived from B. Nash, 'A Study of the Freeman and Apprenticeship Registers of Letter Book D (1309–1312): The Place Name Evidence' (Royal Holloway, University of London, MA thesis 1990).

[32] *LBE*, 13.

[33] A. Sutton, 'The Silent Years', 140.

[34] *Historical Charters and Constitutional Documents of the City of London*, ed. W. de Gray Birch (rev. edn. London, 1887), 46–7.

[35] Between 1391 and 1464, 1,047 men were admitted to the freedom through the mercers' company: 69 (7%) bought the freedom and 978 (93%) came via apprenticeship, J. Imray, '"Les bones gentes de la Mercerye de Londres": A Study of the Membership of the Medieval Mercers' Company' in A. E. J. Hollaender and W. Kellaway (eds.), *Studies in London History Presented to P. E. Jones* (London, 1969), 155–78, esp. 159.

of the city, whether wholesalers or artisans, had secured for themselves an impregnable position in city government in the firm control of access to the freedom whether by apprenticeship or by purchase.[36] In practice the achievement was of particular significance for the artisans, because the wholesale dealers, as aldermen, had already exercised considerable influence in the city. By this charter 'the crafts had won that measure of control over citizenship which was to colour the whole history of late medieval London', and one contemporary saw it as a time when 'many men of the crafts in London were clothed in their liveries, and a good time was about to begin'.[37]

THE SEARCH FOR LEGITIMATION: CRAFT FRATERNITIES IN THE FOURTEENTH AND FIFTEENTH CENTURIES

Most craft or trade groupings had, at their core, a fraternity or religious association dedicated to a saint (e.g. St Dunstan for the goldsmiths or St Eloy for the blacksmiths), and committed to honouring the saint's day, feasting together in Christian fellowship and, usually, requiring contributions from members to fund religious services and commemorative masses for the brothers and sisters. Such fraternities (or guilds) were ubiquitous in late medieval society and, by the fifteenth century, there were probably more than two hundred in London.[38] Most fraternities were localized and focused on a parish church and so were comprised of neighbours. When those who practised the same craft tended to live close to each other a neighbourhood fraternity could easily evolve into a craft fraternity. In this way a fraternity which was founded in 1342 to repair a chapel in the church of All Hallows at London Wall 'in honour of Jesus Christ who hanged on the Cross' had evolved, by the time of the royal inquiry into fraternities and guilds in 1388–9, into a fraternity run by, and probably for, brewers. In the same way the salters came to dominate the guild of Corpus Christi in the church of All Hallows Bread Street and the poulters adopted the fraternity of Corpus Christi in the church of St Mildred in the Poultry.[39] The religious fraternity was particularly prominent and important in some craft associations: for example the tailors' fraternity of St John the Baptist attracted members from a range of other crafts and, indeed, the almshouses run by the fraternity were the gift of John Chircheman who had been a grocer.[40] On the other hand the mercers seem not to have had a fraternity and

[36] Year 1312, *LBE*, 13.

[37] G. A. Williams, *Medieval London from Commune to Capital* (London, 1963), 283; *Croniques de London depuis L'An Hen.III jusqu'à l'an 17 Edw.III*, ed.,G. Aungier (Camden Society, 1844), 41, 'En cele temps multz des gentz de mesters en Loundres furent vestuz de suite, et fut bon secle comensaunt'.

[38] See C. Barron, 'The Parish Fraternities of Medieval London', in C. Barron and C. Harper-Bill (eds.), *The Church in Pre-Reformation Society: Essays in Honour of F. R. H. Du Boulay* (Woodbridge, 1985), 13–37.

[39] Ibid. 14–17.

[40] M. P. Davies, 'The Tailors of London: Corporate Charity in the Late Medieval Town', in R. Archer (ed.), *Crown, Government and People in the Fifteenth Century* (Stroud, 1995), 161–90, esp. 182–6.

had no clear religious affiliation until, in the course of the later fourteenth century, the company took over the church of St Thomas of Acre.[41] Sometimes crafts moved their fraternity to a different church. The haberdashers seem originally to have located their fraternity dedicated to St Katherine in the Cathedral church of St Paul but they later moved the fraternity into the parish church of St Mary Staining near their company hall.[42] The saddlers, whose original affiliation in the twelfth century had been with the church of St Martin le Grand, in the course of the fourteenth century formed an association with the parish church of St Vedast in the area where many saddlers lived, and by the fifteenth century their fraternity was dedicated to the Virgin.[43] Since these associations were religious as well as secular in their purposes their ordinances are sometimes to be found among the records of the Commissary Court (e.g. the glovers, blacksmiths, or the shearmen) and in these cases the religious and social concerns of the group are particularly prominent.[44] More often the rules governing the activities of the association are to be found copied into the city's records where the organizational and economic aspects of the group tend to be emphasized.

Few craft associations appear to have drawn up ordinances in the thirteenth century, but the need for corporate action to deal with entries to the freedom led the crafts to become more organized and to create rules for their self-government. Between 1322 (armourers) and 1396 (coopers) at least thirty-seven crafts brought ordinances to the mayor and aldermen for ratification and enrolment.[45] All these ordinances were drafted either in Anglo-Norman or in Latin, although it seems clear that some crafts did have rules written in English from the mid-fourteenth century, but those that were presented to the mayor and aldermen were written in the more legal, or formal, languages.[46] This would reinforce the suggestion that these ordinances were normative, and drawn up to secure the approval of the city's rulers.[47]

The ordinances varied from craft to craft but they usually contained provisions for the election of masters or wardens (varying in number from two to six), and for the search, subject to the overall authority of the mayor and aldermen, for defective goods. There were regulations about the making and the marketing of goods and about the acceptance and training of apprentices. Usually there was some provision for maintaining a monopoly and for excluding non-members from working in the craft. In effect, by approving such ordinances, the mayor and

[41] Keene, 'Introduction', in Imray, *The Mercers' Hall*, 7–15. Although the mercers used a maiden's head on their seal, it is unlikely that this was supposed to represent the Blessed Virgin, see A. Sutton, *I Sing of a Maiden: The Story of the Maiden of the Mercers' Company* (The Mercers' Company, London, 1998).

[42] I. Archer, *The History of the Haberdashers' Company* (Chichester, 1991), 10.

[43] Oliver, *Company of Saddlers*, 27–8.

[44] *Index to the Testamentary Records in the Commissary Court of London, 1375–1488*, ed. M. Fitch (London, 1969), 208.

[45] Unwin, *Guilds and Companies*, 88.

[46] C. Barron and L. Wright, 'The London Middle English Guild Certificates of 1388–9', *Nottingham Medieval Studies*, 39 (1995), 108–45, esp. 111–14.

[47] H. Swanson, *Medieval Artisans: An Urban Class in Late Medieval England* (Oxford, 1989), 112–13.

aldermen were handing over to what may have been a self-appointed group the right to regulate all those working in that craft. It is noteworthy that the groups who brought their ordinances for ratification were all artisan crafts who, in this way, were seeking the approval of a court of aldermen that was composed almost entirely of merchants. The mercers, grocers, drapers, or vintners, for example, did not feel the need to bring their rules into court for ratification: they comprised the court and that was sufficient. It was not that these mercantile groups did not have their own rules: the grocers had ordinances from 1345–8, the mercers from 1348 and the goldsmiths from 1364, but they saw no need to have them approved by 'higher authority'.[48] This distinction, between the governing role played in the city by the merchants and the governed role played by the artisans, is notable and was to contribute significantly to the instability of civic government in the late fourteenth century.

Some craft and trade groups sought approval not from the church, nor from the mayor and aldermen, but from the Crown. As we have seen the weavers and bakers among others had sought royal approval as early as the twelfth century but this seems to have been comparatively infrequent. However, it becomes much more common in the course of the fourteenth century: in 1327 the skinners, the girdlers, and the tailors all secured royal charters and there was a steady trickle throughout the reign of Edward III.[49] Often these charters were really no more than licences to allow the craft or trade group to hold land in mortmain. But on occasion these royal charters appeared to circumvent the mayor and aldermen by granting to the crafts direct power to regulate their own affairs, rather than by authority delegated to them from the mayor and aldermen. In 1377 the mayor, Nicholas Brembre, required all crafts that had received royal charters to hand them over to the mayor and chamberlain at Guildhall on the grounds that the privileges they contained infringed the powers vested in the mayor.[50] This uneasy tension between the authority of the Crown and that of the mayor could be exploited by disaffected crafts when it suited them.

The activities of guilds and fraternities became of increasing concern to the Lords and Commons in Parliament in the aftermath of the revolt of 1381. As a result of a Parliamentary petition, in 1388 the Crown instigated an inquiry into the activities of all religious and craft guilds, which were required to send into Chancery details about their purposes, organization, and property-holding. Over 500 guild certificates, constructed in response to this inquiry, now remain and of these forty-two come from London. Either some of the London returns have been lost or many guilds in the city ignored the royal writ. The London returns were

[48] Nightingale, *Mercantile Community*, 247; A. Sutton, 'The Mercery Trade and the Mercers' Company of London, from the 1130s to 1348' (University of London Ph.D. thesis, 1995), 372–9; T. F. Reddaway and L. M. Walker, *The Early History of the Goldsmiths' Company, 1327–1509* (London, 1975), 33.

[49] *Memorials*, 153–6; *LBF*, 52. It is worth noting that all three crafts thought it expedient to have their royal charters copied into the London Letter Books.

[50] *CPMR 1381–1412*, 148–9; Barron and Wright, 'London Guild Certificates', 117.

written in Latin, Anglo-Norman, and English and covered a range of associations: small religious fraternities; religious fraternities with 'economic' clauses (e.g. about apprenticeship) which betray a craft affiliation, such as the return of the incipient brewers fraternity in All Hallows church; fraternities of craftsmen whose ordinances contain no 'economic' clauses at all (such as the whitetawyers or the pouchmakers); and straightforward and clearly defined craft guilds.[51] These returns provide an excellent example of the variety of associations that in fourteenth-century London could be covered by the single word 'guild'. If these associations were seditious, as the Commons feared, then the members were careful to conceal this aspect of their activities in their returns. But they were not so successful at concealing the fact that much land was being held by and for fraternities by groups of trustees or feoffees, which meant that they had been able to avoid the expense of buying a royal licence to enable them to hold land in mortmain (i.e. in perpetuity). This legal loophole was closed by the second Statute of Mortmain in 1391 which extended to urban and mercantile corporations (including those guilds and fraternities that held lands) the provisions of the earlier statute of Edward I's reign which had required them to secure a royal licence before receiving such endowments in perpetuity.

As a result of this statute several trade and craft associations in London sought the security of a royal charter: the skinners and grocers in 1393, the goldsmiths and mercers in 1394, and the saddlers in the following year.[52] In fact these new royal charters did more than simply grant a licence to hold land in mortmain: they granted to these guilds the right to have a 'perpetual commonalty' or, in the words of the tailors' charter of 1408, 'a sound, perpetual and corporate fraternity' and to plead and be impleaded in common. It is therefore from the 1390s that some of the London guilds or fraternities can properly be called companies since it is at that time that they became incorporated bodies. This development was extremely important in enabling the companies to develop their spiritual and charitable functions and, in this respect, to challenge the church as the appropriate administrator of perpetual benefactions. These royal charters also enabled companies, by a form of delegated legislation, to draw up rules for the administration of their craft or trade that might cut across, or challenge, civic regulations. It was for this reason, therefore, that the Commons promoted a petition in the Parliament of 1437 to ensure that Letters Patent and charters should be shown to the governors of cities and towns and that no ordinances should be promulgated before they had

[51] Barron, 'Parish Fraternities', 16–17; the craft guilds from which returns survive are: glovers, cordwainers, saddlers, curriers, minstrels, barbers, cutlers, girdlers, painters, and goldsmiths: Barron and Wright, 'Guild Certificates', 115.

[52] Unwin, *Guilds and Companies*, ch. 11; E. Veale, *The English Fur Trade in the Later Middle Ages* (Oxford, 1966), 109; Nightingale, *Mercantile Community*, 400, 404 (in fact the grocers' first charter did not include a licence to alienate into mortmain, which the company did not secure until 1429); Reddaway and Walker, *Goldsmiths' Company*, ch. 4; A. Sutton, *The Mercers' Company's First Charter 1394* (The Mercers' Company, London, 1994); Oliver, *Company of Saddlers*, ch. 2.

been approved and enrolled by them.[53] Doubtless in response to this new regulation, the tailors and the saddlers were ordered to bring their charters to the mayor, Stephen Broun, in 1438–9 'to be examined by the counsel of the city to ascertain whether they were contrary to the city's liberties or not'.[54] It may well have been the activities of the tailors that provoked this particular legislation. They were an artisan company with a prestigious fraternity but they had comparatively little influence within the court of aldermen where there was only one tailor, Ralph Holland. The tailors needed men of influence to support them in their attempt to break into the profitable London market for the sale of cloth, and to fight off the powerful drapers who were claiming the right to search the cloth offered for sale in the city by tailors. Although the drapers could number several aldermen among their company, the tailors had been able to counter this advantage by their support among members of the aristocracy (their customers?) and from the Crown. They had secured a number of wide-ranging royal charters. The statute of 1437 forced them back under the authority of the mayor and aldermen. When the tailors' alderman, Ralph Holland, lost the mayoral election for the third time in 1441 to the draper, Robert Clopton, a riot broke out in Guildhall and sparked off the most serious challenge to the authority of the city's rulers in the fifteenth century.[55] But the purchase of a royal charter was not cheap: the mercers' costs in 1394 amounted to over £87; the tailors paid over £79 for their Letters Patent in 1439 and the pewterers' new charter in 1468 cost more than £100.[56] Yet such charters secured for the companies rights that were important: legal incorporation, a common livery, power to hold assemblies and elect officers to rule the company and carry out rights of search, the right to make ordinances and to hold land of a specified annual value in perpetuity. In theory these rights were held subject to the overriding authority of the mayor, but in practice power was slipping away from the city's rulers, and when there was further trial of strength between the tailors and the court of aldermen in 1504 over another royal charter that the tailors had secured, the city not only failed to get the tailors' charter annulled but provoked Parliament into deciding that the statute of 1437, which had been favourable to mayoral authority over guilds and companies, had lapsed.[57] Not surprisingly, therefore, the London crafts began increasingly to seek the security of a royal charter. Between 1462 and 1515 at least sixteen of the 'middle class' crafts and trades of the city

[53] That the governors of London played an active role in promoting this petition is suggested by the fact that it is copied into a city's Letter Book, see *LBD*, 311; W. Herbert, *The History of the Twelve Great Livery Companies of London*, 2 vols. (London, 1834), i. 106–7; *RP* iv. 507; *The Statutes of the Realm*, 10 vols. (London, 1810–28), ii. 298–9, 15 Henry VI. C.6.

[54] *CPMR 1337–57*, 33–4; Unwin, *Guilds and Companies*, 170.

[55] See C. Barron, 'Ralph Holland and the London Radicals, 1438–1444' in R. Holt and G. Rosser (eds.), *The Medieval Town: A Reader in Urban History 1200–1540* (London, 1990), 160–83.

[56] Sutton, 'Mercers' Company's First Charter', 10; Barron, 'Ralph Holland', 166; Unwin, 'Guilds and Companies', 164.

[57] H. Miller, 'London and Parliament in the Reign of Henry VIII', *BIHR* 35 (1962), 128–49; M. P. Davies, 'The Tailors of London and their Guild, *c.*1300–1500' (University of Oxford, D.Phil. thesis, 1994), 130–2.

bought royal charters.[58] A few companies sought the extra glamour of a grant of arms to embellish their new corporate status: the drapers (1438), the tallow chandlers (1456), and the cooks (1461 and 1467).[59]

But by no means all craft or trade associations felt the need to seek a royal charter of incorporation. Some continued simply to seek the approval of the mayor and aldermen. In the last forty years of the fifteenth century at least sixteen crafts had their ordinances enrolled in the city's Letter Book: indeed that Letter Book is almost entirely taken up with such ordinances.[60] In 1487 it was reiterated that all craft and trade ordinances in the city were to be approved by the mayor and aldermen, and those ordinances that had not been so approved were to be cancelled. The saddlers took the opportunity to revise and expand their ordinances, which had originally been drawn up in 1363. Not only were the saddlers now concerned to regulate the trade as a whole but it is interesting to note that, like all the company ordinances of this period, the new rules were drawn up in English and not in the Anglo-Norman of Edward III's reign.[61]

JOURNEYMEN AND YEOMEN

It is unlikely that the craft and trade groupings that emerged during this period and were recognized by the Crown or by the city's rulers represented all those who practised such a trade or craft in London. The mayor and aldermen may have come to recognize particular groups as representative of their fellow practitioners because it suited them to do so. At the end of the thirteenth century groups of wage workers (servants, i.e. not householders and probably not citizens) in the crafts of the skinners and the cordwainers had attempted to form their own associations to secure better terms from their employers, whether for higher wages or better prices for their goods. At about the same time there appears to have been associations of dissident (or alternative) groups among the carpenters, the blacksmiths, the spurriers, and the coppersmiths.[62] The economic dislocations that followed in the wake of the Black Death encouraged groups of wage labourers (servants, *vadlets*, or journeymen) to form associations to press for higher wages or better working conditions. There is evidence for such groups among the shearmen

[58] Unwin, *Guilds and Companies*, 163. Of these sixteen, four crafts, the tallowchandlers, dyers, cooks, and waxchandlers, took the precaution of having their charter enrolled in the city's Letter Book, see *LBL*, 101, 193–4, 211, 313.

[59] A. R. Wagner, *Heralds and Heraldry in the Middle Ages* (Oxford, 1956), ch. 8.

[60] Unwin, *Guilds and Companies*, 171. To Unwin's list of thirteen sets of ordinances copied into Letter Book L may be added those of the fishmongers (1462), the brewers, (1482) and the cutlers (1488), *LBL*, 16, 200–2, 256.

[61] Oliver, *Company of Saddlers*, 46–8.

[62] *CEMCR 1298–1307*, 25, 33, 52, 65. A. H. Thomas translated *servientibus operariis* as journeymen, literally workers who were paid by the day. But this word came later to have a slightly different connotation in the medieval period. In 1327 the sheathers attempted to control the work contracts of their servants or *vallets*: *CPMR 1323–64*, 39.

(1350), skinners (1368), saddlers (1380), spurriers (1381), and cordwainers (1387).[63] It is interesting that in three cases, the skinners, the cordwainers, and the spurriers there seems to have been some continuity of a subsidiary, or protest, association from the earlier part of the century. Although the mayor and aldermen often characterized such meetings as 'congregations, unions (*alligaciones*) and covins in taverns and other places' yet the members claimed that their associations were social and fraternal and not damaging to the common good.[64] That working men needed to form such associations may be explained by their exclusion from the inner secrets, and workings, of the craft. The ordinances of the bladesmiths drawn up in 1408 specifically required that 'no-one of the trade shall teach his journeyman the secrets (sciences) of his trade, as he would his apprentice'.[65] In these circumstances it is not surprising to find that these groups of workers turned to the church for support. As their members were bound together by a common oath, then those who failed to keep the oath could be summoned before the church courts.[66] The journeymen of the saddlers met in St Mary le Bow; the servingmen of the spurriers in St Bartholomew's Hospital and the servingmen of the cordwainers at the Blackfriars. Clearly such groups sought the support of the church when the hierarchy of civic government denied them recognition. The 'servingmen, called yomen' of the saddlers had formed a fraternity in honour of the Virgin's Assumption and on her feast day (August 15) they met at Stratford dressed in a common livery and processed into the city to the church of St Vedast in Foster Lane where they heard mass. Moreover they had a beadle who summoned members to attend the vigils of dead brothers. The masters of the saddlers asserted that the servingmen met 'under colour of sanctity' and that their real purpose was to take common action to raise their wages. The masters were also annoyed at finding that their workers would absent themselves without permission in order to attend the vigils. The mayor and aldermen decided that the servingmen were to hold no more meetings at Stratford nor anywhere else, and they were to be under the governance of the masters of the craft 'as the servingmen of the other trades in the city'. The masters, however, were enjoined to behave properly towards their servingmen, which suggests that faults had been found in the way they treated their workers.[67]

The servingmen of the tailors' craft provide a good example of a group of disaffected workers who were reintegrated into the 'main' company as, indeed, had been the hope of the mayor and aldermen in the case of the saddlers. By 1415 groups of 'yoman taillours' had taken to living together in houses around the city, holding their own assemblies, and wearing a common livery. The mayor and aldermen forbade them to do this in future and instructed them to accept the

[63] *Memorials*, 247–8, 251; *CPMR 1364–81*, 88–9; ibid. 264; ibid. 291–4; *Memorials*, 495.

[64] *CPMR 1364–81*, 89.

[65] *Memorials*, 570.

[66] E.g. the smiths in 1298–9: *CEMCR 1298–1307*, 33; the spurriers in 1381: *CPMR 1364–81*, 291.

[67] *Memorials*, 542–4; the saddlers ordinances of 1362 had expressly prohibited joint action by their employees but by 1380 such journeymen were meeting at St Mary le Bow: *CPMR 1364–81*, 264; Oliver, *Company of Saddlers*, 25–6.

'governance and rule of the masters and wardens of the trade, the same as other serving men of other trades in the city'.[68] Two years later the yeomen tailors made another bid for recognition and asked that they might be allowed to meet together annually on the feast of the Decollation of St John the Baptist (29 August: the 'main' tailors' guild was dedicated to St John the Baptist and celebrated his Nativity on 24 June) in the Hospitallers' church of St John at Clerkenwell to make offerings for the deceased brothers and sisters of the fraternity and for other rites. The mayor and aldermen, remembering the earlier problems, refused to sanction this association unless the meetings were held in the presence of the masters of the trade.[69] But this decision does not seem to have killed the fraternity of yeomen tailors but, rather, to have encouraged the 'parent' company to draw the yeomanry into the 'legitimate' guild. By 1437 the yeomen were allowed to celebrate their annual feast and to wear liveries and to celebrate the feast of the Decollation of St John, first with a mass at the church of St Martin Outwich next to the tailors' hall and then to go out to St John's Clerkenwell for their assembly, followed in the evening by an election dinner to be held in the company hall, to whose kitchen roof the yeomen tailors had contributed £6 13*s.* 4*d.* five years earlier.[70]

It seems to have been the case that the fraternity of the yeomanry of the tailors was composed both of men who were employed as servants by other tailors, and also of young men who had recently completed their apprenticeships but were not yet sufficiently established to enter the livery of the company. For them it simply marked a stage in their life cycle. The purposes of the fraternity were predominantly religious and the diversity of its membership meant that the group was unlikely to develop a coherent set of grievances or objectives.[71] Many of the young men who acted as wardens of the yeomen fraternity went on to be successful practitioners of their craft. Davy Brecknock and John Stanbury, the leaders of the yeomanry in 1415, both had distinguished careers in the service of John duke of Bedford. Stanbury was, by 1431, the keeper of Bedford's robes and jewels in France and Brecknock had extensive responsibilities as Bedford's wardrober with the charge not only of his chapel goods, furs, and domestic furnishings, but also of the papers and the books that Bedford had acquired from the Louvre library. By the end of his life he was a prosperous 'esquire and gentleman' with property in London and in Buckinghamshire.[72] In the same way the young men 'out of the livery' of the goldsmiths in 1477 made trouble for the wardens and were imprisoned for their pains. But all of them went on to take apprentices themselves, three became liverymen, and two were to hold the positions of renter and warden. They were young men in their twenties, impatient at the authority and practices of the rulers of the craft.[73] Likewise the skinners' company was, by the fifteenth century, composed of two fraternities, the fraternity of the liverymen dedicated to Corpus Christi and the fraternity of the yeomanry dedicated to the Virgin's Assumption

[68] *Memorials*, 609–12.
[69] 5 August 1417, *LBI*, 187–8.
[70] See M. P. Davies, 'The Tailors of London and their Guild', 147–56.
[71] Ibid. 155.
[72] J. Stratford, *The Bedford Inventories* (Society of Antiquaries, London, 1993), 407–8, 423.
[73] Reddaway and Walker, *Goldsmiths' Company*, 154.

and based on the church of St John Walbrook. This fraternity was prosperous and prestigious with its own wardens and clerk and store of linen and plate. Its members wore a common livery, attended each other's funerals, and relieved each other in need. The fraternity also attracted members from outside London, including members of the royal family and high-ranking ecclesiastics. But it had no governing role to play in the craft: that was carried out by a select group from within the Corpus Christi fraternity.[74] But not all fraternities of servants got on so harmoniously with their masters as did the tailors and skinners. In 1441 the masters of the bakers complained about the activities of the 'servauntis of the crafte' who had formed a brotherhood, wore a common livery, refused to work unsociable hours and supported each other against their employers. In spite of a spirited and reasoned defence put up by nine leaders and 'alle the company of the servauntes Bakeres of the said Citee', the mayor and aldermen supported the masters and told the servants to accept their governance and forbade them to wear any common 'clothing or livery'.[75]

These lesser associations might be called fraternities of yeomen, or 'bachelors', or journeymen, or servants, and in different crafts the associations were differently comprised. Almost always they were, in some way, subordinate to the ruling group composed primarily of masters and employers who were on almost every occasion supported by the mayor and aldermen in their attempts to keep the lesser/younger men, or servants, under their control. Apart from the tailors and the skinners, yeomanry fraternities were to be found in the curriers by 1388, cordwainers by 1423, blacksmiths by 1434, carpenters by 1468, and ironmongers by 1493.[76] Usually such lesser companies emerged when, as in the case of the tailors, the guild was very large, or when there was a sharp distinction, as in the case of the skinners, between the artisan workers and the merchant importers. In the course of the fifteenth century the distinctions between these different groups within companies became sharper: the prosperous, merchant, employer groups were distinguished from their lesser, younger, employee, artisan colleagues by the wearing of a distinctive livery: they were the liverymen of the company and recognized by the mayor and aldermen as the rulers of their craft.

THE EMERGENCE OF THE LIVERY COMPANIES

In the course of the fifteenth century in most of the larger companies the more substantial members were distinguished from the ordinary members by the wearing of the company livery. Earlier, as at the reception for Edward I's second wife Margaret in 1300, the citizens of London had all worn a common livery of red and white with the cognizances of the different crafts emblazoned on their sleeves.[77]

[74] Veale, *English Fur Trade*, 111–15.

[75] *LBK*, 263–6.

[76] Barron and Wright, 'English Guild Certificates', 115, 124; *A Book of London English 1384–1425*, eds. R. W. Chambers and M. Daunt (Oxford, 1931), 148; Unwin, *Guilds and Companies*, 225–7.

[77] See Ch. 1.

Clearly by the time of the royal inquiry into guilds in 1388 it had become the practice for the more prosperous associations, whether predominantly religious or craft, to wear a common livery or, at least, a common hood. The joiners' guild at the church of St James at Garlickhithe required that members 'every yer, shul be clothed in suyt, and every man paye for that he hath'.[78] The royal inquiry had particularly required guilds to state whether they wore a common livery and in the charters of the 1390s that right was specifically granted to the new companies. It seems to have been the practice for the livery cloth to be bought communally and then each member paid his share and had his cloth made up to fit. In 1418–19 the brewers spent £185 on livery cloth for their numerous members.[79] Some of this cloth might be given out to 'friends' of the company: the tailors gave hoods to most of the city officers and also to Richard Whittington every year between 1399 and 1414.[80] Although Whittington lived for a further eight years he ceased to receive a hood from the tailors because in 1415 the mayor and aldermen decided that no city officer was in future to 'take any livery or vestment from any craft or fraternity within the city, save only that one craft of which he has been made free'.[81]

In the larger and wealthier companies it was becoming the practice for the wearing of the craft livery to be restricted to a select group of the more prosperous members or, as in the case of the tailors, to those who were members of the fraternity within the craft. Indeed, if they had to pay for their share of the livery cloth this restriction may have been understandable. In 1428 the grocers' company was composed of sixty-eight members who wore the full livery, eighteen who wore only the hood and forty-nine householders or servants who were outside the livery.[82] In the period 1394–1461 covered by the account book of the mercers' company, 1,047 men entered the company of whom 456 (44%) reached the livery.[83] In 1404 there were 102 goldsmiths in the livery and eighty out of it, although by 1462 the company was reduced in size with sixty-three in the livery and forty-nine outside it.[84] The members of the founders' company in 1490 were divided into three categories: brothers of the clothing, householders keeping shop and not of the clothing, and journeymen.[85]

It was these brothers of the clothing, or the liverymen, who came to govern the crafts. In 1466 the mayor and aldermen decided that the election of the wardens in

[78] Chambers and Daunt, *London English*, 45; cf. the ordinances of the pouchmakers, ibid. 54.

[79] J. M. Bennett, 'Women and Men in the Brewers' Gild of London. ca.1420', in E. B. DeWindt (ed.), *The Salt of Common Life: Individuality and Choice in the Medieval Town, Countryside and Church: Essays Presented to J. Ambrose Raftis* (Kalamazoo, Mich., 1995), 181–232, esp. 201 n. 31, where Bennett corrects some earlier misunderstandings. It appears that women did not, as Unwin believed, wear livery cloth, *Guilds and Companies*, 191.

[80] C. Barron, 'Richard Whittington: The Man behind the Myth', in *Studies in London History*, 197–248, 234 n. 2.

[81] *Memorials*, 612.

[82] Nightingale, *Mercantile Community*, 421.

[83] Imray, 'Membership of the Mercers' Company', 174.

[84] Reddaway and Walker, *Goldsmiths' Company*, 79, 139; in 1477 there were fifty-seven in the livery and sixty-two 'young men': ibid. 138 .

[85] *LBL*, 272; cf. a similar threefold division in the cutlers' company in 1488: ibid. 256.

the butchers' company should in future be confined to those in the livery.[86] The evolution of an elite group within most companies gave tangible expression to the inchoate idea that some citizens were more worthy, more respectable than others. It was also more convenient to consult with a worthy few rather than the less biddable many. In 1467 the liverymen of the companies were recognized as a separate class when common council decided that to them would fall the responsibility of electing the mayor and the sheriffs at Guildhall each year.[87] In this way the stamp of official recognition was given to the separation of the liverymen from the other members of the craft, and the mere citizen was excluded from the elections of those who governed him.

COMPANY HALLS

More than liveries, however, it was the adaptation, or building, of company halls that provided the visible evidence of these new associations within the life of the city. Before the charters of incorporation in the late fourteenth century, few companies had their own halls, although some crafts, such as the goldsmiths, seem to have held land corporately but did so by the use of feoffees or trustees (and so avoided, until 1391, the need to acquire a royal licence). But this was rare. The precise stages by which groups of merchants or craftsmen acquired land and a common hall are far from clear, but by 1400 perhaps only six companies had taken this step, and all of them merchant, rather than artisan, associations (see Table 9.1). By 1500, however, a further thirty-one had built or bought halls, and by 1540 there were forty-seven company halls.

Why did these companies want to acquire halls? It was an expensive way to accommodate the annual feast and, in any case, it was possible to rent halls for such occasions. The brewers had built their hall early in the fifteenth century and in 1423 they were able to make money by letting it to fifteen different companies, including the 'footballpleyers' who hired the hall twice for 20*d.* and the yeomen of the cordwainers who hired it just once for 3*s.* 4*d.* The brewers also let the hall twice to the 'fraternity of the Cross' and four times to the 'fraternity of the Trinity', and once for the holding of the wardmote inquest.[88] In all they let their hall on forty-seven occasions in 1423 which netted a total income of £3 4*s.* 2*d.* (or an average of 1*s.* 4*d.* for each letting). By 1540, ten of the crafts that had hired the brewers' hall in 1423 had acquired halls of their own. Those who had not were the footballplayers (who were probably a club rather than a craft), the pointmakers (makers of fastenings for clothes), the ferrours (farriers, as opposed to the smiths), and the galochemakers (wooden shoe makers). None of these survived as an independent craft association in the city. On the other hand, the barbers who hired the hall nine

[86] *LBL*, 67; cf. the exclusion of the journeymen from the elections of the wardens to govern the weavers' company in 1444, *LBK*, 290.

[87] *LBL*, 73, and see Ch. 7.

[88] Chambers and Daunt, *London English*, 148.

times in 1423, and the girdlers and parish clerks who each hired it five times, must have become acutely aware of the need, and the advantage, of having a hall of their own. It is also apparent that crafts needed a hall more frequently than simply for their annual feast. A hall was becoming the increasingly necessary centre for the nascent administration of the crafts. It was the place where their records were compiled and stored, and their funds and treasures were hoarded. When a company acquired or built a hall it became the focus for the loyalties, and the common remembrances, of its members. It was in the hall that members (and their wives) might enjoy the style of communal living that members of the retinue of a great lord might experience in his household.

In one significant respect the company halls in London differed from the great houses or castles of the aristocracy: very few of them had chapels. The grocers' hall had a small chapel on the first floor, but it was very modest and the company retained its original close links with the parish church of St Antholin near Soper Lane.[89] The mercers, who had not had any particular association with a parish church, gradually took over the chapel of the house of St Thomas of Acre in Cheapside and then built themselves a new chapel there in the 1520s.[90] The hall of the merchant tailors seems to have had a chapel from the time when it was first built in the early fifteenth century but the company remained loyal to its fraternity chapel dedicated to St John the Baptist in St Paul's cathedral and also to the parish church of St Martin Outwich, next to their hall where, by 1548, the tailors were responsible for funding no fewer than ten obits or chantries.[91] Most companies did not have chapels within their new halls, but continued to use a conveniently situated parish church where they might adopt an altar or a chapel and fund one or more priests to pray particularly for their members. It has been argued that in the later medieval period the aristocracy and gentry in England went 'private' in their religious practices and tended to abandon their parish churches for their domestic chapels.[92] This was certainly not the case with the London companies whose religious habits remained distinctly public. The magnificent funeral palls that the companies acquired (those belonging to the fishmongers, the saddlers, the merchant tailors, and the brewers still survive) bear witness to this public life: the dead brothers and sisters of the craft would be buried in their own parish church, but the coffin would be covered with the richly embroidered cloth of the company, thus symbolizing the way in which the companies complemented parish life and did not supplant it.[93]

[89] Nightingale, *Mercantile Community*, 410–15.

[90] Imray, *Mercers' Hall*, 13–15.

[91] *London and Middlesex Chantry Certificate 1548*, ed. C. Kitching (London Record Society, 1980), 87–8; M. P. Davies, 'The Tailors of London and their Guild', 50.

[92] C. F. Richmond., 'Religion and the Fifteenth-Century English Gentleman', in R. B. Dobson (ed.), *The Church, Politics and Patronage in the Fifteenth Century* (Gloucester, 1984), 193–208.

[93] Unwin, *Gilds and Companies*, 214–16; Oliver, *Company of Saddlers*, 63 and endpapers; K. Staniland, *Embroiderers* (London, 1991), 60–1; P. Wallis, 'London, Londoners and Opus Anglicanum', in L. Grant (ed.), *Medieval Art, Architecture and Archaeology of London* (British Archaeological Association, 1990), 135–9, esp. 137–8.

TABLE 9.1: *Crafts and companies in some civic lists, 1328–1518*

	Craft	1328	1364	1376	1377(a)	1377(b)	1381	1445	1447
Armaments	Bowyers		✓	✓	✓	✓	✓	✓	
	Fletchers			✓	✓	✓	✓	✓	
Building	Carpenters								
	Glaziers								
	Limemen								
	Marbelers								✓
	Masons			✓	✓	✓	✓		
	Painters	✓		✓	✓		✓		✓
	Paviours								
	Plasterers								
	Stainers								✓
	Tilers								
Chandlers	Tallowchandlers		✓	✓	✓		✓	✓	✓
	Waxchandlers		✓	✓	✓		✓	✓	✓
Clothing	Broiderers			✓	✓	✓	✓	✓	
	Cappers	✓		✓					
	Girdlers	✓	✓	✓	✓		✓	✓	✓
	Glovers		✓					✓	✓
	Hatters				✓	✓	✓		
	Hosiers	✓							
	Hurers	✓		✓	✓	✓	✓		✓
	Netters								
	Tailors	✓	✓	✓	✓	✓	✓	✓	
	Upholders								✓
Leather/Furs	Bottlemakers								
	Cobblers								
	Cofferers	✓							
	Corders	✓							
	Cordwainers	✓	✓	✓	✓		✓		
	Curriers		✓	✓	✓	✓	✓		
	Leathersellers			✓	✓	✓	✓	✓	✓
	Pouchmakers		✓	✓	✓	✓	✓		
	Pursers								
	Saddlers	✓	✓	✓		✓	✓	✓	✓
	Skinners	✓	✓	✓	✓	✓	✓		✓
	Tanners		✓	✓	✓	✓	✓		
	Tawyers				✓	✓	✓		

1448	1449	1453(a)	1453(b)	1454	1456(a)	1456(b)	1461	1485	1488	1504	1518	Hall by 1540
			✓			✓	✓	✓	✓	✓	✓	✓
			✓			✓	✓	✓	✓	✓	✓	✓
			✓			✓	✓	✓	✓	✓	✓	✓
	✓		✓			✓		✓	✓			✓
										✓		
	✓								✓			✓
	✓		✓			✓	✓	✓	✓	✓	✓	✓
	✓		✓			✓	✓	✓	✓	✓	✓	✓
						✓			✓			✓
										✓		
	✓		✓			✓		✓	✓	✓	✓	
								✓	✓	✓	✓	✓
			✓			✓	✓	✓	✓	✓	✓	✓
✓			✓			✓	✓	✓	✓	✓	✓	✓
	✓		✓			✓		✓	✓	✓	✓	✓
✓			✓		✓	✓	✓	✓	✓	✓	✓	✓
								✓	✓	✓		
	✓							✓		✓		
			✓			✓		✓		✓		
	✓							✓	✓			
✓			✓	✓	✓	✓	✓	✓	✓	✓	✓	✓
✓			✓			✓	✓	✓	✓	✓		
	✓											
	✓											
	✓											
			✓		✓	✓	✓	✓	✓	✓	✓	✓
✓	✓		✓			✓		✓	✓	✓	✓	✓
✓		✓	✓	✓		✓	✓	✓	✓	✓	✓	✓
✓									✓			
									✓	✓		
✓		✓	✓	✓	✓	✓	✓	✓	✓	✓	✓	✓
✓		✓	✓	✓	✓	✓	✓	✓	✓	✓	✓	✓
✓								✓	✓			

Table 9.1 (cont.)

	Craft	1328	1364	1376	1377(a)	1377(b)	1381	1445	1447
Mercantile	Drapers	✓	✓	✓	✓	✓	✓	✓	✓
	Felmongers								
	Haberdashers	✓		✓	✓	✓	✓	✓	✓
	Linendrapers								
	Mercers	✓	✓	✓	✓	✓	✓	✓	✓
	Woolmongers	✓							
Metal	Armourers		✓	✓	✓		✓	✓	
	Bladesmiths								
	Braziers		✓	✓	✓				
	Cardmakers				✓	✓			
	Coppersmiths								
	Cutlers	✓	✓	✓	✓	✓	✓	✓	
	Ferrours								
	Founders			✓	✓	✓	✓	✓	
	Goldsmiths	✓	✓	✓	✓	✓	✓	✓	✓
	Ironmongers	✓	✓	✓	✓	✓	✓		
	Latteners								
	Lorimers				✓	✓	✓		✓
	Pewterers		✓	✓	✓		✓	✓	✓
	Pinners			✓	✓	✓	✓	✓	
	Plumbers			✓	✓	✓	✓		
	Smiths			✓	✓	✓	✓		
	Spurriers		✓	✓	✓	✓	✓		
	Wiresellers								
Textiles	Dyers			✓	✓		✓	✓	
	Fullers			✓	✓		✓	✓	
	Shearmen			✓	✓	✓	✓	✓	✓
	Tapissers			✓	✓	✓	✓		
	Weavers			✓	✓	✓	✓		
Transport	Carters								
Victualling	Apothecaries	✓							
	Bakers			✓	✓	✓	✓		
	Brewers		✓	✓	✓	✓	✓	✓	✓
	Butchers	✓	✓	✓	✓	✓	✓	✓	
	Cheesemongers	✓							
	Cooks							✓	
	Fishmongers	✓	✓	✓	✓	✓	✓	✓	✓
	Fruiterers								
	Grocers	✓	✓	✓	✓	✓	✓	✓	✓
	Pastillers								

1448	1449	1453(a)	1453(b)	1454	1456(a)	1456(b)	1461	1485	1488	1504	1518	Hall by 1540
✓		✓	✓	✓	✓	✓	✓	✓	✓	✓	✓	✓
								✓	✓	✓		
✓		✓	✓	✓	✓	✓	✓	✓	✓	✓	✓	✓
								✓	✓	✓		
✓		✓		✓	✓	✓	✓	✓	✓	✓	✓	✓
								✓	✓	✓		
✓			✓			✓	✓	✓	✓	✓	✓	✓
	✓		✓					✓	✓	✓		
	✓								✓			
✓	✓							✓	✓			
✓			✓		✓	✓	✓	✓	✓	✓	✓	✓
✓	✓								✓			
✓	✓		✓		✓	✓	✓	✓	✓	✓		
✓		✓	✓	✓	✓	✓	✓	✓	✓	✓	✓	✓
✓			✓	✓	✓	✓	✓	✓	✓	✓	✓	✓
	✓											
✓			✓			✓		✓	✓	✓		
✓	✓		✓		✓	✓		✓	✓	✓	✓	✓
			✓			✓		✓	✓			✓
	✓					✓	✓	✓	✓	✓	✓	
✓	✓		✓			✓	✓	✓	✓	✓	✓	✓
	✓		✓			✓		✓	✓	✓	✓	
								✓	✓	✓	✓	
			✓	✓	✓	✓	✓	✓	✓	✓	✓	✓
			✓		✓	✓	✓	✓	✓	✓	✓	✓
✓	✓		✓	✓		✓	✓	✓	✓	✓	✓	✓
	✓					✓		✓	✓			
	✓		✓					✓	✓	✓	✓	✓
											✓	
	✓		✓			✓	✓	✓	✓	✓	✓	✓
✓			✓	✓		✓	✓	✓	✓	✓	✓	✓
✓			✓		✓	✓	✓	✓	✓	✓	✓	✓
								✓	✓			
✓			✓									✓
✓		✓		✓	✓	✓	✓	✓	✓	✓	✓	✓
			✓			✓		✓	✓			
✓		✓	✓	✓	✓	✓	✓	✓	✓	✓	✓	✓
						✓	✓	✓	✓		✓	

Table 9.1 (cont.)

	Craft	1328	1364	1376	1377(a)	1377(b)	1381	1445	1447
	Poulters		✓						✓
	Salters		✓	✓	✓		✓	✓	
	Stockfishmongers								
	Vintners	✓	✓	✓	✓	✓	✓		✓
Wood	Coopers								
	Fusters	✓			✓	✓	✓		
	Joiners			✓	✓	✓	✓		
	Pattenmakers								
	Shipwrights								
	Turners								
	Wheelwrights								
	Woodmongers			✓	✓		✓		
Other	Barber Surgeons								✓
	Barbers								
	Beaders	✓							
	Clerks								
	Corsers								
	Horners			✓	✓	✓	✓		✓
	Innholders								✓
	Organmakers								
	Scriveners							✓	✓
	Stationers								
	Surgeons								✓
	Woolpackers								
	Writers Court Han								

1328 Masters of crafts sworn, *LBE*, 232–234
1364 Crafts contributing to a loan to the king, *LBG*, 171–2
1376 Crafts sending representatives to the common council, *LBH*, 42–44
1377(a) Crafts sending representatives to the common council, *CPMR* 1364–81, 243
1377(b) Crafts sending representatives to the common council, ibid., 256
1381 Crafts sending representatives to the common council, *CPMR* 1381–1412, 29
1445 Crafts sent to meet the queen, CLRO, Journal 4, fo. 72^{v}
1447 Crafts contributing to Guildhall chapel, ibid., fo. 192–99
1448 Crafts contributing to peace-keeping, ibid., fo.217^{v}
1449 Crafts paying for soldiers, CLRO, Journal 5, fo.11
1453(a) Crafts going to meet the queen, ibid., fo. 120
1453(b) Crafts contributing to peace-keeping, ibid., fos 131–131^{v}

1448	1449	1453(a)	1453(b)	1454	1456(a)	1456(b)	1461	1485	1488	1504	1518	Hall by 1540
✓			✓				✓	✓	✓	✓	✓	
			✓	✓		✓	✓	✓	✓	✓	✓	✓
										✓		
		✓	✓	✓	✓	✓	✓	✓	✓	✓	✓	✓
	✓		✓			✓		✓	✓	✓	✓	✓
	✓					✓		✓	✓			
			✓			✓	✓	✓	✓	✓	✓	✓
✓			✓			✓		✓				
								✓	✓			
	✓						✓	✓	✓			
								✓	✓			
								✓	✓	✓	✓	
									✓			
✓			✓		✓	✓	✓	✓	✓	✓	✓	✓
	✓											✓
	✓								✓			
			✓			✓		✓	✓			
✓						✓		✓	✓	✓	✓	✓
									✓			
			✓			✓		✓	✓	✓		
			✓					✓	✓	✓		✓
	✓		✓				✓	✓	✓	✓		
	✓										✓	
						✓						

1454 Crafts patrolling the Thames, ibid., fos 187v–188
1456(a) Crafts consulted about a tax, CLRO, Journal 6, fo. 5
1456(b) Crafts contributing soldiers, ibid., fo. 106
1461 Crafts appointed to guard the city, ibid., fo. 35
1485 Lists of crafts from Trinity College, Cambridge, MS 0.3.1, fos 62v–63
1488 Crafts contributing to a loan to the king, Bodleian Library, Oxford, Digby Roll 2, fo. 28v
1504 Crafts contributing to Guildhall kitchens, CLRO, Rep., 1 fos. 181–182v. In this list the Hurers/Hattermerchants, Painters/Stainers and Glovers/Pursers are listed as joint companies
1518 Crafts appointed to keep the watch, CLRO, LBN, fo. 79
1540 Crafts with halls by this date

It is clear that the company halls varied considerably in grandeur and in cost. The grocers' magnificent new hall built of stone in the years 1427–41 cost a total of £1,750, including the cost of the site and legal fees,[94] whereas the pinners in the 1470s simply adapted a building at a cost of £7 6*s.* 0*d.* with a mere 5*s.* 4*d.* spent on the furnishings: a table, two trestles and four forms.[95] The larger companies added extra rooms to their halls, such as a parlour or kitchens. The drapers provided a room especially for the use of ladies and several of the company halls had elaborate gardens.[96] It seems as if the grocers took particular trouble over their garden which boasted not only herb and rose beds, but archery butts and a fruitful vine which provided two or three bunches of grapes daily for the members.[97] In 1379 the goldsmiths feasted Isabel, the daughter of Edward III and her daughter Philippa, the countess of Oxford, Lord Latimer, John Hales, the prior of the Hospitallers at Clerkenwell, John Philipot, the mayor of London, and six other 'good folks of the city'.[98] It was in its hall that the company could provide impressive entertainment, and the craftsmen and suppliers could make friends and influence customers.

Just as a nobleman's hall was the centre of his administration, so it was for the city companies. The accounts that have survived bear witness to the developing bureaucracy of the crafts. Almost every company had its own beadle who looked after the records, collected quarterage, organized feasts, kept lists of members, summoned them to meetings, and acted as the caretaker for the hall and garden.[99] At the end of the fourteenth century, when the beadle may well have been the only company employee, the mercers paid theirs £4 p.a. and the tailors theirs £3 p.a. In 1463 the pewterers were able to pay their beadle only 24*s.* and the lowly pinners paid a meagre 6*s.* 8*d.*, but at least they were able to pay something for a 'common servant'.[100] The larger companies, however, by the mid-fifteenth century were also employing skilled clerks to keep their records and to provide legal advice. One of the first such clerks was the energetic and assiduous William Porlond, who kept the records of the brewers' craft from 1418 until his death twenty years later. The tailors employed three clerks between the late 1450s and 1512: the most remarkable of them, Henry Mayour, had been employed by the goldsmiths' company before he moved to the clerkship of the tailors who paid him the substantial annual salary of £5.[101] Some companies employed a rent-collector and, in a few cases, also a gardener and a cook.

94 Nightingale, *Mercantile Community*, 398–421, esp. 420.

95 Unwin, *Guilds and Companies*, 187.

96 A. H. Johnson, *The History of the Worshipful Company of the Drapers of London*, 4 vols. (Oxford, 1914–22), i. 113.

97 Nightingale, *Mercantile Community*, 417–20.

98 Herbert, *Twelve Great Livery Companies*, ii. 235; Reddaway and Walker, *Goldsmiths' Company*, 44.

99 Unwin, *Guilds and Companies*, 188.

100 Ibid. 187–9; Reddaway and Walker, *Goldsmiths' Company*, 137.

101 Bennett, 'Women and Men in the Brewers' Gild', 184–5; M. P. Davies, *The Merchant Taylors' Company of London: Court Minutes 1486–1493* (Stamford, 2000), 8–12, 253.

THE CHARITABLE ACTIVITIES OF THE COMPANIES

The incorporation of the London guilds led to another development of great significance: they were now able to become the repositories of charitable trusts and in this way they came to administer large estates bequeathed to them in trust to fulfil religious and charitable purposes. By the time of the dissolution of the monasteries and the chantries in 1534–48, the city companies had largely replaced the religious houses as the recipients of land to be used to fund charitable purposes and prayers for the donor. Incorporation made the city companies as immortal as religious houses and, as events turned out, more so. London benefactors appear to have had more faith in the business acumen of their fellows than in the religious communities of an earlier period. The concern for pious commemoration and for social security which had led men to form and to join religious fraternities now found concrete expression in the endowment of trusts, run by companies, to respond to spiritual, social, and educational concerns. It was only incorporated companies that could administer trust funds in this way. In 1437 the vintners were seeking a charter of incorporation from the king but when Richard Meryvale, a vintner, drew up his will on 5 April, the company had not yet secured the charter and so Meryvale left them lands and tenements in the parish of St Edmund in Lombard Street to fund relief for the poor of the mistery, provided that they secured incorporation within the next two years.[102] In fact the vintners secured their charter on 22 August that year and so were able to accept the Meryvale bequest. When Guy Shuldham, another vintner, drew up his will in 1446 he was able to leave to the company the site in the Vintry on which they built not only their hall but also thirteen almshouses 'for poor and needy men and women of the said mistery' or, if there were none among the vintners, then any poor and needy men and women of good fame were to live in the almshouses and receive one penny a week out of the profits of Shuldham's lands.[103] In return the company was to observe certain obits in the church of St Martin Vintry and to maintain a chantry there. By the time of the chantry inquiry in 1548, the vintners' company received £7 p.a. from the Shuldham lands out of which they paid 15*s.* for an obit and had £6 12*s.* clear profit.[104] The company may well have used this money for the poor in the almshouses, but this is not made clear.

By the sixteenth century most city companies were administering some trust funds, and the larger companies had very large property portfolios. Their responsibilities covered the provision of obits, the maintenance of chantries, the relief of the poor, the running of almshouses and the oversight of schools. The tailors were responsible for a grammar school in Wolverhampton founded by Sir Stephen Jenyns; the goldsmiths administered the schools at Stockport and at Cromer, both

[102] *HW* ii. 487–8.

[103] Ibid. 596; CLRO, HR 224(17) for details of Shuldham's bequest; for almshouses generally, see Ch. 11.

[104] *London Chantry Certificate*, 83.

established by wealthy goldsmiths, and the mercers looked after the endowments that funded an elementary school at Farthinghoe in Northamptonshire as well as the famous school at St Paul's which was reorganized by John Colet early in the sixteenth century.[105] It is clear that the responsibilities of the city companies as trustees extended far beyond London itself. By 1548 the grocers were responsible for paying priests to say memorial masses in Biddenham, Bedfordshire, Lullingstone, Kent, Thorpe Salvin in Yorkshire, Glynde in Sussex, and at the chapel at Halliwell in Middlesex. In addition they funded priests and obits in nine churches in London. In all the grocers had a 'charitable' property portfolio that produced over £150 p.a. and from which the company, after paying for priests and giving the stipulated amounts to the poor, had a clear profit of nearly £65 which could be used as they saw best. In addition the company looked after two cash funds amounting to £180 out of which they paid annual salaries to priests, presumably until the money was used up.[106] Even a modest company such as the waxchandlers was responsible for maintaining obits in two parish churches in London for which they had received lands worth £11 3*s.* 4*d.* and, after paying for the obits, for lights, a quitrent to the king and £2 13*s.* 4*d.* for the poor, cleared £5 18*s.* 1*d.* in profit.[107] Of course, much of this land and the income was confiscated by the Crown in 1548 and the companies had difficulty even in holding on to the land which had been given for 'non-superstitious' purposes such as the relief of the poor, for education, the maintenance of church fabric, or the upkeep of the company hall.

THE ADMINISTRATION OF THE COMPANIES

The responsibility for administering these substantial property portfolios, the choice of fraternity priests and of schoolmasters, the organization of commemorations, funerals, and feasts, the employment and payment of company servants, and the adjudication of disputes between members, all fell to the masters and wardens of the company. Although the terminology differed somewhat between crafts, by the end of the fifteenth century, most companies were governed by a master and two or four wardens. The pinners, however, had two wardens and an umpire seen, perhaps, as an adjudicator should the wardens not agree. These men (never women) were selected not by the whole body of the craft, nor by the livery, but by their predecessors. In 1516 the drapers had a master and four wardens who chose their successors by handing over garlands at the company feast.[108] These 'honorary' officers were, in most companies, helped by a group of senior members

[105] C. Barron, 'The Expansion of Education in Fifteenth-Century London', in J. Blair and B. Golding (eds.), *The Cloister and the World: Essays in Medieval History in Honour of Barbara Harvey* (Oxford, 1996), 219–45, esp. 236–7.

[106] *London Chantry Certificate*, 88–9.

[107] Ibid. 84.

[108] Unwin, *Gilds and Companies*, 197; cf. Imray, 'Membership of the Medieval Mercers' Company', 176–7.

of the company who were known as 'assistants' and they, together with the master and wardens, constituted the court of assistants.[109] The master and wardens needed help and advice in carrying out their multifarious and onerous duties. They also needed the reassurance of spreading responsibility rather more widely. As early as 1376 the grocers were selecting six men to act as auditors and advisers to their wardens.[110] The shearmen had twelve assistants, whereas the mercers had a more informal committee of ex-wardens and those mercers who were currently serving as aldermen in the city. But in 1463 they decided

> That for the holding of many courts and congregations of the fellowship, it is tedious and grievous to the body of the fellowship and especially for matters of no great effect. That hereafter yearly shall be chosen and associated to the Wardens for the time-being, 12 other sufficient persons to be assisting to the said wardens so being, when and as often as they shall be duly required if need be, and all matters by them, or the most part of them finished, to be held firm and stable and the fellowship to abide by them.[111]

In 1486 the carpenters decided that every Friday the master and wardens might summon such members of the fellowship as they thought fit to help them in the 'support and continuance' of the good rules of the craft and in the 'reformacion, repressyng and punysshement of Rebellious or mysdoers ayenst the same Rules and ordenaunces'.[112] In fact the records of meetings of such company courts of assistants rarely survive from the fifteenth century, and most of the surviving company material is financial. There are minute books for the goldsmiths' company from the late fourteenth century, and for the mercers from 1453, and the remains of two books covering the years 1486–93 survive from the archives of the merchant tailors.[113] Although the mercers' volume is an edited transcript made in the second quarter of the sixteenth century, the other records seem to have been compiled near to the time of the meetings of the courts they record. It may be that William Newbold, the mercers' clerk who compiled the transcript, edited out matter which seemed to him of little significance. Thus, whereas the mercers appear to have been largely preoccupied with 'political' matters and with the rate of the subsidy on exported wool and cloth, the records of the goldsmiths and tailors are more domestic, concerned with entries into apprenticeship and the freedom, disputes arising between masters and apprentices, and the contributions to be made by the companies to civic ceremonial. Moreover, different clerks (as can be clearly seen in the case of the tailors' minute book) recorded meetings and events in very different ways.[114] Not all craftsmen belonged to such well-organized companies: when the makers of points, the galochemakers, or the farriers—craftsmen who

[109] Unwin, *Guilds and Companies*, 218.

[110] Nightingale, *Mercantile Community*, 249 and n. 7.

[111] *Acts of Court of the Mercers' Company 1453–1527*, eds. L. Lyell and F. D. Watney (Cambridge, 1936), 58.

[112] *LBL*, 241 and n. 3.

[113] Reddaway and Walker, *Goldsmiths' Company*, *Acts of Court of the Mercers' Company*, ed. Lyell and Watney; *Merchant Taylors Court Minutes*, ed. Davies.

[114] *Merchant Taylors Court Minutes*, ed. Davies, 8–12.

never associated sufficiently formally to draw up ordinances, let alone acquire a hall—quarrelled among themselves, then it is likely that they would resort to the mayor's court to settle disputes which, in the larger and more organized crafts, would be the business of the weekly court of assistants.

The range of business covered by the companies' courts of assistants was very considerable. There was a growing responsibility for lands and for the charitable purposes that the lands supported. There were legal battles to be fought and potential benefactors to be wooed and won. The hall and all its outbuildings had to be maintained and furnished. Increasingly the mayor and aldermen expected the companies to provide men for the watch and money for civic enterprises and to take responsibility for the good behaviour of their members. On occasion additional levies had to be raised from members, whether for civic or company purposes. Some companies, like the mercers, might be in direct negotiation with the Crown, or with the Royal Council, about economic policy and indirect taxation. The pretensions of rival craftsmen, and of non-citizens and aliens, had to be challenged and defeated. The right to search for defective goods had to be defended when it was challenged by other crafts, by the mayor and aldermen, or by the Crown. It might be necessary to organize petitions to Parliament. All aspects of apprenticeship and entries to the freedom were regulated, and disputes resolved, by the company courts. The sanctions the courts could impose were physical chastisement (in the case of apprentices), fining (often hard to collect), and, in the last resort, expulsion from the company, which could carry with it loss of citizenship and its attendant economic privileges unless, or course, the recalcitrant man could find another company to adopt him.

CRAFT RIVALRIES AND AMALGAMATIONS

Although the companies might attempt to settle disputes with other crafts within their own courts, it was to the mayor and aldermen that jurisdiction ultimately belonged. Much of the time of the court of aldermen was taken up with such disputes and this was particularly the case in the early fourteenth century when the structures for governing the crafts were not yet formalized and groups of men who worked in related, or sometimes interdependent, crafts fought to secure a share of the market, or to monopolize it, or to dominate (or escape the domination of) another craft. There were conflicts between burellers (cloth salesmen) and weavers,[115] between tailors and tawyers,[116] between girdlers and saddlers,[117] between skinners and tawyers,[118] and between bowyers and fletchers,[119] to mention only a few of the more bitter disputes. The demand for luxury goods created a need for specialized crafts: in 1365 Robert Leg was described as an 'ageletmakere',

[115] Year 1300, *CEMCR 1298–1307*, 53–5.

[116] Years 1305, 1321, *Calendar of London Trailbaston Trials under Commission of 1305 and 1306*, ed., R. B. Pugh (London, 1975), 95; *Eyre 1321*, i. 77.

[117] Year 1356, *LBG*, 67, 70.

[118] Year 1365, *Memorials*, 330–1.

[119] Year 1371, ibid. 348–50.

i.e. a maker of the metal tags on shoelaces. Not surprisingly he fell into dispute with the wiredrawers who may well have supplied his raw materials.[120] In the same way, the fusters, who made wooden saddle trees became dependent upon the saddlers who were the sole purchasers of their products.[121] These conflicts were particularly sharp in the fourteenth century when the luxury market was expanding and craft structures were fluid and less hierarchical. Although there were some notable craft disputes in the fifteenth century, such as that between the drapers and the tailors in the 1430s and between the cobblers and the cordwainers more continually, yet the general shortage of labour after 1350 ensured that there was enough work to go round.[122] The sharpest battles were not for work, but for workmen.

In the second half of the fifteenth century as the population began once more to rise, so there was shortage of work and this led crafts into disputes but, most frequently, into amalgamations. That the manufacturing crafts in London were feeling under pressure can be seen from the increasingly protectionist ordinances that they presented to the mayor and aldermen, and in their plaintive petitions to Parliament in which they complain about the massive imports of manufactured goods flooding the home market and leaving English workers unemployed.[123] The response to these pressures was for groups of craftsmen to amalgamate to form larger and more secure groupings. The leathersellers (whose earliest ordinances date from 1372) absorbed the tawyers in 1479, the glovers and pursers (who had already combined forces in 1498) in 1502, and the pouchmakers in 1517. It is likely that the leathersellers (who had established a hall by 1445) were already buying up the products of the smaller craftsmen and acting as indispensable middlemen.[124] The horners and bottlemakers joined forces in 1476 because they had become 'so distressed and impoverished', and in 1497 the wiremongers amalgamated with the pinners to form the wiresellers because of their poverty and decay and, even so, they then fell under the sway of the girdlers.[125] At the turn of the sixteenth century the expansionist haberdashers' company absorbed the older, but struggling, craft groups of hatters and cappers.[126] The surgeons finally agreed to link up with the inferior, but more numerous, company of barbers to form the barber-surgeons company, and the fullers and shearmen joined forces in 1528 to form the clothworkers' company. These are only some of the many amalgamations that characterize the activities of city crafts and trades at the end of the fifteenth century. In

[120] E. Veale, 'Craftsmen and the Economy of London in the Fourteenth Century', in Holt and Rosser (eds.), *The Medieval Town*, 120–40, esp. 131.

[121] Oliver, *Company of Saddlers*, 18–24; cf. D. Keene, 'Metalworking', 98–9; G. Rosser, 'Crafts, Guilds and the Negotiation of Work in the Medieval Town', *Past and Present*, 154 (1997), 3–31, esp. 14.

[122] Barron, 'Ralph Holland', in Holt and Rosser, *The Medieval Town*; *Memorials*, 571–4; *LBL*, 146–7.

[123] *LBL*, p. xxxvi; C. Barron, 'London and Parliament in the Lancastrian Period', *Parliamentary History*, 9 (1990), 343–67, esp. 360–1; for the volume and type of goods imported into London, see *The Overseas Trade of London: Exchequer Customs Accounts 1480–1*, ed. H. S. Cobb (London Record Society, 1990), pp. xxxv–xxxviii.

[124] Unwin, *Gilds and Companies*, 167–8.

[125] Ibid. 163; *LBL*, 138, 319–20.

[126] Archer, *Haberdashers' Company*, 16.

1422 the brewers' clerk listed 111 crafts used in the city of London in the past or at the present. He included crafts such as burlesters and basketmakers, which we know lacked any formal organization, and he omitted well-organized crafts such as the coopers, fusters, masons, and bladesmiths.[127] The fact is that from the 1370s when there were about fifty crafts sufficiently organized to elect men to represent them at the common council, the number of such organised crafts remained fairly constant (see Table 9.1).[128] Fifty-three crafts were summoned to assist the mayor and aldermen in safeguarding the city in 1453, and fifty-six crafts were expected to provide, or finance, soldiers three years later.[129] The forty-eight companies that kept the watch in 1518 were not all the same crafts who had elected men to the common council in the 1370s: gone, for example, are the cappers, glovemakers, pouchmakers, tawyers, tanners, braziers, tapissers, hatters, hurers, lorimers, fusters, and horners. Instead new crafts have emerged, the pastillers, wiresellers, carpenters, stainers, tilers, coopers, barbers, and innholders.[130] In general the changed listings reflect a shift from the manufacturing crafts to the building, food, and service industries. The crafts of the 1370s were probably still practised in the city but, as we have seen in the case of the hatters and hurers, now within larger and more secure associations.

But the varying winds of economic prosperity also affected the 'great twelve'. An analysis of the men of the different companies who were elected to the court of aldermen in the period 1300–1550 shows that whereas the drapers, mercers, and fishmongers dominated the court in the early fourteenth century, the grocers were most prominent in the later part of the century. The fishmongers and the vintners both declined sharply in influence in the fifteenth century. Meanwhile the marketing trades represented by the merchant tailors and the haberdashers began to make their presence felt in the court of aldermen only at the end of the fifteenth century, and then much more strongly in the sixteenth. The artisan crafts are noticeably absent: whereas corders and cordwainers were elected as aldermen in the early fourteenth century, this was not the case later until a member of the new leathersellers' amalgamated company was elected in 1546. In the period of annual elections of aldermen between 1376 and 1394, a move intended to broaden the constituency from which aldermen were elected, only two artisans were selected, a broiderer and a waxchandler. Henry Pountfreyt, a saddler, was the only craftsman to serve as an alderman in the fifteenth century: he was alderman for the ward of Bishopsgate from 1403 to 1411.[131] When in the sixteenth century, a broiderer, a brewer, a tallowchandler, and a painter-stainer were elected as aldermen, they transferred to one of the 'greater' crafts. But by this date the association between

[127] Unwin, *Gilds and Companies*, 167, 370; Veale, 'Craftsmen and the Economy', 128.

[128] See *CPMR 1364–81*, 243, 256; *CPMR 1381–1413*, 29; see Table 9.1.

[129] CLRO, Journal 5, fo. 120; ibid. 6, fo. 106; see Table 9.1.

[130] Unwin, *Gilds and Companies*, 371; of the forty-eight companies keeping the watch, nine are not known to have had a hall by 1540, although several acquired one not long afterwards, see table 9.1.

[131] A. B. Beaven, *The Aldermen of the City of London*, 2 vols. (London, 1908–13), ii. 2; Oliver, *Company of Saddlers*, 51.

the name of a company and the activities of those who were its members was becoming much less close.

Such discrepancies in political influence between the greater trading groups and the lesser artisan associations were bound to create tensions within the city, between those who exercised power and influence and those who did not. Contemporaries were aware of these differences although they were not always described in the same way. In 1299 William de la Foreste claimed that he was an *operarius* (handicraftsman) and not a merchant; in the proclamation that followed the murder of Bishop Stapledon in November 1326 the good men of the city whether 'working with their hands or trading' were enjoined to keep the peace.[132] John Bale, the organization man behind the tailors' struggle with the drapers in the 1430s and 1440s told the court of aldermen that the prosperity of the city depended upon the artisans (*artifices*) and not upon the merchants (*mercatores*).[133] Of course this was not the only economic fissure between groups in medieval London. One difference between the merchant traders and the artisans was that the artisans tended to form groups of men who were carrying out the same craft. Merchants, on the other hand, in spite of their company associations, tended to be general traders, often (but not exclusively) engaged in overseas trade, and their spheres of influence overlapped. In the fourteenth century, while grocers were primarily involved in the import of spices, mercers in the import of linens, silks, and expensive textiles, and drapers primarily in the export of cloth, all three companies were in fact engaged in exporting and importing a wide range of products. It was the rivalries among the merchant classes that produced the bitter struggles of the 1370s and 1380s. In the earlier fourteenth century, whereas the drapers had provided a significant component of the court of aldermen, by the reign of Richard II the grocers had overtaken them in influence (and doubtless in prosperity also).[134] There were different factions within the drapers' craft, and John of Northampton championed one group and looked for support among the 'small people' of London. He presented himself as a radical leader aiming to bring down the price of food and to broaden the representation of the smaller crafts in city government. When he was mayor he relied on the support of men from crafts such as the armourers, girdlers, lorimers, pinners, wiredrawers, cardmakers, curriers, horners, tilers, smiths, dyers, fullers, shearmen, haberdashers, and cordwainers.[135] By the 1390s the unity of the mercantile class was largely restored and so, although the rift between the merchants and the artisans remained, the stability of city government was not seriously threatened when the tailors challenged the dominance of the drapers in the 1430s and 1440s.[136] It is of significance, however, that the

[132] *CEMCR 1298–1307*, 49; *CPMR 1323–64*, 16.

[133] CLRO, Journal 4, fo. 10.

[134] For a discussion of the causes of the acute rivalries of this period, see R. Bird, *The Turbulent London of Richard II* (London, 1949); P. Nightingale, 'Capitalists, Crafts, and Constitutional Change in Late Fourteenth-Century London', *Past and Present*, 124 (1989), 3–35; I. Archer, *The Pursuit of Stability: Social Relations in Elizabethan London* (Cambridge, 1991), 21–4; Quinton, 'The Drapers and the Drapery Trade', 36–82.

[135] E. Powell and G. M. Trevelyan (eds.), *The Peasants' Rising and the Lollards* (London, 1899), 27.

[136] See Barron, 'Ralph Holland'; Davies, 'The Tailors of London and their Guild', 120–7.

tailors in 1503 sought incorporation from the Crown as 'merchant tailors' and the haberdashers also persuaded Henry VII to incorporate them under the name of 'merchant haberdashers' (which annoyed the court of aldermen and was later dropped, although the tailors clung to their hard-won merchant title).[137]

THE COMPANIES AND THE CITY

On the whole, although the crafts and trades were anxious to play a part in London government, the city's rulers were largely content to leave them to settle their own disputes and control their own workmen and standards.[138] In the fourteenth century the crafts made serious attempts to form the electorate for the common council: twenty-five crafts elected councilmen in 1328 and thirteen in 1350.[139] After the changes of 1376, between thirty-nine and fifty crafts elected men to the common council until the older system of election by the wards was restored in 1384.[140] Even if this route to participation in civic government was cut off, yet in the course of the fifteenth century the crafts, whether artisan or trading, were increasingly summoned by the court of aldermen to play a part in governing the city. Between 1445 and 1456 the city companies were called upon at least nine times to raise money or soldiers, to help the mayor to keep the peace, to patrol the Thames, or to contribute to the ceremonial entry of Queen Margaret on her arrival from France.[141] Sometimes their masters and wardens were summoned to meet the court of aldermen simply to give advice.[142] It is true that these were particularly difficult years for the city's rulers, but it is also the case that by this date the crafts were sufficiently well governed, and sufficiently wealthy, to be in a position to assist the mayor and aldermen in their tasks. Moreover, many of the companies now had halls to which they could summon their members, whereas it was much more difficult for an alderman to summon the men of his ward for he had to use a church or his own house. So these vigorous new organizations with their burgeoning bureaucracies, records, and common purposes were ideal vessels into which the city's governors could pour their concerns. It was not, therefore, surprising that by 1467 the right to elect the mayor had passed finally from the citizens as a whole to the men of the crafts and, most specifically, the liverymen of the crafts.[143] It was, moreover, the men of the crafts, dressed in their distinctive liveries, who accompanied the mayor when he rode to take his oath to the king at the Exchequer on 29 October. Men were fined for failing to turn up to support their craft on these civic occasions: twelve drapers 'that fayled at the mayris rydynge' in

[137] Davies, 'The Tailors of London and their Guild', 130; Archer, *Haberdashers' Company*, 16–18.

[138] See Rosser, 'Crafts, Guilds and the Negotiation of Work', 13; Unwin, *Guilds and Crafts*, 67.

[139] *LBE*, 232–4; *LBF*, 238–9.

[140] Forty-seven in 1376: *LBH*, 41–4; fifty in 1377: *CPMR 1364–81*, 243; thirty-nine in 1377: ibid. 256; forty-nine in 1381–2: *CPMR 1381–1413*, 29; see Ch. 6.

[141] For the lists of crafts summoned during these years, see Table 9.1; as early as 1327 the wardens of the crafts had been made responsible for the behaviour of their members, see *CPMR 1323–64*, 35.

[142] 26 January 1456, CLRO Journal 6, fo. 5.

[143] See Ch. 7.

1434–5 were fined sums ranging from 8*d.* to 24*d.*, and ninety-four yeomen and thirty-nine liverymen of the tailors' company were fined for failing to turn out to greet Margaret of Anjou in 1445.[144] When a member of their own company was elected as mayor, then the members of his craft made a particular effort and laid out sums to provide minstrels for the procession and contributed to the costs of the feast which followed. This, in the fifteenth century, tended to be held not in the new mayor's own house but in his company hall.

CONCLUSION

The years between 1200 and 1500 saw the formation and consolidation of the craft and trading associations in London. The informal clusters of men who practised the same craft and lived near to each other gradually crystallized into more permanent and more structured groupings, which in the fourteenth century struggled to define their relationship to other groups that practised related skills (whether craft or trade ones) and to the overarching authority of the mayor and aldermen and the central civic bureaucracy. The 1319 charter, which secured for the crafts control of entries to citizenship, was crucial in propelling the informal associations towards more formal structures. At some points during the fourteenth century it looked as if the guilds might replace the wards as the essential units of civic government, but their inevitable rivalries made this an unstable solution to the problems of urban government. The more colourless, more disinterested wards, which represented geographical fact rather than economic speculation, provided a more neutral constituency for civic government.

The craft and trade associations grew and prospered, seeking coherent internal structures, and struggling to reconcile the rivalries and conflicting interests of employers and employees, rich wholesalers and poor craftsmen, and battling to maintain the interests of their members against the threats posed by workers in related crafts, foreigners, and aliens. The keeping of records, the development of a system of taxation (quarterage), a common livery, or hood, or cognizance, a shared saint and a hall of their own, all these contributed coherence and stability to these craft and trade groupings. As the crafts found ways in which to organize themselves, so the mayor and aldermen came to use them as agents for civic administration: to raise money, control workmanship and prices, provide men, organize civic pageantry, and give advice. In the fourteenth century the crafts lost the battle to elect the common council but in the fifteenth century they won a place within the governing structure of the city as advisers to the court of aldermen and as electors of the mayor.

In the sixteenth century the companies were strengthened by amalgamations and bolstered by greater formality and regulation, yet power, if not prestige, was

[144] Johnson, *History of the Drapers*, i. 334; M. P. Davies, 'Artisans, Guilds and Government in London' in R. Britnell (ed.), *Daily Life in the Middle Ages* (Stroud, 1998), 125–50, esp. 137.

slipping away from them. Their control over the economic activities of their members (and over those who remained outside their membership) became more difficult to enforce as London swelled beyond its jurisdictional borders and the task of searching for illegal practitioners or defective workmanship became impossible.[145] Moreover, the new trading companies, such as the Levant company, the Spanish company, and the East India company, all challenged the role in overseas trade that had been played earlier by such companies as the mercers, drapers, and grocers. The complexity of the emerging capitalist methods of production could not be easily contained or controlled by the old craft company structures. The Reformation, in its turn, removed the spiritual or fraternal *raison d'être* of the companies and, for all their economic importance, that had been at their heart. Their social and charitable role remained (indeed still remains) but the loss of economic control and spiritual significance in the sixteenth century were blows from which the companies would not recover. Thus the years between 1440 and 1540 probably witnessed the city companies at the height of their power and influence.

[145] See J. R. Kellett, 'The Breakdown of Gild and Corporate Control over the Handicraft and Retail Trade in London', *EconHR* 10 (1958), 386–94; W. F. Kahl, *The Development of the London Livery Companies* (Boston, Mass., 1960), 25–32.

PART 4

The Practice of Civic Government

CHAPTER TEN

The Urban Environment

By 1500 London had developed a reasonably sophisticated system of civic government. The lack of written records from the early part of the period may tend to exaggerate the differences between the system in place in 1200 and that 300 years later. But there certainly had been developments, not least in the plurality of agencies that had now come to play a part in civic government. The scope and effectiveness of this governing plurality will now be examined in two areas where, in modern times, city councils (in conjunction with central government) expect to play a prominent role: namely, the control of the urban environment and the provision of welfare services. In medieval London the city government shared responsibility for these matters with the Crown, the church (religious houses and parishes), the organized craft guilds and, above all, with individual Londoners. The divisions of responsibility were customary and *ad hoc* rather than regulated and specific and, on occasion, the regulators or providers failed to work together effectively. On the other hand, in some instances, such as in the provision and management of the city's water supply, or in the care of the orphan children of citizens, the arrangements in medieval London worked remarkably well.

POPULATION AND PLAGUE

There is no doubt that the population of London was larger than that of any other town in medieval England; but that is more or less the only statement about the population of the medieval city that can be made with any certainty since there are no parish registers before the sixteenth century and no national census before the nineteenth. Indeed it may not matter very much what the overall population of London was at any given date, but the population *trends* of the city must be important to the historian, as they were, unconsciously perhaps, to the civic authorities at the time. A contracting or expanding population will pose different problems for, and elicit different responses from, the governors of London.

Attempts have been made to reconstitute the population of the city in 1086 by using Domesday Book, in spite of the fact that London is not covered by that great survey. The resulting figure of 17,850 cannot be much more than an inspired guess.[1] In 1545 the king commissioned an inquiry into the priestly personnel and

[1] J. C. Russell, *British Medieval Population* (Albuquerque, 1948), 45–51; Russell based his estimate on the assumption that there were eighty-five parishes in London in 1086; a more recent estimate of the

goods of all the parish churches in England. In his returns the rector or vicar was required to state how many communicants there were in his parish. The figures, if they were accurate, would provide parish-by-parish totals of the population over the age of about 12. But these parochial figures are, in many cases, clearly no more than rough estimates although they have been used to calculate a total population for London (the 113 parishes lying all, or partly, within the liberty, or jurisdiction, of the mayor) of between 56,000 and 70,000 in the late 1540s.[2]

There are indications that the earlier years of the thirteenth century saw rapid population growth and pressure on space in London. The royal inquiries of 1244, 1276, and 1279 revealed lengthy lists of those accused of encroaching on the common soil or of blocking public rights of way. Robert of Assendene, for example, was accused of occupying a plot in the king's highway and building a house there.[3] The profusion of these cases suggests considerable pressure on space within the city. By 1321, however, when a similar inquiry took place, there are comparatively few indications of such demand for land and no long lists of offenders to compare with those of the previous century.[4] The evidence of the inquests suggests that the population of London may have reached a plateau by about 1300.

An intensive study of property-holding in five parishes around Cheapside has revealed that in this area, admittedly the prime commercial street in the city, there may have been as many as 400 shops by the end of the thirteenth century, some as small as six feet wide and twelve feet deep. Moreover in the selds, or covered markets, opening off Cheapside there may have been a further 2,000 trading sites. This level of building density was not reached again until *c.*1600 when the population within the walls was *c.*100,000 (200,000 including the extramural suburbs). If building densities in other parts of London in 1300 mirror those of 1600, we shall have to accept that the population of the city in 1300 may have been as high as 100,000, i.e. the rival of Florence or Paris. It seems likely that the minimum figure for the population of London in 1300 was 50,000 and that the likely size was nearer to 80,000.[5]

number of parishes calculates that there were ninety-five which would expand the population figure to 19,950: C. N. L. Brooke with G. Keir, *London 800–1216: The Shaping of a City* (London, 1975), 66.

[2] Russell, *Medieval Population*, 298, and see R. Finlay, *Population and Metropolis: The Demography of London 1580–1650* (Cambridge, 1981), 51, where he estimates the population of London to have been 50,000 in 1500 and 70,000 by 1550, i.e. he agrees in general terms with Russell. The Chantry returns for London are printed in *London and Middlesex Chantry Certificate 1548* (London Record Society, 1980). For discussion of these figures, see V. Harding, 'The Population of London, 1550–1700: A Review of the Published Evidence', *London Journal*, 15 (1990), 111–28, esp. 115–117.

[3] *The London Eyre of 1244*, ed. H. M. Chew and M. Weinbaum (London Record Society, 1970), 131–153; *The London Eyre of 1276*, ed. M. Weinbaum (London Record Society, 1976), 89–98; M. Weinbaum, *London unter Eduard I und II*, 2 vols. in 1 (Stuttgart, 1933), ii. 138–54. See G. A. Williams, *Medieval London from Commune to Capital* (London, 1963), 200–1. For Robert Assendene, see *Eyre 1276*, 95.

[4] *The Eyre of London, 14 Edward II AD 132*, ed. H. M. Cam, 2 vols. (Selden Society, 1968–9), i. pp. cxxxiv–cxxxv.

[5] D. Keene, 'A New Study of London before the Fire', *Urban History Yearbook* (1984), 11–21, esp. 20, and, id., 'London from the Post-Roman Period to 1300', in D. Palliser (ed.), *The Cambridge Urban History of Britain*, 3 vols. (Cambridge, 2000), i. 187–216, esp. 194–6; Nightingale has argued that the population of London *c.*1300 was no higher than 60,000, see P. Nightingale, 'The Growth of London in the Medieval English Economy', in R. Britnell and J. Hatcher (eds.), *Progress and Problems in Medieval England: Essays in Honour of Edward Miller* (Cambridge, 1996), 89–106 .

Whether the devastating bubonic plague that reached London at the end of 1348 attacked a static or a rising population is not certain, but there is no doubt about the dramatic short-term effects.[6] Robert Avebury, a registrar in the archbishop of Canterbury's court who lived in London, wrote that between February and April 1349 the death toll reached such proportions in the city that a new graveyard had to be consecrated near Smithfield.[7] Here, at the height of the epidemic, as many as two hundred were buried in a day.[8] Although Avebury's figures may be a little exaggerated, there can be no doubt that the plague struck rapidly and with devastating, if brief, effect.[9] This may be judged from the enrolment of wills in the Husting Court of London. In the years 1338–48 an average of twenty-three wills were enrolled annually; in the years 1351–9 the average was seventeen. But in 1349 no fewer than 352 wills were enrolled in a single year, i.e. the death rate in London at the height of the plague was sixteen times greater than usual.[10] In the worst of the plague epidemics of the sixteenth and seventeenth centuries, that of 1562, the death rate was only eight times the normal.[11] When the plague returned again in 1361–2 the will enrolments again soared to 130, i.e. about eight times the normal rate.[12] This would suggest that, since in normal conditions 3 per cent of the population dies each year, then 48 per cent of the population of London may have died in 1348–9, and 24 per cent in the course of the later outbreak. Moreover those who enrolled their wills in the Husting court were freemen of London and therefore the most prosperous section of the population, so it is likely that the increase in the death rate for London was even higher than the figure calculated from the Husting wills.

There is no evidence that the government of London took any initiative in coping with the crisis: they could not have been expected to have anticipated mortality on such a scale and, once it had struck, there was little that could be done to contain the outbreak. Perhaps the main tasks of the governors were to maintain the government of the city and to prevent a social disaster from escalating into a complete breakdown of law and order. Between 1348 and October 1349 eight aldermen (a third

[6] The evidence of tax returns and the 1321 Eyre suggests a static population, but Keene points out that land in Cheapside continued to be in demand until the mid-fourteenth century: 'A New Study', 18. See R. Britnell, 'The Black Death in English Towns', *Urban History*, 21 (1994), 195–210, 196.

[7] *Adae Murimuth Continuatio Chronicarum: Robertus de Avesbury, De Gestis Mirabilibus Regis Edwardi Tertii*, ed. E. M. Thompson (Rolls Series, 1889), p. xxii; *HW*, ii. 7.

[8] *Robert of Avesbury*, 407.

[9] Stow, *Survey*, ii. 81, records that 50,000 were buried in the new graveyard: his information came from the Latin inscription on a cross in the churchyard. The London Charterhouse was later founded on the site of the graveyard and its register records that 60,000 were buried there, W. S. Hope, *The History of the London Charterhouse* (London, 1925), 8; Britnell, 'Black Death', 198–9.

[10] *HW*, i. 508–632; the number of wills enrolled in 1350 was 49, i.e. just over twice the normal number, see B. Megson, 'Mortality among London Citizens in the Black Death', *Medieval Prosopography*, 19 (1998), 125–33; Britnell, 'Black Death', 201.

[11] I. Sutherland, 'When was the Great Plague? Mortality in London, 1563 to 1665', in D. V. Glass and R. Revelle (eds.), *Population and Social Change* (London, 1972), 287–320, esp. 299.

[12] The number of wills enrolled in 1362 was thirty-seven, i.e. about twice the usual number. The number of enrolments again jumped to thirty-six in 1375 which may indicate that some kind of epidemic was abroad in London in that year also.

of the court) died and were replaced;[13] eight wardens of the cutlers' company died between August and November 1349, the six wardens of the hatters between December 1347 and July 1350, and all the wardens of the goldsmiths' company in the two years 1347 to 1349.[14] Numerous holders of city offices died including the chamberlain, Thomas de Maryns, but all were replaced within a month or two.[15] This in itself is a testament to the effectiveness of civic government. Guardians were appointed for the large number of city orphans, and the city's rulers took measures to control the dramatic rise in wages and prices that followed the outbreak. Walter Turke, the mayor elected in October 1349, and his fellow aldermen issued a long and disorganized ordinance covering the wages of building workers and household servants, the charges tailors, shearmen, and cooks might make for their work, and the prices at which wine, furs, wheat, barley, shoes, and horseshoes might be sold. The haphazard structure of the ordinance is testimony to the troubled times, and its final clause delegates legislative power to their successors 'the mayor, aldermen and good folks of the wards sworn, or others in their places, if any of them have been taken by God unto himself': at this date an all too likely event.[16]

The most immediate concern, of course, was the need to bury the bodies of the dead as quickly as possible. This was a health hazard, but there was also a pressing spiritual problem: those who had not been able to make their final confession before dying stood in mortal danger. The bishop of London bought three acres of land outside Aldersgate and dedicated it as a churchyard: he was assisted by Sir Walter Manny, a Flemish knight who had grown rich in the service of Edward III, who purchased a much larger piece of adjoining land that belonged to St Bartholomew's hospital, also used for burials, and there established a chapel where priests might pray for those buried so hastily in this newly consecrated ground. Twenty years later his small college of priests was developed into the famous London Charterhouse.[17] The health hazard posed by decaying corpses had been solved by the concerns of the bishop and a pious layman troubled that 'many were compelled to bury their dead in places unseemly and not hallowed or blessed; for some, it was said, cast the corpses into the river'.[18] In the same way a clerk, John Corey, encouraged by a group of substantial men of the city, persuaded the prior of Holy Trinity to sell a plot of land lying to the east of the Tower which was then walled and consecrated as a burial ground by the bishop of London. Here 'innumerable bodies of the dead were afterwards buried, and a chapel built in the same place to the honour of God'.[19] It was on this site that Edward III, soon afterwards,

13 A. B. Beaven, The *Aldermen of the City of London*, 2 vols. (London, 1908–13), i. 386–7.

14 Britnell, 'Black Death', 205; T. F. Reddaway and L. M. Walker, *The Early History of the Goldsmiths' Company* (London, 1975), 323.

15 Britnell, 'Black Death', 205; B. Masters, *The Chamberlain of London 1237–1987* (London, 1988), 107.

16 *Memorials*, 253–8.

17 Hope, *The London Charterhouse*, 3–21; B. Barber and C. Thomas, *The London Charterhouse* (London, 2002), 12–14.

18 Hope, *The London Charterhouse*, 7.

19 Stow, *Survey*, i. 124—5; *The Cartulary of Holy Trinity Priory Aldgate*, ed. G. Hodgett (London Record Society, 1971), 186; see D. Hawkins, 'The Black Death and the New London Cemeteries of 1348', *Antiquity*, 64 (1990), 637–42; Barber and Thomas, *Charterhouse*, 14–15.

established his new Cistercian house, St Mary Graces. So, by the combined efforts of individual Londoners, churchmen, and the mayor and aldermen, the surviving Londoners were able to bury their dead, find clerks to pray for them, and secure food and services at reasonable prices. In due course the city's rulers would begin to take some preventive measures to avert another such catastrophe: the link between overcrowding and dirt and the spread of the disease seems to have been understood, and the greater concern about the cleanliness of the city in the second half of the fourteenth century was the result of this realization.[20]

In spite of the magnetic power of London to attract immigrants from other parts of England, there can be little doubt that the city in the later Middle Ages suffered from substantial and long-term population decline. Mayoral instructions to the aldermen in 1378 and 1380 enjoin them to enquire not only into all tenements which were 'let and inhabited' but also into those which were 'empty and void'.[21] Holdings were amalgamated so that tenements became larger and some rows of shops, like those in Soper Lane off Cheapside, were completely demolished.[22] In response to this population dearth, in 1381 it was decided to reduce the £3 entry fee for those taking up the freedom of the city because many houses in the city stood empty and 'the number of citizens had diminished'.[23] It is difficult to tell how effective this measure was: the signs are that the population of the city reached its lowest point, about 40,000, at the end of the fourteenth century and then stabilized until it began to grow again a hundred years later.

The dramatic drop in population was accompanied by a rise in real wages, in per capita wealth and in the living standard of the working population. It is not hard therefore to understand why the last quarter of the fourteenth century was the most restless in the history of the city during the later Middle Ages.[24] Plague remained endemic in the urban populations of medieval England and slowed down the rate of recovery. There were dramatic outbreaks of disease, such as the sweating sickness of 1485 that carried off two mayors and four aldermen within the space of two months; but there are signs that from the last quarter of the fifteenth century pressure on land in some parts of the city or the suburbs was beginning to intensify once more. Although the demand for property in the Cheapside area remained sluggish until the mid-sixteenth century yet in suburbs outside the city walls—for example in Westminster—the demand for land seems to have been buoyant from *c.*1470.[25] It seems likely that the population of London within the twenty-five wards (but excluding areas further afield) had reached 50,000 in 1500.[26] Nothing either in recent

[20] E. Sabine, 'City Cleaning in Mediaeval London', *Speculum*, 12 (1937), 19–43.

[21] *LBH*, 84, 155.

[22] Keene, 'A New Study', 18; cf. C. Barron, *The Parish of St Andrew Holborn* (London, 1979), 50; Britnell, 'Black Death', 206.

[23] *LBH*, 162.

[24] See Chs. 1 and 6.

[25] G. Rosser, *Medieval Westminster: 1200–1540* (Oxford, 1989), 81–92; M. Carlin, *Medieval Southwark* (1996), 143–4.

[26] Finlay, *Population and Metropolis*, 51; Creighton calculated from the bills of mortality of 1532–5 that the population of London in these years was 62,400: C. Creighton, 'The Population of Old London', *Blackwood's Magazine*, 149 (1891), 477–96, esp. 486.

experience or collective memory could have prepared the citizens for the population explosion that was to hit the city in the sixteenth century. Between 1500 and 1600 the number of people living in London and the immediate suburbs quadrupled and the medieval garden city moved rapidly closer to the 'infernal wen' of later centuries.

WALLS AND BUILDINGS

Until the population explosion rendered the wall of London redundant, it was an extremely important element in the city's topography. There were three miles of it to be kept in repair. The responsibility for this lay jointly with the citizens and the king. In the east Edward I enlarged and strengthened the Tower of London in the years 1275–85, not to protect the city from riverborne attack but, rather, to tighten his grip on London itself. To the citizens the Tower always symbolized the hostile power of the king. It was at the Tower that the king's judges sat in the great judicial inquiry of 1321 to investigate every aspect of the city's privileges. Tower officials such as William Brigis and his man John could harass the inhabitants of the surrounding area by charging them for access to the Thames to collect water and wash their clothes, by rounding up their horses and cattle and driving them away into the security of the Tower, or by seizing barges and boats and forcing their owners to buy them back.[27] The Tower, indeed, brooded over the eastern part of the city, menacing and hostile. In the west the private castles of Montfichet and Baynard disappeared in the thirteenth century.[28] These had epitomized the private franchises that once dominated the city, but had given way to communal government and jurisdiction. Edward I did not intend to allow the citizens to occupy the vacuum created by the disappearance of the private strongholds. Acting decisively and with the support of the Dominican Archbishop Kilwardby, in the years following 1275, Edward I moved the Blackfriars from Holborn where they had established a house in the 1220s and planted them on a new site south of Ludgate and east of the Fleet River, where Montfichet and Baynard's castles had once stood. In return for the site the friars agreed to rebuild and extend the western section of the city wall, for which they then remained responsible.[29] The use of the new urban religious orders of friars to maintain sections of civic walling may be observed elsewhere in Europe, and it is noteworthy that the three largest friaries in London were sited along, or near, sections of the city wall.[30]

27 *CPMR 1413–36*, 141, 156.

28 For the history of these two western castles in the thirteenth century see M. D. Lobel (ed.), *Historic Towns Atlas: The City of London from Prehistoric Times to c.1520* (Oxford, 1989), 65, 81.

29 W. A. Hinnebusch, *The Early English Friars Preachers* (Rome, 1951), 35–55; *CPR 1272–81*, 258; *LBA*, 222. The London citizens were also expected to contribute to this work which was still not completed by 1315: *LBE*, 63.

30 Cf. the siting of the two friary churches in Dubrovnik. Although the precinct of the Austin Friary in Broad Street appears not to have extended to the city wall, yet the king and the city governors in the fifteenth century were concerned about the friary walls, *PPC*, ii. 168–9; B. Masters, 'The City Surveyor, the City Engineer and the City Architect and Planning Officer', *The Guildhall Miscellany*, 4 (1983), 237–55, esp. 238.

If at its eastern and western extremities the Roman wall of London had been strengthened in the thirteenth century, yet in between it was a thing of shreds and patches. By the middle of the twelfth century the Roman riverside wall had keeled over into the encroaching tidal mud and had not been rebuilt. But the king required the citizens to keep the remaining lengthy stretches of the wall in good repair. When, in 1257, Henry III ordered the citizens to repair the walls there were complaints about the cost.[31] The Roman core—still visible today, for example at Tower Hill—continued to be patched and strengthened, but the wind, the rain, and the quarryers continually eroded the good work.[32] The king empowered the citizens to raise money for the walls by a special tax on the sale of certain goods. This tax came to be known as murage, but, if we may judge by the surviving accounts in 1331 and 1332, only a small proportion—about a sixth—of the money raised was actually spent on the walls.[33] Later in the fourteenth century the citizens experimented with novel ways of raising money for the walls, for example by the sale of the monopoly on retailing sweet wine in the city: this was extremely unpopular, and taxes on tenement values and the search for 'free gifts' followed.[34] In 1379 it was decided that every householder should provide a labourer to work on the walls one day in every five weeks.[35] After this flurry of repair work in the later fourteenth century concern for the state of the walls and ditch seems to have lapsed until the 1470s. But in May 1477 all householders were required to contribute fivepence towards the cleaning of the city and ditches and the mayor Ralph Josselyn 'of his zele' provided bricks and lime for repairing the walls.[36]

The fourteenth century repairs took the form of tile or brick courses between layers of Kentish ragstone. The more extensive rebuilding of the 1470s was carried out entirely in brick, decorated in places (as can still be seen in the section preserved at St Alphege gardens) with a diaper pattern. In some sections the wall was reinforced with massive brick arches; there was a wall walk reached by several staircases, and loopholes for firing missiles.[37] Inside—in theory at least—a 16-foot-wide girdle of land was kept clear of building 'for the perambulation of the city', with the intention, presumably, of ensuring that men could have easy access

[31] Matthew Paris, *Chronica Majora,* ed. H. R. Luard, 7 vols (Rolls Series, 1872–83), v. 634, 663.

[32] 6 December 1310, royal proclamation against evildoers who maliciously removed stone from the city walls and timber from the city gates: *Memorials,* 79; Hugh of Croyden in 1344 was accused of removing stones from Newgate: *London Assize of Nuisance 1301–1431,* ed. H. M. Chew and W. Kellaway (London Record Society, 1973), 95.

[33] Murage grants 1279, 1284: *LBA,* 222–4, *LBB,* 55–6; 1307 murage farmed for £14 13*s.* 4*d.* p.a.: *LBC,* 161–2, *LBE,* 63; 1319 murage discontinued: *LBE,* 104, 146–7; 1329 murage again collected: *LBE,* 237; 1331, murage farmed for £166 13*s.* 4*d.* p.a.: *LBE,* 257. The murage accounts for 1331–2 are printed in *Memorials,* 186–7.

[34] *LBG,* 199. For the political repercussions of the sweet wine monopoly see C. Barron, *Revolt in London: 11th to 15th June 1381* (London, 1981), 13–14, 18–19.

[35] *LBH,* 127–8.

[36] *LBL,* 149, *CPMR 1458–82,* 110–11 and n. 1; April 1478, Edward Stone was chosen as master of the works of the city, to see to the repair of the works and the cleansing of the city ditch, see Ch. 8.

[37] W. F. Grimes, *The Excavation of Roman and Medieval London* (London, 1968), 81–3; F. J. Forty, 'London Wall', *Guildhall Miscellany,* 5 (1955), 1–39; J. Schofield, *The Building of London from the Conquest to the Great Fire* (London, 1984), 66–8.

to the wall in order to defend it. Outside there lay the city ditch, 80 feet wide and filled by the waters of the Fleet, the Walbrook, and the Thames. In spite of the best efforts of the city governors, however, it was extremely difficult to prevent Londoners from building up against the walls or gardening the edges of the city ditch. The ordinance of 1386 that forbade the leasing of gardens or vacant spaces adjoining the gates, walls, or ditches of the city, seems to have been largely ignored.[38] By the time Stow wrote at the end of the sixteenth century, the wall and ditch had become an anachronism with the result that the ditch

> which of olde time was used to lie open, alwayes from time to time cleansed from filth and mud, as neede required, of great breadth, and so deepe that divers watring horses, where they thought it shallowest, were drowned both horse and man. But now of later time, the same ditch is inclosed, and the banks thereof let out for garden plots, carpenters' yardes, bowling allies, and diverse houses thereon builded, whereby the citie wall is hidden, the ditch filled up, a small channell left, and that verie shallow.[39]

The medieval walls of London must have been kept in sufficiently good repair to act as a deterrent to would-be attackers. No foreign army then, or since, ever attempted to take London. Although a riverborne attack from the French was expected in the 1330s and 1340s it never materialized.[40] The rebels in 1381 penetrated the city only because Aldgate and the gate on London Bridge were opened to them and, on most occasions during the Wars of the Roses, the city governors reckoned discretion to be the better part of valour. Only in 1471, when the Lancastrian 'Bastard of Fauconberg' attempted to take London, did the citizens decide to resist an attacking army, and held the city instead for Edward IV. Their success in doing so (although it is true that it is not clear how formidable an opposition Fauconberg presented) suggests that even before mayor Josselyn's repairs the city walls were defensible.[41] It was, in fact, the good internal peace established by the Tudors, the decline of baronial feuds, and the harmonious relations between the Crown and the city that finally made the city walls redundant and led to the deterioration of the defences that Stow described.

At six points the medieval city wall was breached by gates, Aldgate, Bishopsgate, Cripplegate, Aldersgate, Newgate, and Ludgate; all of them ancient and probably Roman. Two of the gates, Newgate and Ludgate, served as prisons while the other four were all sufficiently substantial structures to contain rooms or houses above the actual gate. These apartments were much sought after and were usually let out to honoured civic officers.[42] Aldgate was usually leased to the mayor's serjeant but

[38] *Memorials*, 489.

[39] Stow, *Survey*, i. 126, cf. 20, 129, 164. Stow may have had an unduly romantic view of the old city ditch which was often blocked, infrequently scoured, and constantly encroached upon.

[40] Year 1338, *LBF*, 28; in 1380 John Philipot at his own expense built a defensive tower on the Thames to protect the city: *LBH*, 155.

[41] C. Barron, 'London and the Crown 1451–61', in J. R. L. Highfield and R. Jeffs (eds.), *The Crown and the Local Communities in England and France in the Fifteenth Century* (Gloucester, 1981), 88–109; C. F. Richmond, 'Fauconberg's Kentish Rising of May 1471', *EHR* 85 (1970), 673–92; Stow, *Survey*, i . 30.

[42] See Ch. 8.

in 1374 'the whole of the dwelling house above the gate, with the rooms built over, and a certain cellar under the south side of the gate' was leased to Geoffrey Chaucer. The poet agreed to keep the building in good repair and the city undertook, in return, not to turn any part of the gate into a prison while Chaucer lived there.[43] Whereas the city officers lived *above* the gates, the actual keeper of the gate, as might be expected, lived at ground level in a small apartment tucked next to the gate.[44] Exceptionally, Bishopsgate, since 1292, had been the collective responsibility of the Hanse merchants; in 1318 John le Long 'the Easterling' was granted for his life the rooms above Bishopsgate, a 'tourelle' on the wall lying to the east of the gate and a garden running between the two.[45] It seems likely that the responsibility for Bishopsgate rested lightly on Hanseatic shoulders and as their relations with London deteriorated in the fifteenth century, so did Bishopsgate. In the 1460s the London aldermen finally took possession of the gate, installed William Calbeck, a city serjeant-at-mace, in the rooms above the gateway and embarked upon repairs to the whole building.[46]

The city gates appear to have looked much like other town gates, with a central opening for carts and a passage for those on foot on either side (the narrower gates of Aldgate and Cripplegate had only a single postern gate). There are engravings of the main city gates in the early eighteenth century but by this date all but two of them had been rebuilt since the medieval period. Here again the overall responsibility of the city's governors for the fabric of the gates was supplemented by the charitable enterprise of individuals: Cripplegate was rebuilt in 1491 by the executors of the wealthy goldsmith Edmund Shaa who left the substantial sum of 400 marks for the work, which was to bear his arms and those of his company.[47] Bishopsgate was adorned on its north façade with statues that represented, as the eighteenth-century antiquarian Strype supposed, the Norman Bishop William of London flanked by King Alfred and his son-in-law Aethelred of Mercia.[48] If these statues date from the late fifteenth century rebuilding, and if Strype is correct in his identifications, then it is interesting to speculate about what led the city governors of the time, to choose those particular heroes to adorn the gate. The bishop of London is not a surprising choice for Bishopsgate, and perhaps the king of Wessex and the ealdorman of Mercia were selected to suggest the extent of 'London's region' in the early tenth century.

43 Year 1305, *LBC*, 144; 1467, *LBL*, 70; *Memorials*, 377–8; see Ch. 7.

44 New houses were built for the keepers of Cripplegate and Aldersgate in 1337, *LBF*, 9, 15; *Memorials*, 206–7.

45 *LBC*, 41, 111; *Memorials*, 127; *LBK*, 46. Long's house was, however, later leased to a London vintner and to the retired ward beadle: *LBG*, 203; *LBH*, 83; see Ch. 5.

46 C. Barron, 'The Government of London and its Relations with the Crown 1400–1450', (University of London Ph.D. thesis, 1970), 365–72; *LBL*, 13–14.

47 Reddaway and Walker, *History of the Goldsmiths*, 176–7, 306–7; for its design, see J. Schofield and A. Dyson, *Archaeology of the City of London* (London, 1980), 47.

48 J. Strype, *Survey of the Cities of London and Westminster*, 2 vols. (London, 1720), i. 14–21; J. Schofield, *Medieval London Houses* (New Haven, Conn., 1994), 9–12. For the history of individual gates see H. Harben, *A Dictionary of London* (London, 1918) s.n.; T. Friedman, 'The Rebuilding of Bishopsgate 1723–35', *Guildhall Studies in London History*, 4 (1980), 75–90.

Although these six gates were the main access points to the city throughout the medieval period they were not, in fact, the only breaches in the three miles of London's wall. Just north of the Tower was a postern gate, dating from Edward I's rebuilding of the city, in the late fourteenth century, leased out to 'men of good credit', such as the mayor's swordbearer, in order that it should be maintained and guarded.[49] But its upkeep seems to have lapsed and in 1440 the gate fell down and was not rebuilt properly in stone, much to Stow's disgust since 'the weak and wooden building' that succeeded it was inhabited by 'persons of lewde life'.[50] Here it would seem that the weak gate did not pose a sufficient threat for the city corporately to spend money on its repair, nor was it prestigious enough to attract private charity. One entirely new gate was, however, built in the medieval period. In 1415 the mayor, Thomas Fauconer, appears to have initiated a number of 'public works', most of them concerned to improve the drainage and sewage in the city. Moorfields, which lay to the north of the city, was frequently flooded with unwholesome results for those living nearby. So it was decided by the mayor and aldermen, 'and an immense congregation of very reputable men of the city' that the moor should be divided up into gardens to be let out to the profit of the city chamber, in accordance with a plan set out on a sheet of parchment and shown to those present at the meeting. The little postern gate was to be rebuilt and enlarged, to enable easier access from the city out to the new allotments.[51] The initiative in this venture seems, clearly, to have lain with the mayor, but it is not clear who paid for the new gate. It was, however, 're-edified' in 1472 by the then mayor, Sir William Hampton.[52] Moorgate was never an important gate in the medieval period and no roads led to or away from it.[53] It was probably simply an enlarged pedestrian gate created out of one of the twenty or so small turrets that studded London's wall between the gates.[54] Although one or two of these turrets seem to have been leased out by the commonalty, most of them were probably not inhabited.[55] The fact, however, that rooms over the city's gates were sought after as residences suggests that fear of siege warfare was not an ever-present anxiety in the minds of the citizens.

[49] *LBH*, 277, 288, 443.

[50] Stow, *Survey*, i. 28. It would appear that both Holy Trinity Priory and the Greyfriars were allowed to open up small postern gates from their precincts through the city wall, *Archaeology of the City of London*, 60.

[51] *LBI*, 101; *Memorials*, 614–15; CLRO, Journal 2, fo. 53; see E. Levy, 'Moorfields, Finsbury and the City of London in the Sixteenth Century', *London Topographical Record*, 26 (1990), 78–96.

[52] Stow, *Survey*, i. 32. Hampton's will does not survive, so it is not possible to assess the extent of his contribution.

[53] Moorgate was rebuilt in 1672 as a carriage gate with two posterns, but it was demolished with the other gates in 1762.

[54] H. L. Turner, *Town Defences of England and Wales* (London, 1971), 156. The eastern turrets were probably Roman, whereas the western ones were medieval, possibly constructed in the thirteenth century, Schofield, *Building*, 68.

[55] The 'turella' lying to the north of Aldgate was leased in 1338, 1353: *LBF*, 20, *LBG*, 24; another tower near Bishopsgate was leased in 1314: *LBE*, 39. The tower to the north of Ludgate was leased to Mary, countess of Pembroke before 1377: *CPMR 1364–8*, 242 and n.

The gates and turrets, being built of stone or brick, were considerably more substantial than the homes of most medieval Londoners. Communal action had, from an early date, tried to ensure that those who built houses in London should do so in a way that was neither a nuisance, nor a danger, to their neighbours. Probably from the late twelfth century—possibly earlier—there had been building regulations in force in London. The earliest of these civic rules were those that dealt with party walls: they were to be built of stone, three feet wide and sixteen feet high. If one of the parties could not afford to build such a wall then he might contribute merely his one and a half feet of land.[56] The frequent fires in the city in the eleventh and twelfth centuries, culminating in a particularly serious fire in July 1212,[57] provoked the mayor, Henry fitz-Ailwyn, into promulgating a series of building regulations, known as the Assize of Buildings, intended to inhibit the construction of wooden buildings in the city. Roofs of thatch or straw were to be plastered and new roofs were to be made of tiles, shingles, or boards. Potentially dangerous buildings were to be inspected and either repaired or destroyed.[58] In the course of the thirteenth century the scope of the Assize of Buildings was enlarged to deal with communal problems that arose from disputes about cesspits, leaking gutters, blocked lights, or corbels and joists that rested on party walls.[59] An individual who believed that his neighbour had contravened the civic regulations could demand an assize; and although the records of these complaints and inspections survive only from 1306, it is clear that by that date the procedure was well established. In fact it was customary for six aldermen to inspect the 'nuisance'.[60] As the centuries wore on the range of nuisances covered by the assize procedure seems to have been more widely interpreted; moreover the mayor and aldermen came, increasingly, to delegate their duties to a panel of professional viewers that included carpenters and masons.[61] In its way the assize was a remarkably sophisticated civic response to the problems caused by crowded living conditions; an attempt to ensure that neighbourly nuisances did not give rise either to danger or to brawls.

Private protests found redress through the assize of nuisance; communal protests were aired at wardmotes. The freemen who met once or twice a year in the wardmote were encouraged to present offenders against all civic ordinances. From as early as 1311, and probably earlier, the members of the wardmote were expected to present hearths that were built in the wooden parts of houses, chimneys that

[56] M. Bateson, 'A London Municipal Collection of the Reign of John', *EHR* 17 (1902), 506–7; *Assize of Nuisance*, pp. x–xi.

[57] For fires in London see Brooke with Keir, *Shaping of a City*, 212 n. 4; *Assize of Nuisance*, p. ix and n. 1.

[58] Bateson, 'A London Municipal Collection', 730; *Assize of Nuisance*, p. xi. The articles of the assize are translated in T. H. Turner, *Some Account of Domestic Architecture in England*, 4 vols.(Oxford, 1851–9), i. 18–24. These regulations, which were also concerned with the rebuilding of the city after the fire, fixed the wages of carpenters, masons, tilers, plasterers, and ditchers.

[59] For the regulation for the Assize of Nuisance *c.*1270, see *Liber de Antiquis Legibus seu Chronica Maiorum et Vicecomitum Londoniarum*, ed. T. Stapleton (Camden Society, 1846), 206–11.

[60] *Assize of Nuisance*, pp. xii–xx.

[61] Ibid. pp. xix–xx; *London Viewers and their Certificates 1508–1558*, ed. J. Loengard (London Record Society, 1989).

were not constructed of stone, tiles, or plaster, dangerously overhanging or obstructive buildings, and householders who did not provide barrels of water and ladders ready to deal with fires.[62] So in the wardmote inquests of 1422 the men of the parish of St Andrew Holborn declared that fifteen cottages in Chancery Lane were covered in straw and dangerous to their neighbours; the men of Walbrook claimed that there was no ladder, grappling hook, or ropes to use in the ward for fire-fighting and the men of Bishopsgate grumbled about the inns that had jettied first floors overhanging the streets 'whereby horsemen and carts are hindered and incommoded'.[63] The long catalogue of offences presented by the wardmotes suggests, perhaps, a high degree of negligence but also of communal self-consciousness. Moreover the absence of any serious and widespread fires in the city between the twelfth and seventeenth centuries testifies to the effectiveness of the fire precautions. Obviously there were many leaking privies, and obstructive and dangerous buildings, yet through the assize of nuisance and the wardmote inquests, these antisocial structures were contained and the decencies of communal living were preserved.

Virtually none of the housing of medieval Londoners has survived and we have to rely largely on documentary and archaeological evidence. The 'great houses' in the city, since they were built of stone, tended to survive longest and are best recorded.[64] A rough chronological building pattern may be observed: in the thirteenth century the grand new houses belonged to the bishops and great abbots who needed London inns for political and commercial reasons; in the next century the merchant princes of the city built homes for their own enjoyment, and in the fifteenth century the city companies either adapted older houses or constructed their own great halls, or mansions. Houses were interchangeable between these groups because they shared a basic architectural structure, namely a version of the courtyard plan.[65] Decorative details and building techniques might change with the centuries but there was no impetus (e.g. overcrowding) to inspire architectural innovation.

Before 1200 few ecclesiastics had town houses, although the archbishop of Canterbury and the bishop of Rochester were established at Lambeth and the bishop of Winchester at the northern extremity of his diocese in Southwark. By 1300 six abbots or priors had inns near Winchester house, and two had houses north of Cripplegate, but the great majority (the archbishop of York, twelve bishops and seven abbots) had built their town houses in the western suburb, between the city itself and Westminster. Most of these houses lay on, or near, the Strand and Holborn. This rash of inn-building by bishops and heads of religious houses in the thirteenth century is both witness and contributory to the development of

[62] For the wardmote ordinances, see Ch. 6.

[63] *CPMR 1412–36*, 123, 125, 135.

[64] For a comprehensive survey of what it is possible to know about building in London between the Conquest and the Great Fire see Schofield, *Building*.

[65] J. Schofield, 'Medieval and Tudor Domestic Buildings in the City of London', in L. Grant (ed.), *Medieval Art, Architecture and Archaeology in London* (British Archaeological Association, 1990), 16–29, esp. 17–21.

London as a capital city. The siting of so many inns in the area between the city and Westminster exemplifies the role played by the king's government in that development. These bishops and abbots needed to visit London to buy supplies for their houses, to attend the king's court and to offer him counsel in Parliament.[66] Towards the end of the thirteenth century they would also be able to seek in London the expert advice of a professional lawyer. But only a few of these aristocratic town houses were built within the mayor's jurisdiction and so most were not subject to the scrutiny of the assize of nuisance. In any case, these grand houses would have been built of stone and less likely to cause a nuisance to their neighbours. On occasion the aristocratic owners of houses in London would be called to account by Londoners using the assize of nuisance procedures and they, in turn, complained about the failure of their London neighbours to repair walls or clean out shared watercourses.[67]

One town house built within the city walls belonged to the abbot of Waltham, in the parish of St Mary at Hill in the eastern part of the city, which was more accessible from Essex.[68] The abbot had established his inn comparatively early, in the late twelfth century. It was not a large inn but, by the time of the Dissolution, it had a gatehouse, stable, courtyard leading to a great hall, dormitory, chapel, kitchen, and other domestic offices. Some of these medieval walls survived into the twentieth century.[69] There is no record of trouble between the abbot and his urban neighbours: when the parishioners of the nearby church of St Mary at Hill in the late fifteenth century wanted to extend the south aisle of their church, the abbot sacrificed his kitchen to them in return for an annual rent of ten shillings.[70]

Most of the houses within the city walls were built by Londoners themselves. John Gisors, a vintner and member of one of the great thirteenth-century London dynasties, bequeathed his 'new hall' to his son Thomas in his will in 1296. Gisors hall (or Gerard's hall as it was later called) was a great house in the parish of St Mildred Bread Street which later became a prosperous hostelry when the family parted company with it later in the fourteenth century. The substantial vaulted undercroft carried on a row of four central columns, supported a great house built in part at least of Caen stone (or so Stow believed). The undercroft, which presumably served simply as a warehouse (it lacked either a hearth or chimney), is suggestive of the grandeur of the building as a whole.[71]

[66] C. Barron, 'Centres of Conspicuous Consumption: The Aristocratic Town House in London 1200–1550', *London Journal*, 20 (1995), 1–16.

[67] *Assize of Nuisance*, 13, 54, 136, 145, 170.

[68] *The Early Charters of the Augustinian Canons of Waltham Abbey, Essex 1062–1230*, ed. R. Ransford (Woodbridge, 1989), 378–97.

[69] M. Honeybourne, 'The Abbot of Waltham's Inn', *London Topographical Record*, 20 (1952), 34–46. Honeybourne's conclusions have been revised in D. Gadd, 'The London Inn of the Abbots of Waltham: A Revised Reconstruction of a Medieval Town House in Lovat Lane', *TLMAS* 34 (1983), 171–7.

[70] *The Medieval Records of a London City Church (St Mary at Hill) 1420–1559*, ed. H. Littlehales (EETS, 1905), 240, 391.

[71] *HW*, i. 128; Stow, *Survey*, i. 348; Turner, *Some Account of Domestic Architecture in England*, ii. 185–6; Williams, *Medieval London*, 69–70, 325–6; S. Thrupp, *The Merchant Class of Medieval London* (Michigan, 1948), 345–6; Schofield, *Building*, 78.

Nearly two hundred years later, in the 1460s, John Crosby, an outstandingly successful grocer, of Yorkist sympathies and sound business sense, built himself a fine town house on the east side of Bishopsgate. In fact he enlarged the already substantial house of the Italian merchant, Cataneo Pinelli, and created a mansion of not one, but two courtyards, extensive gardens and outbuildings, an apartment with a vaulted crypt that may have been used as a chapel, and a remarkable great hall and parlour: two fine rooms each with tall bay windows and elaborately carved and gilded wooden ceilings. The hall has been transplanted to Chelsea, having escaped both the Great Fire and the Victorian redevelopments, and is the sole surviving reminder of the grandeur of the medieval London merchant's house. In Crosby hall Richard III stayed when he was still only eyeing the Crown, and several foreign ambassadors were accommodated there. Indeed there is little except size to choose between John Crosby's hall and the palace built by King Edward IV himself at Eltham in the 1470s; the only difference is that the king had several palaces and Crosby only one: but their tastes, and perhaps also their masons and carpenters, may have been shared.[72]

It is likely that Gisors hall and Crosby hall were among the finest London houses built in their time. John Stow wrote of Gisors hall that it was 'one great house, of old time builded upon arched vaults and with arched gates of stone' and that Crosby hall 'was builded of stone and timber, verie large and beautifull, and the highest at that time in London'.[73] Clearly there had been developments both in design and in building techniques during the two hundred years that separate the two mansions. Crosby's new hall employed the new building material of brick: not where it could be seen (where ashlar stone was used), but in the undercroft. Bricks were rarely used in thirteenth-century London and their use became widespread only in the fifteenth century; but they were cheap and could be manufactured on the spot (e.g. from brick earth in Moorfields), which was especially important for a city far from good quarries.[74] Gisors hall had fronted directly onto the street, but between Crosby's main courtyard and Bishopsgate there lay a row of six tenements, which not only produced a useful rent income but also provided some privacy for the great mansion which was thus cut off from the noise of the road by its plebeian screen.[75] Such rows of 'rents' along road frontages became much more common in the later period.

The majority of moderately prosperous Londoners would have lived in the kind of houses that Crosby rented out in Bishopsgate Street. We can attempt to reconstruct these houses from the few surviving building contracts and the archaeological remains. In 1417 Richard Hercy, a draper, had built for himself a house and a

[72] P. Norman, *Crosby Place, with an Architectural Description* (London, 1908); Schofield, *Building*, 123–4. Crosby Hall, removed to Chelsea, has lately been re-equipped with a surrounding 'palace'.

[73] Stow, *Survey*, i. 172, 348.

[74] Schofield, *Building*, 126–9.

[75] Cf. the eleven shops built in 1373 along the street frontage of the town house of the prior of Lewes in Southwark; D. Harrison, 'The Surrey Portion of the Lewes Cartulary', *Surrey Archaeological Collections*, 43 (1935), 84–112 esp. nos. 32 and 33. A similar fringe of shops separated Asselynes wharf (or Browne's Place) from Thames Street: C. L. Kingsford, 'A London Merchant's House and its Owners', *Archaeologia*, 74 (1923–4), 137–58.

shop on the north side of Paternoster Row; the cellar was to be of stone and the shop on the ground floor and two further storeys were to be constructed 'of good and sufficient timber under one roof'.[76] Archaeologists have found the cellars of similar houses on the south side of Thames Street, usually two rooms deep with quays on the waterfront. At New Fresh wharf the houses seem to have been divided by internal alleys that ran down to the quays. These houses had privies, and cesspits for rubbish, and the cellar of one of them was carefully faced in flint and chalk chequerwork.[77] But there must have been great numbers of Londoners for whom even comparatively modest houses of this kind would have been far beyond their pockets. At worst the poor would have lived in hovels or cottages, such as the 'cote' on Cornhill where the poet William Langland lived with his wife and daughter.[78] Such cots would have been well below the dignity of a deed or lease and none has been excavated. Many Londoners probably squatted in parts of larger, broken-down houses. There is considerable evidence for the division of tenements (not always with due regard to structural safety) and such shared occupancies often led to disputes that the mayor and aldermen attempted to resolve through the assize of nuisance.[79] Even in the thirteenth century, however, there seems not to have existed the acute pressure on the housing stock that caused constant anxiety to the city governors in the later sixteenth century. There was still space in medieval London for those who had the money to take advantage of it.

Between 1200 and 1500 there are increasingly numerous references to privies and cesspits, to purpose-built chimneys of tile, to water gutters, pipes, and sewers; to tile floors and tile roofs, which all suggest a degree of structural sophistication and comfort. Window-glazing seems to have come in during the thirteenth century, although the glass was opaque rather than clear.[80] It is possible to judge the degree of comfort in a London home of this period from the few surviving inventories. Thomas Mocking, a fishmonger, died in 1372 and left his house—the Castle on the Hoop, in the parish of St Magnus near London Bridge—together with its contents to his wife and son. The listed contents, suggest a welcome degree of comfort: in the chamber there were two beds with their hangings, chests and counters (or tables). The hall was furnished as the main reception room with two trestle tables, stools, fire dogs for the hearth, washing bowls and basins, candelabra, and cushions. The storehouse contained barrels (for ale and wine), jugs, plates, salt cellars, silver cups, mazers, and table linen. Upstairs in the parlour, which was the

[76] *CPMR 1413–37*, 61; in 1383 John Wolfey, carpenter, agreed to build five shops in Addle Street, each with two jettied storeys above, for Thomas Carleton, an embroiderer. It is likely that a separate contract was made with the mason to construct the stone cellars, M. Tatchell, 'A Fourteenth Century London Building Contract', *Guildhall Miscellany*, 2 (1962), 129–31. For a survey of London house-types in the medieval period, see Schofield, *Building*, 86–92.

[77] *Archaeology of the City of London*, 56.

[78] *Piers Plowman by William Langland: An Edition of the C-text*, ed. D. Pearsall (London, 1978), Passus V, line 3.

[79] *CPMR 1298–1307*, 177–8; *CPMR 1364–81*, 183 and n. The city's measures to deal with the repair of shared properties were not always successful as the dispute between John Derke, a joiner, and his downstairs neighbour Robert Mildenhale indicates: *CPMR 1437–57*, 57; cf. *Assize of Nuisance*, 43.

[80] Ibid. 17, 55, 88.

more private reception room, there was a wall hanging, a table, a counting table and a cupboard; and in a room near the parlour there were chairs, still quite rare in ordinary houses where people customarily sat on stools and benches. The room for the workmen and apprentices had a chest, tables, and forms (benches) and the kitchen was equipped with tubs, tankards for water, tripods, spits, cooking utensils, brass pots and cauldrons (probably imported from the Low Countries).[81] Mocking's house may have been more lavishly furnished than many, but most citizens would have been likely to possess wooden furniture, a bed with hangings, brass and pewter pots and dishes, iron kitchen utensils, and some silver.

Although some shops such as that which Richard Hercy had built were quite substantial, others appeared to have been no more than enclosed stalls. From the mid-thirteenth century covered bazaars appear in Cheapside: these were known as 'selds' where a trader rented a small plot with a chest or bench, perhaps twenty or thirty such plots within a single seld.[82] John le Botonner had a very small corner shop lying between Soper Lane and Cheapside which was open on two sides, and the upper floor was supported by a strong corner post. At night Botonner attached his shutters to iron hooks fixed to the timber of the floor above.[83] Since many shops were also workrooms where goods were made, light was essential. John Beaufront, a woolmonger, and his wife Margery complained when their neighbour in Wood Street built a forge with an overhanging pentice in the road. This cut off the light from their shop so that their workmen could no longer see to card and prepare wool. The mayor and aldermen viewed the nuisance and ordered the forge to be removed within forty days. [84]

GARDENS AND LIVESTOCK

Medieval London was a city of gardens and open spaces. Many London houses had gardens attached to them, and for those Londoners who had no private garden there were plenty of green open spaces. Most of the city churches had churchyards where people could meet for business or pleasure.[85] To the north of the city the moor was used for sport, although part of it was leased out as allotments in the fifteenth century;[86] and further north still at Halliwell and Finsbury there were fields where elms and reeds and willows grew in abundance.[87] It was here, to the north of the city, where the land began to rise and, perhaps, form natural theatres, that open-air plays were performed at Clerkenwell and Skinnerswell, by the

[81] *CPMR 1364–81*, 154–6. Mocking's will is enrolled 1 February 1372, also that of his own son Thomas, a clerk: *HW*, ii. 153, 448–449.

[82] Keene, 'A New Study', 14; id., 'Shops and Shopping in Medieval London', in Grant, *Medieval Art, Archaeology and Architecture in London*, 29–46, esp. 38–40.

[83] *Assize of Nuisance*, 43. Botonner's shop was acknowledged to be 'very small'; it was only about 5 feet square and 6 feet high. In the early thirteenth century a shop in the west fishmarket had a frontage on the street of 7 feet and a depth of about 10, Hodgett, *Cartulary of Holy Trinity Aldgate*, 584.

[84] *Assize of Nuisance*, 138.

[85] Ibid. 13; *LBG*, 265.

[86] See p. 246 above.

[87] *LBC*, 239; *LBE*, 7, 28, 118, 165; *CPMR 1328–64*, 185; *Memorials*, 39.

fraternity of the parish clerks of London.[88] The city appears corporately to have owned much of the land immediately outside the city walls, beyond the ditch, and to have leased this out for gardens, or smallholdings.[89] Some gardens lay further away: John of Beverley, 'gardiner', leased a piece of wasteland near the hospital of St Mary Bishopsgate from the city for an annual rent of 3*s.* 4*d.* in 1374.[90] Although some of the city's gardeners had their own smallholdings, others such as Adam Vynour, in charge of the bishop of Ely's great estate in Holborn, marketed the produce from their masters' gardens. These gardeners customarily sold their produce, 'pulse, cherries and vegetables', near St Augustine's gate at the south-east corner of St Paul's churchyard, but by 1345 they made so much noise that they disturbed the services and their market was moved westwards along Carter Lane.[91] Fruiterers, on the other hand, in the fifteenth century sold their wares in Cheapside outside St Thomas of Acre hospital.[92] Figs, blackberries, pears, and apples appear to have been common in the thirteenth century but archaeologists have found that by the fourteenth century grapes, plums, cherries, and strawberries had been added to the Londoners' diet.[93]

All the religious houses—and there were over thirty of them in or near London—had gardens of their own, although they were not all as enclosed and private as they might have been. A man was murdered in the garden of St Bartholomew's priory in 1325 and the Greyfriars complained that because of the negligence of the canons of St Martin's next door in failing to repair their fence, the friars' garden was ruined and the plants and fruit were stolen.[94] The city's assize of nuisance dealt with neighbourly problems in this area also. The Austin friars had a complaint similar to that of the Greyfriars: again owing to the negligence of their neighbours, dogs, pigs, and poultry, as well as humans, had damaged their prior's garden. The mayor and aldermen in this case judiciously decided that, 'since decorum particularly requires that the enclosure between religious and others should be strong and well-founded', the parties should pool their resources and build a stone wall.[95] The great town houses all had gardens. In the bishop of Ely's estate in Holborn, where Adam Vynour grew onions, garlic, turnips, leeks, parsley, herbs, and beans in the pod, men and women were employed to dig the

[88] *The Westminster Chronicle 1381–1394*, ed. L. C. Hector and B. F. Harvey (Oxford, 1982), 94–5; I. Lancashire, *Dramatic Texts and Records of Britain: A Chronological Topography to 1558* (Toronto, 1984), 112–13. The public well at Clerkenwell has been excavated and preserved *in situ*, see Museum of London Archaeology Service, *The Archaeology of Greater London* (Museum of London, 2000), 224–5.

[89] e.g. *c.*1300, Robert de Meldebourne leased a garden near London wall at Aldersgate from the city Chamber for 12*d.* p.a.: *LBC*, 237.

[90] *LBG*, 329.

[91] *Memorials*, 228–9.

[92] *CPMR 1458–82*, 118–19.

[93] C. Thomas, B. Sloane, and C. Phillpotts, *Excavations at the Priory and Hospital of St Mary Spital, London* (Museum of London, 1997), 238–44.

[94] *Calendar of Coroners' Rolls of the City of London 1300–1378*, ed. R. R. Sharpe (London, 1913), 113; *Assize of Nuisance*, 7.

[95] 1328, *Assize of Nuisance*, 67. The Austin friars had earlier replaced the hedge and ditch around their garden with an earth wall, which had led to flooding since the ditch had been useful for drainage: ibid. 188. The prior of Holy Trinity and the prioress of St Helen's Bishopsgate also complained about defective earthen walls which allowed their communities to be spied upon and their fruit stolen: ibid. 46, 129.

vines, weed, remove thorns and plant new hedges.[96] Doubtless the scale of Vynour's operation was greater than that of most town gardeners: it is clear that many Londoners expected to grow their own produce. When Robert de Stratford and his wife Dionisia assigned the lease of their house in All Hallows London Wall to John Pritewelle in 1348 they reserved for themselves half the fruit growing on the trees on the premises.[97] Some gardens were quite small: a shop in the goldsmithery in St Peter Wood Street had a herb garden that had to be drained through another shop, and a house in Hosier Lane appears to have had a roof garden.[98] Many of the cases that came to the attention of the mayor and aldermen in the assize of nuisance concerned the damage done to gardens by broken walls or blocked drainage ditches. John Hankyn complained bitterly about his waterlogged garden in 1369; 'the vines and other plants which used to grow and bear fruit, are withered and barren'.[99]

With the gardens, of course, there came livestock: not all city gardens were oases of quiet shade and orderly rows of leeks. Many Londoners kept poultry, and there were numerous ducks splashing around in the marshy waters of the moor outside Cripplegate. Not surprisingly neighbours complained of the 'discomfort and nuisance' caused by these ducks.[100] At least the ducks were outside the wall, but pigs seem often to have been kept within the city and caused frequent complaints. By civic ordinance all pigs had to be penned or kept securely in gardens except those belonging to the hospital of St Anthony; these were marked out by a distinguishing bell. Roaming pigs were to be killed, or their owners fined 4*d.* a day.[101] Pigs were a nuisance: when they broke into the churchyard of St Benet Fink, they ate the plants and 'committed other enormities in contempt of God'. But they were also dangerous.[102] In 1322 a sow strayed through an open shop door and mortally bit a baby girl lying in her cradle.[103] Not surprisingly Londoners were unenthusiastic about their neighbours' pigsties. Rose le Hert was compelled to move her pigsties away from the party wall, and David of Kingston, who had ingeniously constructed his pigsties over the Walbrook, was ordered to remove them.[104] Although there are occasional references to goats and cattle kept in the city, it is likely that most cattle were kept outside the wall and nearer to pastures.[105] Adam le Eyre and his wife Denise had a cowhouse and garden in the extra-mural parish of St Andrew Holborn, and John Stow as a child collected milk for his family from a herd of thirty or forty cows kept by 'one Trolop' at a farm near the house of the Minoresses outside Aldgate.[106] Most oxen and beef cattle were fattened on the

[96] E. Williams, *Early Holborn and the Legal Quarter of London*, 2 vols. (London, 1927), i. 423. In the bishop of Winchester's garden in Southwark there was a vineyard, an orchard containing pear, apple, and peach trees, a herb garden, and a vegetable garden that produced leeks, beans, garlic, and other vegetables: M. Carlin, *Medieval Southwark* (London, 1996), 43 and n.

[97] *LBF*, 186.

[98] *Assize of Nuisance*, 15; cf. 12; *CPMR 1413–37*, 127.

[99] Ibid. 138; cf. 45, 61.

[100] Ibid. 67, 156; *CPMR 1413–37*, 119.

[101] *LBA*, 216, 217, 220; *LBC*, 5; *LBD*, 251. In 1365 William Baldwyn entered into a £100 obligation not to rear pigs in the city, *CPMR 1364–81*, 39.

[102] *Assize of Nuisance*, 13; cf. 62, 67.

[103] *Coroners' Rolls* 56–7.

[104] *Assize of Nuisance*, 58, 93.

[105] Ibid. 524; *CPMR 1413–37*, 141.

[106] *Possessory Assize*, 96; Stow, *Survey*, i. 126.

pasturelands of manors some way from London and then brought to Smithfield market for immediate sale and slaughter.[107]

Animals could be dangerous: an insecurely bridled horse kicked a Londoner to death and another savage horse bit off the ear of John de Radcliff.[108] In 1307 a fight between two dogs led to the death of one of their masters and it was claimed that one dog alone in 1366 had managed to bite fifty-four sheep.[109] The mere fact that a man kept dogs in his house led to his being presented by his neighbours at the wardmote.[110] Many keen gardeners complained at the assizes of nuisance about the havoc wrought by dogs. In the interests of hygiene and safety the mayor and aldermen decided in 1387 that no dogs except *chiens gentilz* were to be allowed to wander at large in the city. By *chiens gentilz* the civic authorities may have had in mind lapdogs such as those belonging to Chaucer's genteel prioress:

> of smale houndes had she, that she fedde
> with rosted flesh, or milk and wastel breed.

When this ordinance was reiterated in 1475 it was agreed that butchers' dogs, except bitches on heat, should also be allowed to roam freely.[111] Since most of the roaming dogs would have been 'masterless hounds' it would have been virtually impossible to impose the 40*d.* fine on their owners. The ordinances are, perhaps, a measure of the problem rather than the solution.

WATER AND SEWAGE

This attempt by the city authorities to confine dogs within safe bounds was simply one aspect of a general concern to improve the environment within which Londoners lived and worked. Other measures were, perhaps, more positive. The rulers of London understood the need for fresh water, for effective drainage and sanitation, and for street cleaning. There is no reason to suppose that medieval London was unduly squalid; the worst problems developed with the burgeoning population in the sixteenth century.

The Thames was originally the main source of water in the city but it was apparent that the river was contaminated both by sewage and rubbish. In spite of this Thames water was extensively used both for washing and drinking.[112] Little Eleanor Gubbe was sent down to the Thames in October 1324 to fill two earthenware pitchers with water. It was curfew time and when she slipped and fell in no

[107] *Eyre 1244*, 79. It would appear that many of the fields of the manors at Tottenham, north of London, were used for pasturing cattle, see D. Moss and I. Murray, 'A Fifteenth-Century Middlesex Terrier', *TLMAS* 25 (1974), 285–294, esp. 293–4; D. Moss, 'The Economic Development of a Middlesex Village', *Agricultural History Review*, 28 (1980), 104–14, esp. 109–10, 114.

[108] *Eyre 1244*, 61–7; *Calendar of Letters from the Mayor and Corporation of the City of London c.1350–1370*, ed. R. R. Sharpe (London, 1885), 125.

[109] *Coroners' Rolls*, 26; *CPMR 1364–81*, 68–9.

[110] Ibid. 252–3.

[111] *LBH*, 311; *LBL*, 130–1.

[112] D. Keene, 'Issues of Water in Medieval London', *Urban History*, 28 (2001), 161–79, esp. 169.

one saw her until her father came later and found her drowned.[113] Those who could afford it purchased *bouges* (leather pouches) of water from water-carriers who would take up water at Dowgate or at Castle Baynard, and then sell it throughout the city.[114] There were private wells, but the cases of death from asphyxiation while cleaning them do not speak well for their purity.[115]

Probably because of the dubious quality of the water obtained from these sources, it was decided early in the thirteenth century that the Londoners should have their own supply of fresh water to be piped from springs in Tyburn (north of Oxford Street) into the city itself. Access to the Tyburn waters was bought by the city in 1237 and work began on the pipes in 1245.[116] The water was brought south to Charing Cross and then along the Strand, up Fleet Street and thence to Cheapside.[117] The foreign merchants from the north French towns of Amiens, Corbie, and Nesle in 1237 gave £100 'to the water conduit from the fountains at Tyburn to be brought into the city of London'.[118] The conduit, sited at the east end of Cheapside outside the house of St Thomas of Acre, was constructed in the 1230s or 1240s.[119] It has been suggested that the siting of the conduit at the house of St Thomas (rather than in the centre of Cheapside) 'may have been associated with a significant stage in the development of the cult of St Thomas within the city, endowing the charitable provision of water by the community of the citizens with a profound religious and symbolic significance'.[120] When the Cheapside conduit was completed, a warden was appointed to guard and maintain the new city water supply. It had been intended to supply this water freely to all London inhabitants but when, in 1312, the pipes were in need of repair, it was decided to raise the necessary money by charging brewers, cooks, and fishmongers who used the water for business.[121] Names of wardens, and their accounts, appear intermittently in the city's Letter Books until 1368 when it was decided to lease out the city's water supply.[122] The lessee, who paid the city 10 marks annually for ten years, was

[113] *Coroners' Rolls*, 100; the men of the Tower ward were accustomed to collect water from the Thames: *CPMR 1413–37*, 141.

[114] *LBG*, 206 and n. 2; *HW*, i. 509 and n. The prices that water-carriers could charge were regulated in 1350: *Memorials*, 254. By 1496 the waterbearers were organized into a fraternity dedicated to St Christopher and based on Austin Friars: H. C. Coote, 'The Ordinances of Some Secular Guilds of London 1354–1496', *TLMAS* 4 (1871), 55–9.

[115] *LBB*, 276–7; *Coroners' Rolls*, 198–9. Sometimes wells were used for dumping rubbish, e.g. a case in 1390: *Memorials*, 516–17.

[116] *LBA*, 14–15; the best account of the city's water supply is to be found in Keene, 'Issues of Water', 174–8.

[117] For the route of the pipes see *Memorials*, 503–4; A. M. Davies, 'London's First Conduit System: A Topographical Study', *TLMAS* 2 (1913), 9–59.

[118] Year 1237, *Liber Custumarum*, ii. 64–6; for these woad merchants, see Ch. 5.

[119] The Great Conduit House was recorded by archaeologists in 1994: P. Treveil and P. Rowsome, 'Number 1 Poultry – the Main Excavation: Late Saxon and Medieval Sequence', *London Archaeologist*, 8 (1998), 283–91.

[120] Keene, 'Issues of Water', 178.

[121] *Memorials*, 77–8, 107.

[122] Year 1310, *LBD*, 236; 1325, *LBE*, 204; 1327, *LBE*, 220–1; 1333–5, *LBF*, 28–9; 1350, *LBF*, 303–4; 1353, *LBG*, 2, 11. In 1337, Richard de Gaunt, lately the keeper of the conduit, was accused of stealing lead and money: *CPMR 1327–64*, 144. The accounts record the sums paid by those who used tins and tankards (i.e. brewers and artisans) to collect the water, 1333–5, 1350, 1353, *LBF*, 28–9, 303–4; *LBG*, 11.

responsible for the upkeep of the conduits and pipes above ground but the city remained responsible for the underground pipes.[123] When the lease ran out in the 1370s the more public-spirited rulers who prevailed in city government in the years 1376–84 decided not only to repair the existing water supply but also to extend the piping up Cornhill.[124] Although the extension was not achieved, a further city conduit or 'standard' in the centre of Cheapside was built by 1395.[125] From about this date Londoners began to make bequests in their wills for the upkeep of the city water supply; it now qualified as a pious work, like bridge-building and the maintenance of roads.[126] In the fifteenth century, it was decided that the whole supply system was in need of a major overhaul. It may be that the springs at Tyburn were drying up, for the city leased further land at Oxlese, near Paddington, from the abbot of Westminster. Wellheads were constructed and the water was piped southwards to Tyburn to link up with the existing system. All the old piping was renewed in the years between 1439 and 1455 and many of the wellheads were repaired. The total cost of this operation may have been about £5,000 which was raised largely by special civic taxes but also by bequests.[127] John Welles, who was mayor of London in 1431–2 and died ten years later, may have been responsible for this initiative: the 'standard' in the centre of Cheapside, which had originally been made of wood, was rebuilt in stone by his executors and displayed 'wels imbraced by angels'.[128] The main conduit was rebuilt owing to the generosity of Thomas Ilome[129] and the project of a century earlier was finally realized when the supply was extended eastwards up Cornhill to the intersection with Gracechurch Street, where a new conduit was built to serve the needs of those living in the eastern part of the city.[130]

The public water supply was carefully guarded, although groups of local inhabitants were sometimes licensed to take spurs off the main pipeline provided that this did not impede the flow of water elsewhere.[131] Those who siphoned off the public water supply without licence were severely punished. William Campion, a brewer in Fleet Street, who tapped the conduit pipe and so brought water into his

[123] Although the commonalty were to pay the usual charges, the mayor, aldermen, and sheriffs were to receive their water free, *LBG*, 223.

[124] 24 November 1378, *LBH*, 108, also 116, 128, 215–16.

[125] *Annales Londonienses*, in *Chronicles of the Reigns of Edward I and II*, ed. W. Stubbs, 2 vols. (Rolls Series, 1882–3), 44; *CChR*, ii. 38; H. A. Harben, *A Dictionary of London* (London, 1918), 270, 545; the water supply was repaired, but not extended, *LBH*, 343, 354, 358.

[126] *HW*, ii. 218, 301, 307, 430; *LBH*, 358.

[127] Barron, 'Government of London', 266–77 and App. 38; *LBL*, 158.

[128] Harben, *Dictionary*, 545; *HW*, ii. 499; Stow, *Survey*, i. 26.

[129] Year 1467, £100 was allocated for the repair of the conduit: ibid. 71. In 1479 Thomas Ilome, sheriff, 'newly builded the Great Conduit in West Cheap', Stow, *Survey*, ii. 177.

[130] Year 1491, licence to Dame Elizabeth Hill to turn up the soil in Grace Church Street for a conduit: *LBL*, 280; Stow records that Thomas Hill, mayor in 1485, had 'the conduit of Grasse streete builded', Stow, *Survey*, i. 110.

[131] In 1388 the inhabitants of Fleet Street were allowed to draw off the water for a new conduit near Salisbury inn; in 1398 the inhabitants of the area around the church of St Michael le Querne were licensed to erect a private conduit: *Memorials*, 503–4; 531. This conduit is illustrated in *The London Surveys of Ralph Treswell*, ed. J. Schofield (London Topographical Society, 1987), plate 1.

own home was condemned to a singular punishment. He was to be paraded around on a horse 'with a vessel like unto a conduit full of water upon his head, the same water running by small pipes out of the same vessel, and that when the water is wasted, new water to be put in the said vessel again'.[132] It must have taken some time to construct the apparatus with which to punish Campion.

Not everyone, of course, depended upon the public water supply for fresh water. Grand houses may well have piped in their own supplies from fields around London. Those we know about were religious houses. Westminster Abbey used water brought from its manor at Hyde (now Hyde Park) and the Greyfriars and Dominicans derived their water from wells in Bloomsbury.[133] St Bartholomew's priory and hospital had water piped from Canonbury and in 1436–42 the grocer Thomas Knolles obtained the prior's permission to divert some water from this supply for the use of the prisoners at Newgate and Ludgate.[134] The priory and hospital of St Mary Bishopsgate brought water from a spring in Lollesworth Field in underground pipes, which supplied drinking water and was then used to flush out the kitchens and the latrine in the infirmary. The system was still working in the late sixteenth century.[135] When the London Charterhouse was founded in the fourteenth century water was piped across the fields from Islington to an elaborate wellhead built in the centre of the large quadrangle.[136]

Water was needed not only for drinking and cooking, but also, of course, for washing. Poorer people washed themselves and their clothes in the Thames, especially in the ditches around the Tower.[137] Wealthier Londoners would wash in the privacy of their own homes, using basins and ewers made of copper or brass imported from the Low Countries. Household inventories refer also to 'Lavatoria', which consisted of containers of pewter or lead raised on a stand and fitted with an exit pipe and a plughole. Such a modern convenience was expensive—one was valued at 2*s.* 6*d.* in 1393—and would be placed in the hall for the use, particularly, of guests.[138] From the middle of the fourteenth century there are references to white soap imported in cases from Spain, which was expensive and was known, even then, as 'Castille' soap.[139] Most Londoners, however, used a much rougher

[132] Year 1478, *LBL*, 160.

[133] H. Colvin (ed.), *The History of the King's Works*, 3 vols. (London, 1963), i. 549–50; P. Norman, 'On an Ancient Conduit-Head in Queen Square, Bloomsbury', *Archaeologia*, 6 (1899), 257–66; Keene, 'Issues of Water', 176–7.

[134] N. J. Kerling, 'Note on Newgate Prison', *TLMAS* 22 (1968–70), 21–2; *LBL*, 4, 130; CLRO, Journal 6, fo. 153^{v}; *CPMR 1458–82*, 92–3.

[135] Thomas, Sloane, and Phillpotts, *Hospital of St Mary Spital*, 43.

[136] W. S. Hope, 'The London Charterhouse and its Old Water Supply', *Archaeologia*, 8 (1902), 293–312. The hospitallers and the nuns of St Mary Clerkenwell were also linked to the Charterhouse supply: W. O. Hassall, 'Conventual Buildings of St Mary Clerkenwell', *TLMAS* 8 (1940), 234–7; WAM, 9182.

[137] Reference to bathing in the moat around the Tower: *Memorials*, 7, 260–1; in the Thames: *Coroners' Rolls*, 59; *Letters*, 85; in Houndsditch: *Coroners' Rolls*, 190; clothes washing in the Thames at St Katherines: *CPMR 1413–37*, 120.

[138] See inventory of house of Richard Toky, grocer, 1393: *CPMR 1381–1412*, 209; cf. *CPMR 1363–81*, 91, 155. In 1373 a pewter 'lavatory' was deemed defective by a jury of pewterers, *CPMR 1323–64*, 264.

[139] *Letters*, 56; *CPMR 1363–81*, 77; *CPMR 1423–37*, 215–16; *CPMR 1437–57*, 65, 83–4.

soap fabricated simply of ashes and oil in 'sope houses' set up along the Thames.[140] Londoners had access to public bathhouses which were known by the unprepossessing name of 'stews'. These, as early as the thirteenth century, were notorious: 'Bathestereslane' (lane of the female bathkeepers) is recorded from the mid-thirteenth century.[141] Although a ban on stews in the city was attempted by the civic authorities early in the fifteenth century, it was impossible to enforce and so there developed, instead, a system of licensed stews. It was believed that the immoral bathhouses had been run by aliens (especially Flemings) and that the immorality would cease when free-born London citizens were in control. After this reform, in 1428, the complaints, if not perhaps the immorality, came to an end. But given the reputation of these bathhouses it is anyway doubtful they contributed much to public health.[142]

Although few London houses would have had a private supply of piped water, many did have private privies. The building regulations of the city required private cesspits to be two and half feet away from neighbouring land if they were built of stone, or three and a half feet if they were not so lined.[143] As might be expected, leaking and unneighbourly privies were a constant source of complaint and dispute.[144] Moreover, these private privies had to be regularly cleaned. City regulations required that this 'ordure' should not be dumped in the streets but should be thrown into the Thames or deposited well outside the city.[145] Soon professional privy cleaners appeared. William Wombe, described as 'a cleaner of latrines', drowned at Haywharf while he was washing himself after a day's work in 1338.[146] City customs also required that privy cleaning should be done at night when it would be less inconvenient for the vigorous street life of the city. In 1466 John Lovegold was awarded a monopoly of privy-cleaning in the city. He was to be allowed to charge 2*s.* 2*d.* for every tun of 'ordure' he removed and this, one may guess, he then sold to the gardeners living in the city suburbs.[147] Doubtless John Lovegold grew rich from plying his essential but unattractive trade. When Thomas Mason, 'ordure voider', cleaned out ordure at night from tenements belonging to the Bridge in the 1530s, he charged only 18*d.* a tun; at the annual cleaning, he had sixty-six tuns to take away from two tenements in Wood Street.[148]

Not all private latrines ran into cesspits; many were constructed over the city's various watercourses, especially the Walbrook, the Fleet, and the city ditch. The governors of London waged continual war against these private privies: eleven

[140] Dispute in 1414: *CPMR 1413–37*, 16–18.

[141] Keene, 'Issues of Water', 169.

[142] Barron, 'Government of London', 260–1; R. Karras, *Common Women: Prostitution and Sexuality in Medieval England* (New York, 1996), 17–18.

[143] *Assize of Nuisance*, p. xxv; some private privies seem to have had pipes leading to cesspits and even some rudimentary water flushing system, E. Sabine, 'Latrines and Cesspools of Medieval London', *Speculum*, 9 (1934), 303–21, esp. 313–15.

[144] e.g. *Assize of Nuisance*, 1.

[145] *Memorials*, 67–8.

[146] *Coroners' Rolls*, 221.

[147] Sabine, 'Latrines and Cesspools', 306–7, 316; *LBL*, 67–8.

[148] *London Bridge: Selected Accounts and Rentals 1381–1538*, ed. V. Harding and L. Wright (London Record Society, 1995), 186, 195, 212–13. The Bridgewardens usually paid another man to check up on Thomas Mason 'to see him fill the tuns'.

were removed from the foss around the Fleet prison in 1355 and others were swept away from the Tower ditch in 1369.[149] The rector of St Botolph Aldgate who had built a latrine over Houndsditch was ordered to remove it in 1357, although the Minoresses were given permission to retain their 'easement' into the city ditch at Aldgate.[150] For quite a long time, however, the city tolerated the private latrines that were built over the Walbrook. Rents were charged for such privies and a keeper of the Walbrook was appointed to prevent the stream from becoming blocked.[151] But in 1463 it was decided that all lavatories overhanging the Walbrook should be abolished and fourteen years later the ban was extended to privies over the city ditch.[152] So by the end of the period the only private latrines were the cesspits, because the open sewers of the Walbrook and ditch were no longer tolerated: indeed the Walbrook was covered in brick and paved with stone so that, as Stow observed, 'no man may by the eye discerne it'.[153]

For those who had no access to a private latrine the city provided several public lavatories. Some of these drained into the city ditch, for example at Ludgate, or into the Walbrook at Moorgate,[154] but most of the common privies were on the banks of the Thames: at the Temple (a latrine of four seats maintained at the expense of the landlords), at Castle Baynard, and at Queenhithe.[155] There was also a public privy on London Bridge which appears to have had two entrances, for a debtor was able to give his creditor the slip there in 1306. When the privy later fell into decay it was decided that the bridgewardens should be responsible for its repair.[156] It must have been considered that the provision of public latrines in the city was inadequate, for Richard Whittington, or his executors, provided a new 'house of easement' for the city in the parish of St Martin Vintry on the Thames. This benefaction was known as Whittington's long house since it provided sixty-four seats each for men and women overhanging a narrow inlet that was cleaned out by the tidal ebb and flow of the Thames.[157]

The attitude of Londoners to the necessary human functions was practical and matter-of-fact, yet they did not lack a sense of decency or appropriateness. It was the generally held view that nature should be relieved in private and in the places provided; men and women were expected to use the common privies and not the

[149] *Memorials*, 279–80, 338.

[150] *Assize of Nuisance*, 118; *LBG*, 266–7.

[151] In 1374 a keeper of the Walbrook was appointed and a rent of 12*d*. charged: *LBG*, 324; *Memorials*, 379–80. In 1383 the rent for a privy over the Walbrook was doubled to 2*s*.; stables over the stream were forbidden as was rubbish tipping: ibid. 478–9.

[152] *LBL*, 21, 149.

[153] Stow, *Survey*, i 119.

[154] The latrine at Moorgate was reconstructed when the new gate was made in 1415, *Memorials*, 614–16. The common privy at Ludgate was defective and perilous in 1421: *CPMR 1413–37*, 124. For public latrines in London see Sabine, 'Latrines and Cesspools', 307–9.

[155] Temple privy: *Memorials*, 306; Castle Baynard privy: *CPMR 1413–37*, 132; Queenhithe privy: *Assize of Nuisance*, 214; *LBG*, 266–7. In 1466 it was decided that the inhabitants of Queenhithe ward should have the toll from a boat using the public dock to pay for cleaning the common 'lystoft' of the ward: *LBL*, 67.

[156] *CPMR 1298–1307*, 247; *CPMR 1364–87*, 237–8; *LBH*, 212. There is no reference to this public privy on the Bridge in the published accounts of the Bridgewardens, *London Bridge*, ed. Harding and Wright.

[157] P. E. Jones, 'Whittington's Longhouse', *LTR* 23 (1974) 27–34. Above the privies there were five or six almshouses for the parish poor.

city streets and open spaces.[158] Joan and Andrew de Aubrey complained that the neighbour with whom they shared a privy had removed the partition 'so that the extremities of those sitting upon the seats can be seen, a thing which is abominable and altogether intolerable'. The assize committee sympathized with the de Aubreys' complaint and ordered the offending neighbour to restore the partition 'according to civic custom'.[159]

STREET-CLEANING

The city authorities tackled the problem of street-cleaning from two angles: in the first place the streets had to be well paved and in the second they had to be kept clean. During the mayoralty of Gregory de Rokesle (1274-81) each ward had been instructed to elect four men to look after the pavements and remove rubbish. In the last resort it was the responsibility of the aldermen to ensure that the streets in his ward were in good condition.[160] In spite of this it would appear that the city accepted some communal responsibility: early in the fourteenth century, four paviours were sworn to look after the pavements throughout the city and, on occasion, carts and goods brought into the city would be assessed for pavage (i.e. a tax levied for the upkeep of the city streets).[161] It may be that certain areas, e.g. around the city gates and the markets, were particularly the responsibility of the city commonalty, but it was clearly also the responsibility of each householder to maintain the pavement in front of his own house.[162] When the rector of St Bartholomew the Less failed to repair the pavement outside his house in Broad Street, the mayor ordered Thomas Gardiner, a paviour, to carry out the work and send the bill to the rector. When the bill for 18*s.* 4*d.* arrived the rector responded that the pavement was not his responsibility since his house, although lying on Broad Street, was actually entered from the churchyard. The jury were not impressed with his ingenious plea and he was ordered to pay the bill.[163] The rector may, however, have been overcharged since a whole boatload of paving stones had been sold for only seven shillings thirty years earlier.[164] It was almost impossible to ensure that householders kept their pavements in good order; many tenements were vacant and ironshod wheels were constantly damaging the road surfaces. The wardmote returns of 1421 are full of complaints about broken and neglected pavements, and

[158] In 1307 two men upbraided a man who failed to use the common privy and a brawl ensued, *CEMCR 1298–1307*, 255. Urinating in a public place in 1384 was deemed to be provocative, see P. Strohm, 'Hochon's Arrow', in *Hochon's Arrow: The Social Imagination of Fourteenth-Century Texts* (Princeton, NJ, 1992), 11–31, esp. 25–6.

[159] *Assize of Nuisance*, 79.

[160] *LBA*, 183. In 1311 four surveyors of pavements were sworn for Langbourn ward, *LBD*, 312; see Ch. 6.

[161] Paviours appointed, *LBC*, 115; *LBD*, 55, 116; *CPMR 1323–64*, 219–20. In 1344 there were repairs to the pavement at Aldgate and elsewhere: ibid. 160–1. Pavage levied in 1356, *Memorials*, 291–2; 1377, 1380, 1384, *LBH*, 63, 145, 155.

[162] *Assize of Nuisance*, 29, 39, 89. In 1469 the responsibility of the individual householder was reiterated: *LBL*, 84–5.

[163] *CPMR 1364–81*, 144–5.

[164] *CPMR 1323–64*, 139.

Italian visitors commented on the poor road surfaces and ever-present mud, which led to the development of particularly strong double leather shoes.[165]

The better the pavement the easier it was to clean. From the thirteenth century the city had attempted to enforce the clearing and cleaning of streets and by 1332, if not earlier, it appears to have been the ward beadle, equipped with a cart, on whom the responsibility for street-cleaning rested.[166] Soon he had underlings, scavengers who looked after the pavements and rakers who actually collected up the rubbish and dumped it outside the city (although some took it no further than the next ward!).[167] To assist the rakers in their task the city provided twelve communal carts (with twenty-four horses) for ten of the inner city wards.[168] But even these dung carts were insufficient to deal with all the rubbish, and so all the carts that came into the city with loads of sand, gravel, or loam were commandeered to take away dung (although the city authorities had the sense to specify that other carts were not to be used for this purpose).[169] As a measure of the importance attached to the problem of street-cleaning, the city in 1385 appointed its first sanitary officer, the serjeant of the channel; with a general brief to oversee the work of the ward beadles, scavengers and rakers and to be responsible for the cleanliness of the city streets.[170] But Londoners were both lazy and ingenious. Fines had to be levied on those who simply dumped their rubbish, and double fines exacted from those who dumped it outside the house of their neighbour. Some householders placed their rubbish outside their houses so early that it was scattered over the street before the rubbish carts came.[171] Another difficulty was that the carts would be overloaded and thus spill their contents onto the street as they went to the city dumps. It was decided, therefore, that rubbish carts should have backboards at least two and a half feet high.[172] The problem could be contained but not solved; civic regulations were hard to enforce, ward officers could be bribed or might be negligent, and the appointed dumping places were, inevitably, some distance away. But the continuing efforts of the city authorities to introduce new regulations and new solutions bears witness to their concern to create a healthy and pleasant civic environment.

[165] Ironshod wheels were banned from 1277: *CPMR 1364–81*, 196 and n.; *CPMR 1413–37*, 154; *LBL*, 220; C. Barron, C. Coleman, and C. Gobbi, 'The London Journal of Alessandro Magno 1562', *London Journal* 9 (1983), 136–52, 148.

[166] *LBA*, 183, 216; *Memorials*, 67; *LBF*, 125; *LBG*, 33, 75, 92; *CPMR 1323–64*, 97–8; see E. Sabine, 'City Cleaning in Medieval London', *Speculum*, 12 (1937), 19–43. See Ch. 6.

[167] Scavengers first appear in 1364: *LBG*, 198, 208; rakers first appear in 1357: *CCR 1349–54*, 391; *CPMR 1364–81*, 164; *LBH*, 108. For a case in 1384 of a raker who swept his rubbish into the next ward see *CPMR 1381–1412*, 71; see Ch. 6.

[168] Year 1372, *CPMR 1364–81*, 147. This move seems to have been part of a concerted campaign to clean up the city: *ibid.* 164, 150; *LBG* 300.

[169] Year 1379, *Memorials*, 435–6.

[170] *LBH*, 275. When Nicholas Foche was admitted and sworn in 1390 his range of duties was extended to include the killing of stray pigs and geese, ibid. 355. In the fifteenth century oath of the serjeant of the channel it is clear that there was anxiety not only about the cleanliness of the city but also about possible extortion by the serjeant: *LBD*, 201; Barron, 'Government of London', 140, 568; see Ch. 8.

[171] *LBH*, 255, 275.

[172] Year 1405 *LBI*, 45; the men of Cripplegate ward complained in 1421 that their 'tumbrel cart' was defective: *CPMR 1413–37*, 133.

INDUSTRIAL ACTIVITY

London was not, however, simply a city in which people lived: it was a great industrial city and a place where goods were produced on a scale massive by comparison with any other town in England. There were problems, therefore, not only of human but of industrial waste. Animals were reared, roamed, and were killed in city streets; their carcasses had to be skinned or plucked, their hides tanned, and their bones carved into utensils. Food had to be prepared and cooked, and beer brewed. Houses had to be built, cloth had to be woven and fulled and dyed, iron had to be worked into armour, or tools, or horseshoes, or cartwheel rims. Lead had to be fashioned into pipes. Much of this industrial activity depended to a greater or lesser extent upon heat generated partly by wood, but largely by coal. Smoke, dirt, and noise enveloped the homes of Londoners. It was the task of the city governors to prevent, or at least limit, the most antisocial of these activities and to attempt to ensure that the profit of one Londoner was not made at the expense of his neighbour.

Poulters were forbidden to pluck birds in the streets and butchers, in the course of the fourteenth century, were subject to increasingly stringent regulations about the slaughtering of beasts.[173] In 1343 the city had granted the butchers a quay on the Fleet River outside the city walls where they were instructed to clean carcasses before sale.[174] The butchers' market lay in the parish of St Nicholas Shambles in Newgate near the Greyfriars precinct. Clearly the transport of slaughtered beasts along Newgate Street and down to the Fleet for cleaning was not popular with the local inhabitants who protested to the king. Richard Bayser, a butcher, and his wife Emma had built a 'skaldynghous' in the Shambles and as a result water, mixed with the blood and hair of slaughtered animals, flowed along the street gutter and thence to the friars' garden 'causing a stench in many places'.[175] The king was sympathetic to the complaints and it was decided in 1371 that cattle should be slaughtered well away from the city, at Knightsbridge in the west and at Stratford in the east.[176] The prohibition was not entirely effective and the aristocratic householders in the western suburbs complained about the continuing slaughter of beasts at Holborn Bridge and all along the Fleet River.[177] The difficulty was that, if beasts were slaughtered further away, the price of fresh meat then rose; so in 1393 a new inner-city slaughterhouse was provided near Queenhithe, although the butchers

173 E. Sabine, 'Butchering in Medieval London', *Speculum*, 8 (1933), 335–53, where the author links the increasingly numerous proclamations dealing with butchering with the outbreaks of plague. The proclamations may, however, simply reflect the rapid development of a comparatively new industry that, in its turn, depended on the increased *per capita* wealth brought about by the plague. See also P. E. Jones, *The Butchers of London* (London, 1976), esp. ch. 4. In 1365 there was a proclamation about poulterers: *LBG*, 207.

174 *Memorials*, 214.

175 *Assize of Nuisance*, 142; Sabine, 'Butchering', 339–42.

176 *LBG*, pp. xxvii–viii; *Memorials*, 356–8; *LBH*, 301.

177 *LBH*, 372, 375, 376, 392, 394; C. Barron, 'The Quarrel of Richard II with London 1392–7' in C. Barron and F. R. H. Du Boulay (eds.), *The Reign of Richard II: Essays in Honour of May McKisack* (London, 1971), 173–201, esp. 175–6.

had to agree to cut up the offal and take it in boats out into the Thames at mid-stream to dump it.[178] The problems caused by the rapid increase in the demand for fresh meat in the second half of the fourteenth century seem not to have been so acute later.

Early in the fourteenth century tanners had been forbidden to practise their craft within the city walls and, in the subsidy rolls of this period, they are to be found living either in Cripplegate ward outside the walls or, similarly, in the ward of Farringdon Without.[179] The parishioners of St Andrew Holborn and St Sepulchre complained about the tanners who obstructed the Turnmill Brook (the name for the northern section of the Fleet River) by tying their hides to stakes in the stream.[180] At the end of the period whitetawyers were also prevented from working in the city and were banished either to Southwark or Bermondsey.[181] It seems unlikely that the Londoners consulted the inhabitants of Southwark or Bermondsey before promulgating this ordinance: a good example of the cavalier attitude that the city adopted towards its outlying neighbours.

Some of the most noxious crafts practised in the city were those of the smiths and metalworkers of all kinds. As early a 1299 a blacksmith agreed not to work at night because of the unhealthiness of the coal smoke and the general inconvenience to his neighbours.[182] It was the general opinion that coal smoke was more poisonous than that of charcoal, and the city was still able to secure enough firewood at this period not to have to rely as heavily on imported coal as was to be the case in the sixteenth century.[183] It was still inconvenient to have an armourer as a nextdoor neighbour even if he did not work at night. Alice and Thomas Yonge complained about the blows of the sledgehammers, the shaking of the house walls, and the stench of smoke from the forge next door, which penetrated all their rooms and even spoiled the wine and ale in their cellars.[184] One poet was moved to write graphically about the horrors of a blacksmith's forge:

> Swart smoky smiths smutted with smoke
> Drive me to death with the din of their dints
> Such noise at night heard no man ever,
> Such crying of knaves and clattering of knocks
> The pug-nosed bumpkins cry for 'Coal! Coal!'
> And blow with their bellows till their brains are all bursting.[185]

[178] Year 1393, *LBH*, 392; cf. *LBL*, 104.

[179] *CPMR 1298–1307*, 161–2 and n.; *Two Early London Subsidy Rolls*, ed. E. Ekwall (Lund, 1951), 86–7; see D. Keene, 'Tanners' Widows, 1300–1350', in C. Barron and A. Sutton (eds.), *Medieval London Widows 1300–1500* (London, 1994), 1–27.

[180] Year 1422, *CPMR 1413–37*, 125–6.

[181] Year 1478, *LBL*, 155.

[182] *CEMCR 1298–1307*, 33–4; 1394 blacksmiths' ordinances, *Memorials* 537–39; wiremongers' ordinances in 1481, 1497: *LBL*, 185–6, 319–20.

[183] References to imported coal from 1235: *Eyre 1244*, 44; *Letters*, 94; *CPMR 1364–81*, 246–7; see J. Galloway, D. Keene, and M. Murphy, 'Fuelling the City: Production and Distribution of Firewood and Fuel in London's Region', *EconHR* 49 (1996), 447–72.

[184] *Assize of Nuisance*, 160–61.

[185] Modern English rendering by E. Rickert, *Chaucer's World* (New York, 1948), 16–17, from BL, Arundel Ms 292, fo. 72^{v}.

Some blacksmiths had their forges out in the street and although this may have been less dangerous for their neighbours' wine yet the inconvenience to traffic was just as great.[186] Not surprisingly, perhaps, a great many metalworkers were to be found in the early fourteenth century living in the ward of Farringdon outside the walls and the bell founders settled in the parish of St Botolph outside Aldgate.[187] The difficulty faced by the city authorities in dealing with industrial nuisances is exemplified in their response to a complaint about the 'great damage and peril of death' faced by all those who breathed the smoke from a plumber's forge in the parish of St Clement, Candlewick Street. The mayor and aldermen pointed out that the plumber must be allowed to practise his craft but they enjoined him to raise the height of his furnace shaft to minimize the danger of fire and the nuisance caused by the smoke.[188] Neighbours complained about the harmful fumes caused by burning plaster of Paris, and the antisocial habits of dyers also caused trouble:[189] they blocked up the inlets on the Thames at Dowgate when they discarded the bark and peel from their dyes and kept dangerous pits where they put the hot cloth after it had been dyed. A panel of arbitrators decided that Thomas Newbolt should not use the pit outside his front door for dyeing cloth when it was hot, but might use it when the cloth was cold.[190]

It is, perhaps, surprising to find that the civic authorities were concerned not only about the dangerous and evil-smelling crafts but also about noisy ones. The blacksmiths were prohibited from working at night; so were the wiredrawers who were not to carry out 'knokkyng, filyinng or any other noyfulle werk whereby his neighbours might be noyed or diseased' between the hours of eight at night and five in the morning.[191] Horners were not to work at night for the same reason.[192] From the thirteenth century metalbound cartwheels had been prohibited in the city not only because they damaged the pavements but also because of the noise they made.[193] In the wardmote inquests of 1421 there were complaints about men who illegally used ironbound cartwheels, and the men of Bassishaw ward complained that William Bracy who hired out carts 'on diverse nights beyond the proper hour causes his servants to drive out of a gate, bumping and striking the sides of the gate so roughly that all the neighbours are disturbed and grieved of their repose and quiet at night'.[194]

186 *Assize of Nuisance*, 117, 138.

187 *Subsidy Rolls*, ed. Ekwall, 87; J. C. L. Stahlschmidt, *Surrey Bells and London Bellfounders* (London, 1884); C. Barron, 'Johanna Hill (d.1441) and Johanna Sturdy (d.*c.*1460), Bell-Founders', in Barron and Sutton, *Medieval London Widows*, 99–111.

188 *Memorials*, 355–6.

189 *CPMR 1364–81*, 166.

190 *CPMR 1413–37*, 62, 134.

191 *LBL*, 320; 1345, the spurriers were also banned from night-working: *Memorials*, 226–7.

192 *LBH*, 363–4; for the text of the Horners' ordinances see F. J. Fisher, *A Short History of the Worshipful Company of Horners* (London, 1936), 20–2. On the other hand it was decided in 1310 that tailors and skinners who needed to scour furs in the street were to do so *only* at night; otherwise they impeded the traffic. If they had too much work to do to complete it during the night, they were to use a blind alley, *Memorials*, 77.

193 *LBA*, 217; *LBH*, 352.

194 *CPMR 1413–37*, 117–18, 154.

CONCLUSION

The management of the urban environment in which the inhabitants of London lived was a matter of concern to the king, to the city's governors and to individual Londoners. The church intervened only in times of crisis such as the extreme mortality caused by the Black Death. The interests of the Crown were comparatively remote but where the city's rulers appeared to be negligent, as in the repair of the walls or in keeping the city clean, the king would intervene to stir them into action. Individual Londoners, and later the city companies, were often the providers of the capital needed to finance major civic improvements. It was the charity of wealthy individuals that rebuilt the city prisons, constructed the new Guildhall, extended the water supply, rebuilt the gates, and provided public lavatories. Only rarely was the cost of new, or improved, civic amenities borne by the city chamber or met by civic taxation. The overhaul, and extension, of the city's water supply in the middle of the fifteenth century was unusual in being a joint public and private enterprise: about half the cost was raised by civic taxation, and the other half was raised by charitable subscription.[195] Once the improvements were in place, then the maintenance of these civic facilities was the responsibility of the city's governors. In addition they were expected to have a general oversight of the practicalities and problems of urban living. It was they who drew up and implemented the regulations governing building disputes between neighbours, livestock control, sewage and drainage, industrial activities, and street-cleaning. Specific tasks would be passed down the line, via the aldermen, to the inhabitants and officers of the wards. But the mayor and aldermen bore the ultimate authority for ensuring that civic regulations were observed, that transgressors mended their ways, and that the common good was promoted.

The records that have survived are largely the chronicles of complaints and failures, of injunctions and punishments. Such is the nature of medieval judicial and administrative records. Yet, it would seem that from the early thirteenth century the needs of the community were able to restrain selfish individuality. Of course, all was not sweetness and light, and yet one cannot read the records of medieval London without being made aware of a restless pursuit of high communal standards of public health and safety.

[195] Barron, 'Government of London', 268–78, and app. 38.

CHAPTER ELEVEN

Welfare Provision

William beveridge and the other creators of the 'welfare state' in England in the twentieth century would not have been impressed by the extent to which medieval Londoners were expected to be corporately responsible for the well-being of those who were not able to look after themselves.[1] The courts of alderman and common council did not take up much time in dealing with 'social' problems, nor did they expect to impose taxation on London citizens to pay for welfare benefits, yet there was a common, unofficial expectation that those well endowed by God in this world should accept the obligation to care for their less fortunate neighbours. By and large welfare in medieval London was provided by the church or by wealthy Londoners responding to ecclesiastical injunctions. Over the period it is possible to detect two developments. In the first place the city governors became responsible for increased welfare provision in the city; by 1485 the court of aldermen not only had official responsibility for the orphan children of citizens, but also the problems of the aged merited their attention. Already in the twelfth century the citizens had oversight of the suburban leper houses and from the mid-fourteenth century they began to intervene in the government of the religious house of St Mary Bethlehem (Bedlam) where lunatics were confined. Moreover, although the city governors had no direct responsibility for the care of the poor, and no shelter was provided for them at the city's expense, yet indirectly they exercised responsibility in the control of food prices in the city, and they attempted to break the price-enhancing practices of forestallers and monopolists.

The second development which may be observed is the increasingly secular provision of help to those in need: wealthy Londoners who cared for their fellow men decided to establish institutions that were not staffed by members of religious orders. This is particularly noticeable in the foundation of almshouses for the old from the early fifteenth century onwards, and in the almost completely secular structure devised for the administration of Henry VII's great hospital of the Savoy early in the sixteenth century. Most almshouses were to be governed by a city company or, occasionally, by the churchwardens and a parish fraternity. By implication the prayers of the grateful recipients must have been considered as efficacious as the prayers of the religious, and the testator avoided the expense of endowing a religious house alongside his almshouse or hospital. Moreover the maladministration

[1] For a discussion of the ideas behind the Beveridge report of 1942 and of the various acts that implemented some of the ideas and thereby created the 'welfare state', see P. Thane, *Foundations of the Welfare State* (London, 1982).

of the temporalities of many London (and other) religious houses in the later Middle Ages by men who, if not deliberately dishonest, were clearly incompetent stewards, must have discouraged merchants from entrusting their hard-won fortunes to those who were incapable of conserving them. If the poor and needy were to receive any benefit from these bequests they had to be administered by good businessmen, and the newly incorporated city companies provided obvious expertise in this new approach to the posthumous relief of poverty.

THE CARE OF ORPHANS

It was orphan children who first attracted the corporate attention of London's rulers. At some time between 1244 and 1276 the city formalized its responsibility for the orphaned children of the freemen (or citizens) of London. In a disputed case about the guardianship of a city orphan in 1244, the king's judges asked the mayor and citizens to whom, after the death of the father and mother, the guardianship of their children should belong. The answer was that a citizen might choose whom he liked to look after his children and care for their goods, but that if no guardian had been named by the parents, then the custody of the child should be entrusted to a relative who would not stand to profit by the child's death.[2] At this date the parental choice was paramount and the concern of the mayor and aldermen was simply residual. But by 1276 the mayor and reputable men of London committed the three orphan children of Alan Godard to a woman named Sarah Haberdas, who seems not to have been their mother. Sarah was to have custody of the goods, tenements, and rents that belonged to the children; she was to feed and clothe them and, when they came of age, render account for their possessions. Five men, including her father, acted as pledges for Sarah.[3] By this date it is clear that the mayor and citizens of London were accepting, and exercising, an overall responsibility for the orphaned children of citizens, although the competing claims of rival guardians could not always be easily resolved.[4] By about 1340 the mayor and aldermen claimed, according to the custom of the city, to have the wardship and marriage of all orphans of citizens of London; the children, together with their lands and goods, were to be entrusted under suitable security to appropriate guardians selected by the mayor and aldermen, unless the parent had

[2] *The London Eyre of 1244*, ed. H. M. Chew and M. Weinbaum (London Record Society, 1970), no. 184, and for more details of this case J. Strype, *Survey of the Cities of London and Westminster*, 2 vols. (London, 1720), ii., bk. 5, 327.

[3] *LBA*, 4; Alan Godard's will, enrolled February 1275, mentioned a wife Johanna and three children, William, Mathilda. and Mary to whom he bequeathed rents: *HW*, i. 22.

[4] In 1300, John Potrel complained to the mayor and aldermen that the guardianship of Robert de Garthorp had been granted to Joce and Joanna de Spaldyngge although Joanna stood to inherit Robert's property. In answer to this challenge Joce produced a letter under the king's seal appointing him guardian. The mayor and aldermen were 'unadvised' about the matter and decided to leave Robert with Joce for the time being. It is not clear whether Robert's father, Hugh de Garthorp, had specified a guardian for his son in his will or not: *LBE*, 121.

specifically designated a guardian.[5] On the other hand, the guardianship of children whose parents were not citizens of London was not the responsibility or concern of the mayor and aldermen even if the parent had possessed land in the city.[6] The efficiency and, one may presume, popularity and success of the overall guardianship exercised by the court of aldermen may be judged, perhaps, from the number of orphanage cases which appear in city records from 1300 onwards. In the fourteenth century there were about seventy-eight cases a decade, or eight a year; in the fifteenth century, eighty-eight cases a decade or nine a year, although the population was certainly smaller in the fifteenth century than it had been a century earlier.[7] In 1420 when the guardianship of the son of the ex-sheriff John Bryan was disputed, the alderman William Sevenoke declared that, by the immemorial custom of the city, when a freeman or woman of London died leaving an heir under age, then the guardianship of the heir belonged to the mayor, aldermen, chamberlain, and citizens of London: to them belonged the task of finding a suitable guardian.[8]

Orphanage matters were usually dealt with by the court of aldermen who would sometimes summon the chamberlain to assist them, since he acted as the official guardian of the property of city orphans.[9] It was, however, the common serjeant-at-law who acted as the spokesman of behalf of orphans and, when necessary, prosecuted cases on their behalf.[10] It was not until 1492 that a separate court of orphans emerged, presided over by the common serjeant (or, sometimes, the chamberlain).[11] At first this court was little more than an annual roll-call, held on the fourth Sunday after Shrove Tuesday, when all those who had stood surety for orphans' goods appeared in court to prove that they were still alive and living in the city, and so still able to answer to their obligations. But as the sixteenth century

[5] *The Maire of Bristol is Kalender by Robert Ricart*, ed. L. Toulmin Smith (Camden Society, 1872) pp. xx–xxi, 92–113, esp. pp. 99–100. Ricart, who was town clerk of Bristol in 1479, copied some London material into his calendar from a book that had belonged to Henry Darci, mayor of London 1337–9. Darci's custumal is now lost, see *ECMR 1298–1307*, pp. xxv–xxvii; W. Kellaway, 'John Carpenter's Liber Albus', *Guildhall Studies in London History*, 3 (1978), 67–84, esp. 72–3. The mayor and aldermen also claimed that if lands and goods in the city were bequeathed to a child of a London citizen, even if the father were alive, the lands and goods should be committed to the mayor and aldermen exactly as if the child were an orphan. The father could act as guardian of the lands etc. if he provided sufficient security: *Maire of Bristol*, 100. In 1379 a case of this kind occurred when the bequest of a maternal grandfather to two little girls was entrusted to their father as guardian, their mother being dead: *LBH*, 119. For a study of the operation of the custody of orphans in London and Bristol, see E. Clark, 'City Orphans and Custody Laws in Medieval England', *American Journal of Legal History*, 34 (1990), 168–87.

[6] See the case of Stephen, son of Richard at Hulle, whose guardianship in 1369–73 was disputed between Andrew d'Oo, Sir Robert Geddynge, and the mayor and aldermen: *LBG*, 239; *CPMR 1364 –81*, 171.

[7] C. Carlton, *The Court of Orphans* (Leicester, 1974), figures derived from table 1, p. 20.

[8] *LBI*, 220–2. A more detailed study of the orphan children of citizens in the years 1375 and 1399 found that the court of aldermen dealt with 301 children, 159 boys and 142 girls, i.e. about thirteen children a year, see B. Megson, 'Life Expectations of the Widows and Orphans of Freemen in London 1375–1399', *Local Population Studies*, 57 (1996), 18–29, esp. 25.

[9] *CPMR 1323–64*, 123 and n.: 138; see Ch. 8.

[10] C. Barron, 'The Government of London and its Relations with the Crown, 1400–1450' (University of London, Ph.D. thesis, 1970), 213; see chapter 8.

[11] *LBL*, 286; Barron, 'Government of London', 214 and n.

progressed, and the population of London grew, so the business of the court of orphans (first so called in 1529) expanded and the procedures became more regulated.[12]

In the medieval period, when a freeman died leaving heirs under age, those lands and goods destined for the heirs passed to the city chamberlain. The chamberlain, together with the aldermen, had a threefold task: to commit the care of the child to a suitable guardian (usually in accord with the wishes of the testator), to entrust the child's inheritance to a suitable warden (usually, but not always the same person as the guardian of the child), and to keep a supervisory eye on the activities of the guardian to ensure that the orphan was appropriately educated or apprenticed or married. This oversight came to an end when the orphan was 21 or, in the case of a girl, when she married someone who was at least 21. No apprenticeship bonds or marriage contracts might be entered into without the permission of the court of aldermen.[13]

It was customary to entrust orphaned children to the custody of their mother, or to the man who married the widowed mother. In this way families were kept together and continuity not only of family life, but also of the family business, was secured. Sometimes testators selected their parents to act as guardians: in 1320 Stephen de Coventry specified that his mother was to have charge of his children and their legacies, and only after her death was his widow Isabella to take over the responsibility.[14] Joanna, the widow of John of Oxford, wanted the guardianship of her two sons to go to her father.[15] The new guardian was usually entrusted with the orphan's patrimony, together with any lands, rents, or goods bequeathed to the child. He was expected to put the money to work to earn interest and, from the profits, to be reimbursed for the costs of the child's upkeep. Robert de Brynkeleye, a mercer, in 1374 received £300 when he took on the guardianship of Thomas atte Boure. In the thirteen years of his guardianship he put the money to work so that it increased to £1,080 i.e. he made a profit of £780. He was allowed to keep half this profit (i.e. £390) 'for his trouble' and was also allowed just under £120 for the costs of maintaining and educating Thomas for thirteen years. So at the end of his guardianship Brynkeleye handed over to the young man about £570.[16] All guardians were required to provide sureties for the due administration of the goods of orphans and, at the end of their term, the accounts would be audited and the orphan would acknowledge receipt of his patrimony in court and declare that he was satisfied.

It was the duty of the guardian to see to the education or training of the orphan in his charge. In 1306 William de Caustone, a mercer, agreed to act as guardian to

[12] Carlton, *Court of Orphans*, esp. ch. 2.

[13] Ibid. 21; Barron, 'Government of London', 215.

[14] *LBE*, 78.

[15] Year 1357, *LBG*, 95. In 1368 Alice Pecham was committed to her uncle as guardian; seven years later she was dead: *LBG*, 229–30.

[16] *Memorials*, 378–9; see also the case of Alice Reyner: her guardian received £66 13*s.* 4*d.* and looked after her for five years. He made a profit of £66 13*s.* 4*d.* of which he was entitled to half. Her education, keep, clothes and marriage contract cost £20 and so, out of a total of £133 6*s.* 8*d.* (capital plus growth), Alice received £80: ibid. 446–7.

Nicholas de Paumer who was 12 years old and to teach him for eight years.[17] In 1354 William and Alice Horwode asked to be relieved of the guardianship of John Fabe because they had no trade or craft that they could teach him; so he was transferred to a pewterer.[18] The supervision exercised by the court of aldermen in these matters was not remote. For example in 1420 the court was consulted before 17-year old John Stapleford was apprenticed to a grocer for ten years (a long apprenticeship since Stapleford would be 28 before he was free), and Richard Arghton was apprenticed to a fishmonger on the same occasion.[19]

The consent of the court had also to be obtained before orphans might be married. Sometimes events moved too quickly for the court to control them. Henry Sutton carried off Alice, the orphan daughter of John atte Marsh, and took control of her property. The little girl, who was only 7, had been quickly married off (doubtless at a price) to Thomas de Staunesby, a tailor, while the action was pending.[20] Nicholas Mokking came to court in 1354 and complained that his guardian had appropriated his property and taken money to marry him off to Margery Malewayn. The guardian counterclaimed that the marriage was not a disparaging one and that he was ready to render account. When the auditors found that he was £100 in debt to the orphan, the guardian paid the money on the spot in silver and gold. The court then decided that since young Nicholas 'did not appear to be of full age nor able to take care of himself' he should be committed to the care of his father-in-law as his guardian. This may not have been the happy outcome for which Nicholas was hoping.[21] Sometimes guardians married the girl orphans in their charge. When she was 7 years old, Agnes atte Holt, the daughter of a timbermonger who died in the plague, was committed to the care of John de Berholte, a carpenter. Six years later, when she was 13, John came to court and asked to be discharged since he had married Agnes.[22] In the fifteenth century the court of aldermen was frequently consulted about projected marriages for orphan girls. Margaret Beaumond who married the mercer John Everard without first seeking the court's permission was fined, and her sister Dionysia was refused permission to marry the mercer (later mayor) Hugh Wiche.[23] Sometimes orphans were married to the children of their guardians. Henry, the orphan son of the alderman John Perneys, was asked by the court whether his master, John Selby, had arranged a marriage for him. He told the court that, although his master had done nothing in the matter, his master's wife had arranged for him to marry their daughter,

[17] *LBC*, 200–1. Caustone took the boy's £50 cash patrimony and agreed to hand over £60 at the end of the eight years.

[18] *LBG*, 32.

[19] CLRO, Journal 1 fo. 77v.

[20] Year 1342, *CPMR 1323–64*, 205–6; Sutton was sent to prison, but he managed to avoid producing Alice in court.

[21] *LBG*, 38–9.

[22] Ibid. 243–4.

[23] Barron, 'Government of London', 216: similarly in 1393 Idonea Camber was fined £4 for marrying John Hake, mercer, without permission: *LBH*, 211. Sometimes the man paid the fine: William Cotgrave in 1373 was fined £21 17*s*. for marrying the orphan Isabella de Poulesholt without permission, a fine that amounted to a third of Isabella's inheritance: *LBG*, 321–2.

although he had not yet done so.[24] There is a ring of truth about this candid response. Some city orphans chose the religious life in preference to marriage: Mathilda Toky became a nun at the priory of Kilburn and her inheritance of nearly £90 was handed over to Lady Emma de Saint Omer, the prioress, who came in person to the court to collect it.[25] Similarly John, the orphan son of Thomas Frenshe, decided to become a monk in the house of the Austin Canons at Merton in Surrey.[26]

Obviously, the supervision of the court of aldermen was not perfect: on occasion orphans were abducted or, perhaps, apprenticed or married, against their inclinations or interests. In 1315 the court managed to prevent 8-year-old Agnes from being married off to the 11-year-old son of her mother's new husband; she was taken out of her mother's care and placed in the charge of the city chamberlain.[27] In another case an orphan, Ralph Hubbard, was abducted from his guardian and married off to Agnes, the daughter of the famous master mason, William Ramsey. The court pointed out to the boy that the marriage could not be annulled, but he was asked whether he would prefer to remain with his new wife and father-in-law, or return to his guardian. He chose to live with his new family, which may suggest that he was not abducted against his will.[28] There is no doubt that the court of aldermen spent considerable time and trouble over orphanage matters, as the Letter Books and Journals indicate, and their concern was not solely with questions of property but extended to the well-being of the child. Wealthy orphans were desirable because the guardian, in taking charge of the child, also took possession of what could be quite a sizeable capital sum, which he was free to employ in his own concerns for a period of years, and from which he might legitimately derive profit, provided that the orphan also ultimately profited. Goods and tenements which were not handed over to guardians were administered by the chamberlain who might in this way accumulate a considerable orphans' fund. In February 1391 the mayor and aldermen borrowed £400 from the orphans' fund to buy imported grain to be stored against the possibility of dearth in the city the following summer.[29]

Although the civic responsibility for orphans devolved upon the court of aldermen, the chamberlain, and the common serjeant, yet there was an underlying assumption that all citizens had a responsibility to protect those too young to look after themselves. This communal responsibility is apparent in the wardmote

[24] 14 June 1437, CLRO, Journal 3 fo. 201ᵛ. Henry did in fact marry and have a family: S. Thrupp, *The Merchant Class of Medieval London* (Michigan, 1948), 360.

[25] Year 1393, *Memorials*, 535.

[26] Year 1393–1406, *LBH*, 441.

[27] The city had to defend this action in the face of a royal writ to restore Agnes to her mother: *LBE*, 47.

[28] Year 1331, *LBE*, 266–7; see J. Harvey, *English Medieval Architects: A Biographical Dictionary to 1550* (rev. edn, 1984), 242.

[29] *CPMR 1381–1412*, 174–5; cf. *LBH*, 361–2. This occurrence was sufficiently unusual for it to be noted by the chronicler, Henry Knighton, who recorded that 2000 marks (or £1333 13*s.* 4*d.*) had been borrowed 'de communi sista orphanorum' and that the aldermen had each contributed a further £20, *Knighton's Chronicle 1337–1396*, ed. G. Martin (Oxford, 1995), 538.

inquests in 1421 where men of the ward provided information about the property of orphans that was being concealed, and also brought to the attention of the court of aldermen orphan children who were in need of proper guardianship.[30]

In the comparatively small community of late-medieval London—and the freemen whose children alone were subject to these procedures comprised only about a third of the adult male population of the city—the system appears to have worked reasonably well and there were few complaints. But, of course, many children, indeed the majority, lay outside this pool of official communal concern, and when they were orphaned their fate is largely unrecorded: since they had few goods, they were not very important. Their fate would depend upon neighbourly or religious charity.[31] But, unlike in many Continental cities (such as Florence where the *Ospedali degli Innocenti* had been founded in 1410), there appears to have been no need for an orphanage in London until the 1550s.[32] Until then, communal charity and the population dearth ensured that orphaned children in London found homes. It was in the sixteenth century, with expansion of the population of London as a whole, and with the rising proportion of citizens within that population, that the administration of the court of orphans collapsed under the pressure of work and over-extended credit.[33] In the reign of Edward VI Christ's Hospital was founded where 'the innocent and fatherless' might be 'trained up in the knowledge of God and some virtuous exercises, to the overthrow of beggary'.[34]

THE POOR

In the case of orphans the citizens accepted a measure of communal responsibility: a responsibility which cost them time but not money, for the children of citizens were unlikely to have been left penniless. But in the case of the poor, the city accepted no communal responsibility and no municipal care was provided. In so far as the poor were relieved in medieval London, that relief was provided by the church in its broadest sense, and by private charity, responding in part to ecclesiastical injunctions.

The existence of the poor was officially recognized by exemption from taxation on their personal property: no one was to pay taxes unless the value of their goods reached a certain sum. There was a differential between rural and urban taxation; the cut-off rate was almost always lower in boroughs than in the countryside, thereby recognizing, perhaps, the greater poverty of those who lived in towns. In

[30] *CPMR 1413–37*, 132, 140, 158. The court did, later, concern itself with the fate of the children of William Flete and one of them, Joanna, was committed to the charge of her new stepfather in 1428: *LBK*, 85.

[31] On the effectiveness of households, kin, and neighbours as providers of care see, P. Horden and R. Smith (eds.), *The Locus of Care: Families, Communities, Institutions and the Provision of Welfare Since Antiquity* (London, 1998), esp. chs. 1 and 2.

[32] P. Gavitt, *Charity and Children in Renaissance Florence: The Ospedale degli Innocenti 1410–1535* (Michigan, 1990). In Florence many children were not officially orphaned, but abandoned.

[33] Carlton, *Court of Orphans*, esp. ch. 2.

[34] Strype, *Survey of London*, i. bk. 3, 131.

the years 1322 and 1332, in the countryside tax was to be paid only by those whose goods were worth a minimum of ten shillings, and in the towns the limit was six shillings.[35] In 1334 the basic method of assessing royal taxes was changed and block sums were paid by counties and boroughs. It was left to the local assessors to decide who should contribute and who might legitimately be excused taxation. When the novel poll taxes were introduced in 1377, 1379, and 1381, which levied per capita sums from all lay adults, 'genuine paupers' were again exempted, and in 1381 the rich were enjoined to help the poor to pay their contributions of one shilling a head.[36] In the same way a century later the poor in London were exempted from paying the benevolence demanded by Edward IV.[37]

But there were obviously problems in defining 'the poor'. Not all those who escaped taxation in the subsidies of the early fourteenth century were truly destitute. As has been pointed out, 'there must have been in London a considerable number of people who economically held a position just on the line of the taxable minimum and who in one year may have had sufficient property to be taxed, in another year had sunk below the minimum and had been exempted'.[38] In the 1319 subsidy rolls for London several names have been crossed out and the word *pauper* or *nihil* written against them; at first presumably the assessors believed they should contribute and then reconsidered their earlier assessment.[39] It was generally accepted that widows were poor and should be exempt, and yet many London widows were quite prosperous and did, in fact, contribute to taxation.[40]

It is impossible to establish how many poor there were in London: it is not known how many people did not contribute to the taxes of the early fourteenth century, let alone how many of those were truly destitute and dependent upon the charity of others. The royal household was, particularly in the thirteenth century, a very important source of such charity. Henry III provided for meals for 3,500 poor people every week and in 1244, 6,000 paupers came to Westminster to receive dole: the children were put in the Queen's chamber, the aged and infirm in the greater and lesser halls, and the rest in the King's chamber.[41] Whether so many

[35] See J. F. Willard, *Parliamentary Taxes on Personal Property 1290–1334* (Medieval Academy of America, 1934), esp. 87–92.

[36] *The Poll Taxes of 1377, 1379 and 1381*, ed. C. Fenwick, 2 vols. (British Academy, 1998), i. pp. xvi, xxiii–xxv.

[37] Year 1481, *LBL*, 176.

[38] *Two Early London Subsidy Rolls*, ed. E. Ekwall (Lund, 1951), 78–9; cf. Willard, *Parliamentary Taxes*, 174–8.

[39] *Early London Subsidy Rolls*, ed., Ekwall, 79.

[40] Eighteen London widows contributed to the 1436 tax on lands and rents: Thrupp, *Merchant Class*, 378–385. In 1268 Henry III had exempted widows from taxation and in 1392 the widows of London complained at having to contribute to the sum granted by the city to Richard II: *LBC*, 36–7; C. M. Barron, 'The Quarrel of Richard II with London' in F. R. H. Du Boulay and C. Barron (eds.), *The Reign of Richard II: Essays in Honour of May McKisack* (London, 1970), 173–201, 195 and n. 89; Willard, *Parliamentary Taxes*, 88; see C. Barron, 'Introduction' in C. Barron and A. Sutton (eds.), *Medieval London Widows, 1300–1500* (London, 1994), pp. xiii–xxxiv, esp. xxiii.

[41] H. Johnstone, 'Poor Relief in the Royal Households of Thirteenth Century England', *Speculum*, 4 (1929), 149–67. When Queen Eleanor refounded the Hospital of St Katherine by the Tower in 1273 she provided that 1,000 poor men should each receive ½*d.* on the anniversary of the death of Henry III:, *VCH, London*, 526.

poor people really crowded into Westminster Palace on one occasion may be doubted, but the almoner paid out a penny a meal, as if they had. Not all the poor who thronged to Westminster for royal alms would have been Londoners, but that there were indeed a great many poor in London is suggested by the will of Robert de Lincoln enrolled in 1318; he left £10 to be distributed among 2,000 poor persons so that each might receive a penny (the customary cost of a meal for a poor person).[42] It seems clear that in the early fourteenth century there were at least hundreds (if not thousands) of paupers seeking alms in the city. A monastic chronicler recorded that in a heatwave in London in 1258, 20,000 people died.[43] In 1322 about fifty people were crushed to death in the throng at the gateway to the Blackfriars house at Ludgate, when the door was opened in the morning for the distribution of alms.[44] Whether other religious houses in London distributed alms generously to the poor of the city is hard to know; it would appear that the monks of Westminster spent only very modest amounts on the relief of poverty and even those sums diminished in the fifteenth century.[45]

We can catch only glimpses of the poor of medieval London, for they had no goods to bequeath and no lands to record, and were not relieved by the city in its corporate capacity. Their sad and hopeless deaths on occasion fleetingly caught the attention of the coroners or justices: in the 1260s two men died from hunger in the London streets; in 1336 Emma, who suffered from epilepsy and was described as a 'pauper and mendicant' fell into the Tower ditch while collecting water and drowned.[46] On occasion people were sufficiently desperate to murder a woman simply to get hold of her clothes.[47] Many of the poor population of London would have been vagrants, pilgrims, or poor travellers: men perhaps in search of work or, sometimes, escaping from villeinage or a criminal record elsewhere. In 1276 William from Lindsey killed a man in a brawl and fled leaving behind his goods, a tabard worth tenpence, a hatchet and bow with three arrows worth twopence, and a sheet valued at fourpence; in all, his worldly goods were worth sixteen pence 'beyond which he had no goods or chattels'.[48] The most compelling description of the inwardness of poverty comes from the pen of William Langland, the presumed author of *Piers Plowman*, who lived in the later fourteenth century in a 'cote' on Cornhill with his wife and daughter, among the second-hand clothes markets that took place there every evening.[49]

[42] *HW*, and i. 277. In fact £10 would have provided meals for 2,400 people.

[43] *Annales Monastici*, ed. H. R. Luard, 5 vols. (Rolls Series, 1864–9), i. 166.

[44] *Calendar of Coroners' Rolls of the City of London 1300–1378*, ed., R. R. Sharpe (London, 1913), 61.

[45] B. F. Harvey, *Living and Dying in England 1100–1540: The Monastic Experience* (Oxford, 1993), ch. 1.

[46] *The London Eyre of 1276*, ed. M. Weinbaum (London Record Society, 1976), 136, 165: *Coroners' Rolls*, 178, and cf. similar cases, 194, 220.

[47] Year 1322, *Coroners' Rolls*, 68–9. In 1373 Alice de Sainsbury, a beggar, kidnapped Margaret, daughter of John Oxwyk, grocer, both for her clothes and to use her as a begging tool: *Memorials*, 368.

[48] *Memorials*, 5.

[49] These were known as 'evechepynges', 1369: *LBG*, 248; 1393, *Memorials*, 532–3. Langland's most vivid account of poverty is to be found in the C-text, Passus IX, lines 70–87: see B. White, 'Poet and Peasant' in du Boulay and Barron (eds.), *The Reign of Richard II*, 58–74.

The Black Death of 1348–9 seems to have thrown the poor into greater prominence. This may seem paradoxical for the plague, as is well known, by killing about a third of the population, created a shortage of labour and led therefore, indirectly, to an improvement in the wages and conditions of labourers, both in the countryside and in the towns. But these improvements were neither uniform nor universally welcomed. The shortage of labour and rising prices provoked a series of restrictive measures, the ordinance of labourers of 1349, followed by the statutes of 1351 and 1388. It became necessary to draw a distinction between the worthy poor, namely widows and children, the sick and maimed and old, those who through no fault of their own could not work, and the unworthy poor, the 'sturdy beggars' who should be compelled to work and not take up the alms that ought to go to those who were really in need.[50] The Commons in Parliament also become increasingly concerned to stabilize the labourforce and ensure that municipal authorities arrested and repatriated vagrant labourers.[51] The city of London had already by this date devised a system of local peacekeeping and vagrant control.[52]

Although the 1349 ordinance of labourers had recognized, by implication, that there were two classes of poor people, the worthy who were impotent and the unworthy who were sturdy, this distinction was explicitly recognized in the city's proclamation of 1359, ten years after the Black Death. Those beggars who were able to work were to leave the city under threat of being put in the stocks on Cornhill; on the other hand poor folks, lepers, the blind, the halt, and persons oppressed with old age and other maladies, were alone to enjoy the alms available in the city.[53] In 1366 the aldermen were instructed to set sturdy beggars to work, but in the following year it was decided that all vagrants, whether sturdy or impotent, were to leave the city.[54]

The court of aldermen appears to have pursued a double policy: either sturdy beggars should be made to work or they would be driven from the city so that those who were genuinely helpless should not be deprived of alms. This policy continued to be pursued in the fifteenth century but with less intensity. In August 1418 beggars were enjoined to leave London under pain of arrest and to go 'uplande' (i.e. into the countryside) where labour was needed to bring in the harvest.[55] Although the fifteenth-century proclamations lack the vehemence of those

[50] In 1349 the ordinance of labourers makes this distinction by implication: *The Statutes of the Realm*, 10 vols. (London, 1810–28), i. 307–8. There is no attempt to define different classes of poor in the Statute of 1351: ibid. 311–13. The statute of 1388 follows the 1349 distinction but further requires genuine beggars, scholars, pilgrims and travelling beggars (e.g. discharged soldiers) to have testimonial letters: ibid. ii. 56.

[51] See K. Anderson, 'The Treatment of Vagrancy and the Relief of the Poor and Destitute in the Tudor Period, Based upon the Local Records of London to 1552 and Hull to 1576' (University of London, Ph.D. thesis, 1933), esp. 93–101.

[52] Ibid. 102.

[53] *Memorials*, 304–5.

[54] *LBG*, 208, 217. In 1372 it was proclaimed in the city that no one who was capable of maintaining himself by his art or his labour should pretend to be poor and beg: ibid, 301. This proclamation was repeated in 1375 and 1378: *Memorials*, 389–90; *LBH*, 110.

[55] This proclamation was repeated in 1440, and in 1475, vagabonds and 'masterless people' were once more banished from the city: *LBK*, 240; *LBL*, 136.

of the previous century, yet a consciousness of the distinction between the worthy poor and those who were poor through *malam gubernationem* (bad management) continued to be apparent in the wills of fifteenth-century London testators.[56] Almsgiving is much more carefully directed than in the days when Robert of Lincoln indiscriminately distributed £10 among 2,000 poor people.

It would seem that the social and economic dislocations caused by the plague were particularly acute in the second half of the fourteenth century. Certainly it is the case that in this period there are recorded a number of convictions for counterfeiting property; men posed as invalids, war veterans, and returning pilgrims.[57] Two imposters, one from York and the other from Somerset, managed to persuade the Londoners that they had been robbed and their tongues torn out so that they were now mutes. To prove the point they roared horribly and even demonstrated where their tongues had been cut out.[58] Another enterprising labourer had pretended to be an official alms collector for Bethlehem Hospital outside Bishopsgate and managed to secure quite a tidy sum with his iron-bound collecting box.[59] But why did men pretend to poverty if there was work available for them to do in London? Perhaps the work-shy, like the poor, are always with us, but the general shortage of labour certainly rendered their activities particularly obnoxious to the authorities. It may also be the case that there was a disproportionately large number of genuinely poor people in London in the second half of the fourteenth century, attracted from the countryside by the prospect of greater freedom and opportunity than was offered on most manorial estates. Some, like Richard Lyons, were successful and rose from nothing to great wealth, but many must have sunk to the bottom of the heap, unable to find reasonably paid work, with no money to purchase an apprenticeship and no resources to weather the fluctuations in prices and wages.[60] Such men, and women, must have lived on intermittent daily wages, some buying and selling of cheap goods and produce, their wits, and the hope of alms from the rich or the religious. During the mayoralty of John de Northampton (1381–3) the court of aldermen took measures to ensure cheaper food in the city. Bakers and brewers were ordered to sell their goods by farthing measures, and to ensure that this was possible the mayor had £80 worth of farthings (i.e. nearly 77,000 farthings) specially minted at the Tower so that there could be no excuses about not having the right change.[61] There was also an attempt to break down monopolies in the food trades (especially that of the fishmongers) and to crack down on those who bought up food supplies before they reached the open market and then raised the price.[62] Perhaps these measures were to some degree successful; perhaps the economy settled down after

[56] See cases cited in J. A. F. Thomson, 'Piety and Charity in Later Medieval London', *Journal of Ecclesiastical History*, 16 (1965), 178–95, esp. 182–3.

[57] *CPMR 1323–64*, 256; *CPMR 1364–81*, 5; *Memorials*, 479, 584.

[58] Year 1380, ibid. 445–6.

[59] Year 1412, ibid. 586–7.

[60] A. R. Myers, 'The Wealth of Richard Lyons', in T. A. Sandquist and M. R. Powicke (eds.), *Essays in Medieval History presented to Bertie Wilkinson* (Toronto, 1969), 301–29.

[61] Year 1382, *LBH*, 183. The clergy were also enjoined to accept farthings as offerings at mass.

[62] Year 1383, ibid. 209–10.

the disasters of 1348–9 and 1361; perhaps the average labourer began to be able to profit by his scarcity.

Londoners began to seek for solutions to poverty together in fraternities or brotherhoods. Sometimes the purpose of these fraternities, as in the case of the journeymen (or day labourers) who worked for shearmen, was to push up wages by withdrawing labour;[63] sometimes the purpose was to honour a saint and provide mutual support and charity in times of trouble.[64] Charitable Londoners in their wills established loan funds, which might be used to tide people over difficult periods.[65] In the relief of poverty, however, the role of mayor and aldermen was not conspicuous. Apart from the measures implemented by the mayor, John de Northampton, in the 1380s the court of aldermen did little beyond controlling the price of essential foods and punishing or expelling sturdy paupers and beggars. For the rest it was left to the religious houses and to the charity of the wealthy—and not so wealthy—individuals to implement the seven Christian acts of mercy and to relieve, in ways that were often imaginative as well as humanitarian, the 'poor folk who are our neighbours'.[66]

MEDICAL CARE

The same somewhat laissez-faire policy was apparent in the attitude of the mayor and aldermen towards medical care in the city. They could attempt to prevent fraudulent medical practice and to ensure some reasonable standards of competence (as in any other city craft) amongst the various 'healers' at work in the city;[67] they also tried to ensure a decent water supply and a measure of cleanliness in the streets and other public places.[68] But, unlike many Italian towns, the mayor and aldermen did not expect to provide medical personnel or hospitals for the comfort of sick Londoners, although in the case of certain hospitals the city came to displace the religious orders as hospital managers, and so inaugurated a policy that was to be greatly expanded in the sixteenth century.[69]

[63] Year 1350, *Memorials*, 250–1. Cf the journeymen fraternity of the saddlers in 1396: ibid. 542–4; see Ch. 9.

[64] See C. Barron, 'The Parish Fraternities of Medieval London', in C. Barron and C. Harper-Bill (eds.), *The Church in Pre-Reformation Society: Essays in Honour of F. R. H. Du Boulay* (Woodbridge, 1985), 13–37, esp. 26–7.

[65] Michael Northburgh, bishop of London 1354–61, in his will left 1,000 marks to establish a loan chest at St Paul's Cathedral which was accessible to Londoners as well as the clergy of the cathedral: *HW*, ii. 62; loan chests had been established at Cambridge University since the end of the thirteenth century, see G. Pollard, 'Medieval Loan Chests at Cambridge' *BIHR* 17 (1939–40), 113–29. Henry Crosse, rector of St John Walbrook (d.1469), bequeathed £40 as a loan fund for his parishioners: BL, Add. MS 73945; and Robert Parys, an ironmonger, in 1469 left £40 to be kept in an iron-bound chest in the parish of St Michael Queenhithe to provide loans for poor parishioners and others: *HW*, ii. 561–2; see J. A. F. Thompson, 'Piety and Charity', 185–6.

[66] See the case of Nicholas Alwyn who left £10 to buy 200 quart-sized pewter pots, two each to be given to 100 poor girls at their marriages: ibid. 186.

[67] See F. Getz, *Medicine in the English Middle Ages* (Princeton, 1998), 83–4.

[68] See Ch. 10.

[69] See K. Park, *Doctors and Medicine in Early Renaissance Florence* (Princeton, 1985), 87–99.

There is no lack of evidence for the existence of illness and pain in medieval London. Accidents damaged limbs and set up infection; there were pulmonary disorders and dysentry, contagious diseases such as fevers and plague, and there were illnesses whose causes, even today, are uncertain, such as epilepsy, paralysis, and gout. Recent analysis of medieval skeletons excavated in London cemeteries has, so far, revealed little about diseases, not because 'the population as a whole was particularly healthy, but merely that the ailments suffered were generally such as did not leave obvious traces upon the bones'.[70] The skeletons show signs of nutritional deficiencies, chronic anaemia, osteoporosis and osteoarthritis caused by hard physical labour, and several bone tumours, all benign. Several of the bones had fractures, but had healed well. The ever-present hazards of childbirth were also evident in some of the skeletons where unborn babies were found lodged in the pelvis.[71] On the other hand medieval men and women were comparatively free from the great scourges of modern society, cancer in all its forms, venereal disease, and AIDS.[72]

Most sick people must have been treated at home. The wealthy might turn for assistance to the healing professions and it is certainly true that there were more 'doctors' in London than anywhere else in England.[73] The modern word 'doctor' covers a wide range of medical practitioners in medieval London: physicians, surgeons, barber-surgeons, apothecaries, and leeches. Their areas of competence were not clearly defined, and they had frequently to fight each other as well as to ward off the complaints of dissatisfied customers.

At the top of the social scale were the physicians, men with university degrees, usually clerks, who were barred by their cloth from practising surgery.[74] They were never numerous either in London or elsewhere, and their learning was intensely academic as can be seen in the case of Chaucer's physician who knew all the works of Aesculapius, Hippocrates, Galen, Avicenna, and Averroes, and

> he knew the cause of everich maladye
> were it of hoot or cold, or moiste, or drye
> and where engendred, and of what humour.
> He was a verrey parfit practisour.[75]

[70] W. White, *Skeletal Remains from the Cemetery of St Nicholas Shambles, City of London* (LMAS, 1988), 48.

[71] Ibid. 37–51; C. Thomas, B. Sloane, and C. Philpotts, *Excavations at the Priory and Hospital of St Mary Spital, London* (Museum of London, 1997), 39–40, 230–1.

[72] On venereal disease see M. Pelling, 'Appearance and Reality: Barber Surgeons, the Body and Disease', in A. L. Beier and R. Finlay (eds.), *London 1500–1700: The Making of the Metropolis* (London, 1986), 82–112, esp. 97–103. In 1547–8 a quarter of the patients admitted to St Bartholomews hospital suffered from the French pox or syphilis.

[73] See C. Rawcliffe, 'Medicine and Medical Practice in Late Medieval London', *Guildhall Studies in London History*, 5 (1981), 13–23. For the numbers of those practising healing in England, see C. H. Talbot and E. A. Hammond, *The Medical Practitioners of Medieval England* (London, 1965). For additions to this listing, see F. Getz., 'Medical Practitioners in Medieval England', *Social History of Medicine*, 3 (1990), 245–83.

[74] G. N. Clark, *A History of the Royal College of Physicians of London*, 2 vols. (London, 1964), i. 17.

[75] Geoffrey Chaucer, prologue to *The Canterbury Tales*, lines 419–22.

Master Gregory 'physicus' appears in London as early as 1226 and in 1276 two 'medics', Master John de Hexham and his brother Master Semman prescribed pills for a man suffering from fever: they were probably physicians.[76] Although more physicians appear in the London records in the fourteenth and fifteenth centuries, the numbers were always very small. There is evidence, in the fifteenth century, of laymen becoming physicians but since the majority were clerks they perhaps did not feel the need for the protection of a craft or guild association.[77] The physicians comprised a very small, select, and learned group who ministered particularly to the court and to the wealthy. Most Londoners would have had little experience of their skills and not all those who did thought highly of their services. Margaret Paston wrote to her son, 'Also, fore Goddys sake be ware what medesynys ye take of any fysissyanys of London. I schal never trust to hem because of yowre fadre and myn onkle, whous soulys God assoyle.'[78]

Although the number of physicians practising at any one time in the city was small, yet in the fifteenth century some attempt was made at corporate organization. In 1423 Master Gilbert Kymer, described as rector of the 'medicyne' in the city of London, and Master John Somerset and Master Thomas Southwell, described as 'surveyors of the faculty of physic in the city', joined with the two masters of the craft of surgery in London to petition the mayor and aldermen to establish a community (which we would now call college), in order to ensure higher standards among physicians and surgeons practising in the city.[79] In seeking to control the personnel and practice of sophisticated medicine, Kymer and his colleagues were acting in the same spirit as any other civic craft which sought incorporation.[80] But there was

[76] *Eyre, 1244*, 14; Talbot and Hammond, *Medical Practitioners*, 67; *Eyre, 1276* no. 257; the man who was suffering from fever and his valet who had charge of the pills both ate so many of them that they died.

[77] Thomas Franke 'doctor in medicine' claimed to be a clerk so that he could hold the rectory of Brightwell in Suffolk. His claim was contested on the grounds that he was a physician, a Greek, and not ordained, and he ultimately gave up the living to pursue his medical career at the French court, J. Harris, *Greek Emigrés in the West 1400–1520* (Camberley, 1995), 90–3. There are references also to Thomas Creke, physician, *c.*1416, who was paid £13 4*d.* for attending John, son of Robert Tatersale draper (d.1429), and to William Hurtebyse, physician, in 1448; PRO, Eton College Unpublished Records Calendar, vol. 47 no. 130, *CPMR 1437–57*, 14. Neither of these is noted by Talbot and Hammond.

[78] 8 June 1464, *Paston Letters and Papers of the Fifteenth Century*, ed. N. Davis, 2 vols. (Oxford, 1971–6), i. 291.

[79] *LBK*, 11; Clark, *College of Physicians*, 26–7. For the text of the petition see J. F. Smith, *Memorials of the Craft of Surgery in England*, ed. D'Arcy Power (London, 1886), app. B, 299–303. Kymer was sworn as rector of the faculty of physicians in London in 1423 and 1424, but seems then to have left his London practice, perhaps to join the household of Humphrey, duke of Gloucester, and, later, to become dean of Salisbury: *LBK*, 14, 41; Talbot and Hammond, *Medical Practitioners*, 60–3; John Somerset was physician to Henry VI, and a layman who held offices that ranged from warden of the royal mint to surveyor of the King's Works: ibid. 184–5, but see H. Colvin (ed.), *The History of the King's Works*, 6 vols. (London, 1963), i. 191 n. 8; Thomas Southwell was an Oxford graduate who became rector of St Stephen's Walbrook, but was convicted of practising witchcraft and died the night before his execution: Talbot and Hammond, *Medical Practitioners*, 356; A. B. Emden, *A Biographical Register of the University of Oxford to AD 1500*, 3 vols. (Oxford, 1957), 1734–5.

[80] On this point see C. Webster, 'Thomas Linacre and the Foundation of the College of Physicians', in F. Maddison, M. Pelling, and C. Webster (eds.), *Essays on the Life and Work of Thomas Linacre c. 1460–1524* (Oxford, 1977), 198–222.

more to their proposal than mere craft control: while it is true that they were to have the power to search apothecaries' shops and the rector (presumably Kymer) was to be consulted about particularly difficult medical cases, yet the members of the community were also to have a house where they could meet for readings and disputations 'in philosophy and medicine'. Rooms were to be set aside where the surgeons could practise and, most remarkably of all, the poor could come there for free advice either in physic or in surgery. This impressive attempt both to raise the standards in the profession and to diffuse medical help lower down the social scale may have owed its inception to the enthusiasm and skill of Gilbert Kymer. Not surprisingly, perhaps, the scheme had foundered within two years. It may be that Kymer left London to accompany the duke of Gloucester to Hainault in *c.*1424 and with his departure the driving spirit went out of the enterprise. Apart from Kymer, the other members of what can never have been a very large group may have been drained away to serve with the English armies in France. It is possible, also, that the exclusiveness of the group may have aroused the competitive hostility of the 'paramedics' in the city, for example the barbers and apothecaries. So it was not until 1518 that Thomas Linacre successfully founded the College of Physicians in London, modelling his new institution upon Italian prototypes. This new college 'was not able to bring about a substantial improvement in the health of the citizens of London, [but] it created an elite corps of physicians, pledged to support a rigorous code of medical ethics'.[81] Unlike the abortive institution of a hundred years earlier, provision of free medical advice for the poor does not feature in the statutes of Linacre's college.

The two surgeons who joined with the physicians to propose a 'community' in 1423 were 'masters of the craft of surgery' in the city. This craft seems to have begun to define itself in the middle years of the thirteenth century.[82] The skilled practice of surgery probably originated in the royal household from where it spread outwards to the wealthy. In 1300 the mayor and aldermen first recorded their competence to supervise the practice of surgery in London. Peter the Surgeon had undertaken to cure Ralph de Mortimer and all the surgeons in the city were to attend to assess Peter's competence. [83] This evidence for surgeons acting as a corporate group is matched by increasingly frequent references to them in the city's records.[84] In 1354 four surgeons, all described as 'master', were sworn before the mayor and aldermen to give evidence about a wounded jaw that had failed to heal

[81] Ibid 221. For Kymer as chancellor of Oxford University from 1431, see A. B. Emden, *A Biographical Register of the University of Oxford to A. D. 1500* (Oxford, 1957–9), ii, 1068–9.

[82] There are no surgeons recorded in the Eyre of 1244 and only two, Alfred le Surgien and Master Thomas le Surigien, appear in the records of the 1276 Eyre, *Eyre 1276*, nos. 16, 260, 573. For Master Thomas see Talbot and Hammond, *Medical Practitioners*, 331.

[83] *CEMCR 1298–1307*, 81; Talbot and Hammond, *Medical Practitioners*, 243–4.

[84] Year 1305 Godfrey the Surgeon: *Calendar of London Trailbaston Trials under Commission of 1305 and 1306*, ed. R. B. Pugh (London, 1975), no. 235; 1307, Master Gilbert the Surgeon: *London Assize of Nuisance 1301–1431*, ed. H. M. Chew and W. Kellaway (London Record Society, 1973), 26, presumably to be identified with the London surgeon who died in 1312: Talbot and Hammond, *Medical Practitioners*, 57; 1312, William Mabeley surgeon: *Assize of Nuisance*, 38–9, Talbot and Hammond, *Medical Practitioners*, 407; 1321, Master Ralph Surgeon: *The Eyre of London, 14 Edward II AD 1321*, ed. H. M. Cam, 2 vols. (Selden Society, 1968–9), 221.

under the care of John le Spicer (presumably an apothecary). Their considered opinion—not perhaps a totally disinterested one—was that if John had taken skilled advice the jaw would have healed, but it had now become incurable. [85] In the same way four master surgeons were summoned in 1365 to advise the mayor and aldermen whether a man was in danger of death or not.[86] Some of these London surgeons were extremely prosperous. Philip of Beauvais, who succeeded his father Simon as royal surgeon in about 1285, had a very large house in London at La Ryole;[87] and the wills of other surgeons suggest that surgery and poverty were not close companions.[88] John Nicole, a London surgeon, had three horses, thirty-six pieces of cloth, and seven stone of wool seized by a bailiff in 1366.[89]

In 1369 for the first time three London surgeons appeared before the mayor and aldermen and swore to act as master surgeons in the city, to serve the people faithfully, charge reasonable prices, inspect the work of those who undertook cures, be ready to attend the maimed and wounded, and give expert advice to the city officers.[90] Although such a formal appearance by the master surgeons is not again recorded until 1390 it is likely that the masters were sworn annually. The oath is the same in 1390 as on the earlier occasion except that their supervision is specifically stated now to include all those undertaking cures 'both men and women'.[91] One of the surgeons who took the oath as master on this occasion was John Bradmore who was to have a distinguished career not only in royal, but also in civic, service. In 1402 he was called in to treat the monks of Westminster Abbey, and at the battle of Shrewsbury in 1405 he successfully extracted an arrowhead from the nose of the future Henry V.[92] He and his wife, in 1377, were members of the Holy Trinity

[85] *Memorials*, 273–4. Two of the four surgeons consulted on this occasion were not Englishmen, the Prior of Hogges (possibly St Vaast la Hogue) and Master Pascal de Bologna; the other two were Adam de la Poletria (Poultry) and David of Westmoreland: Talbot and Hammond, *Medical Practitioners*, 6, 34, 238.

[86] *CPMR 1364–81*, 27–8; the four surgeons on this occasion were Master Adam Rous (the royal surgeon); Master David (possibly David of Westmoreland); Master Henry de Wotton, Master William Taunton: Talbot and Hammond, *Medical Practitioners*, 7, 32, 88, 417–18.

[87] Ibid. 254–6; Getz, *Medicine in the English Middle Ages*, 27. In 1321, Philip's son was not allowed to inherit La Ryole on the grounds that his father had come from France and was not a citizen and so could not claim the privilege of a Londoner: *Eyre 1321*, i. pp. cxxix–x.

[88] See e.g. the wills of Master Gilbert (d.*c.*1312) and Adam Rous (d.1369): *HW*, i. 234; ii. 207–8. For medical fees in London in the medieval period see Rawcliffe, 'Medicine and Medical Practice', 21–2.

[89] *Calendar of Letters from the Mayor and Corporation of the City of London c.1350–1370*, ed. R. R. Sharpe (London, 1885), no. 270: John Nicole, otherwise unrecorded as a London surgeon, perhaps traded in cloth and wool more enthusiastically than he practised surgery.

[90] *Memorials*, 337. The surgeons on this occasion were Master John Donhead, Master John Hyndstoke, and Nicholas Kyldeby: Talbot and Hammond, *Medical Practitioners*, 141, 157, 227.

[91] *Memorials*, 519–20; the surgeons on this occasion were Master John Hyndstoke, Master Geoffrey Grace, Master John Bradmore, and Master Henry Sutton, Talbot and Hammond, *Medical Practitioners*, 53, 84, 123–4, 157. The activities of women as surgeons, or as midwives, is very obscure in the medieval period. Thomas Gate estimated that there were sixty women practitioners in London in 1560; this figure probably included midwives, M. Pelling and C. Webster, 'Medical Practitioners', in C. Webster (ed.), *Health, Medicine and Mortality in the Sixteenth Century* (Cambridge, 1979), 165–235, esp. 183–4; and see A. L. Wyman, '"The Surgeoness"', the Female Practitioner of Surgery 1400–1800', *Medical History*, 28 (1984), 22–41. In fact midwives were not licensed in London until the sixteenth century and not organized until the seventeenth, see J. Donnison, *Midwives and Medical Men* (London, 1977), ch. 1.

fraternity established in the church of St Botolph Aldersgate: he was a churchwarden in 1400 and a master of the fraternity in 1409–10. At his death in 1412 Bradmore was in possession of a large house in Aldersgate Street which passed to his second wife Margaret and, ultimately, to the Holy Trinity guild. To his brother Nicholas, who was also a surgeon, Bradmore bequeathed a 'black paper book', which doubtless contained some of the secrets of his craft, and to Philip Brycheford, a surgeon who was later on the staff of Thomas Morstede at the battle of Agincourt, he bequeathed a 'a black book of surgery'. Brycheford may at one time have been his apprentice. The will of Bradmore, with bequests not only of books, but also of silk cloths, silver plate, daggers, and rings, as well as substantial London tenements, is further indication of the wealth and status to which skilled surgeons could aspire.[93]

Surgeons 'proper' like Bradmore were always few in number. Like the physicians they were a small and elite profession whose skills may have been more practical than those of the physicians, and yet these skills were derived in part, as Bradmore's will suggests, from 'book learning'. Their relationship to the more numerous craft of barbers and barber-surgeons was not always harmonious and it may have been pressure from the barbers that drove the surgeons 'proper' into the short-lived alliance with the physicians in 1423 already described. After the failure of this 'community' the surgeons continued to maintain their separate identity and masters of the fellowship of surgeons were sworn before the mayor and aldermen in 1423, 1428, 1431, and 1438.[94] Moreover, in 1435 when the membership apparently numbered seventeen, new ordinances were drawn up to organize the fellowship and provide for four, rather than two, masters.[95] But, as we shall see, in the later fifteenth century, the elitist fellowship of surgeons was finally absorbed by the more numerous, if more plebeian, craft of the barbers and barber-surgeons.

For most Londoners it would be to the more lowly barbers that they would have recourse for simple medical help. Barbers were skilled, not simply in shaving, but also in drawing teeth, minor surgical acts where life and limb were not at stake, cauterization, and, above all, in blood-letting.[96] The rise of the barbers' craft can be traced in the judicial inquiries of 1244 and 1276; two barbers are recorded in 1244

[92] See B. F. Harvey, *Living and Dying in England 1100–1540: The Monastic Experience* (Oxford, 1993), 86, 234–5.

[93] Talbot and Hammond, *Medical Practitioners*, 123–4, 256: *Parish Fraternity Register: The Fraternity of the Holy Trinity and SS Fabian and Sebastian in the Parish Church of St Botolph Without Aldersgate* (London Record Society, 1982), 22, 37, 72, 100. See C. Rawcliffe, 'The Profits of Practice: The Wealth and Status of Medical Men in Later Medieval England', *Bulletin of the Society for the Social History of Medicine*, 1 (1988), 61–78.

[94] *LBK*, 30, 98, 143, 222.

[95] See J. Dobson, *Barbers and Barber Surgeons of London* (London, 1979), 26–27. These ordinances do not survive among the city's records but were copied into the late fifteenth-century ordinance book of the fellowship of surgeons (now at Barbers' Hall), see R. T. Beck, *The Cutting Edge* (London, 1974) where the ordinances are transcribed.

[96] For a description of the range of barbers' skills in the sixteenth century see M Pelling, 'Appearance and Reality: Barber-Surgeons, the Body and Disease', in Beier and Finlay (eds.), *London 1500–1700*, 82–112, esp. 94–5.

and thirteen in 1276.[97] In 1308 the London barbers chose Richard le Barbour to supervise the craft and, in particular, to ensure that barbers did not take up as brothel-keepers nor act in other ways that might discredit the craft.[98] The terms of Richard's oath suggest that at this point barbers were operating at the very bottom of the medical market. In 1376 the barbers' first ordinances were presented to the mayor and aldermen: no one was to practise barbery in the city until he had been examined by two masters of the craft. The purpose of such provision was twofold: to prevent outsiders from practising and also to ensure a reasonable standard of professional service.[99] From this date onwards the names of the wardens of the barbers' craft are found quite frequently recorded in the city's Letter Books.

The struggle between the surgeons and the barbers was fought out in the course of the fifteenth century. Clearly the barbers had become increasingly resentful of the attempts by the surgeons to supervise barbers practising surgical skills. In 1410 the barbers secured an exemplification of their 1376 ordinances which made it clear that only barbers were to supervise the surgery practised by barbers, e.g. shaving, making incisions, or phlebotomy (or bleeding).[100] The growing popularity of the barbers is attested by the volume of business that came their way, and led to their keeping their shops open on Sundays, which provoked the displeasure of the archbishop of Canterbury.[101] In order to meet possible complaints from the surgeons' fellowship, the barbers decided in 1415 that they would elect two of their members who practised surgery to act as inspectors of that aspect of their craft. In the following year the mayor and aldermen stipulated that no barber-surgeon should take anyone into his care who was in danger of death or maiming, without showing the case within three days to these masters of the barber-surgeons.[102] It was the seemingly unstoppable incursions by the barbers into the fields traditionally monopolized by the master surgeons that probably pushed the surgeons into the alliance with the physicians in the early 1420s. The civic authorities may, indeed, have encouraged the barbers to develop their simple surgical skills in order to provide a wider and, perhaps, cheaper range of medical services in the city.

The continuing success of the barber-surgeons was marked by their acquisition of a company hall in 1441–5 on a site lying between Monkwell Street and the city wall in the north-west corner of the city,[103] and this success was followed by

[97] It was presumably the overenthusiasm of a barber that led to the death, through excessive bleeding, of William le Pannere, a skinner, in 1278, *Memorials*, 14–15.

[98] Ibid. 67.

[99] Ibid. 393–4. The barbers' fraternity return to the royal guild inquiry of 1388–9 survives in PRO, C47/42/214.

[100] *LBI*, 5.

[101] Year 1413, *Memorials*, 593–4; the mayor and aldermen responded to the archbishop's complaints by imposing fines of 6*s*. 8*d*. on barbers who opened their shops on Sundays, *LBI*, 116.

[102] *Memorials*, 606–8. Simon Rolf and Richard Wells were chosen to act as masters for the barbers practising surgery: Talbot and Hammond, *Medical Practitioners*, 283, 325. The oath taken by these two masters of the barber-surgeons closely resembles that taken by the master surgeons in 1369.

[103] Dobson, *Barbers and Barber-Surgeons*, 77–8.

further ordinances in 1451.[104] Their rise was then crowned by a royal charter of incorporation granted to the 'barbers of the city of London using the faculty or mistery of surgery' by Edward IV in 1462.[105] The elevated status of the barber-surgeons is reinforced in the provisions in their ordinances of 1482 that members were not to accept as apprentices those who were 'avexed or disposed to be lepur or gowty maymed or disfigured in any parties of his body whereby he shall fall in disdeyn or lothefulnesse'.[106] So barbers were to be handsome and wholesome in order that they might inspire confidence in their clients.

The expanding business of the barber-surgeons threw the fellowship of master-surgeons onto the defensive. Since they were such a small group (in 1492 there were only eleven surgeons) they accepted the inevitable and began the process of merging with the barber-surgeons, by drawing up articles of agreement in 1493. Four wardens were to be appointed, two by the surgeons and two by the barber-surgeons, and these four were to examine all those who wished to practise surgery in the city or suburbs. Those who satisfied the wardens were to receive a licence under the common seal of both guilds.[107] This agreement paved the way for important developments in the licensing and education of surgeons. By 1497 the barber-surgeons were employing a doctor of 'physick' to instruct and examine apprentices in the more theoretical aspects of their craft, and in 1530 new ordinances made it compulsory for those barbers who practised surgery to come to the company hall to hear lectures on surgery whenever they were given, and to be prepared to lecture themselves.[108] When the final act of union between the surgeons and the barber-surgeons came in 1540, the result was to confirm the strength of the company and the more academic approach to the craft.[109] The act of union even assigned four corpses a year to the company 'for anatomies'.[110] The barbers had come a long way from the early fourteenth century when their activities could be barely distinguished from keepers of bathhouses and brothels, to the practice of the healing arts under the supervision, and by the licence, of their incorporated fellowship of barber-surgeons.

Lower down the medical hierarchy stood the apothecary, the man who supplied and made up the medicaments and medicines prescribed by physicians or, more rarely, by surgeons. In the reign of King John a man named William was described as *speciarius regis* and from this time onwards a succession of prosperous spicers

[104] Year 1451, *LBK*, 333; S. Young, *The Annals of the Barber-Surgeons of London* (London, 1890), 44–7. These ordinances aimed to restrict the practice of barbery (of all kinds) to those who were members of the company or their apprentices. Strangers who wished to practise the craft were to be examined by the master and wardens, and six or eight 'cunning' persons of the craft.

[105] Ibid. 51–60.

[106] Ibid. 61–2.

[107] Dobson, *Barbers and Barber-Surgeons*, 28–9. A copy of such a licence granted to Robert Anson in 1497 is preserved in the ordinance book at Barbers' hall.

[108] Young, *Annals of the Barber-Surgeons*, 70; Dobson, *Barbers and Barber-Surgeons*, 23.

[109] Ibid. 34; Young, *Annals of the Barber-Surgeons*, 78–80 and app. C. See M. C. Erler, 'The First English Printing of Galen: The Formation of the Company of Barber-Surgeons', *Huntington Library Quarterly*, 48 (1985), 159–73.

[110] For the history of the sixteenth-century fortunes of the barber-surgeons see Pelling and Webster, 'Medical Practitioners', in Webster (ed.), *Health, Medicine and Mortality*, 165–235, esp. 173–8.

may be traced in the royal household accounts.[111] Many spicer-apothecaries in the thirteenth century came from Italy, particularly Lucca: Robert from Montpellier was appointed spicer-apothecary to Henry III while he was in Gascony in 1242–3 and then followed his royal master to London.[112] Joseph, the spicer who supplied the royal household in the 1230s, had a house in Bread Street; Robert of Montpellier had a large house in Milk Street and a seld in West Cheap.[113] Indeed, in the 1270s this part of Cheapside was known as *Spiceria* and the Montpellier family monopolized most of the royal business.[114] The royal apothecary not only made up the drugs and medicines prescribed by the royal physician, but acted also as a purveyor of fresh fruit and was responsible for making the spiced wine drunk on special royal occasions such as Christmas, or the feast of St Edward. It was also the apothecary's task to provide the substances (aloes, myrrh, and musk) that would be used to embalm the sovereign when the time came.[115] Apothecaries performed similar services, if on a reduced scale, for other households.

The spicer-apothecaries appear to have been content to remain as a specialized group within the greater company of the grocers (rather as the barber-surgeons remained as a subgroup within the barbers' company).[116] Not only grocers, however, dealt in many goods used by apothecaries: the wealthy fishmonger Stephen Forster in 1445 stocked barrels of ginger, green ginger root, wormseed (used against intestinal worms), scamonia (a purgative) and also 'storax calamita' which is gum resin.[117] In the course of the fifteenth century treacle came to be used increasingly in pharmaceutical preparations and this was also stocked by grocers.[118] The apothecaries, therefore, however distinguished and skilled, were men who had learnt their craft through an apprenticeship and their knowledge was empirical rather than acquired through books. Moreover the apothecaries were not only a subgroup within the grocers' company but they were also very much subordinate to the physicians whose prescriptions they made up.[119] Chaucer's

[111] L. G. Matthews, *The Royal Apothecaries* (London, 1967), ch. 1; G. E. Trease, 'The Spicers and Apothecaries of the Royal Household in the Reigns of Henry III, Edward I and Edward II', *Nottingham Medieval Studies*, 3 (1959), 19–52.

[112] Ibid. 24.

[113] Ibid. 24–7; for selds see Ch. 10.

[114] *HW*, i. 38; Richard of Montpellier in 1284 was the first spicer to be described as 'apothecary': Trease, 'Spicers and Apothecaries', 32.

[115] See J. R. H. Moorman, 'Edward I at Lanercost Priory 1306–7', *EHR* 263 (1952), 162–74. Edward I was ill while at Lanercost and the total bill for drugs supplied by apothecaries on the instructions of Master Nicholas de Tyngenyk was £134 16*s.* 4*d.* Richard of Montpellier was paid a further £164 14*s.* 9*d.* for 2196¼ lb of diverse medicines bought at a flat rate of 18*d.* a pound. In happier times we find Queen Isabella in 1311–12 supplied with 'sweetmeats in tablet form' along with other spices by her apothecary, Peter of Montpellier, see *The Household Book of Queen Isabella of England*, ed. F. D. Brackley and G. Hermansen (Edmonton, 1971), 108–9.

[116] In 1365 men were appointed to act as surveyors of the mistery of 'Grossers, Pepperers and Apothecaries', *LBG*, 204.

[117] *CPMR 1437–57*, 83–4.

[118] Matthews, *Royal Apothecaries*, 42–3. In 1471 some treacle in London was certified as unwholesome by two physicians, Roger Marshall and Wolford Cook, together with seventeen apothecaries: *LBL*, 103.

[119] In the fifteenth century the royal apothecary clearly worked in the household as a subordinate of the royal physician: Matthews, *Royal Apothecaries*, 54.

physician had apothecaries at his beck and call 'for ech of hem made other for to winne'. It is clear that physicians tended to use the services of a particular apothecary. William Goldwyn, at one time a fellow of All Souls College, Oxford, who acted as domestic chaplain to the Stonor family in Oxfordshire, wrote in 1480 to John Byrell 'poticary' who lived in Bucklersbury and ordered considerable quantities of spices to be used in making up prescriptions for 'a special mistress of mine'. Goldwyn expressed the hope that he would soon be in London when he would tarry with Byrell, and, two years later, we find Byrell acting as Goldwyn's executor.[120]

But the advent of printing may have contributed to the hostility that developed in the sixteenth century between the apothecaries and the physicians. It became harder to keep book learning and pharmaceutical recipes out of the hands of the apothecaries (and indeed the patients).[121] When, therefore, the physicians established their college in 1518 they were anxious to control the free-ranging activities of the apothecaries. In 1524 it was agreed that no physician who was member of the college would make or sell medicines and, in return, the apothecaries agreed not to make up prescriptions for physicians who were not members of the College. In 1538 the physicians secured the right to search apothecaries' shops which meant that the apothecaries found themselves subject to the masters both of the physicians and the grocers. The struggle was resolved only when, in 1617, the apothecaries secured their own charter.[122]

The apothecaries may have offered informal medical help but most Londoners could not have afforded the services of a physician such as Master William Goldwyn, or the range of spices and herbs supplied by an apothecary such as John Byrell. Although there was, perhaps, more expert help to be found in London than elsewhere, it was the complaint of moralists such as Langland that physicians (and surgeons) charged excessive fees for their services. Not only was medical advice and care expensive, but there were lacking in London those empirical general practitioners, usually known as 'leeches', who were frequently to be found in the countryside.[123]

[120] *Kingsford's Stonor Letters & Papers 1290–1483*, ed. C. Carpenter (Cambridge, 1996), no. 271; Talbot and Hammond, *Medical Practitioners*, 395–7. Goldwyn, like many in the medical profession, lived in the parish of St Stephen Walbrook where Thomas Southwell (see n. 79) had been rector; see J. McConica, 'The Early Fellowship', in J. McConica (ed.), *Unarmed Soldiery: Studies in the Early History of All Souls College* (All Souls College, Oxford, 1996), 33–64, esp. 43–4.

[121] On the question of the development and dissemination of printed medical advice see P. Slack, 'Mirrors of Health and Treasures of Poor Men: The Uses of Vernacular Medical Literature of Tudor England', in Webster (ed.), *Health, Medicine and Mortality*, 237–73.

[122] R. Roberts, 'The London Apothecaries and Medical Practice in Tudor and Stuart England' (University of London, Ph.D. thesis, 1964), esp. ch. 1, pp. 33 *et seq.* See also Pelling and Webster, 'Medical Practitioners', in Webster (ed.), *Health, Medicine and Mortality*, 177–9.

[123] Roberts, 'The London Apothecaries and Medical Practice', 9. Very few 'leeches' appear in the London records: in 1324 Nicholas Walsh, goldsmith, was taken after a brawl to the house of Robert le Leche in Cornhill to be medically treated, *Coroners' Rolls*, 91; on two other occasions recorded in the coroners' rolls friends secured medical help for injured parties: ibid. 97, 117; in 1397 William Stanes 'leche' was discharged from jury service on the grounds of old age: *LBH* 442; in 1431 Geoffrey Constantyn 'leche' brought a suit in the sheriffs' court: *CPMR 1413–37*, 252. For country medical men, probably rather more skilled than leeches, see J. K. Mustain, 'A Rural Medical Practitioner in

There seems to have been little charitable provision of free medical advice although the mercer John Don left £5 p.a. for five years for a surgeon to treat the poor 'lakkyng helpe and money to pay for their lechcrafte'.[124] In these circumstances men and women were bound to treat themselves and their families.[125] Conscientious clerics may sometimes have provided rudimentary medical help for their needy neighbours or parishioners. William Palmer, the rector of St Alphage's who died in 1400, bequeathed medical books in his will.[126] On the other hand some clerics seem to have used their superior position merely to deceive the gullible. William, the rector of St Margaret Lothbury, imported wolves' flesh to use as a cure for a disease from which he claimed to be suffering, namely 'Le Lou'. The learned medical men who gathered to examine the case could find 'no disease' in their medical or surgical writings against which the flesh of wolves might be effective and they further discovered that William was not, in fact, ill.[127] The parson of St Leonard, Foster Lane, was presented at the wardmote by his own parishioners 'because he presented himself as a surgeon and physician to deceive the people with his false cunning, that he showeth unto the people, by the which craft he hath slain many a man'.[128]

On occasion the informal help that was offered was simply insufficiently skilled, as in the case of Richard Cheyndut who failed to cure the leg of Walter del Hull, although he was not accused of deception.[129] But on other occasions it is clear that quacks simply resorted to sorcery or black magic. Roger Hacche paid Roger Clerk of Wandsworth 12*d.* to cure his wife Joanna. The 'cure' consisted of a leaf of a book, tied up in a piece of gold cloth hung around Joanna's neck. When the cure failed to work, Roger Clerk claimed that the paper had written on it a charm that was good for curing fevers. When the deception was discovered, however, he was condemned to be paraded through the city with the parchment hung around his neck together with a whetstone to indicate lies, and urinals (the symbol of the medical profession) slung before and after him.[130] The advent of printing may, however, have helped the poor man to help himself, and the popularity in the sixteenth century of explanatory textbooks and collections of remedies suggests that these books met a real need.[131]

Fifteenth-Century England', *Bulletin of the History of Medicine*, 46 (1972), 469–76, and P. M. Jones. 'Thomas Fayreford: An English Fifteenth-Century Medical Practitioner', in R. French, J. Arrizabalaga, A. Cunningham, and L-M. Ballester (eds.), *Medicine from the Black Death to the French Disease* (Aldershot, 1998), 156–83.

[124] Year 1480, cited by Thomson, 'Piety and Charity', 187. For the free advice to be given to the poor by the physicians and surgeons in 1423 see above p. 281.

[125] Several Londoners grew their own herbs; see case in 1293: *LBA*, 182.

[126] R. A. Wood, 'A Fourteenth-Century London Owner of Piers Plowman', *Medium Aevum*, 53 (1984), 83–90.

[127] Year 1299, *CEMCR 1298–1307*, 51; see Getz, *Medicine in the English Middle Ages*, 76.

[128] Year 1421, *CPMR 1413–37*, 127.

[129] Year 1377, *CPMR 1364–81*, 236.

[130] Year 1382, *Memorials*, 464–6. Most prosecutions for sorcery in the city concerned cases of lost or stolen articles that the sorcerer was paid to reveal, but in most cases he resorted to accusing innocent people, see cases in 1375, three in 1382, another in 1390, *Memorials*, 462–3, 472–3, 475–6, 518–19; *CPMR 1364–81*, 189 and n. 3.

[131] Slack, 'Mirrors of Health', 243–6; P. M. Jones. 'Medicine and Science', in L. Hellinga and J. B. Trapp (eds.), *The Cambridge History of the Book in Britain* (Cambridge, 1999), iii. 433–48, esp. 446–8.

HOSPITALS

One way, of course, in which a Londoner could cope with illness was to gain admission to a hospital. In the medieval period this term covered a wide variety of institutions, almshouses, leper isolation colonies, lodging houses for poor travellers, and hospices for the dying, as well as places where medical help and some slight hope of recovery might be offered. Only five of the thirty or so medieval hospitals in London fell into the last category; these were St Bartholomew's in Smithfield (founded 1123); St Thomas's in Southwark (founded in the 1170s); St Mary outside Bishopsgate (founded 1197); St Mary Bethlehem (founded 1247), and the hospital dedicated to St John the Baptist and usually known simply as The Savoy (founded 1505–17).[132]

The first three of these hospitals were houses of Augustinian canons, founded in the twelfth century. By the thirteenth century it would seem that they all offered a little more than simply peace and quiet to the dying. St Bartholomew's had an infirmary where the sick were cared for and it is likely that most of the nursing was carried out by sisters, although in 1316 the master was ordered to visit the sick frequently and provide for their needs.[133] It is possible that the skilled expertise of surgeons or physicians may have been provided for the patients: certainly in the later fourteenth century John of Mirfield, a clerk and scholar, who 'found himself . . . in the circle of the Priory and Hospital of St Bartholomew' in about 1390 compiled his medical compendium, the *Breviarium Bartholomei* there.[134] This massive work contained chapters dealing with every kind of complaint from leprosy to stomach ache and from nightmares to pregnancy. It seems likely that Mirfield had observed the ailments at close quarters in the hospital infirmary and applied some of his knowledge to relieve the suffering of 'a population that was poor, secular, often transient and sometimes women or children'.[135] The hospital in the fourteenth and fifteenth centuries appears also to have had a maternity ward for 'yong wymmen that have mysse done that ben whythe chylde'. Here a mother could stay after her baby was delivered, and be cared for and fed until her purification. Moreover if the mother died in childbirth the hospital cared for the child until it was seven years old.[136] At the time of the dissolution St Bartholomew's appears to have had about fifty beds for the sick poor.

[132] For a survey of the range of hospitals in medieval London see C. Rawcliffe, 'The Hospitals of Later Medieval London', *Medical History*, 28 (1984), 1–21.

[133] *Cartulary of St Bartholomew's Hospital*, ed. N. Kerling (London, 1973), 7, 9; *VCH, London*, 521.

[134] Getz, *Medicine in the English Middle Ages*, 50.

[135] Ibid. 52; Kerling, *Cartulary*, 9.

[136] *The Historical Collections of a Citizen of London*, ed. J. Gairdner (Camden Society, 1876), pp. viii–ix. In the fourteenth century the master of the hospital claimed that the brothers and sisters cared for the sick poor until they were healed, for pregnant women until they were delivered, and for the children born there for seven years, if the mother died: *CCR 1349–54*, 414–15. The brothers seem also to have tried to rescue babies from Newgate prison, see N. Kerling, 'A Note on Newgate Prison', *TLMAS* 22 (1968), 21–2.

The picture of St Thomas's hospital is very like that of St Bartholomew's. By 1295 the hospital catered for forty sick inmates who were cared for by five sisters.[137] In 1387 it was necessary for William of Wykeham, the bishop of Winchester, to issue reforming ordinances that included the requirement that the sick should be visited every day, provided with decent food, and housed in a peaceful environment.[138] Originally the patients slept in the nave of the church where they could look upon the altar but later in the sixteenth century a large new ward was built at the northern end of the hospital precinct.[139] From the late thirteenth century there were maternity patients in the hospital and a maternity ward for unmarried mothers appears to have been added in the fifteenth century. In this case the donor was Richard Whittington who provided a chamber with eight beds, and strictly enjoined that what went on there should be kept secret so that the young women's chances of marriage should not be impaired.[140]

The third of the Augustinian houses was St Mary outside Bishopsgate, which had been founded expressly to care for the poor and the sick. Not all those who found refuge there were in fact sick and poor. Mathilda, the wife of Sir Robert Aleyn, stayed at the hospital for two years and ran up considerable bills for food and drink for herself and two servants, not to mention the loans she extracted from the prior for which her husband was subsequently sued.[141] But there is also evidence that sisters at the hospital did care for the sick, and at the time of the Dissolution there were said to be 180 beds there, set out in an open ward and each illuminated with its own lamp.[142]

The hospital of St Mary of Bethlehem, just outside Bishopsgate, was founded by a Londoner, Simon fitz-Mary, in 1247; it was attached to the military order of St Mary of Bethlehem and, although the foundation deed did not specifically enjoin the brothers and sisters to care for the poor and the sick, yet a hospice of some kind may have been envisaged from the outset.[143] Almost a century after its foundation, in 1346, the mayor and aldermen took the hospital under their patronage and agreed to appoint two aldermen to act each year as governors and overseers at the house.[144] When, in 1366, the bishop of Bethlehem threatened to farm the house the mayor urged him not to do this on the grounds that the charitable work of

137 M. Carlin, *Medieval Southwark* (London, 1996), 75–85, esp. 78.

138 Ibid. 78–9.

139 Ibid. 81–2; Rawcliffe, 'Hospitals', 12.

140 Gairdner, *Historical Collections*, p. xi; Carlin, *Medieval Southwark*, 78, 81.

141 *CPMR 1381–1412*, 47–9; Elizabeth Despenser, Lady Zouche, may well have died in the Hospital in 1408, see P. Payne and C. Barron, 'The Letters and Life of Elizabeth Despenser, Lady Zouche (d.1408)', *Nottingham Medieval Studies*, 41 (1997), 126–56, esp. 142, 144.

142 *VCH, London*, 531–2; fresh water for the hospital came from a spring belonging to the bishop of London at Stepney. The hospital, with an annual income of £504, was the best endowed of any London hospital apart from the Savoy. For a detailed study of the hospital, see C. Thomas, B. Sloane, and C. Phillpotts, *Excavations at the Priory and Hospital of St Mary Spital, London* (London, 1997), esp. ch. 4.

143 J. Andrews, A. Briggs, R. Porter, P. Tucker, and K. Waddington, *The History of Bethlem* (London, 1997), 27–33; P. Allderidge, 'Management and Mismanagement at Bedlam 1597–1633', in Webster (ed.), *Health, Medicine, Mortality*, 141–64 esp. 142. The priory was also to receive the bishop of Bethlehem when he should chance to come to London; for the foundation deed of 1247, see Strype, *Survey*, i. pt. ii, 94–5.

144 *LBF*, 154–5; Andrews et al., *History of Bethlem*, 56–9.

the house was important to the city.[145] John Gardyner, chaplain, was appointed by the mayor and aldermen as warden, or master, of the hospital in 1381,[146] but by the end of the century the king appears to have gained control of the appointment.[147] The civic interest in the hospital is reflected, perhaps, in the existence of at least three fraternities of lay people associated with it. In 1361 a group of drapers living in Cornhill, together with 'other good men and women', decided to join together to honour St Mary of Bethlehem 'where Jesus Christ was born for the Salvation of all people, where the star appeared to the shepherds and gave light to the three kings of Cologne'.[148] This enterprise was encouraged by William Tytte, one of the brothers, whose enthusiasm brought him in due course the mastership of the hospital.[149] The fraternity of pouchmakers, dedicated to the Virgin, chose to celebrate the feast of the Annunciation in the hospital chapel and to provide two tapers to burn there, and the yeomanry of the skinners' craft also met there.[150] But neither of these fraternities appears to have continued to thrive into the fifteenth century.

The explanation for this waning enthusiasm may be that, perhaps from the 1370s and certainly by 1403, the violently insane were being housed at Bethlehem hospital. Six lunatics and three sick persons were housed there in 1403 and the hospital was provided with keys, manacles, chains, and stocks for restraining those who were violent. For this sophisticated care a fee of 6*s.* 8*d.* a quarter (sometimes 12*d.* per week) was charged. Some of the patients were kept in the hospital through the generosity of their neighbours.[151] The visitations of 1403 found that the day-to-day running of the hospital had been left to the porter, Peter the Taverner, who had embezzled the goods of the hospital and abused the patients. Clearly the current master (by this date a royal nominee) was infrequently present and not only did Taverner's depredations go unchecked, but divine service was maintained only intermittently in the chapel. Moreover the house was not well endowed: in the early sixteenth century its income was only £90 a year, whereas most of the London hospitals had lands producing hundred of pounds' worth of income. The Bethlehem house had to survive precariously on alms collections and offerings. The visitation may have done some good. Brothers and sisters at the hospital

[145] *Letters*, 145–6.

[146] *LBH*, 165: this appointment was disputed by the king who attempted to appoint Robert Lyncoln as keeper in 1389, ibid. 338. While resisting the king's claims, the city seized some of the hospital's tenements on the grounds that the hospital was forty shillings in arrears with the rent, *LBH*, 343.

[147] *VCH, London*, 496; Andrews et al., *History of Bethlem*, app. 1, 723.

[148] Guild ordinances, in French, PRO, C47/42/202. Apart from the dedication, the ordinances closely resemble those of other London fraternities of the time. There were bequests to the guild from a jeweller in 1364, a vintner in 1371, and four drapers: *HW*, ii. 90, 159, and E. Quinton, 'The Drapers and the Drapery Trade of Late Medieval London *c.*1300–*c.*1500' (University of London, Ph.D. thesis, 2001), 31–5. Poor members were to be buried at the cost of the fraternity in the churchyard of the hospital, which had been granted this privilege in 1362: *VCH, London*, 495–6.

[149] Brother Tytte of 1361 occurs as master in 1370–1 and 1380, ibid. 497. See also *The Church in London 1375–1392*, ed. A. K. McHardy (London Record Society, 1977), 3, 27.

[150] PRO, C47/46/464, printed in *A Book of London English 1384–1425*, eds, R. W. Chambers and M. Daunt (Oxford, 1931), 53–7; Andrews *et al.*, *History of Bethlem*, 72; E. Veale, *The English Fur Trade in the Later Middle Ages* (Oxford, 1966), 112.

[151] *VCH, London*, 496; Rawcliffe, 'Hospitals', 4, 11.

were again in evidence in 1424, and in 1436 William Mawere, tailor, was excused jury service because of his 'constant attention to the poor mad inmates of the hospital'.[152] The author of 'Gregory's Chronicle' in the 1460s, wrote of Bethlem

> and in that place been found many men that been fallen out of their wits. And full honestly they been kept in that place; and sum been restored unto their wits and health again. And some been abiding therein for ever, for they been fallen so much out of themselves that it is uncurable unto man[153]

This may perhaps be an over-optimistic view of what went on in the Bethlehem hospital in the second half of the fifteenth century. The masters were probably appointed by the Crown but it is interesting that a few of them appear to have been men with some medical training. Thomas Denman, for example, who was a university-trained physician, was master of the hospital in 1494–1504 and requested burial in the chapel there, which suggests, perhaps, that he had an active rather than a remote interest in the hospital.[154]

The city appears to have continued to take an interest in the Bethlehem house and in 1523 Stephen Jenyns, mayor and merchant tailor, left £40 to the city to be used for the outright purchase of the patronage of the house from the Crown.[155] Even when the dissolution of the religious houses put Bethlehem, along with St Thomas's and St Bartholomew's, onto the market the Crown did not sell the hospital outright to the city, but only its 'custody, government and order'.[156] This chronicle of the house of St Mary of Bethlehem, sorry as it is in several respects, yet contains some interesting pointers for the future. To all intents and purposes by the end of the fourteenth century the house was no longer one of professed brothers and sisters who belonged to a religious order. Indeed by 1403 no one wore the distinctive dress of the order and, indeed, there were no brothers or sisters. The 'care' that was offered to the insane in the hospital was increasingly secular. In the same way the masters were, by the end of the period, not only not members of a religious order, they were not even clerks. Finally we can detect the efforts, not always successful by any means, of the mayor and aldermen to gain control of this house so that they could run it for the benefit of Londoners. They were thwarted in this instance by the competitive needs of the Crown, but the attempt to admin-

[152] *LBK*, 194. It is not clear whether Mawere held an official position at the hospital; he was not the master.

[153] Gairdner, *Historical Collections*, p. ix.

[154] Talbot and Hammond, *Medical Practitioners*, 339–40. Other medical men who were associated with St Mary Bethlehem were William Hobbes, a physician and surgeon who was appointed to the mastership of the hospital in 1479: ibid. 401–2; Thomas Browne who was appointed to the mastership in 1459–70 may have been a barber surgeon: ibid. 336; John Smeathe or Sneethe 1470–9 may have been a royal surgeon: ibid. 182; Andrews et al., *History of Bethlem*, 85. Rawcliffe argues that the appointment of these distinguished physicians led to absenteeism and may have aggravated the administrative problems of the hospital, 'Hospitals', 8–9.

[155] Stow, *Survey*, i 164–5; Allderidge shows that the court of aldermen had been attempting to gain control of the house from the Crown since at least 1504, 'Management and Mismanagement', 147.

[156] Ibid. 148–9. The management of the hospital, which was supervised by the governors of Bridewell, was very lax, and the keepers paid little attention to the needs of the inmates. There were twenty-one patients in the hospital in 1598 and thirty-one in 1624, ibid. 152–60.

ister and control one aspect of medical work in the city, the care of the insane, was to provide an important precedent in the sixteenth century.

Not surprisingly, perhaps, it was a totally new foundation that made the first clear and specific provision for sick patients in a hospital. The Savoy, which was projected by Henry VII in 1505 (but not completed until 1517), was not attached to a religious order although the staff included a chaplain and other priests.[157] A matron and twelve sisters were to tend 100 poor men and they had the expert advice of a physician, a surgeon, and an apothecary;[158] money was allocated to provide the prescribed drugs. Here the hospital was influenced by the Florentine hospital of Santa Maria Nuova: the dormitory was built in cruciform shape and each of the inmates was provided with a separate cubicle containing a bed and the necessary linen.[159] When the city finally gained control of the two hospitals of St Bartholomew's and St Thomas's in the 1550s, their administration was modeled on that of the Savoy (although, paradoxically, the Savoy hospital ceased to provide for the poor and sick and became a decrepit sinecure).[160] The new civic hospitals were to be run by committees of reputable Londoners and the patients were to have the services of surgeons, physicians, apothecaries, and nursing sisters. Whereas in 1500 the London hospitals might have been places of refuge, where men and women could live and die in a degree of comfort, cleanliness, and peace (there may have been 350–400 beds for the sick in the five London hospitals before the Dissolution), by 1600 some of the London hospitals, notably St Bartholomew's, had become places where people went to be cured of their illnesses. By the 1590s, 200 people a year passed through the hospital and a high proportion of these could take up their beds and walk. The Dissolution had served finally to break the hold the religious orders had had upon medical care and hospitals and, in this respect, the new secular order was able to bring new learning to bear upon the problems of disease and pain.

Leprosy presented a particular problem for medieval urban societies: it was thought to be highly infectious and there was no cure for the disease.[161] The only solution, therefore, which a caring community could offer was to separate the leprous from the healthy members of society. Pious founders had established two places of refuge for lepers in the twelfth century, the hospitals of St Giles in Holborn (founded 1100–18) and of St James at Westminster (founded by 1189).[162] In 1276 the mayor and aldermen banned lepers from entering the city and it may

[157] *VCH, London*, 497.

[158] The physician was to receive £20 *p.a.*, the surgeon and the apothecary £10 each.

[159] Colvin (ed.), *History of the King's Works*, iii. pt. 1, 198–9; R. S. Somerville, *The Savoy* (London, 1960) 29, 32; see also K. Park and J. Henderson, '"The First Hospital among Christians": The Ospedale di Santa Maria Nuova in Early Sixteenth-Century Florence', *Medical History*, 35 (1991), 164–88, esp. 168.

[160] *VCH, London*, 547.

[161] This did not deter the gullible from seeking cures: John Clotes in 1408 handed over some valuable jewels to John Luter, 'leche', in the hope of being cured of leprosy. In court Luter argued that, although he had not cured the leprosy, he had taught Clotes how to make balsam and other medicines: *CPMR 1381–1413*, 289.

[162] See M. Satchell, 'The Emergence of Leper Houses in Medieval England 1100–1250' (University of Oxford, D.Phil. thesis, 1998), esp. 102–7, 155–6, 312–13, 388–9.

be that it was at this time that the city's own leper houses were established, although it is not known by whom. These were the Lock at Southwark and a house at Kingsland near Hackney. By the early sixteenth century there were four further leper houses in the vicinity of London, at Mile End, Holloway (Highgate), Knightsbridge, and Hammersmith.[163] All these were established well away from the city, but on main roads so that the inmates might beg alms from passing travellers.[164]

From as early as the twelfth century the city appears to have assumed a measure of supervision over the leper houses around the city, as was to be found in other English towns, such as Norwich.[165] The names of overseers, always substantial London citizens, survive from 1191.[166] In the fifteenth century the supervisors swore 'well and truly to oversee and govern' the lepers at St Giles, the Lock, and Hackney, and these three houses seem always to have been the most important of the London leper colonies in the later medieval period.[167] In the fourteenth century the city had asserted a claim to send fourteen lepers to the St Giles hospital, and to manage, through the city's two leper overseers, the revenue of the house.[168] To all intents and purposes St Giles became a civic leper house like the Lock and the Hackney hospital. But these houses may have been very small: in 1451 there were only five lepers at St Giles and it is unlikely that the other houses were larger.[169] Although the city had some responsibility for the buildings, at least of the Lock and Hackney, it was expected that this work of charity would be supported by pious benefactions. Between 1359 and 1400, fifty-seven wills enrolled in the Husting court recorded bequests to lepers, but between 1400 and 1450 there were only four wills with such bequests (although there were far fewer wills enrolled in this court in the later period). This might suggest that the existing provision was thought to be adequate. It is generally accepted that the incidence of leprosy began to decline in England from the fourteenth century onwards.[170] But in the 1340s two royal writs addressed to the mayor of London urgently insisted that lepers were to be banished from the city 'to solitary field places' and they were also to be

[163] For a full description of leprosy and leper houses in London see M. Honeybourne, 'The Leper Hospitals of the London Area', *TLMAS* 21 (1963–7), 1–61; for a rather fuller account of the hospital of St James, which was originally founded to house leprous maidens but was no longer caring for the lepers by the mid-fourteenth century, see G. Rosser, *Medieval Westminster* (Oxford, 1989), 300–10.

[164] Satchell, 'Emergence of Leper Houses', 171–6.

[165] C. Rawcliffe, *Medicine for the Soul: The Life, Death and Resurrection of an English Medieval Hospital* (Stroud, 1999), 203–4.

[166] See the list in Honeybourne, 'Leper Hospitals', 10–11; Satchell, 'Emergence of Leper Houses', 130, n. 64. To this list may be added in 1449 the names of John Bracy, tallowchandler, and Reginald Derlington, fishmonger, CLRO, Journal 5, fo. 4^{v}.

[167] February 1447, CLRO, Journal 4, fo. 168.

[168] *LBL*, 343.

[169] Honeybourne, 'Leper Hospitals', 24; see the will of John of Gaunt (d.1399) where the testator left five nobles to each leper house within five miles of London that had five lepers, and three nobles to those with fewer, cited ibid. 8.

[170] See e.g. the argument that the increase of tuberculosis in the community induced, in those who survived, an immunity to leprosy: K. Manchester, 'Tuberculosis and Leprosy in Antiquity: An Interpretation', *Medical History*, 28 (1984), 162–73.

forbidden to beg along the roads that linked the city with Westminster.[171] As late as 1472 Edward IV was sufficiently concerned to issue a writ banishing lepers from the city, and he specifically stated that the disease was on the increase.[172] Several references to lepers appear in the city's fifteenth-century journals, including the case of Robert Sewale who was many times convicted of leprosy and exiled to a leper house only to return again to the city. He was finally banished under threat of losing a limb if he reappeared.[173] By the sixteenth century, when the six outlying leper hospitals were handed over to be administered by St Bartholomew's in 1549, the disease does appear to have been in retreat. Patients suffering from incurable diseases were sent from St Bartholomew's to one of these houses, but they were by no means all leprosy sufferers. In fact the last recorded case of leprosy in London occurred in 1557 when two leprous patients were sent to the Lock hospital.[174]

The history of the London leper hospitals shows that, as the religious foundations of St Giles in the Fields and St James in Westminster failed to fulfil their original purpose of offering refuge to lepers, so the citizens stepped in and founded small hospitals to function as civic leper colonies, managed by lay overseers, responsible to the mayor and aldermen. [175] Here, even more clearly than in the case of St Mary Bethlehem hospital for the insane, we find the governors of the city taking control of a situation in order to maintain an essential social service that the church was failing to supply. The medieval policy of inflicting segregation upon lepers, although inhumane, may have helped to control the spread of the disease.[176] The successful implementation of this policy in medieval London was the achievement of the citizens, not the church.

OLD AGE

In a society where private pensions were rare and state pensions unknown, how did men and women cope with the prospect and problems of old age? For those who survived infancy, life expectancy was about 37; so the proportion of old and impotent people within the population would have been much smaller than now.

[171] Honeybourne, 'Leper Hospitals', 7; *Memorials*, 230–1. It may be that it was the king's dislike of lepers in his vicinity that led to the decline of St James as a leper hospital.

[172] *LBL*, 102. William Pole, who had been a yeoman to the Crown under Edward IV, was smitten with leprosy and in 1473 persuaded the king to grant him a piece of land at Highgate to build a leper hospital: Honeybourne, 'Leper Hospitals', 16–19.

[173] Barron, 'Government of London', 261–4.

[174] Honeybourne, 'Leper Hospitals', 9: the six hospitals handed over to St Bartholomew's were Hackney, the Lock, Mile End, Highgate, Knightsbridge, Hammersmith.

[175] The history of both these hospitals is a sorry tale of disputed claims to patronage and the dissipation of the lands and goods of the communities: in both cases the financial demands of the Crown were largely to blame, Rosser, *Medieval Westminster*, 306–9; Honeybourne, 'Leper Hospitals', 20–31.

[176] See Manchester, 'Tuberculosis and Leprosy', 171. The wardmote inquests of 1421–2 presented Maud Hoke as a leper in St Sepulchre's parish, and Nicholas Yonge in Candlewick Street: *CPMR 1413–37*, 125, 132.

The task of providing for those who were too old to work was undertaken jointly by the church, by individual acts of charity, and by the civic authorities.

Jobs within the city's own bureaucracy sometimes carried pensions; serjeants of the chamber received forty shillings p.a. when they retired, provided that they had served the city well.[177] John Blyton who had been the mayor's swordbearer at the fateful meeting with Wat Tyler in June 1381, retired fourteen years later with a pension of £5 p.a. and the grant of a house over Aldersgate, together with its garden.[178] In 1477 John Bandy, a chamber serjeant who resigned because of his age, received a gown, food, and drink such as the mayor's serjeants enjoyed in the mayor's house.[179]

But most jobs did not carry the prospect of a pension and middle-aged Londoners, like everyone else, had to take thought for the morrow. In the countryside manorial court rolls reveal that ageing customary tenants secured, by *pre-mortem* transfer of their holdings to children or relatives or friends, a measure of care and security in old age.[180] These transfers, which were enforceable in the manorial court, ensured that the lord's land was worked, his dues paid, and the old maintained.[181] Together, those who were retired and those who were employable 'implemented a private system of support defined by shared resources'.[182] To take an example of such an agreement: in the reign of Edward III, at Gressenhall in Norfolk, Henry son of Stephen made over to Henry son of Richard and Emma and his wife, a third part of a messuage together with five acres of meadow. In return the younger couple agreed to give him twenty shillings a year, forty bushels of grain (barley, wheat, and rye), fodder, three shillings to have his clothes washed, one pair of shoes, two pairs of stockings, and two pairs of sheets every year.[183] Not all agreements were as specific as this and their terms varied from area to area. After the Black Death such agreements became rarer, they are less frequently drawn up between kin, and they tend to cover transactions involving cash rather than goods.[184]

It is likely that similar agreements were made in London but they were not regularly written down in any of the records that have survived. In 1276 Denise la Vileyn complained that Henry Greneford of Gracechurch Street had broken the agreement they had made, whereby in return for all Denise's lands in Distaffe Lane Henry was to provide her with all her necessities in food and clothing as long as she lived and then ensure that she was honourably buried in the nun's priory at

[177] *LBG*, 204; *LBH*, 355; see Chs. 7 and 8.

[178] Year 1395, *LBH*, 433.

[179] Year 1477, *CPMR 1458–82*, 108, and see B. Masters, 'The Mayor's Household before 1600', in W. Kellaway and A. Hollaender (eds.), *Studies in London History Presented to P. E. Jones* (London, 1970), 95–114, esp. 108–9.

[180] E. Clark, 'Some Aspects of Social Security in Medieval England', *Journal of Family History*, 7 (1982), 307–20.

[181] R. M. Smith, 'The Manorial Court and the Elderly Tenant in Late Medieval England', in M. Pelling and R. M. Smith (eds.), *Life, Death and the Elderly: Historical Perspectives* (London, 1991), 39–61, esp. 46, 55–7.

[182] Clark, 'Social Security in Medieval England', 316.

[183] Ibid. 318.

[184] Smith, 'Manorial Court and the Elderly', 49, 51–2.

Clerkenwell.[185] In 1381 Alice Smale agreed to provide her old father with food, clothing, bed, shoes, and 14*d.* a week pocket money in return for all his goods and chattels.[186] Stephen Piers, a London tailor, and his wife in 1467 drew up an agreement with their son John and his wife, which they had ratified before the master and wardens of the tailors. Stephen handed over his house, business, servants, apprentices, and goods to his son in return for two rooms in the house and a pension of £10 yearly. If one of the parents died, then the amount to be paid was reduced, but the agreement was to remain in force until both Stephen and his wife were dead.[187] It is possible that other Londoners made such arrangements and used the authority of their companies to secure publicity and legitimation for them.

It was perhaps because of the mobility of the population of the city that Londoners looked not to their families but to the numerous religious houses for support in old age. As early as the late twelfth century we find Ralph de Quatremarns and his wife Aubrey granting a tenement and orchard in All Hallows Bread Street to St Bartholomew's: in return the hospital agreed to look after them in their own home or, if necessary, to receive them into the community for care.[188] In the same way a widow, Alice de Chalvedon, made over all her lands to St Thomas's hospital in 1253 in return for a 'suitable bed' there for life, and 5*s.* 6*d.* a year for her food and clothing.[189] Such arrangements were known as corrodies (although corrodies could take many different forms) and they were much criticized for two reasons. First they contributed to the financial impoverishment of many religious houses in the fourteenth and fifteenth centuries and, second, they often intruded an element of inappropriate worldliness into the monastic precinct.[190] Sometimes the foundation ordinances of a religious house included provision for the poor and elderly to live in the community. At St Katharine's hospital ten bedeswomen or almswomen lived in the house and wore a special outfit of grey caps and cloaks.[191] But in the early sixteenth century the master of

[185] *Eyre 1276*, no. 505. Henry had not provided Denise with necessities for the past three years: the parties agreed that Henry should pay Denise forty shillings to cover the past three years and, in the future, twenty-four shillings p.a. in lieu of food and clothing.

[186] *CPMR 1364–81*, 294.

[187] See *The Merchant Taylors' Company of London: Court Minutes, 1486–1493*, ed. M. P. Davies (Stamford, 2000), 277–81.

[188] Kerling, *Cartulary*, no. 726.

[189] Rawcliffe, 'Hospitals', 3 n. 11.

[190] For a discussion of corrodies, see Harvey, *Living and Dying*, ch. 6, where the author points out that not all corrodians were old, and that the monks of Westminster may have had sound economic interests in selling corrodies. See also R. I. Harper, 'A Note on Corrodies in the Fourteenth Century', *Albion*, 15 (1983), 95–101. In 1316 the bishop of London condemned the granting of corrodies at St Bartholomew's hospital and forbade any future grants without his permission: *VCH, London*, 521; in 1324 the bishop of Winchester placed a similar embargo on the sale of corrodies at St Thomas's hospital, Hampshire Record Office, Bishops Stratford's Register fo. 171; I owe this reference to the kindness of Dr Martha Carlin. For the abuse of corrodies at St Giles Hospital, see Honeybourne, 'Leper Hospitals', 22–3. The problem was made particularly acute by the grants of corrodies by the Crown or monastic patrons (or their descendants) to aged retainers or domestics who thereby depleted the resources of the house while contributing nothing: Rawcliffe, 'Hospitals', 3–4 .

[191] *VCH, London*, 525–30. In 1273 Queen Eleanor enjoined that there should be twenty-four poor people living in the hospital of whom six were to be poor scholars; by 1412 there were only ten poor women living there and these, by 1535, each received 10½*d.* a week.

the hospital, William Skeyngton, decided to institutionalize the corrody system and make it pay. Since the late fourteenth century there had been a fraternity at the hospital dedicated to St Katherine.[192] This appears to have lapsed in the fifteenth century but a new fraternity dedicated to St Barbara was established in 1528. In return for a down payment of 10*s.* 4*d.*, an enrolled brother or sister who fell on hard times or became old and feeble could bring his letter of membership to the hospital and receive 12*d.* a week, house room, bedding, and a woman to wash his clothes and dress his meat, until his death.[193]

But what happened to those old people who had not made provision for their old age by doing some sort of deal either with a religious house or with younger relatives or friends? In the countryside the lord of the manor could intervene and, where an old person was incapable of working his holding, it could be assigned to kinsmen or others who would be expected to work the land and use the produce, in part at least, to maintain the elderly person. Obviously it was in the lord's interest to have his land worked and the dues paid.[194] In the same way on occasion the mayor and aldermen acted as 'lords' to safeguard the interests of those who were no longer able to look after themselves, even though the corporate interests of the city were not as directly involved as those of the lord in the countryside. In 1381 Floria de Shaldeford complained in the mayor's court that her husband's aunt, Maud Grene, 'who was very aged and had little sense or discretion to look after herself', was not being appropriately maintained by John Donyngton who had taken possession of her and of her property. The court decided to commit Maud, and her property, to another couple who had no financial interest in her rents or tenements, and they agreed to maintain her 'well and honestly according to her condition'.[195] In a similar case an old carpenter, Nicholas Pays, who had become senile and unable to manage his affairs, was entrusted, together with his property, by the mayor and aldermen to the care of his son-in-law who agreed to provide food, clothing, a bed, shoes, and all necessaries. A watching brief was given to neighbours (who included the old man's brother John) to warn the mayor if anything went amiss with the arrangement.[196] So, just as the mayor and aldermen assumed responsibility for those too young to look after themselves, so also in a less formalized way they provided, on occasion, for those who were too old or senile to look after their own interests.

By the fifteenth century, however, a new kind of foundation appeared on the London scene to provide shelter and comfort for the old, namely the almshouse. The first such house, for seven men of the tailors' company, was built from money bequeathed to the company by John Chircheman (d.1413).[197] This was the first

192 Return of guild of St Katherine, PRO, C47/42/216; see also *HW*, ii. 209, 268, 343.

193 Strype, *Survey*, i. pt. ii, 6–7.

194 Clarke, 'Social Security in Medieval England'; see Z. Razi, 'Intrafamilial Ties and Relationships in the Medieval Village: A Quantitative Approach, Employing Manor Court Rolls', in Z. Razi and R. M. Smith (eds.), *Medieval Society and the Manor Court* (Oxford, 1996), 369–91, esp. 383–5.

195 *CPMR 1381–1412*, 4–5.

196 Ibid. 104–5.

197 M. P. Davies, 'The Tailors of London: Corporate Charity in the Late Medieval Town', in R. Archer (ed.), *Crown, Government and People in the Fifteenth Century* (Stroud, 1995), 161–90, esp. 181–6.

actual almshouse to be administered by a city company, although such companies had already been administering charitable funds for the relief of poor and old members or those incapacitated by accident or misfortune.[198] Once John Chircheman and the tailors had led the way, however, other companies, encouraged by their wealthy and charitable members, followed suit: the skinners (1416 and second almshouse in 1523), the brewers (1423), the cutlers (1422), the mercers (1424 and a second almshouse founded in Croyden by Elias Davy in 1445),[199] the grocers (1433), the vintners (1446), the salters (1455), the parish clerks (by 1529), the drapers (1534 and the second almshouse in 1540), the haberdashers (1539), the clothworkers (1540), and the coopers (between 1536 and 1554). [200] Most of the almshouses were established within London itself but some were outside the city: the coopers' almshouses were at Ratcliffe in Middlesex.[201] Those admitted to Whittington's almshouses, administered by the mercers' company, were principally to be poor, feeble men of the craft of mercery, but not members of the livery who were otherwise provided for. There is no specific mention of old people, but those who were poor and feeble were likely to be the old.

Most of the company almshouses were, like Whittington's, places of refuge for decayed but respectable members of the company and their widows. But it was not only within crafts and companies that this sense of communal responsibility for the old was evoked. Parishes, sometimes working through a fraternity, established almshouses: sixteen poor people were housed by the brotherhood of Our Lady in St Giles Cripplegate and the guild of the Virgin's Assumption in St Margaret's Westminster provided cottages for four poor widows.[202] The parishioners of St Clement Danes had built a hall in the churchyard with rooms underneath, let to the poor rent-free.[203] John Tate, a mercer (d.1515) gave land for an almshouse for thirteen poor men to be attached to St Anthony's hospital and this may also have been intended for the benefit of parishioners but, because it was attached to a religious foundation it was, unlike the others, destroyed at the Dissolution.[204] But when Henry VII and his mother, Margaret Beautfort, wished to found two almshouses at Westminster, one for thirteen poor men and the other for poor

[198] J. Imray, *The Charity of Richard Whittington* (London, 1968), 10–11.

[199] See M. Groom, 'Piety and Locality: Studies in Urban and Rural Religion in Surrey *c.*1450–*c.*1550' (University of London, Ph.D. thesis, 2001), 82–3, 96–105.

[200] For the London almshouses see the gazetteer to M. D. Lobel (ed.), *Historic Towns Atlas: The City of London from Prehistoric Times to c.1520* (Oxford, 1989); W. K. Jordan, *The Charities of London 1480–1660* (London, 1960), 135–9; V. Snelling, 'The Almshouses of Medieval London 1400–1550' (Royal Holloway, University of London, MA thesis, 1997).

[201] The almshouse for fourteen poor men and women was established at Ratcliffe in 1536 by Avice and Nicholas Gybson, grocer, who bequeathed them to the coopers' company at his death in 1540. Avice died in 1554 when the coopers took possession, see P. Maryfield, "*Love as Brethren*": *A Quincentennial History of the Coopers' Company* (London, 2000), 35–9.

[202] *London and Middlesex Chantry Certificate 1548*, ed. C. Kitching (London Record Society, 1980); 18. Rosser, *Medieval Westminster*, 320–1.

[203] *Chantry Certificate*, ed. Kitching, 152.

[204] Stow, *Survey*, i. 183; *VCH, London*, 583; Jordan, *Charities*, 137 and n. where he confuses St Anthony's with St Antholin's.

women, they saw no need to place these establishments within the context of a religious order.[205] All that was believed to be necessary in this case was to set a priest in charge of the establishment; in this way costs were reduced, for the endowment had to support only the poor and not also a group of religious. But in this we observe a reversal of the priorities of the twelfth century: then the main purpose was to found a house of religious; the care of the sick and old was but incidental to the main work of the foundation. By the early sixteenth century the charitable purposes were now uppermost and patrons sought out new ways to relieve the problems of poverty, pain, and old age: these had become the primary objectives.

One group within society posed particular problems when they became old, namely secular priests.[206] Members of religious orders were cared for by their communities, but secular priests who had neither families nor communities had no one to care for them in their old age. William Elsing in 1331 founded a hospital near Cripplegate (Elsyng Spital) which was originally intended to care particularly for blind priests although it later became an 'ordinary' Augustinian house and hospital. A century later, in 1442 the fraternity of St Augustine Papey was established to provide shelter, food, and warmth for sixty poor priests who were to live together in a house near to the church of St Augustine Papey, which now became their chapel; here mass was said daily and the inmates received 14*d.* a week, together with the services of a 'barber and launder and one to dresse and provyde for hyr mete and drynke'.[207] This later fraternity, which included lay brothers and sisters in its society, was modest and self-governing, and many Londoners bequeathed money to the brotherhood in return for prayers.[208]

Thus Londoners, in the fifteenth century, choosing to work through a number of organizations—the religious house, the city company, the parish fraternity—had made available before the 1520s some 250 or 300 places in almshouses for those who were too ill, maimed, or old to be able to work any more. Whether this charitable provision was provoked by an increase in poverty or merely by a heightened perception of possible solutions to the problem, it is difficult to tell. What seems certain, however, is that the remarkable almshouse provision by Londoners in the sixteenth century was not the result of Protestant teaching. After the 1540s and the official abolition of the doctrine of purgatory, London testators could focus their charity on institutions for the relief of their fellow Londoners. Almshouses, by now

[205] D. Knowles and R. N. Hadcock, *Medieval Religious Houses: England and Wales* (rev. edn., 1971), 402; Colvin, *History of the King's Works*, iii. 206–10.

[206] See N. Orme, 'The Sufferings of the Clergy: Illness and Old Age in Exeter Diocese, 1300–1540', in Pelling and Smith (eds.), *Life, Death and the Elderly*, 62–73.

[207] Gairdner, *Historical Collections*, p. viii.

[208] For Elsyngspital see *VCH, London*, 535–6; A. Bowtell, 'Elyngspittal' (Royal Holloway, University of London, MA thesis, 2001); for St Augustine Papey, *VCH, London*, 550 and T. Hugo, 'The Hospital of Le Papey in the City of London', *TLMAS* 5 (1881), 183–221. In the fifteenth century Jesus (or Doctors') Commons was established in Dowgate as a college where secular priests might live together: Stow, *Survey*, i. 231; G. Squibb, *Doctors' Commons* (Oxford, 1977).

a tried and tested solution to the problems of the elderly poor, multiplied in London itself, and in towns and villages all over England.[209]

The Black Death and other endemic diseases may have reduced the population by 50 per cent, from a 'high' of 80,000 in 1300 to 40,000 by 1400. In the century following 1375 there is remarkably little reference to poor people, particularly to poor people *en masse*, in the surviving London records, although there are many such references earlier in the thirteenth century, and certainly later in the sixteenth. It may be suggested that the gap between the needs of the old, sick, poor, and young and what was available for their relief, was narrower in London in the later medieval period than at any other time. This relief was secured by a series of measures, some provided by the city corporately, some by religious houses, some by fraternities and companies, and much by charitable individuals working through these institutions, or independently. From the late fifteenth century, however, the rising population began to gnaw away at the prosperity that had underpinned the comparatively successful welfare provision in London, which had been one of the hallmarks of the city in the late-medieval period.

[209] See Jordan, *Charities*, 136–9; Thomson argues that the rise in the number of almshouses in the sixteenth century was due not to Protestantism, but to an increase in the problem of poverty, 'Piety and Charity', 184.

Epilogue

In 1339 at a congregation of the mayor, aldermen and 'an immense commonalty' it was asserted that rioting was inappropriate in London which was the mirror, and set the example, for the whole realm.[1] Although this assertion comes comparatively early in the period, it well expresses the 'school prefect' tone that the city of London came to adopt as the centuries wore on. It was necessary for the city to be better governed and more law-abiding because it was the premier city of the realm, the king's chamber, and the model for all other towns in England. There is no doubt that London became a more peaceful, salubrious, and orderly city in the course of the three hundred years that have been under review here. But it was not a steady development and there were losses along the way. The Londoner probably had less say in how the city was governed in 1500 than he had had in 1200, although he could play a part in other governing structures such as those of his craft, his parish, or his religious fraternity. Protest was possible but the surviving records do not suggest that it often led to changes in policy.[2] Yet the possibility of protest, and the existence of channels for expressing alternative opinions, tended to moderate extreme self-interest on the part of the governors. Changes in the way London was governed had to be negotiated—they could not be imposed. And there is no doubt that in the three hundred years reviewed here there were changes.

In the first place there was a significant change in the nature of the relations between the Londoners and the Crown. The thirteenth century was characterized by constant friction over the payment of arbitrary royal tallage and yet, in the changed circumstances of the fifteenth century, the financial issue revolved instead around loans rather than taxation, and the discussions about these were conducted in a comparatively calm and formulaic manner. The intervening period had seen two significant assertions of royal power: Edward I's seizure of the city's liberties in 1285–97 and a similar seizure by Richard II in 1392. For all the financial and political weakness of the Lancastrian kings, there was never any doubt where ultimate power lay, however important the presentational role the citizens might be required to play in converting *de facto* kings into *de iure* ones.

It is surely right to see the years when Edward I ruled London directly through his appointed warden as crucial in breaking the power of the comparatively small

[1] *CPMR 1323–1364*, 107, 'qest merour et en sanple de tute la terre'.

[2] See T. F. Reddaway and L. M. Walker, *The Early History of the Goldsmiths' Company 1327–1509* (London, 1975), ch. 6; C. Barron, 'Ralph Holland and the London Radicals, 1438–1444', in R. Holt and G. Rosser (eds.), *The English Medieval Town: A Reader in English Urban History 1200–1540* (London, 1990), 160–83.

number of families who had ruled London for the previous hundred years.[3] In this period it is clear that the aldermen began to find it useful to associate with them in their decision-making other tried and trusted men from the different wards. In this way some form of representative assembly, comparable to the commons meeting together in Parliament, began to emerge, and would develop in the course of the fourteenth century into the common council. The way in which this council should be selected, whether by crafts or by wards, was a matter of intense debate in the fourteenth century and that this should have been of such concern bears witness to the importance of the new body. Alongside this important development there emerged also a civic bureaucracy, able to advise the court of aldermen and the court of common council, and to provide the secretariat necessary to make effective the decisions taken by the elected assemblies. New officers came to be created to meet new needs, such as the serjeant of the channel first appointed in 1385 to oversee the cleanliness of the city in the aftermath of outbreaks of plague.[4]

The plague that struck London in 1348–9, and again in 1361–2, had halved the population of the city by the end of the century.[5] This dramatic drop in the population of London created massive problems in the short term and great opportunities over the longer term. Those Londoners who survived the outbreaks, or who were drawn to the city from the countryside, enjoyed higher wages, greater opportunities for work, and a higher standard of living. It is noticeable how few references there are to mass poverty in London in the period 1350–1500.[6] It seems, indeed, as if the survivors were at considerable pains to create and fund new, but more selective, institutions such as almshouses, chantry colleges, and schools to provide help and opportunities to improve the lot of the young, the sick, and the old. They now had the means to endow such institutions and this creative 'social' charity is characteristic of London benefactions in the later part of the period.

The Black Death arrived close on the heels of the dramatic bankruptcies of the Italian bankers who had largely funded royal government since the 1290s. The plague and the bankruptcies created opportunities for native English merchants, most of whom became Londoners even if they were not born in the city, to create considerable fortunes. In some cases it is possible to chart the careers of men such as Adam Fraunceys, John Pyel, and Richard Lyons or, in the next generation, Richard Whittington and John Heende.[7] Their rapidly made fortunes created

[3] G. A. Williams, *Medieval London from Commune to Capital* (London, 1963), esp. 74, 262 and app. B. In the thirteenth century eighteen families produced two or more aldermen over several generations; in the period 1350–1450 there were only two families (Wotton and Reynwell) that produced an alderman in successive generations.

[4] See Ch. 8.

[5] See B. Megson, 'Mortality Among London Citizens in the Black Death', *Medieval Prosopography*, 19 (1998), 125–33.

[6] See Ch. 11.

[7] *A Calendar of the Cartularies of John Pyel and Adam Fraunceys*, ed. S. O'Connor (Camden Society, 1993); id., 'Finance, Diplomacy and Politics: Royal Service by Two London Merchants in the Reign of Edward III', *Historical Research*, 67 (1994), 18–39; A. R. Myers, 'The Wealth of Richard Lyons', in T. A. Sandquist and M. R. Powicke (eds.), *Essays in Medieval History Presented to Bertie Wilkinson* (Toronto, 1969), 301–29; C. Barron, 'Richard Whittington: The Man behind the Myth', in

sharp personal rivalries such as that between the grocer Nicholas Brembre and the draper John of Northampton in the 1370s and 1380s.[8] These personal conflicts, however, had a new significance. Whereas in the thirteenth century they arose simply between wealthy and competitive individuals, by the end of the fourteenth century such men tended to lead, or to use, groupings of men who shared common economic interests. In the century following the accession of Edward I, craft and trade groupings in London developed as increasingly formal associations, drawing up rules, electing officers, controlling the work and trading practices of members, and attempting to exercise monopolies. Such groups were by no means always homogeneous in the later fourteenth century, but they could be used by ambitious men with wider political agendas of their own. These new craft associations tried, and failed, to form the constituencies for elections to the common council but the less contentious wards were favoured instead. Although the groupings of craftsmen and merchants did not achieve a formal place within the civic constitution they did, in 1319, secure control over entries to the freedom. No man might exercise a craft or trade in London as a citizen unless he had been first accepted by the men whose craft he intended to practise. Moreover, in the fifteenth century, the masters and wardens of the crafts came to be frequently consulted by the mayor and aldermen about matters of taxation and public order. In the same way they came to be used also as agents to carry out the decisions of the courts of aldermen and common council.

The economy of London seems always to have been diversified and comparatively buoyant. The years between 1200 and 1500 saw some marked changes. The manufacturing base of the city's economy grew and became more specialized, albeit challenged in the later fifteenth century by the influx of alien craftsmen and manufactured goods from the Continent, especially the Low Countries. The early export of English cloth through London had given way, by the late thirteenth century, to the export of wool and the import of cloth from the Low Countries. In part as a result of Edward III's policy of war with France and his interference in the wool trade for political ends, English cloth began to be manufactured on a larger scale and to a higher standard. From the mid-fourteenth century it was exported abroad in ever-increasing amounts. Not only were the aliens squeezed out of the English overseas trade but London came increasingly to dominate exports, so that by 1540 about 75 per cent of all England's overseas trade was passing through London.[9] Since a wide range of goods was imported into London and, moreover, many goods were also manufactured in or near the city, it is not surprising that many London fortunes were made in the distributive trade. As the great fairs declined (from the beginning of the fourteenth century) men began to travel to London to supply their local needs and to carry back to their castles, manors, and

A. E. J. Hollaender and W. Kellaway (eds.), *Studies in London History Presented to P. E. Jones* (London, 1969), 197–248; J. Stratford, 'John Hende', in *New DNB* (forthcoming).

[8] See P. Nightingale, 'Capitalists, Crafts and Constitutional Change in Late Fourteenth Century London', *Past and Present*, 124 (1989), 3–25 .

[9] See Ch. 5.

monasteries the consumer goods that, increasingly, were only to be found in the city.

There is no doubt that in this period London increased its lead over other English towns: it sent four members to Parliament when other boroughs sent only two, and it virtually monopolized English overseas trade. The Hanse merchants in the course of the fifteenth century increasingly focused their attention on the London Steelyard. The king spent more time at Westminster and in his other palaces in the Home Counties. Whereas London paid 1.9 per cent of the national taxation in 1334, by 1524 it was contributing 11 per cent.[10] In the thirteenth century perhaps 1.5 per cent of the population of England lived in London, but by 1540 it may have risen to 3.5 per cent and the figure rose to nearly 11 per cent by 1700.[11] There may seem to be something unjustifiably Whiggish in this analysis which finds in the medieval period the seeds of later greatness. But in some ways the fifteenth century marked the apogee of London's success: not in terms of population, nor in terms of wealth, but in its ability to exercise effective self-government. As the population began once more to grow in the late fifteenth century, and yet more dramatically after 1540, and as the centralizing authority of the Tudors began to take a grip on the English kingdom, so the autonomy of the city of London began to be eroded. The city grew out beyond the limits of the mayor's jurisdiction and this made effective government virtually impossible without royal support. The Tudor monarchs used Parliament, and parish vestries, in ways that came to undermine the powers of the mayor and aldermen. Moreover the Reformation, and the consequent parliamentary statutes, deprived the city companies of their important *raison d'être* as associations gathered together to pray for past and present members. Much of their landed wealth, which had been given to them for these 'superstitious' purposes, was confiscated. More important than this, however, was the fracturing of the vital link between members that had been based not only upon a shared craft or trade but also upon common religious concerns. The functions of the companies began to atrophy and they fossilized into the respectable charitable institutions that we know today. The twin forces of rapid demographic growth, and a rupture in the religious underpinning of many (albeit not all) the social institutions in the city, meant that London in 1600 was very different from the city of a hundred years earlier, as John Stow was among the first to point out.[12]

10 See R. E. Glasscock, *The Lay Subsidy of 1334* (London, 1975), p. xvi, 187, and J. Sheail, *The Regional Distribution of Wealth in England as Indicated by the 1524/5 Lay Subsidy Returns* ed. R. W. Hoyle, 2 vols. (List and Index Society, 1998), ii. 208, 438.

11 These figures are calculated from R. M. Smith, 'Demographic Developments in Rural England, 1300–1348: A Survey', in B. M. Campbell (ed.), *Before the Black Death* (Manchester, 1989), 49; D. Keene, 'A New Study of London before the Great Fire', *Urban History Yearbook* (1984), 11–21; E. A. Wrigley and R. S. Schofield, *The Population History of England, 1541–1871: A Reconstruction* (London, 1981), 207–8. P. J. Corfield, 'Urban Development in England and Wales in the Sixteenth and Seventeenth Centuries', in D. C. Coleman and A. H. John (eds.), *Trade, Government and Economy in Pre-Industrial England: Essays Presented to F. J. Fisher* (London, 1976), 214–47, esp. 217. I am very grateful to Miss Barbara Harvey for help in putting together these figures.

12 See I. Archer, 'The Nostalgia of John Stow', in D. L. Smith, R. Streier, and D. Bevington (eds.), *The Theatrical City: Culture, Theatre and Politics in London 1576–1649* (Cambridge, 1995), 17–34.

The conflicts with the Crown, and between Londoners themselves, that characterized the city in the thirteenth century and much of the fourteenth, created a city that, in the fifteenth century, was notably well governed and prosperous. While the nobles fought each other to extinction on the rural battlefields of England, no one was lynched or summarily executed in London in this century, which was no mean achievement when one considers the acts of retributive barbarity meted out in Paris, Ypres, or Ghent in the same period. Increasingly those who governed London came to reflect upon their responsibilities as well as on their opportunities. There is a world of difference between the sharp sectarian viewpoint of alderman Arnold fitz-Thedmar who wrote his contemporary chronicle in the mid-thirteenth century and the detached, almost amused, viewpoint of Robert Fabyan who compiled his account of London in the early years of the sixteenth.[13] Gone is the passion of fitz-Thedmar, and his anger. Perhaps these qualities had been beaten out of London's governors by both the Crown and the demands of those they governed. The aldermen and the 'civil servants' who ruled London in the late-medieval period took their tasks seriously and reflected upon their role. Andrew Horn, the city chamberlain in the early fourteenth century, copied some of Brunetto Latini's treatise on civic government, his *Trésor*, into his *Liber Custumarum* which he bequeathed to the city at his death and where it still remains.[14] John Carpenter, the common clerk of London in the early fifteenth century, collected one of the most extensive private libraries to be found in fifteenth-century London; it included works by Aristotle and Seneca. Many of these books he bequeathed to the new public library at Guildhall for the common profit of the students there.[15] City aldermen commissioned handbooks to help them to carry out their tasks. Thomas Carleton, an embroiderer and alderman in 1382–3 and again in 1388 (in the period of annual elections of aldermen) had compiled a book into which he had copied, dutifully if not very accurately, Fitz-Stephen's account of London in the twelfth century.[16] Thomas Cook, draper and alderman from 1456 to 1471, had composed for him a handbook in which was written out all that he needed to know about holding wardmotes, administering oaths to ward officials, or presiding over the sheriffs' court; but he chose also to include a good deal of information about the radical protests, and proposed reforms,

[13] fitz-Thedmar's Latin chronicle was edited by T. Stapleton as *Liber de Antiquis Legibus seu Chronica Maiorum et Vicecomitum Londoniarum* (Camden Society, 1846), and translated by H. T. Riley in his *Chronicles of the Mayors and Sheriffs of London, A.D. 1188 to A.D. 1274* (London, 1863); Fabyan's chronicle was edited by A. H. Thomas and I. D. Thornley as *The Great Chronicle of London* (London, 1938).

[14] Printed in *Munimenta Gildhallae Londoniensis: Liber Albus, Liber Custumarum et Liber Horn*, ed. H. T. Riley, 3 vols. (Rolls Series, 1859–62), ii. p. 1, 16–25; see also S. Reynolds, 'Medieval Urban History and the History of Political Thought', *Urban History Yearbook* (1982), 14–23; and J. Catto, 'Andrew Horn: Law and History in Fourteenth-Century England', in R. H. C. Davis and J. M. Wallace-Hadrill (eds.), *The Writing of History in the Middle Ages: Essays Presented to R. W. Southern* (Oxford, 1981), 367–91.

[15] See T. Brewer, *Memoir of the Life and Times of John Carpenter, Town Clerk of London* (London, 1856), where his will is printed in full and the books described, 121–44.

[16] BL, Additional MS 38131; see H. Kleineke, 'Carleton's Book: William FitzStephen's "Description of London" in a Late Fourteenth-Century Common-Place Book', *Historical Research*, 74 (2001), 117–26.

dating back to the reign of Richard II a hundred years earlier.[17] These men, and others like them, were reflecting upon the tasks that they had been elected to carry out.

In the sixteenth century London faced massive problems caused by rapid population growth, poverty, shortage of work, endemic plague, threatened famine, and religious controversy. In these circumstances, and with an eye to urban disorder in continental towns, the Tudor monarchs and their counsellors feared the worst. But, to the surprise of all, stability was maintained. There were many reasons for this but, in part, it was due to the maturity of those who governed the city and who had come to realize that to govern London was a responsibility and a duty, and not simply a golden opportunity for personal gain. That the rhetoric of the 'common good' had penetrated the world of action can be seen in the countless acts of charitable altruism chronicled by John Stow. The failed experiments and hard lessons of the years between 1200 and 1500 created the governing structures that underpinned the remarkable prosperity and stability of sixteenth-century London.

[17] Trinity College, Cambridge, MS O.3.11.

Appendix 1: The Mayors and Sheriffs of London 1190–1558

Compiled by Anne Lancashire

The base list used for the mayor and sheriffs for each year is that provided in C. L. Kingsford's 2-volume edition (1908) of John Stow's *A Survey of London* (here cited as Stow, *Survey*), ii. 150–83. Kingsford has corrected Stow, and provides useful name and spelling alternatives in footnotes; the non-obvious alternatives have also been provided here in footnotes. Kingsford's names have been checked against, and corrected according to, A. B. Beaven's *The Aldermen of The City of London*, 2 vols. (London, 1908–13); all corrections other than spelling changes have been footnoted. For sheriffs, A. Hughes's *List of Sheriffs for England and Wales* (PRO, London, 1898, rev. edn. with corrections and additions, New York, 1963), in a Corporation of London Records Office copy with handwritten annotations made apparently at the PRO,[1] has also been consulted, and, for mayors, a *c.*1970s CLRO typescript handlist. Table 2 of S. Reynolds's 'Rulers of London' article in *History*, 57 (1972) has been used as well, for the specific time period 1190–1216, and also C. N. L. Brooke with G. Keir's *London 800–1216: The Shaping of a City* (London, 1975). Any information taken from Hughes, the CLRO handlist, Reynolds, or Brooke with Keir has been footnoted. All first names have been normalized (as generally also in both Stow, *Survey*, and Beaven); surnames have been spelled as in Beaven, both for Beaven's listed aldermen and for non-aldermen also referred to in Beaven's volumes; for aldermen, where there is a choice of Beaven surname spellings, that (including any alternative) found in the chronological listing of aldermen is used, including any in the text immediately preceding the start of the chronological listing in volume 1, and for non-aldermen, the index form is used. For names not in Beaven, the Stow, *Survey*, main surname spellings are followed (with 'Fitz' reproduced as 'fitz-', as in Beaven) except where footnoted otherwise; and S. (for 'Saint') is reproduced as St, 'filius' as 'fitz-'. For names not in either Beaven or Stow, *Survey*, the surname spellings followed are from the indexes of the relevant volumes of R. R. Sharpe's eleven-volume *Calendar of Letter-Books A–L* (London, 1899–1912).

The companies (or, in early years, trades/occupations) to which the various mayors and sheriffs belonged have been provided in all cases possible: from Stow, *Survey* (unmarked if from the edition's list of mayors and sheriffs, footnoted if from elsewhere in the volumes or in cases of disagreement), from Beaven (unmarked if from the chronological listings of aldermen, footnoted if from elsewhere in the volumes or in cases of disagreement), and from other primary sources (for example, City Letter Books, Journals, and Repertories, and livery company MSS), as footnoted, where neither Stow, *Survey*, nor Beaven provides them, or in cases of disagreement. Where neither Stow, *Survey*, nor Beaven provides the information, and a Letter Book, Journal, and Repertory agree on a mayor's or sheriff's company, and also where a Journal and/or Repertory is absent or silent, only the Letter Book is cited; if only a Journal or a Repertory provides a company, that source is cited (the Repertory only if Journal information is lacking); disagreements among Letter Books, Journals, and

[1] Personal communication, CLRO.

Repertories are noted.[2] Stow, *Survey*, rarely provides sheriffs' companies, but supplies most mayors' companies from 1308. Most mayors served first as sheriff; but a sheriff's company is taken from Beaven or footnoted from elsewhere even where Stow, *Survey*, provides the company once that sheriff has become mayor. A number of early chronicles and a few selected secondary works have also been used, and cited as sources of company designations, where no designations have been found in Stow, *Survey*, Beaven, or primary manuscript sources, or where primary-source designations disagree or seem to require reinforcement. To avoid a proliferation of largely misleading footnotes, however, where one or more chronicles, only, disagree with Stow, *Survey*, with Beaven, or with primary manuscript sources, such disagreements have not normally been noted (the chronicles being in large part the less reliable sources). A conservative approach to company designations has included not identifying a sheriff by company where the same name occurs in the records with a company designation but without the person so named being also clearly identified as the individual who served as sheriff (although company possibilities are provided in a few such cases: for example, where more than one source is involved). Names are much repeated in this period, and the same (or nearly the same) name cannot be assumed always to belong to the same individual, nor can members of the same family be assumed always to have belonged to the same trade or company. Even with this conservative approach, the list will not be fully accurate in the company designations supplied, in part because—given all of human error, the possibility at some periods for individuals to belong to more than one company, and the occasional later incorrect claiming by a company of a earlier mayor or sheriff—even the specific primary sources consulted (as well as the identifications made by Beaven, Stow, *Survey*, etc.) will not always be correct, and in part because an individual's trade and his company, where not the same, may cause a misidentification. Also part of the problem, as noted by George Unwin, is that trade specialization among elite Londoners largely began only in the fourteenth century.[3]

Dates of the death of a mayor or sheriff in office, and of the election etc. of a replacement mayor or sheriff, are taken from Beaven where he provides them, and otherwise from the Letter Books, Journals, Repertories, or other primary or secondary sources, in that order of priority; only the first source in that order is cited, unless primary sources disagree. Where more than one source is provided, without disagreement having been noted, this is because the combination of sources is required for the full information here given. For the period before 1275, various kinds of information are also supplied (and footnoted) from Riley's edition (1863) of fitz-Thedmar's *Chronicles of the Mayors and Sheriffs of London.*

The City Letter Books, Journals, and Repertories, from 1347 (for the Letter Books), often specify, for a given year, which sheriff was chosen by the mayor, the other being elected by the commonalty. An asterisk after a sheriff's name indicates that one or more of these specific civic records series identify him as the mayor's choice; where such an identification has been found only outside these civic records series it is footnoted. A bold arabic numeral of 2, 3, or 4 with an m or s, at the right of a mayor's or sheriff's listing, indicates that the individual concerned is serving as mayor or as sheriff for a non-consecutive second, third, or fourth time between 1190 and 1558 (possible pre-1190 service is not noted[4]). Where this information has not come from Stow, *Survey*, or from Beaven, the source is footnoted. An

[2] Letter Books, Journals, and Repertories have largely been searched, for company memberships of mayors and sheriffs, only in their election listings.

[3] G. Unwin, *The Gilds and Companies of London* (London, 1908), 58.

[4] For such possible service see e.g. Brooke with Keir, 234 and n. 3.

apparent non-consecutive recurrence of a name is not treated as another term for the mayor or sheriff concerned unless Stow, *Survey*, and/or Beaven (neither being footnoted), or another footnoted source, has indicated that this is indeed the same individual. Names are not included of individuals elected sheriff or mayor but for one reason or another never sworn into office; this includes sheriffs who served for only a few days before being rejected by the king and replaced.

Grocers were originally called Pepperers; the company appears to have emerged as Grocers in 1372;[5] and the Merchant Taylors were until 6 January 1503 the Tailors and Linen Armourers. For both companies the original name is used until the year of the change, and then the new name, regardless of whether the sources consulted use the old or the new designation. The Fishmongers and the Stockfishmongers were originally different companies which, after one union which did not succeed, were finally united on a permanent basis in 1536.[6] The two different names are here reproduced until 1536, from which year only the Fishmonger designation is used, regardless of the readings of the sources.

The years under which the mayors and sheriffs are listed are basically (with some fluctuations in some early years) the years of the normal term of office, throughout most of this period, of a mayor and of a sheriff: 28/29 Oct.–28/29 Oct. for a mayor, 28 Sept.–28 Sept. for a sheriff.[7] Election and initial oath-taking for both mayors and sheriffs was at Guildhall; subsequently mayors also swore an oath, and sheriffs were presented, at Westminster or at the Tower of London. Dates are provided, where available, for elections of mayors and sheriffs who replaced others who died or were removed from office.

In the listings themselves, (W) identifies an appointed warden (or *custos*: Stow, *Survey* uses C). A bold Arabic numeral of 2 or 3 with a w, at the right of a warden's listing, indicates that the individual named is serving for a second or third non-consecutive time as warden. All footnoted information, such as company membership, for a mayor serving consecutive years in office is supplied only at his first year; it is resupplied, however, at the start of a subsequent non-consecutive term. (For sheriffs, footnoted information is repeated even in consecutive years, as consecutive years in sheriffs' listings do not stand out as clearly as in mayors' listings.) For abbreviations used in the footnotes, see the list of abbreviations. I am grateful, for generous provision of access to manuscripts and permission to cite them, to the Corporation of London Records Office, to the Guildhall Library (Corporation of London), and to the livery companies whose manuscripts are cited below: in alphabetical order, the Worshipful Companies of Clothworkers, Drapers, Goldsmiths, Grocers, Ironmongers, Mercers, Merchant Taylors, Pewterers, and Skinners.

[5] See P. Nightingale, *A Medieval Mercantile Community: The Grocers' Company & the Politics and Trade of London 1000–1485* (New Haven, Conn., 1995), 237.

[6] For the 31 March 1536 date, see GL MS 6750 (2 separate, dated copies of the relevant company charter). See also CLRO Rep. 9 fos. 172ᵛ–175ᵛ (30 March).

[7] The mayor assumed office in the city on 28 Oct., but was not fully mayor until sworn before the king or the king's representatives on (at first) 28 or (later; from before 1300) 29 Oct. See Beaven, ii. p. xxviii and *Liber Albus*, 18–23; also *Chronicles of the Mayors and Sheriffs of London, A.D. 1188 to A.D. 1274*, ed. and trans. H. T. Riley (London, 1863), 12, 21, 22, 74. For the sheriffs' 28 Sept. date of assumption of office see *Liber Albus*, 39-40. (Beaven also provides, ii. pp. xxviii and xxxiii, the changing dates of the mayors' and sheriffs' elections during this period.) The sheriffs did not have to be presented to the king or his representatives before their term of office formally began; see also *The Historical Charters and Constitutional Documents of the City of London*, ed. W. de Gray Birch (London, 1887), 16, 21, 56. See also the City Letter Books (CLRO), from Letter Book C onwards.

Year	**Mayor** (W = Warden)	**Sheriffs**
1190–1	Henry fitz-Ailwyn[8]	William de Haverell (or Haverill)
		John Bokointe (or Bucuint)
1191–2	Henry fitz-Ailwyn	Nicholas Duket
		Peter Nevelun
1192–3	Henry fitz-Ailwyn	Roger le Duc
		Roger fitz-Alan
1193–4	Henry fitz-Ailwyn	William fitz-Isabel (or fitz-Sabel)
		William fitz-Alulf
1194–5	Henry fitz-Ailwyn	Robert Besaunt
		Jukel (or Jokel)
1195–6	Henry fitz-Ailwyn	Godard de Antioche
		Robert fitz-Durand
1196–7	Henry fitz-Ailwyn	Nicholas Duket **2s**
		Robert Blund (or fitz-Bartholomew)[9]
1197–8	Henry fitz-Ailwyn	Constantine fitz-Alulf[10]
		Robert de Bel[11]
1198–9	Henry fitz-Ailwyn	Ernulf fitz-Alulf[12]
		Richard Blunt[13]
1199–1200	Henry fitz-Ailwyn	Roger de Deserto
		James 'Alderman' (or fitz-Bartholomew)
1200–1	Henry fitz-Ailwyn	Simon de Aldermanbury
		William fitz-Alice[14]
1201–2	Henry fitz-Ailwyn	Norman Blund
		John de Cayo (or Cay)
1202–3	Henry fitz-Ailwyn	Walter Brun
		William Chamberleyn
1203–4	Henry fitz-Ailwyn	Thomas de Haverell[15]
		Hamond Brond
1204–5	Henry fitz-Ailwyn	John Waleran
		Richard Winchester
1205–6	Henry fitz-Ailwyn	John fitz-Elinandi[16]
		Edmund fitz-Gerard[17]

[8] Fitz-Ailwyn has traditionally been identified as a draper, but without sufficient evidence; see Beaven, ii. 225 and also A. H. Johnson, *The History of The Worshipful Company of the Drapers of London*, 5 vols. (Oxford, 1914–22), i. 75 n. 1.

[9] See n. to Richard Blunt, sheriff 1198–9.

[10] See n. to Ernulf fitz-Alulf, sheriff 1198–9.

[11] Or le Bel: Stow, *Survey*, ii. 150 n. 12, and *Mayors and Sheriffs*, 2.

[12] Brother of Constantine fitz-Alulf, sheriff 1197–8 (Beaven, i. 365).

[13] Or Richard fitz-Bartholomew: see Stow, *Survey*, ii.150 n. 14, and *Mayors and Sheriffs*, 2; Beaven, i. 364–5 gives this as the alternative surname for 1196–7 sheriff Robert Blund, and Reynolds, 356, lists the sheriffs 1196–7 and 1198–9 as brothers.

[14] Brother of Martin fitz-Alice, sheriff 1213–14 (Reynolds, 356)?

[15] Son of William de Haverell, sheriff 1190–1 (Beaven, i, 365).

[16] Or John Heliland: see Stow, *Survey*, i. 151 n. 8, and *Mayors and Sheriffs*, 3.

[17] Or Edmund de la Hale: see Stow, *Survey*, i. 151 n. 9, and *Mayors and Sheriffs*, 3.

1206–7	Henry fitz-Ailwyn	Henry of St Alban's Serlo le Mercer *Mercer*[18]
1207–8	Henry fitz-Ailwyn	William Hardel *Vintner? Draper?*[19] Robert Winchester
1208–9	Henry fitz-Ailwyn	Peter Duke[20] Thomas Nele[21]
1209–10	Henry fitz-Ailwyn	Peter Nevelun[22] William Blund[23]
1210–11	Henry fitz-Ailwyn	Adam de Witebi Stephen le Gras
1211–12	Henry fitz-Ailwyn died 19 Sept. 1212[24] Roger fitz-Alan replaced fitz-Ailwyn[25]	Joce fitz-Peter John Garland
1212–13	Roger fitz-Alan	Ralph Helyland Constantine "juvenis" (or fitz-Alulf[26])
1213–14	Roger fitz-Alan	Martin fitz-Alice[27] Peter Bate
1214–15	Serlo le Mercer[28] *Mercer*[30]	Salomon de Basing[29] Hugh Basing
1215–16	William Hardel *Vintner? Draper?*[31]	John Travers Andrew Nevelun[32]

[18] Beaven, i. 337 identifies as a mercer the later mayor Serlo le Mercer, who is the same individual as this sheriff (see Reynolds, 356).

[19] See n. to William Hardel, mayor 1215–16 (who is the same individual as this sheriff: see Reynolds, 356–7, who also suggests that Ralph Hardel, mayor 1254–5, is this William Hardel's son).

[20] Reynolds, 356–7 names him Peter le Duc and suggests that his father was a sheriff [Roger le Duc sheriff, 1192–3?].

[21] Or Thomas alderman (or Thomas fitz-Nigel): Reynolds, 356–7, Hughes, 200 (Thomas Aldermannus); or Thomas fitz-Neal: *Mayors and Sheriffs*, 3.

[22] Probably a son of Peter Nevelun, sheriff 1191–2 (Stow, *Survey*, ii, 51 n. 15); perhaps instead the sheriff 1191–2 in another term (Reynolds, 356); father of Andrew Nevelun, sheriff 1215–16 (Beaven, i. 365).

[23] Or William Wite: see Stow, *Survey*, ii. 151 n. 16, and *Mayors and Sheriffs*, 3.

[24] Stow, *Survey*, ii. 152 n. 4.

[25] Beaven, i. 365.

[26] See Beaven, ii. 227; Reynolds, 356–7 suggests he may be the son of Constantine fitz-Alulf, sheriff 1197-98.

[27] Brother of William fitz-Alice, sheriff 1200–1 (Reynolds, 356)?

[28] Mayor in 1215 [not 1214–15], 1216–22: Beaven, i. 337 n. *The Great Chronicle of London*, ed. A. H. Thomas and I. D. Thornley (London, 1938), 5, has Roger fitz-Alan mayor for part of this year and Serlo le Mercer mayor for part, as does *A Chronicle*, 8; *Annales Londonienses*, 17 dates fitz-Alan's removal in May 1215. Brooke with Keir, 376, however, list Serlo le Mercer as mayor 1214–15.

[29] Stow, *Survey*, ii. 152 has no 'de', but presumably this is the mayor of 1216–17 (also without a 'de' in Stow, *Survey*) who is de Basing in Beaven, i. 366.

[30] Mercer: Beaven, i. 337 n.

[31] Williams, 54, speaks of this mayor in terms of a vintner family dynasty; *A Chronicle*, 8, calls him a draper.

[32] Also called Andrew fitz-Peter (Beaven, i, 365); brother of Peter Nevelun, sheriff 1209–10 (Reynolds, 356).

1216–17[33]	James Alderman until 21 May 1217 Salomon de Basing replaced James Alderman	Benedict Senturer[34] *Goldsmith*[35] William Blund[36]
1217–18	Serlo le Mercer[37] **2m** *Mercer*	Thomas Bukerel Ralph Eiland[38] **2s**
1218–19	Serlo le Mercer *Mercer*	John Viel Joce le Spicer[39]
1219–20	Serlo le Mercer *Mercer*	John Viel[40] Richard de Wimbledon
1220–1	Serlo le Mercer *Mercer*	Richard Renger Joce Juvenis (or Junior)[41]
1221–2	Serlo le Mercer *Mercer*	Richard Renger Thomas Lambart
1222–3	Richard Renger	William Joynier Thomas Lambart
1223–4	Richard Renger	John Travers **2s** Andrew Bukerel[42]
1224–5	Richard Renger	John Travers Andrew Bukerel[43]
1225–6	Richard Renger	Roger le Duc[44] Martin fitz-William
1226–7	Richard Renger	Roger le Duc[45] Martin fitz-William
1227–8	Roger le Duc[46]	Stephen Bukerel Henry Cocham
1228–9	Roger le Duc	Stephen Bukerel Henry Cocham
1229–30	Roger le Duc	Walter de Winton[47] Robert fitz-John

[33] Stow, *Survey*, ii. 153 does not explain why one mayor replaced the other in this year. *Mayors and Sheriffs*, 4, says that James Alderman lost the mayoralty on Holy Trinity [21 May 1217] and that Salomon de Basing was immediately made mayor. Reynolds, 356–7, and Brooke with Keir, 376, indicate that William Hardel continued as mayor into 1216–17, until Easter 1217.

[34] Only 'Benedict' in Beaven, i. 366, but Benet Senturer in Stow, *Survey*, ii. 152, and in Hughes, 199 (hand-written annotation), and Benedict le Seynter in *Mayors and Sheriffs*, 4.

[35] Goldsmith: *A Chronicle*, 9.

[36] Same as William Blund, sheriff 1209–10?

[37] Beaven, i. 337, begins his second mayoralty in 1216.

[38] Same as Ralph Helyland, sheriff 1212–13 (*Mayors and Sheriffs*, 188; Reynolds, 356).

[39] Or Josce Ponderator: Hughes, 200, and see also Stow, *Survey*, ii. 152 n. 17; Joce le Pesur: *Mayors and Sheriffs*, 4.

[40] Or John Vitalis: Hughes, 200; and see also Stow, *Survey*, ii. 153 n. 1.

[41] Or Josce filius Willelmi: Hughes, 200; and see also Stow, *Survey*, ii. 153 n. 2.

[42] Andrew Bukerel's traditional identification as a pepperer (see Beaven, i. 371) has been denied by Nightingale, 47.

[43] See n. to Andrew Bukerel, sheriff 1223–24.

[44] See n. to Roger le Duc, mayor 1227–8.

[45] See n. to Roger le Duc, mayor 1227–8.

[46] Son of Roger le Duc, sheriff 1192–3? (Reynolds, 355 and 357); same individual as sheriff 1225–7 (see Beaven, i. 371).

[47] Or Walter de Winchester: *Mayors and Sheriffs*, 6; and see also Stow, *Survey*, ii. 154.

1230–1	Roger le Duc	Richard fitz-Walter John de Woborne
1231–2	Andrew Bukerel[48]	Michael de St. Helena Walter le Bufle
1232–3	Andrew Bukerel	Henry de Edmonton[49] Gerard Bat *Vintner?*[50]
1233–4	Andrew Bukerel	Simon fitz-Mary Roger le Blund
1234–5	Andrew Bukerel	Ralph Eswy (or Aswy) *Mercer* John Norman *Draper?*[51]
1235–6	Andrew Bukerel	Gerard Bat **2s** *Vintner?*[52] Robert Hardel
1236–7	Andrew Bukerel	Henry Cocham **2s**[53] Jordan of Coventry
1237–8	Andrew Bukerel died 1237[54] Richard Renger **2m** replaced Bukerel[55]	John Tulesan (or Tolosan) *Draper* Gervase Chamberlain (or Barn) *Cordwainer*
1238–9	Richard Renger died 1239[56] William Joynier replaced Renger[57]	John de Coudres John de Wylhale
1239–40	Gerard Bat *Vintner?*[58] from 13 Jan. 1240[59]	Reginald de Bungheye Ralph Eswy (or Aswy) **2s** *Mercer*
1240–1[60]	Reginald de Bungheye	John Gisors *Pepperer? Vintner?*[61] Michael Tovi *Goldsmith*[62]

48 See n. to Andrew Bukerel, sheriff 1223–4.

49 Or Henry de Edelmeton: Stow, *Survey*, ii. 154 n. 6, and *Mayors and Sheriffs*, 6.

50 See n. to Gerard Bat, mayor 1239–40 (the same individual: see Beaven, i. 372).

51 Draper?: see Williams, 61.

52 See n. to Gerard Bat, mayor 1239–40 (the same individual: see Beaven, i. 372).

53 Second time as sheriff: see 1227–9, and *Mayors and Sheriffs*, 7.

54 Beaven, i. 371.

55 Stow, *Survey*, ii. 154. Although Beaven, i. 371, states that Bukerel died in 1237, he also (i.371) lists Renger as having been mayor in 1238 (not including 1237). No months are given.

56 Beaven, i. 371.

57 Stow, *Survey*, ii. 154; see also Beaven, i. 372.

58 Vintner?: see Fabyan, 331 n. 4.

59 No mayor earlier, because of a dispute with the king (Stow, *Survey*, ii. 155 n. 3).

60 Gerard Bat was elected mayor but not admitted (Stow, *Survey*, ii. 155 n. 5). See *Mayors and Sheriffs*, 8–9.

61 Pepperer: Beaven, i. 372, Williams, 68 and 325; vintner: Nightingale, 126 and 620 (index). Nightingale, 47 states there is no evidence for the traditional association of the Gisors family with the pepperers. She associates the family with the wine trade.

62 Williams, 206, calls the mayor of 1244–5 a goldsmith; this sheriff is the same individual (see Beaven, i. 372).

1241–2	Ralph Eswy (or Aswy) *Mercer*	Thomas de Dunelm (or Durham) John Viel[63]
1242–3	Ralph Eswy (or Aswy) *Mercer*	Robert fitz-John **2s** Ralph Ashwye *Goldsmith*[64]
1243–4	Ralph Eswy (or Aswy) *Mercer*	Hugh Blunt *Goldsmith*[65] Adam de Basing[66] *Draper*[67]
1244–5	Michael Tovi *Goldsmith*[68]	Ralph de Arcubus *Spicer* Nicholas Bat
1245–6[69]	John Gisors *Pepperer? Vinter?*[70] from 11 or 12 Jan. 1246	Nicholas Bat until 14 Dec. 1245 John Gisors **2s** *Pepperer? Vintner?*[71] replaced Bat until 11 or 12 Jan. 1246 Robert de Cornhill replaced Gisors[72] Adam of Bentley *Goldsmith*[73]
1246–7	Peter fitz-Alan	Simon fitz-Mary **2s** Laurence de Frowyk
1247–8[74]	Michael Tovi **2m** *Goldsmith*[75]	William Viel *Draper?*[76] Nicholas Bat **2s**
1248–9	Michael Tovi *Goldsmith*	Nicholas fitz-Joce Geoffrey de Winton (or Winchester)
1249–50[77]	Roger fitz-Roger	Ralph Hardel *Draper? Vintner?* [78] John Tulesan (or Tolosan) **2s** *Draper*

[63] Possibly the son of John Viel, sheriff 1218–20? Recorded in Stow, *Survey*, ii. 155 n. 7 as 'John son of John Viel', and in *Mayors and Sheriffs*, 9, as 'John Fitz-John Vyel', and ibid. 189, as 'John Viel the Younger'.

[64] Goldsmith: Stow, *Survey*, ii. 155 n. 10.

[65] Goldsmith: *Mayors and Sheriffs*, 10, 189.

[66] Or Adam de Giseburne: Stow, *Survey*, ii. 155 n. 12, *Mayors and Sheriffs*, 10.

[67] Draper: Williams, 323.

[68] Goldsmith: Williams, 206.

[69] Stow, *Survey*, ii. 155 n. 16: Michael Tovi was elected mayor (and Beaven, i. 372 lists him as mayor 1244–6, although only 1244–5 at i. 374 n. 3) but the king refused to admit him and John Gisors was sworn in his place on 12 Jan. 1246 [11 Jan., *Mayors and Sheriffs*, 16]; Nicholas Bat was chosen sheriff, but rejected [14 Dec., *Mayors and Sheriffs*, 12], and was succeeded first by John Gisors and then by Robert de Cornhill. See *Mayors and Sheriffs*, 12–13.

[70] See n. to John Gisors, sheriff 1240–1.

[71] See n. to John Gisors, sheriff 1240–1.

[72] Elected 22 Jan. 1246: *Mayors and Sheriffs*, 13.

[73] Goldsmith: *Mayors and Sheriffs*, 12.

[74] According to *Mayors and Sheriffs*, 15, the city was briefly put by the king into the hands of William de Haverille and Edward de Westminster, 23 Aug.–6 Sept. 1248.

[75] Goldsmith: Williams, 206. [76] Draper?: see Williams, 61.

[77] In this year, 18–24 May 1250, the city was again in the king's hands: see *Mayors and Sheriffs*, 17–18.

[78] Draper: Beaven, i. 372; vintner: Williams, 209.

1250–1	John Norman *Draper?*[79]	Humphrey le Feure William fitz-Richard *Draper*[80]
1251–2	Adam de Basing *Draper*[81]	Laurence de Frowyk **2s** Nicholas Bat **3s**
1252–3	John Tulesan (or Tolosan) *Draper*	William de Durham (or Dunelm) Thomas de Wymburne *Goldsmith*
1253–4	Nicholas Bat	John de Norhampton *Tailor? Skinner?*[82] Richard Pickard
1254–5[83]	Ralph Hardel *Draper? Vintner?*[84]	William Eswy (or Aswy) *Mercer* until Feb. 1255 Robert de Linton *Draper*[85] until Feb. 1255 Henry de Walemunt from *c.* 15 Feb. 1255 Stephen de Oystergate (or Doo) *Fishmonger*[86] from *c.* 15 Feb. 1255
1255–6[87]	Ralph Hardel *Draper? Vintner?*	Matthew Bukerel John le Minur
1256–7	Ralph Hardel *Draper? Vintner?*	Richard de Ewell William Ashwie *Draper*[88]
1257–8[89]	Ralph Hardel *Draper? Vintner?* until 1 Feb. 1258 William fitz-Richard *Draper*[90]	Robert de Cateloigne died Oct. or Dec. 1257 Matthew Bukerel **2s** replaced Cateloigne until 1 Feb. 1258

79 Draper?: see Williams, 61.

80 Draper: Williams, 61. (Same individual as later mayor and warden: see Beaven, i. 372.) See also *Annales Londonienses*, 45. 'Le Prestre' (the priest) in *Mayors and Sheriffs*, 19.

81 Draper: Williams, 323.

82 Tailor?: Beaven, i. 374 (the query mark is his); skinner: Williams, 63.

83 Hardel, according to *Mayors and Sheriffs*, 22–3, did not immediately become mayor, because the city was taken into the king's hands (under John Gisors) until 19 Nov. Sheriffs Eswy and Linton, temporarily out of office also with Hardel (*Mayors and Sheriffs*, 22–3), were removed in Feb. 1255 for neglect involving the gaols and were replaced by Walemunt and Oystergate: see Stow, *Survey*, ii. 156 n. 10, and *Mayors and Sheriffs*, 23–4.

84 Draper: Beaven, i. 372; vintner: Williams, 209.

85 Draper: *A Chronicle*, 18.

86 Fishmonger: Williams, 220 and 228.

87 The city was briefly in the king's hands in Nov.; see *Mayors and Sheriffs*, 24–5.

88 'Drapparius': Stow, *Survey*, ii. 156 n. 15; *Mayors and Sheriffs*, 25.

89 For the details of removals and replacements, and one death, during 1257–8 see Stow, *Survey*, ii. 157 n. 1. An appointed warden served between Hardel and fitz-Richard. Beaven, ii. p. xxxix, however, gives Cateloigne's death as in Dec. 1257, and *Mayors and Sheriffs*, 31 gives 14 Dec., while Stow, *Survey* gives 19 Oct. 1257 as the date upon which Bukerel succeeded Cateloigne. Beaven, i. 373, lists fitz-Thomas as sheriff only in 1258. See also *Mayors and Sheriffs*, 33–9.

90 Draper: Williams, 61.

	replaced Hardel 13 Feb. 1258	Thomas fitz-Thomas *Draper*[91] until 1 Feb. 1258 Michael Tovi[92] *Goldsmith*[93] from 1 to 13 Feb. 1258 John Adrien (or Adrian) *Draper*[94] from 1 to 13 Feb. 1258 Thomas fitz-Thomas *Draper*[95] from 13 Feb. 1258 William Grapefige *Pepperer*[96] from 13 Feb. 1258
1258–9	John Gisors **2m** *Pepperer? Vintner?*[97]	John Adrien (or Adrian) **2s** *Draper*[98] Robert de Cornhill **2s**
1259–60	William fitz-Richard **2m** *Draper*[99]	Adam Bruning *Fishmonger*[100] Henry de Coventre *Vintner*
1260–1	William fitz-Richard *Draper*	John de Norhampton **2s** *Tailor? Skinner?*[101] Richard Picard[102]
1261–2	Thomas fitz-Thomas *Draper*[103]	Philip le Taillour *Mercer*[104] Richard de Walebrook (or Walebrock) *Pepperer*[105]
1262–3	Thomas fitz-Thomas *Draper*	Robert de Mountpiler *Spicer*[106] Osbert de Suffolke

[91] Draper: Williams, 216.

[92] 'Probably the son of (though possibly identical with) the . . . Mayor in 1244–5 and in 1249' (Beaven, i. 374 n. 3; on i. 372 he has Tovi as mayor not just in 1249 but in 1247–9, as accepted in this list–see above). Williams, 220, identifies two individuals named Michael Tovi: the mayor in the 1240s and his son, a goldsmith, a popular leader at this time.

[93] Goldsmith: see Williams, 206 (the earlier mayor) and 220 (the mayor's son).

[94] Draper: Beaven, i. 373. Vintner: Stow, *Survey*, ii. 158 (when mayor in 1270–1).

[95] Draper: Williams, 216.

[96] Pepperer: Williams, 220 and 244; and see also Nightingale, 77 (though she has Grapefige as sheriff in 1252).

[97] See n. to John Gisors, sheriff 1240–1.

[98] See n. to John Adrien, sheriff 1257–8.

[99] Draper: Williams, 61.

[100] Fishmonger: Williams, 63.

[101] See n. to John de Norhampton, sheriff 1253–4.

[102] Same as Richard Pikard, sheriff 1253–4?

[103] Draper: Williams, 216.

[104] Mercer: Williams, 58 and 332.

[105] Pepperer: Nightingale, 77.

[106] Spicer: Nightingale, 76–7.

1263–4	Thomas fitz-Thomas[107] *Draper*	Gregory de Rokesle *Goldsmith?*[108] Thomas de Ford
1264–5	Thomas fitz-Thomas *Draper*	Edward le Blund *Draper* Peter Aungier
1265–6[109]	Hugh fitz-Otho (W)[110] replaced by Linde/Walrauen	John Adrien (or Adrian) **3s** *Draper*[111] until 28 Nov. 1265? Walter Hervi[112] until 28 Nov. 1265? John de la Linde (S and/or W) replaced Adrien/Hervi[113] John Walrauen (S and/or W) *Clerk*[114] replaced Adrien/Hervi[115] William fitz-Richard (S and/or W)[116] **3m/w**[117] *Draper*[118] from 6 May to 11 Nov. 1266
1266–7[119]	Alan de la Souche (W)	John Adrien (or Adrian) **4s**

[107] Not admitted by the king but nevertheless remained in office for the year (*Mayors and Sheriffs*, 62, 74).

[108] Goldsmith: Beaven, i. 374; but Nightingale associates the Rokesle family in general with the trade of roper, and on Gregory de Rokesle see her p. 89.

[109] Beaven, i. 374, lists Gregory de Rokesle and Simon de Hadestok as sheriffs in 1265, not specifying whether in the 1264–5 or the 1265–6 sheriffs' year. This would be a second time for Rokesle as sheriff (see 1263–4). *Mayors and Sheriffs*, 81, places them under 1265–6 and states that they were not admitted; an explanatory note is provided. Adrien and Hervi became sheriffs, with fitz-Otho as warden; see *Mayors and Sheriffs*, 81–4. Stow, *Survey*, ii. 157 provides the 28 Nov. date given here for Adrien and Hervi.

[110] Stow, *Survey*, ii. 157–8 names fitz-Otho as warden; Hughes, 201 lists him as sheriff. He was apparently, like sheriffs Adrien and Hervi, replaced by Linde and Walrauen; see *Mayors and Sheriffs*, 84, and Additions, 190.

[111] See n. to John Adrien, sheriff 1257–8.

[112] Beaven, i. 374, lists as bailiff (i.e. sheriff) 1265–6 (not just in 1265).

[113] From 28 Nov. 1265 according to Stow, *Survey*, ii. 157 and Hughes, 201; on 7 Dec. 1265 according to *Mayors and Sheriffs*, 84.

[114] Clerk: *Mayors and Sheriffs*, 84.

[115] From 28 Nov. 1265 according to Stow, *Survey*, ii. 157 and Hughes, 201; on 7 Dec. 1265 according to *Mayors and Sheriffs*, 84.

[116] Stow, *Survey*, ii. 157 n. 10 states fitz-Richard was sheriff 6 May to 11 Nov. 1266; Hughes, 201 also lists him as a sheriff; Beaven, i. 372 lists him as warden in 1266. *Mayors and Sheriffs*, 89–90, places fitz-Richard's election—as both warden and sheriff—and Guildhall oath-taking on Ascension Day 1266 / the Feast of 'Saint John Port Latin' [6 May] and a St Paul's presentation to the Exchequer barons on 7 May (pp. 90–1).

[117] Mayor twice previously.

[118] Draper: Williams, 61.

[119] Stow, *Survey*, ii. 158 n. 1 (following *Mayors and Sheriffs* [p. 93]) gives the 11 Nov. 1266 date for the start of Adrien's and Batencourt's terms (the same date given for the end of fitz-Richard's here, under 1265–6), Hughes, 201, gives 12 Nov. for Adrien and Batencourt. See n. to William fitz-Richard, sheriff and/or warden 1265–6. *Mayors and Sheriffs*, 95–6, states that Robert de Lintone and Roger Marshal were elected as sheriffs by the people after Easter [17 Apr.] 1267, and Richard de Culeworth by the earl of Gloucester, and that (97) Adrien and Batencourt were restored *c.*18 June.

	from 23 June 1267[120]	*Draper*[121] from 11 Nov. Lucas de Batencourt from 11 Nov.
1267–8[122]	Alan de la Souche (W) until 2 or 7 Apr. 1268 Thomas de Eppegrave (W) from 2 or 7 Apr. 1268 until 26 July 1268 Stephen de Edeworth (W) from 26 July 1268	John Adrien (or Adrian) *Draper*[123] until 2 or 7 Apr. 1268 Lucas de Batencourt until 2 or 7 Apr. 1268 Walter Hervi **2s** from 2 or 7 Apr. 1268 William de Durham (or Dunelm) **2s** from 2 or 7 Apr. 1268
1268–9[124]	Stephen de Edeworth (W) until *c.*6 Feb. 1269[125] Hugh fitz-Otho (W) **2w** from *c.*6 Feb. 1269[126]	Walter Hervi until 3–6 May 1269 William de Durham (or Dunelm) until 3–6 May 1269 Robert de Cornhill **3s** from 3–6 May 1269 Thomas de Basinge *Woolman*[127] from 3–6 May 1269
1269–70[128]	Hugh fitz-Otho (W)[129] until 6 or 16–18 July 1270 John Adrien (or Adrian) *Draper*[131]	Thomas de Basinge *Woolman*[130] until 6 or 18 July 1270 Robert de Cornhill

[120] Stow, *Survey*, ii. 158, lists Alan de la Souche as warden in 1266–7 but also cites p. 158 n. 2 of *Mayors and Sheriffs* [see its p. 97] as a source for his appointment on 23 June 1267.

[121] See n. to John Adrien, sheriff 1257–8.

[122] The various replacements, including dates, are noted in Stow, *Survey*, ii. 158 nn. 3 and 4 and, for the sheriffs only, in Hughes, 201: but Stow, *Survey*'s (and also Hughes's) 7 Apr. is 2 Apr. in *Mayors and Sheriffs*, 106.

[123] See n. to John Adrien, sheriff 1257–8.

[124] Replacements are listed in Stow, *Survey*, ii. 158 nn. 5 and 6, which specifies 3 May for the sheriffs' change date; *Mayors and Sheriffs*, 114 (and see also ibid. 191) has 4–6 May for Cornhill and Basinge. Hughes, 201, includes fitz-Otho in his list of sheriffs (from 17 Feb. 1269) and has all four of the sheriffs here named as 'custodes' from 17 Feb. 1269.

[125] In the first week of Lent: *Mayors and Sheriffs*, 113. Ash Wed. was 6 Feb. in 1269.

[126] In the first week of Lent: *Mayors and Sheriffs*, 113. Ash Wed. was 6 Feb. in 1269.

[127] Woolman: Beaven, i. 374; Ekwall, 168 no. 83 suggests perhaps also a draper.

[128] Replacements, effective 6 July (the date also used by Hughes, 201), are listed in Stow, *Survey*, ii. 158 n. 7; but see also *Mayors and Sheriffs*, 120 and 129–30 (new mayor and sheriffs chosen at the beginning of June; mayor presented to king and admitted 16 July, sworn before king 18 July; sheriffs presented and admitted at Exchequer 18 July). Beaven, i. 235, lists le Poter as sheriff 1270–1, but i. 375, as sheriff only in 1270.

[129] Listed as a sheriff by Hughes, 201.

[130] See n. to Thomas de Basinge, sheriff 1268–9.

[131] See n. to John Adrien, sheriff 1257–8.

	from 6 or 16–18 July 1270	until 6 or 18 July 1270 Philip le Taillour **2s** *Mercer*[132] from 6 or 18 July 1270 Walter le Poter from 6 or 18 July 1270
1270–1	John Adrien (or Adrian) *Draper*	Gregory de Rokesle **2s**[133] *Goldsmith?*[134] Henry le Waleys
1271–2	Walter Hervi	Richard Paris *Cordwainer*[135] John de Bodele
1272–3	Walter Hervi[136] Henry Frowike (W) *Pepperer*[137] from 11 to *c*.18 Nov. 1272[138]	John Horn Walter le Poter **2s**
1273–4	Henry le Waleys	Peter Cosyn until 27–30 Nov. 1273[139] Robert de Meldeburne until 30 Nov. 1273[140] Nicholas fitz-Geoffrey de Winchester (or Winton) replaced Cosyn/Meldeburne[141] Henry de Coventre **2s** *Vintner* replaced Cosyn/Meldeburne[142]
1274–5	Gregory de Rokesle *Goldsmith?*[144]	Lucas Batencorte **2s?**[143] Henry de Frowyk *Pepperer*
1275–6	Gregory de Rokesle *Goldsmith?*	John Horn **2s** Ralph le Blund *Goldsmith*

[132] Mercer: Williams, 58 and 332. Listed among the merchant taylors by Beaven, i. 345, but not so identified (i. 374) in his chronological listing of aldermen.

[133] See n. to year 1265–6. [134] See n. to Gregory de Rokesle, sheriff 1263–4.

[135] Cordwainer: *French Chronicle*, 236.

[136] Not confirmed until *c*.18 Nov. 1272; see n. below to Frowike's dates.

[137] Pepperer: Stow, *Survey*, ii. 159; but not in Nightingale. This wardenship is not listed in Beaven as a position held by the 1274–5 pepperer sheriff.

[138] Stow, *Survey*, ii. 159 n. 2 (10 Nov.-13 Jan.); *Mayors and Sheriffs*, 153–60. Hervi's election was disputed for a time, as the aldermen wanted Philip le Taillour.

[139] Both Cosyn and Meldeburne were removed for taking bribes: Stow, *Survey*, ii. 159 n. 3, *Mayors and Sheriffs*, 167–8.

[140] See immediately preceding n.

[141] Elected 1 Dec. 1273: *Mayors and Sheriffs*, 168; Nov.: Hughes, 201.

[142] Elected 1 Dec. 1273: *Mayors and Sheriffs*, 168; Nov.: Hughes, 201.

[143] Is this the same individual who was sheriff 1266–8? (Stow, *Survey*, ii. 158 and 159 uses different spellings, as reproduced here, in 1266–8 and in 1274–5.)

[144] See n. to Gregory de Rokesle, sheriff 1263–4.

1276–7	Gregory de Rokesle *Goldsmith?*	Robert de Arras (or Araz) Ralph le Fevre (or Faber)[145] *Goldsmith*
1277–8	Gregory de Rokesle *Goldsmith?*	John Adrien (or Adrian) *Draper*[146] Walter l'Engleys (or Cornwaleys) *Vintner*
1278–9	Gregory de Rokesle *Goldsmith?*	Robert de Basinge William le Mazeliner *Pepperer*
1279–80	Gregory de Rokesle *Goldsmith?*	Thomas Box[147] *Corder* Ralph de la More
1280–1	Gregory de Rokesle *Goldsmith?*	William de Farndone *Goldsmith* Nicholas fitz-Geoffrey de Winchester (or Winton) **2s**
1281–2	Henry le Waleys **2m**	William le Mazeliner **2s** *Pepperer* Richard de Chigwell *Fishmonger*
1282–3	Henry le Waleys	Anketin de Betevile *Draper* Walter le Blund
1283–4	Henry le Waleys	Jordan Goodcheape[148] Martin Box *Woolman*
1284–5	Gregory de Rokesle **2m** *Goldsmith?*[150] until 29 June 1285[151]	Stephen Cornhill[149] Robert de Rokesle *Corder?*[152]

145 Hughes, 201, notes that he 'apparently died in office'; but Beaven, i. 375, lists his death as in 1278.

146 His father was also an alderman and draper: see e.g. LBA, fos. 6^r, 7^r, 29^v, and 108^r, Beaven, i. 236 and 405–6, and above, sheriff 1257–8 (in 1258 only), 1258–9, 1265–6 (in 1265 only), 1266–8, mayor 1269–70 (in 1270 only), 1270–1.

147 According to LBA, fo. 101^v he was briefly deposed for a trespass (at Easter according to *Annales Londonienses*, 89) but restored as sheriff the Saturday before St John Baptist: i.e. on 22 June 1280 (but on the eve of St John Baptist, i.e. 23 June, *Annales Londonienses*, 89).

148 Removed from office (after 25 July: *Annales Londonienses*, 92) because implicated in a murder: see *French Chronicle*, 240 nn. 6 and 8, and Stow, *Survey*, i. 254–5; also *A Chronicle*, 31 (Goodcheape imprisoned in the Tower) and *Annales Londonienses*, 92–3.

149 Beaven, i. 238, refers to a Stephen de Cornhulle as sheriff in 1294–5, dying *c.*1295 (will enrolled March 1295). 1294–5 would seem to be a misprint for 1284–5 (other sheriffs are listed for 1294–5 in Stow, *Survey*, and by Hughes, 201; and Beaven does not include Cornhulle in his list, ii. xxxix, of sheriffs who died in office); but I have not here emended the Stow, *Survey* spelling. Beaven's index gives the surname as de Cornhill.

150 See n. to Gregory de Rokesle, sheriff 1263–4.

151 See Stow, *Survey*, ii. 160 n. 1, citing LBF, [fo. 232^r], and *LBF*, 281, where n. 4 explains that the king took the city into his hand in June and Rokesle was removed from office.

152 Corder?: see Ekwall, 164 no. 33.

	Ralph de Sandwich (W)[153] replaced Rokesle[154]	
1285–6	Ralph de Sandwich (W)[155]	Walter le Blunt[156] *Stockfishmonger*[157] John Wade *Blader*[158]
1286–7	Ralph de Sandwich (W)[159]	Walter Hauteyn *Mercer* Thomas Cros[160] *Fishmonger*
1287–8	Ralph de Sandwich (W)	William de Hereford *Goldsmith*? *Pepperer*?[161] Thomas de Estanes (or Stanes)
1288–9[162]	Ralph de Sandwich (W)/Ralph Barnauars (W)?/John le Breton (W) **2w**?[164]	William de Betoyne *Pepperer, Mercer,* or *Goldsmith*[163] John de Canterbury *Blader* or *Pepperer*[165]

[153] Draper according to *A Chronicle*, 32.

[154] LBF, fo. 232ʳ, and *LBF*, 281 n. 5.

[155] LBF, fo. 232ʳ states that Sandwich was warden until 3 Feb. 1286, when he was replaced by John le Breton until 20 July 1287 (and see also *LBF*, 281 and n. 5 (first part)); but Stow,*Survey*, ii. 160 lists Sandwich as warden until 1288–9; and see also *LBF*, 281 n. 5 (second part), and Stow, *Survey*, ii. 385 n. to ii. 160 line 19.

[156] Hughes, 201, states that he was appointed 3 Oct. Same as Walter le Blund, sheriff 1282–3?

[157] Stockfishmonger: *Annales Londonienses*, 95.

[158] Blader: Ekwall, 183 no. 25. 'Wadeblad' in *Annales Londonienses*, 95 (cited by Ekwall).

[159] But see n. to Ralph de Sandwich, warden 1285–6.

[160] Thomas Gros: Hughes, 201.

[161] Goldsmith: Beaven, i. 225, 377; but Nightingale, 95, identifies him as a pepperer.

[162] Stow, *Survey*, ii. 385 provides a long note (to ii,160 line 19): that in [BL], Cotton MS. Julius B.II and in LBF, [fo. 232ʳ] Sandwich is said to have been *custos* [i.e. warden] until the day after [12 June] St. Barnabas Apostle, 1294, but that in the *Liber Custumarum* Sandwich is said to have been removed before the Feast of the Purification [2 Feb.] 1289, with Ralph de Berners [Barnauars, Stow, *Survey*, ii. 160] appointed in his place, and then in turn replaced as warden within a few days by John le Breton. Then in 19 Edward I [20 Nov. 1290–19 Nov. 1291] Sandwich was reinstated: around the feast of St. Margaret [20 July 1291], according to the *Liber Custumarum*. (Both Sandwich and le Breton are here spelled as in Beaven, although in his three uses of the name le Breton Beaven once, i. 370, uses the form 'de Breton'.) *Annales Londonienses*, 96–7, has Sandwich first deposed as constable of the Tower before 2 Feb. 1289, with Berners replacing him there, and then replaced as warden of the city by le Breton the Monday after 2 Feb., with both Berners and le Breton removed and Sandwich reinstated as constable [and presumably also as warden?] *c.*20 July 1289. Sandwich is then again listed as warden, with le Coteler and St. Edmond as sheriffs, in 1290. A CLRO handlist of mayors, dating from the late 1970s or earlier (personal acquisition *c.* 1977–8), lists Sandwich as warden 1285–9 and 1289–2, and le Breton as mayor in 1289. It also indicates that le Breton's 1289 mayoralty was his second (and see n. to Sandwich, warden 1285–6), although his name does not appear on the list earlier; but it then repeats the second-time designation for le Breton as warden in 1293–8.

[163] Pepperer (Beaven, i. 338), goldsmith (Beaven, i. 189); neither in Beaven's chronological listing, i. 377; pepperer, mercer, or goldsmith: Ekwall, 147; and see Nightingale, 93, 109–10, 121 (William de Bethune, mercer).

[164] Possible second non-consecutive term for both Sandwich and le Breton; see n. to Ralph de Sandwich, warden 1285–6 and n. to 1288–9.

[165] Blader or pepperer: Beaven, i. 197 (blader), 338 (pepperer), 377 (blader or pepperer[?]); Nightingale, 95, identifies him as a pepperer.

1289–90[166]	John le Breton (W)?/Ralph de Sandwich (W)?[168] **?w**	Solomon le Coteler[167] *Cutler*[169] Fulk St. Edmond *Bureller*[170]
1290–1[171]	Ralph de Sandwich (W)?/ John le Breton (W)? **?w**	Thomas Romeyn *Pepperer* William de Leyre *Pepperer*
1291–2	Ralph de Sandwich (W)[172] **?w**	Ralph le Blund **2s** *Goldsmith* Hamo Box *Corder/Roper*[173]
1292–3	Ralph de Sandwich (W) until 12 June 1293[175] John le Breton (W)? **w**[176] replaced Sandwich[177]	Henry le Bole[174] Elias Russell *Draper*
1293–4	John le Breton (W)[178]	Robert Rokesley the younger[179] Martin Amersbury *Goldsmith*[180]
1294–5	John le Breton (W)	Henry Box[181] Richard de Gloucester *Draper*[182]
1295–6	John le Breton (W)	John de Dunstaple *Skinner* Adam de Hallingberi *Skinner*

166 See n. to 1288–9.

167 Also known as Salomon de Laufare (Beaven, ii. 160); see LBA, fo. 102ʳ, LBF, fo. 232ʳ, and also Stow, *Survey*, ii. 160 n. 9 (including a suggested association with a Salomon de Lanvare, cutler; see Stow, *Survey*, ii. 330 n. to i. 262 line 18).

168 See n. to Ralph de Sandwich, warden 1284–5.

169 Beaven omits the company designation in his chronological list of aldermen (i. 377) but places le Coteler in his list of cutler aldermen (i. 351).

170 Bureller: LBA fo. 102ʳ, Fulk de St. Edmund, 'buriler', elected sheriff 1289. Bureller = maker of burel (coarse woollen cloth; see *OED* s.v. Burel, 1, and also *LBB*, 20 n. 1).

171 See n. to 1288–9.

172 See n. to Ralph de Sandwich, warden 1284–5.

173 Corder: Williams, 157–8; roper: Nightingale, 88; perhaps corder: Ekwall, 164, no. 35.

174 Hughes, 201, lists both le Bole and Russell as appointed 27 May 1293 by the chancellor of the Exchequer; but LBC, fo. 4ᵛ records their election in September 1392. Both Stow, *Survey*, ii. 160, and Beaven, i. 377 also list both as sheriffs 1292–3.

175 LBF, fo. 232ʳ (under *anno* 15) states that Sandwich's wardenship ceased on 12 June 1294; and Stow, *Survey*, ii. 160–1 lists Sandwich as warden for 1292–3 and 1293–4 (with a note incorrectly citing LBF for le Breton as becoming warden on 11 June 1294). But elsewhere (see LBF, fo. 232ʳ under *anno* 21, and *LBF*, 282 n. 5) the ending year given for Sandwich is 21 Edward I [20 Nov. 1292-19 Nov. 1293]; and in LBA le Breton is named as warden in all of late June 1293, July 1293, and March 1294 (fos. 87ᵛ, 88ʳ, 96ᵛ). (The CLRO handlist of mayors also gives le Breton as warden 1293–8.)

176 See n. to 1288–9.

177 See n. to end-of-term date for Ralph de Sandwich, warden 1292–3.

178 See n. to end-of-term date for Ralph de Sandwich, warden 1292–3.

179 Son of Robert de Rokesle, sheriff 1284–5 (see Ekwall, 167, no.68).

180 Goldsmith: LBA, fo. 102ʳ.

181 Perhaps a timber merchant: Ekwall, 198, no.53.

182 Draper: Beaven, ii. 227 (in the Addenda and Corrigenda, for i. 378).

1296–7	John le Breton (W)	Thomas of Suffolke *Skinner*[183] Adam le Blund de Foleham (or Fulham) *Fishmonger*
1297–8	John le Breton (W) until Apr. 1298[184] Henry le Waleys **3m** replaced le Breton	William de Storteford *Pepperer*[185] John de Storteford[186]
1298–9	Henry le Waleys	Richer le Refham *Mercer* Thomas Sely *Skinner*
1299–1300	Elias Russell *Draper*	John de Armentiers *Draper* Henry de Fyngrie *Fishmonger*[187]
1300–1	Elias Russell *Draper*	Lucas de Hauering *Corder*[188] Richard Champs
1301–2	John le Blund *Draper*	Robert le Callere *Mercer* Peter de Bosenho *Skinner*[189]
1302–3	John le Blund *Draper*	Hugh Pourte *Stockfishmonger* Simon de Paris *Mercer*
1303–4	John le Blund *Draper*	William de Combemartyn John de Bureford *Pepperer*
1304–5	John le Blund *Draper*	Roger de Paris *Mercer*

183 Skinner: Ekwall, 170 no. 14.

184 According to LBB, fo. 93r (and *Liber Albus*, 16), the king and his council granted to London on 9 Apr. 1298 the election of the mayoralty; and Henry le Waleys was elected mayor on 11 Apr., presented to the king at Fulham on 16 Apr., and sworn at Westminster on 17 Apr. Sharpe (*LBB*, 212 n. 2) says that the charter of restitution of the city's liberties is dated 11 April 1298, and correctly notes (213 n. 1) that LBC, fo. 24v shows the king's writ to the barons of the Exchequer, notifying them of the restitution, as dated 28 May 1298 from York, with le Waleys elected and presented to the king at Fulham the following day. See also *LBB*, 217 and n. 1; and the writ here (LBB, fo. 94r) is said to have been sent to the Exchequer in June.

185 Pepperer: Ekwall, 176 no. 6.

186 He apparently died in 1298: see Hughes, 201, and *HW* i. 134–5. If so, it was presumably late in 1298, as he is not included in Beaven's list (ii. p. xxxix) of sheriffs who died in office.

187 Fishmonger: *Mayors and Sheriffs*, Additions, 220; see also *Annales Paulini*, 304. (*CEMCR's* index provides two separate lines for this name, as though possibly concerning two individuals, one line specifying fishmonger and the other specifying sheriff; Ekwall, 149 no. 35 uses *CEMCR*.)

188 Corder: Ekwall, 164 no. 38.

189 Skinner: LBA, fo. 101r and LBC, fo. 62v.

		John de Lincoln *Draper*[190]
1305–6	John le Blund *Draper*	William Cosyn *Roper? Woolman?*[191] Reginald Thunderley[192]
1306–7	John le Blund *Draper*	Geoffrey de Conduit[193] Simon Bolet
1307–8	John le Blund *Draper*	Nicholas Pycot *Mercer* Nigel Drury
1308–9	Nicholas de Farndone *Goldsmith*	William de Basinge[194] *Woolstapler*[195] James le Boteler *Draper*[196]
1309–10	Thomas Romeyn *Pepperer*	Roger le Palmer[197] *Skinner*[198] James of St. Edmond *Bureller*[199]
1310–11	Richer le Refham *Mercer*	Simon Corp *Pepperer* Peter de Blakeneye *Draper? Woolmonger?*[200] died 1 Aug. 1311[201] John Cambridge *Mercer* replaced Blakeneye[202]
1311–12	John de Gisors *Pepperer*	Simon Merwod *Bureller*[203] Richard de Welleford *Draper* and *Hosier*[204]
1312–13	John de Gisors *Pepperer*	John Lambyn *Fishmonger*

[190] Beaven, ii. 227 notes that Lincoln is called a vintner in the *Liber de Antiquis Legibus*; see *Mayors and Sheriffs*, 222.

[191] Roper: see Nightingale, 120; woolman: see Ekwall, 165 no. 45.

[192] A Reginald de Thunderle, wealthy 'immigrant draper,' is mentioned by Williams, 113 but without further identification; see also Ekwall, 167 no. 67.

[193] *Liber Custumarum*, 73, names a 'Galfridus de Conductu, taverner' (1295–6), and Williams, 125, writes about a major vintner of this name; in neither case, however, is a term as sheriff noted.

[194] William de Basinge: *LBC*, index; W. Basing in Stow, *Survey*, ii. 162.

[195] Woolstapler: *Mayors and Sheriffs*, 213; see also Williams, 338. (woolmonger).

[196] Draper: *Mayors and Sheriffs*, 213, Ekwall, 168 no. 81.

[197] Beaven, ii. 227 corrects his i. 381 listing of this name as de Palmer.

[198] Skinner: Beaven, i. 381; blader: *Mayors and Sheriffs*, 213.

[199] Bureller: *Mayors and Sheriffs*, 213. Son of Fulk de St. Edmund (*Annales Londonienses*, 158 [the 1289-90 sheriff?]).

[200] Draper: *A Chronicle*, 43; woolmonger: *Mayors and Sheriffs*, 214.

[201] LBD, fo. 2ᵛ.

[202] See LBD, fo. 2ᵛ for Cambridge's name, company, and 3 Aug. date of appointment; his name is also given in Stow, *Survey*, ii. 162 n. 4.

[203] Bureller: *Mayors and Sheriffs*, 213.

[204] Draper and hosier: Ekwall, 179 no. 45.

		Richard de Welleford *Draper* and *Hosier*[205] died 23 Dec. 1312[206] Adam Lutkin[207] replaced Welleford[208]
1313–14	Nicholas de Farndone **2m** *Goldsmith*	Robert Burdeyn *Goldsmith*[209] Hugh de Gartone *Mercer*
1314–15	John de Gisors **2m** *Pepperer*	Stephen de Abyndon *Draper* Hamo de Chigwell *Fishmonger*[210]
1315–16	Stephen de Abyndon *Draper*	Hamo de Godchep *Mercer* William Bodelay *Vintner*[211]
1316–17	John de Wengrave[212]	William de Caustone *Mercer* Ralph Belancer *Pepperer*[213]
1317–18	John de Wengrave	John Priour[214] *Woolmonger* William Furneis *Pepperer*[215]
1318–19	John de Wengrave	John Poyntel *Leatherseller* (or *Cordwainer*) John Dalling *Mercer*[216]
1319–20	Hamo de Chigwell *Fishmonger*[217]	Simon de Abyndon *Draper* John de Prestone *Corder*[218]

[205] Draper and hosier: Ekwall, 179 no. 45.

[206] LBD, fo. 3^r; Beaven, ii. p. xxxix says 28 Dec.

[207] An Adam Lutkin is footnoted in *CEMCR*, 63 n. 1 as mentioned in the Letter Books as a blader or cornmonger, but there is no Adam Lutkin in indexes to *LBA–C*, and the indexed Adam Lutkin in the *LBD–E.* is not identified by company.

[208] Elected Wed. 3 Jan. 1313, Westminster 20 Jan. (LBD, fo. 3^r).

[209] Goldsmith: LBD, fo. 3^v.

[210] Fishmonger: Beaven, i. 380. Stow, *Survey*, ii. 163–4, lists him as a pepperer when he is mayor in 1319–20 (see also Fabyan, 424 n. 1), 1321–2 to 1326–7 (in 1326 only), 1327–8 (see also Fabyan, 439 n. 2); but Nightingale (see 614, Index) calls him a fishmonger, and see also Ekwall, 332 no.1, and *Annales Londonienses*, 232.

[211] Vintner: LBD, fo. 4^r.

[212] Clerk and lawyer: Ekwall, 222 no. 1.

[213] Pepperer: Nightingale, 137.

[214] John Priour Senior: LBD, fo. 5^r.

[215] Pepperer: LBD, fo. 5^r (William de Fourneys); Stow, *Survey*, ii. 163, lists W. Furneis and no company identification.

[216] Mercer: Ekwall, 275 no. 90. A John de Dallynges is also listed among other mercers *c.*1328 in LBE, fo. 190^r. Beaven, i. 266 lists a John de Dallyng, mercer, as a representative of London in Parliament 1340 (and, i. 286, as dying in 1349: see *HW* i. 618): possibly a son of the 1318–19 sheriff (see Ekwall).

[217] See n. to Hamo de Chigwell, sheriff 1314–15.

[218] See n. to John de Prestone, mayor 1332–3.

1320–1	Nicholas de Farndone **3m** *Goldsmith* until Jan. 1321[219] Robert de Kendale (W) replaced Farndone until May 1321[221] Hamo de Chigwell **2m** *Fishmonger*[222] replaced Kendale[223]	Reginald de Conduit *Vintner* William Produn *Fishmonger*[220]
1321–2	Hamo de Chigwell *Fishmonger*	Richard Costantyn *Draper* Richard de Hakeneie *Woolmonger*[224]
1322–3	Hamo de Chigwell *Fishmonger* until 4 Apr. 1323[225] Nicholas de Farndone **4m** *Goldsmith* replaced Chigwell[227]	John de Grantham *Pepperer* Richard Elie *Fishmonger*[226]
1323–4	Nicholas de Farndone *Goldsmith* until 7 Dec. 1323[228] Hamo de Chigwell **3m** *Fishmonger*[229] replaced Farndone[230]	Adam de Salisbury *Pepperer* John de Oxenford *Vintner*
1324–5	Hamo de Chigwell *Fishmonger*	Benedict de Folesham *Pepperer* Alan Gille[231]

219 See *LBE*, 214 n. 1. The city was taken into the king's hand.

220 William Prodhomme, fishmonger: LBD, fo. 6^r; Stow,*Survey*, ii. 153 lists W. Produn. A William Prodomme is also listed among other fishmongers *c.*1328 in LBE, fo. 190^r; and see also Ekwall, 332 no. 2.

221 For Kendale's name and appointment, see *LBE* 214 n. 1. In May 1321 the city recovered its liberties.

222 See n. to Hamo de Chigwell sheriff, 1314–15.

223 For Chigwell's name and election see *LBE* 214 n. 1.

224 Woolmonger: Beaven, i. 382. Fishmonger: Stow, *Survey*, i. 209 (probably confusing this Richard de Hakeneie with an earlier fishmonger one, for whom see Ekwall, 148 no. 22).

225 LBD, fo. 6^v. Removed by the king.

226 Fishmonger: *Mayors and Sheriffs*, 210; *French Chronicle*, 256; *Annales Paulini*, 304. Both a Robert de Ely and a Roger de Ely are listed among other fishmongers *c.*1328 in LBE, fo. 190^r, but no Richard.

227 See LBD, fo. 6^v for Farndone's appointment by the king.

228 See LBD, fo. 6^v, and *LBE*, 214 n. 1. Removed by the king.

229 See n. to Hamo de Chigwell, sheriff 1314–15.

230 Admitted Westminster Wed. 7 Dec. 1323; see LBD, fo. 6^v, LBE, fo. 148^r, and *LBE*, 214 n. 1. LBE, fo. 148^r states the date of the appointment Letters Patent as 29 Nov.

231 According to LBD, fo. 6^v, John de Caustone was originally elected but did not take up the election, and on 29 Sept. Alan Gille was elected and sworn in his place, and admitted at Westminster on Mon. 1 Oct. But on 29 Oct. Caustone, who had been stripped of the freedom of the city and of his aldermanship, asked to be reinstated, and replaced Gille; Caustone was elected and sworn 29 Oct. at the Guildhall, and admitted 30 Oct. at Westminster. (Beaven mentions Gille and his election situation, ii. xxxii.) An Alan Gille is listed among other bladers *c.*1328 in LBE, fo. 90^v; and see also Ekwall, 329 no. 27, although he says nothing about his listed Alan Gille (blader/cornmonger) as having been sheriff.

		until 29 Oct. John de Caustone *Mercer* replaced Gille
1325–6	Hamo de Chigwell *Fishmonger*	Gilbert Mordon *Fishmonger? Stockfishmonger?*[232] John Cotun *Skinner*
1326–7	Hamo de Chigwell *Fishmonger* until Nov. 1326[233] Richard de Betoyne *Pepperer*[235] replaced Chigwell[236]	Richard de Rothyng *Vintner* Roger Chaunteclere[234]
1327–8	Hamo de Chigwell **4m** *Fishmonger*[237]	Henry Darci *Draper* John Hauteyn *Mercer*
1328–9	John de Grantham *Pepperer*	Simon Fraunceys*[238] *Mercer* Henry de Combemartyn *Woolmonger*
1329–30	Simon de Swanlond *Draper*	Richard le Lacer *Mercer* Henry de Gisors *Vintner*
1330–1	John de Pulteney *Draper*	Robert de Ely *Fishmonger* Thomas Harewolde (or Harrewode) *Pepperer?*[239]
1331–2	John de Pulteney *Draper*	John de Mockyng *Fishmonger* Andrew Aubrey *Pepperer*

[232] Fishmonger: *Mayors and Sheriffs*, 210; stockfishmonger: Ekwall, 212 no. 16.

[233] A writ of 6 Nov. 1326 restored the mayoralty to the city and called for an election within eight days: LBE, fo. 171^{r}.

[234] Wool exporter: Ekwall, 313 no. 102.

[235] Beaven, i. 382 n. 7c, says he was a pepperer in 1316, and so lists him as such (but as a goldsmith at i. 343, though see also i. 411); but Stow, *Survey*, ii. 164 lists him as a goldsmith—as which, Beaven says, he is generally described. For pepperer see Nightingale (Richard de Bethune), e.g. 121 (and see index).

[236] *LBE*, 214 n. 1.

[237] See n. to Hamo de Chigwell, sheriff 1314–15.

[238] Mayor's choice: *CPMR 1323–64*, 69.

[239] A Thomas de Horewold is listed as a grocer, with one other, *c.*1328 in LBE, fo. 190^{r}. See also Nightingale, 176, 197, and 161 n. 2.

1332–3	John de Prestone	Nicholas Pike
	Corder[240]	*Skinner*[241]
		John Husbond
		Cornmonger[242]
1333–4	John de Pulteney **2m**	John Hamond
	Draper	*Pepperer*
		William Haunsard
		Fishmonger?[243]
1334–5	Reginald de Conduit	John de Hyngston
	Vintner	*Goldsmith*
		Walter Turke
		Fishmonger
1335–6	Reginald de Conduit	Walter de Mordone
	Vintner	*Stockfishmonger*
		Ralph de Uptone
		Draper
1336–7	John de Pulteney **3m**	John de Northall[244]
	Draper	*Skinner*
		William (Curteys) de Bricklesworth
		Woolmonger
1337–8	Henry Darci	Walter Neel
	Draper	*Blader*[245]
		Nicholas Crane
		Butcher[246]
1338–9	Henry Darci	William de Pountfreyt
	Draper	*Skinner*
		Hugh Marberer[247]
1339–40	Andrew Aubrey	William de Thorneye
	Pepperer	*Pepperer*
		Roger de Forsham
		Mercer
1340–1	Andrew Aubrey	Adam Lucas*[248]

[240] Stow, *Survey*, ii. 164 calls him a draper (as also does Fabyan, 442 n. 2), and LBF, fo. 232^{v}, a girdler. Beaven, i. 357 provides a lengthy footnote pointing out that there were two John de Prestones contemporary with one another, one a corder and one a girdler, and argues convincingly for the mayor [and sheriff in 1319–20] as the corder. See also Nightingale, 186 and 205 (roper).

[241] Skinner: LBF, fo. 232^{v}.

[242] Cornmonger: Ekwall, 270 no. 33. (A John Husebonde is listed among other bladers *c.*1328 in LBE, fo. 190^{v}.)

[243] Fishmonger?: see Beaven, i. 266 and 286. A William Haunsard is also listed among other fishmongers *c.*1328 in LBE, fo. 190^{r}; and see Ekwall, 344 no. 9.

[244] Stow, *Survey*, ii. 165 lists John Clarke but footnotes name alternatives as John le Clerk of North halle and John de Northalle.

[245] Stow, *Survey*, ii. 165 has bladesmith, but corrects this to blader on ii. 385, and has blader on i. 245 and 249. See Stow,*Survey*'s nn. at ii. 325 and 385.

[246] Butcher: Ekwall, 327 no. 169.

[247] Perhaps a draper. A Hugh le Marberer, draper, in 1337 along with other Londoners lent a very large sum of money to the city for presents to royalty etc.; see LBF, fo. 4^{v}.

[248] Mayor's choice: *CPMR 1323–64*, 129.

	Pepperer	*Stockfishmonger*[249] Bartholomew Deumars *Corder*
1341–2	John de Oxenford *Vintner* died 18 June 1342[250] Simon Fraunceys *Mercer* replaced Oxenford[252]	Richard de Berkynge *Draper* John de Rokele *Corder (?Pepperer)*[251]
1342–3	Simon Fraunceys *Mercer*	John Lovekyn *Stockfishmonger*[253] Richard de Kislingbury *Draper*
1343–4	John Hamond *Pepperer*	John Syward *Stockfishmonger* John de Aylesham *Mercer*
1344–5	John Hamond *Pepperer*	Geoffrey de Wychingham *Mercer* Thomas Leggy *Skinner*
1345–6	Richard le Lacer[254] *Mercer*	Edmond Hemenhall[255] John de Gloucester *Fishmonger*
1346–7	Geoffrey de Wychingham *Mercer*	John de Croydon *Fishmonger* William Claptus
1347–8	Thomas Leggy *Skinner*	Adam Brabazon* *Fishmonger* Richard de Basyngstoke *Goldsmith*
1348–9	John Lovekyn *Stockfishmonger*[256]	Henry Picard *Vintner* Simon Dolseley *Pepperer*

249 Stockfishmonger: see Beaven, i. 286 and 266.

250 LBF, fo. 60^{v}. Beaven, i. 383 has 17 June; but LBF's date is Tues. the morrow of St. Botolph, not the feast day itself (17 June). See also *LBF*, 285 n. 4, and Stow, *Survey*, ii. 165 n. 9.

251 Corder (?pepperer): Beaven, i. 386; for pepperer see also *French Chronicle*, 289. Nightingale (spelling his name Rokesley) states (p. 89) that he remained a roper although several other ropers joined with the pepperers in the 1340s.

252 Elected Tues. 18 June 1342, Westminster [Wed.] 19 June (LBF, fo. 60^{v}).

253 See also n. to John Lovekyn, mayor 1358–9 for a pepperer association.

254 Richard Leget in Stow, *Survey*, ii. 165.

255 A well-off Edmund de Hemenhale, mercer, died in 1348, *HW* i. 608).

256 Stockfishmonger: Beaven, i. 386; fishmonger: Stow, *Survey*, ii. 166; stockfishmonger: LBF, fo. 233^{r}. See also n. to John Lovekyn, mayor 1358–9, for a pepperer association, and also (for this year) Fabyan, 460 n. 2.

1349–50	Walter Turke *Fishmonger*	Adam de Bury *Skinner* Ralph de Lenne *Stockfishmonger*
1350–1	Richard de Kislingbury *Draper*	John Nott *Pepperer* William Worcester[257]
1351–2	Andrew Aubrey **2m** *Pepperer*	John Wroth *Fishmonger* Gilbert Stayndrop* *Goldsmith*[258]
1352–3	Adam Fraunceys *Mercer*	John Pecche *Fishmonger* John de Stodeye *Vintner*
1353–4	Adam Fraunceys *Mercer*	William de Welde *Draper* John Little *Fishmonger*
1354–5	Thomas Leggy **2m** *Skinner*	William de Todenham *Mercer* Richard Smelt *Fishmonger*
1355–6	Simon Fraunceys **2m** *Mercer*	Walter Forster *Skinner* Thomas Brandon
1356–7	Henry Picard *Vintner*	Richard de Notyngham* *Mercer* Thomas Dolseley *Pepperer*
1357–8	John de Stodeye *Vintner*	Stephen Cavendisshe (or Caundisshe) *Draper* Bartholomew de Frestlyng *Pepperer*[259]
1358–9	John Lovekyn **2m** *Stockfishmonger*[260]	John de Bernes *Mercer* John Buris *Draper*[261]

257 William de Worcestre, LBF, fo. 233r; W. Worcester in Stow, *Survey*, ii. 166.

258 Goldsmith: LBF, fo. 233r. A Gilbert de Steyndrop is also listed as a Goldsmiths' warden in 1342–3 and 1350–1 (Goldsmiths' MS 1518, 6 and 9).

259 Nightingale states (see e.g. 205) that he began as a roper.

260 Stockfishmonger: Beaven, i. 386 and (for this year) Stow, *Survey*, ii. 167; LBF fo. 233r, however, lists Lovekyn in this year as a pepperer, though in 1348 as a stockfishmonger. Fabyan, 468 n. 2 has grocer (i.e. pepperer). Nightingale, 221, suggests a possible association with the grocers/pepperers. Stockfishmonger in *HW*, ii. 117–18.

261 Draper: LBF, fo. 233r.

1359–60	Simon Dolseley *Pepperer*	Simon de Benyngton[262] *Draper*[263] John de Chichester *Goldsmith*
1360–1	John Wroth *Fishmonger*	John Denis *Ironmonger*[264] Walter de Berneye *Mercer*
1361–2	John Pecche *Fishmonger*	William Holbech *Draper* James de Thame *Goldsmith*
1362–3	Stephen Cavendisshe (or Caundisshe) *Draper*	John de St Albans James Andreu *Draper*
1363–4	John Nott *Pepperer*	Richard de Croydon *Fishmonger* John Hiltoft *Goldsmith*[265]
1364–5	Adam de Bury *Skinner*	John de Mytford *Draper* Simon de Mordone *Stockfishmonger*
1365–6	Adam de Bury *Skinner* until 28 Jan. 1366[266] John Lovekyn **3m** *Stockfishmonger*[267] replaced Bury[268]	John de Briklesworth* Thomas Irlond *Skinner*
1366–7	John Lovekyn *Stockfishmonger*	John Warde *Pepperer* Thomas of Lee
1367–8	James Andreu *Draper*	John Tornegold *Fishmonger*[269] William Dikeman *Ironmonger*[270]

[262] Or Simon de Bedyngton: see Beaven, i. 286, where Beaven also states the correct form to be 'almost certainly' Benyngton.

[263] Draper: LBF, fo. 233^{r}; also Beaven, i. 267 (Simon de Bedyngton; see also i. 286).

[264] Ironmonger: LBF, fo. 233^{r}.

[265] Goldsmith: LBF, fo. 233^{r}; and see Beaven, i. 286 and 267. Company warden in 1345–6, 1349–50, 1353–4, 1359–60 (Goldsmiths' MS 1518, 7, 9, 11, 23).

[266] Adam de Bury was removed from office 28 Jan. 1366 by the king. See LBG, fo. 175^{r}; also LBF, fo. 233^{r}.

[267] Stockfishmonger: Beaven, i. 386. Fishmonger: Stow, *Survey*, ii. 167. See also n. to John Lovekyn, mayor 1358–9, for a pepperer association.

[268] Elected 28 Jan. 1366 (LBG, fo. 175^{r}; also LBF, fo. 233^{r} [though identifying Lovekyn as a pepperer]).

[269] Fishmonger: Beaven, i. 389. Mercer: LBF, fo. 233^{r}.

[270] Ironmonger: Stow, *Survey*, i. 281.

1368–9	Simon de Mordone *Stockfishmonger*	Robert Girdelere Adam Wimondham*[271]
1369–70	John de Chichester *Goldsmith*	John Pyel *Mercer* Hugh Holbech*
1370–1	John de Bernes *Mercer*	William Walworth *Fishmonger* Robert Geyton
1371–2	John de Bernes *Mercer*	Adam Stable *Mercer* Robert Hatfield* *Pepperer*
1372–3	John Pyel *Mercer*	John Philipot *Grocer? Fishmonger?*[272] Nicholas Brembre *Grocer*
1373–4	Adam de Bury **2m** *Skinner*	John Aubrey* *Grocer*[273] John Fyfhide *Mercer*
1374–5	William Walworth *Fishmonger*[274]	Richard Lyons* *Vintner*[275] William Wodehous *Skinner*
1375–6	John Warde *Grocer*	John Hadle* *Grocer* William Neuport *Fishmonger*
1376–7	Adam Stable *Mercer* until 21 March 1377[277] Nicholas Brembre *Grocer* replaced Stable[278]	John (Comberton) de Northampton* *Draper*[276] Robert Launde *Goldsmith*

[271] There is an Adam (de) Wymondham, mercer, in *CPMR 1323–64*, 259 (1362) and *CPMR 1364–81*, 76 (1367).

[272] Grocer: Beaven i. 390; but Nightingale, 184, states that, although closely associated with the grocers, Philipot never became a company member. Fishmonger: see *HW* ii. 275 n. 1.

[273] Grocer: Beaven, i. 225, though not in his chronological listing, i. 389. A John Aubrey is listed in Grocers' GL, MS 11570, 45, as a company member in 1373; his name has subsequently been crossed out, as have others in the same list (largely marked as dead), but the deletion date is unknown. Beaven, i. 389, records the sheriff Aubrey as alderman 1370–7 and as dying *c.*Dec. 1380. The next list of company members in GL, MS 11570 is dated 1383 and no Aubrey is included. Nightingale (see e.g. 231–2) discusses a grocer John Aubrey who sought election as an alderman in 1370, though she does not mention any term for him as sheriff. A John Aubrey is listed as a pepperer, and as a cordwainer, in *CPMR 1364–81*, 71 (1367), 200 (1375).

[274] Fishmonger: Beaven, i. 389; Stockfishmonger: LBF, fo. 233^{v}.

[275] Vintner: Beaven, i. 390, though he puts Lyons among the goldsmiths at i. 343.

[276] See n. to John de Northampton, mayor 1382–3.

[277] Stable was discharged 21 March 1377 by the king; see LBH, fo. 59^{r} and LBF, fo. 233^{v}.

[278] Elected and sworn, Guildhall and Tower, Sat. 21 March 1377 (LBH, fo. 59^{r}; see also LBF, fo. 233^{v}).

1377–8	Nicholas Brembre *Grocer*	Nicholas Twyford *Goldsmith* Andrew Pykeman* *Fishmonger*
1378–9	John Philipot *Grocer*[279]	John Boseham* *Mercer* Thomas Cornwaleys *Goldsmith*
1379–80	John Hadle *Grocer*	John Heylesdon* *Mercer* William Baret *Grocer*
1380–81	William Walworth **2m** *Fishmonger*[280]	Walter Doget* *Vintner* William Knyghtcote *Mercer*
1381–2	John (Comberton) de Northampton *Draper*[281]	John Rote *Skinner* John Heende* *Draper*
1382–3	John (Comberton) de Northampton *Draper*[282]	Adam Bamme *Goldsmith* John Sely* *Skinner*
1383–4	Nicholas Brembre **2m** *Grocer*	Simon Wynchcombe *Armourer* John More* *Mercer*
1384–5	Nicholas Brembre *Grocer*	Nicholas Exton *Fishmonger*[283] John Fresshe* *Mercer*
1385–6	Nicholas Brembre *Grocer*	John Organ* *Mercer* John Chircheman *Grocer*
1386–7	Nicholas Exton *Fishmonger*[284]	William More* *Vintner*

[279] See n. to John Philipot, sheriff 1372–3.

[280] Fishmonger: Beaven, i. 389. Stockfishmonger: LBF, fo. 233^{v}.

[281] See n. to John de Northampton, mayor 1382–3.

[282] Draper: Beaven, i. 391. Draper or skinner: Stow, *Survey*, ii. 168 (though not given for the 1381–2 mayoralty)

[283] Fishmonger: Beaven, i. 397. Goldsmith: LBF, fo. 233^{v}; fishmonger: *HW*, ii. 352 n. 2.

[284] Fishmonger: Beaven, i. 397. Goldsmith: LBF, fo. 233^{v}; fishmonger: *HW*, ii. 352 n. 2.

		William Staundon[285] *Grocer*
1387–8	Nicholas Exton *Fishmonger*	William Venour* *Grocer* Hugh Fastolf *Grocer*
1388–9	Nicholas Twyford *Goldsmith*	Thomas Austyn *Mercer* Adam Karlill* *Grocer*
1389–90	William Venour *Grocer*	John Walcote *Draper* John Loneye (or Loveneye)* *Mercer*
1390–1	Adam Bamme *Goldsmith*	John Fraunceys *Goldsmith* Thomas Vynent* *Mercer*
1391–2[286]	John Heende *Draper* until 25 June 1392 Edward Dalyngregge (W) replaced Heende until 22 July 1392 Baldwin de Radyngton (W) replaced Dalyngregge	John Shadworth* *Mercer* until 25 June 1392 Henry Vanner *Vintner* until 25 June 1392 Gilbert Maghfeld (or Maunfeld) *Ironmonger* replaced Shadworth/Vanner Thomas Newenton (or Neuton) *Mercer* replaced Shadworth/Vanner
1392–3	William Staundon *Grocer*	Gilbert Maghfeld (or Maunfeld)* *Ironmonger* Thomas Newenton (or Neuton) *Mercer*
1393–4	John Hadle **2m** *Grocer*	Drugo (or Drew) Barentyn *Goldsmith* Richard Whytyngdone (or Whittington)* *Mercer*

[285] William Staman: Hughes, 202.

[286] All three originally elected officers—Heende, Shadworth, and Vanner—were deprived of office 25 June 1392 and imprisoned for a short time: see LBF, fo. 233^{v}, LBH, fo. 270^{v}, *LBF*, 289–90 and n. 2, and Beaven, i. 401. Appointed by the king in their places were sheriffs Gilbert Maghfeld and Thomas Newenton (Letters Patent 25 June, sworn 1 July: LBH, fo. 270^{v}) and, as warden, first Edward Dalyngregge (Letters Patent 25 June, sworn 1 July: LBH, fo. 270^{v}), and then Baldwin de Radyngton (Letters Patent 22 July: LBH, fo. 273^{v}). See also LBF, fo. 233^{v}. According to *LBH*, 379, n. 1 (citing Higden, i.e. monk of Westminster), during the interval between the removal of Heende and the appointment of Dalyngregge, the city was ruled by William Staundon.

1394–5	John Fresshe *Mercer*	William Brampton* *Stockfishmonger* Thomas Knolles *Grocer*
1395–6	William More *Vintner*	Roger Elys* *Wax Chandler* William Shyringham *Mercer*
1396–7	Adam Bamme **2m** *Goldsmith* died June 1397[287] Richard Whytyngdone (or Whittington) *Mercer* replaced Bamme[288]	Thomas Welford* *Fishmonger* William Parker *Mercer*
1397–8	Richard Whytyngdone (or Whittington) *Mercer*	John Wodecok *Mercer* William Askham* *Fishmonger*
1398–9	Drugo (or Drew) Barentyn *Goldsmith*	John Wade *Fishmonger* John Warner* *Ironmonger*
1399–1400	Thomas Knolles *Grocer*	William Walderne* *Mercer* William Hyde *Grocer*
1400–1	John Fraunceys *Goldsmith*	John Wakele* *Vintner* William Evote *Draper*
1401–2	John Shadworth *Mercer*	William Venour[289] *Grocer* William Framlyngham[290] *Skinner*
1402–3	John Walcote *Draper*	Robert Chichele *Grocer* Richard Merlawe *Ironmonger/Fishmonger*[291]
1403–4	William Askham *Fishmonger*	Thomas Fauconer *Mercer*

287 LBH, fo. 314r.

288 Appointed 8 June by Letters Patent; see LBH, fo. 314r.

289 Not the same individual as the 1389–90 mayor: see e.g. Beaven, i. 338.

290 John in Stow, *Survey*, ii. 170, but William in Beaven, ii. 2, and in Skinners' GL, MS 31692 fo. 4r.

291 Beaven, i. 234 notes that Merlawe appears to have been both an ironmonger and a fishmonger (and incorrectly states that he is described as an ironmonger in the LBI notice [fo. 204] of his election to the mayoralty in 1417). Merlawe is an ironmonger as both sheriff and (twice) mayor in LBF, fo. 234; and see *HW*, ii. 428–9.

		Thomas Polle* *Goldsmith*
1404–5	John Heende **2m** *Draper*	William Louthe* *Goldsmith*
		Stephen Speleman *Mercer*
1405–6	John Wodecok *Mercer*	William Crowmere *Draper*
		Henry Barton *Skinner*
1406–7	Richard Whytyngdone (or Whittington) **2m** *Mercer*	Nicholas Wotton *Draper*
		Geoffrey Broke *Grocer*
1407–8	William Staundon **2m** *Grocer*	Henry Pountfreyt *Saddler*
		Henry Halton* *Grocer*[292]
1408–9	Drugo (or Drew) Barentyn **2m** *Goldsmith*	William Norton *Draper*
		Thomas Duke* *Skinner*[293]
1409–10	Richard Merlawe *Ironmonger/Fishmonger*[294]	William Chichele *Grocer*
		John Lane* *Mercer*
1410–11	Thomas Knolles **2m** *Grocer*	John Penne* *Skinner*
		Thomas Pyke *Draper*
1411–12	Robert Chichele *Grocer*	Walter[295] Cottone *Mercer*
		John Reynwell* *Fishmonger*[296]
1412–13	William Walderne *Mercer*	William Sevenoke *Grocer*[297]
		Ralph Lobenham* *Draper*

[292] Grocer: Beaven, ii. 4. Mercer: Stow, *Survey*, ii. 171; but grocer: Stow, *Survey*, i. 252. See also Grocers' GL MS 11570, 102 (the company pays for minstrels for the oath-taking of Halton as a grocer sheriff).

[293] Skinner: *A Chronicle*, 91; and a Thomas Duk, skinner, died 1411, *HW* ii. 429.

[294] See n. to Richard Merlawe, sheriff 1402–3.

[295] William in Stow, *Survey*, ii. 171.

[296] Fishmonger: Beaven, ii. 5; identified as an ironmonger in 1433 in LBK, fo. 127, as noted by Beaven, ii. 229; fishmonger in LBF, fo. 234^r. (Cf. Richard Merlawe, sheriff 1402–3, mayor 1409–10 and 1417–18.)

[297] Grocer: Beaven, ii. 4. Nightingale, 344, records that Sevenoke originally went through his apprenticeship to, and became free as, an ironmonger. See also n. to John Michell, sheriff 1414–15.

1413–14	William Crowmere *Draper*	John Sutton* *Grocer*[298] John Micholl *Vintner*[299]
1414–15	Thomas Fauconer *Mercer*	John Michell* *Stockfishmonger*[300] Thomas Aleyn *Mercer*
1415–16	Nicholas Wotton *Draper*	Alan Everard *Mercer* William Cauntbrigge* *Grocer*[301]
1416–17	Henry Barton *Skinner*	Robert Widyngton *Grocer* John Coventre *Mercer*
1417–18	Richard Merlawe **2m** *Ironmonger/Fishmonger*[302]	John Gedney *Draper* Henry Read*[303] *Armourer*[304]
1418–19	William Sevenoke *Grocer*[305]	Ralph Barton *Skinner* John Bryan* *Fishmonger*[306] died 10 Oct. 1418[307] John Perneys (or Perveys) *Fishmonger* replaced Bryan[308]

298 Grocer: LBI, fo. 126r; and see also the Grocers' GL MS 11570, 111 and 112 (the company pays for minstrels for a grocer sheriff). See also Beaven, i. 287 and 270, and the Grocers' GL MS 11592A (Admissions) under 1383, Jankyn Sutton. (Stow, *Survey*, i. 305 has goldsmith.) Sutton was a company warden in 1406–7: see the Grocers' GL MS 11570, 102.

299 Vintner: LBI, fo. 126r. A. Crawford, *A History of the Vintners' Company* (London, 1977), 35–6, also mentions a prominent early fifteenth-century vintner of this name; and see also *CPMR 1413–37*, 9 (1413), for a John Micholl, vintner.

300 Stockfishmonger: Beaven, ii. 4. Grocer: LBI, fo. 135r (as sheriff 1414–15); fishmonger: LBF, fo. 234r (as mayor 1424–5, 1436–7) and Stow, *Survey*, ii. 172 and 173 (as mayor 1424–5, 1436–7). Beaven, ii. 4 n. 7 cites his own *Notes & Queries* article on the company concerned: S.10, 12 (6 Nov. 1909), 361–2. Nightingale states (see 379–381) that all three of John Michell (fishmonger), William Sevenoke (ironmonger) and William Cauntbrigge (ironmonger) became grocers, that Cauntbrigge called himself both ironmonger and grocer, and that Michell eventually chose the fishmongers over the grocers.

301 See n. to John Michell, sheriff 1414–15.

302 See n. to Richard Merlawe, sheriff 1402–3.

303 For Read's first name see LBI, fo. 203v and also LBF, fo. 234r; Stow, *Survey*, ii. 171, lists H. Read.

304 Armourer: see LBI, fo. 203v and also LBF, fo. 234r.

305 Grocer: Beaven, ii. 4. See n. to John Michell, sheriff 1414–15.

306 Fishmonger: LBI, fo. 220r; see also Beaven, i. 287 and 270.

307 LBI, fo. 220r. He was drowned in the Thames, supposedly as he went to relieve himself; see *Chronicles of London*, ed. C. L. Kingsford (Oxford, 1905), 297–8.

308 Elected Tues. 11 Oct. 1418, sworn Guildhall and to Westminster Wed. 12 Oct. (LBI, fo. 220r–v).

1419–20	Richard Whytyngdone **3m** (or Whittington) *Mercer*	Robert Whytingham *Draper* John Botiler (or Boteler)* *Mercer*[309]
1420–1	William Cauntbrigge *Grocer*[310]	John Boteler* *Draper*[311] John Welles *Grocer*
1421–2	Robert Chichele **2m** *Grocer*	Richard Gosselyn *Ironmonger* William Weston* *Draper*[312]
1422–3	William Walderne **2m** *Mercer*	Robert Tatersale *Draper* William Estfeld* *Mercer*
1423–4	William Crowmere **2m** *Draper*	Nicholas Jamys *Fishmonger*[313] Thomas Wandesford* *Mercer*
1424–5	John Michell *Stockfishmonger*[314]	Simon Seman* *Vintner* John atte Water (or Bithewater) *Goldsmith*
1425–6	John Coventre *Mercer*	John Brokle *Draper* William Melreth* *Mercer*
1426–7	John Reynwell *Fishmonger*[316]	Robert Arnold*[315] *Grocer*

[309] Beaven, ii. 6 n. 12 notes that another John Boteler, draper, became sheriff in 1420 (but was never an alderman).

[310] Grocer: Beaven, ii. 5. See n. to John Michell, sheriff 1414–15.

[311] Draper: see Beaven, ii. 6 n. 12; also Stow, *Survey*, i. 235, and LBI, fo. 254^{r}, and *CPMR 1413–37*, 109 (draper and sheriff, 1421). A John Botiller appears in the early parts of the Drapers' earliest extant accounts, Drapers' MS +140.

[312] Draper: LBI, fo. 270^{r} (John Weston); see also Beaven, i. 287 and 270. A William Weston appears frequently, as a warden and otherwise, in Drapers' MS +140.

[313] Beaven, ii. 229 corrects his ii. 6 designation of ironmonger (a designation also given in Stow, *Survey*, i. 207 and in LBK, fo. 9^{r}).

[314] See n. to John Michell, sheriff 1414–15.

[315] John Arnold in Stow, *Survey*, ii. 172; but Robert Arnold, grocer, in LBK, fo. 39^{v}; Robert Arnold in Jor. 2, fo. 84^{r}. *A Chronicle*, 115, also has Robert Arnold, though identifying his company as the haberdashers. Nightingale, 359, calls Arnold originally a haberdasher and forced to become a grocer. The grocers pay 'diuersez costages' in respect to him during their 1426–7 accounting year (Grocers' GL MS 11570, 162), i.e. during the year he was sheriff, and he is listed (175) as a member of the livery in 1428. See also Grocers' (20th century) GL MS 11592A (Admissions) under 1426, Robert Arnold.

[316] See n. to John Reynwell, sheriff 1411–12.

		John Higham *Draper*[317]
1427–8	John Gedney *Draper*	Henry Frowyk *Mercer* Robert Otele* *Grocer*
1428–9	Henry Barton **2m** *Skinner*	Thomas Dufthous (or Dufhous)[318] *Fishmonger*[319] John Abbot* *Mercer*[320]
1429–30	William Estfeld *Mercer*	William Russe* *Goldsmith* Ralph Holland *Tailor* and *Draper*[321]
1430–1	Nicholas Wotton **2m** *Draper*	Robert Large *Mercer* Walter Chertsey* *Draper*[322]
1431–2	John Welles *Grocer*	Stephen Broun *Grocer* John Hatherle (or Atherle)* *Ironmonger*
1432–3	John Perneys (or Perveys) *Fishmonger*	John Paddesle *Goldsmith* John Olney *Mercer*
1433–4	John Brokle *Draper*	Thomas Chalton* *Mercer* John Lynge *Draper*[323]
1434–5	Robert Otele *Grocer*	Thomas Bernewell* *Fishmonger*

317 Draper: LBK, fo. 39^{v}; see also Beaven, i. 287 and 271. A John Higham appears, as a warden and otherwise, in the Drapers' earliest extant accounts, Drapers' MS +140, *passim*.

318 Beaven corrects to Dufhous at ii. 218 his previous spelling (i. 90) of Dufthons, and uses 'Dufthous (or Dufhous)' in his index.

319 Fishmonger: LBK, fo. 55^{v}.

320 Mercer: LBK, fo. 55^{v}. See also Mercers' MS Wardens' Accounts 1347–1464, fos. 98^{v} and 100^{r} (the Mercers receive and pay money for Abbot as a mercer sheriff). See also Beaven, i. 287 and 271.

321 Draper: Stow, *Survey*, i. 253; but see Merchant Taylors' GL MS 34048/1 fo. 211^{r} (expenses for a tailor sheriff in 1429). For Holland's membership in both companies see C. Barron, 'Ralph Holland and the London Radicals, 1438–1444', in R. Holt and G. Rosser (eds.), *The Medieval Town: A Reader in English Urban History 1200-1540* (London, 1990), 162–3. His name appears a number of times in the Drapers' earliest extant accounts, Drapers' MS +140, *passim*.

322 Draper: Stow, *Survey*, ii. 173; and a Walter Chertsey, draper, also appears in the early parts of the Drapers' earliest extant accounts, Drapers' MS +140, and in *CPMR 1413–37*, 102 (1421), 145 (1422), 171 (1424), 260 (1431), 276–77 (1435).

323 See Drapers' MS +140 fos. A1^{r}, D2^{v}, G1^{v}, and G2^{v} (the company pays oath-taking expenses for Lynge as a draper sheriff).

		Simon Eyre *Draper*
1435–6	Henry Frowyk *Mercer*	Robert Clopton *Draper*
		Thomas Catteworth *Grocer*
1436–7	John Michell **2m** *Stockfishmonger*[324]	William Gregory *Skinner*
		Thomas Morstede* *Fishmonger*[325]
1437–8	William Estfeld **2m** *Mercer*	William Hales* *Mercer*[326]
		William Chapman *Tailor*[327]
1438–9	Stephen Broun *Grocer*	Nicholas Yoo *Draper*
		Hugh Dyke* *Mercer*[328]
1439–40	Robert Large *Mercer*	Philip Malpas *Draper*
		Robert Marshal* *Grocer*[329]
1440–1	John Paddesle *Goldsmith*	John Sutton *Goldsmith*
		William Whetenhall* *Grocer*
1441–2	Robert Clopton *Draper*	William Combes* *Stockfishmonger*
		Richard Rich *Mercer*[330]

[324] See n. to John Michell, sheriff 1414–15.

[325] Fishmonger: LBK fo. 162ᵛ. Draper: *A Chronicle*, 123, but not found in Drapers' MS +140 (earliest extant accounts). A Thomas Morsted, fishmonger, is in *CPMR 1437–57*, 160 (1438).

[326] Mercer: LBK, fo. 171ʳ; see also Mercers' MS Wardens' Account 1347–1464, fos. 127ʳ and 130ʳ (the mercers are receiving and paying money for Hales as a mercer sheriff).

[327] LBK, fo. 171ʳ has draper; but the Merchant Taylors pay for minstrels this year at the sheriffs' oath-taking. A William Chapman was master of the tailors 1428–9 (see Merchant Taylors' GL MS 34048/1 fo. 191ᵛ); and no William Chapman is listed in the Drapers' earliest set of wardens' accounts running *c.*1413–41 (Drapers' MS +140). Chapman was probably a tailor only, though possibly he was connected also with the drapers; see n. to Ralph Holland, sheriff 1429–30, and cf. John Derby, sheriff 1445–6.

[328] Mercer: Jor. 3, fo. 171ᵛ; also Mercers' MS Wardens' Account 1347–1464, fos. 131ʳ and 133ᵛ (the mercers are receiving and paying money for Dyke as a mercer sheriff). Beaven, i. 145, lists a Hugh Dyke, mercer, as a nominee for alderman in 1437.

[329] Grocer: LBK, fo. 178ᵛ; see also Grocers' GL MS 11570, 238, 258 and 260 (the Grocers receive and pay money for Marshal as a grocer sheriff).

[330] Mercer: Stow, *Survey*, i. 110, 275; also Mercers' MS Wardens' Account 1347–1464 fos. 139ᵛ–140ʳ (the mercers receive and pay money for Rich as a mercer sheriff), although Rich's mercer identity has been deleted in LBK, fo. 197ᵛ.

1442–3	John Hatherle (or Atherle) *Ironmonger*	Thomas Beaumond* *Salter*[331] Richard Nordon *Tailor*[332]
1443–4	Thomas Catteworth *Grocer*	John Norman *Draper* Nicholas Wyfold* *Grocer*
1444–5	Henry Frowyk **2m** *Mercer*	Stephen Forster* *Fishmonger*[333] Hugh Wiche *Mercer*
1445–6	Simon Eyre *Draper*	John Derby* *Draper* and *Tailor*[334] Geoffrey Feldynge *Mercer*
1446–7	John Olney *Mercer*	Robert Horne* *Fishmonger*[335] Geoffrey Boleyn *Mercer*
1447–8	John Gedney **2m** *Draper*	Thomas Scott *Draper* William Abraham* *Vintner*
1448–9	Stephen Broun **2m** *Grocer*	William Cantelowe *Mercer* William Marowe* *Grocer*
1449–50	Thomas Chalton *Mercer*	Thomas Canynges *Grocer* William Hulyn[336]* *Fishmonger*
1450–1	Nicholas Wyfold *Grocer*	William Dere* *Pewterer*?[337]

331 Salter: *HW* ii. 533.

332 Tailor: see Merchant Taylors' GL MS 34048/1 fos. 358ʳ and 365ᵛ (the company is receiving and paying money for the oath-taking of a tailor sheriff).

333 Nightingale, e.g. 453, describes him as also a grocer.

334 Beaven, i. 330 n.2, notes that Derby is described in his will (1479) as a draper [*HW*, ii. 579–80] but that he appears to be identical to the John Derby who was master of the tailors and linen armourers in 1461–2. See also Beaven, i. 82 and 345, and ii. 9. In LBK, fo. 283ᵛ, Derby is identified as a draper, and also in Drapers' MS +140, *passim*. Barron (see n. to Ralph Holland, sheriff 1429–30) cites Derby (162 n. 8) as unusually both a draper and a tailor. Cf. 1429–30 Holland and 1437–8 Chapman.

335 Beaven, ii. 9 n. 14, corrects his brewer designation of i. 56, 329 (which he calls 330).

336 William Aulyn: Hughes, 203.

337 Pewterer: suggested by Beaven, ii. 164 and 229. A William Dere is included in the first quarterage payment list in the Pewterers' GL MS 7086/1 fo. 14ᵛ, for 1456–7, but his name has been crossed out and does not appear in subsequent quarterage lists, the next two being on fo. 18ᵛ (for 1458–9) and fo. 21ʳ (for 1459–60). Beaven lists sheriff William Dere as an alderman 1451–6, with a will dated June 1459 and proved February 1464.

		John Middleton *Mercer*
1451–2	William Gregory *Skinner*	Matthew Philip* *Goldsmith*
		Christopher Warter *Skinner*
1452–3	Geoffrey Feldynge *Mercer*	Richard Alley *Skinner*
		Richard Lee* *Grocer*
1453–4	John Norman *Draper*	John Walderne* *Grocer*
		Thomas Cook[338] *Draper*
1454–5	Stephen Forster *Fishmonger*[339]	John Feelde *Stockfishmonger*[340]
		William Taillour* *Grocer*
1455–6	William Marowe *Grocer*	Thomas Oulegrave *Skinner*
		John Yonge* *Grocer*
1456–7	Thomas Canynges *Grocer*	Ralph Verney *Mercer*
		John Steward* *Chandler*[341]
1457–8	Geoffrey[342] Boleyn *Mercer*	William Edward* *Grocer*
		Thomas Reyner *Goldsmith*[343]
1458–9	Thomas Scott *Draper*	Ralph Josselyn* *Draper*
		Richard Nedeham *Mercer*[344]
1459–60	William Hulyn *Fishmonger*	John Stokker *Draper*

[338] Thomas Cook, Junior: LBK, fo. 274^{r}.

[339] See n. to Stephen Forster sheriff 1444–5.

[340] Stockfishmonger: Beaven, ii. 11. Fishmonger: LBK, fo. 278^{v}.

[341] Chandler: Caroline Barron, personal card file at CLRO. A John Steward was master of the Tallow Chandlers in June 1467 and in Dec. 1472 (see R. Monier-Williams, *The Tallow Chandlers of London*, 4 vols. (London, 1973), iii. 53), and was also a company benefactor; and for a John Styward, chandler, in an Oct. 1455 entry see Jor. 5, fo. 267^{v}, and also (1460) *CPMR 1458–82*, 155 (tallow chandler).

[342] Godfrey in Stow, *Survey*, ii. 175.

[343] Goldsmith: Jor. 6, fo. 177^{v}. A Thomas Reyner the elder was a Goldsmiths' warden in 1455–6, 1460–1, and 1464–5 (Goldsmiths' MS 1520, 67, 83, 97), and in several earlier years as well, and a Thomas Rayner the younger, in 1459–60 (Goldsmiths' MS 1520, 79).

[344] Mercer: Mercers' MS Wardens' Accounts 1347–1464, fos. 193^{v} and 194^{r} (the Mercers are receiving and paying money for Nedeham as a mercer sheriff). See also Beaven, i. 288 and 272.

Year	Mayor	Sheriffs
		John Plummer (or Plomer)*[345] *Grocer*
1460–1	Richard Lee *Grocer*	Richard Flemyng *Ironmonger* John Lambarde* *Mercer*
1461–2	Hugh Wiche *Mercer*	George Irlond *Grocer* John Lok* *Mercer*[346]
1462–3	Thomas Cook *Draper*	William Hampton *Fishmonger* Bartholomew James* *Draper*
1463–4	Matthew Philip *Goldsmith*	Robert Bassett *Salter* Thomas Muschampe* *Mercer*[347]
1464–5	Ralph Josselyn *Draper*	John Tate* *Mercer* John Stone *Tailor*[348]
1465–6	Ralph Verney *Mercer*	William Constantyn *Skinner* Henry Waver* *Draper*
1466–7	John Yonge *Grocer*	John Bromer* *Fishmonger* Henry Bryce (or Brice) *Fuller*[349] died 20 June 1467[350] John Stokton *Mercer* replaced Bryce[351]
1467–8[352]	Thomas Oulegrave *Skinner*	Humphrey Hayford *Goldsmith*

345 Nightingale, 499 and 534, states that his original name was John Leynham.

346 Mercer: Beaven, ii. 12. Vintner: LBL, fo. 5^{v}, but for mercer see also Jor. 6, fo. 21^{r}, and Mercers' MS Wardens' Accounts 1347–1464, fos. 201^{v} and 202^{r} (the mercers receive and pay money for Lok as a mercer sheriff).

347 Mercer: Jor. 7, fo. 39^{r}; see also Mercers' MS Wardens' Account 1347–1464, fos. 207^{v} and 208^{r} [my count; leaves are unfoliated] (the mercers are receiving and paying money for Muschampe as a mercer sheriff).

348 Tailor: LBL, fo. 33^{v}; see also Davies, 57 n. 38. See also Beaven: the aldermanic nominee sheriff J. Stone (i. 138 and 154) is presumably the same as the aldermanic nominee John Stone, tailor (i. 231)

349 Fuller: LBL, fo. 46^{v}.

350 LBL, fo. 52^{r} and LBF, fo. 234^{v}; Beaven, ii. p. xxxix; Jor. 7 fo. 150^{r} (died at dawn 20 June).

351 Elected Sat. 20 June 1467, Westminster Mon. 22 June (LBL, fo. 52^{r}). LBF, fo. 234^{v} gives the Westminster date as 21 June.

		Thomas Stalbrook* *Draper*
1468–9	William Taillour *Grocer*	William Haryot *Draper*
		Simon Smyth* *Grocer*[353]
1469–70	Richard Lee **2m** *Grocer*	Robert Drope *Draper*
		Richard Gardyner* *Mercer*
1470–1	John Stokton *Mercer*	John Warde *Mercer*
		John Crosby* *Grocer*
1471–2	William[354] Edward *Grocer*	John Aleyn *Goldsmith*[355]
		John Shelley* *Mercer*[356]
1472–3	William Hampton *Fishmonger*	John Browne *Mercer*
		Thomas Bledlowe* *Grocer*
1473–4	John Tate *Mercer*	William Stokker* *Draper*
		Robert Billesdon *Haberdasher*
1474–5	Robert Drope *Draper*	Edmund Shaa *Goldsmith*
		Thomas Hill* *Grocer*
1475–6	Robert Bassett *Salter*	Robert Colwyche *Tailor*
		Hugh Bryce* *Goldsmith*
1476–7	Ralph Josselyn **2m** *Draper*	Richard Rawson *Mercer*

[352] Nicholas Marchall (ironmonger) is listed as sheriff 1467–8 by Beaven, ii. 12, but is not named as sheriff in any of Stow, *Survey*, Hughes, LBL, or Jor. 7. In the Ironmongers' mid-fifteenth-century accounts (in GL, MS 16988/1) he is a prominent company member, and a warden in both 1455–8 and the early 1460s. The accounts contain no reference to him as sheriff and no unusual expenses such as might be made for a company sheriff. Beaven, ii. 12–13 also lists both Hayford and Stalbrook as sheriffs, 1467–8.

[353] See Grocers' GL MS 11570A, 29 (money received for sheriff's minstrels), and GL MS 11571/2, e.g. fos. 150^{r}, 172^{r}–173^{r}. (On both fos. 172^{v} and 180^{r}, GL MS 11571/2, he is called 'Symkyn' Smith, and also when a company warden in 1461–2, see fo. 2^{r}.)

[354] Willey in Stow, *Survey*, ii. 176.

[355] Goldsmith: LBL, fo. 77^{v} and LBF, fo. 234^{v}. See also Goldsmiths' MS 1520, 155 col. b (costs relating to a company member being sheriff at Midsummer 1472), and 177 and 201 (Aleyn as a goldsmith).

[356] Mercer: LBL, fo. 77^{v} and LBF, fo. 234^{v}; also Mercers' MS Acts of Court, 1, fo. 26^{r}.

		William Horne* *Salter*
1477–8	Humphrey Hayford *Goldsmith*	Henry Colet *Mercer* John Stokker* *Draper*
1478–9	Richard Gardyner *Mercer*	Robert Hardyng* *Goldsmith* Robert Byfeld *Ironmonger*[357]
1479–80	Bartholomew James *Draper*	John Warde *Grocer* Thomas Ilome* *Mercer*
1480–1	John Browne *Mercer*	William Bacon *Haberdasher* Thomas Danyell* *Dyer*[358]
1481–2	William Haryot *Draper*	Robert Tate* *Mercer* William Wyking *Skinner* died 19 Oct. 1481[359] Richard Chawry *Salter* replaced Wyking[360]
1482–3	Edmund Shaa *Goldsmith*	John Mathewe *Mercer* William White* *Draper*
1483–4	Robert Billesdon *Haberdasher*	Thomas Northland (or Norlonde)* *Grocer* William Martin *Skinner*
1484–5	Thomas Hill *Grocer* died 23 Sept. 1485[361] William Stokker *Draper*	Thomas Breteyn* *Ironmonger* died *c.*Sept. 1485[362] Richard Chester *Skinner*

[357] Ironmonger: LBL, fo. 136^{r}; see also the Ironmongers' GL MS 16988/1 fo. 41^{v} (the company pays the oath-taking costs of Byfeld as an ironmonger sheriff) and fo. 42^{r-v}. See also Beaven, i. 199, 190, 154.

[358] Dyer: LBL, fo. 156^{r} and LBF, fo. 234^{v}.

[359] Beaven, ii. 16.

[360] LBL, fo. 168^{v} and LBF, fo. 234^{v}. Elected and sworn Sat. 20 Oct. 1481, Westminster Mon. 22 Oct. (LBL, fo. 168^{v}).

[361] Beaven, ii. 15.

[362] Beaven, ii. 17. Apparently not replaced. Beaven does not include him in his list (ii. xxxix) of sheriffs who died in office. LBL, fo. 212^{r-v} has Breteyn at common council on 23 Sept. and absent from 24 Sept.

	replaced Hill; died 28 Sept. 1485[364]	died 6 Feb. 1485[363]
	John Warde	Ralph Astry
	Grocer	*Fishmonger*
	replaced Stokker[365]	replaced Chester[366]
1485–6	Hugh Bryce	John Swan
	Goldsmith	*Tailor*
		John Tate*
		Mercer
1486–7	Henry Colet	John Percyvale*
	Mercer	*Tailor*
		Hugh Clopton
		Mercer
1487–8	William Horne	William Remyngton
	Salter	*Fishmonger*
		John Fenkyll (or Fynkell)*
		Draper
1488–9	Robert Tate	Ralph Tilney
	Mercer	*Grocer*
		William Isaak*
		Draper
1489–90	William White	William Capel*
	Draper	*Draper*
		John Broke
		Grocer
1490–1	John Mathewe	Henry Cote*
	Mercer	*Goldsmith*
		Robert Revell
		Grocer
		died 23 Feb. 1491[367]
		Hugh Pemberton
		Tailor
		replaced Revell[368]
1491–2	Hugh Clopton	Thomas Wood*
	Mercer	*Goldsmith*
		William Browne
		Mercer[369]
1492–3	William Martin	William Purchase*
	Skinner	*Mercer*

[363] Beaven, ii. 17.

[364] Beaven, ii. 14. Elected and sworn Guildhall [Sat.] 24 Sept. 1485, Tower Mon. 26 Sept. (LBL, fo. 212^{v}).

[365] Elected and sworn Guildhall [Thurs.] 29 Sept. 1485, Westminster [Fri.] 30 Sept.—with sheriffs (LBL, fos. 212^{v}–213^{r}).

[366] Elected Mon. 7 Feb. 1485, sworn Guildhall Thurs. 10 Feb., Westminster Fri. 11 Feb. (LBL, fo. 203^{r}).

[367] Beaven, ii. 18.

[368] Elected and sworn Guildhall Thurs. 24 Feb. 1491, Tower Wed. 2 March (LBL, fo. 283^{v}).

[369] Not William Browne, mercer, sheriff 1504–5, mayor 1513–14. See Beaven, ii. 20 and 21.

		William Welbeck *Haberdasher*
1493–4	Ralph Astry *Fishmonger*	Robert Fabyan* *Draper*
		John Wynger *Grocer*
1494–5	Richard Chawry *Salter*	Nicholas Ailwyn* *Mercer*
		John Warner *Armourer*[370]
1495–6	Henry Colet **2m** *Mercer*	Thomas Kneseworth* *Fishmonger*
		Henry Somer *Haberdasher*[371]
1496–7	John Tate *Mercer*	John Shaa* *Goldsmith*
		Richard Haddon *Mercer*
1497–8	William Purchase *Mercer*	Bartholomew Rede* *Goldsmith*
		Thomas Wyndout *Mercer*
1498–9	John Percyvale *Tailor*	Stephen Jenyns *Tailor*
		Thomas Bradbury* *Mercer*
1499–1500	Nicholas Ailwyn *Mercer*	James Wilforth (or Wylford)* *Tailor*
		Richard Bronde[372] *Fishmonger*[373]
1500–1	William Remyngton *Fishmonger*	John Hawes* *Mercer*
		William Stede *Grocer*
1501–2	John Shaa *Goldsmith*	Lawrence Aylmer* *Draper*
		Henry Hede *Ironmonger*[374]
1502–3	Bartholomew Rede *Goldsmith*	Nicholas Nynes *Tailor*

[370] He was translated to the grocers in 1503 (Beaven, ii. 20).

[371] Haberdasher: LBL fo. 316^{v}.

[372] Thomas Brond in Stow, *Survey*, ii. 179, but referred to by Beaven (ii. p. xxxvii) as Richard Bronde; also Richard Bronde in LBF, fo. 235^{r}; Richard Brande in LBM, fo. 18^{v}, in Jor. 10 fo. 163^{r}, and in Hughes.

[373] Fishmonger: LBM, fo. 18^{v} (Richard Brande).

[374] Ironmonger: LBM, fo. 34^{v}; also LBF, fo. 235^{r}; and the Ironmongers' GL MS 16988/1, fos. 86^{v}–87^{v} identifies him as sheriff 1501–2 and records the various costs of having a company member as sheriff. Beaven, i. 91, lists a Henry Hede, ironmonger, as an aldermanic nominee (and also i. 35, H. Hede).

		Henry Kebyll* *Grocer*
1503–4	William Capel *Draper*	Christopher Hawes* *Mercer* Robert Watts *Draper*[375] died Nov. 1503[376] Thomas Graunger *Skinner* replaced Watts[377]
1504–5	John Wynger *Grocer*	Roger Acheley* *Draper* William Browne *Mercer*[378]
1505–6	Thomas Kneseworth *Fishmonger*	Richard Shore* *Draper* Roger Grove *Grocer*
1506–7[379]	Richard Haddon *Mercer*	William Copynger* *Fishmonger* William Fitz William *Merchant Taylor*
1507–8	William Browne *Mercer*[380] died 22 March 1508[381] Lawrence Aylmer *Draper* replaced Browne[383]	William Boteler (or Butler)* *Grocer* John Kirkby *Merchant Taylor*[382]

[375] Draper: LBM, fo. 78^{v}; also LBF, fo. 235^{r}; and see Beaven, i. 199, 3, 109. The Drapers pay for trumpeters (and their hats etc.) for him as a draper sheriff (Drapers' MS + 403 fo. 77^{r}); and he was a company warden in 1494–5 (fo. 58^{v}).

[376] LBM, f. 82^{v}. LBF, fo. 235^{r} gives 9 Nov.

[377] Elected and sworn Guildhall Sat. 11 Nov. 1503 (LBM, fo. 82^{v}), Westminster [Mon.] 13 Nov. (Raphael Holinshed, *Chronicles of England, Scotland, and Ireland,* [ed. Henry Ellis], 6 vols. [London, 1807–8], iii. 531).

[378] Not William Browne, mercer, sheriff 1491–2, mayor 1507–8. See Beaven, ii. 20 and 21.

[379] In this year Robert Johnson, goldsmith, was elected sheriff, along with Copynger (the mayor's choice: Jor. 10, fo. 364^{v}), but the king refused to admit Johnson. See Stow, *Survey*, ii. 179 (Thomas Johnson) n. 2. Johnson appears, however, in the Stow, *Survey*, main listings; and Beaven, ii. 21 lists him as sheriff in 1506. LBM's entry for the election of sheriffs in 1506 (fo. 124^{r}) is unfinished. The Mercers' MS Acts of Court, 1, records (fo. 137^{v}, assembly of 8 Oct.) the dismissal of Johnson and the admitting of William Fitz William, who is listed by Beaven (ii. 21) as sheriff 1506–7.

[380] Not William Browne, mercer, sheriff 1504–5 and mayor 1513–4. See Beaven, ii. 20 and 21.

[381] Beaven, ii. 20.

[382] Merchant Taylor: LBM, fo. 133^{v}; also LBF, fo. 235^{r}. Probably the John Kirkby, merchant taylor, mentioned in Stow, *Survey*, i. 145 as a sheriff but without a date given. See also Beaven, i. 91, 155, and Davies, e.g. 295.

[383] Elected and sworn Guildhall Mon. 27 March 1508, Tower Wed. 29 March (LBM, fo. 142^{r}).

1508–9	Stephen Jenyns *Merchant Taylor*	Thomas Exmue (or Exmewe)* *Goldsmith* Richard Smyth *Merchant Taylor*[384]
1509–10	Thomas Bradbury *Mercer* died 11 Jan. 1510[385] William Capell **2m** *Draper* replaced Bradbury[387]	George Monoux* *Draper* John Doget *Merchant Taylor*[386]
1510–11	Henry Kebyll *Grocer*	John Rest *Grocer* John Milborne* *Draper*
1511–12	Roger Achele *Draper*	Thomas Mirfyn *Skinner* Nicholas Shelton* *Mercer*
1512–13	William Copynger *Fishmonger* died 7 Feb. 1513[388] Richard Haddon **2m** *Mercer* replaced Copynger[389]	Robert Fenrother *Goldsmith* Robert Aldernes (or Holdernes)* *Haberdasher*
1513–14	William Browne *Mercer*[391] died 3 June 1514[392] John Tate **2m** *Mercer* replaced Browne[394]	John Brugge (or Bruges)[390] *Draper* John Dawes* *Grocer* died 15 June 1514[393] Roger Basford *Mercer* replaced Dawes[395]
1514–15	George Monoux *Draper*	James Yarford (or Yerford)* *Mercer* John Mundy *Goldsmith*
1515–16	William Boteler (or Butler) *Grocer*	Henry Worley* *Goldsmith*

384 Merchant Taylor: LBM fo.146^{v}; also LBF fo. 235^{v}; and this Smyth is also presumably the Richard Smyth, merchant taylor, listed as an aldermanic nominee in Beaven, i. 218. See Davies, e.g. 301.

385 Beaven, ii. 20.

386 Merchant Taylor: LBM, fo. 163^{r}; also LBF, fo. 235^{v}, and Stow, *Survey*, i. 351. See Davies, 288–9.

387 Elected [Sat.] 12 Jan. 1510 (LBM, fos. 166^{v}–167^{v}).

388 Beaven, ii. 21.

389 Elected [Tues.] 8 Feb. 1513 (LBM, fo. 202^{r}).

390 John Bridges: Stow, *Survey*, ii. 180 (alternate spellings of Brugges and Bruge also given). But Stow, *Survey*, ii. 181, uses Brugge when the same individual becomes mayor in 1520.

391 Not William Browne, mercer, sheriff 1491–2, mayor 1507–8. See Beaven, ii. 20 and 21.

392 Beaven, ii. 21.

393 Beaven, ii. 23. LBF, fo. 235^{v} gives 14 June 1514.

394 Elected [Tues.] 6 June 1514 (LBM, fo. 221^{r}).

395 Elected Fri. 16 June 1514 (LBF, fo. 235^{v}).

		Richard Grey *Ironmonger* died 20 Oct. 1515[396] William Bayley *Draper* replaced Grey[397]
1516–17	John Rest *Grocer*	John Thurston *Goldsmith*[398] Thomas Semer (or Seymour)* *Mercer*
1517–18	Thomas Exmue (or Exmewe) *Goldsmith*	Thomas Baldry* *Mercer* Ralph Symonds *Fishmonger*
1518–19	Thomas Mirfyn *Skinner*	John Aleyn (or Alen)* *Mercer* James Spencer *Vintner*
1519–20	James Yarford (or Yerford) *Mercer*	Nicholas Partryche *Grocer* John Wylkynson* *Draper*
1520–1	John Brugge (or Bruges) *Draper*	John Kyme* *Mercer* John Skevynton *Merchant Taylor*
1521–2	John Milborne *Draper*	Thomas Pargeter *Salter* John Breton* *Merchant Taylor*[399]
1522–3	John Mundy *Goldsmith*	John Rudstone* *Draper* John Champneys *Skinner*
1523–4	Thomas Baldry *Mercer*	Michael Englysshe* *Mercer* Nicholas Jenyns *Skinner*
1524–5	William Bayley *Draper*	Ralph Dodmer* *Mercer*[400] William Roche *Draper*

396 LBM, fo. 255^{v}, and Beaven, ii. p. xxxix.

397 Elected Mon. 22 Oct. 1515, sworn Guildhall Sat. 27 Oct., Westminster Mon. 29 Oct.—with mayor (LBM, fo. 255^{v} and LBF, fo. 235^{v}; Rep. 3, fos. 52^{v}–53^{r}, 55^{r}).

398 Formerly a broiderer, Thurston was translated to the Goldsmiths 30 Aug. 1515 (see Beaven, ii. 23).

399 Merchant Taylor: LBN, fo. 171^{v}, LBF, fo. 236^{r}.

400 Formerly a brewer, translated to the Mercers 7 Nov. 1521 (Beaven, ii. 25).

1525–6	John Aleyn (or Alen) *Mercer*	John Cawnton* *Haberdasher* Christopher Ascue *Draper*
1526–7	Thomas Semer (or Seymour) *Mercer*	Nicholas Lambarde (or Lambert) *Grocer* Stephen Pecocke* *Haberdasher*
1527–8	James Spencer *Vintner*	John Hardy* *Haberdasher* William Hollyes *Mercer*
1528–9	John Rudstone *Draper*	Ralph Warren* *Mercer* John Long *Salter*
1529–30	Ralph Dodmer *Mercer*[402]	Michael Dormer*[401] *Mercer* Walter Champyon *Draper*
1530–1	Thomas Pargeter *Salter*	Richard Choppyn *Tallow Chandler*[403] William Dauntsey* *Mercer*
1531–2	Nicholas Lambarde (or Lambert) *Grocer*	Richard Gresham* *Mercer* Edward Altham *Clothworker*[404]
1532–3	Stephen Pecocke *Haberdasher*	Richard Reynolds* *Mercer*[405] Nicholas Pyncheon *Butcher*[406] died 8 Mar. 1533[407] John Martyn *Butcher*[408] replaced Pyncheon died Sept. 1533[409]

[401] Michael Wormer: Hughes, 204.

[402] See n. to Ralph Dodmer, sheriff 1524–5.

[403] Choppyn was later (20 June 1532) translated to the grocers (Beaven, ii. 27).

[404] Clothworker: LBO, fo. 232^{v}; also Clothworkers' MS Wardens' Accounts, 1, fo. 4^{v} of no. 10 (company receipts and expenses at Midsummer because a company member is sheriff).

[405] Mercer: LBO, fo. 263^{v}; see also Mercers' MS Acts of Court, 2, fos. 48^{v} 53^{v} (the company is attending its own member as sheriff).

[406] Butcher: LBO, fo. 263^{v}; a prominent early sixteenth-century member of the company, see P. E. Jones, *The Butchers of London* (London, 1976), 144.

[407] LBP, fo. 6^{v}.

[408] Butcher: LBP, fo. 6^{v}; see also LBF, fos. 48^{r} 236^{r}, and Stow, *Survey*, i. 246.

[409] Elected [Wed.] 12 March, sworn Guildhall and to Tower Wed. 12 or 19 Mar. (LBP, fo. 6^{v}, Jor. 13 fo. 365^{v}); died Sept. (LBP, fo. 22^{v}), by 16 Sept. (Rep. 9, fo. 25^{r}).

		John Preest *Grocer*[410] replaced Martyn[411]
1533–4	Christopher Ascue *Draper*	William Forman* *Haberdasher* Thomas Kytson *Mercer*
1534–5	John Champneys *Skinner*	William Denham *Ironmonger* Nicholas Leveson* *Mercer*[412]
1535–6	John Aleyn (or Alen) **2m** *Mercer*	Humphrey Monmouth* *Draper* John Cotes *Salter*
1536–7	Ralph Warren *Mercer*	Robert Pagett* *Merchant Taylor* William Bowyer *Draper*
1537–8	Richard Gresham *Mercer*	Thomas Lewen *Ironmonger* John Gresham* *Mercer*
1538–9	William Forman *Haberdasher*	Nicholas Gybson *Grocer* William Wilkenson* *Mercer*[413]
1539–40	William Hollyes *Mercer*	John Fayrey* *Mercer*[414] Thomas Huntlowe *Haberdasher*[415]
1540–1	William Roche *Draper*	William Laxton* *Grocer* Martin Bowes *Goldsmith*

[410] Grocer: LBP, fo. 22^{v}. A John Preest is listed as three times a warden of the company (1526, 1534, 1537) in *List of the Wardens of the Grocers' Company from 1345 to 1907* (London: [Grocers' Company,] 1907); see e.g. Grocers' GL MS 11571/4 fo. 233^{v} (Preest as warden in 1526–7). The Grocers' accounts for 1533–4 (Preest's year as sheriff) are missing in the company's series (GL MS 11571/3–5) for the early sixteenth century.

[411] Elected and sworn Guildhall and to Tower Thurs. 18 Sept. 1533 (LBP, fos. 22^{v}–23^{r}).

[412] Mercer: LBP, fo. 46; also LBF, fo. 236^{v}, and Stow, *Survey*, i. 145; and see also Mercers' MS Acts of Court, 2, fo. 80^{r} (the company is attending its own member as sheriff).

[413] Mercer: LBP, fo. 167^{r}; also LBF, fo. 236^{v}; see also Mercers' MS Acts of Court, 2, fo. 117^{r-v} (the company intended to attend its own member as sheriff).

[414] Mercer: LBP, fo. 194v; also LBF, fo. 236^{v}; see also Mercers' MS Acts of Court, 2, fo. 128^{r} (the company is attending its own member as sheriff).

[415] Haberdasher: LBP, fo. 194^{v}; also LBF, fo. 236^{v}; see also Beaven, i. 218.

1541–2	Michael Dormer *Mercer*	Rowland Hill* *Mercer* Henry Suckley *Merchant Taylor*[416]
1542–3	John Cotes *Salter*	Henry Huberthorn* *Merchant Taylor* Henry Amcotts (or Hamcotts) *Fishmonger*[417]
1543–4	William Bowyer *Draper* died 13 Apr. 1544[418] Ralph Warren **2m** *Mercer* replaced Bowyer[419]	John Tolos* *Clothworker* Richard Dobbys *Skinner*
1544–5	William Laxton *Grocer*	John Wylford* *Merchant Taylor* Andrew Judde *Skinner*
1545–6	Martin Bowes *Goldsmith*	Ralph Aleyn[420] *Grocer* George Barne*[421] *Haberdasher*
1546–7	Henry Huberthorn *Merchant Taylor*	Richard Gerveys* *Mercer* Thomas Curtes *Pewterer*[422]
1547–8	John Gresham *Mercer*	Thomas Whyte* *Merchant Taylor* Robert Chertsey *Mercer*
1548–9	Henry Amcotts (or Hamcotts) *Fishmonger*[423]	William Lok* *Mercer* John Ayliffe *Barber-Surgeon*[424]
1549–50	Rowland Hill *Mercer*	Richard Turke* *Fishmonger*

416 Merchant Taylor: LBQ, fo. 36^{v}; also LBF, fo. 236^{v}, and Stow, *Survey*, i. 347; see also Mercers' MS Register of Writings, 2, fo. 138^{v}.

417 The goldsmiths, however, agree to provide forty armed men for him at the Midsummer Watch in 1543 (Goldsmiths' MS 1524, Book G, 74), which suggests a goldsmiths' affiliation. (Only seven bowmen are to be provided by the goldsmiths for the mayor, 80.)

418 Beaven, ii. 28.

419 Elected Thurs. 17 Apr. 1544 (Jor. 15, fo. 86^{r-v}, LBQ, fo. 105^{r-v} [Thurs. 27 April an error for Thurs. 17 April]); Mon. 21 Apr. Westminster (LBQ, fo. 105^{r}).

420 Ralph Alley in Stow, *Survey*, ii. 182 (but Allen, i. 322).

421 George Barons: Hughes, 204.

422 Later (22 Sept. 1556) translated to the fishmongers (Beaven, ii. 33).

423 See also n. to Henry Amcotts, sheriff 1542–3.

424 Later (17 July 1550) translated to the grocers (Beaven, ii. 33). See also Stow, *Survey*, i. 289.

		John Yorke *Merchant Taylor*[425]
1550–1	Andrew Judde *Skinner*	Augustine Hynde* *Clothworker* John Lyon *Grocer*
1551–2	Richard Dobbys *Skinner*	John Lambarde (or Lamberd)* *Draper* John Cowper *Fishmonger*
1552–3	George Barne *Haberdasher*	William Garrarde* *Haberdasher* John[426] Maynard *Mercer*[427]
1553–4	Thomas Whyte *Merchant Taylor*	Thomas Offley* *Merchant Taylor* William Hewet *Clothworker*
1554–5	John Lyon *Grocer*	David Woodroffe* *Haberdasher* William Chester *Draper*
1555–6	William Garrarde *Haberdasher*	John Machell[428] *Clothworker* Thomas Leigh* *Mercer*
1556–7	Thomas Offley *Merchant Taylor*	William Harper* *Merchant Taylor* John Whyte *Grocer*
1557–8	Thomas Curtes *Fishmonger*[429]	James Altham *Clothworker* Richard Malorye* *Mercer*
1558–9	Thomas Leigh *Mercer*	John Hawes (or Halse)* *Clothworker* Richard Champyon *Draper*

425 Merchant Taylor: LBR, fo. 24v. A John York is admitted to the merchant taylors in 1545–6 (Merchant Taylors' GL MS 34048/4 fo. 3r).

426 Thomas in LBR, fo. 205r and Jor. 16, fo. 201r, but John in Stow, *Survey*, ii. 183 and in the Mercers' MS Acts of Court, 2, fo. 262v.

427 Mercer: LBR, fo. 205r (Thomas Maynarde); see also Mercers' MS Acts of Court, 2, fo. 262v (the sheriff, John Maynard, is borrowing from his own company).

428 John Macham: Hughes, 204.

429 Translated 22 Sept. 1556 from the pewterers (Beaven, ii. 33).

Appendix 2: Civic Office Holders *c.* 1300–*c.* 1500

(i) Recorders of London

1298	Geoffrey de Norton	*LBB*, 218–19
1304	John de Wengrave	*LBC*, 132–3
1320	Geoffrey de Hertpole	*LBE*, 11–12
1320	Robert de Swaclyve	*LBE*, 12
1329	Gregory de Norton	Strype, *Survey*, bk. 5, 160
1339	Roger de Depham	Strype, *Survey*, bk. 5, 160
*c.*1359	Hugh de Sadelyngstanes	*LBG*, 105
1362	Thomas Lodelowe	Strype, *Survey*, bk. 5, 160; *LBG*, 138
1365	William de Haldene	*LBG*, 193
1377	William Cheyne	Strype, *Survey*, bk. 5, 160; *LBH*, 54
1390	John Tremayne	*LBF*, 273; *LBH*, 355
1392	William Makenade	*LBH*, 385
1394	John Cokeyn/Cokayne	*LBH*, 417
1398	Matthew de Southworth	*LBH*, 444
1404	Thomas Thornburgh	*LBI*, 32
1406	John Prestone	*LBI*, 51
1415	John Barton	*LBI*, 143
1420	John Fray	*LBI*, 248, 272
1426	John Symond	CLRO, Jor. 2, fo. 86
1436	Alexander Anne	*LBK*, 194
1438	Thomas Cokayne	CLRO, Jor. 3, fo. 163^{v}
1440	John Bowys/Bowes	CLRO, Jor. 3, fo. 46
1442	Robert Danvers	CLRO, Jor. 3, fo. 141
1450	Thomas Billing	CLRO, Jor. 5, fo. 46^{v}
1454	Thomas Urswyk	CLRO, Jor. 5, fos. 196, 210^{v}
1471	Humphrey Starky	CLRO, Jor. 7, fo. 243; 8, fo. 7
1483	Thomas Fitz William	CLRO, Jor. 9, fo. 26
1496	Sir Robert Sheffield	*LBL*, 308
1508	John Chaloner (Chalyner)	Strype, *Survey*, bk. 5, 160; CLRO, LBM, fo. 146^{v}

This list includes unpublished information from a file compiled by B. Masters, 'The City's Law Officers and Counsel to *c.*1600' (1999), at CLRO.

(ii) Undersheriffs of London

1298	William Londoneston		*CEMCR*, 236–7
1309	John de Camera 'clerk'		*LBC*, 181
1374/5	John de Mordon		*CPMR 1364–81*, 266, 272–3
1379/80	?John Levyngton		CLRO, MC1/1
1383	William de Cressewyk		*Poss.Ass.* 46
1391	William Sysel (Cecil)		PRO, C1/7 m. 18
1392	John Edmond		CLRO, HR CP/117 m. 8v
1394/5	John Weston	Thomas Colrex	CLRO, HR CP/120 m. 4
1402	John Selman		CLRO, HR CP/128 m. 9
1405	John Bartone senior		CLRO, HR CP/131 m. 3
1411	John Fray		GL, MS 25,125/53
1412	William Ashton		GL, MS 25,125/54
1416	John Fray	William Ashton	CLRO, Jor. 1, fo. 1v
1417	John Fray	William Ashton	CLRO, Jor. 1, fo. 39v
1419	William Enderby		*LBI*, 209–10 (dismissed from office for extortion)
1423	Alexander Anne		*Poss.Ass.* 100 n. 1
pre 1427	John Fortescue		*Poss.Ass.* 105; CLRO, Jor. 2, fo. 64
1429/30	[Gilbert] Hotoft		*Poss.Ass.* 107
1430/1	John Forster		CLRO, HR CP/155 m. 3
1431/2	John Forster	John Wilton	*Poss.Ass.* 108, n. 5
1432/3	John Forster		*Poss.Ass.* 111
1433/4	John Markham		*Poss.Ass.* 113, n. 4
1434/5	Thomas Burgoyne		*Poss.Ass.* 114, n. 2
1437	John Wilton		CLRO, Jor. 3, fo. 89
1439	Robert Heyworth		CLRO, Jor. 3, fo. 25
1441	Thomas Burgoyne	John Wilton	CLRO, Jor. 3, fos. 88v, 89; *LBK*, 257
1442	Thomas Burgoyne	John Wilton	*Poss.Ass.* 117, 119
1443		John Wilton	*Poss.Ass.* 118 n. 1
1446	Thomas Burgoyne		*Poss.Ass.* 122 n. 3
1449	Thomas Burgoyne	Thomas Billing	CLRO, Jor. 5, fo. 13; *Poss.Ass.* 123

This list is largely derived from information supplied by Dr Penny Tucker and Dr Hannes Kleineke. It also includes unpublished information from the file compiled by B. Masters, 'The City's Law Officers and Counsel to *c.*1600' (1999) at CLRO, and from N. Ramsay, 'The English Legal Profession *c.*1340–*c.*1450' (University of Cambridge Ph.D. thesis, 1985), pp. xliv–xlv. The two London sheriffs had three undersheriffs, two with responsibility for London, and one for Middlesex.

1450	Thomas Burgoyne	Roger Birkes	CLRO, Jor. 5, fo. 47^{v}: *Poss.Ass.* 121, 124, 125, 128, 129 n.3
1453	Thomas Burgoyne	Roger Birkes	*LBK*, 350, 359; *Poss.Ass.* 126
1454	Thomas Burgoyne	Roger Birkes	CLRO, Jor. 5, fo. 47^{v}
1455	Thomas Burgoyne	Roger Birkes	*LBK*, 370
1459	Thomas Burgoyne	Guy Fairfax	CLRO, Jor. 6, fos. 138^{v}
1460	Thomas Burgoyne	Thomas Rigby, *loco* Fairfax	CLRO, Jor. 6, fos. 263; *CPMR 1458-82*, 20, 23
1461	Thomas Burgoyne	Thomas Rigby	CLRO, Jor. 6, fo. 22^{v}
1463	Thomas Burgoyne	Thomas Rigby	*LBL*, 35–6
1467	Thomas Burgoyne	Thomas Rigby	*CPMR 1458–82*, 48; PRO, C254/150/53
1469	Thomas Burgoyne	Thomas Rigby	*CPMR 1458–82*, 66, 118
1470	John Watno		*CCR 1468–76*, no. 482
1478	John Watno	Thomas Rigby	*CPMR 1458–82*, 118; PRO, SC6/1140/27, m. 2
1484	John Watno	Thomas Rigby	CLRO, Jor. 9, fo. 58^{v}
1485	John Watno	Thomas Rigby	CLRO, Jor. 9, fo. 87^{v}; *LBL*, 227
1485	John Haugh/Hawes *loco* John Watno, dec.		*LBL*, 227
1486	Richard Higham	Thomas Rigby	CLRO, Jor. 9, fo. 122
1487	Richard Higham	Thomas Salle	CLRO, Jor. 9, fos. 156^{v}, 209, 237^{v}, 257^{v}, 278^{v}; Jor. 10, fos. 35, 58^{v}
1496	Thomas Marowe	Thomas Salle	CLRO, Jor. 10, fo. 77^{v}
1497	Thomas Marowe	Edmund Dudley	CLRO, Jor. 10, fos. 105, 138, 163^{v}, 195, 233^{v}
1502	Ralph Legh	Richard Broke	CLRO, Jor. 10, fos. 293^{v}, 365

(iii) Common Serjeants-at-Law (Common Pleaders)

*c.*1293–1301	Ralph Pecok	*London Assize of Nuisance*, p. xxix
1319	Gregory de Norton	*LBE*, 20; *London Assize of Nuisance*, 57
*c.*1328	Reginald Wolleward	*London Assize of Nuisance*, p. xxix
1330	William de Iford	CLRO, HR CP, 54 m. 6v; *LBE*, 270
*c.*1347	William de Ford	Strype, *Survey*, bk. 5, 102
1351	Adam de Acres	*LBF*, 234; *London Assize of Nuisance*, 110
by 1356	Thomas Morice	*LBG*, 79, 114
by 1365	John de Briclesworth	*LBG*, 163, 176
1365	John de Wentbrigge	*LBG*, 199
1373	Ralph Strode	*LBG*, 317; *LBH*, 15, 83
1382	John Reche	*LBH*, 23, 305
1388	John Tremayne	*LBH*, 52, 76
*c.*1390	Robert Peek	*CPMR 1381-1413*, 201; *LBH*, 412
*c.*1402	John Weston	*LBI* 19; *CPMR 1413-37*, 43
by 1421	John Fray	*CPMR 1413-37*, 99–102, 106
1423	Alexander Anne	CLRO, Jor. 2, fo. 4; *CPMR 1413-37*, 286
1436	John Mettele	CLRO, Jor. 3, fo. 127^{v}
1437	John Wilton	CLRO, Jor. 3, fo. 188 *facie inversa*
1441	Robert Danvers	CLRO, Jor. 3, fo. 97
1442	Richard (recte, Walter)[1] Moyle, of Gray's Inn	CLRO, Jor. 3, fo. 142^{v}
1443	Thomas Billing (Belling)	CLRO, Jor 4, fo. 9
1449	John Nedeham, *loco* Billing	CLRO, Jor. 5, fos. 13^{v}, 212
1453	Thomas Ursewyk, *loco* Nedeham	CLRO, Jor. 5, fo. 113^{v}
1454	Robert Ingleton, *loco* Ursewyk	CLRO, Jor. 5, fo. 210^{v}
1456	Guy Fairfax	CLRO, Jor. 6, fo. 65^{v}
1459	Thomas Rigby, *loco* Fairfax	CLRO, Jor. 6, fo. 138^{v}
1460	Thomas Bryan	CLRO, Jor. 6, fo. 263
1463	John Baldwin, *loco* Bryan	CLRO, Jor. 7, fo. 40^{v}
1469	Robert Molineux, gentleman	CLRO, Jor. 7, fo. 194^{v}
1485	John Haugh, gentleman, *loco* Molineux, dec.	CLRO, Jor. 9, fo. 86^{v}
1485	Richard Higham	Strype, *Survey*, bk. 5, 162
pre-1492	Thomas Frowyke, *loco* Higham	*LBL*, 280–1

Taken from B. Masters, ' The Common Serjeant', *Guildhall Miscellany*, 2 (1967), 379–89, at 383–5; additional information from unpublished file compiled by B. Masters, 'The City's Law Officers and Counsel to c. 1600' (1999), at CLRO.

[1] I owe this correction to Dr Hannes Kleineke.

1492	Thomas Marowe (Marwe), gentleman, *loco* Frowyke	*LBL*, 280–1
1495	John Greene	CLRO, Jor. 10, fo. 50b^{v}
1521	Henry White, *loco* Greene	CLRO, Jor. 12, fo. 154

(iv) Chamberlains

1237	John de Woborne and John le Wachere	CLRO, LBC, fo. 45b^{v}; *Liber Horn*, ff. 292–3; *Munimenta Gildhallae Londoniensis*, i, 418[1]
*c.*1274–77	Stephen de Mundene, goldsmith, and Hugh Motun	*LBA*, 134, 226, 7
*c.*1277–85	Hugh Motun, pepperer	*LBA*, 26–9, 226
*c.*1288	William de Bettoyne, pepperer	*LBC*, 24–5, 30, 63
*c.*1298/9?	Geoffrey de Norton	*Liber Albus*, 14
1298	John de Dunstaple, skinner,	*LBB*, 70; *LBC*, 65
	and Simon de Paris, mercer	*LBC*, 31, 145
1300	Nicholas Pycot, mercer	*LBC*, 64–5
1304	Richard Poterel, cornmonger/blader	*LBC*, 176
1310	Luke de Haveryng, corder and merchant	*LBD*, 237
1311	John le Mazeliner, pepperer (and goldsmith?)	*LBD*, 79
1313	John Dode, ironmonger	*LBD*, 23; *LBC*, 182
1318	Thomas Prentiz, woolmonger	*LBD*, 28
1320	Andrew Horn, fishmonger	*LBD*, 30
1328	Henry de Seccheford, mercer	*LBE*, 231
1336	Thomas de Maryns, apothecary	*LBE*, 291
1349	Thomas de Waldene, apothecary	*LBF*, 191
*c.*1359	John de Cantebrigge, fishmonger	*LBG*, 58
1374	William (de) Eynesham, pepperer	*LBG*, 320
1378	John Ussher	*LBH*, 103
1380	Richard Odyham, grocer (pepperer)	*LBH*, 149
1391	Stephen Speleman, mercer	*LBH*, 390
1404	John Proffyt, fishmonger	*LBI*, 34
1416	John Hill, fishmonger	*LBI*, 147
1420	John Bederenden, draper	*LBI*, 245
1434	John Chichele, grocer	*LBK*, 183
1449	John Middleton, mercer	*LBK*, 329
1450	John Sturgeon, mercer	*LBK*, 332
1454	Thomas Thornton, draper	*LBK*, 366
1463	Robert Colwyche, tailor	*LBL*, 35
1474	William Philip, goldsmith	*LBL*, 123
1479	Miles Adys, goldsmith	*LBL*, 166

Unless indicated otherwise, this list is from B. Masters, *The Chamberlain of the City of London 1237–1987* (London, 1988), 105–9.

[1] From W. Kellaway, 'The Coroner in Medieval London', in A. Hollaender, and W. Kellaway, (eds.), *Studies in London History Presented to P. E. Jones* (London, 1969), 75–91, at 76 n. 6.

1484	William Purchase, mercer	*LBL*, 215
1492	William Milbourne (Milbroude, Milbronde, Melborne), painter	*LBL*, 289
1506	Nicholas Mattok, fishmonger	CLRO, Jor. 10, fo. 364^{v}
1517	John Barnard	CLRO, Jor. 12, fo. 194^{v}; *LBL*, 279

(v) Chamber Clerks/Controllers

*c.*1294	John of the Chamber	*LBB*, 57
1311	David de Cotesbroke	*LBD*, 275
1319/20	John de Burton	*LBE*, 20
*c.*1332	John de Ilford	*LBE*, 6, 270
1335	Richard de Waltham, *loco* John de Ilford	*LBE*, 6
1380/1	John Marchaunt	*LBH*, 163
*c.*1382	John Dunstone	*LBH*, 197
1400	Richard Osbarn	*LBI*, 6
1437	William Chedworth	CLRO, Jor. 3, fo. 191
1450	Robert Langford (appointed)	CLRO, Jor. 5, fo. 47
1454	Robert Langford (sworn)	CLRO, Jor. 5, fo. 194^{v}
1478	John Hert	*LBL*, 160
1505	Richard Gough, fishmonger	CLRO, Rep. 1, fo. 169^{v}

This list includes unpublished information from notes compiled by Betty Masters on the Comptroller of the Chamber (ACCN/1999/89/2) at CLRO.

(vi) Common Clerks

1274	Ralph Crepyn, *alias* de Alegate or Aldgate	*Rotuli Hundredorum*, 428, 415
1284	John de Bauquell (Batequell, Banquell, Bankwell)	*LBA*, 161
1311	Hugh de Waltham	*LBD*, 275
1335, Jan	Roger de Depham *loco* Waltham, deceased	*LBE*, 5
1335, Aug	John de Shirbourne	*LBE*, 290
1364	John Lucas	*LBG*, 169
1368	Henry de Padingtone	*LBG*, 232
1375	Henry Perot	*LBH*, 8
*c.*1399	John Marchaunt	*LBI*, 19
1417	John Carpenter *loco* Marchaunt	*LBI*, 19; *LBK*, 242 n.
1438	Richard Barnet	CLRO, Jor. 3, fo. 172
1446	Roger Spicer *alias* Tonge	CLRO, Jor. 4, fo. 149; Jor. 6, fo. 46
1461	William Dunthorne	CLRO, Jor. 6, fo. 7^{v}
1490	Nicholas Pakenham	CLRO, Jor. 9, fo. 213^{v}
1510	Walter Stubbe *loco* Pakenham	CLRO, Jor. 11, fo. 113
1514	William Paver *loco* Stubbe, deceased	CLRO, Jor. 11, fo. 190^{v}

List taken from B. Masters, 'The Town Clerk', *Guildhall Miscellany*, 3 (1969), 55–74, at 71–2.

(vii) Mayors' Esquires/Swordbearers

1381	John Blyton	*A Chronicle*, 74; *LBH*, 229, 433
*c.*1394	John Credy	*LBI*, 66; *LBH*, 433
1419 (still)	John Credy	*LBI*, 226
1421	John Hastings	*LBI*, 259
1426	John Pencriche	CLRO, Jor. 2, fo. 78^{v}
1442	Richard Power	CLRO, Jor. 3, fo. 136
1464	John Wellisbourne	CLRO, Jor. 7, fo. 68^{v}
1465	John Morley, gentleman	*LBL*, 68; CLRO, Jor. 7, fo. 104
1467	John Medford (Metford)	CLRO, Jor. 7, fos. 154, 197
1485–1489	Walter Thomas	CLRO, Jor. 9, fo. 81
1504	Valentine Mason	CLRO, Rep. 1, fo. 166
1522	Richard Barwick (Berwyck)	CLRO, Rep. 5, fo. 293

List taken from T. K. Collett, 'The Swordbearer', *Guildhall Historical Association*, 3 (1963), 39–45, at 44–5; includes unpublished information from file compiled by B. Masters, 'Officers of the Mayor's Household before 1600' (1989), at CLRO.

(viii) Common Serjeants-at-Arms/Common Criers

1291	Thomas Juvenal	*LBC*, 123, 161
1309	Thomas de Kent	*LBD*, 14
1327/8	Robert Flambard	CLRO, HR CP/51, fo. 1d
1338	John Bevyn, deputy to Robert Flambard	*LBF*, 30
1343	Nicholas de Abyndone	*LBF*, 87
1369	Robert de Kaytone (Cayton)	*Calendar of Letters of Mayor*, 132; *LBG*, 242
1370	John de Watlyngton	*LBG*, 265; *LBH*, 252
1390	Hugh Batisford (Battesford)	*LBH*, 375; *CPMR 1381–1412*, 233; *LBI*, 65
1407	John Pychard	*LBI*, 54
1417	John Combe	*LBI*, 189
1460	John Asshe (Aisshe)	CLRO, Jor. 6, fo. 203; *LBK*, 401
1485	Thomas Cambrey	CLRO, Jor. 9, fos. 91^{v}, 229
1489	Thomas Say	CLRO, Jor. 9, fo. 229
c.1504	Richard White	CLRO, Rep. 1, fo. 159

List taken from P. E. Jones 'Common Crier and Serjeant at Arms', *Transactions of Guildhall Historical Association*, 3 (1963), 80–87, at 86–87; includes unpublished information from file compiled by B. Masters, 'Officers of the Mayor's Household before 1600' (1989), at CLRO.

(ix) Waterbailiffs

1385	John Salesbury	*CPMR 1381–1412*, 119
1387	John Besouthe	*LBH*, 314
1396	Alexander Boner	*CPMR 1381–1412*, 273; *LBH*, 426
1413	William Talworth	*LBI*, 120–21; *CPR 1413–16*, 94; CLRO, Jor. 2, fos. 21^{v}, 25^{v}
1431	John Houghton	*LBK*, 133
1445	William Veyse(y)	*LBK*, 303–03; CLRO, Jor. 4, fo. 59^{v}
1457	John Goode	CLRO, Jor. 6, fo. 188
1486	Henry Snowe	CLRO, Jor. 9, fo. 118
1496	Geoffrey Moreton	CLRO, Jor. 10, fo. 75
1522	Thomas Brugge(s)	CLRO, Rep. 4, fo. 181^{v}, 5 fo. 265^{v}

This list includes unpublished information from file compiled by B. Masters, 'Officers of the Mayor's Household before 1600' (1989), at CLRO.

(x) Common Hunts

1379	John Charneye	*LBH*, 121
1387	Thomas Biringtone, *loco* Charney	*LBH*, 309
1392	James Ormesby, esquire[1]	*LBH*, 388
by 1401	Nicholas Brincheslee	*LBI*, 179
1417	John Courteney, gentleman	*LBI*, 179
1423	John Russell	CLRO, Jor. 2, fo. 8^{v}
1448	John Tyler, gentleman	*LBK*, 321, 325
1457	John Green, gentleman	CLRO, Jor. 6, fo. 118
1459	William Sudbury	CLRO, Jor. 6, fo. 223
1463	John Stokker, gentleman	*LBL*, 36
1500	Arnold Babington, draper	CLRO, Jor. 10, fo. 181^{v}

See *Guildhall Historical Association*, 6, article 6, pp. 6–7; this list includes unpublished information from file compiled by B. Masters, 'Officers of the Mayor's Household before 1600' (1989), at CLRO.

[1] Ormesby held the office of Common Hunt until his death, which occurred between summer 1400 and January 1401, see J. S. Roskell, L. Clark, and C. Rawcliffe, *The House of Commons 1386–1421*, 4 vols. (Stroud, 1992), iii. 879.

(xi) Serjeants of the Channel (Surveyor of Streets and Lanes)

1385	John —	*LBH*, 275
1390	Nicholas (*recte* Richard) Foche	*LBH*, 355
1418	Henry Waleys	CLRO, Jor. 1, fo. 14
1422	William Horn	*LBK*, 5; CLRO, Jor. 2, fo. 1
1444	John Holden	*CPMR 1437–57*, 59
1457	John Horncastle	CLRO, Jor. 6, fo. 188; *LBL* 11
1468	— Rowland	CLRO, Jor. 7, fo. 180
pre-1472	Henry Snowe	CLRO, Jor. 8, fo. 32^{v}
1472	John Hall	CLRO, Jor. 8, fo. 32^{v}
1477	John Malpas	CLRO, Jor. 8, fo. 161^{v}
by 1487	John Purcas	CLRO, Jor. 9, fo. 159
1499	John Swyft, *in loco* John Purcas	CLRO, Rep. 1, fo. 47^{v}; Rep. 3, fo. 141
1517	John Herbert/Herberd	CLRO, Rep. 3, fos. 141, 159^{v}

This list includes unpublished information from file compiled by B. Masters, 'Officers of the Mayor's Household before 1600', (1989), at CLRO.

(xii) Coroners

Occurs 1225–26	Thomas de Blunnville	CLRO, Misc. Roll AA, m. 1
Occurs 1225–26	Henry fitz Archer	*CCR 1227–31*, 123
*c.*1227	?Peter de Rivalle	CLRO, Misc. Roll AA, m. 1
1228	Gervaise le Cordwainer	*CPR 1225–32*, 226; *CCR 1227–31*, 123; CLRO, Misc. Roll AA, mm. 1–2d
1232–33	Simon fitz-Mary	CLRO, Misc. Roll AA, m. 2d
1234	John de Colmere	*CPR 1232–47*, 62; CLRO, Misc. Roll AA, mm. 1–3
Occurs 1235	John de Gisors	CLRO, Misc. Roll AA, m. 3
1236	Ralph Asshwy and John de Gisors	*CPR 1232–47*, 167; CLRO, Misc. Roll AA, mm. 1, 3
1236	William de Haverhulle	*CPR 1232–47*, 172; CLRO, Misc. Roll AA, mm. 1, 3; *CLibR 1245–51*, 13
1249	William de Plessetis	*CCR 1247–54*, 139, 159–60; *CPR 1247–58*, 35.
1249	Arnold de Geraudum	*CPR 1247–58*, 46
1251	Thomas Esperun and Arnold (de) Geraudum	*CPR 1247–58*, 117; BL, Add. Ch. 5153, mm. 1–1d;
1253	John de Gisors	*CPR 1247–58*, 180, 451; BL, Add. Ch. 5153, mm. 1d, 3–4
1256	William de Haselbeche	*CPR 1247–58*, 482; BL, Add. Ch. 5153, m. 4
1256	Matthew Bokerel and Thomas Esperun	*CPR 1247–58*, 505, 614; BL, Add. Ch. 5153, mm. 4–5
1258	Peter de Gisors	*CPR 1247–58*, 618; BL, Add. Ch. 5153, mm. 4d–6d; *CLibR 1260–67*, 80
Occurs 1262	John de Swineford	*CLibR. 1260–67*, 102; BL, Add. Ch. 5153, mm. 6d–7
Occurs 1263	William de Porstok	*CPR 1260–67*, 258; *CLibR. 1260–67*, 129; BL, Add. Ch. 5153, m.7
1264	Reynold de Suffolk	*CPR 1260–67*, 305; BL, Add. Ch. 5153, mm. 8–9d; *CPR 1266–72*, 189
1268	Walter de Capeles	*CPR 1266–72*, 189; BL, Add. Ch. 5153, m. 10; *CLibR. 1267–72*, 45

Up to 1475 this list is taken from W Kellaway, 'The Coroner in Medieval London', in A. Hollaender and W. Kellaway (eds.), *Studies in London History Presented to P. E. Jones* (London, 1969), 75–94 at 87–9. The names of coroners after 1483 have been kindly provided by Dr Hannes Kleineke and Dr Jessica Freeman.

1268	Stephen de Edeworth	*CPR 1266–72*, 296; BL, Add. Ch. 5153, m. 10; *CLibR. 1267–72*, 66
Occurs 1269	Hugh fitz Otto	BL, Add. Ch. 5153, mm.10, 10d; *CCR 1268–72*, 153, 157; *CLibR. 1267–72*, 126
1270	Walter Hervy	BL, Add. Ch. 5153, m. 11d–12
?1272–4	Poncius de Mora	*CPR 1266–72*, 715; *CCR 1268–72*, 43–520 *passim; CCR 1272–79*, 93; *CLibR. 1267–72*, 205
1275	Gregory de Rokesle	*MGL* ii. pt. i. 239
1278	Matthew de Columbariis	*MGL* ii. pt. i. 239
1299	Adam de Rokesle	*MGL* ii. pt. i. 243; *CPR 1292–1301*, 408
1302	William Trente	*CPR 1301–07*, 74; *MGL*, ii. pt. i. 243
1307	Henry de Say	*CPR 1307–13*, 9; *MGL*, ii. pt i. 244
1309	Walter de Waldeshef	*CPR 1307–17*, 209; *MGL*, ii. pt i. 113–4, 244–5
1316	Stephen de Abindon	*CPR 1313–17*, 520; *CCR 1313–18*, 355; *MGL* i. 245–6; *Cron. Ed. I & II* (Rolls series, 1882-83), i. 236
1325	Benedict de Fulsham	*CPR 1324–27*, 184; *CCR 1323–27*, 411; *CCR 1327–30*, 34
1327	Richard de la Pole	*CFR 1327–37*, 33, 235, 359; *CCR 1327–30*, 129
1331	Arnold Micol	*CFR 1327–37*, 235, 359
1338	Michael Mynyot	*CFR 1337–47*, 65
1339	Hugh de Ulseby	*CFR 1337–47*, 121
1339	Reymund Seguyn	*CFR 1337–47*, 154
1347	John de Wesenham	*CPR 1345–8*, 220; *CPR 1348–50*, 570
1350	Henry Picard	*CPR 1348–50*, 570
1359	John de Stodeye	*CPR 1358–61*, 252
1361	William (de) Strete	*CPR 1358–61*, 580; *CPR 1374–77*, 443–4
1376	Geoffrey de Newetone	*CPR 1374–77*, 352; *CFR 1369–77*, 363
1377	Thomas Tyle	*CPR 1377–81*, 60
1382	John Slege	*CPR 1381–5*, 176
1395	Thomas Brounflete	*CPR 1391–6*, 583, 608
1399	John Payne	*CPR 1399–1401*, 15
1402	Thomas Chaucer	*CPR 1401–5*, 170;
1407	Sir John Tiptoft	*CPR 1405–8*, 327, 334
1407	Thomas Chaucer	*CPR 1405–8*, 380
1418	Nicholas Merbury (d.1421)	*Rot.Normann*, 284
1421–2	Thomas Chaucer	*CPR 1422–9*, 7
1435	Ralph Butler, lord Sudeley	*CPR 1429–36*, 447
1458	John Talbot, earl of Shrewbury	*CPR 1452–61*, 428
1460	Sir John Wenlock, lord Wenlock	*CPR 1452–61*, 644
1471	John Stafford, earl of Wiltshire	*CPR 1452–61*, 262
1475	Anthony Woodville, earl Rivers	*CPR 1476–77*, 415, 103

In 1478 the City purchased the right to elect its own coroner as soon as the present coroner ceased to hold office; this occurred when Earl Rivers was executed in 1483.

1483	Robert Cartleage	PRO, KB 9/951, no. 14
Sept. 1485	John Green	CLRO, Jor. 9, fo. 88b
Dec. 1485	Thomas Butside, *loco* Green (later Secondary)	CLRO, Jor. 9, fo. 93b PRO, KB 9/369, no. 39
by 1488	William Karkeke/Carkeke	PRO, KB 9/377, no. 44
1494	William Slade	PRO, KB 9/401, no. 6
by 1495	Thomas Bradshaw (also Secondary)	PRO, KB 9/404, no. 38
by 1502	Thomas Squyer	PRO, KB 9/425, no. 47
1504	Giles Cleybroke (later Secondary)	PRO, KB 9/1062, no. 9
1509	Thomas Barnewell	PRO, KB 9/452, no. 90

(xiii) Deputy Coroners

*c.*1278	John Horn	*MGL* ii. pt. i. 239; *LBB* 280
1280/1	John de Gisors	*MGL* ii. pt. i. 240
1285	Nicholas de Wynton	*CPR 1281–92*, 194; *MGL* ii. pt. i. 240
1286	William le Mazerer	*CCR 1288–96*, 89; *MGL* ii. pt. i. 241
1290	John le Clerk, of the Vintry	*MGL* ii. pt. i. 241–4
1299	John le Clerk, after the death of Matthew de Columbariis	*CCR 1296–1302*, 251–2
1302	John le Clerk, *in loco* William Trente	*MGL* ii. pt i. 113; *CCR 1302–7*, 3; *LBC*, 116
1307–*c.*1315	Robert de Gunthorpe	*LBD*, 179-80; *CCR 1307–13*, 5, 169; *MGL* ii. pt. i. 113
*c.*1309	with John de Wengrave	*MGL* ii. pt. i. 244–6
*c.*1309–*c.*1320	John de Wengrave, with Robert de Gunthorpe	*MGL* ii. pt. i. 244–6
*c.*1316	John de Wengrave, with John de Shirbourne	*MGL* ii. pt. i. 244–6; *CCR 1313–18*, 252, 355; PRO, JUST 2/94a
1316–*c.*1320, 1325–41	John de Shirbourne, with John de Wengrave	*CCR 1313–18*, 355; *MGL* ii. pt. i. 245-6; *CCR 1323–37*, 426; *CCorR*, 130, 136; *CCR 1327–30*, 34, 129; *1330–33*, 210; *1337–39*, 301, 565; *1339–41*, 8, 324; *CCorR*, 209, 248–9; *LBF*, 255
1320	Robert de Barsham, with John de Ilford	*CCR 1318–23*, 276; *MGL*, ii. pt. i. 246
1320	John de Ilford, with Robert de Barsham	*CCR 1318–23*, 276
1325–41	John de Shirbourne	*CCR 1318–23*, 413; *LBE*, 165-6; *CCorR*, 150, 136; *CCR 1323–37*, 411
1325–41	John de Foxton	*CCR 1341–43*, 168; *1346–49*, 135; *Poss.Ass.* 65
*c.*1349	Henry de Sutton	*Poss.Ass.* 46, 20–68; *LBG*, 118; *CCR 1354–60*, 598
1367	William de Hockele	*CCorR*, 272, 274–5; *CCR 1369–74*, 403; *LBG*, 296
1369	Thomas de St Albans	*Poss.Ass.* 46–9; *LBG*, 277
1375	Henry de Morton	*CCR 1374–7*, 158, 393; *LBH*, 4, 50, 69, 81
1377	Henry Shelford, temporarily replacing Henry de Morton	*LBH*, 81
1377	Nicholas Symcok	*CCR 1377–81*, 34, 401, 405; *LBH*, 81–2

This list is taken from W. Kellaway, 'The Coroner in Medieval London', in A. Hollaender and W. Kellaway (eds.), *Studies in London History Presented to P. E. Jones* (London, 1969), 75–91 at 89–91.

1380–88	John Charneye	*CCR 1377–81*, 401, 405; *LBH*, 154; *CCR 1381–5*, 165, 188, 255, 506; *CPR 1385–9*, 532
1382	Richard Wellesbourne,	*LBH*, 201; *CCR 1381–5*, 178, temporarily replacing John Charneye 188
1383, 1384	Henry Shelford, temporarily replacing John Charneye	*CCR 1381–85*, 196, 255, 506; *LBH*, 201–2, 254
1390	John de Scardeburgh	*CCR 1389–92*, 115
1392	John Clos, deputy for John de Scardeburgh	*CCR 1392–6*, 35
1395	Robert Newenton, deputy for John de Scardeburgh	*CCR 1392–6*, 321; *LBH*, 398
1395	John Michel	*CCR 1392–6*, 435; *LBH*, 423
1398	Robert Newenton, deputy for John Michel	*LBH*, 352, 445; *CCR 1396–99*, 80
1399	Nicholas Symcok	*LBH*, 5
1400	Robert Newenton, deputy for Nicholas Symcok	*CCR 1399–1402*, 80
1400	Robert de Brounflete (?deputy for William de Brounflete)	*CCR 1399–1402*, 232; *Poss.Ass.* 84, 89
1402	John Ballye	*CCR 1402–4*, 11; *LBI*, 21
1403	John de Pokelyngtone	*CCR 1402–5*, 46; *LBI*, 24
1405	Nicholas Clent	*CCR 1405–9*, 2
1406, 1407–21	Richard Alfelde	*CCR 1405–9*, 26; *LBI*, 45, 61, 115, 240, 241; *CCR 1413–19*, 498; *LBK*, 8
1421	John Combe	*CCR 1419–22*, 166; CLRO, Jor. 1, fo. 94
1423	Richard Alfeld	PRO, KB 9/ 218/2, no. 5
1425	Adam May	*LBK*, 19
1429	Thomas Haseley	*LBK*, 92
1435	John Combe	PRO, KB 9/227/1, nos. 121, 8
1435	John Forthey	*CCR 1429–35*, 332; *LBK*, 186
1438	Thomas Beaufitz	*CCR 1435–41*, 147; CLRO, Jor. 6, fo. 89
by 1459	Robert Beaufitz	CLRO, Jor. 6, fo. 148ᵛ
1461	John Laweley	*CCR 1461–68*, 9; Jor. 6, fo. 45ᵛ
1471	Richard Burton	*LBD*, 2
1473	John Maxey	PRO, KB 9/334, no. 53
1474	William Fyssher	PRO, KB 9/945, nos. 18, 19; *CCR 1468–76*, 287; PRO, KB 9/358, no.7
by 1482	Andrew Dymmock	PRO, KB 9/359, no. 61; 360, no. 18

Bibliography

MANUSCRIPT SOURCES CITED

Cambridge, Trinity College
MS o.3.11, Fifteenth-Century Miscellany

London, British Library
Additional Charter 5153, Pleas of the Crown, 1276
Additional Charter 73945, award relating to bequest of Henry Crosse, 1485
Additional MS 38131, Statutes of England (Thomas Carleton's book)

London, Corporation of London Records Office
Liber Horn
Liber Fleetwood
Liber Dunthorne

Letter Books, A–R
Journals, 1–16 (The foliation of Journal 6 is that of the manuscript as incorrectly rebound and renumbered in the nineteenth century. Since my work on the volume, it has now been photographed and the pages reordered correctly. A concordance between the nineteenth-century foliation and that of the photographic copy is available at the CLRO.)
Repertories, 1–9

Book of Fines 1517–1628

Mayor's Court Plea and Memoranda Rolls
Mayor's Court Files of Original Bills MC1/1–3A

Husting Court Rolls of Deeds and Wills
Husting Pleas of Land
Husting Common Pleas
Husting Roll of Outlawries, 1415–1417, Misc. Roll KK
Calendar of Husting Rolls, 1327–76, Misc. Roll MM

Sheriffs Court Rolls, 1318, 1320, Misc. Roll CC
Sheriffs Court Rolls, 1406–08
Sheriffs' Register 1458–9

Portsoken Ward Presentments

Pleas held before the Justices at the Tower, 1244–6, Misc. Roll AA
Fines and amercements relating to the London Eyre, 1276, Misc. Roll BB

'Officers of the Mayor's Household before 1600', compiled by B. Masters (1989)
'The City's Law Officers and Counsel to c. 1600', compiled by B. Masters (1999)

London, Clothworkers' Hall
Quarter and Renter Wardens' Accounts, vol. i (1528–58)

London, Drapers' Hall
MS + 140, Wardens' Accounts 1413–41
MS + 403, Wardens' Accounts 1475–1509

London, Goldsmiths' Hall
MS 1518, Minute Book AA, 1334–42
MS 1520, Minute Book A, 1444–1516
MS 1524, Minute Books G, H, I, 1543–57

London, Guildhall Library
MS 1499, Aldersgate Wardmote Inquest, 1510
MS 2050, Aldersgate Wardmote Minute Book, 1467 onwards
MS 4600, Ordinances of the Fraternity of St Simon and St Jude, 1595–1782 (Shipwrights)
MS 5440, Brewers' Company Memorandum Book
MS 7086, Pewterers' Company Wardens' Accounts, 1451 onwards
MS 9051, Registers of Wills proved in the Archdeaconry Court of London
MS 9171, Registers of Wills proved in the Commissary Court of London
MS 11570, Grocers' Company Memorandum and Ordinance Book, 'The Black Book'
MS 11570A, Grocers' Company Wardens' Accounts, 1463–1557
MS 11592, Grocers' Company Freedom Admissions, 1516 onwards
MS 16988, Ironmongers' Company Wardens' Accounts, 1454–1752
MS 25125, St Paul's Cathedral, Rent Collectors' Account Rolls, 1315
MS 31692, Skinners' Company, Fraternity of the BVM, Register 1472

London, Mercers' Hall
Wardens' Accounts 1348, 1398–1464
Acts of Court vol. i, 1453–1527
Acts of Court, vol. ii, 1527–1560
Register of Writings, vol. ii

London, Public Record Office
C1, Chancery: Early Proceedings
C47, Chancery Miscellanea
C244, Chancery: Corpus cum Causa Files
C254, Chancery Files: Dedimus Potestatem
E101, Exchequer Accounts Various
E122, Exchequer Customs Accounts
E159, Exchequer King's Remembrancer Rolls
E199, Exchequer Sheriffs Accounts
E401, Exchequer Receipt Rolls
E403, Exchequer Issue Rolls
E404, Exchequer Warrants for Issues
JUST 2, Coroners Rolls and Files
KB9, King's Bench Indictments
SC6, Ministers and Receivers Accounts
SP, State Papers

London, Westminster Abbey Muniments
MS 9182, Licence for aqueduct, 1431
MS 13184, Agreement between St Martin le Grand and Saddlers

Oxford, Bodleian Library
Digby Roll 2

Oxford, Magdalen College
Fastolf Estate Papers

Truro, Cornwall Record Office
AR37, Dinham Family Papers

Winchester, Hampshire Record Office
Register of Bishop Stratford (11/191)

Worcester, Record Office
009:1, Box 175, no. 92475, Bishop of Worcester, Receiver's Account

PRIMARY PRINTED SOURCES

Account Rolls of the Abbey of Durham, ed., J. T. Fowler, 3 vols. (Surtees Society, 1898–1901).

Acts of Court of the Mercers' Company 1453–1527, ed. L. Lyell and D. Watney (Cambridge, 1936).

Adae Murimuth Continuatio Chronicarum: Robertus de Avesbury, De Gestis Mirabilibus Regis Edwardi Tertii. ed. E. M. Thompson (Rolls Series, 1889).

Anglo Norman Letters & Petitions, ed. M. D. Legge (Oxford, 1941).

Annales Londonienses, in *Chronicles of the Reigns of Edward I and II*, ed. W. Stubbs, 2 vols. (Rolls Series, 1882–3).

Annales Monastici. ed. H. R. Luard, 5 vols. (Rolls Series, 1864–9).

Annales Paulini. in *Chronicles of the Reigns of Edward I and II*, ed. W. Stubbs, 2 vols. (Rolls Series, 1882–3).

The Anonimalle Chronicle 1307–1334, ed. W. R. Childs and J. Taylor (Yorkshire Archaeological Society, 1991).

A Book of London English 1384–1425, ed. R. W. Chambers and M. Daunt (Oxford, 1931).

The Brut, or the Chronicles of England, ed. F. W. Brie (EETS, 1906).

A Calendar of the Cartularies of John Pyel and Adam Fraunceys, ed. S. O'Connor (Camden Society, 1993).

Calendar of Charter Rolls.

Calendar of Close Rolls.

Calendar of Coroners' Rolls of the City of London 1300–1378, ed. R. R. Sharpe (London, 1913).

Calendar of Early Mayor's Court Rolls 1298–1307, ed. A. H. Thomas (Cambridge, 1924).

Calendar of Fine Rolls.

Calendar of Letters from the Mayor and Corporation of the City of London c.1350–1370, ed. R. R .Sharpe (London, 1885).

Calendar of the Letter Books of the City of London A–L, ed. R. R. Sharpe, 11 vols. (London, 1899–1912).
Calendar of Liberate Rolls, 6 vols. (London, 1916–64).
Calendar of London Trailbaston Trials under Commission of 1305 and 1306, ed. R. B. Pugh (London, 1975).
Calendar of Patent Rolls.
Calendar of Plea and Memoranda Rolls, ed. A. H. Thomas, vols. 1–4; ed. Philip E. Jones, vols. 5–6 (Cambridge, 1924–1961).
Calendar of Wills Proved and Enrolled in the Court of Husting, London 1258–1688, ed. R. R. Sharpe, 2 vols. (London, 1889–90).
Capital Histories: A Bibliographical Study of London, ed. P. Garside (Aldershot, 1998).
The Cartulary of Holy Trinity Priory Aldgate, ed. G. Hodgett (London Record Society, 1971).
The Cartulary of Launceston Priory, ed. P. L. Hull (Devon and Cornwall Record Society, 1987).
Chamber Accounts of the Sixteenth Century, ed. B. Masters (London Record Society, 1984).
Chronica Johannis de Oxenedes, ed. H. Ellis (Rolls Series, 1859).
Chronicle of London, ed. H. N. Nicolas (London, 1827).
Chronicles of London, ed. C. L. Kingsford, (Oxford, 1905).
'Chronicle of Thomas Wykes', in *Annales Monastici*, ed. H. R. Luard (Rolls Series, 1864), iv.
Chronicles of the Mayors and Sheriffs of London, A.D. 1188 to A.D. 1274, ed. and trans. H. T. Riley (London, 1863).
The Church in London 1375–1392, ed. A. K. McHardy (London Record Society, 1977).
The Church Records of St Andrew Hubbard Eastcheap c.1450–c.1570, ed., C. Burgess (London Record Society, 1999).
The Coronation of Richard III, ed. A. Sutton, and P. Hammond (Gloucester, 1983).
Croniques de London depuis l'an 44 Hen.III jusqu'à l'an 17 Edw.III, ed. G. Aungier (Camden Society, 1844).
The Early Charters of the Augustinian Canons of Waltham Abbey, Essex 1062–1230, ed. R. Ransford (Woodbridge, 1989).
Elenchus Fontium Historiae Urbanae, ed. S. Reynolds, W. de Boer, G. Mac Niocaill (Leiden, 1988).
English Historical Documents 1189–1327, ed. H. Rothwell (London, 1975).
English Historical Documents 1327–1485, ed. A. R. Myers (London, 1969).
The Eyre of London, 14 Edward II AD 1321, ed. H. M. Cam, 2 vols. (Selden Society, 1968–9).
Fabyan, Robert, *The New Chronicles of England and France*, ed. Henry Ellis (London, 1811).
Facsimile Account of the First Volume of the Ms Archives of the Worshipful Company of Grocers of the City of London 1345–1463, ed. J. A. Kingdon, 2 vols. (London, 1886).
The Fifty Earliest English Wills in the Court of Probate, ed. F. J. Furnivall (EETS, 1882).
The French Chronicle of London in *Chronicles of the Mayors and Sheriffs of London A.D. 1188 to A.D. 1274*, ed. and trans. H. T. Riley (London, 1863), 229–95.
Gesta Henrici Quinti. ed. F. Taylor and J. S. Roskell (Oxford, 1975).
The Great Chronicle of London, ed. A. H. Thomas and I. D. Thornley (London, 1938).
Historical Charters and Constitutional Documents of the City of London, ed. W. de Gray Birch (rev. edn. London, 1887).
The Historical Collections of a Citizen of London, ed. J. Gairdner (Camden Society, 1876).
Holinshed, Raphael, *Chronicles of England, Scotland, and Ireland* [ed. Henry Ellis], 6 vols. (London, 1807–8).
The Household Book of Queen Isabella of England, ed. F. D. Brackley and G. Hermansen (Edmonton, 1971).

Hugh Alley's Caveat: The Markets of London in 1598, ed. I. Archer, C. Barron, and V. Harding (London Topographical Society, 1988).

Index to Testamentary Records in the Commissary Court of London 1374–1488, ed. M. Fitch (London, 1969).

Kingsford's Stonor Letters & Papers 1290–1483, ed. C. Carpenter (Cambridge, 1996).

Knighton's Chronicle 1337–1396, ed. G. Martin (Oxford, 1995).

Letters and Papers Illustrative of the Wars of the English in France during the Reign of Henry Vi. ed. J. Stevenson, 2 vols. (Rolls Series, 1861–4).

Letters of Queen Margaret of Anjou, Bishop Beckington and others, ed. C. Munro (Camden Society, 1863).

The Libelle of Englyshe Polycye, ed. G. Warner (Oxford, 1926).

Liber Albus: The White Book of The City of London, ed. and trans. H. T. Riley (London, 1861).

Liber de Antiquis Legibus seu Chronica Maiorum et Vicecomitum Londoniarum, ed. T. Stapleton (Camden Society, 1846).

London Assize of Nuisance 1301–1431, ed. H. M. Chew and W. Kellaway (London Record Society, 1973).

London Bridge: Selected Accounts and Rentals, 1381–1538, ed. V. Harding and L. Wright (London Record Society, 1995).

London Consistory Court Wills 1492–1547, ed. I. Darlington (London Record Society, 1967).

The London Eyre of 1244, ed. H. M. Chew and M. Weinbaum (London Record Society, 1970).

The London Eyre of 1276, ed., M.Weinbaum (London Record Society, 1976).

London and Middlesex Chantry Certificate 1548, ed. C. Kitching (London Record Society, 1980).

London Possessory Assizes: A Calendar, ed. H. M. Chew (London Record Society, 1965).

The London Surveys of Ralph Treswell, ed. J. Schofield (London Topographical Society, 1987).

London Viewers and their Certificates 1508–1558, ed. J. Loengard (London Record Society, 1989).

The Maire of Bristol is Kalender by Robert Ricart, ed. L. Toulmin Smith (Camden Society, 1872).

Medieval Records of a London City Church (St Mary at Hill) 1420–1559, ed. H. Littlehales (EETS, 1905).

Memorials of London and London Life, ed. H. T. Riley, (London, 1868).

The Merchant Taylors' Company of London: Court Minutes 1486–1493, ed. M. P. Davies, (Stamford, 2000).

Munimenta Gildhallae Londoniensis: Liber Albus, Liber Custumarum et Liber Horn, ed. H. T. Riley, 3 vols. (Rolls Series, 1859–62).

The Overseas Trade of London: Exchequer Customs Accounts 1480–1, ed. H. S. Cobb (London Record Society, 1990).

Parish Fraternity Register: The Fraternity of the Holy Trinity and SS Fabian and Sebastian in the Parish Church of St Botolph without Aldersgate, ed. P. Basing (London Record Society, 1982).

Paris, Matthew, *Chronica Majora*, ed. H. R. Luard, 7 vols. (Rolls Series, 1872–83).

Paston Letters and Papers of the Fifteenth Century, ed. N. Davis, 2 vols. (Oxford, 1971–6).

Piers Plowman by William Langland: An Edition of the C-Text, ed. D. Pearsall (London, 1978).

The Plumpton Correspondence, ed. T. Stapleton (Camden Society, 1839).

Political Poems and Songs, ed. T. Wright, 2 vols. (Rolls Series, 1859–61).

The Poll Taxes of 1377, 1379 and 1381, ed. C. Fenwick, 2 vols. (British Academy, London, 1998–2001).
The Proceedings and Ordinances of the Privy Council of England, ed. H. Nicolas, 6 vols. (London, 1834–37).
The Red Book of the Exchequer, ed. H. Hall, 3 vols. (Rolls Series, 1896).
Regesta Regum Anglo-Normannorum: The Acta of William I (1066–1087), ed. D. Bates (Oxford, 1998).
A Relation . . . of the Island of England . . . c.1500, ed. C. A. Sneyd (Camden Society, 1847).
[Record Commission], *Rotuli Hundredorum temp. Hen III & Edw I*, 2 vols. (London, 1812).
Rotuli Normanniae in Turri Londinensi asservati Johanne et Henrici Quinto, ed. T. D. Hardy (London, 1835).
Rotuli Parliamentorum 1278–1503, 6 vols. (London, 1832).
Scriveners' Company Common Paper 1357–1628, ed. F. W. Steer (London Record Society, 1968).
Select Cases Concerning the Law Merchant 1251–1775, ed. H. Hall, 3 vols. (Selden Society, 1932).
Six Town Chronicles of England, ed. R. Flenley (Oxford, 1911).
The Statutes of the Realm, 10 vols. (London, 1810–28).
Stow, John, *A Survey of London*, ed. C. L. Kingsford, 2 vols. (Oxford, 1908).
Testamentary Records in the Archdeaconry Court of London, 1363–1649, ed. M. Fitch (British Record Society, 1979).
Testamentary Records in the Commissary Court of London 1489–1570, ed. M. Fitch (British Record Society, 1974).
Two Early London Subsidy Rolls, ed. E. Ekwall (Lund, 1951).
[Walsingham, Thomas], *Chronicon Angliae 1328–1388*, ed. E. M. Thompson (Rolls Series, 1874).
The Westminster Chronicle 1381–1394, ed. L. C. Hector and B. F. Harvey (Oxford, 1982).
Wills, Leases and Memoranda in the Book of Records of the Parish of St Christopher le Stocks in the City of London, ed. E. Freshfield (London 1895).
The York Mercers and Merchant Adventurers 1356–1917, ed. M. Sellers (Surtees Society, 1918).

SECONDARY SOURCES

For a more complete bibliography of recent writing on medieval London history, see P. Garside, *Capital Histories: A Bibliographical Study of London* (Aldershot, 1998).

Alexander, J., and Binski. P. (eds.), *Age of Chivalry: Art in Plantagenet England 1200–1400* (London, 1987).
Allderidge, P., 'Management and Mismanagement at Bedlam 1597–1633' in C. Webster, (ed.) *Health, Medicine, and Mortality in the Sixteenth Century* (Cambridge, 1979), 141–64.
Anderson, K., 'The Treatment of Vagrancy and the Relief of the Poor and Destitute in the Tudor Period, Based upon the Local Records of London to 1552 and Hull to 1576' (University of London, Ph.D. thesis, 1933).
Andrews, J., Briggs, A., Porter, R., Tucker, P., and Waddington, K. (eds.), *The History of Bethlem* (London, 1997).
Anglo, S., 'The London Pageants for the Reception of Katherine of Aragon in 1501', *Journal of the Warburg and Courtauld Institutes*, 26 (1963), 53–89.

ARCHER, I., *The Pursuit of Stability: Social Relations in Elizabethan London* (Cambridge, 1991).

—— *The History of the Haberdashers' Company* (Chichester, 1991).

—— 'The Nostalgia of John Stow', in D. L. Smith, R., Streier and D. Bevington, (eds.), *The Theatrical City: Culture, Theatre and Politics in London 1576–1649* (Cambridge, 1995), 17–34.

ARCHER, R. (ed.), *Crown, Government and People in the Fifteenth Century* (Stroud, 1995).

AXWORTHY, R., 'The Financial Relationship of the London Merchant Community with Edward III, 1327–1377' (University of London, Ph.D. thesis, 2000).

BALL, M., *The Worshipful Company of Brewers* (London, 1977).

BARBER, B., and THOMAS, C., *The London Charterhouse* (London, 2002).

BARRON, C., 'Richard Whittington: The Man Behind the Myth', in A. Hollaender and W. Kellaway (eds.), *Studies in London History Presented to P. E. Jones* (London, 1969), 197–248.

—— 'The Government of London and its Relations with the Crown 1400–1450' (University of London Ph.D. thesis, 1970).

—— 'The Quarrel of Richard II with London 1392–7', in F. R. H. Du Boulay and C. Barron (eds.). *The Reign of Richard II: Essays in Honour of May McKisack* (London, 1971), 173–201.

—— *The Medieval Guildhall of London* (London, 1974).

—— *The Parish of St Andrew Holborn* (London, 1979).

—— 'London and the Crown 1451–61', in J. R. L. Highfield and R. Jeffs (eds.), *The Crown and the Local Communities in England and France in the Fifteenth Century* (Gloucester, 1981), 88–109.

—— *Revolt in London: 11th to 15th June 1381* (London, 1981).

—— 'The Parish Fraternities of Medieval London', in C. Barron and C. Harper-Bill (eds.), *The Church in Pre-Reformation Society: Essays in Honour of F. R. H. Du Boulay* (Woodbridge, 1985), 13–37.

—— 'The Fourteenth-Century Poll Tax Returns for Worcester', *Midland History*, 14 (1989), 1–29.

—— 'London and Parliament in the Lancastrian Period', *Parliamentary History*, 9 (1990), 343–67.

—— 'Ralph Holland and the London Radicals, 1438–1444', in R. Holt and G. Rosser (eds.), *The Medieval Town: A Reader in English Urban History 1200–1540* (London, 1990), 160–83.

—— 'The Deposition of Richard II', in J. Taylor and W. Childs (eds.), *Politics and Crisis in Fourteenth-Century England* (Gloucester, 1990), 132–49.

—— 'Johanna Hill (d.1441) and Johanna Sturdy (d.*c.*1460), Bell-Founders', in C. Barron, and A. Sutton (eds.), *Medieval London Widows 1300–1500* (London, 1994), 99–111.

—— 'Centres of Conspicuous Consumption: The Aristocratic Town House in London 1200–1500', *London Journal*, 20 (1995), 1–16.

—— 'The Expansion of Education in Fifteenth-Century London', in J. Blair and B. Golding (eds.), *The Cloister and the World: Essays in Medieval History in Honour of Barbara Harvey* (Oxford, 1996), 219–45.

—— 'Richard II and London' in A. Goodman and J. Gillespie (eds.), *Richard II: The Art of Kingship* (Oxford, 1999), 129–54.

—— 'London 1300–1540', in D. Palliser (ed.), *Cambridge Urban History of England* (Cambridge 2000), i. 395–440.

—— 'Lay Solidarities: The Wards of Medieval London', in P. Stafford, J. Nelson and J. Martindale (eds.), *Law, Laity and Solidarities: Essays in Honour of Susan Reynolds* (Manchester, 2001), 218–33.

BARRON, C., 'Chivalry, Pageantry and Merchant Culture in Medieval London', in P. Coss and M. Keen, (eds.), *Heraldry, Pageantry and Social Display in Medieval England* (Woodbridge, 2002), 219–41.
BARRON, C., and HARPER-BILL, C. (eds.), *The Church in Pre-Reformation Society: Essays in Honour of F. R. H. Du Boulay* (Woodbridge, 1985).
BARRON, C., and ROSCOE, J., 'The Medieval Parish Church of St Andrew Holborn', *London Topographical Record*, 24 (1980), 31–60.
BARRON, C., and SAUL, N. (eds.), *England and the Low Countries in the Late Middle Ages* (Stroud, 1995).
BARRON, C., and SUTTON, A. (eds.), *Medieval London Widows 1300–1500* (London, 1994).
BARRON, C., and WRIGHT, L., 'The London Middle English Guild Certificates of 1388–9', *Nottingham Medieval Studies*, 39 (1995), 108–45.
BARRON, C., COLEMAN, C., and GOBBI. C., 'The London Journal of Alessandro Magno 1562', *London Journal*, 9 (1983), 136–52.
BASSET, M., 'Newgate Prison in the Middle Ages', *Speculum*, 18 (1943), 233–46.
BATEMAN, N., *Gladiators at the Guildhall* (London, 2000).
BATESON, M., 'A London Municipal Collection of the Reign of John', *EHR* 17 (1902), 480–511, 707–730.
BEAVEN, A. B., *The Aldermen of The City of London*, 2 vols. (London, 1908–13).
BEIER, A. L., 'Engine of Manufacture: The Trades of London', in A. L. Beier and R. Finlay (eds.), *London 1500–1700: The Making of the Metropolis* (London, 1986), 141–67.
BEIER, A. L., and FINLAY, R., (eds.), *London 1500–1700: The Making of the Metropolis* (London, 1986).
BENNETT, E., 'Debt and Credit in the Urban Economy: London, 1380–1460' (University of Yale, Ph.D. thesis, 1989).
BENNETT, J., 'Women and Men in the Brewers' Gild of London. *c.*1420', in E. B. DeWindt (ed.), *The Salt of Common Life: Individuality and Choice in the Medieval Town, Countryside and Church: Essays Presented to J. Ambrose Raftis* (Kalamazoo, Mich., 1995), 181–232.
BERLIN, M., 'Civic Ceremony in Early Modern London', *Urban History Yearbook* (1986), 15–27.
BINSKI. P., 'Monumental Brasses'. in J. Alexander and P. Binski (eds.), *Age of Chivalry: Art in Plantagenet England 1200–1400* (London, 1987), 171–3.
—— *Westminster Abbey and the Plantagenets: Kingship and the Representation of Power 1200–1400* (New Haven, Conn., and London, 1995).
BIRD, R., *The Turbulent London of Richard II* (London, 1949).
BLAIR, C., 'Copper Alloys', in J. Blair and N. Ramsay (eds.), *English Medieval Industries* (London, 1991), 81–106.
BLAIR, J., 'Purbeck Marble', in J. Blair and N. Ramsay (eds.), *English Medieval Industries* (London, 1991), 41–56.
BLAIR, J., and GOLDING, B. (eds.), *The Cloister and the World: Essays in Medieval History in Honour of Barbara Harvey* (Oxford, 1996).
BLAIR, J., and RAMSAY, N. (eds.), *English Medieval Industries* (London, 1991).
BLATCHER, M., *The Court of King's Bench 1450–1550* (London, 1978).
BOLTON, J. L., *The Medieval English Economy 1150–1500* (London, 1980).
—— 'The City and the Crown , 1456–61', *London Journal*, 12 (1986), 11–24.
—— *The Alien Communities of London in the Fifteenth Century* (Stamford, 1998).

—— review of Natalie Fryde, *Ein mittelalterlicher deutscher Grossunternehmer, Terricus Teutonicus de Colonia in England, 1217–1247* (Stuttgart, 1997) in *German Historical Institute London: Bulletin*, 21 (1999), 30–4.

Bottin, J., and Calabieds, D. (eds.), *Les Étrangers dans la Ville* (Paris, 1999).

Bowtell, A., 'Elyngspittal' (Royal Holloway, University of London, MA thesis, 2001).

Bradley, H., 'The Italian Community in London' (University of London, Ph.D. thesis, 1992), 214–15, 456–7.

—— 'The Datini Factors in London 1380–1410' in D. Clayton, R. Davies, and P. McNiven (eds.), *Trade, Devotion and Governance: Papers in Later Medieval History* (Stroud, 1994), 55–79.

Brewer, T., *Memoir of the Life and Times of John Carpenter, Town Clerk of London* (London, 1856).

Britnell, R., 'The Black Death in English Towns', *Urban History*, 21 (1994), 195–210.

—— 'Rochester Bridge 1381–1530', in N. Yates and J. M. Gibson (eds.), *Traffic and Politics: The Construction and Management of Rochester Bridge AD 43–1993* (Woodbridge, 1994), 43–106.

—— *The Commercialisation of English Society 1000–1500* (2nd edn., Manchester, 1996).

—— (ed.), *Daily Life in the Middle Ages* (Stroud, 1998).

—— 'Urban Demand in the English Economy, 1300–1600', in J. Galloway (ed.), *Trade, Urban Hinterlands and Market Integration c.1300–1600* (Institute of Historical Research, London, 2000), 1–21.

Britnell, R., and Hatcher, J. (eds.), *Progress and Problems in Medieval England: Essays in Honour of Edward Miller* (Cambridge, 1996).

Brooke, C. N. L., with Keir, G., *London 800–1216: The Shaping of a City* (London, 1975).

Brooke, C. N. L., Keir, G., and Reynolds, S., 'Henry I's Charter for the City of London', *Journal of the Society of Archivists*, 4 (1973), 558–78.

Bulst N., and Genet, J.-P., (eds.), *La Ville, la bourgeoisie et la genèse de l'etat moderne (XII–XVIII siecles)* (Paris, 1988).

Burgess, C., 'Shaping the Parish: St Mary at Hill, London in the Fifteenth Century', in J. Blair and B. Golding (eds.), *The Cloister and the World: Essays in Medieval History in Honour of Barbara Harvey* (Oxford, 1996), 246–86.

—— 'London Parishioners in Times of Change: St Andrew Hubbard, Eastcheap, c.1450–1570', *Journal of Ecclesiastical History*, 53 (2002), 38–63.

Burwash, D., *English Merchant Shipping 1461–1540* (Toronto, 1947).

Campbell, B. (ed.), *Before the Black Death* (Manchester, 1989).

Campbell, B., Galloway, J., Keene, D., and Murphy, M., *A Medieval Capital and its Grain Supply: Agrarian Production and Distribution in the London region c.1300* (Geography Research Series, London, 1993).

Campbell, M., 'English Goldsmiths in the Fifteenth Century', in D. Williams (ed.), *England in the Fifteenth Century* (Woodbridge, 1987), 43–52.

—— 'Gold, Silver and Precious Stones', in J. Blair and N. Ramsay (eds.), *English Medieval Industries* (London, 1991), 106–66.

Carlin, M., 'The Urban Development of Southwark, c.1200–1550' (University of Toronto, Ph.D. thesis, 1983).

—— *Medieval Southwark* (London, 1996).

—— 'Fast Food and Urban Living Standards in Medieval England' in M. Carlin and J. Rosenthal (eds.), *Food and Eating in Medieval Europe* (London, 1998), 27–51.

Carlin, M., and Rosenthal, J. (eds.), *Food and Eating in Medieval Europe* (London, 1998).

Carlton, C., *The Court of Orphans* (Leicester, 1974).

Carus-Wilson, E., 'La Guède française en Angleterre: un grand commerce du Moyen Âge', *Revue du Nord*, 35 (1953), 89–105.

—— 'The Origin and Early Development of the Merchant Adventurers Organization in London as Shown in their Own Medieval Records', in E. Carus-Wilson *Medieval Merchant Venturers* (London, 1954; 2nd edn. 1967), 143–82.

—— 'The English Cloth Industry in the Late Twelfth and Early Thirteenth Centuries', in E. Carus-Wilson, *Medieval Merchant Venturers* (London, 1954), 211–38.

—— *Medieval Merchant Venturers* (London, 1954; 2nd edn. 1967).

Catto, J., 'Andrew Horn: Law and History in Fourteenth-Century England', in R. H. C. Davis and J. Wallace-Hadrill (eds.), *The Writing of History in the Middle Ages: Essays Presented to R.W. Southern* (Oxford, 1981), 367–91.

Cherry, J., 'Pottery and Tile', in J. Blair and N. Ramsay (eds.), *English Medieval Industries* (London, 1991), 189–209.

Chew, H. M., 'The Office of Escheator in the City of London during the Middle Ages', *EHR* 58 (1943), 319–30.

Childs, W., *Anglo-Castilian Trade in the Later Middle Ages* (Manchester, 1978).

—— '"To oure losse and hindrance": English Credit to Alien Merchants in the Mid-Fifteenth Century', in J. Kermode (ed.), *Enterprise and Individuals in Fifteenth-Century England* (Stroud, 1991), 68–98.

—— 'Anglo-Portuguese Trade in the Fifteenth Century', *TRHS*, 6th ser., 2, (1992), 195–219.

Clark, E., 'Some Aspects of Social Security in Medieval England', *Journal of Family History*, 7 (1982) 307–20.

—— 'City Orphans and Custody Laws in Medieval England', *American Journal of Legal History*, 34 (1990), 168–87.

Clark, G. N., *A History of the Royal College of Physicians of London*, 2 vols. (London, 1964).

Clayton, D., Davies, R., and McNiven, P. (eds.), *Trade, Devotion and Governance: Papers in Later Medieval History* (Stroud, 1994).

Cobb, H., 'Cloth Exports from London and Southampton in the Later Fifteenth and Early Sixteenth Centuries: A Revision', *EconHR* 31 (1978), 601–9.

Coleman, D.C., and John, A. H. (eds.), *Trade, Government and Economy in Pre-Industrial England: Essays Presented to F. J. Fisher* (London, 1976).

Collett, T. K., 'The Swordbearer', *Guildhall Historical Association*, 3 (1963), 39–45.

Colvin, H. (ed.), *The History of the King's Works*, 6 vols. (London, 1963–82).

Combes, H., 'Piety and Belief in Fifteenth-Century London: An Analysis of the Fifteenth-Century Churchwardens' Inventory of St Nicholas Shambles', *TLMAS* 48 (1997), 137–52.

Consitt, F., *The London Weavers' Company* (Oxford, 1933).

Coote, H. C., 'The Ordinances of Some Secular Guilds of London 1354–1496', *TLMAS* 4 (1871), 55–9.

Corfield, P. J., 'Urban development in England and Wales in the Sixteenth and Seventeenth Centuries' in D. C. Coleman and A. H. John (eds.), *Trade, Government and Economy in Pre-Industrial England: Essays Presented to F. J. Fisher* (London, 1976), 214–47.

Corfield, P. J., and Keene, D. (eds.), *Work in Towns 850–1850* (Leicester, 1990).

Coss, P., and Keen, M. (eds.), *Heraldry, Pageantry and Social Display in Medieval England* (Woodbridge, 2002).

Crawford, A., *A History of the Vintners' Company* (London, 1977).

Creighton, C., 'The Population of Old London', *Blackwood's Magazine*, 149 (1891), 477–96.

Crowfoot, E., Pritchard, F., and Staniland, K., *Textiles and Clothing 1150–1450* (2nd edn., Woodbridge, 2001).

Davies, A. M., 'London's First Conduit System: A Topographical Study', *TLMAS* 2 (1913), 9–59.

Davies, M. P., 'The Tailors of London and their Guild *c.*1300–1500' (University of Oxford, D.Phil. thesis, 1994).

—— 'The Tailors of London: Corporate Charity in the Late Medieval Town', in R. Archer (ed.), *Crown, Government and People in the Fifteenth Century* Stroud, 1995), 161–90.

—— 'Artisans, Guilds and Government in London', in R. Britnell (ed.), *Daily Life in the Middle Ages* (Stroud, 1998), 125–50.

—— 'Dame Thomasine Percyvale, the "Maid of Week" (d.1512)', in C. Barron and A. Sutton (eds.), *Medieval London Widows 1300–1500* (London, 1994), 185–207.

Davis, R. H. C., and Wallace-Hadrill, J. (eds.), *The Writing of History in the Middle Ages: Essays Presented to R. W. Southern* (Oxford, 1981).

Davis, R., 'The Rise of Antwerp and its English Connection 1406–1500', in D. C. Coleman and A. H. John (eds.), *Trade, Government and Economy in Pre-Industrial England: Essays presented to F. J. Fisher* (London, 1976), 2–20.

Deadman, H., and Scudder, E., *An Introductory Guide to the Corporation of London Records Office* (London, 1994).

Dempsey, S., 'The Italian Community in London during the Reign of Edward II', *London Journal*, 18 (1993), 14–22.

DeWindt, E. B. (ed.), *The Salt of Common Life Individuality and Choice in the Medieval Town, Countryside and Church: Essays Presented to J. Ambrose Raftis* (Kalamazoo, Mich., 1995).

Dietz, B., 'The North East Coal Trade 1550–1750: Measures, Markets and Metropolis', *Northern History*, 22 (1986), 280–92.

—— 'Overseas Trade and Metropolitan Growth', in A. L. Beier and R. Finlay (eds.), *London 1500–1700*, (London, 1986), 115–40.

Dobson, J., *Barbers & Barber Surgeons of London* (London, 1979).

Dobson, R. B. (ed.), *The Church, Politics and Patronage in the Fifteenth Century* (Gloucester, 1984).

Donnison, J., *Midwives and Medical Men* (London, 1977).

Douch, H. L., 'Household Accounts at Lanherne', *Journal of the Royal Institution of Cornwall*, 2 (1953), 25–32.

Du Boulay, F. R. H., and Barron C. (eds.)., *The Reign of Richard II: Essays in Honour of May McKisack* (London, 1971).

Dunn, D. E. S., (ed.), *Courts, Counties and the Capital in the Later Middle Ages* (Stroud, 1996).

Duvosquel, J.-M., and Thoen, E. (eds.), *Peasants and Townsmen in Medieval Europe: Studia in Honorem Adriaan Verhulst* (Ghent, 1995).

Dyer, A., 'Ranking Lists of English Medieval Towns', in D. Palliser (ed.), *Cambridge Urban History of England*, 3 vols. (Cambridge, 2000), i. 747–70.

Dyer, C., 'The Consumer and the Market in the Later Middle Ages', in C. Dyer, *Everyday Life in Medieval England* (London, 1994), 257–81.

—— *Everyday Life in Medieval England* (London, 1994).

Eames, E., *Medieval Tilers* (London, 1992).

Emden, A. B., *A Biographical Register of the University of Oxford to AD 1500*, 3 vols. (Oxford, 1957).

Epstein, S. R. (ed.), *Town and Country in Europe 1300–1800* (Cambridge, 2001).

Erler, M. C., 'The First English Printing of Galen: The Formation of the Company of Barber-Surgeons', *Huntington Library Quarterly*, 48 (1985), 159–73.

Finlay, R., *Population and Metropolis: The Demography of London 1580–1650* (Cambridge, 1981).

Fisher, F. J., *A Short History of the Worshipful Company of Horners* (London, 1936).

—— 'The Development of London as a Centre of Conspicuous Consumption in the Sixteenth and Seventeenth Centuries', *TRHS* 30 (1948), 37–50, reprinted in F. J. Fisher *London and the English Economy, 1500–1700*, ed., P. J. Corfield and N. Harte (London, 1990), 105–18.

—— *London and the English Economy, 1500-1700*, ed. P. J. Corfield and N. Harte (London, 1990).

Forty, F., 'London Wall', *Guildhall Miscellany*, 5 (1955), 1–39.

Freeman, J., 'The Mistery of Coiners and the King's Moneyers of the Tower of London, *c*.1340–*c*.1530', *The British Numismatic Journal*, 70 (2001), 67–82.

French, R., Arrizabalaga, J., Cunningham, A., and Ballester, L.-G. (eds.), *Medicine from the Black Death to the French Disease* (Aldershot, 1998).

Friedman, T., 'The Rebuilding of Bishopsgate 1723–35', *Guildhall Studies in London History*, 4 (1980), 75–90.

Friel, I., *The Good Ship: Ships, Shipbuilding and Technology in England 1200-1520* (London, 1995).

Fryde, E., 'The English Cloth Industry and the Trade with the Mediterranean *c*.1370–*c*.1480', in M. Spallanzani (ed.), *Produzione Commercio e Consumo dei Panni di Lana* 2 vols. (Florence, 1976), ii. 343–67.

—— 'Edward III's Wool Monopoly of 1337: A Fourteenth-Century Royal Trading Venture', in E. Fryde, *Studies in Medieval Trade and Finance* (London, 1983), no. VIII, 8–24.

—— *Studies in Medieval Trade and Finance* (London, 1983).

—— 'The English Farmers of the Customs 1343–51', in E. Fryde, *Studies in Medieval Trade and Finance* (London, 1983), no. X, 1–17.

Fryde, N., 'Antonio Pessagno of Genoa, King's Merchant of Edward II of England', in *Studi in memoria di Federigo Melis*, 4 vols (Naples, 1978), ii. 159–178.

Gadd, D., 'The London Inn of the Abbots of Waltham: A Revised Reconstruction of a Medieval Town House in Lovat Lane', *TLMAS* 34 (1983), 171–77.

Galloway, J., 'Market Networks: London Hinterland Trade and the Economy of England', *Centre for Metropolitan History: Annual Report 1997–8* (Institute of Historical Research, London, 1998), 44–50.

—— (ed.), *Trade, Urban Hinterlands and Market Integration c.1300–1600* (Institute of Historical Research, London, 2000).

—— 'Town and Country in England, 1300–1570', in S. R. Epstein (ed.), *Town and Country in Europe 1300–1800* (Cambridge, 2001), 106–31.

—— 'One Market or Many? London and the Grain Trade of England', in J. Galloway (ed.), *Trade, Urban Hinterlands and Market Integration c.1300–1600* (London, 2000), 23–42.

Galloway, J., Keene, D., and Murphy, M., 'Fuelling the City: Production and Distribution of Firewood and Fuel in London's Region', *Econ.HR* 49 (1996), 447–72.

Garside, P. *Capital Histories: A Bibliographical Study of London* (Aldershot, 1998).

Gavitt, P., *Charity and Children in Renaissance Florence: The Ospedele degli Innocenti 1410–1535* (Ann Arbor, Mich., 1990).

Getz, F., 'Medical Practitioners in Medieval England', *Social History of Medicine*, 3 (1990), 245–83.

—— *Medicine in the English Middle Ages* (Princeton, NJ, 1998).

Glass, D., and Revelle, R. (eds.), *Population and Social Change* (London, 1972).

Glasscock, R. E., *The Lay Subsidy of 1334* (London, 1975).

Goldberg, J. P., *Women, Work and the Life Cycle in a Medieval Economy: Women in York and Yorkshire 1300–1520* (Oxford, 1992).

Goodman, A., and Gillespie, J. (eds.), *Richard II: The Art of Kingship* (Oxford, 1999).

Gordan, D., Monnas, L., and Elam, C. (eds.), *The Regal Image of Richard II and the Wilton Diptych* (London, 1997).

Gottfried, R., *Bury St Edmunds and the Urban Crisis: 1290–1539 (*Princeton, NJ, 1982).

Grant, L. (ed.), *Medieval Art, Architecture and Archaeology in London,* (British Archaeological Association, 1984).

Gras, N. B., *The Early English Customs System* (Cambridge, Mass., 1918).

Greaves, D., 'Calais under Edward III', in G. Unwin *Finance and Trade under Edward III* (Manchester, 1918), 313–50.

Grew, F., and de Neergaard, M., *Shoes and Pattens* (London, HMSO, 1988).

Griffiths, R.A., and Sherborne, J. (eds.), *Kings and Nobles in the Later Middle Ages: A Tribute to Charles Ross* (Gloucester,1986).

Grimes, W. F., *The Excavation of Roman and Medieval London* (London, 1968).

Grummit, D., 'The Financial Administration of Calais during the Reign of Henry IV, 1399–1413', *EHR* 113 (1998), 277–299.

Guth, D. J., 'Richard III. Henry VII and the City: London Politics and the "Dun Cow"' in R. A. Griffiths and J. Sherborne (eds.), *Kings and Nobles in the Later Middle Ages: A Tribute to Charles Ross* (Gloucester, 1986), 185–99.

Hanawalt, B., and Reyerson, K. (eds.), *City and Spectacle in Medieval Europe* (Minneapolis, 1994).

Harben, H. A., *A Dictionary of London* (London, 1918).

Harding, V., 'The Port of London in the Fourteenth century: Its Topography, Administration and Trade' (University of St Andrews, Ph.D. thesis, 1983).

—— 'The Population of London, 1550–1700: A Review of the Published Evidence', *London Journal*, 15 (1990), 111–28.

—— 'Cross-Channel Trade and Cultural Contacts: London and the Low Countries in the Later Fourteenth Century', in C. Barron and N. Saul (eds.), *England and the Low Countries in the Late Middle Ages* (Stroud, 1995), 153–68.

—— 'Pageantry on London Bridge', in B. Watson, T. Brigham and A. Dyson, *London Bridge, 2000 Years of a River Crossing* (London, 2001), 114–15.

Harper, R. I., 'A Note on Corrodies in the Fourteenth Century', *Albion*, 15 (1983), 95–101.

Harris, J., *Greek Emigrés in the West 1400–1520* (Camberley, 1995).

—— 'Two Byzantine Craftsmen in Fifteenth-Century London', *Journal of Medieval History*, 21 (1995), 387–403.

Harrison, D., 'The Surrey Portion of the Lewes Cartulary', *Surrey Archaeological Collections*, 43 (1935), 84–112.

Harriss, G. L., 'Aids, Loans and Benevolences', *Historical Journal*, 4 (1963), 1–19.

Harvey, B. F., *Living and Dying in England 1100–1540: The Monastic Experience* (Oxford, 1993).

Harvey, J., *English Medieval Architects: A Biographical Dictionary to 1550* (rev. edn., Gloucester, 1984).

Hassall, W. O., 'Conventual Buildings of St Mary Clerkenwell', *TLMAS* 8 (1940), 234–7.

Hatcher, J., *English Tin Production and Trade before 1550* (Oxford, 1973).

Hatcher, J., 'The Great Slump of the Mid-Fifteenth Century', in R. Britnell and J. Hatcher (eds.), *Progress and Problems in Medieval England: Essays in Honour of Edward Miller* (Cambridge, 1996), 237–72.

Hawkins, D., 'The Black Death and the New London Cemeteries of 1348', *Antiquity*, 64 (1990), 637–42.

Hellinga, L., and Trapp, J. B. (eds.), *The Cambridge History of the Book in Britain* (Cambridge, 1999), vol. iii.

Herbert, W., *The History of the Twelve Great Livery Companies of London* (London, 1834).

Highfield, J. R. L., and Jeffs, R. (eds.), *The Crown and the Local Communities in England and France in the Fifteenth Century* (Gloucester, 1981).

Hillaby, J., 'London: The Thirteenth-Century Jewry Revisited', *Jewish Historical Studies: Transactions of the Jewish Historical Society of England*, 32 (1990–2), 89–158.

Hinnebusch, W., *The Early English Friars Preachers* (Rome, 1951).

Hollaender, A., and Kellaway, W. (eds.), *Studies in London History presented to P. E. Jones* (London, 1969).

Holmes, G., 'Florentine Merchants in England', *EconHR*, 13, 2nd ser., (1960–1), 193–208.

—— 'Lorenzo de'Medici's London branch', in R. Britnell and J. Hatcher, (eds.), *Progress and Problems in Medieval England: Essays in Honour of Edward Miller* (Cambridge, 1996).

Holt, J. C., *Magna Carta* (Cambridge, 1965).

Holt, R., and Rosser, G. (eds.), *The Medieval Town: A Reader in English Urban History 1200–1540* (London, 1990).

Homer, R., 'Tin, Lead and Pewter', in J. Blair and N. Ramsay (eds.), *English Medieval Industries* (London, 1991), 57–80.

Honeybourne, M., 'The Abbot of Waltham's Inn', *LTR* 20 (1952), 34–46.

—— 'The Leper Hospitals of the London Area', *TLMAS* 21 (1967), 1–54.

Hope, W. S., 'The London Charterhouse and its Old Water Supply', *Archaeologia*, 8 (1902), 293–312.

—— *The History of the London Charterhouse* (London, 1925).

Horden, P., and Smith, R. (eds.), *The Locus of Care: Families, Communities, Institutions and the Provision of Welfare since Antiquity* (London, 1998).

Hovland, S., 'Apprenticeship in Later Medieval London, *c.*1300–*c.*1530' (University of London Ph.D. thesis, forthcoming).

Howe, E., *Roman Defences and Medieval Industry* (London, 2002).

Howell, M., 'The Resources of Eleanor of Provence as Queen Consort', *English Historical Review* 102 (1987), 372–393.

Huffman, J., *Family, Commerce and Religion in London and Cologne: Anglo-German Emigrants c.1000–c.1300* (Cambridge, 1998).

Hughes, A., *List of Sheriffs for England and Wales* (PRO, London, 1898; with handwritten corrections and additions, 1963).

Hugo, T., 'The Hospital of Le Papey in the City of London', *TLMAS* 5 (1881), 183–221.

Hunnisett, R. F., 'The Medieval Coroners' Rolls', *The American Journal of Legal History*, 3 (1959), 95–124, 205–221, 324–359, 383.

Hunt, R. W., Pantin, W. A., and Southern, R. W. (eds.), *Studies in Medieval History Presented to F. M. Powicke* (Oxford, 1948).

Imray, J., *The Charity of Richard Whittington* (London, 1968).

—— '"Les bones gentes de la Mercerye de Londres": A Study of the Membership of the

Medieval Mercers' Company', in A. Hollaender and W. Kellaway (eds.), *Studies in London History Presented to P. E. Jones* (London, 1969), 155–178.

—— *The Mercers' Hall* (London, 1991).

JAMES, M. K., *Studies in the Medieval Wine Trade*, ed. E Veale (Oxford, 1971).

JAMES, M., 'Ritual, Drama and Social Body in the Late Medieval Town', *Past and Present*, 98 (1983), 3–29.

JENKS, S., 'Hansische Vermachtnisse in London ca.1363–1483', *Hansische Geschichtsblätter*, 104 (1986), 35–111.

JEWITT, L., and HOPE, W. S., *The Corporation Plate and Insignia of Office*, 2 vols. (London, 1895).

JOHNSON, A. H., *The History of The Worshipful Company of the Drapers of London*, 5 vols. (Oxford, 1914–22).

JOHNSON, D., *Southwark and the City* (London, 1969).

JOHNSTONE, H., 'Poor Relief in the Royal Households of Thirteenth Century England', *Speculum* 4, (1929), 149–167.

JONES, P. E., 'The Court of Hustings', *The Law Journal* 93 (1943), 285–6.

—— 'The City Courts of Law, Mayor's Court and Sheriffs' Courts', *The Law Journal*, 93 (1943), 301–302.

—— 'Some Bridge House Properties', *Journal of the British Archaeological Association*, 3rd ser., 15 (1953), 59–73.

—— 'Common Crier and Serjeant at Arms', *Transactions of Guildhall Historical Association*, 3 (1963), 80–87.

—— *The Worshipful Company of Poulters of the City of London* (2nd edn., London 1965).

—— 'Whittington's Longhouse', *LTR* 23 (1974), 27–34.

—— *The Butchers of London* (London, 1976).

JONES, P. M., 'Thomas Fayreford: An English Fifteenth-Century Medical Practitioner', in R. French, J. Arrizabalaga, A. Cunningham, and L–G. Ballester (eds.), *Medicine from the Black Death to the French Disease* (Aldershot, 1998), 156–83.

—— 'Medicine and Science', in L. Hellinga and J. B. Trapp (eds.), *The Cambridge History of the Book in Britain* (Cambridge, 1999–), iii, 433–48.

JORDAN, W. K., *The Charities of London, 1480–1660* (London, 1960).

JURKOWSKI. M., SMITH, C. L., and CROOK, D., *Lay Taxes in England and Wales 1188–1688* (London, 1998).

KAHL, W. F., *The Development of the London Livery Companies* (Boston, Mass., 1960).

KARRAS, R., *Common Women: Prostitution and Sexuality in Medieval England* (New York and Oxford, 1996).

KEENE, D., 'Shops and Shopping in Medieval London', in L. Grant, *Medieval Art, Architecture and Archaeology in London* (British Archaeological Association, 1984), 29–46.

—— 'A New Study of London before the Great Fire', *Urban History Yearbook* (1984), 11–21.

—— 'The Walbrook Study: A Summary Report' (unpublished manuscript, 1987; copy in Institute of Historical Research).

—— 'Medieval London and its Region', *London Journal*, 14 (1989), 99–111.

—— 'Introduction', in J. Imray, *The Mercers' Hall* (London, 1991), 7–15.

—— 'Tanners' Widows, 1300–1350', in C. Barron and A. F. Sutton, (eds.), *Medieval London Widows 1300–1500* (London, 1994), 1–27.

KEENE, D., 'Small Towns and the Metropolis: The Experience of Medieval England', in J-M. Duvosquel and E. Thoen (eds.), *Peasants and Townsmen in Medieval Europe: Studia in Honorem Adriaan Verhulst* (Ghent, 1995), 223–38.

——'Metalworking in Medieval London: An Introductory Survey', *Journal of the Historical Metallurgy Society*, 30 (1996), 95–102.

——'Guilds in English Towns, AD 1000–1500' in B. Ranson (ed.), *Power, Resistance and Authorities: Aspects of Guild Organisation in England* (Department of Sociology, Hong Kong Baptist University, 1997), 28–43.

——'Du seuil de la Cité à la transformation d'une économie morale: l'environment hanséatique a Londres entre XIIe et XVIIe siècle' in J. Bottin and D. Calabieds (eds.), *Les Étrangers dans la Ville* (Paris, 1999), 409–24.

——'Wardrobes in the City: Houses of Consumption, Finance and Power', in M. Prestwich, R. Britnell, and R. Frame, (eds.), *Thirteenth Century England*, 7 (Woodbridge, 1999), 61–79.

——'Changes in London's Economic Hinterland as Indicated by Debt Cases in the Court of Common Pleas', in J. Galloway (ed.), *Trade, Urban Hinterlands and Market Integration c.1300–1600* (London, 2000), 59–81.

——'London from the Post-Roman Period to 1300', in D. Palliser (ed.), *The Cambridge Urban History of Britain*, (Cambridge, 2000), i. 187–216.

——'Issues of Water in Medieval London', *Urban History*, 28 (2001), 161–79.

KELLAWAY, W., 'The Coroner in Medieval London', in A. Hollaender and W. Kellaway (eds.), *Studies in London History* (London, 1969), 75–91.

——'John Carpenter's Liber Albus', *Guildhall Studies in London History*, 3 (1978), 67–84.

KELLETT, J. R., 'The Breakdown of Gild and Corporate Control over the Handcraft and Retail Trade in London', *EconHR*, 10 (1958), 386–94.

KERLING, N., 'A Note on Newgate Prison', *TLMAS* 22 (1968–70), 21–2.

KERMODE, J., 'Obvious Observations on the Formation of Oligarchies in Late Medieval English Towns', in J. A. F. Thomson (ed.), *Towns and Townspeople in the Fifteenth Century* (Gloucester, 1988), 87–106.

——(ed.), *Enterprise and Individuals in Fifteenth-Century England* (Stroud, 1991).

——'Money and Credit in the Fifteenth Century: Some Lessons from Yorkshire', *Business History Review*, 65 (1991), 475–501.

——*Medieval Merchants: York, Beverley and Hull in the Later Middle Ages* (Cambridge, 1998).

KIMBALL, E., 'Commissions of the Peace for Urban Jurisdictions 1327–1488', *American Philosophical Society*, 121 (1977), 448–74.

KINGSFORD, C., *The Grey Friars of London* (Aberdeen, 1915).

——'A London Merchant's House and its Owners', *Archaeologia*, 74 (1923–4), 137–58.

——*English Historical Literature in the Fifteenth Century* (rpt, New York, 1972).

KIPLING, G., 'The London Pageants for Margaret of Anjou: A Medieval Script Restored', *Medieval English Theatre* (1982), 5–27.

KLEINEKE, H., 'The Dinham Family in the Later Middle Ages' (University of London, Ph.D. thesis, 1998).

——'Carleton's Book: William FitzStephen's "Description of London" in a Late Fourteenth-Century Common-Place Book', *Historical Research*, 74 (2001), 117–26.

KNOWLES, D., and Grimes, W. F., *The London Charterhouse* (London, 1954).

KNOWLES, D., and Hadcock, R. H., *Medieval Religious Houses: England and Wales* (2nd edn., London, 1971).

Kowaleski. M., *Local Markets and Regional Trade in Medieval Exeter* (Cambridge, 1995).
——'Town and Country in Late Medieval England: The Hide and Leather Trade' in P. J. Corfield and D. Keene (eds.), *Work in Towns 850–1850* (Leicester, 1990), 57–73.
Lancashire, A., 'The Problem of Facts and the London Civic Records, 1275–1558', in A. F. Johnstone (ed.), *Editing London Records* (Toronto, 2003).
Lancashire, I., *Dramatic Texts and Records of Britain: A Chronological Topography to 1558* (Toronto, 1984).
Levy, E., 'Moorfields, Finsbury and the City of London in the Sixteenth Century', *London Topographical Record*, 26 (1990), 78–96.
Lindenbaum, S., 'Ceremony and Oligarchy: The London Midsummer Watch' in B. Hanawalt and K. Reyerson (eds.), *City and Spectacle in Medieval Europe* (Minneapolis, 1994), 171–88.
Lindley, P., 'Absolutism and Regal Image in Ricardian Sculpture' in D. Gordan, L. Monnas, and C. Elam (eds.), *The Regal Image of Richard II and the Wilton Diptych* (London, 1997), 61–83.
List of Wardens of the Grocers' Company from 1345 to 1907 (London, 1907).
Lloyd, T. H., *The English Wool Trade in the Middle Ages* (Cambridge, 1977).
——*Alien Merchants in England in the High Middle Ages* (Brighton, 1982).
——*England and the German Hanse* (Cambridge, 1991).
Lobel, M. D. (ed.), *Historic Towns Atlas: The City of London from Prehistoric Times to c.1520* (Oxford, 1989).
McConica, J., 'The Early Fellowship', in J. McConica (ed.), *Unarmed Soldiery: Studies in the Early History of All Souls College* (All Souls College, Oxford, 1996), 33–64.
——(ed.), *Unarmed Soldiery: Studies in the Early History of All Souls College* (All Souls College, Oxford, 1996).
MacCracken, H., 'King Henry's Triumphal Entry into London: Lydgate's Poem and Carpenter's Letter', *Archiv für das Studium der Neuren Sprachen und Literaturen*, 126 (1911), 75–102.
MacGregor, A., 'Antler, Bone and Horn', in J. Blair and N. Ramsay (eds.), *English Medieval Industries* (London, 1991), 355–78.
McKisack, M., 'London and the Succession to the Crown during the Middle Ages', in R. W. Hunt, W. A. Pantin and R. W. Southern (eds.), *Studies in Medieval History Presented to F. M. Powicke* (Oxford,1948), 76–89.
Macleod, R., 'The Topography of St Paul's Precinct, 1200–1500', *London Topographical Record*, 26 (1990), 1–14.
Maddison, F., Pelling, M., and Webster, C. (eds.), *Essays on the Life and Work of Thomas Linacre c. 1460–1524* (Oxford, 1977).
Manchester, K., 'Tuberculosis and Leprosy in Antiquity: An Interpretation', *Medical History*, 28 (1984), 162–73.
Martin, G., 'The Early History of the London Saddlers' Guild', *Bulletin of the John Rylands University Library of Manchester*, 72 (1990), 145–54.
——*The Husting Rolls of Deeds and Wills, 1252–1485* (Cambridge, 1990).
Maryfield, P., "*Love as Brethren*", *a Quincentennial History of the Coopers' Company* (London, 2000).
Masschaele, J., *Peasants, Merchants and Markets: Inland Trade in Medieval England 1150–1350* (London, 1997).
Masters, B., 'The Common Serjeant', *Guildhall Miscellany*, 2 (1967–8), 379–89.
——'The Secondary', *Guildhall Miscellany*, 2 (1967–8), 425–433.

Masters, B., 'The Mayor's Household before 1600', in W. Kellaway and A. Hollaender (eds,), *Studies in London History Presented to P. E. Jones* (London, 1969), 95–114.
——'The Town Clerk', *Guildhall Miscellany*, 3 (1969), 55–74.
——'The City Surveyor, the City Engineer and the City Architect and Planning Officer', *Guildhall Miscellany*, 4 (1973), 237–55.
——*The Chamberlain of the City of London 1237–1987* (London, 1988).
Matthews, L. G., *The Royal Apothecaries* (London, 1967).
Megson, B., 'Life Expectations of the Widows and Orphans of Freemen in London 1375–1399', *Local Population Studies*, 57 (1996), 18–29.
——'Mortality among London Citizens in the Black Death', *Medieval Prosopography*, 19 (1998), 125–33.
Miller, E., and Hatcher, J. (eds.), *Medieval England: Towns, Commerce and Crafts 1086–1348* (London, 1995).
Miller, P., and Stephenson, R., *A Fourteenth-Century Pottery Site in Kingston upon Thames, Surrey* (London, 1999).
Milne, G. (ed.), *From Roman Basilica to Medieval Market* (London, 1992).
Mitchell, S., *Taxation in Medieval England* (New Haven, Conn. 1951).
Monier-Williams, R., *The Tallow Chandlers of London*, 4 vols. (London, 1970–7).
Monnas, L., 'Fit for a King: Figured Silks shown in the Wilton Diptych', in D. Gordon, L. Monnas, and C. Elam (eds.), *The Regal Image of Richard II and the Wilton Diptych* (London, 1997), 165–77.
Moore, E. W., *The Fairs of Medieval England* (Toronto, 1985).
Moorman, J., 'Edward I at Lanercost Priory 1306–7', *EHR* 263 (1952), 162–74.
Moss, D., 'The Economic Development of a Middlesex Village', *Agricultural History Review*, 28 (1980), 104–14.
——and Murray, I., 'A Fifteenth Century Middlesex Terrier', *TLMAS* 25 (1974), 285–94.
Munro, J. H., 'The International Law Merchant and the Evolution of Negotiable Credit in Late Medieval England and the Low Countries', in *Banchi Pubblici. Banchi Privati e monti di pieta nell' Europa preindustriale* (Societa Ligure di Storia Patria) n.s. 31 (Genoa, 1991), 49–80.
Museum of London Archaeology Service, *The Archaeology of Greater London* (Museum of London, 2000).
Mustain, J. K., 'A Rural Medical Practitioner in Fifteenth-Century England', *Bulletin of the History of Medicine*, 46 (1972), 469–76.
Myers, A. R., 'The Wealth of Richard Lyons', in T. A. Sandquist and M. R. Powicke (eds.), *Essays in Medieval History Presented to Bertie Wilkinson* (Toronto, 1969), 301–29.
Nash, B., 'A Study of the Freeman and Apprenticeship Registers of Letter Book D (1309–1312), The Place-Name Evidence' (Royal Holloway, University of London, MA thesis 1990).
Nightingale, P., 'Capitalists, Crafts and Constitutional Change in Late Fourteenth-Century London', *Past and Present*, 124 (1989), 3–35.
——'Monetary Contraction and Mercantile Credit in Later Medieval England', *Economic History Review*, 43 (1990), 560–75.
——*A Medieval Mercantile Community: The Grocers' Company and the Politics and Trade of London 1000–1485* (New Haven and London, 1995).
——'The Growth of London in the Medieval Economy', in R. Britnell and J. Hatcher (eds.), *Progress and Problems in Medieval England* (Cambridge, 1996), 89–106.

——'England and the European Depression of the Mid-Fifteenth Century', *Journal of European Economic History*, 26 (1997), 631–56.

NORMAN, P., 'On an Ancient Conduit-Head in Queen Square, Bloomsbury', *Archaeologia*, 6 (1899), 257–66.

——*Crosby Place, with an Architectural Description* (London, 1908).

NORTH, D. C., 'Transaction Costs in History', *Journal of European Economic History*, 14 (1985), 557–76.

O'CONNOR, S., 'Finance, Diplomacy and Politics: Royal Service by Two London Merchants in the Reign of Edward III', *Historical Research*, 67 (1994), 18–39.

OLDLAND, J., 'London Clothmaking, *c.*1270–c.1550' (University of London, Ph.D. thesis, 2003).

OLIVER, K., *Hold Fast, Sit Sure: The History of the Worshipful Company of Saddlers of the City of London 1160–1960* (Chichester, 1995).

ORME, N., 'The Sufferings of the Clergy: Illness and Old Age in Exeter Diocese, 1300–1540', in M. Pelling and R. M. Smith (eds.), *Life, Death and the Elderly* (London, 1991), 62–73.

PAGE, W. (ed.), *The Victoria History of the Counties of England: London* (London, 1909).

PALLISER, D. (ed.), *Cambridge Urban History of Britain* (Cambridge 2000), i .

PARK, K., *Doctors and Medicine in Early Renaissance Florence* (Princeton, NJ, 1985).

PARK, K., and Henderson, J., '"The First Hospital among Christians": The Ospedale di Santa Maria Nuova in Early Sixteenth-Century Florence', *Medical History*, 35 (1991), 164–88.

PARKER, J. H., and TURNER, H., *Some Account of Domestic Architecture in England* (London, 1853).

PARSONS, E. J. S., *The Map of Great Britain circa AD 1360 known as the Gough Map* (1958, rpt. Oxford, 1996).

PAXTON, C., 'The Nunneries of London and its Environs in the Later Middle Ages' (University of Oxford, D.Phil. thesis, 1992).

PAYNE, P., and BARRON, C., 'The Letters and Life of Elizabeth Despenser, Lady Zouche (d.1408)', *Nottingham Medieval Studies*, 41 (1997), 126–56.

PEARCE, J., and VINCE, A., *A Dated Type-Series of London Medieval Pottery: 4. Surrey Whitewares* (LAMAS, 1988).

PEARSALL, D., *John Lydgate* (Charlottesville, Va., 1970).

PEBERDY, R., 'Navigation of the River Thames between London and Oxford in the Late Middle Ages: A Reconsideration', *Oxoniensia*, 16 (1996), 311–40.

PELLING, M., 'Appearance and Reality: Barber Surgeons, the Body and Disease' in A. L. Beier and R. Finlay (eds.), *London 1500–1700: The Making of the Metropolis* (London, 1986), 82–112.

PELLING, M., and SMITH, R. M. (eds.), *Life, Death and the Elderly* (London, 1991).

PELLING, M. and WEBSTER, C., 'Medical Practitioners', in C. Webster (ed.), *Health, Medicine and Mortality in the Sixteenth Century* (Cambridge, 1979), 165–235

PENDRILL, C., *Old Parish Life in London* (Oxford, 1937).

PERROY, E., 'Le Commerce anglo-flamand au XIIIe siècle: le Hanse flamande de Londres', *Revue Historique*, 252 (1974), 3–18.

PHYTHIAN-ADAMS, C., *Desolation of a City: Coventry and the Urban Crisis of the Late Middle Ages* (Cambridge, 1979).

POLLARD, G., 'Medieval Loan Chests at Cambridge', *BIHR* 17 (1939–40), 113–29.

POWELL, E., and TREVELYAN, G. M., (eds.), *The Peasants' Rising and the Lollards* (London, 1899).

Power, E., *The Wool Trade in English Medieval History* (Oxford, 1941).
Power, E., and Postan, M. (eds.), *Studies in English Trade in the Fifteenth Century* (London, 1933).
Prestwich, M., 'Italian Merchants in Late Thirteenth and Early Fourteenth Century England', in [Centre for Medieval and Renaissance Studies, University of California, Los Angeles], *The Dawn of Modern Banking* (New Haven, Conn., and London, 1979), 77–104.
Prestwich, M., Britnell, R., and Frame, R. (eds.), *Thirteenth Century England* (Woodbridge, 1999).
Pugh, R. B., *Imprisonment in Medieval England* (Cambridge, 1968).
Quinton, E., 'The Drapers and the Drapery Trade of the Late Medieval London, c.1300–c.1500' (University of London, Ph.D. thesis, 2001).
Ramsay, N. 'The English Legal Profession *c.*1340–1450' (University of Cambridge, Ph.D. thesis, 1985).
Rawcliffe, C., 'Medicine and Medical Practice in Late Medieval London', *GSLH*, 5 (1981), 13–23.
——'The Hospitals of Later Medieval London', *Medical History*, 28 (1984), 1–21.
——'The Profits of Practice: The Wealth and Status of Medical Men in Later Medieval England', *Bulletin of the Society for the Social History of Medicine*, 1 (1988), 61–78.
——'"That Kindliness Should be Cherished More, and Discord Driven Out": The Settlement of Commercial Disputes by Arbitration in Later Medieval England', in J. Kermode (ed.), *Enterprise and Individuals in Fifteenth-Century England* (Stroud, 1991), 99–117.
—— *Medicine for the Soul: The Life, Death and Resurrection of an English Medieval Hospital* (Stroud, 1999).
Razi, Z., 'Intrafamilial Ties and Relationships in the Medieval Village: A Quantitative Approach, Employing Manor Court Rolls' in Z. Razi and R. M. Smith (eds.), *Medieval Society and the Manor Court* (Oxford, 1996), 369–91.
——and Smith, R. M. (eds.), *Medieval Society and the Manor Court* (Oxford, 1996).
Reddaway, T. F., and Walker, L. M., *The Early History of the Goldsmiths' Company, 1327–1509* (London, 1975).
Rees Jones, S., 'York's Civic Administration 1354–1464', in S. Rees Jones (ed.), *The Government of Medieval York: Essays in Commemoration of the 1396 Royal Charter*, Borthwick Studies in History, 3 (York, 1997), 108–40.
——(ed.), *The Government of Medieval York: Essays in Commemoration of the 1396 Royal Charter*, Borthwick Studies in History, 3 York, 1997), 108–40.
Reynolds, S., 'The Rulers of London in the Twelfth Century', *History*, 57 (1972), 337–57.
——'Medieval Urban History and the History of Political Thought', *Urban History Yearbook* (1982), 14–23.
Rhodes, W. E., 'The Italian Bankers and their Loans to Edward I and Edward II', in T. F. Tout and J. Tait (eds.), *Historical Essays by Members of the Owen's College* (Manchester, 1907), 137–67.
Richmond, C. F., 'Fauconberg's Kentish Rising of May 1471', *EHR* 85 (1970), 673–92.
——'Religion and the Fifteenth-Century English Gentleman', in R. B. Dobson (ed.), *The Church, Politics and Patronage in the Fifteenth Century* (Gloucester, 1984), 193–208.
Rickert, E., *Chaucer's World* (Oxford, 1948).
Rigby, S., 'Urban "Oligarchy" in Late Medieval England', in J. A. F. Thomson (ed.), *Towns and Townspeople in the Fifteenth Century* (Gloucester, 1988), 62–86.

ROBERTS, R., 'The London Apothecaries and Medical Practice in Tudor and Stuart England' (University of London, Ph.D. thesis, 1964).
ROHRKASTEN, J., 'Londoners and London Mendicants in the Late Middle Ages', *Journal of Ecclesiastical History*, 47 (1996), 446–77.
——'The Origin and Early Development of London Mendicant Houses', in T. R. Slater and G. Rosser (eds.), *The Church in the Medieval Town* (Aldershot, 1998), 76–99.
ROSENFIELD, M., 'Holy Trinity Aldgate on the Eve of the Dissolution', *Guildhall Miscellany*, 3 (1970), 159–73.
ROSKELL, J. S., *The Commons and their Speakers in English Parliaments 1376–1523* (Manchester, 1965).
ROSKELL, J. S., CLARK, L., and RAWCLIFFE, C., *The House of Commons 1386–1421*, 4 vols. (Stroud, 1992).
ROSSER, G., *Medieval Westminster 1200–1540* (Oxford, 1989).
——'Sanctuary and Social Negotiation in Medieval England' in J. Blair, and B. Golding, (eds.), *The Cloister and the World: Essays in Medieval History in Honour of Barbara Harvey* (Oxford, 1996), 57–79.
—— 'Crafts, Guilds and the Negotiation of Work in the Medieval Town', *Past and Present*, 154 (1997), 3–31.
RUBIN, M., *Corpus Christi: The Eucharist in Late Medieval Culture* (Cambridge, 1991).
RUSSELL, J. C., *British Medieval Population* (Albuquerque, 1948).
SABINE, E., 'Butchering in Medieval London', *Speculum* 8 (1933), 335–53.
——'Latrines and Cesspools of Medieval London', *Speculum*, 9 (1934), 303–21.
——'City Cleaning in Medieval London', *Speculum*, 12 (1937), 19–43.
SALZMAN, L. F., *Building in England down to 1540: A Documentary History* (Oxford, 1952).
SAMUEL, M., 'Reconstructing the Medieval Market at Leadenhall', in G. Milne (ed.), *From Roman Basilica to Medieval Market* (London, 1992), 114–25.
SANDQUIST, T. A., and POWICKE, M. R. (eds.), *Essays in Medieval History Presented to Bertie Wilkinson* (Toronto, 1969).
SCHOFIELD, J., *The Building of London from the Conquest to the Great Fire* (London, 1984).
——'Medieval and Tudor Domestic Buildings in the City of London', in L. Grant (ed.), *Medieval Art, Architecture and Archaeology in London* (British Archaeological Association, 1994), 16–29.
——*Medieval London Houses* (London, 1994).
SCHOFIELD, J., and DYSON, A., *Archaeology of the City of London* (London, 1980).
SCOTT, K., *Later Gothic Manuscripts 1390–1490*, 2 vols. (London, 1996).
SEABOURNE, G., 'Controlling Commercial Morality in Late Medieval London: The Usury Trials of 1421', *Journal of Legal History*, 19 (1998), 116–42.
SETON-WATSON, R. W. (ed,), *Tudor Studies Presented to A. F. Pollard* (London, 1924).
SHARPE, R. R., 'Pleas of the Crown in the City of London', *Journal of the British Archaeological Association*, n.s. 3 (1897), 103–12.
SHEAIL, J., *The Regional Distribution of Wealth in England as Indicated by the 1524/5 Lay Subsidy Returns*, ed. R. W. Hoyle, 2 vols. (List and Index Society, 1998).
SLACK, P., 'Mirrors of Health and Treasures of Poor Men: The Uses of Vernacular Medical Literature of Tudor England', in C. Webster (ed.), *Health, Medicine and Mortality in the Sixteenth Century* (Cambridge, 1979), 237–73.
SLATER, T. R., and ROSSER, G. (eds.), *The Church in the Medieval Town* (Aldershot, 1998).
SMITH, D. L., STREIER, R., and BEVINGTON, D. (eds.), *The Theatrical City: Culture, Theatre and Politics in London 1576–1649* (Cambridge, 1995)

SMITH, J. F., *Memorials of the Craft of Surgery in England*, ed. D'Arcy Power (London, 1886).

SMITH, R. M., 'Demographic Developments in Rural England, 1300–1348: A Survey', in B. Campbell (ed.), *Before the Black Death* (Manchester, 1989).

——'The Manorial Court and the Elderly Tenant in Late Medieval England', in M. Pelling and Smith R. M. (eds.), *Life, Death and the Elderly: Historical Perspectives* (London, 1991), 39–61.

SNELLING, V., 'The Almshouses of Medieval London 1400–1550' (Royal Holloway, University of London, MA thesis, 1997).

SOMERVILLE, R., *The Savoy* (London, 1960).

SPALLANZANI. M. (ed.), *Produzione Commercio e Consumo dei Panni di Lana*, 2 vols. (Florence, 1976).

SQUIBB, G., *Doctors' Commons* (Oxford, 1977).

STAFFORD, P., NELSON, J., and MARTINDALE, J. (eds.), *Law, Laity and Solidarities: Essays in Honour of Susan Reynolds* (Manchester, 2001).

STAHLSCHMIDT, J., *Surrey Bells and London Bellfounders* (London, 1884).

STANILAND, K., *Embroiderers* (London, 1991).

STENTON, F. M., 'The Road System of Medieval England', *EconHR*, 7 (1936–7), 1–21.

STEVEN WATSON, J., *A History of the Salters' Company* (London, 1965).

STRATFORD, J., *The Bedford Inventories* (Society of Antiquaries, London, 1993).

——'John Hende' in *New DNB* (forthcoming).

STROHM, P., *Hochon's Arrow: The Social Imagination of Fourteenth-Century Texts* (Princeton, NJ, 1992).

STRYPE, J., *Survey of the Cities of London and Westminster*, 2 vols. (London, 1720).

SUTHERLAND, I., 'When was the Great Plague? Mortality in London, 1563 to 1665', in D. Glass and R. Revelle (eds.), *Population and Social Change* (London, 1972), 287–320.

SUTTON, A., 'Merchants, Music and Social Harmony: The London Puy and its French and London Contexts c.1300', *London Journal*, 17 (1992), 1–17.

——*The Mercers' Company's First Charter 1394* (The Mercers' Company, London, 1994).

——'The Mercery Trade and the Mercers' Company of London, from the 1130s to 1348' (University of London, Ph.D. thesis, 1995).

——'The Silent Years of London Guild History before 1300: The Case of the Mercers', *Historical Research*, 71 (1998), 121–41.

—— *I Sing of a Maiden: The Story of the Maiden of the Mercers' Company* (The Mercers' Company, London, 1998).

——'The Shop-Floor of the London Mercery Trade, *c.*1200–*c.*1500: The Marginalisation of the Artisan, the Itinerant Mercer and the Shopholder', *Nottingham Medieval Studies*, 45 (2001), 12–50.

—— 'The Merchant Adventurers of England: Their Origins and the Mercers' Company of London', *Historical Research*, 75 (2002), 25–46.

SWANSON, H., *Medieval Artisans: An Urban Class in late Medieval England* (Oxford, 1989).

TALBOT, C. H., and HAMMOND, E. A., *The Medical Practitioners of Medieval England* (London, 1965).

TATCHELL, M., 'A Fourteenth Century London Building Contract', *Guildhall Miscellany*, 2 (1962), 129–31.

TATTON BROWN, T., 'Excavations at the Custom House Site, City of London, 1973', *TLMAS* 25 (1974), 117–219.

TAYLOR, J., and CHILDS W. (eds.), *Politics and Crisis in Fourteenth-Century England* (Gloucester, 1990).

Taylor, P., 'The Estates of the Bishop of London from the Seventh Century to the Early Sixteenth Century' (University of London, Ph.D. thesis, 1976).
Thomas, A. H., 'Notes on the History of the Leadenhall, 1195–1488', *London Topographical Record*, 13 (1923), 1–22 .
Thomas, C., Sloane, B., and Phillpotts, C., *Excavations at the Priory and Hospital of St Mary Spittal, London* (London, 1997).
Thomson, J. A. F., 'Tythe Disputes in Later Medieval London', *EHR* 78 (1963), 1–17.
——'Piety and Charity in Later Medieval London', *Journal of Ecclesiastical History*, 16 (1965), 178–95.
——'Wealth, Poverty and Mercantile Ethics in Late Medieval London', in N. Bulst and J. P. Genet (eds.), *La Ville, la bourgeoisie et la genèse de l'État moderne (XII–XVIII siècles)* (Paris, 1988), 265–78.
——(ed.), *Towns and Townspeople in the Fifteenth Century* (Gloucester, 1988).
Thornley, I. D., 'The Destruction of Sanctuary', in R. W. Seton-Watson (ed.), *Tudor Studies Presented to A. F. Pollard* (London, 1924), 182–207.
——'Sanctuary in Medieval London', *Journal of the British Archaeological Association*, 2nd ser. (1933), 293–315.
Thrupp, S., *The Merchant Class of Medieval London* (Michigan, 1948).
——*A Short History of the Worshipful Company of Bakers* (London, 1933).
——'The Grocers of London: A Study of Distributive Trade', in E. Power and M. Postan (eds.), *Studies in English Trade in the Fifteenth Century* (London, 1933), 247–92.
Tout, T. F., and Tait, J. (eds.), *Historical Essays by Members of the Owen's College* (Manchester, 1907).
Trease, G. E., 'The Spicers & Apothecaries of the Royal Household in the Reigns of Henry III, Edward I and Edward II', *Nottingham Medieval Studies*, 3 (1959), 19–52.
Treveil, P., and Rowsome, P., 'Number 1 Poultry—the Main Excavation: Late Saxon and Medieval Sequence', *London Archaeologist*, 8 (1998), 283–91.
Tucker, P., 'Government and Politics, London 1461–1483' (University of London, Ph.D. thesis, 1995).
——'Relationships between London's Courts and the Westminster Courts in the Reign of Edward IV' in D. E. S. Dunn, (ed.), *Courts, Counties and the Capital in the Later Middle Ages* (Stroud, 1996), 117–138.
——'London's Courts of Law in the Fifteenth Century: The Litigants' Perspective', in C. W. Brooks and M. Lobban (eds.), *Communities and Courts in Britain 1150–1900* (London, 1997), 25–41.
——'The Early History of the Court of Chancery: A Comparative Study', *EHR* 115 (2000), 791–811.
Turner, H. L., *Town Defences of England and Wales* (London, 1971).
Turner, T. H., *Some Account of Domestic Architecture in England*, 4 vols. (Oxford, 1851–69).
Unwin, G., *The Guilds and Companies of London* (London, 1908).
——'The Estate of Merchants 1336–1365', in id. *Finance and Trade under Edward III* (Manchester, 1918), 179–255.
——*Finance and Trade under Edward III* (Manchester, 1918).
Valente, C., 'The Deposition and Abdication of Edward II', *EHR* 113 (1998), 852–81.
Veale, E., *The English Fur Trade in the Later Middle Ages* (Oxford, 1966).
——'Craftsmen and the Economy of London in the Fourteenth Century' in R. Holt and G. Rosser (eds.), *The Medieval Town: A Reader in English Urban History 1200–1540* (London, 1990), 120–40.

Veale, E., 'The 'Great Twelve': Mistery and Fraternity in Thirteenth-Century London', *Historical Research*, 64 (1991), 237–63.

Wagner, A., *Heralds and Heraldry in the Middle Ages* (Oxford, 1956).

Wallis, P., 'London, Londoners and Opus Anglicanum', in L. Grant (ed.), *Medieval Art, Architecture and Archaeology of London* (British Archaeological Association, 1990), 135–9.

Watson, B., 'The Construction of the Colechurch Bridge' in B. Watson, T. Brigham and A. Dyson, *London Bridge: 2000 Years of a River Crossing* (London, 2001), 83–92.

Watson, B., Brigham, T., and Dyson, A., *London Bridge: 2000 Years of a River Crossing* (London, 2001).

Webster, C., 'Thomas Linacre and the Foundation of the College of Physicians', in F. Maddison, M. Pelling, and C. Webster (eds.), *Essays on the Life and Work of Thomas Linacre c. 1460–1524* (Oxford, 1977), 198–222.

——(ed.), *Health, Medicine, and Mortality in the Sixteenth Century* (Cambridge, 1979).

Weinbaum, M., *London unter Eduard I und II.* 2 vols. (Stuttgart, 1933).

White, B., 'Poet and Peasant', in F. R. H. Du Boulay and C. Barron (eds.), *The Reign of Richard II: Essays in Honour of May McKisack* (London, 1971), 58–74.

White, W., *Skeletal Remains from the Cemetery of St Nicholas Shambles, City of London* (London and Middlesex Archaeological Society, 1988).

Willard, J. F., *Parliamentary Taxes on Personal Property 1290–1334* (Medieval Academy of America, 1934).

Williams, D., (ed.), *England in the Fifteenth Century* (Woodbridge, 1987).

Williams, E., *Early Holborn and the Legal Quarter of London*, 2 vols. (London, 1927).

Williams, G. A., *Medieval London from Commune to Capital* (London, 1963).

Wood, R. A., 'A Fourteenth Century London Owner of Piers Plowman', *Medium Aevum*, 53 (1984), 83–90.

Wright, R., 'The Shipwrights of Medieval London, 1250–1500' (Royal Holloway, University of London, MA thesis, 2001).

Wrigley, E. A., and Schofield, R. S., *The Population History of England, 1541–1871: A Reconstruction* (London, 1981).

Wylie, J. H., *The Reign of Henry IV*, 4 vols. (London, 1884–98).

Wyman, A. L., 'The Surgeoness', the Female Practitioner of Surgery 1400–1800', *Medical History*, 28 (1984), 22–41.

Yates, N., and Gibson, J. M. (eds.), *Traffic and Politics: The Construction and Management of Rochester Bridge AD 43–1993* (Woodbridge, 1994).

Young, S., *The Annals of the Barber-Surgeons of London* (London, 1890).

CITY OF LONDON *c.*1520

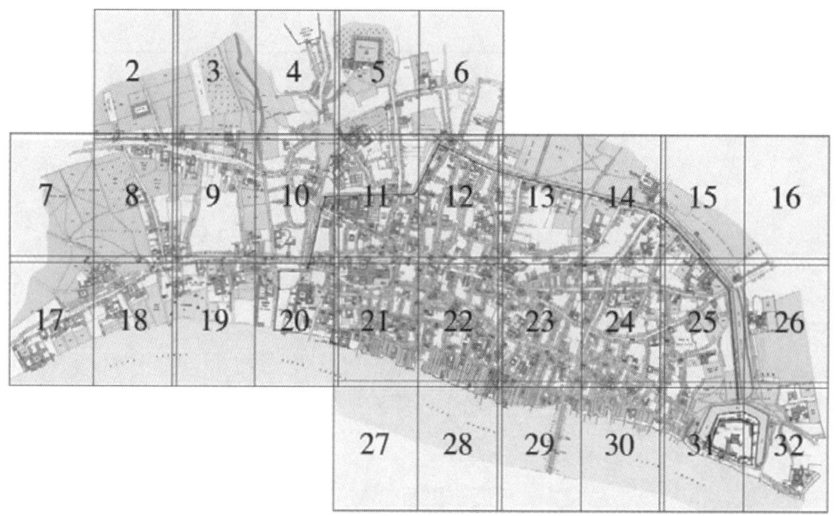

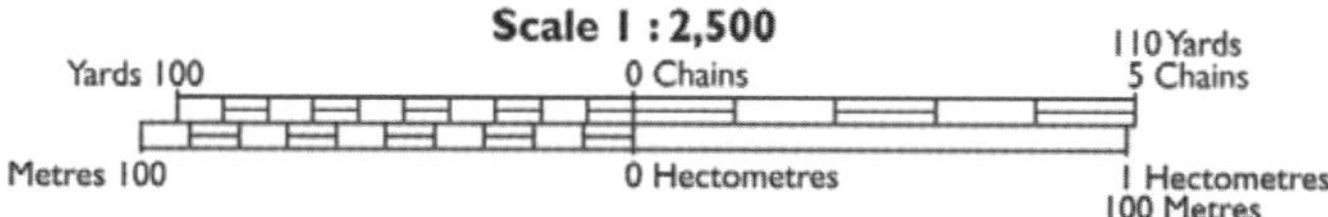

Heights are in metres, these are indicative of ground heights at the late medieval period and are based on the Ordnance Survey datum of c.1870.

This Map was first printed in Mary D. Lobel (ed.), *The City of London: From Prehistoric Times to c.1520* (Oxford, 1989) and is reproduced here with the kind permission of the Historic Towns Trust. The cartography is by Lovell Johns Ltd., Long Hanborough, Oxfordshire OX29 8RU.

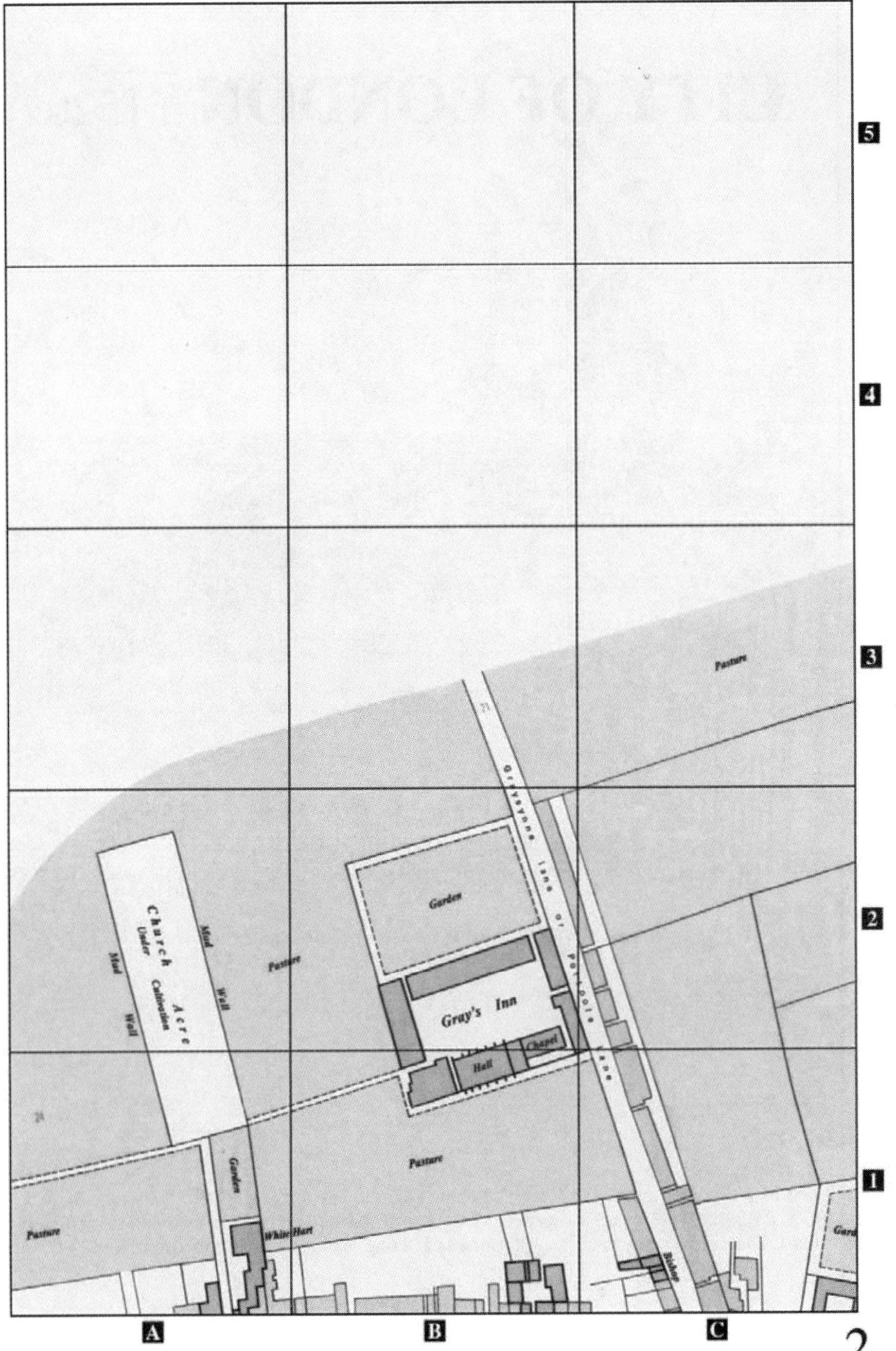
5
4
3
2
1
A
B
C
Pasture
Garden
Gray's Inn
Chapel
Hall
Church Acre
Under Cultivation
Mud Wall
Mud Wall
Pasture
Pasture
Garden
White Hart
Pasture
Bishop
Grayes Inn lane or Portpole lane

2

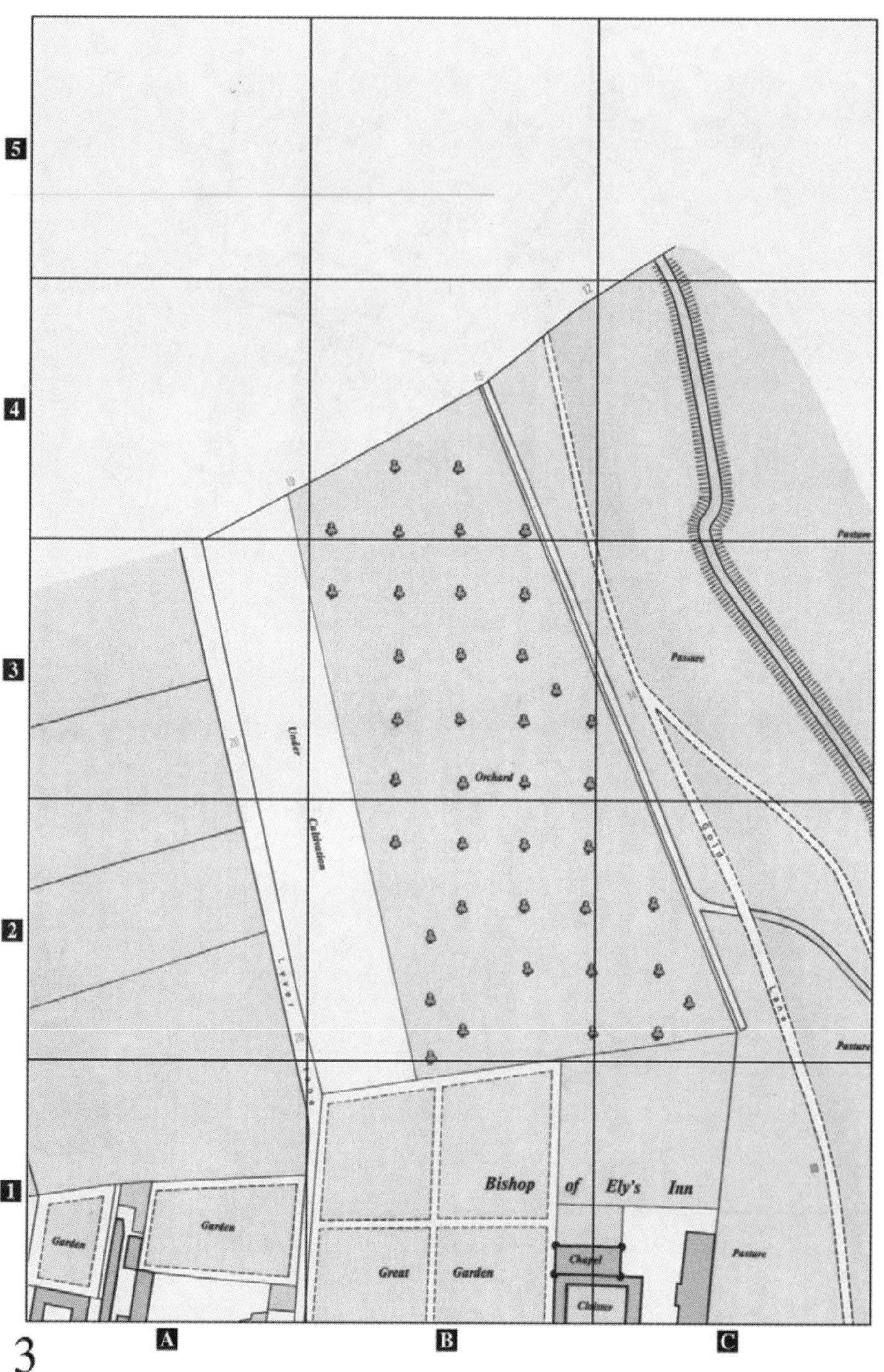
5
4
3
2
1
A
B
C
Pasture
Pasture
Under
Cultivation
Orchard
Gold
Lane
Lyvel
Lane
Pasture
Bishop of Ely's Inn
Garden
Garden
Great Garden
Chapel
Cloister
Pasture

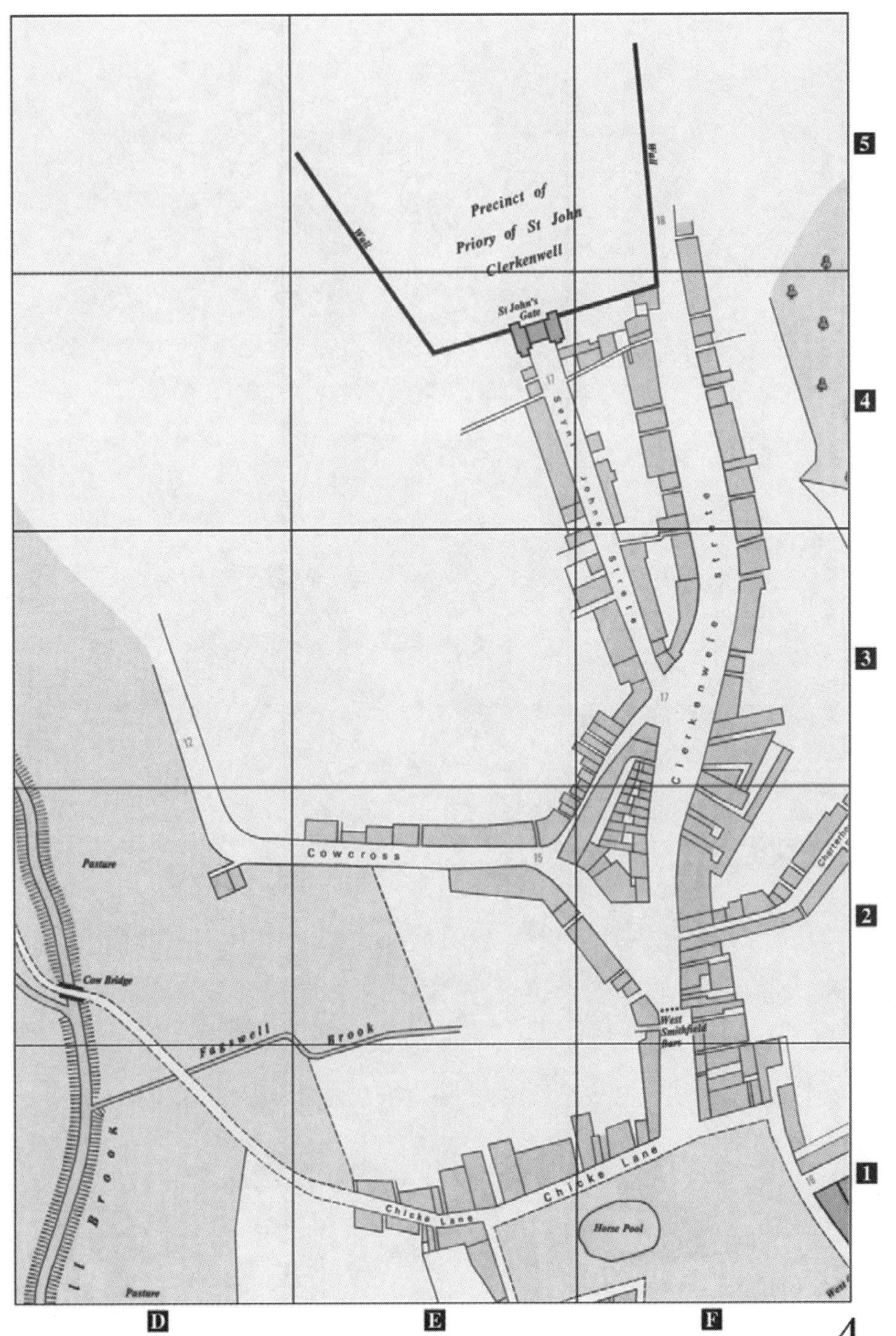

Precinct of
Priory of St John
Clerkenwell
Wall
Wall
St John's Gate
St Johns Streete
Clerkenwele streete
Cowcross
Pasture
Cow Bridge
Fagswell Brook
West Smithfield Bars
Chicke Lane
Chicke Lane
Horse Pool
Pasture
5
4
3
2
1
D
E
F

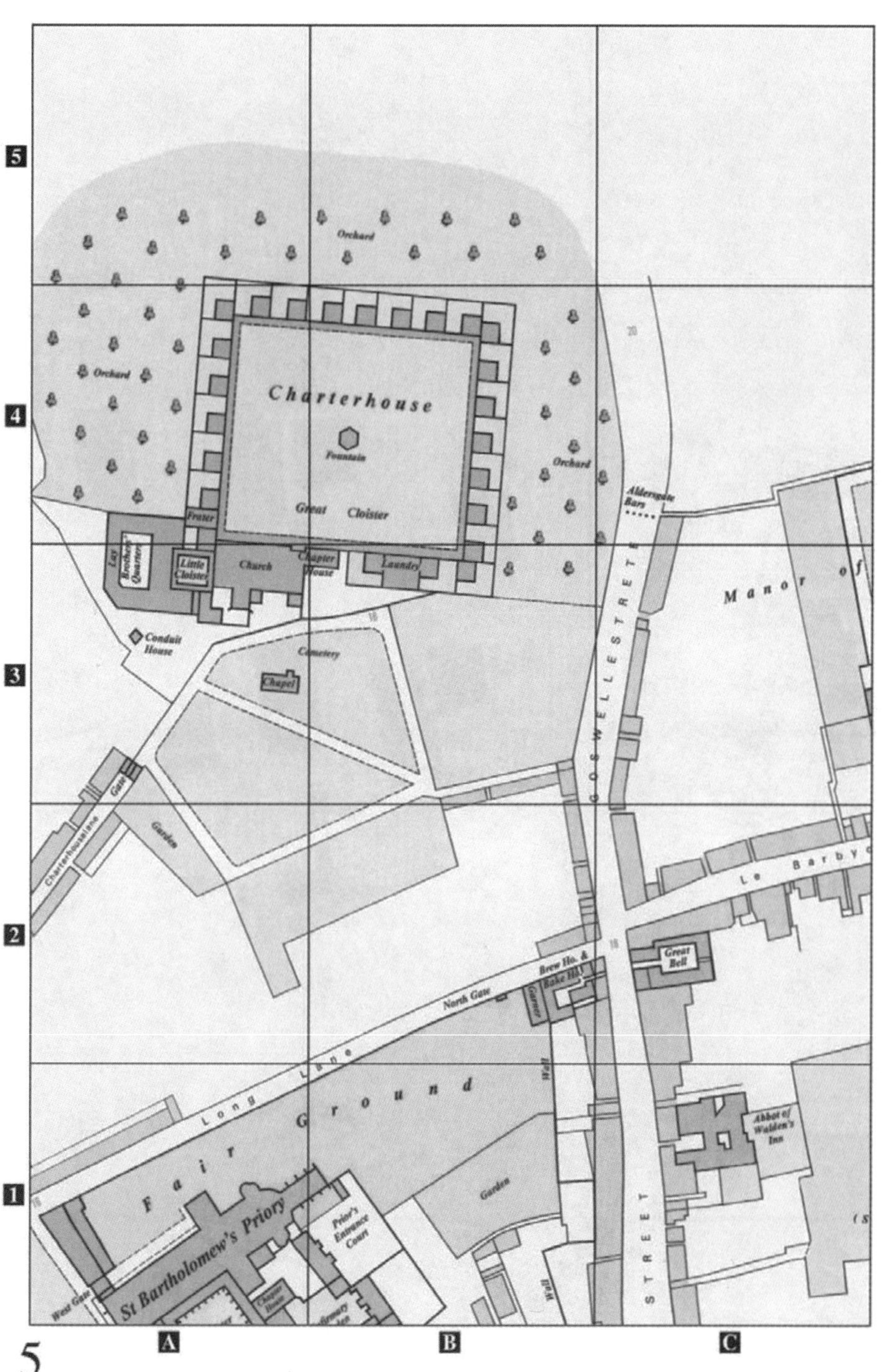
Orchard
Charterhouse
Fountain
Great Cloister
Orchard
Orchard
Frater
Lay Brothers' Quarters
Little Cloister
Church
Chapter House
Laundry
Conduit House
Cemetery
Chapel
Aldersgate Bars
Manor of
GOSWELLESTRETE
Gate
Charterhouselane
Garden
Le Barbyc
Great Bell
Brew Ho. & Bake Ho.
Garner
North Gate
Long Lane
Fair Ground
Wall
Abbot of Walden's Inn
Garden
St Bartholomew's Priory
Prior's Entrance Court
Chapter House
West Gate
Wall
STREET
5
4
3
2
1
A
B
C
5

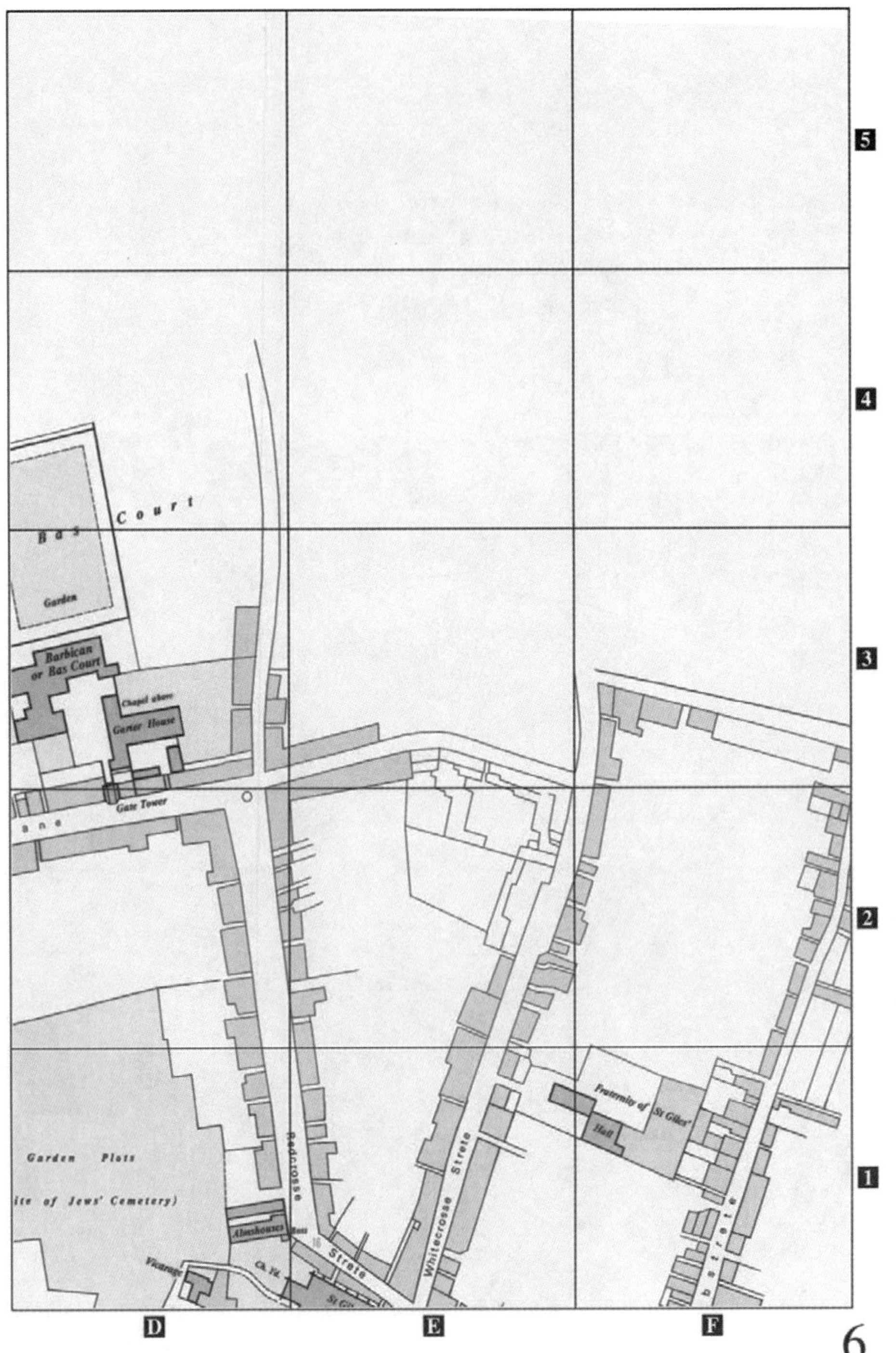
Bas Court
Garden
Barbican or Bas Court
Chapel above
Garter House
Gate Tower
ane
Garden Plots
ite of Jews' Cemetery)
Almshouses
Vicarage
Ch. Yd.
Redcrosse
Strete
Whitecrosse Strete
Fraternity of St Giles'
Hall
5
4
3
2
1
D
E
F

6

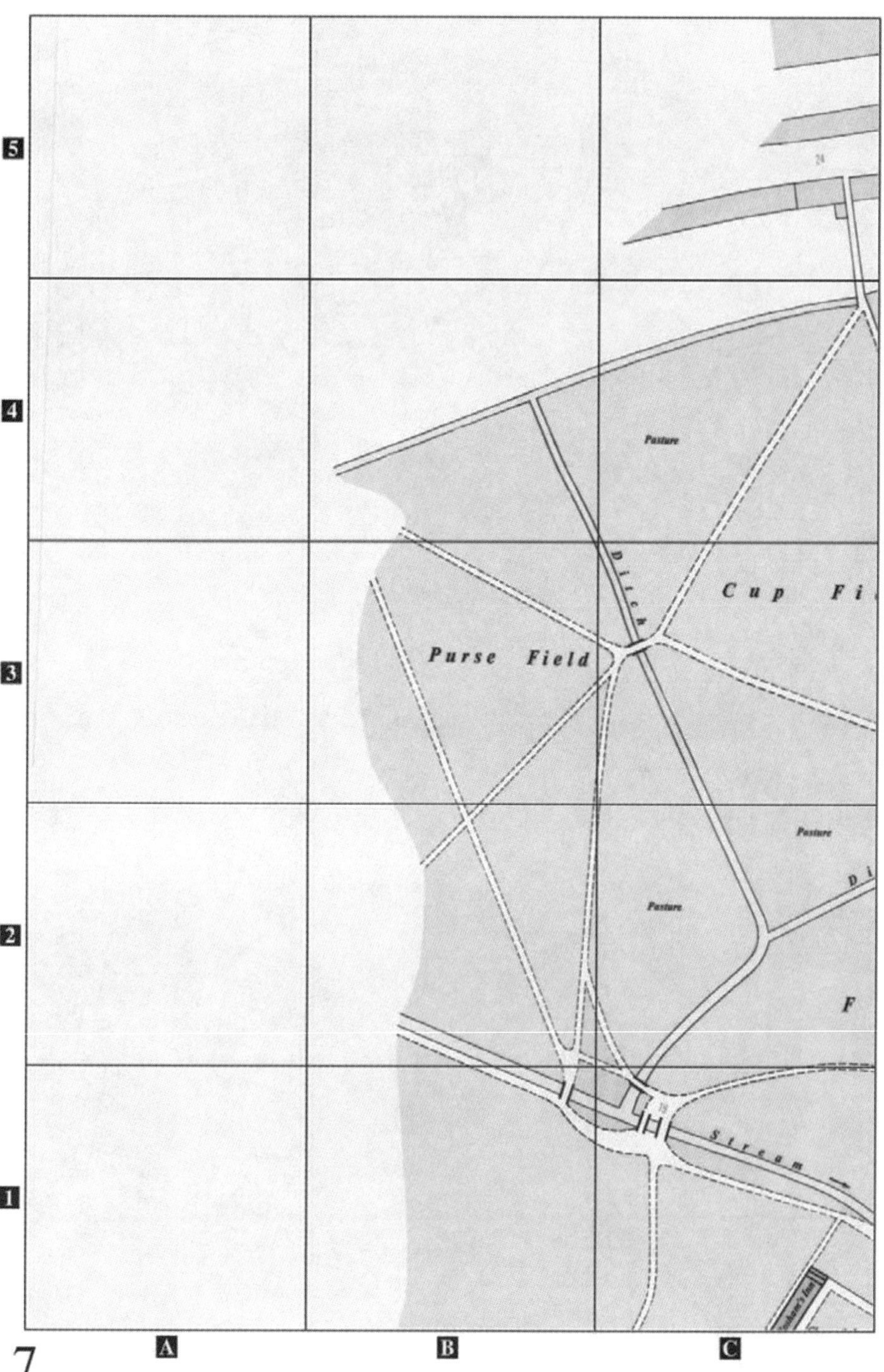
5
4
3
2
1
A
B
C
Pasture
Ditch
Cup Fi
Purse Field
Pasture
Pasture
Di
F
Stream
7

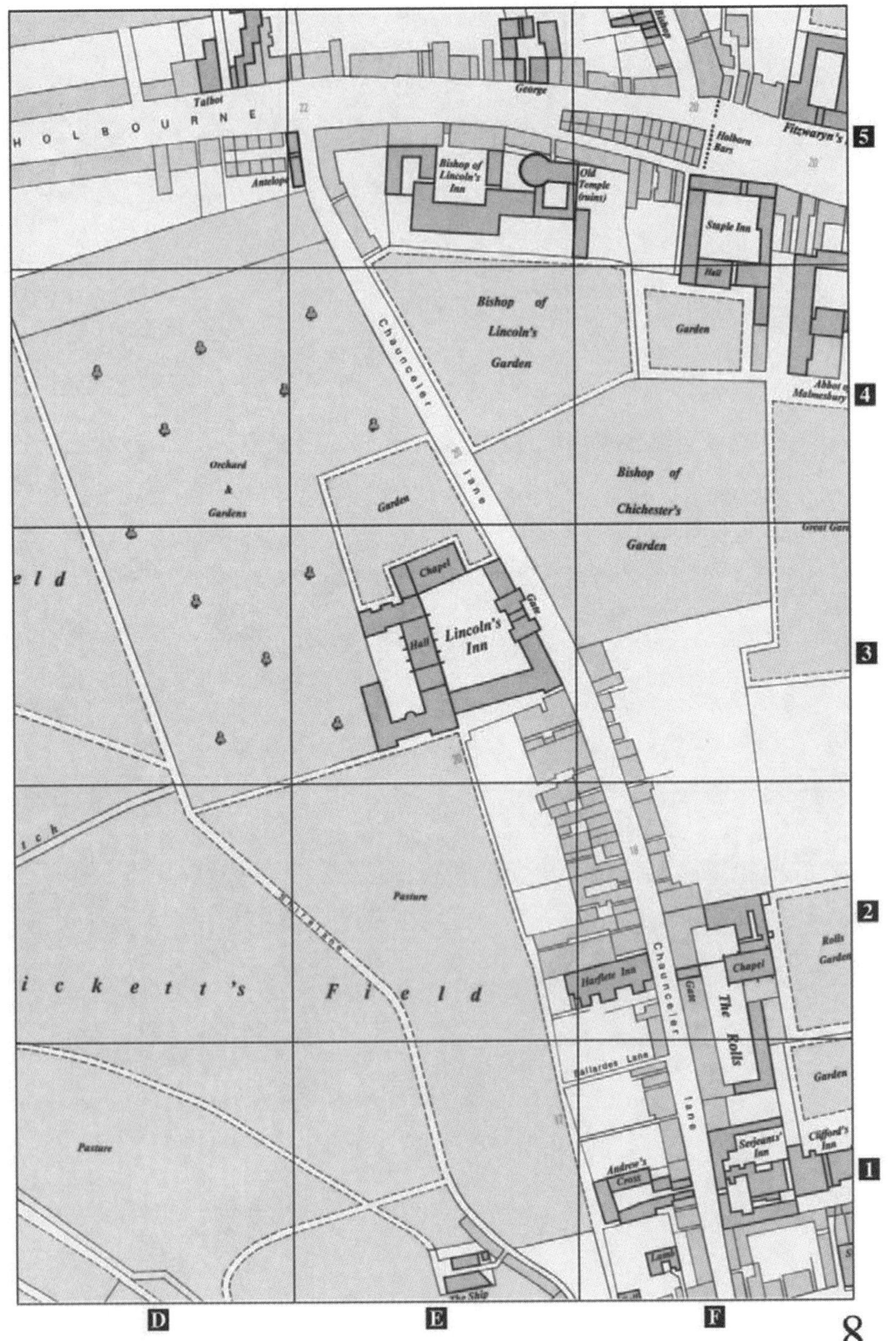
Talbot
HOLBOURNE
George
Bishop
Fitzwaryn's
Holborn Bars
Antelope
Bishop of Lincoln's Inn
Old Temple (ruins)
Staple Inn
Hall
Bishop of Lincoln's Garden
Garden
Abbot of Malmesbury
Chaunceler lane
Orchard & Gardens
Garden
Bishop of Chichester's Garden
Chapel
Gate
Hall
Lincoln's Inn
Pasture
ickett's Field
Harflete Inn
Chapel
Rolls Garden
Chaunceler lane
Gate
The Rolls
Ballardes Lane
Garden
Serjeants' Inn
Clifford's Inn
Andrew's Cross
Pasture
The Ship
5
4
3
2
1
D
E
F

8

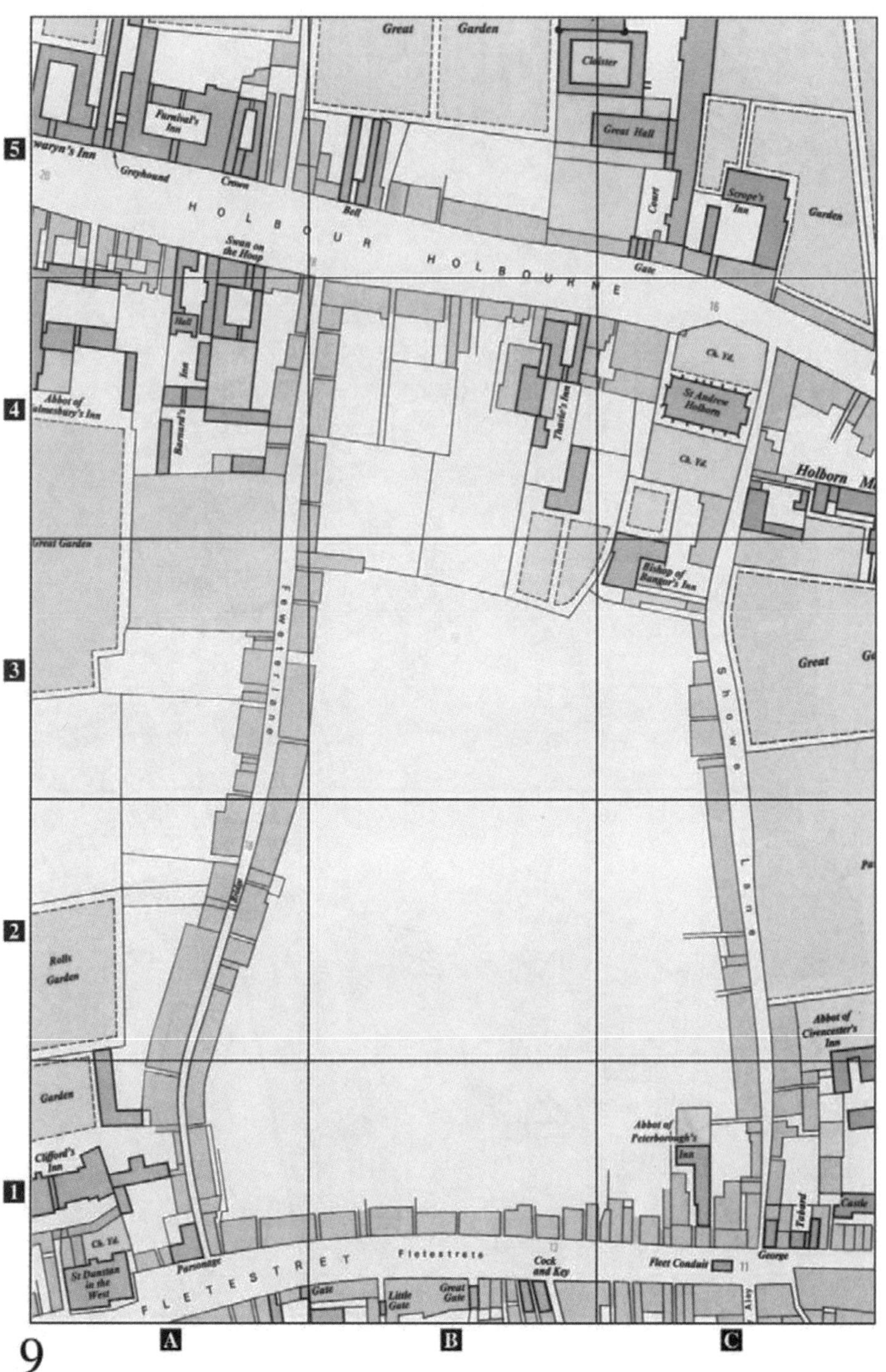
Great Garden
Cloister
Furnival's Inn
Great Hall
Greyhound
Crown
Bell
Court
Scrope's Inn
Garden
HOLBOURNE
Swan on the Hoop
HOLBOURNE
Gate
Hall
Inn
Barnard's
Ch. Yd.
St Andrew Holborn
Thavie's Inn
Ch. Yd.
Holborn
Great Garden
Bishop of Bangor's Inn
Feweterlane
Showe Lane
Great
Rolls Garden
Abbot of Cirencester's Inn
Garden
Clifford's Inn
Abbot of Peterborough's Inn
Tabard
Castle
Ch. Yd.
St Dunstan in the West
Parsonage
Fletestrete
Cock and Key
Fleet Conduit
George
FLETESTRET
Gate
Little Gate
Great Gate
Alley
5
4
3
2
1
A
B
C

9

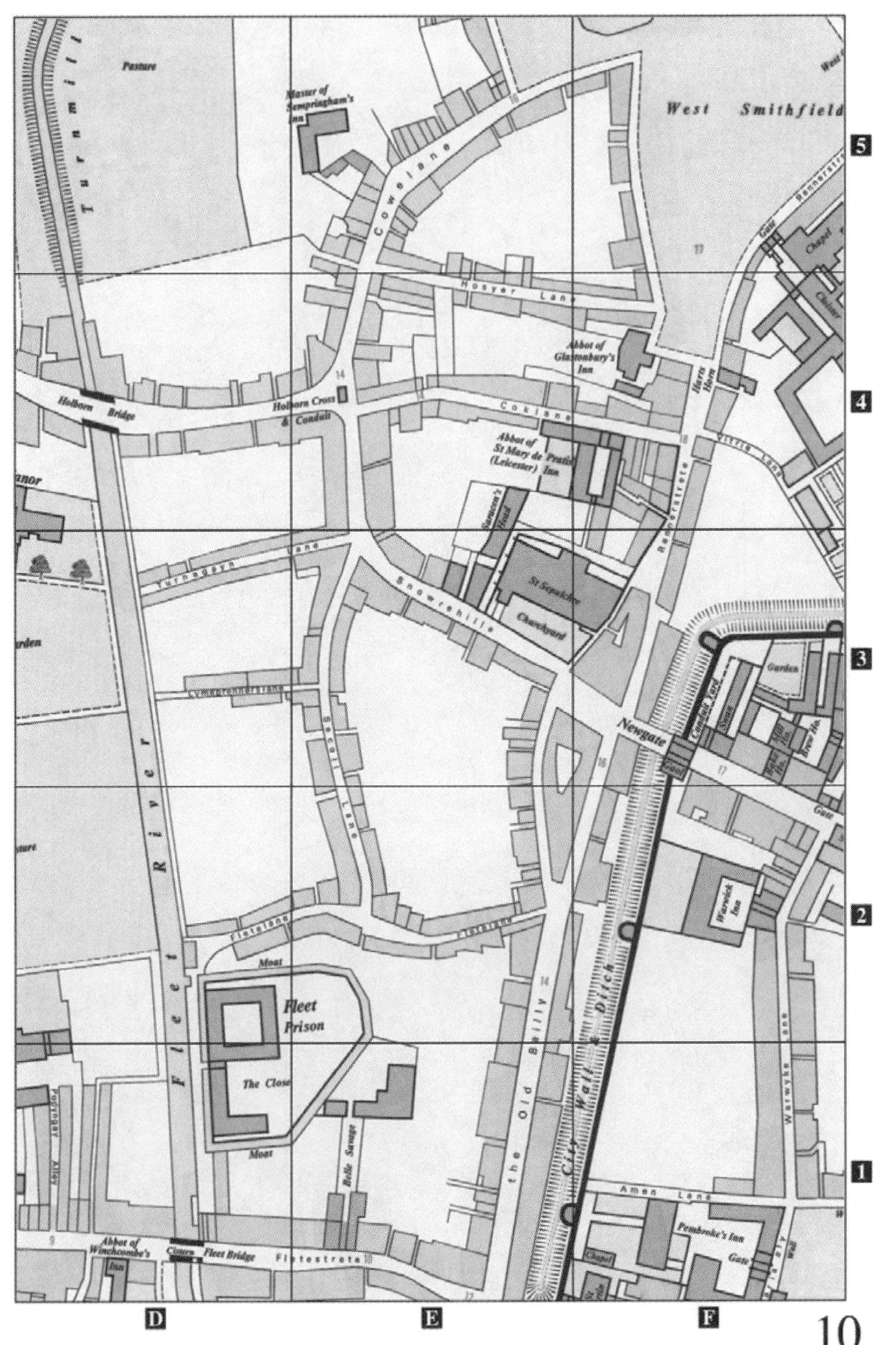

Pasture
Turnmill
Master of Sempringham's Inn
Cowelane
West Smithfield
Hosyer Lane
Abbot of Glastonbury's Inn
Harts Horn
Holborn Bridge
Holborn Cross & Conduit
Coklane
Abbot of St Mary de Pratis (Leicester) Inn
Vitrie Lane
Rennerstrete
Saracen's Head
Chapel
Turnagayn lane
Snowrehille
St Sepulchre
Churchyard
Garden
Newgate
Conduit Yard
Swan
Gaol
Mill Ho.
Brew Ho.
Gate
Lymeburnersiane
Secoll Lane
River
Fleet
Warwick Inn
Warwyke lane
Fletelane
Moat
Fleet Prison
The Close
City Wall & Ditch
the Old Baily
Belle Savage
Amen Lane
Pembroke's Inn
Abbot of Winchcombe's Inn
Cistern
Fleet Bridge
Fletestrete
5
4
3
2
1
D
E
F

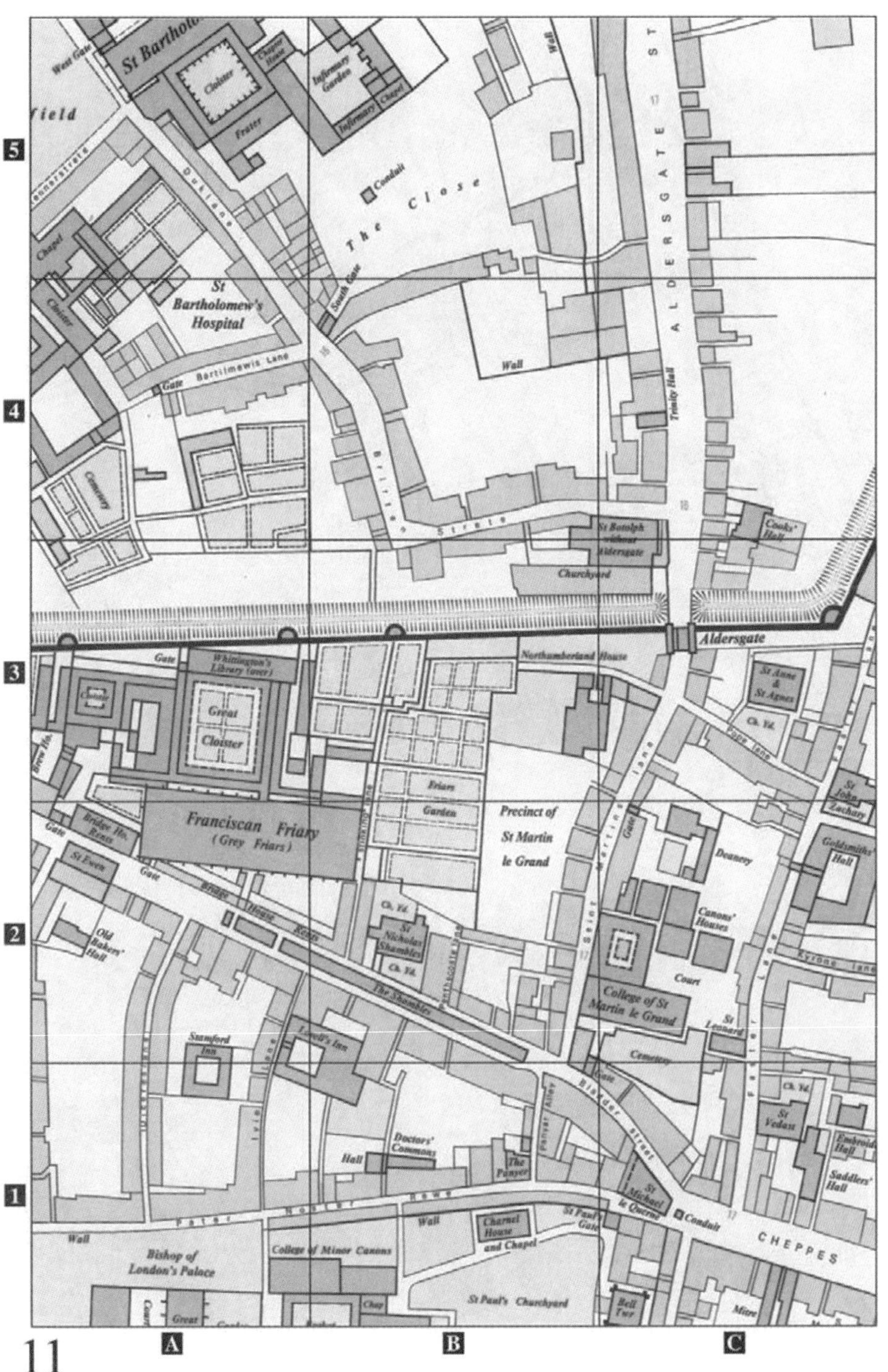
West Gate
Cloister
Chapter House
Infirmary Garden
Infirmary
Chapel
Frater
Conduit
The Close
Wall
Duck lane
South Gate
Chapel
Cloister
St Bartholomew's Hospital
Bartilmewis Lane
Gate
Cemetery
Strete
St Botolph without Aldersgate
Churchyard
Cooks' Hall
Trinity Hall
ALDERSGATE ST
Aldersgate
Gate
Whittington's Library (over)
Great Cloister
Cloister
Brew Ho.
Northumberland House
St Anne & St Agnes
Ch. Yd.
Pope lane
Franciscan Friary (Grey Friars)
Friars Garden
Precinct of St Martin le Grand
Bridge Ho. Rents
Gate
St Ewen
Gate
Bridge House Rents
Old Bakers' Hall
Ch. Yd.
St Nicholas Shambles
Ch. Yd.
The Shambles
Deanery
St John Zachary
Goldsmiths' Hall
Canons' Houses
Court
College of St Martin le Grand
St Leonard
Foster Lane
Stamford Inn
Lovell's Inn
Ivie Lane
Cemetery
Gate
Bladder street
Panyer Alley
Doctors' Commons
Hall
The Panyer
St Michael le Querne
Conduit
Ch. Yd.
St Vedast
Saddlers' Hall
CHEPPES
Wall
St Paul's Gate
Charnel House and Chapel
Wall
Bishop of London's Palace
College of Minor Canons
St Paul's Churchyard
Bell Twr
Mitre
Great
5
4
3
2
1
A
B
C
11

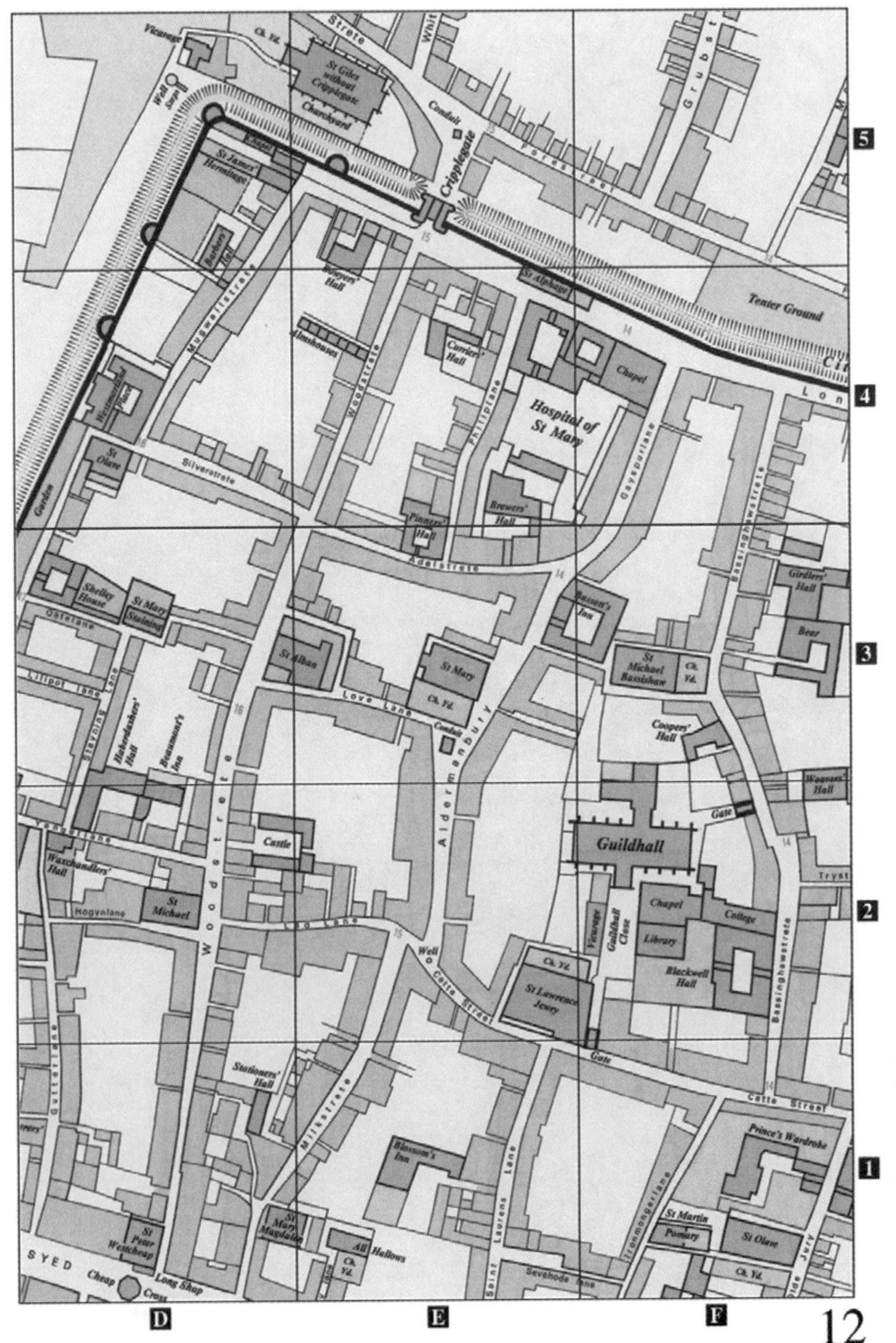
Vicarage
Ch. Yd.
St Giles without Cripplegate
Churchyard
Strete
Whit
Well
Conduit
Cripplegate
Grub st
Forest reet
St James' Hermitage
Chapel
Barbers' Hall
Bowyers' Hall
Almshouses
St Alphage
Tenter Ground
Curriers' Hall
Hospital of St Mary
Chapel
Lon
Westmorland Place
St Olave
Mugwellstrete
Woodstrete
Philipslane
Gayspurlane
Silverstrete
Garden
Brewers' Hall
Pinners' Hall
Adelstrete
Basinghawstrete
Girdlers' Hall
Bear
Shelley House
St Mary Staining
Oatelane
Bassett's Inn
St Alban
St Mary
St Michael Bassishaw
Ch. Yd.
Lilipot lane
Love Lane
Ch. Yd.
Conduit
Coopers' Hall
Haberdashers' Hall
Beaumont's Inn
Steyninglane
Aldermanbury
Weavers' Hall
Gate
Guildhall
Castle
Waxchandlers' Hall
Hogynlane
St Michael
Woodstrete
Tryst
Chapel
College
Library
Blackwell Hall
Guildhall Close
Vicarage
Ch. Yd.
St Lawrence Jewry
Well
Catte Street
Gate
Stationers' Hall
Milkstrete
Catte Street
Prince's Wardrobe
Blossom's Inn
Gutterlane
Saint Laurens Lane
Ironmongerlane
St Martin Pomary
St Olave
St Peter Westcheap
St Mary Magdalen
All Hallows
Ch. Yd.
Ch. Yd.
Sevehode lane
Olde Jury
SYED
Cheap
Cross
Long Shop
5
4
3
2
1
D
E
F
12

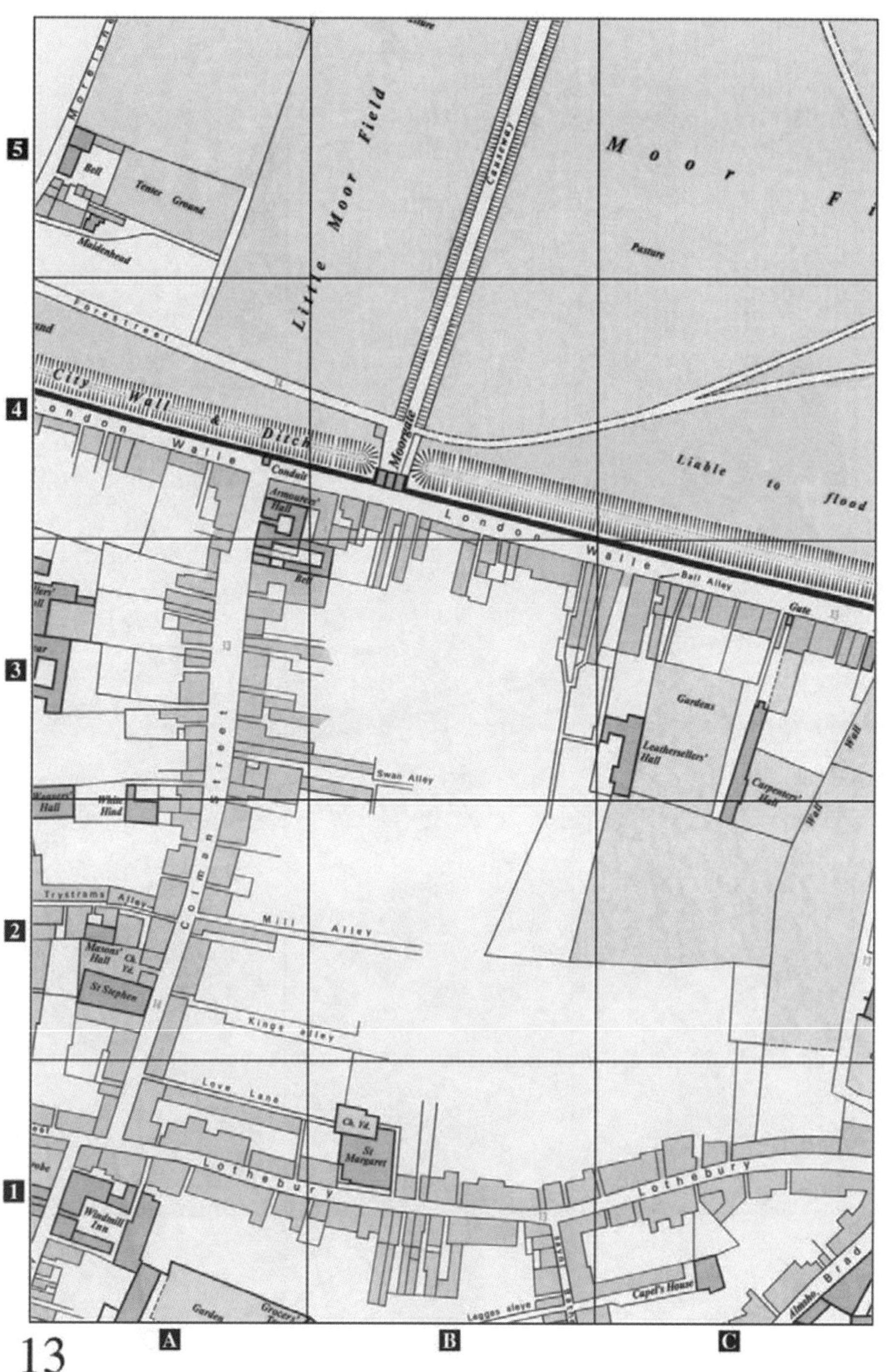
5
4
3
2
1
A
B
C
Bell
Tenter Ground
Maidenhead
Little Moor Field
Causeway
Moor
Pasture
Forestreet
City Wall & Ditch
London Walle
Conduit
Moorgate
Liable to flood
Armourers' Hall
Bell
Ball Alley
Gate
Gardens
Leathersellers' Hall
Carpenters' Hall
Wall
Swan Alley
Colman Street
White Hind
Trystrams Alley
Mill Alley
Masons' Hall
Ch. Yd.
St Stephen
Kings alley
Love Lane
Ch. Yd.
St Margaret
Lothebury
Windmill Inn
Garden
Capel's House
Legges aleye

13

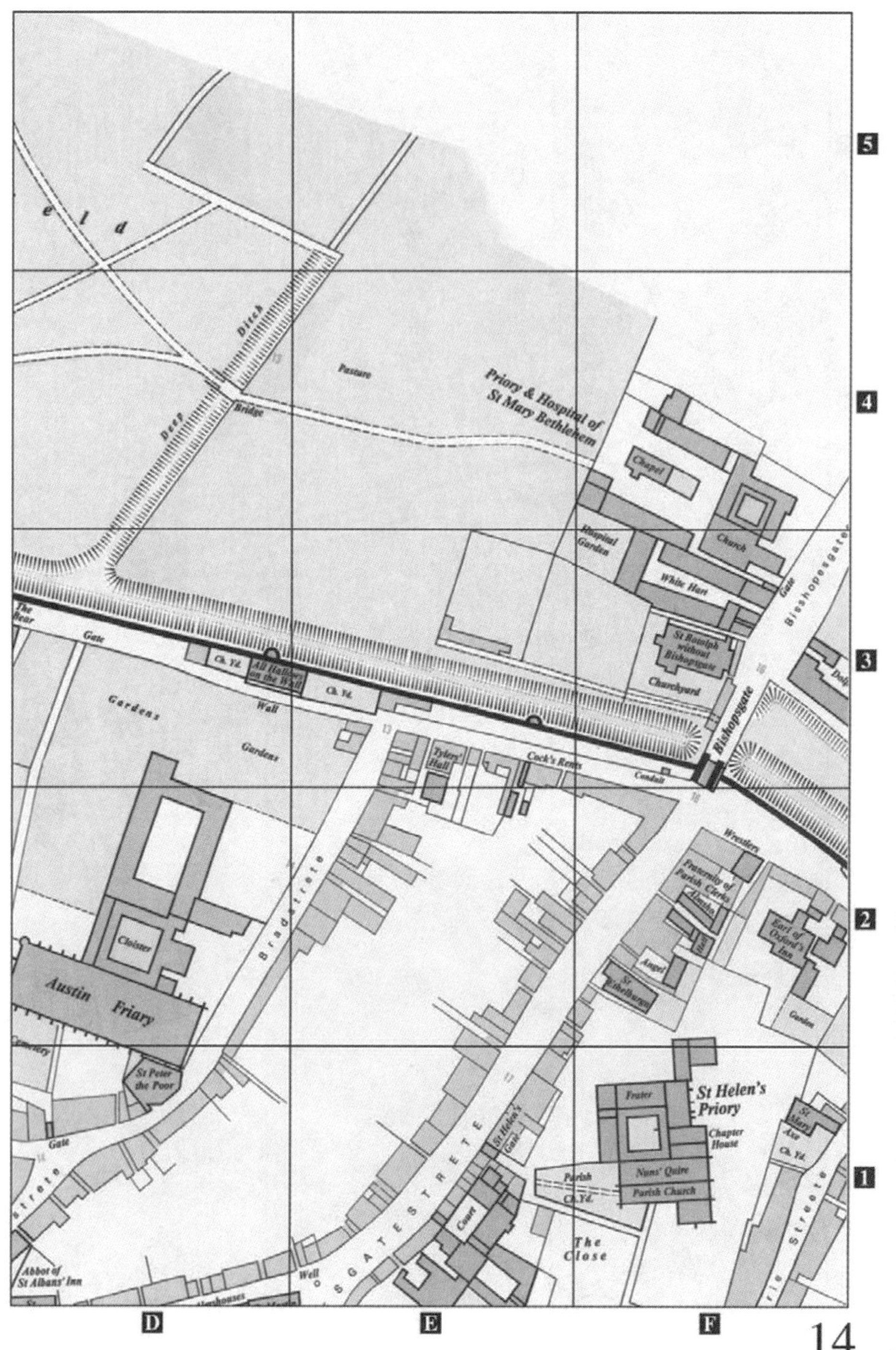
e l d
Ditch
Pasture
Deep
Bridge
Priory & Hospital of
St Mary Bethlehem
Chapel
Hospital
Garden
Church
White Hart
Gate
Bishopesgate
St Botolph
without
Bishopsgate
Churchyard
Bishopsgate
The
Bear
Gate
Ch. Yd.
All Hallows
on the Wall
Ch. Yd.
Gardens
Wall
Gardens
Tylers'
Hall
Cock's Rents
Conduit
Wrestlers
Fraternity of
Parish Clerks
Almsho.
Earl of
Oxford's
Inn
Angel
St
Ethelburga
Garden
Brad strete
Cloister
Austin
Friary
St Peter
the Poor
Gate
strete
St Helen's
Priory
Frater
Chapter
House
St Helen's
Gate
Court
Parish
Ch.Yd.
Nuns' Quire
Parish Church
St
Mary
Axe
Ch. Yd.
The
Close
Streete
Abbot of
St Albans' Inn
Well
S G A T E S T R E T E
5
4
3
2
1
D
E
F

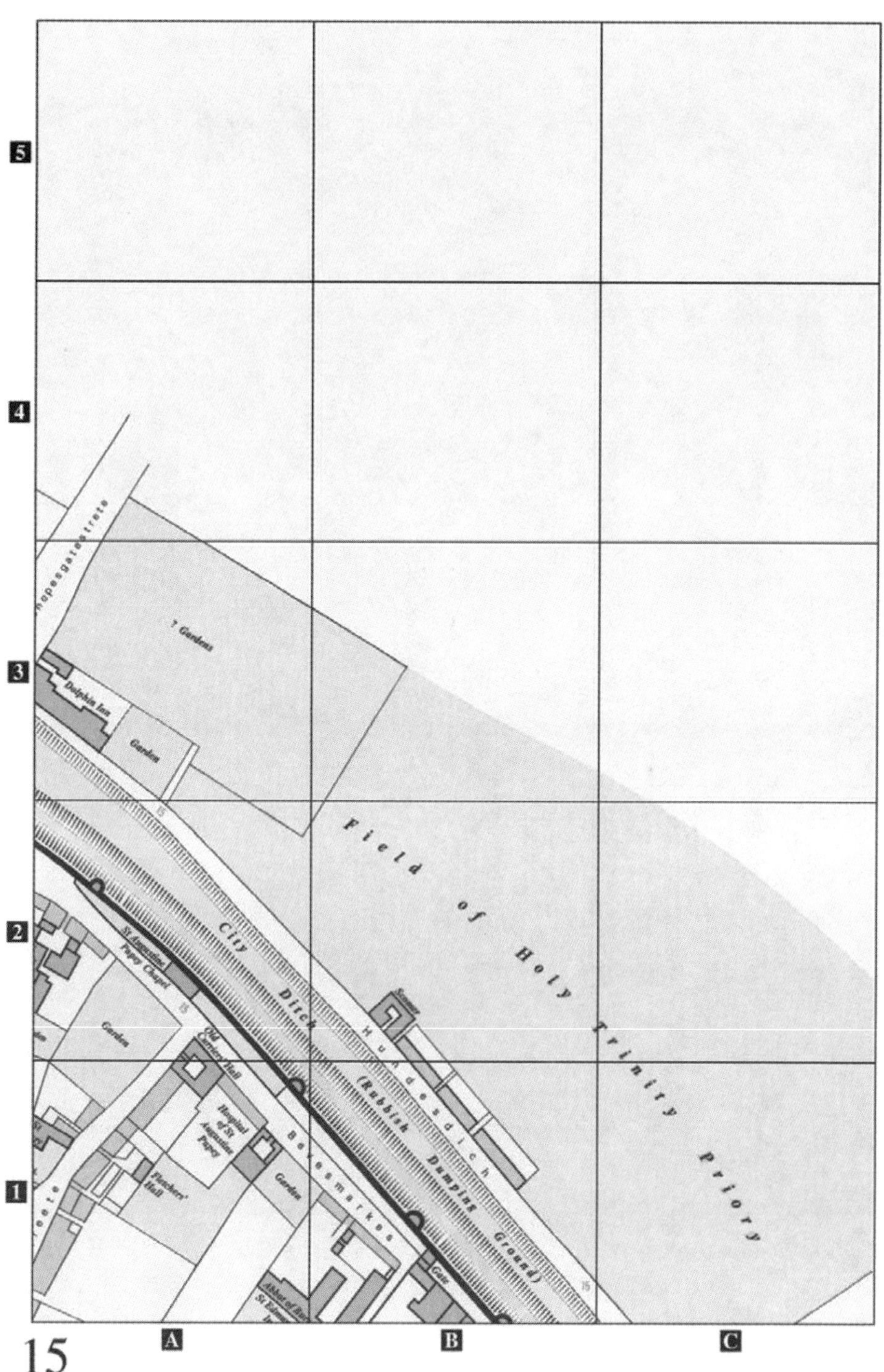
5
4
3
2
1
A
B
C
? Gardens
Dolphin Inn
Garden
Field of Holy Trinity Priory
City Ditch
Hundesdich
(Rubbish Dumping Ground)
St Augustine Papey Chapel
Garden
Hospital of St Augustine Papey
Fletchers' Hall
Bevesmarkes
Garden
Gate

15

Hog Lane
5
4
3
2
1
D
E
F
16

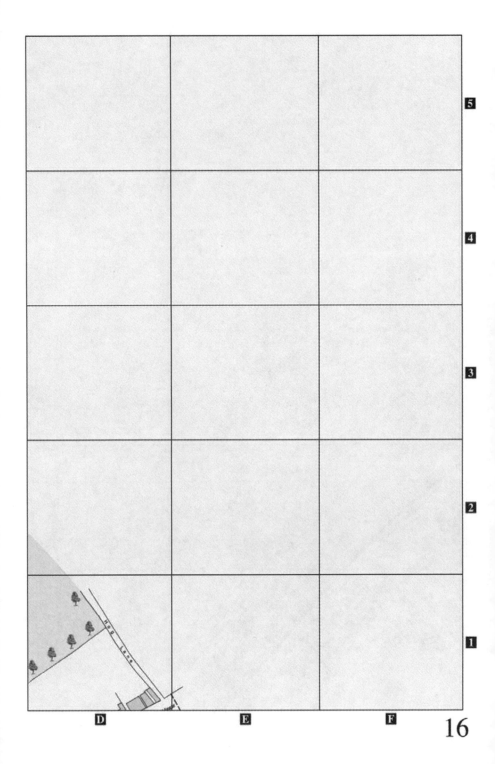

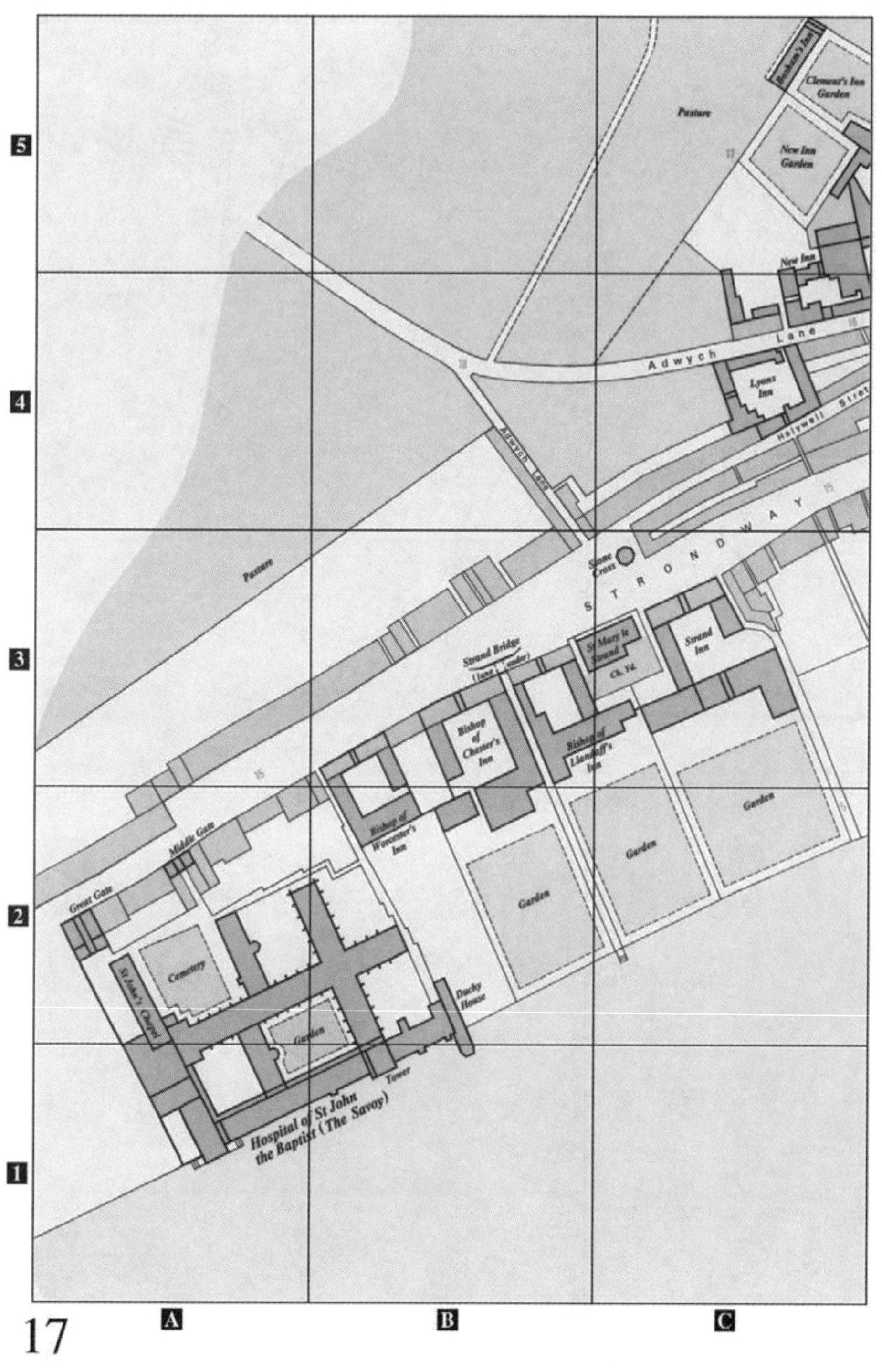

5
4
3
2
1
A
B
C
17
Beckham's Inn
Clement's Inn Garden
Pasture
New Inn Garden
New Inn
Adwych Lane
Lyons Inn
Halywell Strete
Adwych Lane
STRONDWAY
Stone Cross
Pasture
Strand Bridge
St Mary le Strand
Ch. Yd.
Strand Inn
Bishop of Chester's Inn
Bishop of Llandaff's Inn
Bishop of Worcester's Inn
Garden
Garden
Garden
Middle Gate
Great Gate
Cemetery
St John's Chapel
Garden
Duchy House
Tower
Hospital of St John the Baptist (The Savoy)

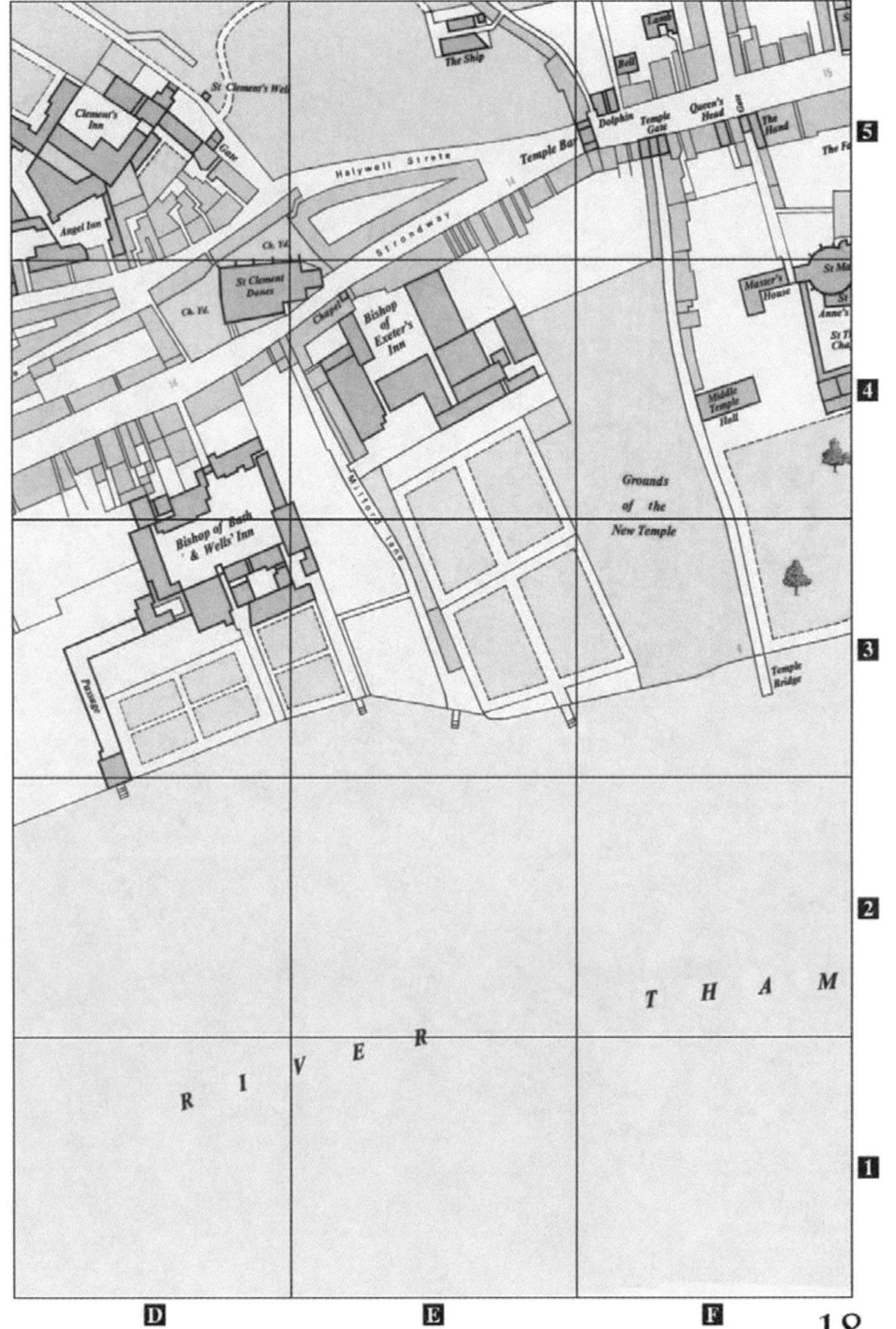
The Ship
St Clement's Well
Clement's Inn
Gate
Angel Inn
Halywell Strete
Strondway
Temple Bar
Ch. Yd.
St Clement Danes
Ch. Yd.
Chapel
Bishop of Exeter's Inn
Lamb
Bell
Dolphin
Temple Gate
Queen's Head
Gate
The Hand
Master's House
Middle Temple Hall
Grounds of the New Temple
Milford lane
Bishop of Bath & Wells' Inn
Passage
Temple Bridge
T H A M
R I V E R
5
4
3
2
1
D
E
F
18

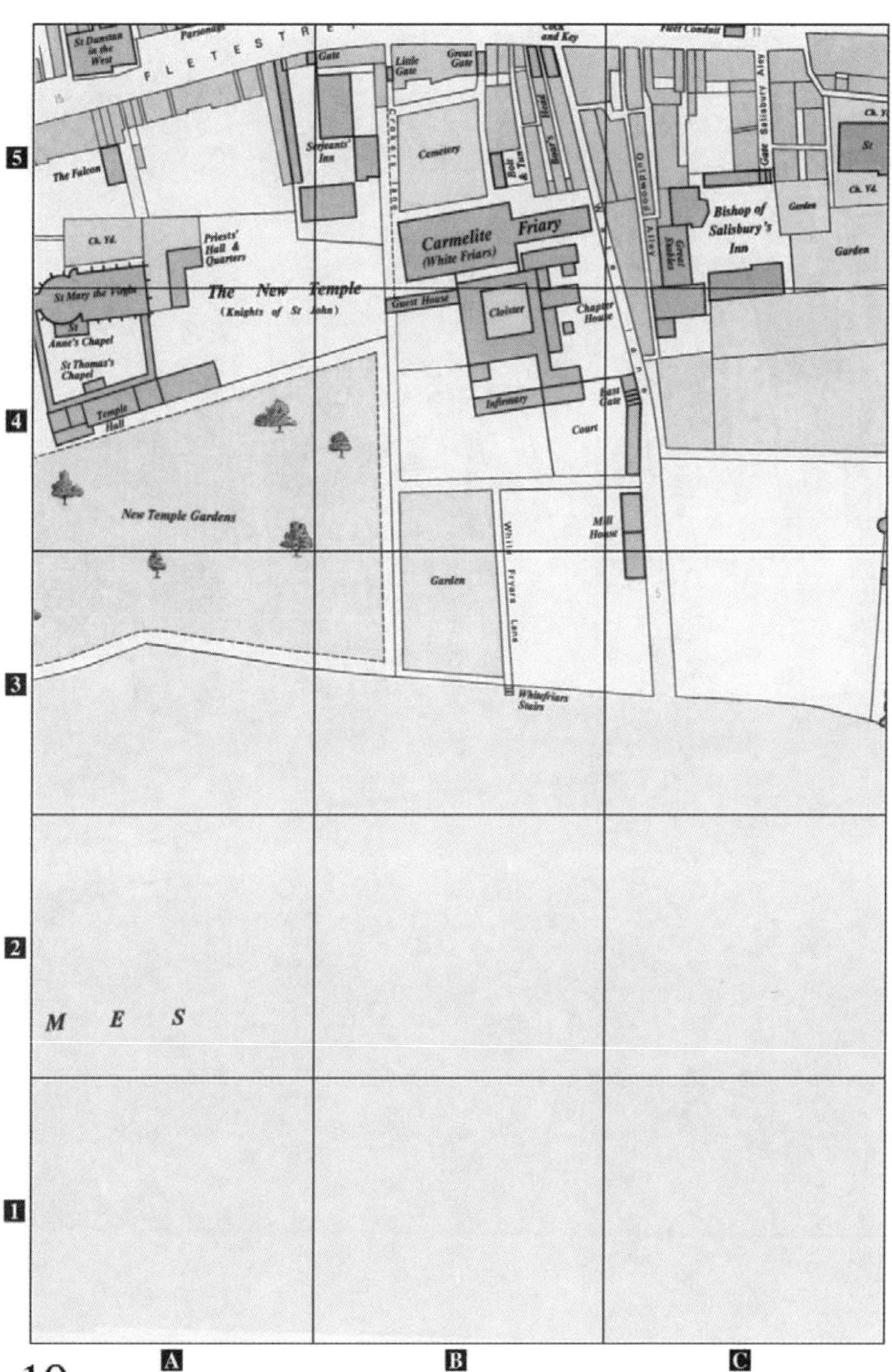

St Dunstan in the West
Parsonage
F L E T E S T R E
Cock and Key
Fleet Conduit
Gate
Little Gate
Great Gate
Serjeants' Inn
Cemetery
Bolt & Tun
Hand
Boar's
Salisbury Alley
Gate
Ch. Yd.
St
The Falcon
Ch. Yd.
Priests' Hall & Quarters
Carmelite Friary
(White Friars)
Great Stables
Bishop of Salisbury's Inn
Garden
Garden
St Mary the Virgin
The New Temple
(Knights of St John)
Guest House
Cloister
Chapter House
St Anne's Chapel
St Thomas's Chapel
Temple Hall
Infirmary
East Gate
Court
New Temple Gardens
Mill House
White Fryars Lane
Garden
Whitefriars Stairs
M E S
5
4
3
2
1
A
B
C

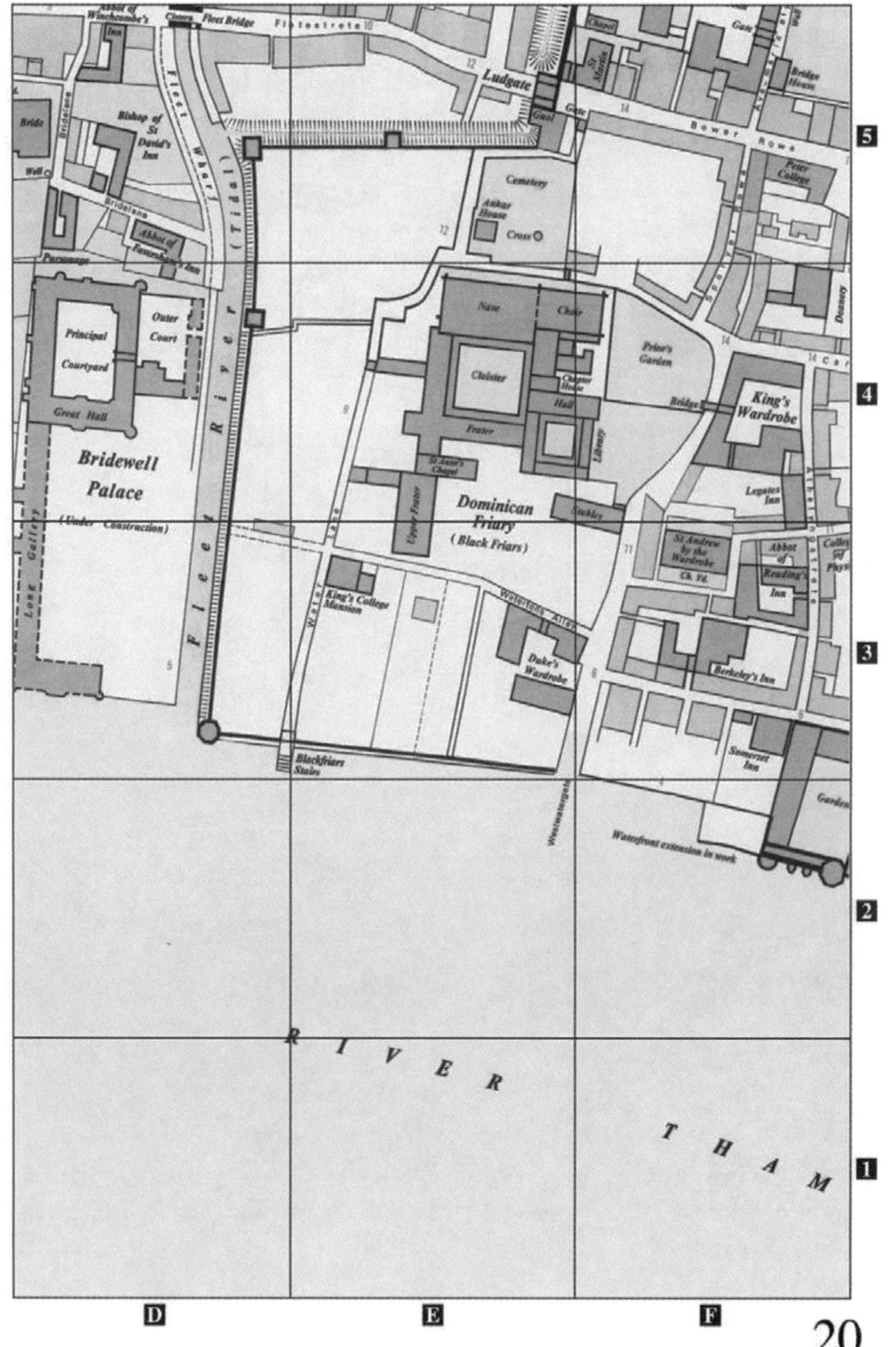
Fleet Bridge
Flete strete
Ludgate
Gaol
Gate
Bower Rowe
Bridge House
Bishop of St David's Inn
Bride
Well
Bridelane
Fleet Wharf (Tidal)
Cemetery
Ankar House
Cross
Peter College
Abbot of Faversham's Inn
Parsonage
Principal Courtyard
Outer Court
Great Hall
Bridewell Palace
(Under Construction)
Long Gallery
Fleet River
Nave
Choir
Cloister
Chapter House
Hall
Frater
Library
St Anne's Chapel
Prior's Garden
Bridge
King's Wardrobe
Deanery
Legates Inn
Dominican Friary
(Black Friars)
Upper Frater
Stables
St Andrew by the Wardrobe
Ch. Yd.
Abbot of Reading's Inn
King's College Mansion
Water lane
Watertons Alley
Duke's Wardrobe
Berkeley's Inn
Somerset Inn
Blackfriars Stairs
Garden
Westwatergate
Waterfront extension in work
RIVER
THAM
5
4
3
2
1
D
E
F

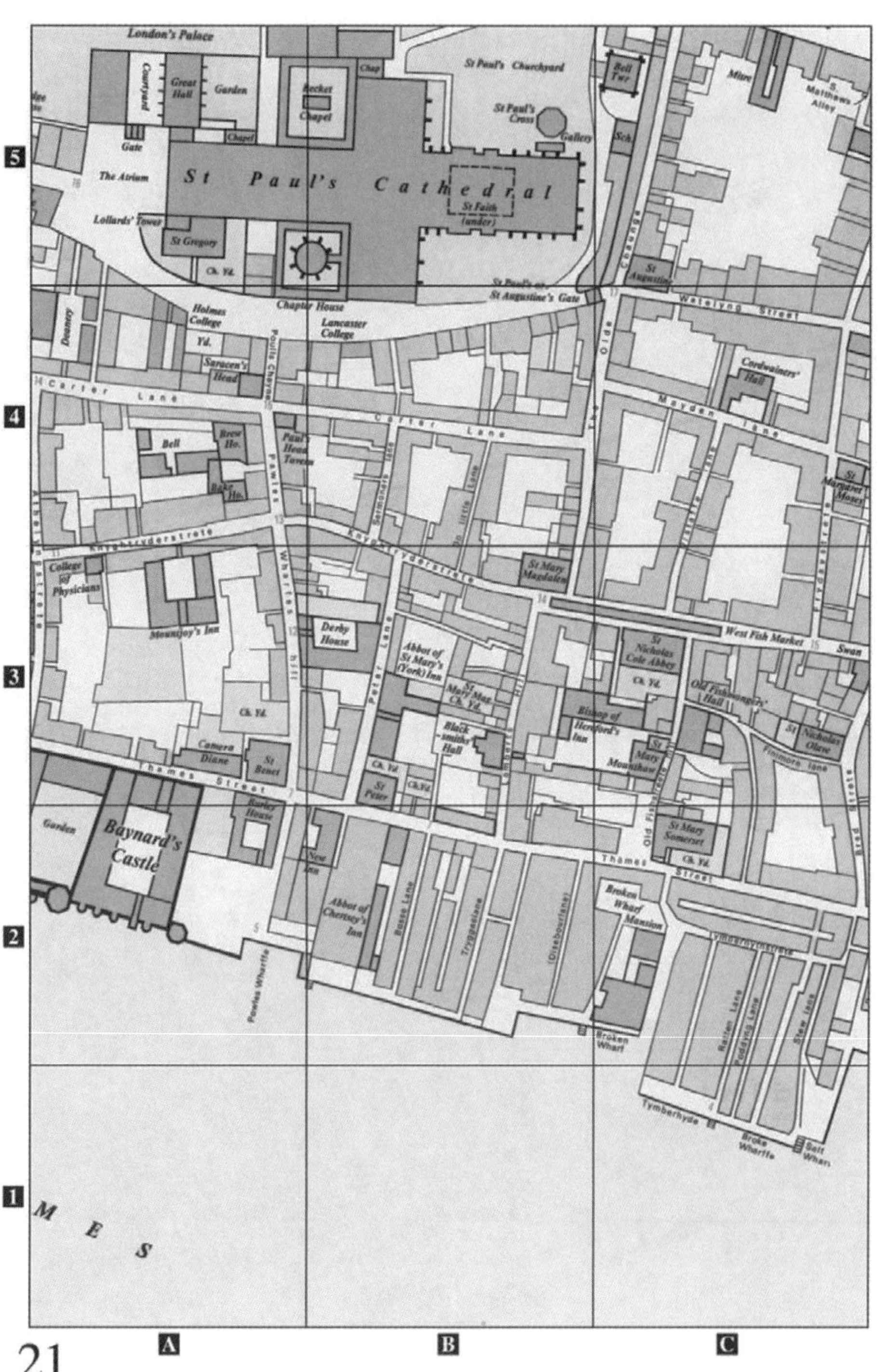
London's Palace
Courtyard
Great Hall
Garden
Becket Chapel
Chap
St Paul's Churchyard
St Paul's Cross
Gallery
Bell Twr
Mitre
St Matthews Alley
Gate
Chapel
Sch
The Atrium
St Paul's Cathedral
St Faith (under)
Lollards' Tower
St Gregory
Ch. Yd.
Chaunge
St Augustine
St Paul's or St Augustine's Gate
Chapter House
Holmes College
Lancaster College
Deanery
Yd.
Saracen's Head
Wetelyng Street
Cordwainers' Hall
Carter Lane
Poulls Cheyne
Mayden lane
Bell
Brew Ho.
Bake Ho.
Paul's Head Tavern
Pawles
Olde
St Margaret Moses
Knyghtryderstrete
College of Physicians
St Mary Magdalen
Mountjoy's Inn
Wharfes hill
Derby House
Peter Lane
Abbot of St Mary's (York) Inn
St Mary Mag Ch. Yd.
West Fish Market
Swan
St Nicholas Cole Abbey
Old Fishmongers' Hall
Bishop of Hereford's Inn
Black smiths' Hall
St Nicholas Olave
Finimore lane
St Mary Mounthaw
Camera Diane
St Benet
Ch. Yd.
St Peter
Thames Street
Barley House
Old Fish street hill
St Mary Somerset
Garden
Baynard's Castle
New Inn
Abbot of Chertsey's Inn
Basse Lane
Tryggeslane
(Oisebournlane)
Broken Wharf Mansion
Pawles Wharffe
Broken Wharf
Retten Lane
Puddyng Lane
Stew lane
Tymberhyde
Broke Wharffe
Salt Wharf
MES
A
B
C
1
2
3
4
5

CHEPPES SYED
Cheap Cross
Long Shop
Standard & Conduit
Goldsmiths' Row
Mermaid
White Bear
Broken Seld
King's Head
St Mary Le Bow
All Hallows
Cow Face
Sevehode lane
Hospital of St Thomas of Acon
Mercers' Hall
Great Conduit
Colechurch
St Mary
Mitre
Crownsild Seld
The Key
Sopers lane
St Pancras
Benet Sherehog
St Pancresse Lane
Bokelerbury
St John the Evangelist
Star Inn
Watelyng Street
All Hallows
Salters' Hall
Chapel
St Mary Aldermary
Romayn's Rent
Bassingslane
The Barge
St Antholin
St Mildred Bread St.
Gerard's Hall
Bowgerowe
Wringwren Lane
Ipres Inn
St Thomas the Apostle
Olde Fysshestrete
Holy Trinity the Less
Knyghtryderstrete
Ormond's Inn
Browne's House
La Riole
Ringed Hall
Cutlers' Hall
St John the Baptist
St Michael Queenhithe
Glaziers' Hall
Whittington's Almshouse
Tallow Chandlers' Hall
Kyronlane
St James Garlickhithe
St Michael Paternoster Royal
College
Skinners' Hall
Thames Street
St Martin Vintry
Jesus Commons
Old Hall
Innholders' Hall
Chequer Inn
Carter lane
Romeland
Queenhithe
The Vyntre
The Vintry
Vintners' Hall & Almshouses
Roperestrete
Hanse Guildhall
The Steelyard
Garlickhythe
Worcester House
Vanours Wharf
Dowgate
D
E
F
1
2
3
4
5

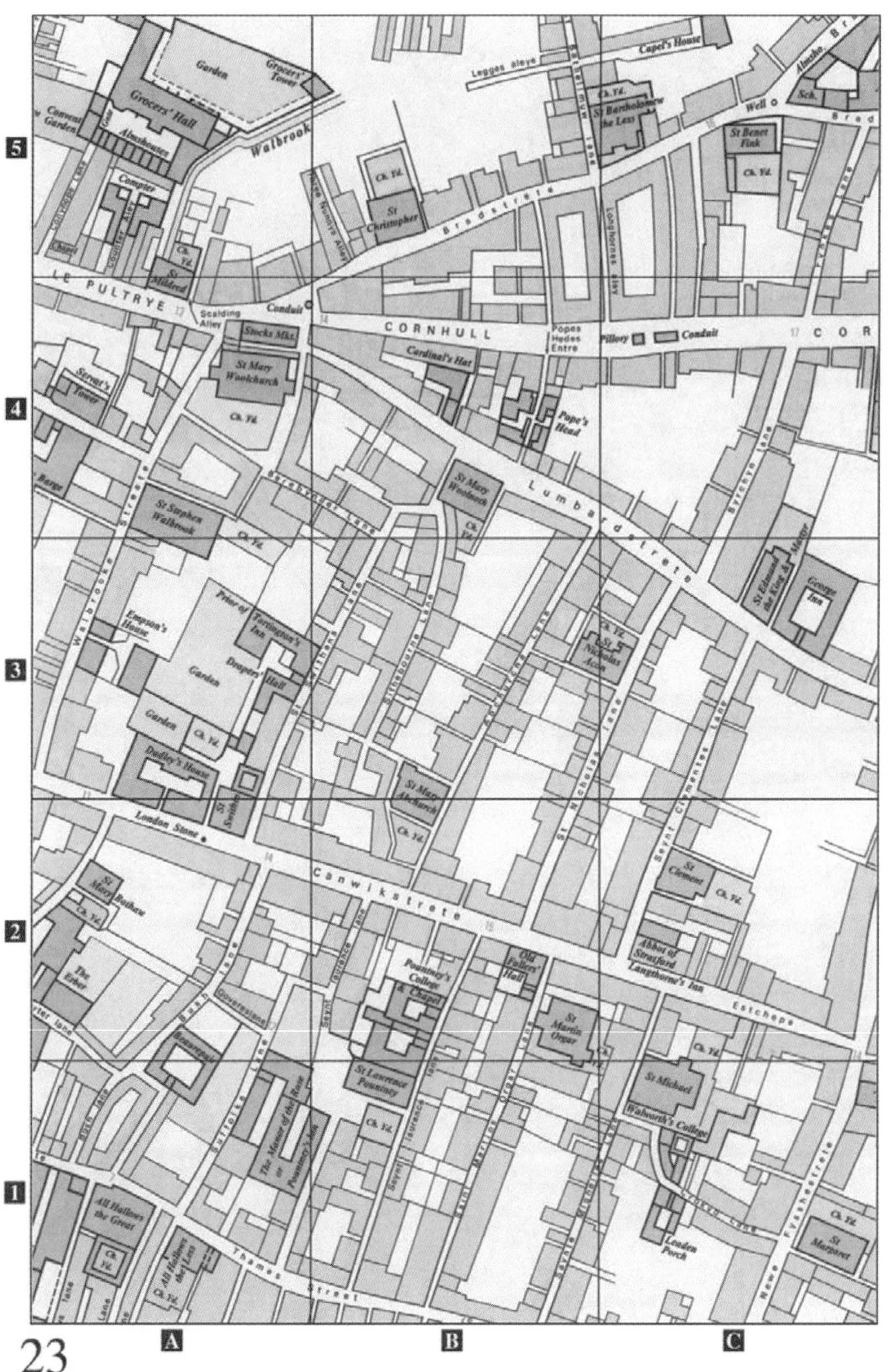

Garden
Grocers' Tower
Grocers' Hall
Convent Garden
Almshouses
Walbrook
Compter
Chapel
Ch. Yd.
St Mildred
LE PULTRYE
Scalding Alley
Conduit
Stocks Mkt.
St Mary Woolchurch
Ch. Yd.
CORNHULL
Cardinal's Hat
Popes Hedes Entre
Pillory
Conduit
COR
Pope's Head
Legges aleye
Capel's House
Ch. Yd.
St Bartholomew the Less
Well
Sch.
St Benet Fink
Ch. Yd.
Ch. Yd.
St Christopher
Bradstrete
Longhornes aley
Servat's Tower
St Stephen Walbrook
Ch. Yd.
St Mary Woolnoth
Ch. Yd.
Lumbardestrete
Walbrooke Strete
Empson's House
Prior of Tortington's Inn
Drapers' Hall
Garden
Garden
Ch. Yd.
Dudley's House
St Swithin
St Swithens lane
Sherborne Lane
St Nicholas Acon
Ch. Yd.
St Nicholas lane
Seynt Clementes lane
St Edmund the King & Martyr
George Inn
St Mary Abchurch
Ch. Yd.
London Stone
Canwikstrete
St Mary Bothaw
Ch. Yd.
The Erber
St Clement
Ch. Yd.
Abbot of Stratford
Langthorne's Inn
Estchepe
Pountney's College & Chapel
Old Fullers' Hall
St Martin Orgar
St Lawrence Pountney
Seynt laurence lane
Bush lane
Suffolke lane
The Manor of the Rose or Pountney's Inn
Beaurepair
St Michael
Walworth's College
Ch. Yd.
Leaden Porch
Newe Fysshestrete
St Margaret
Ch. Yd.
All Hallows the Great
Ch. Yd.
All Hallows the Less
Ch. Yd.
Thames Strete
Saynt Martins Orgar lane
Ch. Yd.
5
4
3
2
1
A
B
C

23

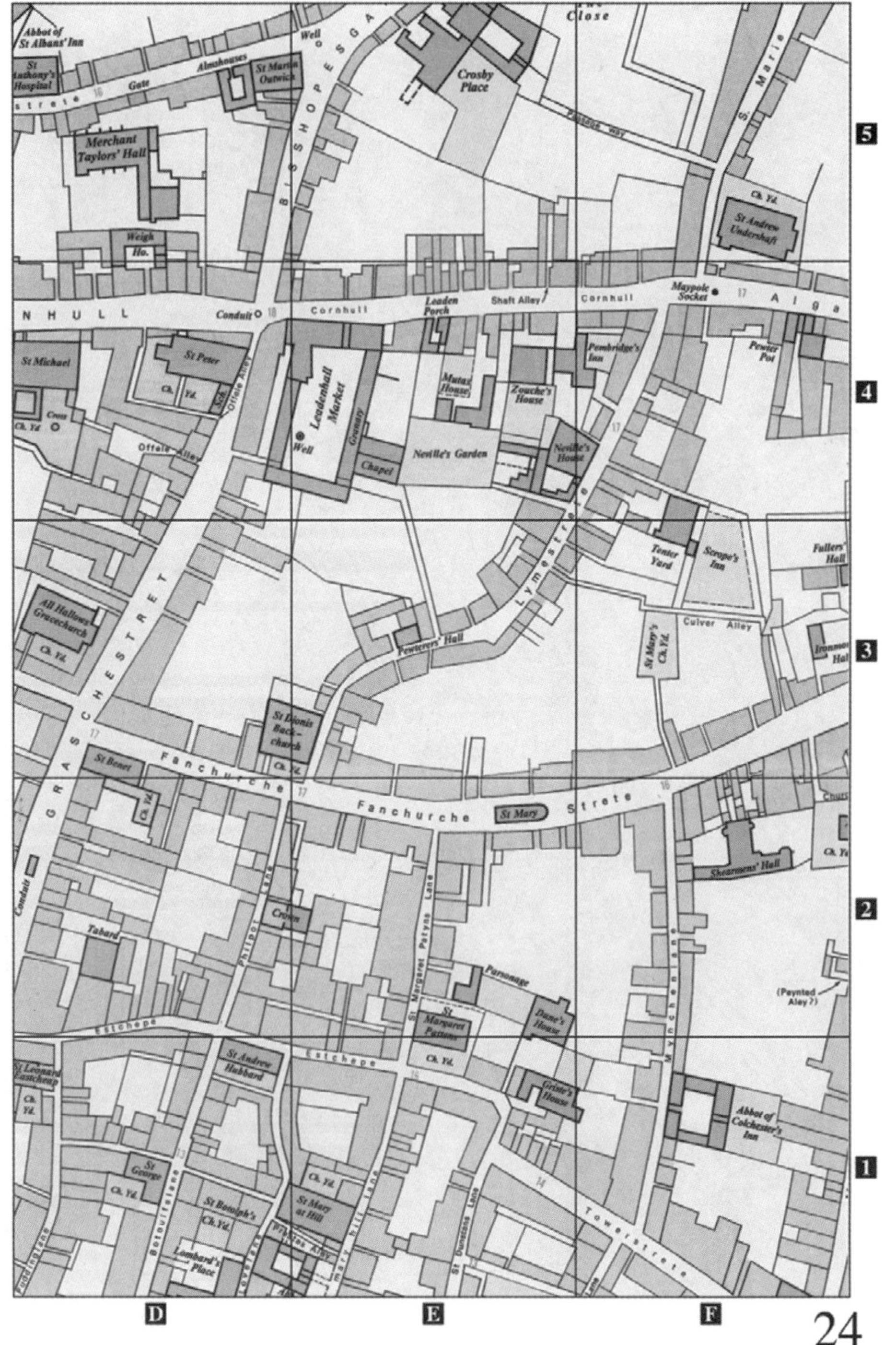
Abbot of St Albans' Inn
St Anthony's Hospital
Gate
Almshouses
St Martin Outwich
Well
BISSHOPESGA
Crosby Place
Close
Merchant Taylors' Hall
Weigh Ho.
Ch. Yd.
St Andrew Undershaft
NHULL
Conduit
Cornhull
Leaden Porch
Shaft Alley
Cornhull
Maypole Socket
Alga
St Michael
St Peter
Ch. Yd.
Offele Alley
Leadenhall Market
Well
Granary
Chapel
Mutas House
Zouche's House
Pembridge's Inn
Pewter Pot
Neville's Garden
Neville's House
Cross
Ch. Yd.
Lymestrete
Tenter Yard
Scrope's Inn
Fullers' Hall
All Hallows Gracechurch
Ch. Yd.
GRASCHESTRET
Pewterers' Hall
Culver Alley
St Mary's Ch. Yd.
St Dionis Backchurch
Ch. Yd.
St Benet
Ch. Yd.
Fanchurche
Fanchurche
St Mary
Strete
Shearmens' Hall
Conduit
Philpot lane
Crown
St Margaret Patyns Lane
Tabard
Parsonage
Dane's House
(Peynted Aley ?)
Estchepe
St Margaret Pattens
Ch. Yd.
Estchepe
Mynchenlane
St Leonard Eastcheap
Ch. Yd.
St Andrew Hubbard
Griste's House
Abbot of Colchester's Inn
St George
Ch. Yd.
St Botolph's Ch. Yd.
St Mary at Hill
Ch. Yd.
Botolfslane
Lombard's Place
St Dunstons Lane
Towerstrete
5
4
3
2
1
D
E
F

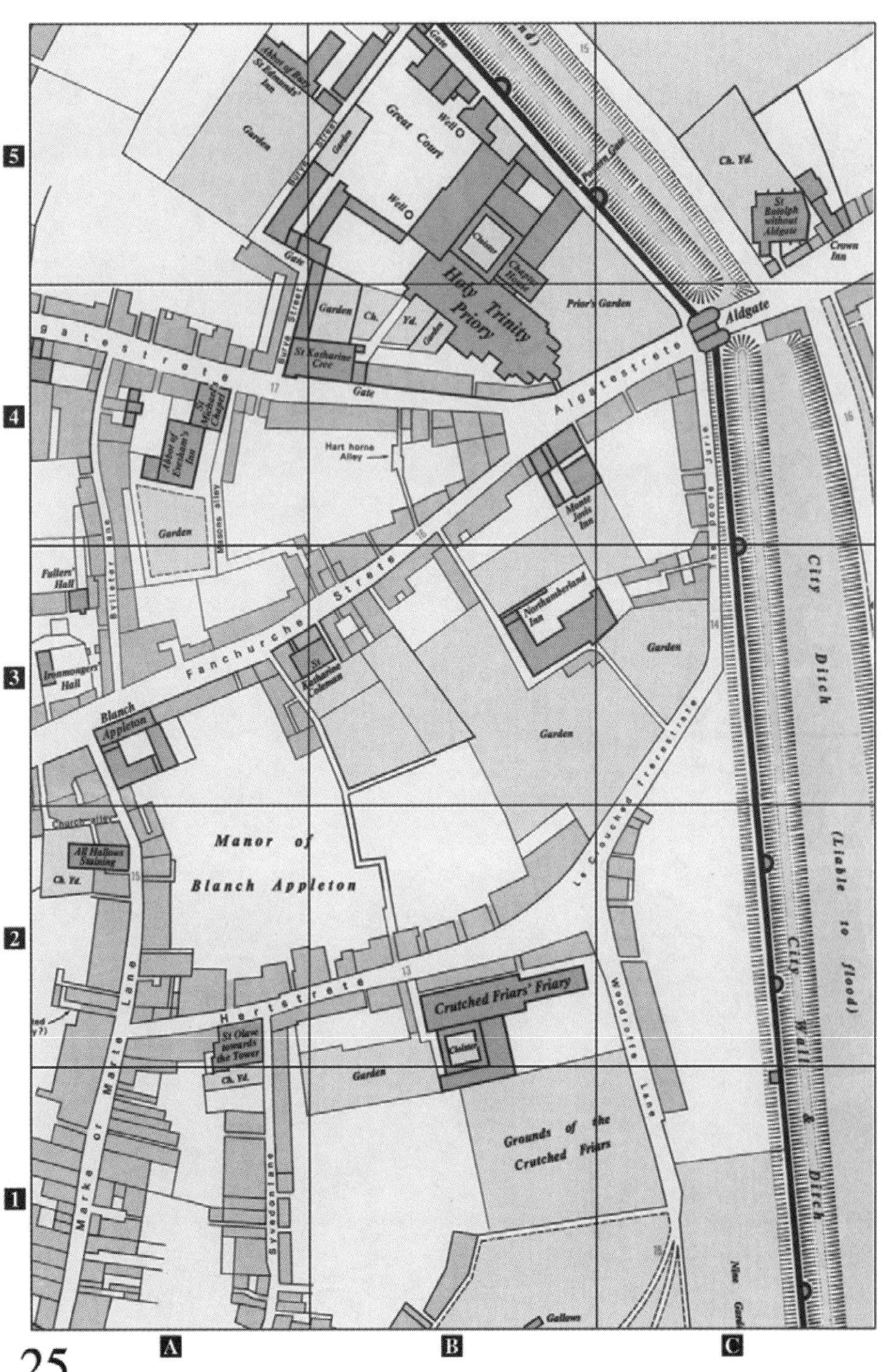
Abbot of Bury St Edmunds' Inn
Garden
Great Court
Well
Well
Postern Gate
Cloister
Chapter House
Holy Trinity Priory
Prior's Garden
Ch. Yd.
St Rotolph without Aldgate
Crown Inn
Aldgate
Gate
Garden
Ch. Yd.
St Katharine Cree
Gate
Algatestrete
St Michael's Chapel
Abbot of Evesham's Inn
Hart horne Alley
Garden
Masons alley
Fullers' Hall
Monte Jovis Inn
Northumberland Inn
Garden
City Ditch
Fanchurche Strete
St Katharine Coleman
Ironmongers' Hall
Blanch Appleton
Garden
Church alley
All Hallows Staining
Ch. Yd.
Manor of Blanch Appleton
Le Crouched frerestrete
(Liable to flood)
City Wall & Ditch
Hertstrete
Crutched Friars' Friary
Cloister
St Olave towards the Tower
Ch. Yd.
Garden
Woodroffe Lane
Grounds of the Crutched Friars
Marke or Marte Lane
Syvedon lane
Gallows
5
4
3
2
1
A
B
C

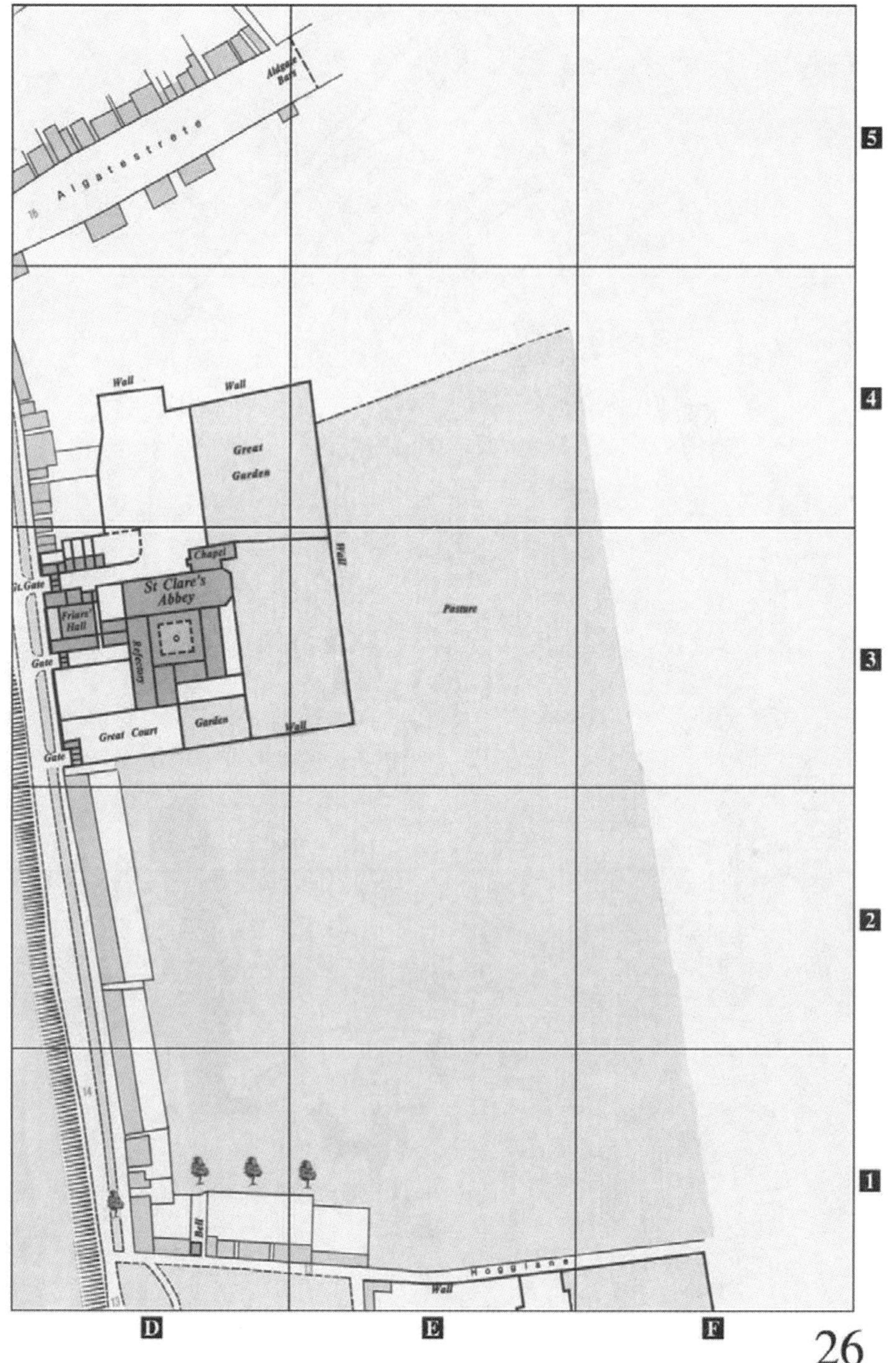

Aldgate Bars
Algatestrete
Wall
Wall
Great Garden
Wall
Chapel
St Clare's Abbey
Gt. Gate
Friars' Hall
Refectory
Pasture
Gate
Great Court
Garden
Wall
Gate
Bell
Hogglane
Wall
5
4
3
2
1
D
E
F
26

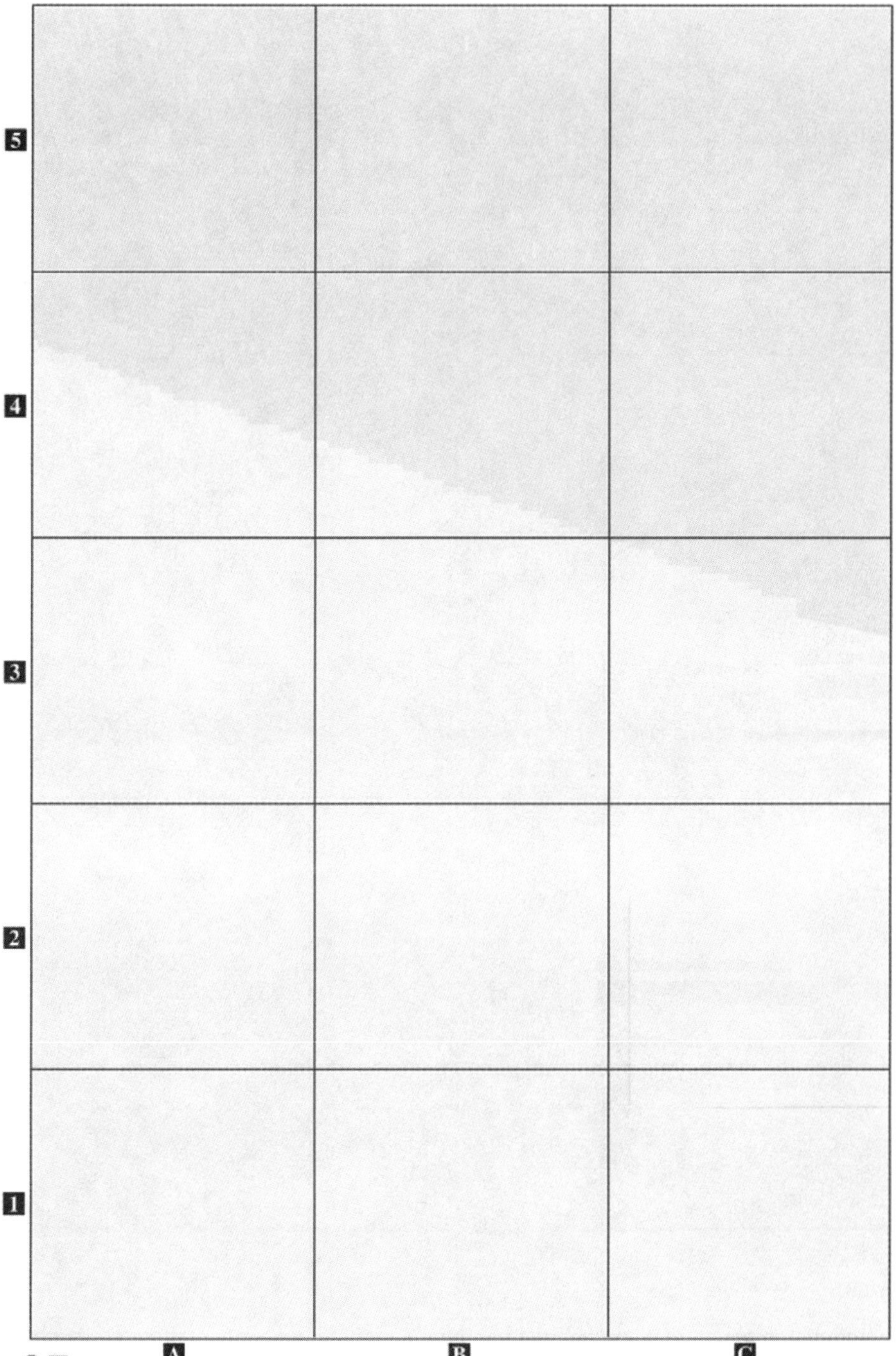

5

4

3

2

1

A B C

27

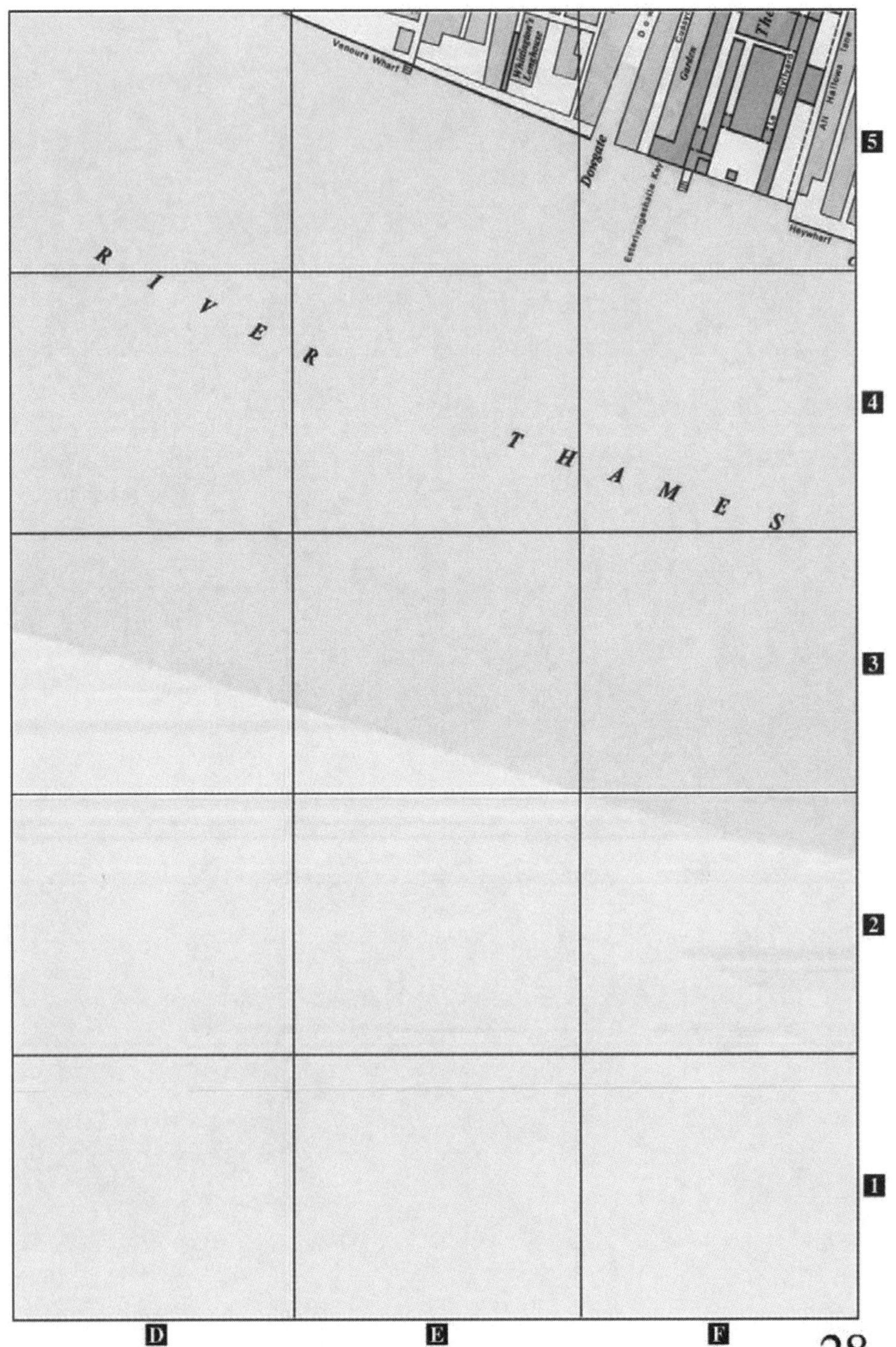
Venours Wharf
Dowgate
Esterlyngeshalle Key
Garden
Heywharf
All Hallows lane
RIVER THAMES
5
4
3
2
1
D
E
F

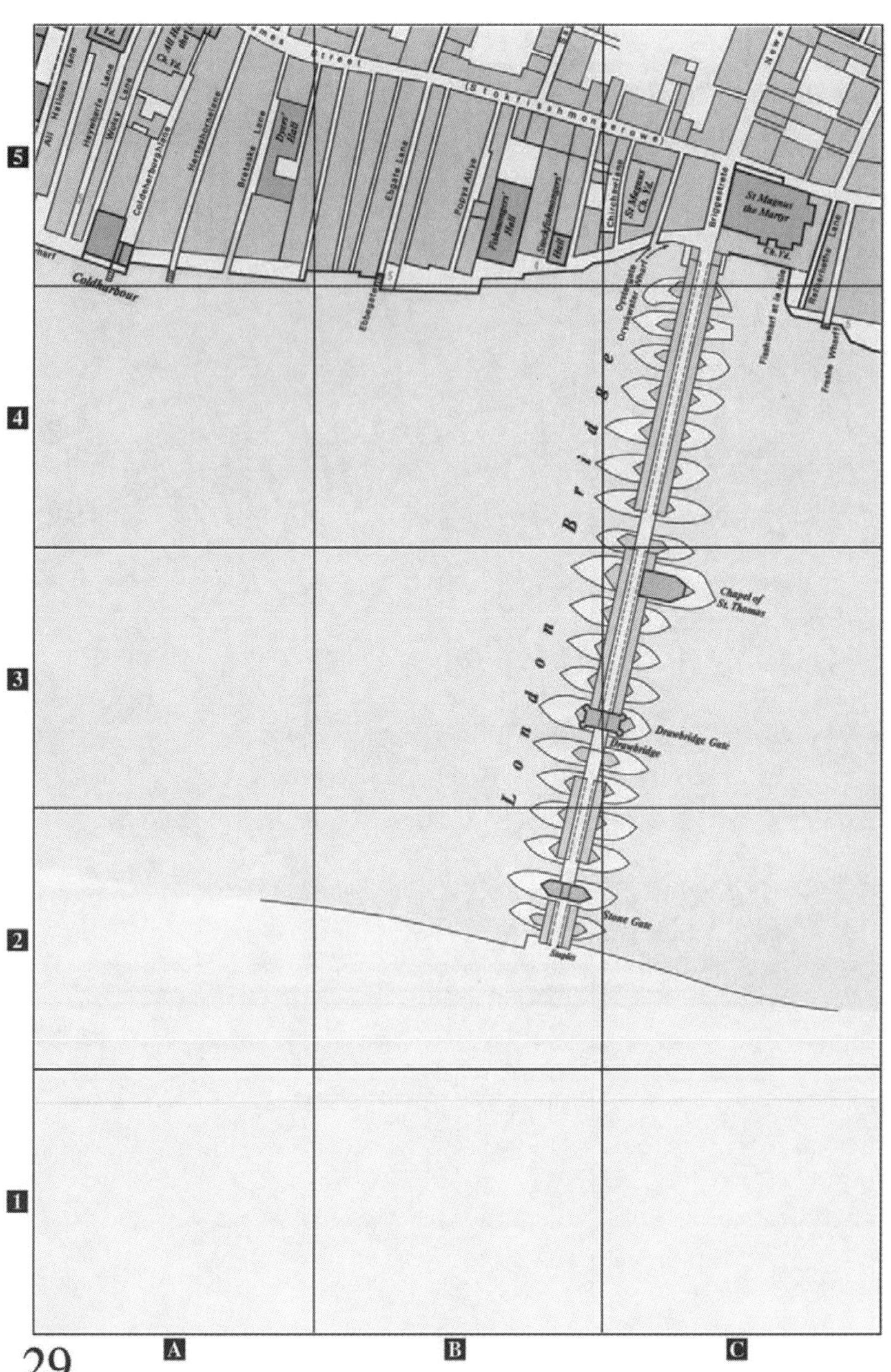

5
4
3
2
1
A
B
C
29
Coldharbour
Ebbegate
London Bridge
Chapel of St. Thomas
Drawbridge Gate
Drawbridge
Stone Gate
St Magnus the Martyr
Ch. Yd.
Fishmongers' Hall
Stockfishmongers' Hall
Dyers' Hall
Ebbgate Lane
Popys Allye
Briggestrete

Lombard's Place
Abbot of Waltham's Inn
St Botolph
Thames Street
Billingsgate Strete
Boss
Billingsgate
Wirehalelane
Botolphswharf
Lyon Key
Holy Roode Wharff
Smarttes Key
Dyceksy
Watergate
St Dunstan in the East
Ch. Yd.
Chapel
St Dunstons Lane
Cokedon Hall
Browne's Place
Browne's Key
Watergate
Sabbis Key
Thames Street
Water lane
Custom House
Hornes Key
Crowne Key
Watergate
Woole Wharfe
R I V E R
5
4
3
2
1
D
E
F
30

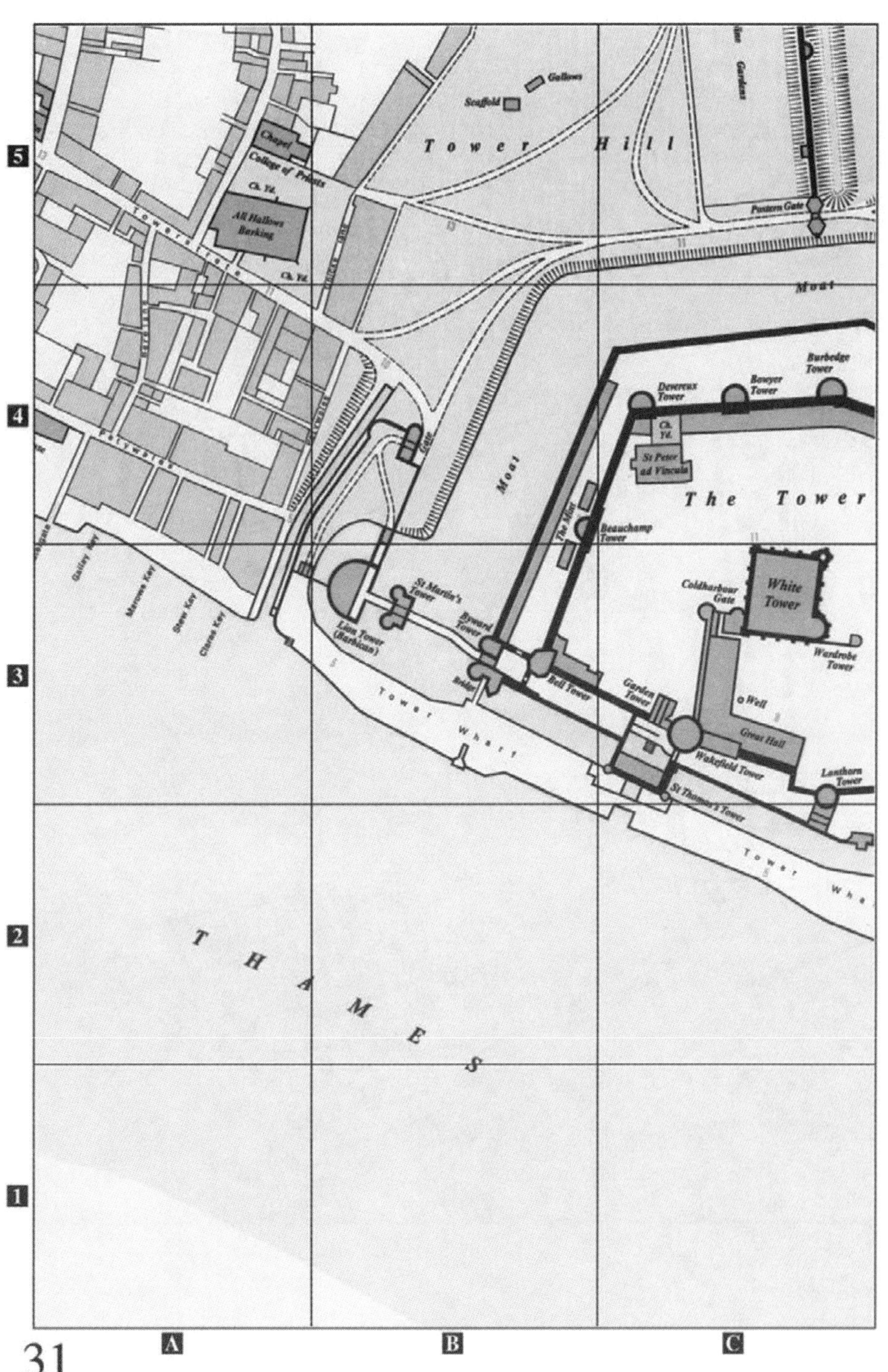
Gallows
Scaffold
Tower Hill
Chapel
College of Priests
Ch. Yd.
All Hallows Barking
Ch. Yd.
Tower Street
Petty Wales
Postern Gate
Moat
Burbedge Tower
Bowyer Tower
Devereux Tower
Ch. Yd.
St Peter ad Vincula
The Tower
Gate
Moat
The Mint
Beauchamp Tower
Coldharbour Gate
White Tower
Wardrobe Tower
St Martin's Tower
Lion Tower (Barbican)
Byward Tower
Bridge
Bell Tower
Garden Tower
Well
Great Hall
Wakefield Tower
Lanthorn Tower
St Thomas's Tower
Tower Wharf
Tower Wharf
Gallery Key
THAMES
5
4
3
2
1
A
B
C

31

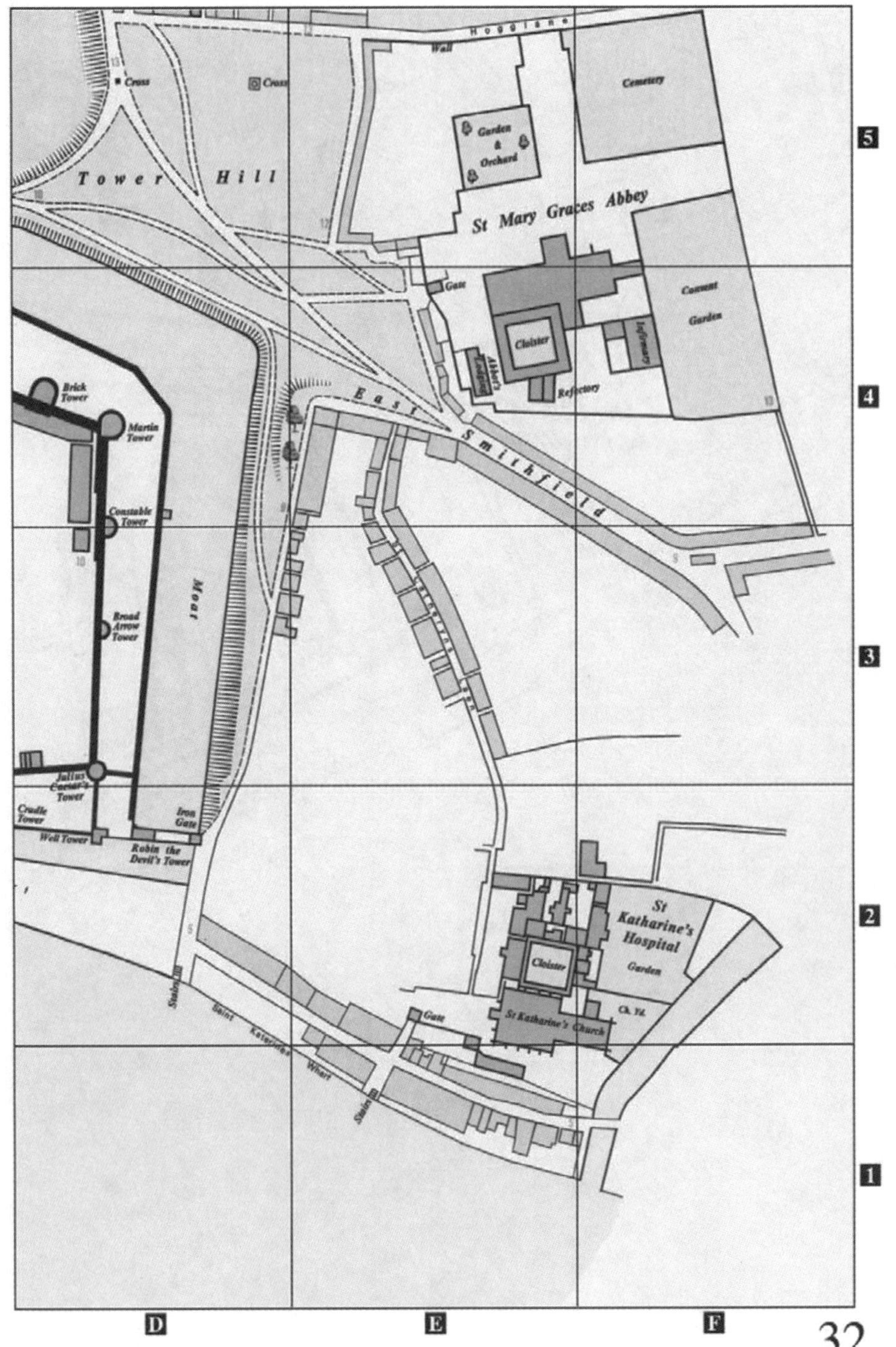
Hogglane
Wall
Cross
Cross
Cemetery
Garden
&
Orchard
Tower Hill
St Mary Graces Abbey
Gate
Convent
Garden
Cloister
Abbot's
Lodging
Infirmary
Refectory
Brick
Tower
Martin
Tower
East Smithfield
Constable
Tower
Moat
Broad
Arrow
Tower
Julius
Caesar's
Tower
Cradle
Tower
Iron
Gate
Well Tower
Robin the
Devil's Tower
St
Katharine's
Hospital
Cloister
Garden
Gate
St Katharine's Church
Ch. Yd.
Stairs
Saint Katherine Wharf
Stairs
5
4
3
2
1
D
E
F

Gazetteer of places named on the City of London *c.*1520 map

Note: this list is derived from the more detailed gazetteer compiled by Martha Carlin and Victor Belcher to be found in M. D. Lobel (ed.), *Historic Towns Atlas: The City of London from Prehistoric Times to c.1520* (Oxford, 1989), 63–99. Contemporary spellings are used for the street names published on the 1520 map and are given here with cross references to modern names where the streets still exist. Buildings are given modern or modernized names. Details about the sources of information will be found in the original publication.

Abchurche Lane 23 B3
Addelane *see* Adelstrete (Cripplegate)
Addle Hill *see* Athelyngstrete
Addle Street *see* Adelstrete (Cripplegate)
Adelstrete (Cripplegate)12 E3
Adwych Lane 17 B4
Aguilon's House *see* Tortington, Inn of the Prior of
Aldermanbury 12 E2
Aldersgate 11 C3
Aldersgate Bars 5 C4
Aldersgate Street 11 C4
Aldewichstrate *see* Adwych Lane
Aldgate 25 C4
Aldgate (street) *and* Aldgate High Street *see* Algatestrete
Aldgate Bars 26 D5
Aldwych *see* Adwych Lane
Algatestrete 26 D5
All Hallows Barking (Barkingchurch, St Mary Barkingchurch), Church of 31 A5
All Hallows Bread Street (Watling Street), Church of 22 D4
All Hallows upon the Cellar *see* All Hallows the Less, Church of
All Hallows Colemanchurch *see* St Katherine Coleman, Church of
All Hallows Fenchurch *see* St Mary Fenchurch, Church of
All Hallows Gracechurch (Cornhill, Lombard Street), Church of 24 D3
All Hallows the Great (at the Hay, Haywharf, in the Ropery, Seaman's Church), Church of 23 A1
All Hallows Honey Lane, Church of 12 E1
All Hallows Lane 28 F5
All Hallows the Less (upon the Cellar, near the Ropery), Church of 23 A1
All Hallows Lombard Street *see* All Hallows Gracechurch, Church of
All Hallows on (*or* by) London Wall, Church of 14 D3
All Hallows in the Ropery *see* All Hallows the Great, Church of
All Hallows near the Ropery *see* All Hallows the Less, Church of
All Hallows Seaman's Church *see* All Hallows the Great, Church of
All Hallows Staining (Stainingchurch), Church of 25 A2
All Hallows Watling Street, *see* All Hallows Bread Street, Church of
Almshouses (Bishopsgate) *see* Parish Clerks, Hall *and* Almshouses of Fraternity of
Almshouses (Cripplegate) *see* St Giles (Cripplegate), Hall *and* Almshouses of Fraternity of
Almshouses (by St Martin Outwich) *see* Merchant Taylors, Almshouses of
Almshouses (Wood Street) 12 E4
Alsies Lane *see* Ivie Lane
Amen Lane 10 F1
Andrew's Cross, The (Chancery Lane) 8 F1
Angel, The (Bishopsgate) 14 F2
Angel Inn (Aldwych) 18 D5
Ankar (Anchorite's) House (Blackfriars) *see* Dominican Friary (Blackfriars)
Ankar Lane 22 D1
Antelope, The (Holborn) 8 D5
Arches les, *see* Bowlane (Dowgate Hill)
Armenterslane *see* Coldeherburghlane
Armourers' Hall 13 A4
Arundelleslane *see* Wolsy Lane
Ass(h)elynes Wharf *see* Browne's Place
Athelyngstrate *see* Watelyng Street
Athelyngstrete (Baynard's Castle) 20 F4
Aubrees watergate *see* Waterlane, le (W. of Browne's Place)
Austin Friary 14 D2
Ave-Maria Aly 20 F5

Babeloyne *see* London Walle (street)
Baggardeslane *see* Old Fishtreete hill
Bailey, The *see* Old Bailly, the

Bake House (St Paul's) 21 A4
Bakers' Hall 30 F5
Bakewell Hall *see* Blackwell Hall
Ball Alley (London Wall) 13 C3
Ballardes Lane 8 F1
Bangor, Inn of the Bishop of 9 C3
Barbecanstret *see* Barbycane, le
Barbers' Hall 12 D5
Barbican or Bas(e) Court 5 C2
Barbycane, Le 5 C2
Barge, The 22 F4
Barkingchurch, -chapel *see* All Hallows Barking, Church of
Barnard's Inn 9 A4
Bars, The *see* Aldersgate Bars, Aldgate Bars, Holborn Barns *and* West Smithfield Bars
Bartholomew Lane (Lothbury) *see* saynt Bathellmuw lane
Bartilmewis Lane (West Smithfield) 11 A4
Bas Court, Manor of (*also called* the Barbican) 6 D3
Basinghall Street *see* Bassinghawstrete
Bassett's Inn 12 F3
Bassinghawstrete 12 F3
Bassinglane 22 D4
Bassisaw *see* Bassinghawstrete
Basyngeslane *see* Wolsy Lane
Bath and Wells, Inn of the Bishop of 18 D3
Bathestereslane *see* Grantham lane
Batoneslane *see* Rattenlane
Batteslane *see* Heywharfe Lane
Baynard's Castle 21 A2
Bear, The (Basinghall Street) 14 D3
Bear, The (London Wall) 14 D3
Beauchamp Inn *see* New Inn
Beaumont Inn *see* New Inn
Beaumont's Inn (Wood Street) 12 D3
Beaurepair 23 A2
Bedlam *see* St Mary of Bethlehem, Priory and Hospital of
Beech Street, *see* Barbycane, Le
Bell, The (Carter Lane) 21 A4
Bell, The (Cripplegate) 13 A5
Bell, The (Coleman Street) 13 A3
Bell, The (Fleet Street) 18 F5
Bell, The (Holborn) 9 B5
Bell, The (Mincing Lane) *see* Colchester, Inn of the Abbot of
Bell, The (Tower Hill) 26 D1
Belle Savage, The (Fleet Street) 10 E1
Bell on the Hoop, The *see* Belle Savage, The (Fleet Street)
Bell Wharf Lane *see* Emperours Headlane, le
Belthotereslan *see* Bylleter lane
Belyeterslane *see* Bylleter lane
Berchervereslane *see* Byrchyn lane
Berebynder Lane 23 A4
Berelane (Great Tower Street) 31 A4
Beremanchurch *see* St Martin Vintry, Church of
Berewardeslane *see* Berelane (Great Tower Street)
Bergavenny House *see* Pembroke's Inn
Berkeley's Inn (*alias* Warwick Inn) 20 F3
Berkyngchapel *see* All Hallows Barking, Church of
Bevesmarkes 15 B1
Bigod's House *see* Broken Wharf Mansion
Billingsgate 30 D4
Billingsgate Strete 30 D5
Billiter Square *see* Culver Alley
Billiter Street *see* Bylleter lane
Birchin Lane *see* Byrchyn lane
Bishop, The (Gray's Inn Road) 2 C1
Bishopsgate 14 F3
Bisshopesgatestrete 14 F3
Blackfriars *see* Dominican Friary (Blackfriars)
Blackfriars Stairs 20 E3
Black Raven Alley *see* Popys Allye
Blacksmiths' Hall 21 B3
Black Swan, The (Holborn) *see* Swan on the Hoop, The (Holborn)
Blackwell Hall 12 F2
Bladder Street 11 C1
Blanch Appleton (house) 25 A3
Blanch Appleton (manor) 25 A2
Bledlowes Key *see* Browne's Place
Blossom's Inn (*or* Bosom's) Inn 12 E1
Boar's Head, The (Fleet Street) 19 B5
Bockyng Wharffe *see* Broke Wharffe
Bogerowe *see* Bowgerowe
Bokelersbury (street) 22 F4
Bolt and Tun, The (Fleet Street) 19 B5
Bordhawlane 22 F4
Bosham's Inn 17 C5
Bosom's Inn *see* Blossom's Inn
Boss (Billingsgate) 30 D5
Boss (Cripplegate) 6 E1
Boss allee *see* Bosse Lane (Paul's Wharf)
Bosse Alye (Billingsgate) 30 E5
Bosse Lane (Paul's Wharf) 21 B2
Botoulfslane 24 D1
Botulphiswharf 30 D4
Bowe, le *see* Bowlane (Dowgate Hill)
Bower Rowe 20 E5
Bowgerowe 22 F3
Bow *or* Bowe Lane (Cheapside) *see* Hosyerlane
Bowlane (Dowgate Hill) 22 F2
Bowlane (S. of St Mary le Bow) *see* Gosselane
Bowyers' Hall 12 E4
Brackel(o)e(s)lane, *see* Grantam lane
Bradstrete 14 D2
Bred Strete 21 C4
Bretaske Lane 29 A5
Brettonestrete, *see* Britten Strete
Brewers' Hall 12 E4
Brew House (St Paul's) 21 A4

Garlickhythe 22 D1
Garlyk Hill 22 D2
Garscherche street *see* Graschestret
Garter House 6 D3
Gayspurlane 12 F4
George, The (Fleet Street) 9 C1
George, The (Holborn, N. side) 8 E5
George Inn, The (Lombard Street) 23 C3
George on the Hoop, The *see* Paul's Head Tavern (Godliman Street)
Gerard's Hall 22 D3
Germayneslane *see* Heywharfe Lane *and* Wynges Lane
Girdlers' Hall 12 F3
Gisor's Hall *see* Gerard's Hall
Glastonbury, Inn of the Abbot of 10 F4
Glaziers' Hall 22 E2
Goderunelane *see* Gutterlane
Godliman Street *see* Pawles Wharfe hill
Goffaireslane *see* Bush Lane
Goldhoper Lane *see* St Pancresse Lane
Gold Lane (Holborn) 3 C2
Goldsmiths' Hall 11 C2
Goldsmiths' Row 22 D5
Gonnepearelane *see* Bush Lane
Gophir Lane *see* Bush Lane
Gosselane 22 E4
Goswellestrete 5 C3
Govereslane *see* Bush Lane
Gracechurch Street *see* Graschestret
Graneswicheslane *see* Grenewiche Lane
Grantam Lane 22 F1
Graschestret 24 D3
Gray's Inn 2 B2
Gray's Inn Road *see* Graysynne lane *or* Portpole Lane
Graysynne Lane *or* Portpole Lane 2 B2
Great Bell, The (Barbican) 5 C2
Great Bell Alley *see* Mill Alley (Coleman Street)
Great Conduit, The (E. end of Cheapside) 22 F5
Great Cross in Cheapside *see* Cheap Cross
Great Seld, The *see* Key, The (Cheapside)
Great Swan Alley *see* Swan Alley
Great Tower Street *see* Towerstrete
Great Wardrobe *see* King's Wardrobe
Greenberries Quay *see* Kneseworth Key
Green Gate, The *see* Mutas House
Grenewiche Lane 22 E1
Gresham Street *see* Catte Street, Lad Lane *and* Yengellane
Grey Friars *see* Franciscan Friary (Grey Friars)
Greyhound, The (Holborn) 9 A5
Grey's Place *see* Serjeants' Inn (Chancery Lane)
Grey's Inn Lane *see* Graysynne Lane
Griste's House 24 E1
Grobbestrate *see* Grub Street
Grocers' Hall and Almshouses 23 A5
Grocers' Hall Court *see* Conyhope Lane
Grope Countlane 22 F4
Grubgatstrete *see* Crepulgate, vicus de
Grubstrete 11 F5
Guildhall 12 F2
Guildhall Chapel 12 F2
Guildhall Close 12 F2
Guildhall College 12 F2
Guildhall Library 12 F2
Guildhall of the Teutons *see* Hanse Guildhall
Guildhall Yard *see* Guildhall Close
Gutterlane 12 D1

Haberdashers' Hall 12 D3
Hacchestrete *see* Hogglane (Tower Hill)
Hadestokeslane *see* Derkelane
Hagge(n)lane *see* Pawles Wharfes hill
Hagin's House *see* Prince's Wardrobe
Hall of the Teutons *see* Hanse Guildhall
Halywell Strete 17 C4
Hand, The 18 F5
Hanging Sword Alley *see* Ouldwood Alley
Hand on the Hoop, The (Holborn) *see* Crown, The (Holborn)
Hanse Guildhall 22 F1
Harbour Lane *see* Brykhil Lane
Hardeleslane *see* Stodies lane
Harflete (*or* Harflu) Inn 8 F2
Harpe, le and Harpe Lane *see* Segeryneslane
Hart Horne Alley (Aldgate) 25 B4
Harts Horn, The (West Smithfield) 10 F4
Hart Street *see* Hertstrete
Hatters Key *see* Kneseworth Key
Haywharf Lane 29 A5
Heggestrete *see* Hogglane (Tower Hill)
Herber Lane *see* Brykhill Lane
Hereford, Inn of the Bishop of 21 B3
Hermitage *or* Anchorite's Cell (London Wall) *see* All Hallows on London Wall, Church of
Herteshornelane 29 A5
Herthstrete *see* Hertestrete
Hertestrete 25 A2
Heywharf 28 F5
Heywharfe Lane 29 A5
High Holborn *see* Holborn
High Timber Street *see* Tymberhythstrete
Hoggan Lane *see* Sporren Lane
Hoggenelane *see* Hogynlane
Hogglane (Tower Hill) 26 E1
Hog Lane (Aldgate) 16 D1
Hogynlane 12 D2
Holborn, The *see* Turnmill Brook
Holborn Bars 8 F5
Holborn Bridge 10 D4
Holborn Cross and Conduit 10 E4
Holborn Manor 9 C4
Holborn Stream *see* Turnmill Brook
Holbourne 8 D5

St Sepulchre without (of) Newgate (in the Bailey, West Smithfield), Church of 10 E3
St Stephen Coleman Street (in the Jewry), Church of 13 A2
St Stephen Walbrook (Bokerel), Church of 23 A4
St Swithens Lane 23 B3
St Swithin London Stone (Candlewick Street), Church of 23 A2
St Sythe *see* St Benet Sherhog, Church of
St Thomas' Chapel *see* London Bridge
St Thomas of Acon *or* Acre, Church of 22 F5
St Thomas The Apostle, Church of 22 E3
St Vedast Foster Lane (*and* St Armand, St Faster), Church of 11 C1
St Wandrille *see* St Mary Magdalen in the Fishmarket, Church of
St Werburga *see* St John the Evangelist Friday Street, Church of
Sakfrerelane *see* Olde Jury
Salisbury, Inn of the Bishop of 19 C5
Salisbury Aley 19 C5
Salters' Hall and Almshouses 22 D4
Salt Wharf 21 C1
Sancti Andree Hubert, venella *see* Philpot Lane
S. Augustini, vicus *see* Watelyng Street
sancti Clementis, vicus *see* Seynt Clementes Lane
Sancti Martini de Otteswyche, vicus *see* Bradstrete
Sancti Martini Orgor' *see* Saint Martin Orgar Lane
sancti Petri, venella *see* Peter Lane
Sancti Swithuni, vicus *see* St Swithens Lane
Saracen's Head, The (Godliman Street) 21 A4
Saracen's Head, The 10 E4
Sarmoneres lane *see* Sermoners lane
Savage's Inn *see* Belle Savage, The (Fleet Street)
Savoy, The (Hospital of St John the Baptist) 17 A2
Sayers lane *see* Coldeherburghlane
Saynt Bathellmuw Lane (Lothbury) 23 B5
Saynte Mighelles Lane 23 B1
Scalding Alley (Poultry) 23 A4
Scalding House *see* Scalding Alley (Poultry)
Schakkeslane *see* Vanners lane
School (Cornhill) *see* St Peter Cornhill, Church of
Scomer, The (Houndsditch) 15 B2
Scrope's Inn (Holborn) 9 C5
Scrope's Inn (Lime Street) 24 F3
Secoll Lane 10 E3
Seething Lane *see* Syvedon Lane
Segeryneslane 30 F5
'Segrave' *see* 'Camera Diane'
Seint Mary Hill Lane 24 E1
Seint uastes lane *see* Faster Lane
Seld *see* Crowned Seld; Key, The; Winchester Seld; Tanners' Seld
Selvernestrate *see* Silverstrete
Sempringham, Inn of the Master of 10 E5
Serjeants' Inn (Chancery Lane) 8 F1
Serjeants' Inn (Fleet Street) 19 B5
Serjeants' Inn (Holborn) *see* Scrope's Inn (Holborn)
Sermoners Lane 21 B4
Servat's Tower 23 A4
Sevehode Lane 12 E1
Sevenfotelane *see* Sevehode Lane
Seynt Clementes Lane 23 C2
Seynt Johns Strete (Clerkenwell) 4 F4
Seynt Laurence Lane (Candlewick Street) 23 B2
Seynt Sythes Lane 22 F4
Shaft Alley 24 E4
Shambles, The (St Nicholas Shambles, the Fleshambles) 11 B2
Shearmens' Hall 24 F2
Shelley House 12 D3
Sherborne Lane *see* Sithebourne Lane
Ship Yard *see* Capel's House
Ship, The (Temple Bar) 18 E5
Shirelane 8 E2
Shitteborwelane *see* Sithebourne Lane
Shoe Lane *see* Showe Lane
Sholond(e) *see* Showe Lane
Showe Lane 9 C3
Silverstrete 12 D4
Sithebourne Lane 23 B3
Sivethenestrate, -lane *see* Syvedon Lane
Skinners' Almshouses *see* Almshouses (Wood Street)
Skinners' Hall 22 F2
Skinners Lane *see* Bowlane (Dowgate) *and* Kyrounlane
Smalelane *see* Fletelane
Smerttes Key 30 E4
Smethefeud, Smithfield *see* West Smithfield
Snore Hylle, Snow Hill *see* Snowrehille
Snowrehille 10 E3
Somerset Inn (*or* Roos Inn) 20 F3
Sommers key *see* Wirehalelane
Soperlane 22 E4
Spital Croft *see* Charterhouse
Sporenereslane *see* Sporyer Rowe
Sporiereslane *see* Water lane (near Custom House)
Sporiereslane in Poletria *see* Pultrye, le
Sporren Lane 22 D2
Sporyer Rowe 20 F4
Sprincle alley *see* Masons alley
Sprottes key *see* Kneseworth Key
Stainingchurch *see* All Hallows Staining, Church of
Staining Lane *see* Stayning Lane
Stamford Inn 11 A2

Index of Personal Names

General Index